A Land of Their Own

Samuel Richard Tickell and the Formation of the Autonomous Ho Country in Jharkhand, 1818-1842.

THE INDIAN EDITION

Paul Streumer
Bluerose

NewDelhi • London

BLUEROSE PUBLISHERS
India | U.K.

Copyright © Paul Streumer 2024

All rights reserved by author. No part of this publication may be reproduced, stored in a retrieval system or transmitted in any form or by any means, electronic, mechanical, photocopying, recording or otherwise, without the prior permission of the author. Although every precaution has been taken to verify the accuracy of the information contained herein, the publisher assumes no responsibility for any errors or omissions. No liability is assumed for damages that may result from the use of information contained within.

BlueRose Publishers takes no responsibility for any damages, losses, or liabilities that may arise from the use or misuse of the information, products, or services provided in this publication.

For permissions requests or inquiries regarding this publication, please contact:

BLUEROSE PUBLISHERS
www.BlueRoseONE.com
info@bluerosepublishers.com
+91 8882 898 898
+4407342408967

ISBN: 978-93-6261-177-2

Cover design & Typesetting: Paul Streumer

Indian Edition: May 2024

A Land of Their Own

Samuel Richard Tickell and the Formation of the Autonomous Ho Country in Jharkhand

1818–1842

The Indian Edition

Paul Streumer read philosophy at the University of Amsterdam, historical anthropology at the University of Utrecht, and development studies at the University of Amsterdam. He obtained his PhD in Languages and Cultures of South Asia from the University of Leiden. He taught sociology of development of South and East Asia at the University of Utrecht, and was a board member of the Friends of the Institute Kern, the Indological Department of the University of Leiden. After his stint in academia, Paul was a consultant on knowledge management to the Dutch Ministry of Infrastructure, respectively for the Directorate General for Civil Aviation and that of Water Affairs. From 2003 till 2023 he was the chairman of the Stichting Buitenlandse Partner, and webmaster of its self-help website for Dutch citizens with partners from outside the EU. He now concentrates on the tribal history of India as an independent researcher.

© Paul Streumer 2016, 2021, 2024

The moral right of the author has been asserted.

All rights reserved. Without limiting the rights under copyright reserved above, no part of this publication may be reproduced, stored in or introduced into a retrieval system, or transmitted, in any form or by any means (electronic, mechanical, photocopying, recording or otherwise), without the prior written permission of the copyright owner.

First published in The Netherlands by Wakkaman, 2016. Second edition 2021.

This Indian edition is published in India by BlueRose Publishers, 2024

To Paul Verweel

In memory to Paul Verweel (1951-2018). Of our student friends' group, he turned out to be the best hunter in the academic jungle—and still came out as more than just an academic manager and professor. Without his support at crucial moments, this book would never have appeared.

...

Contents

Illustrations vii
Preface
(to the Indian edition) .... *xvii*
(to the first edition) .... *xxi*
(to the second edition) .... *xxiii*

Introduction: Individuals and Peoples 1

Prologue: The Independence of the Hos **4**

Part I
Another People's War, 1818–1830

1. Difficult Negotiations 25
2. Attack and Counterattack 44
3. The Mouth of a Gun 57
4. A Champaign Country 65
5. The Return of the Pauri Devi 79

Reflection: Another People's War *84*

Part II
A New Grand Strategy, 1831–1837

6. The Genesis of Wilkinson's System 89
7. Strategic Moves on the Ethnic Frontier 103
8. The Arrival of the Assistant 128
9. Poto Ho's Resistance 140

Part III
The Establishment of the Estate, 1837–1842

10. Post-Conflict Reconstruction 149
11. Consolidation 160

Afterglow: A Complete History of Indian Birds *174*

Part IV
Tickell's Hodésum Articles of 1840

12. The Rude Forefathers 183
13. The Hodésum Articles 193
Reflection: That Tickell Woman *216*

Conclusion: A People in Their Own Land **222**

Appendix: Impact of Tickell's articles 229
Bibliography 232
Notes 264
Index 339

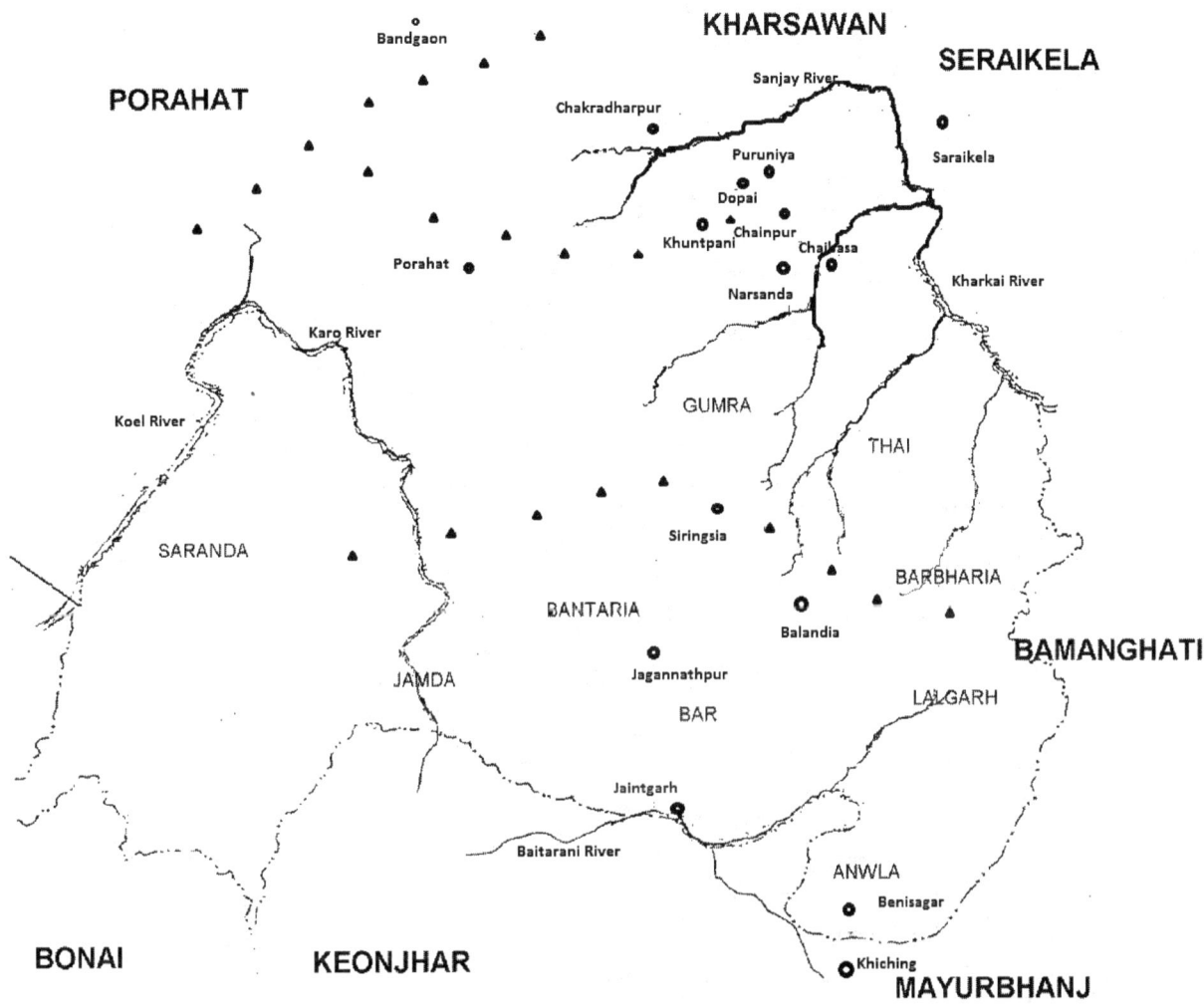

Hodisum and Singhbhum

Adapted from D. N. Majumdar, *The Affairs of a Tribe, A Study in Tribal Dynamics*

(Lucknow: Ethnographic and Folk Culture Society, 1950)

Plate 1. Benisagar ruins

Plate 2. Saraikela palace

This building, which Roughsedge visited in 1820, stands in the courtyard of the new palace.

Plate 3. The field of the Narsanda massacres

Here the Hos stood no chance against the cavalry of Lt. Maillard and Abdullah Khan, resulting in 100-150 dead, 25 March 1820.

Plate 4. Bonga Buru

On 26 March 1820, the Hos of twelve to fourteen villages had retreated here. The Ramgarh Battalion threatened them with immediate annihilation, and they gave up.

Plate 5. *Graucalus Macei*—The greater Cuckoo-Shrike, 1841,

from Samuel Richard Tickell, 'The Zoological Works of Samuel Richard Tickell', illustrated manuscript work in 14 volumes, vol. vii, plate 2, London: Zoological Society of London, [1865-1873]. By permission from the Zoological Society London

Note the 'English park' landscape near Chaibasa, which Tickell mentioned, and the army marching.

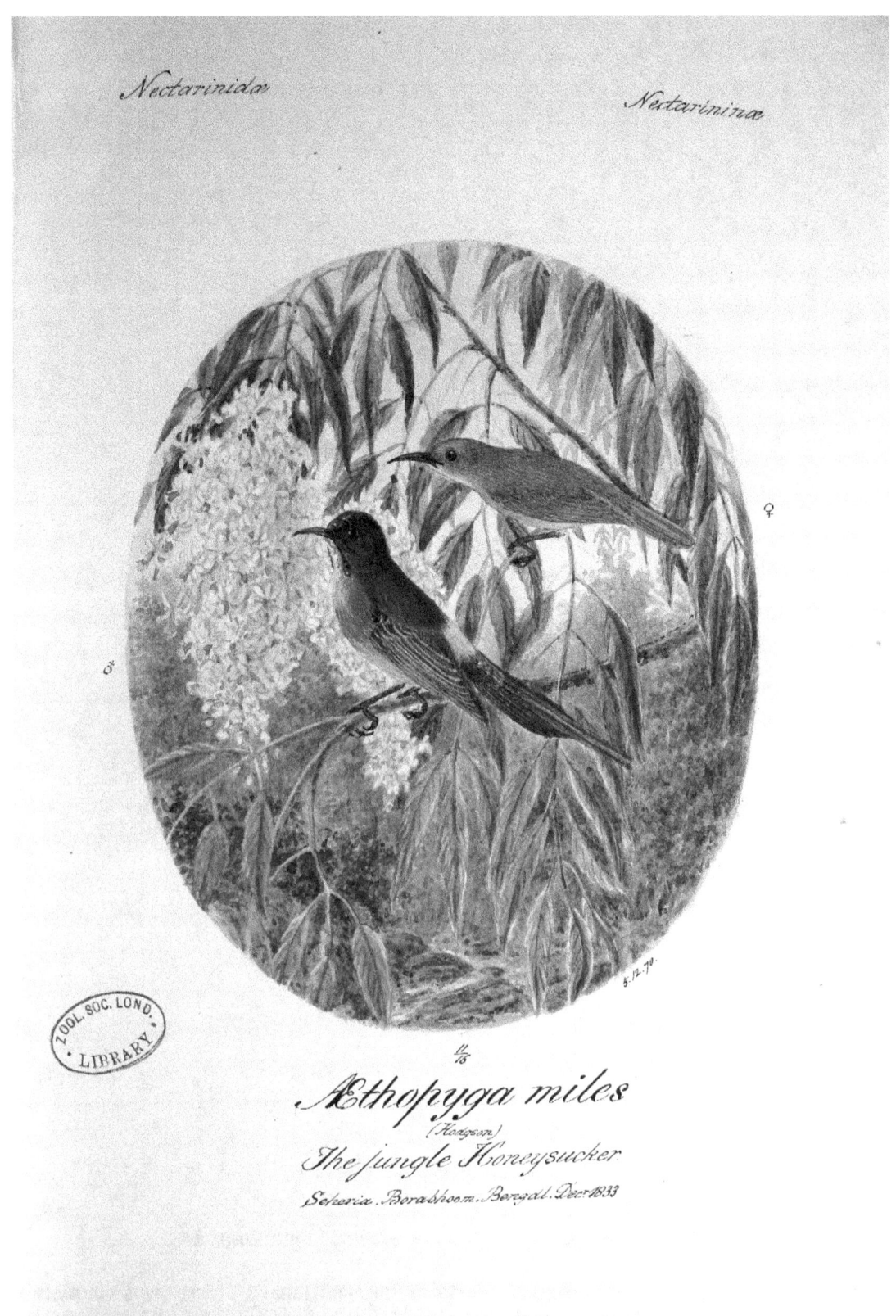

Plate 6. *Aethopyga miles*—The jungle Honeysucker, (Barabhum jungle), 1833,

from Samuel Richard Tickell, 'The Zoological Works of Samuel Richard Tickell', vol. vi, plate 7. By permission from the Zoological Society London

Plate 7. *Artamus fuscus*—The Swallow Shrike, Singhbhum, 1838,

from Samuel Richard Tickell, 'The Zoological Works of Samuel Richard Tickell', vol. vii, plate 1. By permission from the Zoological Society London

An illustration, too, of how the Hos cleared the jungle. Two small houses stand close to the small pond in the foreground. Next to the houses stands a cover for the fireplace. Near the pond are some stumps of trees, and behind these a recently cleared field.

Plate 8. Hodisum countryside

Plate 9. Seringsia Ghat

On 19 November 1837 Hos from the south under the leadership of Poto Ho of Rajabasa ambushed an army column of the East India Company here.

Plate 10. *Ninox scutellatus*—The cooing Hawk Owl, (The village of Urkia), 1842, from Samuel Richard Tickell, 'The Zoological Works of Samuel Richard Tickell', vol. iv, plate 19. By permission from the Zoological Society London

Under the bird streams the river Koel. On the other bank lays the village of Urkia. Here the forest was cleared by circling the trees.

Plate 11. Ho burial place near Jhinkpani

Plate 12. Samuel Richard Tickell

Courtesy of Ms N. Martyn.

This picture, one of the few extant of S. R. Tickell, was probably taken after his departure from India in 1865.

Preface to the Indian edition

...

The first edition of this book was published in 2016 in Europe. Looking back eight years later, the reception of one main character, Poto Ho, has been beyond expectations. At the time, Poto was not completely unknown to the Hos, but much of his life and work was. As a teaser, I published the chapter on Poto and the Battle of Seringsia on my website and repeatedly paid attention to him on Facebook. It caught on. Now, every year the battle of Seringsia (19 November 1837), as well as the memory of his hanging (1 January 1838) are celebrated by an ever-growing crowd before a well maintained memorial on the site of the battle. Poto got a life size statue in Ranchi's tribal museum. As I hoped he would become, Poto Ho is now the symbol of the independent Ho spirit. To see this book published in India is the fulfilment of a deep wish.

The main sources for this period 1818-1842 are from the British officers and administrators, and of course, my book reflects that. From their side, this was a time of first trying to regulate the area through feudal rulers who had dug up ancient claims against the independent Hos. But the Hos did not like that. These feudals did not do much else than trying to tax them to the limit, or employing them as mercenaries in their dynastic and financial quarrels. In a major change of grand strategy, the East India Company took over the land of the Hos in 1837. It became known as the Kolhan Government Estate.

From the Ho side much less is left. They lack sources on paper or on rock. There is lore, but it usually does not go deeper than a few, at most eight, generations. And it is overlaid with the preoccupations of the present. For the Hos, lack of basic information about their history causes confusion, not solved by the school and academic curricula. As a Ho lady from Mumbai wrote me, "Who are we?" To answer that fundamental question of provenance and of place among the many peoples of India, I devoted an extensively documented prologue to the Hos from their earliest times in South East Asia and the Odisha coast up to 1767, when the East India Company arrived at the border of their present abode, the Hodisum in Jharkhand and Odisha.

From then on, the facts of Ho life are easier to come by. Luckily, much contemporary information lays hidden in the British sources. Careful research and close reading have made clear much more about Ho society and its main figures. Contrary to the general feeling of academics and politicians, fighting against the British was not the main activity of the Hos. The Hos were first and foremost agriculturists, fond of an occasional hunt to get more protein, and a raid on another village to satisfy their pride or need for cattle. From time to time, Hos were free lancing for the local feudals. Still, their main concern was keeping their own fields and villages free from outside interference. If the Hos got really worked up and fought back, it was to protect the modesty of their womenfolk, to prevent the plunder of their farms, or to stop attempts by outsiders to lord over them, their family and their neighbours.

Because the Hos were a warned people. In a vague way, through passer-by travellers or through songs, they got the news about feudal suppression, especially up north, of the tribes of Chota Nagpur. They were well aware of it, as the tribals up north were well aware of the inspiring example of that independent tribe called the Larkas (fighters) or Hos.

Among the Chota Nagpur tribals, the Hos stood out. They were free and that showed. From their very first contacts, British were aware of that. When their soldiers came unannounced, they were turned away from the very entrances of the Ho villages; when the Hos fought the East India Company troops, they showed amazing feats of bravery. When Ho leaders met British officers, they often were tough negotiators. Opposite the British administrators Roughsedge, Wilkinson and Tickell, we see Ho statesmen standing, Singrai Tiu of Dopai, Mata Pingua of Balandia, Ghunnoo Manki of Gumuriya. They could fight, but also take a wider view, and negotiate in the knowledge that, as Thomas Sowell famously said, "there are no solutions, only trade-offs". Even when they had conflicts – and there were quite some fierce ones – there was an underlying mutual appreciation between Hos and British.

Fortunately, history is not only politics and war. Near the end of the period treated here, Samuel Richard Tickell caused a quantum jump in the knowledge about Ho life and culture. He gave us a precise – but not very systematic – description of their society and their land. In addition, he wrote a grammar and vocabulary. In the process, he gave us stunning glimpses of their daily life which went as far as poetry and whole dialogues. The treasure trove of Tickell's 1840 articles, too, makes Ho history unique among the Indian tribes.

I set out on researching the history of the Hos with very few preset ideas. Coming to Ranchi, Jharkhand, I was intrigued. Why were the Hos so neglected? They lived far from Ranchi, "in the south", I was told. Which made it sound as if it was very far indeed. That begged for exploration. I visited the Ho country and, crucially, liked the people. That was one requirement to do research fulfilled.

My other personal requirement was that the subject had to be challenging. My aim was to write a history that would meet the highest standards. I soon found that the quality of the few books and articles in which the Hos figured, varied enormously. Most left out crucial information, many were even untrustworthy. The problem was to find out where phantasy, good-sounding but empty phrases, and sloppiness, took over from the cool, hard facts. There was no other way to find out what, in the words of Leopold von Ranke, had "really happened" than to go to the primary sources, and rebuild the story from checked and rechecked facts. Now, we have here a new and authoritative study of those 25 years in which the British established the Kolhan Government Estate, and the Hos largely preserved their autonomy inside their villages.

An early and soon widely admired result of tribal policy, the Kolhan Government Estate was the starting point of the modern development of this area and its largely Ho society. It still exerts its influence today.

This book has been long in the making. It would not have been possible to research and write it in these more than three decennia (with some significant interruptions) without the support from scholars and friends, too many to mention. But my best inspiration was its reception from Hos, way too many to mention. To all of them go out my thanks. With this Indian edition, this story is finally coming home.

Paul Streumer, Houten, 7 March 2024

...

Preface to the first edition

...

The establishment of the Kolhan Government Estate in 1837 is arguably the decisive moment in the history of the Hos, a 1,500,000 strong scheduled tribe in Jharkhand and Odisha. It was the administrative response both to the needs of the modern state and the wish of the Hos to live their life without disturbing outside interference. The Estate was one of the earliest separate tribal areas in India. Although it was abolished in 1952, important elements of it are still there. At present, the Ho people might not have escaped poverty, but, not least due to the Kolhan Government Estate, they have preserved their demographic and cultural cohesion. The story of the establishment of the Kolhan Government Estate gives important clues to what moves the A*divasi* today.

In the garb of a conventional history, a fresh understanding is presented here. It follows from a methodological break. I go way beyond the usual macro-political and socio-economic histories of tribals. That break did not present itself immediately to me. From a great mass and variety of contemporary documents, some of which had only recently been discovered, I meticulously reconstructed the events and developments, and placed these in their context of the emergence of the modern state in East India. So far, I was still in line with my academic education, especially in Utrecht and Amsterdam. History, I was taught, consists of broad movements. The deeper I went into the history of the Hos, the more dissatisfied I became with this approach. Sure, broad movements, if considered sensitively, give one a sense of general direction. It is useful for a swimmer to know that the water of a river ultimately flows down into the sea. But for that particular swimmer the crocodile in the water is more decisive for his actions. On closer inspection, I found that history as it evolves consists of actions taken by individuals. That also agreed more with my own experiences as a social activist, academic, and manager. To present a history that makes sense and to which we can relate, I bring people back in.

Ho people have recognisable names, and their villages, too, are known. Up to now, we are quite well informed about the names of the feudal chiefs in the area and their capitals, and, of course, of the British involved and the seats of their superiors, but not of the Hos and their villages. In the confusion of different spellings in the sources, I have traced the principal Ho participants. To enable the reader to follow them, I have, except where it could cause confusion, standardised their names throughout this book. Come and meet Ho leaders such as Singrai, Mata, Kuntu, Ghunnoo and, of course, Poto. Get to know about the fates of Mahadei and Musammat Birang. Moreover, most Ho places, as they appear in the sources and (if at all) in previous historical writings, lie in a never-never land, not in the Singhbhum we know. I have carefully traced these villages with the help of the excellent maps of the Survey of India. Where a name could not be found, I have retained the spelling as it appeared in the sources. Especially my Singhbhum readers will be pleased to recognise not just Chaibasa and Seringsia, but also other places where major events took place, Narsanda, the Bonga Buru, Balandia, Jaintgarh, Pokharia, Chainpur, and Khuntpani.

Much information on the society and lifestyle of the Hos has survived. Fortunately, the Hos were—and are—talkative and had—and have—definite views. Quite some of these found their way into the archives. Still, these sources were written by outsiders. I treat the contemporary accounts of the Hos as texts, to be understood with the insights of literary criticism, social anthropology and rural economics. Here I am not only interested in the authors' views, but also in what they actually saw.

All this material does not add up to a full-fledged ethnography. But it gives a fair view of what outsiders knew of Ho society and culture in the years up to 1842. I have resisted the temptation to fill in gaps with material from later sources or—even more hazardous—from other peoples in Jharkhand. In the rare instances where I use such material for elucidation or comparison, I do so with extreme caution and added qualifications. Society evolves; so does culture. The Ho of 1840 certainly was a different tiger from the Ho of 1940 or, for that matter, the Ho of 1740. But, like them, and like the Ho of today, he had a full life to defend.

This is the historians' edition. It is extensively documented and states for each fact where one can find it. It gives biographies of the main characters. Moreover, in the notes I correct some —not all— mistakes in earlier literature. If he wants, the non-professional history buff can skip the notes. The main text stands on its own.

This work is a thorough restudy of a field I had covered in my 2003 PhD thesis in Leiden, in which I analysed imperial grand strategies for dealing with the tribal people of eastern India, especially with the Hos. The revisit of the documents was a voyage of discovery. In addition, I found many new sources, got insights from Hos into their culture and life, and was amazed how much I learned. I am deeply grateful to the people who have supported this quest. I cannot mention all, and to select a few seems unfair. It has been my privilege to be inspired and supported by all of you.

I know that more insights are yet to be gained. Still, I trust this work considerably advances our knowledge of this period, and especially of the Ho people and of the Adivasis in general as prime movers in their land. It is essential reading for people who want to understand the historical roots of the situation in eastern India today. Also, I sincerely hope, it will attract the 'tigers of Singhbhum', the Hos. It was my pleasure; it is your story.

Houten, June 2016

Preface to the second edition

In the main text, some spelling errors were corrected. More importantly, the village where Mahadei was outraged was not Puruniya, but Pokharia. I have added a few small items. Samuel Richard Tickell concluded his 1840 'Memoir on Hodésum' with some disapproving sentences on the habits of the "very poorest" of the Hos. This was striking, as in most of his article he was very upbeat about them. At that time, he was staying in Nepal with his brother-in-law Brian Houghton Hodgson, who was critical of the tribals to the south of Nepal. It seems their friction shows here.

I have also added that in 1874-5, the archaeologist J. D. Beglar found Tickells descriptions of archaeological remains "not always reliable". On the authority of the local priest of Khiching, Tickell had mentioned some old temples in Udyapur on the banks of the Baitarani River. Beglar could not discover them. He concluded that either Tickell's informant or his own memory must have misled him. There are few things so illuminating as visiting the places mentioned in the sources.

Or listening to local informants. In the first edition I was under the impression that Poto Ho was a member of the Pingua kili. Luckily, several Ho friends have pointed out the error. This is how tribal history progresses. In this edition I have used the proper name Poto Ho.

Houten, June 2021

Introduction: Individuals and Peoples

Between 1818 and 1842, the Hos had twenty-five odd years to reconsider their ties with the outside world and the modern state. They did so with remarkable success. Although the result was not the independence they wanted, they kept a great measure of internal autonomy inside the Kolhan Government Estate, in present-day West Singhbhum District of Jharkhand. The story of the establishment of the Kolhan Government Estate begins when the local states invited the East India Company in, with the request to subdue the Hos for them. The Company did so, but the area remained highly unstable. The story ends when Samuel Richard Tickell had organised the Ho land as a Government Estate, at village level run by local people. Following the sources, I go from outside in. The political status of the land was the first centre of attention—Who were living in it became clearer only on closer view.

I change the melody to which the Adivasi story usually is sung, and present a counterpoint history. In the unfolding political story, I give primacy to actual meetings between people, belonging to groups such as the local rajas and chiefs, the British officers, and the Hos. Ethnic profiling, so common in books on the pre-Independence history of tribes, would blur their particulars. Here is a story of engagements between individuals of widely differing backgrounds and aspirations. They appear as individuals with a cultural and a family background. Their deliberations and actions are described with empathy and balance. They were not only driven by their assignments, circumstances, or even their interests, but, often decisively, by their feelings. Events and people arise in new detail, showing dynamics not noticed before.

The main concerns of the Singh rulers of Porahat, Saraikela and their fief-holders were their mutual quarrels and pecking order. The Hos did not appear except as enemy groups. The Singhs did not quote a single individual Ho. The British accounts were mostly written by officers on active duty. As military men, they could not afford not to pay attention to what they encountered, but they emphasised military and political aspects. Still, in time, details of Ho life and culture emerged. This trend culminated in the works of Samuel Richard Tickell. He wrote numerous official letters, which shed much light on the establishment of the Kolhan Government Estate and the Ho reactions to its imposition. In the years 1837–40, he collected material for his 'Memoir on the Hodésum' and the first grammar of the Ho language—or, for that matter, of any Jharkhandi tribal language.

Tickell is supremely important for our understanding of this part of eastern India in this period. Therefore I pay quite some attention to his life and works. Through his father and grandfather, Tickell was at one remove from the intense life of the late eighteenth century musicians, theatre players and politicians in Bath and London. He was born in India, though, and liked the jungle with its game, its birds and, in Singhbhum, its people. The Hos stroke a chord with Tickell and he, like his forebears, had the sensitivity to get close to people and the ability to give his experiences shape. His vivid material, often written during or just after the event, constitute most of what we know about the Ho society and culture of his days, and is —in much-dried form—the baseline of the identity of this people as depicted to this day in gazetteers and anthropological writings. In addition, Tickell was a painter. Some of his excellent paintings of jungle birds and village life are reproduced here for the first time.

Individual, but still largely nameless, Hos extensively contributed to Tickell's understanding. Up to a point, they let him participate in their day's routine in the villages, showed him their dances and clothes, told reminiscences and myths, sang songs and spoke with him about their daily life. Some of these dialogues Tickell reproduced in the Ho language as well as in English. It includes the first story in the Ho language to appear in print, also reproduced in this book.

All the main groups that shaped this history, be it the British, the feudal rajas and chiefs, or the Hos, showed major differences of opinion and divergent, often opposing reactions to new circumstances. In the apparatus of the East India Company was a chain of command. So, in the end, its decisions looked as they were arrived at in high places and sent down the line to swing into action the superpower of nineteenth century India. But these decisions were not automatically arrived at. Many times, local officers and administrators had heated discussions about policies and even about strategies, so much that sometimes Calcutta had to intervene to calm passions. On the ground, British officers had considerable freedom to act. When they went too far in the eyes of Calcutta or London, they were censured. But several times these locally operating officers created a situation which the Company had to grudgingly accept.

The people of Singhbhum were the prime movers of their own history. Often, they took the initiative. The rajas and feudal chiefs showed themselves remarkably skilful in furthering their interests. Striving to modernise their often small and weak states, they conducted complicated and lengthy negotiations with the East India Company to get its assistance in expanding their sway and, certainly, their income from taxes. They spent relatively large sums on lobbying in Calcutta or Ranchi. They did not present one front. More often than not, their target was their neighbour or their kinsman. Old rancour and new needs led to mutual aggression. These were major influences on the events—and even on the very introduction of the Kolhan Government Estate.

The Hos were exclusive, but they dealt quite successfully with the outer world. Ho society was a lively political universe with divisions often dating from pre-British times. Some Hos went with the new political configuration; others opposed it. If they opposed, they resisted in carefully forged alliances and planned military actions involving hundreds, sometimes thousands of combatants. These ranged from head-on battles, a seven-day siege to a fort, to well-staged ambushes in jungle warfare. All this was backed up by extensive systems of supply bases. But there also was a sizeable Ho opinion that consistently sided with the East India Company. When the Company was not active, the Hos acted as allies of feudal chiefs who were in conflict with each other. Whatever their political persuasion, the Hos could be tough negotiators, who knew how to press their points, especially on keeping the foreigner and the tax collector out of their villages.

The outcome of all this was that much against the wishes of the local rajas and chiefs, the East India Company took the Ho land under its direct control and organised it as a separate estate. The East India Company thereby reaffirmed, not created, the distinct Ho social and cultural space.

...

Prologue:
The Independence of the Hos

...

A discovery in the jungle; the early states and their peoples; the rise of the Rajput model; Hodisum becomes independent; reflections on the birth of the Ho people

In the cold season of 1839–40, Samuel Richard Tickell, the first Englishman to live in the country of the Hos, proceeded over a road, 'replete with debris of the most melancholy and dreary nature, rank grass waving over tanks, some of great magnitude, which lie on every side', to come to a 'narrow path . . . through dense thickets and forest trees, among which lie, thickly scattered, portions of elaborate sculpture, idols, and alto-relief figures of men in armour on horseback, dancing girls, jugglers, servants'. When he reached the end, he saw an unfinished temple. The building materials for the dome were on the ground around it, 'as if they had been hastily abandoned'. A few kilometres to the north, he found a few extremely poor people in a 'wretched straggling hamlet near the banks of what once was a magnificent tank'. Lying around were idols, some 'buried many feet under a loose reddish soil, having the appearance of decaying bark'. Not one of the local people dared to touch, nor could they tell much about these.[1]

Kutaitundi temple, Khiching

Tickell's was a classic archaeological discovery in the jungle. Thus, it raised more questions than it solved. The people who had made the stone structures were gone; the inhabitants of the hamlet must have moved in sometime. They were Hos. Obviously, their land had a history far beyond what the Benisagar villagers could tell him.

There is preciously little material on the pre-modern period of this area of which the Kolhan Government Estate in West Singhbhum district of Jharkhand is the centre.[2] What we have is quite diverse, and often fragmented. There are the results of linguistic and DNA research, archaeological discoveries and some relatively early recordings of local lore. At several points in time, developments in the often better documented neighbouring districts had an impact on the course of events in the Singhbhum area. Problems of dating and reconciling different findings persist, which is to be expected with such a small volume of research. Still, these findings enable us to establish the history of the Hos and their land Hodisum up to the arrival of the East India Company.

Let us start with the Hos themselves. The name 'Ho' simply means 'a man', in the sense of 'a man of our people'.[3] The Hos share most of their language with the Mundas of Jharkhand.[4] That puts the Ho language in the northern Munda group, together with the Mundas, Santhals and a number of smaller peoples.[5]

Where can we place the Munda speakers linguistically and ethnically? The distant relatives of the Munda languages are Khasi in Meghalaya and, notably, the Mon-Khmer or Austroasiatic tongues of the area from south-east Myanmar (Burma) to Vietnam and the south of China.[6] From that, it appears that South-east Asians carried their language to India. The dates are hotly debated, but here is an indication. The latest date the Austroasiatic language group could have originated would be about 4,000 BC.[7] The earliest Munda speakers could have arrived in India around 2,500 BCE.[8] Genetic analysis points to the earliest Munda, a single male ancestor, living 2,300 BCE (rather, some time between 2,500 and 2,100 BCE).[9] He would have lived in Laos or, more broadly, the area of the Mekong River.

How did this ancestor, or his offspring, arrive in India? The most plausible explanation is that the Austroasiatics, indicated as Proto Mundas, came over sea from Southeast Asia, more specific from the broad area of south Myanmar and Malaysia. The technical means were there. There was an ancient sea route connecting the South-east Asian with the Odisha coast for trade.[10] The route mostly followed the coast, and was seasonal, as the direction of travel had to agree with the monsoons. The foremost authority in Early Austroasiatic Studies, Paul Sidwell places the arrival of the Austroasiatic or even an early form of Munda (Proto Munda) speakers on the Orissa coast in a later time, between in 2,000 to 1,500 BCE.[11]

Here, it is fair to say, opinion is divided. Another school of thought is that the Munda speakers entered mainland India overland from an area in North Burma and then crossed into NE India.[12] But this theory is problematic. Between the Khasi land (Meghalaya) and the Chotanagpur plateau we find no ancient traces of Austroasiatic languages nor even a genetic imprint on the present population.[13] Again, we see a marked difference between the Munda speakers and the Khasis, as the maternal DNA of Munda does not point at all to a connection outside India, whereas one third of Khasi maternal DNA has a South-east Asian connection.[14] That suggests that both areas, though relatively near to each other, must have been peopled from two different directions.[15]

Slightly inland in the hills surrounding the small coastal plains of the Mahanadi delta and the Chilka lake, a new admixture took place now between Austroasiatic immigrants and the local population. At present, the Munda speakers are at first sight outside the South-east Asian racial sphere. Recent DNA research shows that the munda speakers are for 75 per cent descended from the earlier local population.[16] That seems to be true especially on the female side.[17] Most Munda speakers (57%) share one of seven maternal haplogroups in India, which date back to at least 10,000 BCE.[18] Still, the other 25 per cent of their genetic material has a South-east Asian origin and, significantly, is detected exclusively in the male line.[19] The idea of male immigration of Austroasiatic speakers into India is appealing, but we must remember that we cannot assign more than a very vague date and place to this. Certain is that their language prevailed. The sum is that the Munda speakers are genetically quite different and linguistically very different from the Indo-European and Dravidian speakers of east India. These differences, given at the very beginning, would colour their further history.

How did the Munda speakers come from the Mahanadi Basin to the Chota Nagpur plateau? The Munda languages are many, at least 16, the classification of which is unclear. A basic division is that we have the south Munda languages, the central with Korku as a distant outlier to the west, and finally, the northern Kherwarian to which Ho belongs. It is still an open question whether this is a linguistic division or just a geographical.[20] DNA however, provides more clues. The southern branch is the genetically most conservative, established about 1,800 BCE. Which might be close to the date of arrival of the Southeast Asian component in the area. The Northern Munda group has less south-east Asian ancestry, rather mixed more and longer (about 1,000 years) with the local Indian populations, up to 800 BCE. This admixture was not sex specific anymore.[21] Which suggest a more peaceful spread, and mainly northwards. But not in a straight line. That access to the Chotanagpur plateau was blocked by the Bhuiyas – or their ancestors.

This story is quite different from earlier speculations. Up to the 1970s, historical linguists and anthropologists attributed an enormous *Wanderlust* to the Munda people who were thought to have traversed all of northern India. However, evidence for this is rather thin.[22] In Joseph van Troy's view, the Mundas entered the Chotanagpur plateau well to the north of Hodisum in the first millennium BCE. He arrived at that date by assuming that the Mundas were retreating from the Indo-European speakers who after 600 BCE established kingdoms in the eastern Ganges valley.[23] It could well be that retreat was not the main reason. The eastern Ganges valley was hard to reclaim, and Munda presence there must have been very small.[24] They rather settled away from the Ganges in more hilly areas, suitable for their type of agriculture, wet rice cultivation with light implements. Indeed, it is possible that rice cultivation was introduced or even reinvented in north India by Proto-Munda speakers.[25] But they did arrive in the Chotanagpur plateau.[26] In places, as the DNA researches also suggested, they were not the earliest humans to settle there. There are Neolithic flint flakes from Singhbhum which suggest that parts of it were settled by 10,000 BCE or even earlier.[27] That population must have been extremely small; so was their ecological niche along the middle ranges of the rivers and between heights above 700 m and thick forests.[28] The plateau has quite some megalithic remains—which could be Munda, but also could be earlier—and rock paintings—which likely are from the pre-Munda period—but no date has been assigned to these.[29] The Munda colonisation of the plateau progressed slowly,[30] and had far greater ecological consequences,[31] as one can expect from agriculturists. Van Troy assumed that Mundas arrived in the Khunti area down south in the second century or even as late as the fifth century CE.[32] Thus, we see Munda speakers close to present-day West Singhbhum's northern border at a rather unspecified point in time, but well before local records were written.

This triggers the next question: How did the ancestors of the Hos come further south? Barring one time shortly after 1592, there is no evidence that Munda speakers immigrated in considerable numbers at a time into the West Singhbhum area. Large-scale migrations are exceptional events and leave traces in folklore. But the Hos have no tradition about a mass migration.[33] Still, the names of many *kilis* or clans of the Hos are names of villages in the border area of the districts Khunti and West Singhbhum.[34] This suggests that many of the ancestors of the Hos came from there. We are tempted to use the analogy of later migrations of the Hos and imagine a trickle of individual or small groups of Munda-speaking families southwards.[35]

Tickell gave the history of the Singhbhum area as he got it from some unnamed Oraons and Hos.[36] In his rendering, on arrival in Singhbhum the ancestors of the Hos found Bhuiyas there, 'rich in cattle, and industrious cultivators'. The Bhuiyas allowed them to establish villages first in the forests and eventually in the open tracks. At the time, the country was under Sarawak (Sarak) rule. Possibly, these were Jains.[37] Together, the Bhuiyas and the Hos expulsed the Saraks. After some time, the Bhuiyas wanted to have their own raja. They invited people from Marwar, who in alliance with the Bhuiyas fought against the Hos. In the end, however, the Marwaris changed alliance and together with the Hos defeated the Bhuiyas. The Marwaris kept Porahat and the plain to its north. The Hos withdrew from there and 'occupied the remaining tract of open land, ... the Hodésum'. Tickell could not date these events, as 'the narrators ... have no account whatever of time'.[38]

Later, too, serious efforts were made to get the Ho side of the story, but they did not have traditions that threw much light on their past.[39] Indeed, as was stated by A. D. Tuckey in his extensive survey of 1913–18, more than seventy years after Tickell's account, 'seven or eight generations was the farthest back that they put the foundation of a village and could trace their genealogy'.[40] A memory extending over the last two or three generations seemed to have been more common.[41] That put the upper limit of recorded living memory of the Hos at 1725, possibly 1700 CE. There is another limitation, that of historical value. Tuckey's brief was to find founder clans—if any—of originally reclaimed villages, in order to give their members special rights to their land. Contrary to his expectations, the Hos did not make a distinction between the original founders of a village and latecomers. He combined archaeology and, after 'very lengthy and careful cross-examination', local tradition. Thus, he found that many genealogies were concocted.[42] It suggests that the traditions which the Hos narrated to Tuckey had a practical purpose. They were to establish their rights to the land and their relations with their neighbours.[43]

Still, the results of Tuckey's survey broadly confirm Tickell's story. He found that the Hos came from the north or north-west.[44] His conclusion was that the north of the Estate, and that included the northern and central forest areas, was pure Ho country.[45] Most of the names of hills there and in neighbouring Porahat were of Munda origin.[46] Here, Munda speakers must have been the first to clear the jungle. The tracts in the eastern part of Hodisum had been more recently settled and other peoples, such as Santhals and Gonds, lived there, too. In the south, the area where Tickell had made his archaeological discovery, the Hos must have taken over from an earlier population, as there was no break in the occupation of the country.[47] In all, Tuckey found that about 40 per cent of the Ho villages of the Kolhan were taken over from other peoples.[48] They must have moved away, and that is what

Hos had told Tickell, but one should not exclude the possibility that stragglers, small groups as well as individual families had gone over to the Ho ethnicity.

Many of the ancestors of the Hos came from the area inhabited by Mundas. They spoke a dialect of the Munda language and shared many religious beliefs and practices with the Mundas. So, what is the problem? Precisely that the Hos considered (and consider) themselves a separate people. A report of 1908 stated that even where Hos and Mundas lived next to each other, they would not intermarry.[49] Where ethnic indicators fail, we should perhaps look at history, starting with the ruins that Tickell saw.

The Hos might have come from the north, but the oldest datable historical evidence[50] we find in the south of these tracts and it comes from a time before Munda speakers were present there. Two extensive clusters of archaeological remains in the area provide some material backbone for the local history up to the thirteenth century. The first one, which is covered by quite extensive literature, is the 10 sq. km Khiching site in the north of Mayurbhanj district close to the border with West Singhbhum.[51] Eight kilometres to its north, in the extreme south-east of the West Singhbhum District, is the huge Benisagar tank and village, the place Tickell had described (see Plate 1). It is much smaller, containing the remains of some ten temples.[52] There is little literature on it; excavations and repairs are still going on. A seal with an inscription in the Brahmi script, probably from the fifth century, was discovered here. It belonged to Priyangu, who was 'well versed in the four Vedas'. Newspaper accounts of a 'Vedic university' in Benisagar are exaggerated—one scholar does not a university make.[53] The seal does, of course, indicate the presence of a Brahmin. As we have seen, probably at this time, between the second and the fifth centuries CE, groups of Mundas arrived in the Khunti area some 130 km to the north-east and, according to their myths, destroyed the iron industry of the Asuras there. These Munda actions must have made the access to the north more difficult for the inhabitants of Khiching/Benisagar. The area was oriented towards the south.

Rather, it formed the northern fringe of the Bhanja state in present-day Odisha. From about the fourth century onwards, Bhanjas ruled here. But the single name Bhanja covers a more complicated dynastic history. There were successive dynasties called Bhanja. The first Bhanja dynasty ruled the Khiching area in the fourth and fifth centuries.[54] The extent of its sway is not clear. It could be the Keonjhar area only or it could also include Mayurbhanj and Singhbhum.[55]

Moving a few centuries forward, in the first decades of the seventh century, Shashanka, the Shaiva ruler of Bengal, seized the area of Khiching and Benisagar. After his death, the region seemed to have been included in the realm of Harsha, who ruled most of northern India from 606 to 647 CE.[56] Indeed, art styles confirm this connection. Some seventh-century Vishnu statues from Benisagar showed a Bengal influence, probably from the area of Tamralipti, a port on the Bay of Bengal. As the century progressed, a local style developed in Benisagar, as appears from the statue of an unidentified male deity of the end of the seventh century, which was not unlike the late-eighth-century goddess statues from the Saraikela area, north of the present-day West Singhbhum.[57] Thus, reasoning from the artistic towards the political, in the second half of the seventh century, Khiching and Benisagar need not have formed a political unity.[58] That idea is supported by the written sources. In the anarchy after Harsha's demise, another dynasty, also calling itself Bhanja, came to power in the Khiching area,[59] while the local chronicle of the Singhbhum rajas mentioned another dynasty in Venu-garh, not far from Benisagar, and gave a date corresponding to 693 CE.[60]

This second Bhanja house in Khiching originated from the Bamanghati area, some 40 km to the north-east.[61] Again we have artefacts to guide us through this period. A copper plate indicated that Virabhadra established a principality there and that there were many Shaiva ascetics at Khiching.[62] With Kottabhanja, who ruled around 850 CE, we enter a more datable history.[63] Now Khiching saw its first period of temple construction.[64] From that time onwards the Benisagar finds resembled those of Khiching, and we may assume a political unity between the two sites. The Saivite Hindu, Jain and Buddhist faiths inspired the temples and the sculptures. They were definitely Odia in style. The independent kingdom of Khiching encompassed the present-day district of Mayurbhanj, parts of Keonjhar and part of the Ajodhya area in Balasore district.[65]

From 924 to 1050 there was a second wave of temple construction in Khiching town. There lived Jains, Buddhists and Shaivas, possibly the anti-Brahminical Pashupatas,[66] but most new temples were Hindu. Inside the state as a whole, the new developments demanded a new equilibrium. The Bhanjas were prolific donors of villages to Brahmins.[67] They also constructed tanks in Benisagar and Khiching, thereby extending or improving the wet rice cultivation. Not all of this was necessarily foreign investment. The tradition in Benisagar saw the neighbouring village of Keshnagar as the place of origin of the excavator of its huge tank.[68] The stronger economic base and the increased influence of Brahmins integrated these areas further into the wider Odisha setting.[69] Importantly, the import of Brahmins strengthened the apparatus of the Bhanja state.

But the Bhuiyas formed its military backbone. The Bhuiyas, probably of Dravidian stock, were a widespread people with their heartland in a wide stretch to the southern border of present-day West Singhbhum District. In historical times they spoke Odia and had their own political organisation.[70] The new rulers could not bank on the Brahmins and discard the Bhuiyas; they needed both.

There was a religious way out of what could easily have developed into a political and ethnic stand-off. The carriers of both traditions, the Bhuiya and the Brahmin, could be involved in the ritual arrangements of the state. In Odisha, many deities were associated with a certain territory. It made political as well as religious sense to the Bhanjas to adopt Thakurani,[71] the goddess of military peoples such as the Bhuiyas, as the state deity.[72] They nearly completely merged her with their chief family deity, goddess Chamunda, and she got the local name of Khichingeshvari.[73] The construction of a stone temple for her in their capital served a double purpose. It strengthened the prestige of the ruler abroad and attached the Bhuiya military power to him at home.[74] In the Khichingeshvari temple, Bhuiya, not Brahmin, priests performed the rites.[75] The two ritual systems existed side by side.

The archaeological remains and local traditions did not throw light on developments of the next 150 years. From the history of the wider area, the general drift of these can be established. From about 1050, the Bhanja rajas were feudatories of the Somavamsa dynasty. At the beginning of the twelfth century, they came under of the Ganga kings of Odisha. Around 1110, the town of Khiching was destroyed by the Ganga general Purushottam in a war for control of the Sambalpur region.[76] At the end of the twelfth century and in the early thirteenth century, the political constellation in the wider area was unsettled. To the north, Muhammad Bakhtiyar plundered Bihar and Bengal, and threatened Odisha with his Khiljis. In 1206, the Muslims of Bengal invaded Odisha. After 1211, its Ganga king repulsed the Muslims from Odisha and a few decades later, in 1230, expressed his supremacy through the Jagannath cult in the coastal areas. These disturbances had left considerable room for local arrangements. That can be seen in the religious field. The cults of the small kings in the hills continued to respond to more local needs.[77] In the area immediately to the north of Khiching, the response was preceded by a significant political shift.

In Benugarh, the last king of the dynasty[78] died without issue, and the old *divan* (prime minister) of the state, who had trouble controlling the Bhuiya population, invited three Singh brothers who were in the area after serving in Orissa, to come and rule. The local Bhuiya chiefs condoned or supported this move. Tradition gave 1205 as the year in which Darpa Narayan Singh, the first ruler of the Singh dynasty, effectively succeeded to the kingdom.[79]

To understand this development, we must look at the different groups inhabiting the area. Again, the evidence here is mostly, but not exclusively, archaeological. Just north of Khiching, numerous remains were left behind by Sarawaks or Saraks, who are believed to have been Jains. Some 204 old tanks were attributed to the Saraks,[80] and traces of Sarak presence were found in thirty villages.[81] The location of some of these villages suggested colonisation along routes to the north and the north-east.[82] Tuckey also found Dorowas or Gonds to the north of Khiching. They were seen as the oldest inhabitants. Their traces were all over the south of Hodisum, where, it seemed, the Bhuiyas had displaced them.[83] The Bhuiya presence was heaviest in the south-west, though. In historical times, there were also Bhuiya chiefs in the north-west of Singhbhum.[84] In all, more than twenty villages of the Kolhan Government Estate had a presence of Pauri Devi and on that ground could be considered as Bhuiya villages.[85]

The likely chain of events would be that there were Jains (Saraks/Sarawaks), Hindus and Gonds (Dorowas) in the Khiching–Benisagar area. From the south and west, groups of Bhuiyas immigrated, mainly into a virgin territory, but some settled in villages previously inhabited by Dorowas and Saraks. Sometime in this process, at the beginning of the thirteenth century, the old political order to the north of Khiching town collapsed.

The Bhuiyas there invited the Singhs, who founded Singhbhum. Their cooperation was expressed in the cult of the local goddess, not Khichingeshvari of the Bhanjas, but Ma Paudi or Pauri Devi.[86] The chronicle put the mythical advent of Pauri Devi in Singhbhum in 1215, the year the Porahat fort was established. Her definite transfer to the temple in Porahat took place a few years later.[87] One should not take the fort and temple as measures of strength only. Porahat was a bit eccentric place, in the hills off the main road. The plains to its north-east would be—or become—economically and demographically more important. Apparently, Porahat was chosen 'on account of its inaccessibility'.[88] From then on, we know a lot more about the history of the area. The Singh dynasty had a chronicle, the *Vamsa Prabha Lekhana*. From this list of rajas and their exploits, one can tentatively reconstruct local developments.[89]

The Bhuiyas were not the only ones to reckon with in the area. The Singhbhum rajas' chronicle also mentioned 'Kols', the pejorative name the Hindus used for the original population of the Chotanagpur area, especially the speakers of Munda languages.[90] The first time the chronicle mentioned 'Kols' was in the thirteenth century, immediately after the installation of Pauri Devi in Porahat. At that time, the 'Kols' had assembled with the intention of leaving Singhbhum for the neighbouring state of Surguja from where they had come.[91] In the economic conditions of the Middle Ages,[92] the struggle was to keep people on the land.[93] The raja of Singhbhum, Achuta, had to use all his persuasive powers to make them stay. It is possible that they saw the worship of Pauri Devi as an accommodation with the Bhuiyas only and insisted on a similar pact for themselves. They swore an oath, which called for witnesses the grass, the Buru Bonga (the god or spirit of the mountain, one of the main figures of the Munda pantheon), the tiger and the Brahmins.[94] As Brahmins represented the Hindu sphere, apparently the oath was binding on the raja as well.

Singhbhum's history was not a quiet one. In the period from 1270 to 1590, there were eleven uprisings, five by the Bhuiyas, three by the 'Kols', plus two uprisings of the two peoples together and one ethnically unspecified, led by a Tanti (weaver).[95] Every generation there was one major disturbance. The uprisings of the 'Kols' did not always coincide with those of the Bhuiyas. That suggests that the two peoples had their own agendas. After the difficult start in 1215, the relations between the Singh rajas and the 'Kols' remained uneasy. When the latter rebelled, they were, according to the chronicle, 'put down with a stern hand'. The chronicle did not elaborate on these events. It did mention once that the 'Kols' burnt houses and added that after the suppression of these disturbances, many of them went into hiding. The disturbances ended with reconciliation.[96] The chronicle did not dwell on the causes of the disagreements, nor did it mention the terms of the reconciliations. It shows that every thirty years, large parts of the population rejected the rule of the Singhs, which was then renegotiated.

Barring one striking exception to which we shall come shortly, the chronicle was silent about events in the wider area, even when, as in the fourteenth century, these caused major changes. In 1361, the Sultan of Delhi Feroz Shah Tughlaq invaded Odisha and had Khiching destroyed.[97] In 1398, the Bhanja dynasty split into the elder Mayurbhanj and the younger Keonjhar branches.[98] The branches of the Bhanj dynasty remained connected, but the social history of their states diverged slightly.[99] The centre of gravity of the Bhanj kingdom shifted away from the Khiching area. The Bhanjas moved their capital much closer to the coastal plains and changed the name of their kingdom to Mayurbhanj.[100]

In Singhbhum, the second half of the sixteenth century showed increasing tensions. From 1540 up to the 1560s, in a new development, the Singh rajas tried to force Hindu rituals and higher taxes on their subjects.[101] Perhaps these higher taxes were caused by developments in Odisha, again unnoticed by the chronicle. In 1568, during the invasion of the Afghans which destroyed Gajapati rule, a Singhbhum ruler fell fighting the Afghans.[102] This suggested that Singhbhum was obliged to help Mayurbhanj militarily. After their defeat, the Mayurbhanj rulers had to pay the Afghans a heavy tribute to keep their internal autonomy.[103] If the Singhs were feudatories of Mayurbhanj raja, they had to pass on the burden to their subjects.

With Raja Ranjit Singh ascending the throne in 1581, the chronicle became more eloquent. He soon had to face a general popular rebellion in Singhbhum. All the major groups, the Kols, Saraks, Rautias, and Kat Bhuiyas, united to burn the Singh palace. The raja had to hide the Pauri Devi. He fled first to Jodhpur and then to Delhi. There he met Emperor Akbar. In the chronicle, revolts of the Bhuiyas often led to hiding the statue of the tutelary goddess.[104] Even so, the Delhi part was new.

In Delhi, the chronicle continues, Ranjit of Singhbhum made friends with Akbar's general Man Singh. He accompanied him on his expedition to Orissa in 1592.[105] Fortunately, from other sources we are well informed about Man Singh's restructuring of Odisha. Here, the policy of the Mughals was not to ask more from their feudatories than military service or a light rent.[106] The raja of Khurda, the most important state of Odisha, was recognised as the sovereign of more than thirty fiefs and received the title of Maharaja. Man Singh recognised eight other rajas, among these was the raja of Mayurbhanj,[107] which had become an extensive state, comprising much of Odisha's north-east.[108] Singhbhum with only one fort was considered part of Mayurbhanj.[109] As Man Singh did not want to go to Singhbhum in person[110] and as the raja of Mayurbhanj, too, did not show much interest in the area, Ranjit of Singhbhum had to deal with its unruly inhabitants himself. He used this opportunity to put his rule on a firmer base.

Early in the 1590s, the chronicle recorded, Ranjit returned to the south of Singhbhum, took the statue of Pauri Devi from its hiding place and made peace with the insurgents of the south and central parts of Singhbhum.[111] When he sent for his family in Nagpur where they had fled, his brother Bikram brought his bride and '60 families of Ho Bantria' with him. These families came from the Urugaon, a village in Nagpur, and acted as carriers of the dowry. They were settled close to Jagannathpur, where they changed their clan name to Singko 'because they were brought by the Simhas'.[112]

Immigration of Munda speakers was not unique to Singhbhum. In the seventeenth century, the neighbouring states of Bonai, Keonjhar and Mayurbanhj, too, encouraged Mundas, Hos or Kolhas, Santals—and in Bonai also Oraons—to come. The aim was to increase cultivation and, often, these immigrants paid higher rents than the Bhuiyas.[113] The Singhbhum chronicle did not mention the tenure of the Ho Bantria immigrants. Tenures for military service were well known in the Singh area, but these Ho Bantria seemed to have settled on other terms.

Just after 1590 was the earliest date that the chronicle—and as we shall see, this part was written a mere fifty years after the event—used the name 'Hos'. Before, Munda speakers had trickled into the north of the Kolhan, where they cleared its forests. Now, the raja of Singhbhum invited some Mundas or Hos much more south. Sixty families would mean some 300 people; this must have been a fraction of all the Munda speakers in Singhbhum. But these newcomers lived near the power centre of the Singhbhum state. Consequently, the importance of the Munda-speaking groups increased. This was the turning point in the political and ethnic history of Singhbhum.

The first decennia of the seventeenth century saw major changes, even though the chronicle did not always acknowledge this. Ranjit Singh's second successor, Udit Narayan Singh, moved to Champua on the south bank of the Baitarani River. He quelled severe unrest in his area to the north of the river, and here, possibly, we hear for the last time of the Saraks, who together with the Dorowas and Bhuiyas, were indicated as 'the Kols of Benusagar'.[114]

Some vaguely datable proofs of the end of Sarak presence were mango orchards. Mango trees were not integral to the Bhuiya or Ho horticulture. Old mango orchards were mentioned as late as 1868.[115] Mango trees can get as old as 300 years, and some reach 500 years—but with individual trees, one does not talk about orchards. Thus, the approximate end date for a constructive presence of Sarak is a bit after 1600. Even so, their supremacy, if indeed it was ever there, could have ended long before. The evidence points to the desertion of the villages by the Saraks. Their villages were either taken over by the Bhuiyas or left deserted till the Hos repopulated them.[116]

In the north and west of Singhbhum, Udit's successors strengthened their base—and awoke strong resistance. Lal Mohan Singh III rebuilt a temple at Goilkera, 12 km south-east from Porahat, and put down a localised revolt of the Bhuiyas. His successor Mahipat introduced militia, that is, military tenures, in about sixteen places in the northern and western parts of the present-day West Singhbhum.[117] He was succeeded by Kashiram Singh II, who, again turning south-east, conquered Nagra, the main fort of Saranda *pir*.[118] When Kashiram was thus engaged, 'Kols' from Nagpur invaded Singhbhum. In the first instance, 'Hos of Balandia and Dukri drove them back'.[119] That was the second time the chronicle called local Munda speakers Hos, and the first time Balandia was mentioned—the place that was to play a central role in the first half of the nineteenth century. In 1641, the Nagpur 'Kols' once more returned and burnt Porahat. Now the Bhuiyas revolted and again the Pauri Devi was removed.

At that low point in Singh history, the queen gave birth to a son, Chhatrapati. Kashiram II had to flee to Khurda in Odisha. After a few weeks, he returned and after several years had the fortress of Porahat rebuilt.[120] The question is how Kashiram achieved this remarkable change of fortune. Here, we can turn to the story the Hos told Tickell in the 1830s. As with the first 'Kol' invasion, the Singh party turned to the Hos for support.[121] Even then, it took Kashiram Singh II several years to pacify his realm and give it an ideological foundation.

The return to power of Kashiram Singh II seemed the appropriate moment to 'copy' the old *Vamsa Prabha Lekhana*, the Singhbhum chronicle, 'moth eaten and broken in parts'.[122] Kashiram gave this task to Maguni Rout Dogra, who wrote that he completed his task 'with much difficulty' in the month of Vesak (April–May) 1643.[123] Though it contained older material, the chronicle must have been partly rewritten and thus showed the preoccupations of the Singh dynasty at that time.

The ideological kernel of the chronicle was that the Singhs were Rajputs. Maguni Rout Dogra gave a double foundation myth, in which a first Singh dynasty was given a start in the seventh century, and the second, the historical dynasty, a start in 1205.[124] The Rajputhood of each Singh dynasty was stated.[125] This claim of rajas that they were Rajputs was common all over the east of India. Man Singh's successes tied the Odisha states to the Mughal Empire. This heralded a shift in the foundations of princely legitimacy. The rajas, who earlier considered themselves Kshatriyas, the traditional warrior caste, now established themselves as Rajputs.[126] The 1643 rewrite of the chronicle coincided in time and in content with other attempts to 'Rajputisation' of local rulers in the area. With it, the Singhs placed themselves in the wider cultural environment of the Mughal Empire. This was what Kulke has called the 'horizontal or external legitimisation' of new rulers amongst the established rajas of Odisha.[127] So did the Nagbanshis up north in Chotanagpur, who became fief holders of the Mughal emperor.[128]

The recurring internal political message of the chronicle was that the Singhs were rulers over the Bhuiya population.[129] The chronicle showed that with each major rebellion, a priority of the Singh rajas was to keep the statue of Pauri Devi out of the hands of the Bhuiyas. It was the religious charter of Singh supremacy in the area. As for the Hos, the chronicle said little about them.[130] But they had been called 'Hos' for the first time. It could well be that, at least in 1643 when the chronicle was rewritten, there were two types of Munda speakers for the Singhs. One was the 'Kol', the foreign invader or the local who refused to pay taxes. The other was the 'Ho', an ally of some sort, who at the conclusion of the alliance was referred to by his own name: 'Ho' instead of the pejorative 'Kol'.

Finally, in the field of relations further abroad, there was a reference in the chronicle to a visit to Delhi by the thirteenth-century founder of the dynasty, Raja Darpa.[131] It cleared the way for the professions of friendship between the Singhs and the Mughals in the part of the chronicle dealing with the events around 1590. It is probable that Ranjit Singh returned to Singhbhum in 1592 as a largely nominal feudatory of the Mayurbhanj raja. The chronicle was silent on this point. Instead, it moved Ranjit's return to 1590, two years before Man Singh's reorganisation of Orissa. Thus, both Ranjit's relation to Man Singh and the date of his return to Singhbhum pre-empted a claim of Mayurbhanj to the overlordship of Singhbhum. In the chronicle at least, Ranjit was his own man. So was, fifty years later in 1643, Kashiram II who had the chronicle re-edited.

The rule was re-established, the chronicle rewritten. Over the next decades, the Singhbhum rajas continued to do well. Kashiram's son was Chhatrapati the Great, whom we have seen as an infant refugee from foreign invasion. He ruled in the 1650s and 1660s under favourable external circumstances. In 1657–58, the neighbouring states of Keonjhar and Mayurbhanj became weaker, as they joined an unsuccessful rebellion of the Odisha states. When in 1660 the new Mughal governor of Odisha took office, his first act was to treacherously slay the raja of Mayurbhanj, *'den grooten radja Kristna Bens'*, the great king Krishna Bhanj, during an interview.[132] At this time of crisis in Mayurbhanj, Chhatrapati moved his Singhbhum out of its sphere and consolidated his kingdom. Singhbhum reached its greatest expansion.

Chhatrapati's greatest achievement as a ruler, and indicated in some detail in the chronicle, was the introduction of the *pir* or cantonment system. There had been references to individual areas inside or near the Singh countries before. The chronicle mentioned some recognisable areas as *pirs*, such as Singhpukuria (Singh Pokharia, 5 km south of Chaibasa), Chiru in the north and Jamda in the south. Other names such as Khiru and Dasa were not used later on.[133] Chhatrapati, probably building upon the work of his grandfather Mahapit, attempted to make the cantonments/*pirs* parts of a system and connected this with defence requirements. He convened a meeting at Asantalia at which 'all the Nayaks and Paiks' were present.[134] Chhatrapati 'instructed them as to how to keep peace in the country'. Altogether, Chhatrapati employed over 200 soldiers. That was, for the time and place, a huge number.[135] These were not full-time soldiers, but people who got a piece of land on the condition of fulfilling military duties. About 160 of these, he placed in seven small garrisons of ten to thirty persons. Some of these garrisons looked rather isolated and from their orders, it seemed that these were forward barriers to keep out people from neighbouring lands, Rautiyas, Pahari Bhuiyas from Bonai and Dorowas from Mayurbhanj. On the Keonjhar border, where a major trade route entered Singhbhum, the orders were merely to arrest 'any shady person'. The centre of his defensive system was Govindpur, 10 km south-west of Chakradharpur at the northern bank of the Sanjay River. Here was the eighth and largest garrison, with 60 soldiers, and the order was to shoot people coming into Singhbhum, which name probably indicated the cultivated part of the state.[136]

There is no evidence that Hos played a significant part in the *pir* system. The chronicle did not mention 'Kols' as troops of Chhatrapati, but it did mention four mankis. Chhatrapati had to ask leaders of the Munda-speaking villages in the wooded area in the east and south of Hodisum to keep their people from stealing cattle, which does not suggest that he had a firm grip there. It was significant that the *pirs* did not have Ho names.[137] The ideal number of twelve villages indicated the military and revenue function of the *pir* for the Singh state.

Chhatrapati's rule was the high point of Singh power. He was strong in the stretch between Chakradharpur and Porahat, had quite some influence in the north of Hodisum and had garrisons in the south on the borders with Saranda, Bonai, Keonjhar and Mayurbhanj. Chhatrapati was the last ruler to get a detailed treatment in the *Vamsa*. After this towering figure, the chronicle became enumerative and sketchy.[138] We have to augment it with what we can reasonably infer from other sources.

Chhatrapati's son was Arjun Singh II, nicknamed Kala. He further expanded his realm. To the south-west of Porahat and close to Saranda, he conquered Anandpur, which he gave to his youngest son as a fief.[139] Kala Arjun also tried to settle the lands to his east and south-east. In the 1640s, as we have seen, there had been already an alliance of the Hos of Balandia with his grandfather Kashiram, an alliance that superseded that of the Singhs with the Buiyas and, thus, changed the course of the history of these parts.[140] Now, a few decennia later, his grandson Kala Arjun conferred titles of 'Sirdar' (manki) to Hos in places to the east and south-east of Jagannathpur.[141]

Even more ambitious was that Kala Arjun probably[142] destroyed Chamakpur, west of Champua in Keonjhar, and to commemorate his victory (*jaint*) constructed a mud fort (*garh*) on the Singhbhum side of the Baitarani River opposite Champua.[143] Jaintgarh was a strategic site and it commanded what was to become a market place of relative importance. Much later, in the 1830s, in villages around Jaintgarh there were Odia-speaking Hindu cultivators and *paiks*, people who were given rent-free tenures for military service.[144] These tenures could date from Kala Arjun's time, but it is well possible that at least some were given out by his predecessor Chhatrapati when he put twenty soldiers in the area to guard the passage over the river.[145] It suggested that Jaintgarh fort was the military part of a scheme of Hinduisation and possibly commercialisation at the southern border. In it, the Bhuiyas and Hos had a marginal role at best.

The position of the shrines was significant here and could well be an arrangement by Kala Arjun himself. But again, our information comes from much later. In the centre of the fort was a small shrine with the idol of Jatapath. At least till 1910 the Bhuiyas offered small clay horses to this idol. Pauri Devi was also offered toy horses, but her place was only at the entrance of the fort.[146] Apparently, at the time Arjun constructed the fort the worship of Pauri Devi was not his central interest. Nor were the Hos.

Jaintgarh was very important to Singhbhum. The chronicle of Chotanagpur mentioned the place as 'the then seat of the Singhbhum raja' when Kala Arjun's son Jagannath Singh III had a nasty conflict with Ram Shah, the ruler of Chotanagpur (probably 1690–1715).[147] Jagannath refused to take care of the transport of the bride of Ram Shah, traditionally a service rendered by a subordinate. According to the annals of the Nagbhansi family, Ram Shah attacked Jaintgarh and burnt down the town several times. Jagannath did not give in. At the conclusion of peace, Jagannath gave his two sisters in marriage to Ram Shah, but he remained independent.[148] The chronicles did not mention the establishment or re-establishment of Singh authority in the area beyond Jaintgarh. The Fortress of Victory was the *nec plus ultra*[149] of Singh power.

In the first years of the eighteenth century, the death of the next raja Purushottam II of Singhbhum caused a split in the Singh family. This period was very badly covered by the chronicle, and we are mostly dependent on such information as has found its way into British sources. Purushottam II died while his wife was *enceinte*.[150] Bikram, the brother of the deceased king, became the guardian of the newborn boy, Arjun.[151] Around 1720,[152] when Raja Arjun Singh III reached maturity, he donated the town of Saraikela with twelve villages to his uncle.[153] From this base, Bikram extended his lands by force. He defeated neighbouring Patkum, and conquered Kharsawan and Asantalia. Bikram, in turn, donated the small town of Kharsawan to his second son.[154] While Saraikela was growing in strength, the division of the Singh lands had weakened the senior branch in Porahat. Moreover, another player in the field was reinventing himself.

In the crucial period up to 1767, the descendants of the Munda-speaking first inhabitants of the wooded hills of the north and of the retinue of a Chotanagpur bride settled in the centre of Singhbhum, further colonised the southern Kolhan and the west of Bamanghati. Further colonisation, because the chronicle mentioned 'Hos' in that area long before. We have seen the Hos of Balandia as allies of Kashiram in 1641.[155] The pattern of occupation was much less the nuclear village of the northern Munda-speaking parts, but rather individual farmsteads, which suited a rapid colonisation more than a conquest. Bhuiyas continued to live in the area in small numbers.[156] While the Singhbhum state continued to exist, the overall power-shift was clear. The Munda speakers in the present-day Kolhan rendered irrelevant the military function of most of the Singh forts and, with some marginal exceptions, stopped paying taxes to the Singhs. The *pirs* ceased to be effective administrative divisions of the Singh states, though their names continued to be used. The largest of them were furthest from the borders with the Singh states. It could well be that as the Hos moved into virgin lands, they extended the reach of some *pir* names, but in these new lands, they did not always even select a manki, the head of a circle of villages.[157]

In the 1760s it appeared that there was no way the Porahat raja Jagannath Singh IV, the grandson of Arjun Singh III, could regain control over the Ho lands through his own powers. He needed a powerful ally. Mayurbhanj was the traditional big neighbour. However, at that time it was not particularly powerful, as it had suffered from the Afghan–Maratha rivalry of the 1740s.[158] Like the rest of Odisha, Mayurbhanj went to the Marathas in 1751. The new rule heralded an economic decline in the area. The Battle of Panipat of 1761 left both the Afghans and the Marathas seriously weakened.[159] By that time, Mayurbhanj was, as we shall shortly see, engaged elsewhere.

Jagannath Singh had to consider other options. He had many family ties with the rajas in the region, mainly on the route from Chotanagpur to Sambalpur.[160] One of these, the raja of Chotanagpur Dripnath Sahi, ruled just north of Singhbhum.[161] Chotanagpur was a nominal part of the Mughal Empire. It is probable that the Marathas, too, considered it as their tributary. These claims did not, however, make much difference on the ground. Dripnath Sahi took pains to keep his hold on dominions in the area between Ranchi and the Singhbhum border, (which recently had been incorporated into Chota Nagpur by his relative and predecessor Mani Nath Shah), even when he continued to run into serious difficulties with Tamar.[162] His marriage alliance with states such as Keonjhar and Sambalpur spoke of his ambitions.[163]

In 1762, on the invitation of Jagannath of Singhbhum, Dripnath came 'at the head of more than twenty thousand men' for a joint operation against the Hos. This was what Major Roughsedge learned in 1820.[164] The number of 20,000 troops need not be taken literally and might well have been a conventional term of a treaty of alliance.[165] The Hos defeated this large force and caused, as informants told sixty years later, 'immense slaughter'.[166]

A few years after that failure, Jagannath Singh of Singhbhum tried to go at it alone against the Hos.[167] He fought the battle in 'the centre of an extensive and elevated plain'. In 1820, Roughsedge got the story from what he called an eyewitness. It sounded like a Ho song, this noonday heat in the month of May; this pursuit of soldiers of the beaten army running for their lives, collapsing from thirst on the stretch of more than seventeen kilometres to the very border of the Ho country. That was a 'steep ascent', which places the battle on the plains close to Chakradharpur.[168] The rout of this invasion force cost Jagannath 'many hundreds' of men.[169]

Jagannath's power was already weakened by the rise of Saraikela and the failure of his attempt together with Dripnath to retake the Kolhan. The second failure showed that it was beyond repair. He was outclassed in his own Porahat by his cousin Subnath Singh, possibly the *divan* of Singhbhum. He 'leaves him at the enjoyment of his liberty together with the name of ruling, tho' . . . [Subnath] keeps the power in his own hands and obliges [Jagannath] to act in whatever manner he pleases.'[170]

Mayurbhanj gave Jagannath a new idea. In 1764 the Keonjhar and Mayurbhanj rajas had joined an uprising against the Marathas, which failed the next year. Still, in the following years, Damodar Bhanj of Mayurbhanj with some success played the East India Company off against the Marathas.[171] He agreed to pay revenue to the Company for a small territory considered to be part of Midnapur, while he evaded paying taxes to the Marathas. He rightly or wrongly gave the impression that he, as George Vansittart wrote, was 'desirous of shaking off the yoke of the Marathas' and to come under 'the English'.[172] Jagannath, too, turned to the new power on the horizon, the East India Company.

In the 1760s the British East India Company had become a territorial power of consequence in eastern India.[173] In 1765, the Company acquired the *Divani*, the right to rule and to tax Bengal and Bihar. In March 1766, Governor General Harry Verelst ordered Graham, the resident of Midnapur on the south-western border of Bengal, to send an expedition into the hilly jungle tracts to the west of Midnapur.[174] The task of the commanding officer, Ensign John Ferguson,[175] was to see how far the *Divani* extended here and to establish effective overlordship over the local chiefs included in it.[176] It was tough work. Ferguson's troops found themselves opposed by some 2,000 men armed with spears, arrows and swords. They marched over 50 km through dense jungle, continually running into ambushes and sniper fire. In early April 1767, Ferguson captured the ageing Dhalbhum chief who had been the leader of the resistance. He installed his hopefully more pliant young nephew Jagannath Dhal in Ghatsila, the capital of Dhalbhum.

At that moment, representatives of Patkum and Singhbhum visited Ferguson. Both came from countries through which salt merchants made a tax evasion detour. They expressed the wish of their rajas to submit to the East India Company. They gave their reasons; these implied their requests. They were 'constantly oppressed by a neighbour who made a practice and trade of plundering and carrying off their effects'.[177] There was no time to get down to the details of the proposed deal and especially to get more information about that oppressive neighbour lurking in the background.

The question of Singhbhum came up again in December 1767, when the new resident of Midnapur Vansittart found Pitamber Singh, another uncle of Raja Jagannath Singh of Singhbhum, waiting for him. There was more to Singhbhum than just a troublesome neighbour. The palace, too, was in trouble. Pitamber said that Jagannath was 'kept under confinement by his cousin Subnath Singh'.[178] The hard-pressed raja asked for the Company's assistance, in return for which he was 'desirous of putting his territories under their protection and paying them an annual revenue'.

As Pitamber's account is the first modern written information on the Singhbhum tract, it is worth a full quotation.

> It is bounded in the north by Patkum, on the west by Nagpur and Gangpur (Maratha districts) on the south by Keonjhar and Mayurbhanj, on the East by Barabhum and Ghatsila, two districts belonging to these jungles [which are part of the British *Divani*]; and it stretches itself in length from north-east to south-west between 128 and 160 kilometres, and in breadth from north-west to south-east about 26 or 32 kilometres. It formerly contained near 14,000 villages but only about 500 are at present in the raja's possession; of the others some are gone to ruin and the rest are in the hands of the Kols, a tribe of plundering banditti.[179]
>
> The face of the country is in general plain and open: it contains only a few straggly hills, has very little jungle in it, and no fortresses of importance.
>
> The raja is by marriage a distant relation of the Sambalpur raja: there is a constant correspondence between the two districts, and an uninterrupted intercourse of merchants. They are situated from each other about 285 kilometres, and there is a tollerable (*sic*) good road the whole way between them. Singhbhum was never

reduced under the dominion of the Mughals, but for 52 generations been an independent district in the possession of the present family.[180]

The inflated figures were bad marketing. In fact, Pitamber suggested that the East India Company would take on an unknown but militarily able power based in a whopping 13,500 villages. That number was an obvious falsehood. The general drift of his description remained true. The smaller part of Singhbhum was still under the raja. But the main body of his realm with much of a transit route for salt was gone. The Hos had scooped out the state of Singhbhum.

George Vansittart saw a chance here of easier communications with Sambalpur, a buffer state against the Marathas. He explained to Calcutta that he had directed Ferguson to make 'all the inquiries he could' about Singhbhum and had found that Ferguson's findings supported Pitamber Singh's account.[181] Calcutta, anxious to reduce risk, ordered ('recommended') Vansittart to 'send an intelligent person to Singhbhum to acquire knowledge of the country, the strength of the fortresses, and particularly to find out whether the Marathas had any claim, or ever had any pretensions to the country'. Two infantrymen went into the Hodisum, but after about 3.5 km they were forced to go back.[182] Their recce compromised, they did their best while staying at the border. Their findings again confirmed Pitamber's information, except that Jagannath Singh was not confined, even though he was totally in the power of his cousin Subnath. Importantly, the soldiers were 'positive that the jurisdiction of the Marathas never extended to this [area], nor do they receive the smallest revenue from it'.[183] Still, the Marathas were in nearby Odisha, between the important Company possessions of Bengal and Madras. Therefore, Harry Verelst wrote back that he preferred to postpone action in Singhbhum as he hoped 'soon to gain possession of Cuttack' in Odisha.[184] Contrary to what Verelst had in mind in 1768, Cuttack, or rather Odisha, would have to wait until 1803.[185]

The question of Singhbhum was not taken up until 1818. There were local reasons as well as strategic considerations for this. The area to the east of Singhbhum was nominally under the Company, but it was a mess which proved not easy to sort out. The local chiefs had a habit of raiding each other's territory, to which now was added the habit of sticking together when East India Company troops came in to address complaints. At the bottom of this was their inability to raise significant amounts of revenue. Still in 1768, the fighting took to the jungle. What followed was a military nightmare for the East India Company troops, ill-suited to fight a jungle guerrilla. In the classic formulation of Captain Morgan,

> It is all a joke to talk of licking these jungle fellows: they have not the least idea of fighting, they are like a parcel of wasps. They endeavour to sting you with their arrows, and then fly off. It is impossible almost to kill any of them . . . I wish to God this business was over.[186]

The area was restless till the former raja of Ghatsila, Jagannath Dahl, was re-installed in 1777. It remained difficult to get any tribute or tax revenue from the west of Midnapur.[187] It was hard for the Company to assess the ramifications of possible action in the area. Apparently, there was more to Singhbhum than just the Singhs.

And then there was the general strategic situation to be considered. The Maratha states and the East India Company were contenders for supremacy in northern India. Between the territories of these superpowers was a grey zone of tracts and small states, which could be used by either side as buffers.[188] The operative word here is 'could'. Neither the Marathas nor the East India Company needed Singhbhum, nor were they involved in it. The area was a strategic no-man's land. The superpowers' strategy of non-involvement here implied that things ran their own course. That calls for some reflection on the relations between the Hos and the states of Singhbhum.

Ethnogenesis and the state

The Chotanagpur plateau had a dynamic ethnic history. Looking over the centuries, we saw people on the plateau migrating over considerable distances and settling in new areas. Following the nineteenth-century preoccupations, many historians tend to see this as a history of ethnic invasions, replacements and retreats.[189] That explains the question which appears time and again, 'where do the Hos come from?' However, until late in history, one cannot explain the ethnic situation in Chotanagpur in political or military terms. People did not migrate in large ethnic groups, but rather in small groups of a few families organised for the purpose. Though violence was not absent, they more often than not moved into virgin lands where their agricultural skills and organising capacities enabled them to have a decent living. The result was that they formed ethnically quite homogeneous pockets of habitation. For a long time, opportunity defined the ethnic distribution over the land. That was to change but slowly, and against a lot of opposition, with the development of the state on the plateau from the twelfth to the eighteenth century. In the end, it was politics and military strength, not so much opportunity, that defined the ethnic architecture of the land.

In Singhbhum that final supremacy of politics was not the same as the supremacy of the state. Let us, therefore, review the developments there, especially where they concern the Hos. One such fairly homogeneous ethnic pocket was, as we have seen, the north of Singhbhum where the Munda speakers must have been the first to clear the forests. As the names of many of their *kilis* show, the people here came from the area of the Tebo Ghat on the present road to Ranchi. Also more south, in parts of Porahat, were such Munda speaking areas. We have seen that here 'Kols' (Munda speakers) were noticed in one of the earliest entries in the Singhbhum *Vamsa*, referring to the second half of the thirteenth century.

Immigration and expansion of the Munda speaking groups went on. But the development of the state on the plateau, which went slowly, meant increasing demands for taxes and services, and that disturbed the population of these ethnic pockets. After a long series of disturbances, one in each generation, there was a general uprising of the tribals in 1590. When it was quelled, 'Ho Bantria' families were settled near Jagannathpur in the western part of the southern plains. That increased the importance of the Munda speakers already in the area while decreasing the role of the Bhuiyas. We see that the Munda speakers, now called by their own name Hos, were instrumental in restoring Kashiram Singh II against Bhuiya rebellion and foreign tribal invasion around 1640. The Hos were important, and they were armed. But when his successor Chhatrapati reorganised his lands in fiscal and military units, the Hos did not participate much in his scheme. A few decades later, his son Kala Arjun made agreements with Ho villages deep in the jungle such as Balandia. The Hos were now firmly established in the south, as well.

Thus, in the run-up to the eighteenth century, ethnicity became more of an organising idea, especially when it came to resistance against overbearing outsiders. That was not unique to Singhbhum. In many parts of the world, stated Richard Tapper, 'tribes and states have created and maintained each other in a single system, though one of inherent instability'.[190] That was not necessarily a one-way influence emanating from the states, in India often resulting in Hinduisation. On the contrary, a tribe could have a great impact on the states in its neighbourhood. As it had in Singhbhum.

In the eighteenth century, when the Singh states were weak, the Hos consolidated their area in some major battles, and quickly expanded into the southern and eastern areas. In the process, a new awareness came to the Munda speakers in the Kolhan. Their successful defiance and defence added political separation to the considerable cultural and linguistic differences with the Hindu population of the Singh states. There is evidence that the social distance with the Munda speaking population of the area of the Tebo Ghat, still under the Singhs, also grew. As we have seen, the names of many Ho *kilis* refer to that area. But at present, the pronunciation of Ho is closer to that of Naguri Munda spoken closer to Ranchi, than to Hasada Munda spoken around Khunti and north of the Tebo Ghat. Deeney, who drew attention to this, suggested several reasons: the Hasada accent could have changed only after the ancestors of the Hos had left; or the Mundas who are now in the area of the Tebo Ghat had 'come in later through the Northeast', Hasada area.[191] Whatever the cause, a growing difference in accent between groups indicates a growing social and cultural distance.

To become a people, as Pallottino has so eloquently demonstrated, the convergence of cultural, ethnic, linguistic and political elements into a new whole must take place.[192] Thus, in the period between 1717 and 1767, the Hos constituted themselves as a people. They called themselves Hos, just 'people'. The lands from the banks of the Sanjay River in the north to the banks of the Baitarani River in the south, from the hills of Lagra in the east to the hills of Saranda in the west, became Hodisum, 'the land of (our) people'.

Most of the neighbouring Hindu chiefs still claimed parts of Hodisum, but after 1767 they did not even try to enter the Ho lands. Seen from the local states, the Hos' freedom from outside control and taxes was, of course, ultimately political. That is why contemporary commentators called this 'independence'.[193] The Singh rulers and other neighbours recognised that by calling the Hos 'Larka Kols'. Larka Kol meant 'fighting man'. The Hos, too, saw themselves as people who were willing and able to resist interference.[194]

To what extent was Ho society able or willing to set itself up as a political entity that could interact with the states around?[195] Actually, very little. With the retreat of the Singhs, the Chhatrapati *pir* system became defunct in the Ho lands. Their own mankis were not nuclei for a Ho administrative set-up.[196] Even in 1819, more than fifty years after Jagannath's admission of defeat, there was no Ho political or military organisation other than alliances of villages or of members of the same *kili* (clan). The Hos had no need for permanent political consultations or military command structures. Their combined military power made them superior in the area. As far as they could see, they were not threatened from outside.

By 1767, then, the Hos had largely turned their backs towards the outside world. The great majority of the Hos lived outside the reach of the Singh and Bhanja states or, for that matter, any other state. In 1800, they defeated an invasion from Bamanghati to establish effective rule over the eastern part of the Hodisum.[197] When finally, around 1820, the East India Company arrived in the person of Major Edward Roughsedge, people on both sides were very much aware of the ethnic and political border. The Singhs feared the Hos and called their land a 'tiger's den'. In their turn, Hos would warn other Hos to keep the Singhs out.[198]

Independence is not the same as isolation, just like contacts do not necessitate subordination. This fact is easily overlooked by historians of ethnic frontiers. The isolation of Hodisum was not complete. In 1820–21, Ghanshyam Singh and Raghunath Bisi described the political structure of the area as the Singhs saw it. They stressed the territorial aspect.[199] But their accounts also showed that the dividing lines could be blurred. Occasionally, the Singhbhum raja's fief-holder in Chakradharpur collected revenue in some villages of Gumra Pir in the Hodisum. The raja's servants exercised a customary right of passage between Porahat/Jagannathpur and Jaintgarh. Near Chakradharpur and Porahat, and also in Saraikela and Kharsawan, some Ho villages were directly under the local Hindu chief. There were some trade contacts. Inside the Hodisum, there was a demand for salt and cloth met by itinerary merchants. A few times a year, Hos visited the market in Saraikela in a group.[200] Religious or, perhaps better, spiritual beliefs possibly crossed the ethnic border. There was an—easily overstated—influence of Vaishnava beliefs on Ho songs, which could date back to Kala Arjun's time, or even to decennia earlier.[201] Between Ho and Singh areas, there was not a sharp single line.

That did not only follow from the loose organisation of the Hos as a people. It also followed from the nature of the Singh states. These were cellular states, consisting of pockets of direct control connected through a nexus of trade, revenue and family ties. A warning note by the great historian Heesterman is applicable to Singhbhum and Hodisum before the British period. It would be 'misleading', he said, to regard the Indian state of the Mughal period as 'an integrated territorial whole' within sharp boundaries.[202] The new power in the area, the East India Company, had trouble in getting a grip on the claims of the Singhs that they were the legitimate rulers of most of the Hodisum on one side, and, on the other side, the indifference to or even contempt of the most powerful people, the Hos, to these claims. To the local actors, the Singhs and the Hos, it was clear where the other stood. To an external observer from Europe with its Westfalian system of states with clearly defined borders, the lines were blurred. There was one exception in the area. The border between the northern Singh states and Hodisum was a river.[203]

How do we know that the river was the border? The agent to the governor general on the South Western Frontier, Edward Roughsedge, told us so. We started with genetic material and flint flakes as sources, went on to ruined buildings dating from the sixth to the twelfth century and to a chronicle written in 1643. In the end, in 1767, there was a fundamental change. We got the actual words of Pitamber Singh. From then on, the sources were often eye witness accounts, or could speak in the very words of the actors themselves. We enter history proper. So did the Hos.

Part I
Another People's War, 1818–1830

Chapter 1

Difficult Negotiations

...
*Ghanshyam's demands; the states of Singhbhum;
Edward Roughsedge, a biography; difficult negotiations*
...

Ghanshyam Singh, the raja of Porahat, could not be persuaded to sit down on Major Roughsedge's carpet. The carpet was large. Large enough, it soon would appear, for five or six Hos to lay on it at full length, 'and admiring what they saw for a minute or two, [to] prepare to go regularly to sleep'.[1] Both the duration of his travels and the need to uphold his status induced the British officer to go around in style with at least one large tent, a 'dining tent for business', to be transported by an elephant.[2] The carpeted tent was the greatest luxury of Major Edward Roughsedge, the Political Agent to the Governor General on the South Western Frontier.

By January 1820, Ghanshyam's demands from earlier negotiations had diminished to requests, which he made standing. After all, he had little to show but 'ruin and wretchedness',[3] and time was running out. Ghanshyam was the last of the three Singhbhum chiefs whom Roughsedge visited. On 16 January his kinsmen and rivals, the *Kunwar* (chief) of Saraikela and the *Thakur* of Kharsawan,[4] had agreed with Roughsedge to place themselves under 'the British Government' and to obey all its orders.[5] The terms as prescribed in guidelines to Roughsedge were mild.[6] Calcutta demanded only a nominal tribute.[7] The chiefs were to keep their actual possessions.[8] The Company did not want to interfere with their internal administration of the estates. Their rulers mainly were 'to prevent these districts from becoming an asylum for fugitive offenders, or being otherwise turned [in]to an injury of the public peace'.[9] In fact, Calcutta wanted a guarantee for quiet in its own possessions.

Ghanshyam Singh's wishes went further than what the Company was prepared to grant. As Roughsedge informed Calcutta, Ghanshyam 'earnestly solicited' from him the support of the East India Company to reach the following goals: recovery of the image of Pauri Devi from the *Kunwar* of Saraikela, re-establishment of his authority over Kharsawan and Saraikela, and as much assistance 'as might be necessary to check the inroads of the savage race of the Larka Kols'.[10] Roughsedge promised 'all the assistance in his power' to meet Ghanshyam's demands with the exception of the re-establishment of his authority over parts of Saraikela and Kharsawan, which went against the explicit instructions from Calcutta.[11] The dynastic status quo was not to be changed. Both sides speedily dropped discussions on this point. It is good that they did. Roughsedge knew very little about the area.

What Roughsedge had got from the raja and his feuding family in the Singhbhum states in the course of the negotiations was little, vague, and obviously biased. His first and hurried campaign against the Hos in 1820 added some direct impressions and another informant. On 15 April 1820, he compiled a tabulated overview partly with information from Ghanshyam and most probably also from Raghunath Bisi of Jaintgarh.[12] He passed this on to the commander of the Second Kolhan Campaign, Lieutenant Colonel William Richards, on 3 April 1821.[13] This letter forms the base of the following overview.

The Singhbhum group of tiny states, which had escaped the attention of the Company's rivals, the Marathas,[14] was a minor issue in the strategic environment of eastern India. As a group, the Singh states had some value because of their geographical position. They held some passes into Chotanagpur. They could serve as a strategic retreat for the opponents of the Company in the nearby notoriously unruly tracts such as Dhalbhum. The important postal road from Calcutta via Sambalpur and Nagpur to Bombay ran close to its southern borders. This, and the names of the rulers, was about all that the East India Company knew about the Singh states.

The lack of information showed on the maps. In 1778, the best mapmaker in India at the time, Rennell, gave 'Singboom' some mountains on its northern frontier, and two villages or forts.[15] A few years later, in 1818, Roughsedge was involved in the work of Captain James Nesbitt Jackson, who surveyed and built the road from Midnapur to Nagpur.[16] The road was known as 'Captain Jackson's new road'.[17] Jackson also prepared an extensive 'Map of Part of the District of Singhbhoom and the Adjacent Pergunnahs Occupied by and Subject to the Incursions of the Koles'. This first map of the area was dated May 1821, just after the conclusion of the Second Kolhan Campaign. It was precise where it showed the area that skirted the Kolhan in the north, passed through Bamanghati, and went just south of Jaintgarh. Most of the Ho lands and the west of Singhbhum apart from the town of Porahat were left blank.[18] That was about the extent of the East India Company's geographical knowledge of Singhbhum.

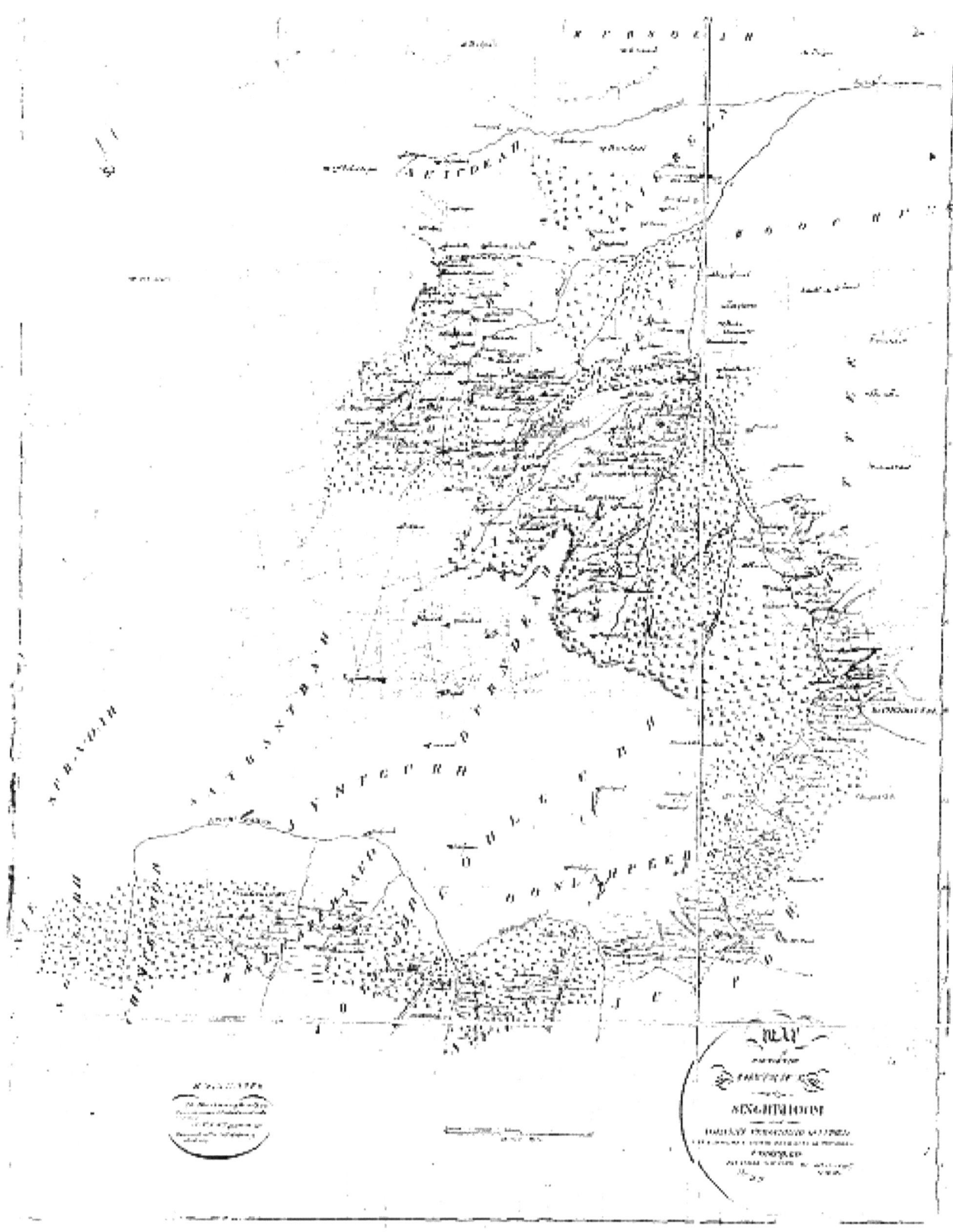

Captain Jackson's map, 1821, National Archives, Delhi.

It is unlikely that Roughsedge himself knew of any event relating to Singhbhum from before 1803.[19] In the first two decades of the nineteenth century, there had been an irregular and sparse correspondence between the East India Company and the heads of the Singhbhum group of states. Outside those rarefied diplomatic and strategic spheres, Roughsedge was but dimly aware of the area. In the season 1808–9 he had mentioned 'Singhbhum or independent territories to the southward [and] ... a range of very high mountains named Larka Pir'.[20] He understood that the territory of the Porahat raja was 'a narrow tract of country' in the south of Singhbhum, 'rapidly diminishing' from the growing power of his relatives and the Hos.[21]

The great unknown to Roughsedge were the Hos. They had figured briefly in a general survey of Central India, made in 1803. This was in Roughsedge's files. It stated that the Hos lived in 'a mountainous and rocky tract of country about 40 miles long and 31 broad'—65–50 km—and were 'perfectly savage' and completely isolated.[22] Five years later, in 1808–9, Roughsedge let his curiosity shine through when he repeated this information and mentioned 'a range of very high mountains ... inhabited by a savage and remarkable race of people with a peculiar language and customs'.[23] At the start of the negotiations some ten years later, Roughsedge instructed his right-hand man, Lieutenant David Ruddell, to collect all information about the country that he could, and 'especially of the extraordinary race called Larkas'. This did not bring much information. Ruddell could not even reach the Hos.[24]

Even with the information provided by Ghanshyam and Raghunath, Roughsedge would have but a hazy notion of the *pirs*, the cantons, inside Hodisum. He heard about Ajodhya (twelve villages) [Aujudeah on Captain Jackson's map], Rajabasa (twenty-four villages) [Rajabassa] and Chiru (twelve villages) [Cherie], all together with 2,500 bowmen. These were on the northern plain and mainly inhabited by Hos. Then there were Gumra [Goomla], containing more than 100 villages with a reputed 4,000 bowmen, and the southern part of Cheri. Roughsedge believed the Thai *pir* [Taiepeer] to the east to be 'very extensive, but [I] have no certain information on the subject.' He further mentioned 'Saint Banteree' or Bantaria [Satbantrah] with sixty villages and Balandia *pir* [Burndeah], 'which last I think touches to the east Thai Pir' and contained twelve villages. The whole of Jaintgarh [Jyntgurh] and Balandia had 3,000 bowmen, and its people were 'amongst the most refractory'.[25]

Actually, there were more *pirs* in the heartland of the Hos. Roughsedge did not mention the Mila, Rela, Latua *pirs* in the west, or the Asantalia, Kanua, Kuldiha and Sidiu *pirs* in the north of the Kolhan. In the centre, he missed Barkela. Besides Thai *pir*, which was an admitted blank in Roughsedge's overview, there were three other Kol *pirs* claimed by Bamanghati [Baumunhattee], and thus outside Singhbhum: the Bharbharia, Lalgarh [Lolgurh], and Anwla [Oonlahpeer]*pirs*. In Roughsedge's rough and incomplete calculation, then, the Hos inhabited at least 316 villages and could mobilise 9,500 men.

Roughsedge feared that the Hos would keep the region in turmoil by enlarging their area. Did the Hos expand their lands? Roughsedge's evidence was not altogether convincing. To the north of the Hodisum, he wrote, 'Larkas' raided Belsia and Basia in Chotanagpur.[26] In Chotanagpur's Sonapur, he was told, they had caused the desertion of forty villages. However, not Hos from the Kolhan conducted these raids, but Mundas living in the northern outer circle of Singhbhum. The raids of the Hos themselves, 'Larkas' from the Kolhan, did not extend to Saraikela and Kharsawan to the north. 'By good management and firmness', both chiefs had stopped encroachment on their area, Roughsedge wrote. Also, they prevented transit by Hos 'in any suspicious shape'.[27]

Although Ghanshyam made a lot of noise, on the Porahat side to the west of the Ho country, too, Roughsedge recorded no recent instances of villages laid waste or even of cattle raids. Here the losses of the raja and his relatives seemed to have occurred many decades earlier. It was difficult to establish the extent of these losses, the more so as there was no sharply drawn border. Quite a few Ho villages in Porahat itself were still under the raja.

The Hos' main attention was to Bamanghati to the east, and the states of Keonjhar, Bonai and Gangpur to the south. To take the south first, after his first invasion of the Kolhan, Roughsedge reached Keonjhar to find more than 160 of its villages ruined.[28] In Gangpur, the Hos had laid waste a number of Brahmin villages.[29] Roughsedge reported destruction, but he mentioned no instances where the Hos had recently taken over villages to live in.[30] The main aim of their raids was to take as many cattle as possible.

'The fine pastorage and abundance of Water in these mountains rendered them a favorite resort of Cowherds, and the quantities of Buffaloes carried off by the Hos of late years is almost incredible.' Roughsedge repeated here the language of an appeal. Indeed, an owner had 'made his way'—there was an attempt to arouse pity even in that, suggesting hardship on this short trip—'to me at Jaintgarh to complain'. He was 'one poor man who lost a herd of one hundred and forty about the 15th March'. Roughsedge pulled some local strings, 'and I found out by the means of some conciliated Hos, that before the end of that month eighty had been devoured, whilst of the remainder there was no chance of recovery'.[31] So the apparently not so poor man remained poorer by 140 head of cattle. Moreover, this was evidence that came too late. This raid was made on 15 March 1820, when Roughsedge had already made up his mind to invade the Hodisum.

The Hos gave serious troubles to their neighbours, but the facts did not add up to a Ho strategy or practice of ethnic expansion by force, and certainly not to one that could be thwarted by strengthening Porahat against the Hos. The troubles on the northern front of Porahat were caused by Mundas living outside the Kolhan. The Hos were troublesome on the eastern front, establishing settlements in the uncleared jungle, and allegedly by threatening the post on Jackson's Road. But they came from the four Kol *pirs* formerly belonging to Bamanghati and outside of Porahat's claims. Strengthening Ghanshyam in the Ho lands could adversely affect the raiding capacity of the Hos only to the south.

Little wonder that Roughsedge had to strike an apologetic note when he reported to Calcutta on his invasion of Hodisum. 'Referring to the length of time during which this state of things [i.e., independence] had existed, and to the line of policy laid down for my guidance in this district, I should have thought myself precluded from all interference in, or support of the raja's pretensions with regard to the Larkas, if their only crime had been the establishment of their independence, and their conduct such as could be with safety tolerated.' By then, both Roughsedge's fear of disruptions by the Hos and his suggested remedy were standard fare. In nearly all his letters on the Singhbhum question, he harped on the necessity to curb Ho power by extending the rule of the raja of Porahat. So he built up the Ho menace: 'In short, it appeared that the Larkas were a dreadful pest to the civilized part of Singhbhum and to all the adjacent chiefs.'[32]

Saraikela was the state to watch. Even Saraikela was not stronger than the Hos. Its *kunwar* Bikram felt very uneasy about his Ho neighbours.[33] But Saraikela together with the small Kharsawan were the only Singh estates that were 'at all productive'.[34] It contained 434 villages with 600 matchlocks (muskets) and 5,000 bowmen.[35] Roughsedge described Saraikela town as 'populous and Stockaded'. He drew attention to 'a few small Guns, mounted on the Walls of the *Kunwar's* House, which have tended no doubt to deter the Hos from attacking it' (see Plate 2).[36] On the negative side, a 'spirit of great animosity' existed between Bikram and the Porahat raja Ghanshyam Singh.[37] That did not bode well for peace in the Singhbhum area.

Since Bikram Singh I set Saraikela up as an independent state in the 1720s, it had been the strongest Singh state. One reason was the stability of its ruling house; unlike in Porahat, here succession had been regular from father to son. The other reason was recent territorial expansion. Around 1800 Kuchang, an outlying part of neighbouring Bamangati (that in its turn was a nominal dependency of Mayurbhanj) was annexed.[38] The oldest letter in Roughsedge's files was written soon after these events, and dated from 1803, the beginning of the war with the Marathas in Odisha. Governor General Wellesley wrote the Saraikela chief 'to make a prayer to your Highness to the effect that your Highness will be gracious enough to take measures to prevent the gang of robbers and the band of adversaries [the Marathas] from passing into the country of the English Company, through your country'. In an enclosed letter, the magistrate of Midnapur, too, addressed himself to 'The Abode of Dignity, Raja Abhiram Singh, Zamindar, District Singhbhum', and reassured him that 'it is never the intention of the British Government to take British troops through your country or to take possession of it.' An inverted threat followed: 'If a little friendship is shown to the Company Bahadur[39] at the time of need, it will do you good for ever. It is therefore proper for you that you should take suitable steps.'[40] In the years that followed, the ruler of Saraikela reacted favourably to Roughsedge's repeated requests to close the passes and apprehend fugitive opponents to the British rule. He received thanks from Roughsedge in 1808, 1810, 1817, 1818 and in June 1819 during the Tamar disturbances.[41]

A bit surprising with this history, that Roughsedge did not count on Abhiram to strengthen the Singh states. It went against his ingrained feeling that the oldest branch of the dynasty, that of Porahat, should have pre-eminence. And he did not like Abhiram's recent (1818) successor Bikram Singh II. When Roughsedge met him in 1819, he found him 'puffed up with the pride of wealth and prosperity, his constitution however is completely worn out, and though under forty he is oppressed with all the infirmities of old age. [He is] kept alive only by the constant use of opium and rapidly declining both in mind and in body.'[42]

Singhbhum

Kharsawan, a mid-eighteenth century offshoot from Saraikela, was the other viable Singh state. Its chief, Chaitan Singh, was Roughsedge's favourite, in fact 'far superior in natural disposition and acquirement to every other Chief in Singhbhum'.[43] He had 'behaved so well on all occasions'. Roughsedge considered him his most useful ally in the area.[44] The state of Kharsawan contained 84 villages with 300 matchlocks and 1,500 bowmen. The small town of the same name was described as 'large and strongly stockaded'.[45]

In Porahat, Raja Ghanshyam Singh's accession had not been in a straight line. His grandfather was Jagannath, the raja who was approaching the Company in 1767. When his grandfather's eldest son, Harihar Singh, died without issue, his second son Raghubar became raja. His son again was Ghanshyam.[46] His realm, the Porahat state, consisted of Porahat, Chakradharpur and outlying tracts. Porahat proper was the dynastic centre. It had, reportedly, well over 160 villages. But if we peel the onion of Ghanshyam's power, we find at its core only 84 villages directly under him.

The most important part of Porahat was Chakradharpur with its 60 villages under Ghasi Singh, a relative of the raja.[47] In addition, Ghasi and Ghanshyam each had a half-share in the Ho Gumra *pir*.[48] This peculiar arrangement was caused by 'the failure of male issue in the younger branch' on which one half had lapsed to the raja of Porahat. But, indeed, 'for a period of fifty [years] antecedent to the month of March 1820, no revenue worth sharing has ever been derived from Gumra'.[49] Apparently, these shares were claims to which the Hos did not pay much attention. Still, Ghasi claimed that he, with two or three servants, did go from village to village to ask for one rupee, about nine kilogrammes

31 | A Land of Their Own

of rice,[50] and two goats.[51] This was a rather relaxed affair. Raja Ghanshyam got but little regard from the Hos of Gumra.[52]

Jaintgarh in the south-east, on the border with Keonjhar, also belonged to Porahat. Roughsedge gave it 120 villages with 4,000 bowmen.[53] These 120 villages referred to the whole area of what was otherwise known as Bar *pir*. As we have seen, Jaintgarh proper was a fort on the banks of the Baitarani River, the principal place on the southern frontier of Singhbhum. Eleven villages in its neighbourhood were 'inhabited by other classes than Kols';[54] most of these were Bhuiyas. Here lived, Roughsedge wrote, 'one family of Brahmans, hereditary descendants' of the ancient commander of the fort. Its head, apparently, was Raghunath Bisi.[55] He claimed that his family had lived amongst the Hos for twenty or twenty-five generations.[56] Whatever the validity of that claim to the long residence, the rise of the family to local eminence was rather recent. From the original title deeds, it would appear that the fort with two-and-a-half villages and some pieces of land elsewhere were granted rent-free to Raghunath's father, Jagannath Das Panigrahi Bisi Mahapatra.[57] That would place the grant sometime in the last two decades of the eighteenth century.

Raghunath was 'permitted though in constant hazard and trepidation to reside [in Jaintgarh], nor would this have been possible but for the ready escape which was open to them in case of danger.'[58] Not all the Hos in this area were actively opposed to the raja and the commander of the fort. The Hos in the *pir* Bantaria, 'far more accommodating than their brethren', allowed unarmed servants and dependents of Ghanshyam Singh to pass through their lands to Jaintgarh.[59] That line of communication did not make the small fort Jaintgarh a secure possession. Roughsedge mentioned 'the few inhabitants' Add that these lived there 'in trepidation' and the impression was not one of strength.

Roughsedge called the tracts to Porahat's north, west, and south 'the outer circle'. It contained an estimated 481 villages, with at least 280 matchlocks and 5,500 bowmen. But the greater part of it, good for 280 matchlocks and 3,500 bowmen, was not directly ruled by the raja of Porahat but consisted of service tenures and grants. In the north, a member of a junior branch of the Singh family ruled Kera. Even further north, on the border with Chotanagpur, was Bandgaon, populated by Mundas. Its fief holder was a Bhuiya.[60] So was Karaikela's ruler. The small fort Chainpur to the east of Chakradharpur was a tenure for military service, also held by a Bhuiya.[61] In the south was Anandpur under Ghanshyam's distant relation Abhai, a Singh 'of whom I (Roughsedge) have but a poor opinion'.[62] Near to it was the sparsely populated and rather isolated Saranda in the south-east corner of Singhbhum. It was overvalued. Roughsedge's overview gave it 2,000 bowmen in 250 villages. In any case, it had escaped from the effective Singh rule. Its Rajput raja, a dependent of Porahat, had been expelled 'some years ago . . . and he now lives in a state of obscurity and indigence in a village of [the neighbouring state of] Bonai'.[63] There were some more small fiefs of Porahat, but 'all the other members of this [Singh] aristocracy, if [I] may use the term', said Roughsedge, 'having two generations ago been expelled from their lands, are exposed to great indigence, and live on the scanty provision of a village or two, generously bestowed upon them by the raja.'[64]

Of the states ruled by members of the Singh family, Porahat was the most run-down. It had 'scarcely anything left', Roughsedge knew.[65] Roughsedge considered its raja 'weak and ignorant'.[66] To this was added Ghanshyam's agony at not producing a son. In the case of further failure in that field, his likely successor would be the third son of Jagannath, his uncle Gajraj, then already well into his sixties.[67] A few years later, Ghanshyam's residence in Porahat would be described as 'dilapidated'. There was 'a listlessness and apathy amongst his household and followers'.[68]

Inside the Singh galaxy, Saraikela's strength showed in the religious sphere, too. The idol of the Pauri Devi, the Singh family goddess, was in Saraikela's palace temple. This was, as we have seen, a major irritant to Ghanshyam. There were different stories of how the idol came in Saraikela. It was stolen, found when thrown away by an apostate raja or bought as a toy.[69] But we do know when it came. A witness account taken by Major Roughsedge corroborates the date as slightly before 1800, a date that nearly all the sources have also mentioned.[70]

In 1795, a dying old Brahmin told a witness from Saraikela about the provenance of the statue. A Kol (that could be a Munda or a Ho) stole the statue of the Pauri Devi from Porahat. Five years later, one Kundra Kumar bought it for a bullock. This Kundra resold the image to one Murburna for Rs 4 or 5. In his turn, Murburna resold it to the Saraikela chief for five villages and the post of the *divan*. This story, which had the strength of a deathbed confession and the weakness of hearsay, placed the disappearance of the image from Porahat at around 1790, and its appearance in the palace of Abhiram Singh at about 1795.[71]

According to Raja Ghanshyam Singh of Porahat, the *Kunwar* of Saraikela had carried off this image.

> One morning however, about May–June 1790, the head priest informed the raja that the lock of the door had been forced and that the Devi was not within. . . . Nothing else, sir, of the materials and ingredients for religious ceremony was touched, the Devi alone was carried off.' A month afterwards intelligence came that the statue was in the house of Abhiram Singh, the father of Bikram Singh of Saraikela. On being asked, 'the babu said at once "the Devi will not be restored". . . . Sometimes the babu used to assert that "the Devi has come of her own accord", sometimes that he had bought her from the thieves, and sometimes [he said] that if the raja felt himself able he better come and take her away himself. By this sort of violence he retained her. At length being helpless the raja assembled a force, as did Abhiram Singh; two actions were fought but the latter remained unsubdued. . . . The result was that the raja died without issue.' Ghanshyam was his young nephew. When he eventually succeeded as raja, he was 'but a nominal raja and the thing [the Devi] which is necessary to constitute a raja was violently retained by Abhiram Singh with the intention of becoming raja himself . . . . This, sir, is a true account of the matter regarding the Devi which is mine from a number of generations.[72]

The counterstatement by Bikram was that 'the claim of the raja upon me, sir, for the Devi is not just. It is a false and calumnious statement':

> You are the master and I am obedient. Raja Arjun Singh [the First] now became raja and worshipped her at Banskata. Soon afterwards she appeared in a dream and directed him to make an image of her, to be placed and worshipped within the Fort [at Porahat]. In conformity to her information, the raja sent for workmen and ordered two images to be made; one of which was worshipped by the raja and the other by the Rani. This sir, is the History of the Devi.' Raja Arjun Singh the Second (actually the third), on reaching maturity gave Saraikela to Bikram Singh I, an earlier Bikram. 'Bikram then taking with him one of the two before

33 | A Land of Their Own

mentioned images repaired to Saraikela. . . . From that day sir . . . five generations continue to worship that image of Pauri Devi. . . . I am in the habit of sending sir, a couple of goats as an offering to the Devi at Banskata.[73]

No matter how and when the event took place, the Singhbhum raja was right to regard the loss of his tutelary image as a severe loss of face. In the pecking order of the branches of the Singh family, this was axiomatic: the one who held the idol of the Pauri Devi was the one who prospered. Even some Hos adhered to this idea.[74] Ghanshyam Singh's anguish could in no small measure be attributed to his firm belief that there existed a connection between the fact that he did not have the idol and that he had not produced a son. He felt ridiculous. On all occasions on which he met Roughsedge, his main demand was the restoration of his tutelary household image. That is, to become the first power among the Singh rulers.

Porahat's own strength did not point in that direction. Roughsedge's figures of villages, often multiples of twelve,[75] have to be taken with more than a grain of salt. If we leave out the fantasy figures for Jaintgarh and Saranda, the figures do, however, indicate a perceived relative strength of the Singh states of, roughly, Saraikela : Kharsawan : Porahat = 4:1:5. But much of Porahat was held as fiefs. If we take as our measure villages directly under the three chiefs, we find a relative strength of the states of Saraikela : Kharsawan : Porahat = 4:1:3. This amounted pretty much to a stalemate.

In a very rough way, taking the first reliable figures in the 1872 census and setting them against the 1820s estimate for the total number of Hos, we can approximate the absolute numbers of inhabitants in the first decades of the nineteenth century. The total for the whole area would have been 110,000. By that time, after the Mutiny, Porahat was reduced in size. Keeping that in mind, a tentative ratio of population strength would be slightly different from what Roughsedge's even rougher figures of villages would suggest. For the years around 1820, we then arrive for the Singh states at a total of 50,000, of which Saraikela had 20,000, Kharsawan 5,000, and Porahat inclusive of its dependencies 25,000 inhabitants. The whole area would have had 65,000 Hos. Of these, possibly 15,000 would reside inside the Singh states in varying degrees of cooperation with the raja and the chiefs, and some 50,000 would live in Hodisum.[76] This gives an idea of the absolute size of the main players. And shows, at the same time, that the restoration of Porahat's pre-eminence would have to come from getting more Hos under its Raja Ghanshyam Singh. Above all, it shows that somebody from outside, that is Roughsedge, would have to do the job.

Given his background, religious interests should have come easily to Roughsedge. In fact, it did not. Born on 21 August 1774, Edward Roughsedge was the eldest son of Reverend Robert Hankinson Roughsedge (1746-1829). Edward had six brothers and five sisters, some of whom died very early. Just after Edward left, his father became Rector of Liverpool in July 1796. The father would survive the son. The major died in 1822, his father seven years later.[77] Although several of the children were mentioned on his father's memorial inscription, Edward was not.[78] Neither was Edward mentioned in his mother's Elizabeth Wareing's short biographical note on his father.[79] That could indicate a troubled relationship.

Edward Roughsedge was appointed Cadet at the age of 21 in March 1796.[80] From the short time between Roughsedge's appointment and his departure to India on 12 April 1796, it is unlikely that he received any military training in England. His social background and his baggage of intellectual and practical skills were typical for officers of the Bengal Army at the time.[81] That did not make him mediocre; Edward Roughsedge was a high performer.

Roughsedge arrived in India on 5 February 1797; he stayed there until his death in 1822.[82] In India, too, there was no special military education for Company officers. After ten months, on 30 October 1797, he was appointed Lieutenant of the 16th Regiment of Native Infantry. He got his training on the job. During his first major assignment in 1798-9 in the border area west of Bengal proper, Roughsedge burned eight villages, for which he felt it necessary to explain himself.[83] This could be taken as overkill by a twenty-four-year-old and inexperienced officer; it did set a pattern for his later career.

In 1804, Roughsedge was transferred to the Ramgarh Battalion. Two years later he became its commander, which he remained for sixteen years with an interruption in 1814-15 when he served as Major of the 26th Regiment of Native Infantry in the Nepal War.[84] He became Major on 6 April 1818.[85] While the military was his proper province, Roughsedge also engaged in non-military tasks such as judicial trials and diplomatic and political interventions.[86]

Many of his insights came, to use the words of Mao Zedong, from his social practice.[87] As officer as well as administrator, Roughsedge was good in human resources management. He could be lavish in his praise of his subordinate officers, local rajas and even of heads of villages.[88] He directed his best social efforts at his colleagues in the army. According to his hagiographic obituary, he had a wide circle of friends as his 'unsparing hospitality has been experienced, at one time or another, by half of his brother officers, and was indeed proverbial throughout India'.[89] The long months of the cold season, especially, were filled with fighting and negotiations, but even then there were occasions for leisure and receiving brother officers. In Spear's convincing words: 'The bottle and the gun were the twin emblems of camp life.'[90] His colleagues were both white British and Anglo-Indians of mixed descent. Many officers of the Bengal Army married or lived together with Indian women.[91] These relationships could mean good access to information about the state and the feelings of the people. Roughsedge himself was not married; the sources were silent on female companions.

Roughsedge learned most of his human resources skills in company, from constant interaction with his troops. For the best part of his career, he commanded the Ramgarh Battalion. Although this was a provincial battalion, its social composition was probably similar to that of the Bengal Army, which was a high-caste preserve.[92] Roughsedge's human resources management stopped outside the spheres of the high caste army, rajas, and village heads. In his direct contacts with the original inhabitants of the South West Frontier Agency, he had a distant style.

It did not help that Roughsedge was not in good health. He regularly referred to the 'precarious state' of his health and to illnesses, which he described in terms of 'attacks', 'severe fits'.[93] He probably suffered from malaria. Roughsedge preferred to travel from October to March, the cold or the campaigning season. In April–May 1820, after the first campaign against the Hos, he had to postpone writing his report due to 'indisposition arising from the fatigue of our march [to Sambalpur], in weather more than ordinarily exhausting'.[94] These bouts of illness increased his inclination for the quick and violent fix.

As he was already doing the work, it was a logical step to appoint him in 1819 as the first Political Agent to Government on the South Western Frontier, the operational area of his Ramgarh Battalion.[95] It covered the present Jharkhand state, the districts of Surguja and Raigarh of Chattisgarh, and Sundargarh and Sambalpur of Odisha. Thus, Roughsedge was the main military and political strategist of government for these areas as well as its hands-on executive. His promotion was bound up with a change in the strategic environment.

Up to 1818, the main contenders of the East India Company for supremacy over the region were the Marathas.[96] In 1780, the Marathas made a Grand Confederacy that covered the best part of the subcontinent below the Ganges. For the East India Company, Chotanagpur and the states on the Odisha frontier were part of a forward defence against the Marathas, especially Nagpur,[97] and groups of frontier freebooters known as Pindaris.[98] Roughsedge, as the representative of the East India Company, interfered in the affairs of these buffer states, sometimes on invitation, sometimes of his own accord. That occupied most of his time. The first twelve years of Roughsedge's career as the commanding officer of the Ramgarh Battalion fell in this era. He must have lived in a tent then. Roughsedge was a central executive in Chotanagpur. Here he spent the best part of his career, here his insights in the administration of the frontier[99] were tested and hardened.

A frontier society of immigrants needs a strong hinterland, preferably a state, to crush resistance by the original inhabitants of the frontier. In Chotanagpur, that strength was not always there. Or, to put it another way, the original population was not invariably the weaker side. Thus, immigration went in stages. So did the often-violent reaction of the original population to it. Chotanagpur state was the frontier of Hindu colonisation from the Ganges plains into the Chotanagpur plateau.

In the fourteenth century, the frontier was in the area immediately south of Gaya.[100] It moved much deeper into the Chotanagpur plateau after the end of the sixteenth century. The Mughals established some control over the tract in 1585 because the area served as a retreat for the Afghan opponents of the Mughal Empire. In addition, the area was attractive as diamonds were found here.[101] In 1615, the governor of Bihar took the Chotanagpur ruler Durjan Sal prisoner and brought him to Delhi.[102] Twelve years later, Durjan returned to Chotanagpur where he emulated the style of the Mughal court. Like the post-Man Singh rulers of the Bhum countries in Bengal and Odisha, he claimed Rajput descent.[103] The needs of the state, or rather of the court, set in train the first major influx of Hindus from the plains.[104] Many of these immigrants obtained gifts of land in exchange for their services. Chotanagpur extended its sway southwards.[105] As we have seen, by the 1760s the Hos stopped short Dripnath Sahi's attempt to bring even Hodisum into its sphere of influence. The Bihari ethnic frontier remained well north of Singhbhum.

Around the same time, in 1765, Chotanagpur was part of the transfer of the *Divani* of Bihar to the East India Company. Here, the *Divani* became effective in 1771 when the raja formally exchanged his bejewelled turban for the hat of Captain Camac and submitted to the Company.[106] The East India

Company's main strategic objective in this area was to control its passes which led into Bihar.[107] In this forward defence strategy against the Marathas, the raja was treated as the chief of a Tributary State.[108] He proved not very trustworthy as a buffer. The Company army had to do the work. On top of this, the raja was slack in paying revenue.[109] This raised the whole question of the nature of Company rule over these tracts. Over the next thirty-five years, the debate continued whether Chotanagpur was primarily a military area of operation, ruled by a tributary raja, or was it British territory ruled by a mere zamindar, to which the Bengal regulations[110] could be applied?[111]

The revenue did not come in and, perhaps worse, Chotanagpur continued to malfunction as a buffer. In the last decade of the eighteenth century alone, there were fresh Maratha invasions in 1792, 1795, 1798, and 1800. Already in 1795, the district officer of Ramgarh W. Hunter pleaded for a battalion to be raised for Chotanagpur. This would shore up the Company's presence in general and, more locally, bring the zamindars and other chiefs into line. It had to be a regular battalion, as the local population were armed and would prove too much for lightly-armed troops. The Ramgarh Battalion was raised.[112]

The precise administrative arrangements here remained unclear. At the bottom of this lay a drawn-out conflict between the military and the civil wing of the administration over the area.[113] And as long as the raja was left to arrange his area's internal matters, he continued to push the zamindari system with its higher taxes and an incipient market. The taxes were a burden on the population, while a proper land market did not exist. In the makeshift arrangements, immigrant zamindars got hold of more and more land without investing in it. That kept economic development very low. The price of this type of development was that the original population lost much of its economic independence and its village organisation. That made Chotanagpur inherently unstable. Both effects were felt very much by the military.

Since Roughsedge became commander of the 600-strong Ramgarh Battalion in 1806, he was plagued by incessant logistical problems. He had to arrange for the Battalion's supply where little or no market existed.[114] At the same time, Roughsedge had to attend to a political situation which often required action shored up by the military. In 1806, the virulently anti-British raja of Chotanagpur Deo Nath Shah died. His son Govind Nath succeeded him. In 1808, the Company sent in Roughsedge to stop Govind's *divan* from taking over the state.[115] Raja Govind Nath now became less intractable and assisted the provision of the Company's army.[116] The next year, Roughsedge proposed to vest Govind Nath with police powers.[117] He aimed to kill two birds with one stone. His first aim was to permanently rope in the raja as an important source of provisions. The second was to ameliorate the disastrous state of public security in Chotanagpur, which prevented the birth of what Roughsedge called a 'market society'. Roughsedge had to tread carefully. His gamble was that the zamindars and the new police would check each other,[118] and this would give the market a chance. Markets were for Roughsedge as many access points to supplies.

As an extra control on the raja and his zamindars, Roughsedge proposed an annual tour:

> ... for some years to come the registrar or assistant of the registrar ... should be directed to make an annual progress through the extensive country for the purpose of receiving and investigating upon the spot such complaints as may be offered. I am guided in this opinion by experience of many journeys through Nagpur in none of which I have failed to receive several hundred petitions.[119]

This annual tour would, he believed, result in a 'comparative cheerfulness' with which the original inhabitants 'would submit to the ... to them novel, restraints of a well regulated police'.[120]

As repeated rebellions were to show, this last remark could hardly have been more wrong. The public peace aspect of the new police system was a disaster. The local population loathed the presence of the police, foreigners from Bihar. The increased presence of the police ensured that the rules of the judicial game changed abruptly, a sure way to a sharp economic downturn. Now, arrears in payment of revenue or debt meant that the land of the defaulter was certain to be seized and sold. The new landlords, often other foreigners from Bihar, used the new concept of private property to exclude the original inhabitants, and were hated by them in return.[121] Already in the winter of 1811-12, there were extensive protests by Mundas and Oraons.

Moreover, after Roughsedge had propped him up, Raja Govind Shah had reverted to his father's way of not paying revenue. Added to these troubles was the threat of an invasion by the Pindaris, groups of freebooters active all over north India. Inside the administration things came to a head in 1812 when Roughsedge ordered the assistant collector, Mr Parry, to meet the extra expenses. Parry protested to Calcutta against what he called Roughsedge's dictatorial style.[122] In turn, Roughsedge struck back by going all out against Parry's proposal to introduce the Bengal regulations in Chotanagpur. He argued that the situation differed vastly from that of the plains of Bengal and Bihar.[123] The raja was largely left free to arrange the internal affairs of his state, including the police,[124] with the Ramgarh Battalion as his backup and the agent as the ultimate arbiter.[125] Roughsedge was more sensitive to the idea of a tributary state that at least would provision his army, than to the mirage of a coffer full of revenue from an area where little or no market existed. He stonewalled proposals for change.

Roughsedge was also responsible for the Company's relations with the Chota Nagpur Tributary States to the south and south-west of Chotanagpur. While the political status of Chotanagpur itself was ambiguous, there was no doubt that these states, like the neighbouring Orissa Tributary States, were independent. Between 1800 and 1820, political control over the Chota Nagpur Tributary States, of which Surguja and Sambalpur were the most important, changed from the Marathas to the East India Company, and back. They had come under Maratha control around 1800. The states resented that and in 1803 agreed to come under the East India Company.[126] However, the Board of Control in London found it advisable to trade some influence and revenue to the Marathas for tranquillity and security.[127] In 1806, part of the new possessions, including Sambalpur, were returned to the Maratha ruler of Nagpur. There was local opposition to this, and only in 1808 Roughsedge actually handed over Sambalpur.[128]

In 1818 the strategic situation in north India changed fundamentally. In June the East India Company had broken the power of the Marathas and become that 'great and supreme power' which a few years earlier former Governor General Hastings had envisaged to bring about 'universal peace and general amity' in India.[129] The sole superpower had to evolve a new grand strategy, a set of policies, in which a state coordinates military and non-military elements to further its long-term interest in relation to other states.[130] Order and quiet on the East India Company's side of the border were partially dependent on the effective 'paramountcy' of the Company over the adjoining tracts.[131] From buffer states, ideally a deterrent strong enough to make the competition think twice before disturbing it, Midnapur, Chotanagpur, Mayurbhanj, and Sambalpur became client states and, ideally, were to be as inconspicuous as possible.[132] Peace enforcement operations in frontier areas of unclear political status were costly in terms of manpower, money and quality time of the topmost administrators in Calcutta and London. There should be a peace dividend. But Roughsedge proceeded as if nothing had changed. Except that the new (1819) South West Frontier agent was the old hand Roughsedge.

After the defeat of the Marathas in 1818, Roughsedge again took Sambalpur under his care.[133] Its nominal independence did not mean that the East India Company could not interfere in its internal affairs. Already the next year Roughsedge interfered in a dynastic dispute. Not evident from the more formal language of the despatches, the agent liked some states more than others. He had cordial relations with the raja and, according to one much later source, also with the younger queen.[134] Sambalpur was important to Roughsedge. The town with its commander's house on the bank of the river was his watering hole in the hot season.[135] This would influence him in 1820 when he became impatient to settle the question of Singhbhum.

Roughsedge would have to find his way in each new case. He was expected not to interfere with the independent states, but also to act proactively where local troubles could spill over the border to areas directly under the Company. The expediency of each measure would be decided in his correspondence with Calcutta, preferably before he would take action. But in the case of Singhbhum, Roughsedge felt he had enough guidance.

In March 1819, Roughsedge sent Lieutenant Ruddell to Porahat to start negotiations.[136] These did not go smoothly. On the Company's side, the bottom line was 'the necessity to enlist your country also under the protection of this Government'.[137] As this was the explicit wish of Ghanshyam Singh of Porahat, in itself this did not pose a serious obstacle. But Ghanshyam asked quite much in return. He demanded that the Company would re-establish his power over the Hos,[138] and restore his pre-eminence among the Singhbhum rulers, also by getting the image of the Pauri Devi back to him.[139] Roughsedge was inclined to comply with these demands. At the end of April, he asked for further instructions. Ghanshyam was pressing hard. In May 1819, the negotiations between Ruddell and Ghanshyam broke off without conclusion.[140]

In the next month, Roughsedge upgraded the Singhbhum question to a strategic consideration. He asked Calcutta to sanction intervention against the 'rapidly increasing power of the Hos'. Captain Jackson was demarcating the new road to Sambalpur and the Hos would, Roughsedge surmised, threaten its security.[141] In the meantime, things in Porahat appeared to have started moving again. In August, Narayan Singh, relation and *vakil* of the raja of Singhbhum, visited Roughsedge in Hazaribagh. Since Narayan had not come with much room to negotiate, Roughsedge asked him to go back to Porahat to obtain 'explicit instructions and fuller powers'.[142]

The exchange had been, in diplomatic terms, frank, in other words, had turned into a furious quarrel. Roughsedge saw Narayan's 'underhand proceedings and evil influence' as the cause of the breakdown of Ruddell's negotiations. He suspected that he had misrepresented Ruddell's remarks to Ghanshyam. The *vakil* immediately ('rather abruptly', wrote Roughsedge) departed, not, as later transpired, to Porahat but to Calcutta, 'where he was no stranger', in order to get the government to recognise the ancient claim of Ghanshyam as having authority over the other chiefs of Singhbhum.[143] Roughsedge wrote to Secretary Metcalfe in Calcutta that Narayan should be ordered to return, as he doubted that as long as Ghanshyam could hope for interference by the government in Calcutta, he would 'willingly close with the terms to his acceptance [of Britsh protection]'.[144]

Meanwhile, the issue of local peace moved to the top of his agenda. A serious rebellion broke out in Tamar, a dependency of Chotanagpur just north of Singhbhum.[145] Its population was closely related to the Mundas and the Hos. There was a drought, which the Tamarians attributed to witchcraft. Foreign tax farmers added to the nuisance and the population rioted against them. A civil investigation into the causes of the rebellion was planned,[146] but Roughsedge had to be ready to step in militarily if need be.[147]

When the Tamar disturbances broke out in earnest in September, Roughsedge asked the government to reconsider negotiations with Singhbhum.[148] On 9 October 1819, Calcutta sanctioned the reopening of negotiations. As before, the government in Calcutta stated that it did not want to reconsider the validity of the title of the chiefs of Saraikela and Kharsawan. Also, it saw no need to re-establish Ghanshyam Singh of Porahat 'in the possessions of his forefathers'.[149] Apparently, Narayan's mission to Calcutta had failed. The process was back at square one, with the difference that negotiations were underway with Singhbhum's local competitors, Saraikela and Kharsawan. These went much more smoothly.

Roughsedge used Kharsawan's Chaitan Singh to forward a letter to the raja. In it, Roughsedge informed Ghanshyam Singh that he would soon come to Porahat to renew the suspended negotiations, and requested him to prepare a meeting on the frontier of his realm. Roughsedge got no reply. Chaitan Singh told him verbally that it 'was received with much want of consideration', and that 'the raja observed that his *vakil* Narayan Singh was in Calcutta and [that] he should decline all intercourse or negotiation except with the Governor General'. Roughsedge believed this to be an exaggerated account and ignored it.[150] At the end of September, he had already requested for an Odia writer because, along with other rajas and chiefs, those of Singhbhum, Saraikela, and Kharsawan 'correspond with me in, and use the Oorea language and character only, and I am obliged to reply to their letters in that language'.[151] So, on 2 December he sent a second letter, now in Odia, to Ghanshyam, pretending that he might not have understood the earlier letter in Hindi. Roughsedge asked again for a meeting and also for supplies for his troops.[152]

Before he could settle the affairs of Singhbhum, he had to protect his rear. He entered Tamar at the head of his troops at the very end of December 1819.[153] Within a week he drove the insurgents from the open country into the jungle. The status quo restored, in military terms a simple task, Roughsedge left Tamar in the first week of 1820. His next aim was to fulfil the more diplomatic task of finalising the negotiations with the Singhbhum states. But it would appear that the troubles in Tamar had not ended and this further delay would influence the course of events in Singhbhum.

At the end of the first week of 1820, Roughsedge packed his tents and carpet to proceed to the Singhbhum group of states. When Roughsedge reached the border of Singhbhum on 14 January 1820, he got Ghanshyam's 'laconic and somewhat singular reply'.[154] Ghanshyam seemed to imply that he had not authorised Narayan to go to Calcutta and that he did not know whether Narayan was with Roughsedge or in Calcutta. In the meantime, Roughsedge concluded negotiations with the other Singh states. The precise terms of the agreements are not known,[155] but Kharsawan itself and the adjoining Asantalia area of Hodisum were granted in perpetuity to the *Thakur*. We may assume like terms for Saraikela.

Roughsedge now marched to the border of Porahat and sent Ghanshyam a confidential letter of invitation. Ghanshyam came immediately 'somewhat singularly' accompanied by . . . Narayan Singh, who was said to have arrived from Calcutta on that same day. That touched a raw nerve. Roughsedge insisted that the *vakil* be sacked forthwith. Narayan was packed off to Jaintgarh, where Roughsedge would meet him a few weeks later.[156]

Ghanshyam had more surprises than just speedy compliance with the demand to sack his *vakil*. Suddenly, he understood Hindi. But, as we have seen, he could not be persuaded to sit down on Roughsedge's carpet. His opening bids were the known points. He added pressure by making them standing. His 'first and evidently chief anxiety' was the recovery of the household image. The second point was to get back his authority over the neighbouring chiefs. The third was assistance to reduce 'the savage race called Larkas which have increased as rapidly of late years, as to render his residence at Porahat extremely hazardous'.[157] The second point, the change of the status quo of the other Singhs, was out of the question and was dropped without much ado. Roughsedge considered the first and third points acceptable under the observance of the principles laid down by the government.

On 1 February 1820, Ghanshyam and Roughsedge reached an agreement on the basis of this verbal understanding. The raja of Porahat signed the written agreement in the presence of Captain Ruddell, who apparently was put in charge of the formalities of concluding the negotiations. In the *kabuliyat* or agreement, Ghanshyam placed himself under the British Government. He bound himself unconditionally to this effect,

> that the Honble Company had taken him under their protection. That he would obey all their orders, truly and faithfully and pay to them an annual tribute of 101 rupees. He bound himself and [his] heirs, in event of acting contrary to the above stipulations to submit to the pleasure of the Governor-General in Council.[158]

To conclude the process, Roughsedge sent him a *pottah* or letter.

> In return for the Engagement which you have executed and delivered to Captain Ruddell, I am authorized and directed by the British Government to assure you of the protection of the Honorable Company, the efficient benefit of which, in your maintenance in all your existing rights, privileges, and possessions, you

and your posterity will continue to enjoy, so long as you and they shall faithfully abide by the stipulations to which you have pledged yourself and them.[159]

It was, perhaps, an indication of Roughsedge's exasperation with the drawn out and often devious negotiations that he mentioned Captain Ruddell, who had been slighted by Ghanshyam during the negotiations of the year before.

It was time to implement the unwritten part of the agreement. Roughsedge returned to Saraikela, accompanied by the raja of Porahat and a *babu* (Hindu gentleman). He arrived on 20 February and without delay started to work on the problem of the Pauri Devi. To persuade Bikram Singh of Saraikela to hand over the statue to the raja proved no easy task.[160] All Roughsedge got were evasive answers from Bikram and contradictory statements from his servants. Bikram used all the tricks and rules of statecraft. He tried to bribe the officers of the Company army; he spread the rumour that he was getting a spurious image made; the image was not even in Saraikela.[161] As we have seen, both sides of the conflict stated their position in writing. For the moment, that left Roughsedge with the restoration of the Porahat raja's rule over his claims in the Hodisum.

From 20 February 1820 onwards, Roughsedge was in Saraikela, where the raja of Porahat joined him. Apart from squabbling over the Pauri Devi idol, Roughsedge devoted his attention to the Ho problem. His enquiries brought him little more than expressions of fear. In the palaces of Kharsawan and Saraikela, it was the general opinion that the Hos 'make no scruple of putting to death any man of respectable caste who presumes to enter their territory'. 'Nor is there', Roughsedge was assured, 'a single Brahmin, Rajput or Muslim in any one of the numerous and well inhabited villages they possess. A traveller would as soon think of entering into a Tiger's den, as of traversing any part of Larka Kol.' Not even troops could try that, Roughsedge was told. 'A party of a hundred armed men would refuse to go the direct road between Bamanghati and Saraikela and all travellers make a circuit of thirty five kilometres to the East to avoid these dreadful savages'. That was true for the Thai *pir* in the north of Hodisum. A bit more to the south, the route from Bamanghati likewise was out of bounds.[162] It was apparent that

> the raja and zamindars of Singhbhum who are in attendance upon me have so formidable an opinion of the power and ferocity of these savages that notwithstanding the considerable force under my command, they are evidently much alarmed and have made formal protests against the danger of the march.[163]

From all this, Roughsedge did learn that these chiefs did not want to risk their own skin in a march through the Ho lands, but he did not get much wiser about the Hos.

Therefore, he sent for some people from the nearby *pir* of Ajodhya. It took him some time and effort, but two important village leaders came. One of them was Singrai Tiu from Dopai.[164] The atmosphere of this meeting was quite different from Roughsedge's previous interviews with Ghanshyam of Porahat or with Bikram of Saraikela. It was on this occasion that four or five of the Hos prepared to go asleep on Roughsedge's carpet. 'Such is their savageness', sighed the Captain.[165] In fact, they had travelled a long way, and sleeping at somebody's house after travel was an established practice in Hodisum.

Back to business, Roughsedge announced his intention to march through the Ho country. He demanded 'amicable treatment' in Ajodhya. He offered what sounded like an amnesty for rebels, when he asked 'whether they were inclined, seeing Singhbhum had now become British Territorium to relinquish their predatory habits and pretensions to independence, and on the assurance of kind treatment return under the ancient and legitimate raja of Singhbhum'.[166] The answer of the Hos, according to Roughsedge 'in a strikingly prompt and manly manner', was that they had 'thrown off their obedience to the raja' because of 'the threats of the southern Hos'. They would 'gladly' return to the Porahat raja's fold. They would receive the troops and the raja himself in their area, 'if he could protect them against the consequences of that step'. In this way, they threw the problem back to the raja. They warned Roughsedge against the Hos of Gumra and the southern Hodisum, who were determined to oppose an invasion by his troops. Roughsedge continued to talk for some time, 'in which I endeavoured to dissipate their shyness and impress upon them the advantage of persevering in such laudable intentions'. Intentions and limitations had become quite clear by now, and he could dismiss the Ajodhya chiefs with 'with trifling presents of a nature calculated to convince the inhabitants [of their area], that [their chiefs] had been very graciously received'.[167] Among the presents were turbans,[168] an attire highly prized by the Hos, but out of the reach of many.

Roughsedge had to go back to Tamar, to address the fallout of the troubles he had thought concluded in early January. As the most important leaders of the Tamar people had escaped, Roughsedge requested the chiefs of Saraikela and Kharsawan to arrest them if they sought shelter in their areas.[169] These weeks in Tamar disturbed his preparations and caused unwanted delay. When he returned to Kharsawan in the Singhbhum area, it was already March.[170] The hot season had started. To make a detour would increase travel time and cause 'very serious inconveniences'.[171] He meant heat and sickness. Travel in the hot season made the troops sick. The commander also had to consider his own malaria. Roughsedge felt he had to take the direct road to Sambalpur. That should be quite possible, as in his meeting with Singrai Tiu and his delegation he had prepared part of the way.

Chapter 2

Attack and Counterattack

...

The First Kolhan Campaign; the Narsanda massacre; the Guntiya massacre; the battle of the Bonga Buru; the burning of Balandia; Mata continues the resistance; Calcutta rebukes Roughsedge; the rape of Mahadei; the Hos sack the fort of Chainpur; capital panic

...

On 18 March[1] Roughsedge, together with the raja and his relatives, set off. Most had claims in the Kolhan, and to that day had never expected to even see these lands and properties. Roughsedge crossed the small Sanjai river into the country which he had been led to believe to be a tiger's den, and experienced with a shock 'the singular spectacle of a well cultivated champaign country studded with large villages, . . . smiling hamlets'.[2]

The first days of the campaign went smoothly. Roughsedge stayed for three days in the *pir* of Ajodhya, where the mundas brought provisions. The rent, to be paid from that moment on to the raja, was 'fixed by themselves'. Roughsedge wanted to minimise delays. He gave each of the mundas a turban and some cloth. They went away 'in great good humour'.[3] One would like to know what they said! Roughsedge could not understand them.

On 22 March, Roughsedge moved to Rajabasa, which, he stated, more than fifty years before was a possession of Saraikela. 'Reports had prevailed in camp the preceding day, that the Hos of Rajabasa and Gumra, the next pir to the southward, were assembled for the purpose of opposing our further progress.' It turned out differently. 'I was agreeably surprized therefore to find myself received at a short distance from the intended encampment by five or six heads of villages. When I reached the ground however, the sight of a large dry excavation where there had been a fine piece of water the day before, naturally excited a suspicion of intended hostility; I did not allow it to appear however.'[4] It looked as if most Hos of Rajabasa at the last moment had dropped the plans to oppose his advance. But now the troops had no water. To avoid trouble, Roughsedge accepted their explanation and moved to a nearby village.[5]

He stayed there for two days (23 and 24 March), during which he was visited by most of the village heads, who submitted to Bikram Singh of Saraikela 'in the same manner as those of Ajodhya did to the raja'.[6] Roughsedge gave them presents and 'encouraged them by every means in power to desist from predatory habits and live peac[e]able for the future'.[7]

This day, 24 March, Roughsedge had a virulent exchange with Bikram Singh of Saraikela. From the investigations into the case of the Pauri Devi in February, he had come to the conclusion that Bikram had no right to the idol because his father had purchased it knowing that it had been stolen. In the meantime, Bikram 'offered bribes to almost everybody in my [Roughsedge's] service to secure a decision in his favour'.[8] Roughsedge lost his temper and in his usual outspoken way made it clear to Bikram that the raja's statement had been correct and his, Bikram's, 'disgraced by contradiction and perjury'. The case would be presented in this fashion to Calcutta if Bikram did not give up on the image at once. If the matter came to a formal investigation, Roughsedge warned, he would not only have to give up the image but would also be exposed to ridicule in the eyes of his relations and his people.[9] Bikram asked for 'a couple of months' time' to get advice from 'some ancient and absent counsellors of his family', and said that then he 'might come to some resolution that was satisfactory with me [Roughsedge]'. Roughsedge saw in this a promise to restore the Devi—and said so. Under the circumstances, he would allow him one month to get his counsel, and dismissed him to Saraikela. Ghanshyam was very disappointed and said that Bikram would use this month to have a 'spurious' Pauri Devi made.[10] That might be or not be, but for the moment Roughsedge had got rid of an important source of friction inside his expeditionary force. He had seen preparations for resistance. There was trouble ahead.

Indeed, hostilities started when Roughsedge moved into the Gumra *pir*, which was claimed by Ghanshyam. The next stop on the troops' march was Chaibasa, which they reached on 25 March. The same morning at 11:00 hrs, the inhabitants of a village not more than 2.5 km from the camp (probably Narsanda), killed a camp follower and severely wounded two more.[11] Passions flared up and the British side considered the attack was made 'wantonly'.[12] 'To have overlooked this conduct would be dangerous as well as disgraceful', Roughsedge stated. He immediately ordered the guard and a troop of horse under the command of Lieutenant John Peter Maillard to attack the Hos. Through a field glass Roughsedge saw the Hos with their bows and battleaxes in full retreat towards the hills.[13]

Lieutenant Maillard with his Rohilla horse under Abdullah Khan[14] made a diversionary movement to the west and then intercepted a party of 300 Hos. As a participant wrote, 'The Hos, on seeing the near approach of L[i]eut. Maillard's party, turned around, drew up in line, and received them with a discharge of arrows. Seeing however that no great impression was made by these weapons, they with the utmost impetuosity and blind courage, rushed on the charge of the horsemen, battleaxe in hand, seemingly seeking rather to kill the horses than the riders, probably from the idea that by dismounting the latter, they should find them an easy prey'.[15] In Roughsedge's own words, 'the Larkas [as]sailed them with a flight of arrows, but finding that they had made no impression, these savages with a degree of harshness and foolhardiness which is scarcely credible met the charge of the troop halfway on a level plane, battleaxe in hand. The result was the immediate slaughter of 40 to 50 men and the pursuit of the remainder, about half of whom effected their escape into the Hills.'[16] The British participant in the battle, with less overview than his commander, had it that the Hos had left 'half of their number dead on the field' (see Plate 3).[17]

Maillard then moved towards the village where the grass cutter had been killed. He found a second party of sixty men standing near the corpse, prepared for action. They behaved with still greater determination, 'rushing upon and striking [with their battleaxes] like furies both horses and men. . . . The chief object of the Larkas appeared to be the horses; they killed one and mortally wounded another with single blow[s] of a battleaxe and seven others were more or less hurt by cuts and arrows.' Two cavalry men were wounded. The savage fight went on till all sixty Hos were sabred. Maillard destroyed Narsanda 'as an example to others', and returned to camp in the afternoon.[18]

Ghanshyam was quick to suggest to Roughsedge that this change to actual hostilities was the result of intrigues by Bikram of Saraikela. Bikram seemed to have good intelligence or a sharp political sense. He sent, by a circuitous road, his son and heir apparent Ajambar with 400 men and thirteen horsemen to assist Roughsedge.[19] Roughsedge, who first saw the reasoning of the raja, was now convinced that Bikram had nothing to do with the Hos.

The day was over with 100 to 200 casualties on the Ho side. The slaughter led to universal outrage. 'I', wrote Roughsedge, 'became convinced that the intention to oppose our progress and cut off our supplies was generally taken up.'[20] Even Hos from villages that had submitted a few days before now stopped others from coming in to the Company forces.

That night the fighting flared up again. The officer commanding a grain escort reported with difficulty that he was surrounded by large bodies of armed Hos. He had taken shelter in the friendly village of Dopai,[21] eight km from Chaibasa, where he expected to be attacked the next morning. And at 10:00 in the evening, news arrived that at the village Guntiya,[22] about six km from Dopai, some Hos had got hold of a postal packet. This had an immediate impact. The postal system was the lifeline of the British officers. Its interruption meant that Roughsedge and his troops were not only surrounded, but also isolated. Roughsedge decided to punch a hole from the inside. He ordered Maillard to first surround Guntiya at daybreak (of 26 March) and to afterwards relieve the surrounded party in Dopai. On arrival in Guntiya, Maillard found the inhabitants of the vicinity ready to oppose him. He was received with 'repeated discharges of arrows'. Four mounted soldiers were wounded, one of these mortally, as well as several horses, and four foot soldiers. Maillard set the village on fire,[23] 'upon which the Larkas (their arrows being nearly expended) rushed furiously upon their foes armed with battle-axes and large stones, by one of which Lieut. Maillard, who behaved very gallantly on the occasion, was nearly killed.'[24] People who continued to resist were killed 'and the remainder throwing down their arrows, received quarters'.[25]

At Narsanda and Guntiya the Hos had met the Ramgarh Battalion's advance with great courage. That could not annul the vast difference between the two sides in armaments and in tactical leadership when it came to battles. In the words of an officer who participated in the Narsanda battle, the Hos were 'are well exercised in the use of weapons . . . , bows and arrows, and battle axes, called tangees'.[26] The Ho long distance bow could cover about 180 m. It had to be spanned with the feet,[27] and therefore would have a long interval between shots. Moreover, because of the position of the shooter, the longbow could not be very accurate. If the long-distance shot hit its target, it made a dreadful wound. For closer quarters, the Hos had a different set of bow and arrows. The arrows for close quarters were 'larger and of different sizes . . . and capable of inflicting very serious wounds'. These were used from 20–30 m from the object.[28] At Narsanda, only the cavalry was put to action, but a mix of cavalry and infantry took on Guntiya.[29]

The trooper of the East India Company had a Land Pattern Musket, also known as the Brown Bess, probably the upgrade called India Pattern. It had a range of up to 160 m with a 75–95 per cent accuracy.[30] In battlefield conditions it was safe to count on one shot a minute but actually, it could go up to four shots.[31] When the shot from the Brown Bess hit target, it inflicted much damage as it used a large soft projectile which would flatten on impact.[32] Thus, the ranges of the Ho long-distance bow and the Brown Bess would be roughly the same.

The infantry on the Company side was trained to be in line and to fire straight.[33] After the initial exchange of fire, the Bengal Army's infantry and cavalry had to cover the distance of 160 m, which could be done in about one-and-a-half minutes. The optimal use for the Brown Bess in that advance was a massed volley at short range, 50 m, which was a useful 20–30 m more than the Ho answer with their short-range bows. Then the Ramgarh Battalion could proceed with infantry and cavalry.

In the battle at close range, the Ho side used *tangees* (battleaxes), and their object was to first hit the horses.[34] The *tangees* were dangerous, but in the end, the Hos killed only two horses.[35] They were at a disadvantage. The mounted troops used their sabres with great effect, slashing down from their high position. The decisive moment was when the Ho ranks broke. Fleeing people could be cut down by unsupported cavalry. The losses of the Hos were debilitating. The Narsanda and Guntiya massacres made a lasting impression. They were remembered even fifty years later.[36]

Maillard lost no time and pushed on. In a dramatic move, one of the prisoners was now sent to a stronghold of the Hos on a neighbouring mountain, probably the Bonga Buru (see Plate 4). Here the grain and the families of twelve to fourteen villages were deposited. He demanded that they deliver up the post that had been carried off, 'with least possible delay' on pain of attack. 'This threat', commented the participant already quoted, 'was principally intended to intimidate them from holding out', as Roughsedge 'felt unwilling to push for further extremities, for enough had been done for example against these ignorant and savage, but brave mountaineers'.[37] It worked. The prisoner came back with a leading Ho, who had witnessed from the mountain the destruction of Guntiya and 'in great trepidation' delivered up the seized post. Roughsedge's allies among the Ajodhya Hos in Dopai, meanwhile, had protected the grain escort from attack by 'a large body of their brethren in arms'.[38] The escort now joined Captain Maillard, who returned to camp at about 2 o'clock in the afternoon.[39] Their initial fury spent, and at a loss as to how to stop Roughsedge's army, the village heads of the area around Chaibasa and of Gumra tendered their submission.[40]

After Narsanda and the Bonga Buru followed three peaceful marches through 'a fine and well cultivated country'. Three days of marches seems much time for a distance of a 40 or 50 km. We have to realise here, that an army on its way to the summer headquarters with all its equipment and retainers would be very slow. In the best of circumstances, an elephant could make 4–6 km an hour, but his upper range for a day was 30 km, a 5–6 hours march. But most of the equipment would be loaded on bullock carts, which moved at an agonising 3–5 km an hour. So probably the army started out very early in the morning, would move for about four hours, and then set up camp. An important reason for these short days was the heat. It was an army going to its hot weather retreat as well as an invading force. It was an impressive force. The officers marched in style, with their tents and stocks of drink carried by up to twenty people, but the common soldiers also had their servants carrying their possessions and kit.[41] For the Ramgarh Battalion of 500 troops, the whole train could well be three times that number.

So Roughsedge took his time. He mentioned the state of cultivation of the country, but maintained an eerie silence about its inhabitants, as if they were not there. He noticed more when he saw the ruined fort in Jagannathpur. It was the chief place of the important Bantaria *pir* of sixty villages. From here the Hos, 'though paying no revenue and professing no obedience', allowed unarmed servants of Ghanshyam Singh passage to and from Jaintgarh. The Hos near Jagannathpur submitted, even though they remained afraid of the Hos of Balandia, Khairpal, and Gumuriya, villages to the north-east and north of Jaintgarh, 'who had threatened with destruction such Hos as should enter into engagements with the raja or myself'. Roughsedge assured them he would take care of the refractory men in question'.[42]

Roughsedge arrived in Jaintgarh, the southernmost place of the Kolhan, on 1 April. His soldiers were collapsing. Here he found Raghunath Bisi and also Narayan Singh, who a few weeks before, on the insistence of Roughsedge himself, had been sacked as *vakil* by Ghanshyam. There was little love lost between the Major and this *babu*. So when Roughsedge tried to get negotiations underway with the Hos in the neighbourhood, he used the good offices of Raghunath, whom Roughsedge trusted. Raghunath did try, but his messengers merely got the answer that 'they should all be killed after the troops had marched'. Driving the message home, the Hos of nearby Gumuria, who were on the Balandia side, attacked a small guard of the bullock drivers and grass cutters of the detachment. The guard suffered two dead and fifteen wounded.[43]

On the request of Ghanshyam, Maillard now took on one of the centres of the resistance, Balandia, 30 km of rough terrain to the north.[44] Here the Hos under the leadership of Mata Pingua were preparing to defend themselves.[45] Maillard's detachment, going probably without camp followers and the luggage train, covered the distance in one night.

> Conformably to your instructions, I marched at midnight on the 6th instant and reached the principal village of Balandia at 7 a.m. on the 7th. I found in it only two to three women and no grain. They informed me that all the male population was in arms in the adjacent jungles, and that they had formed fortified hide outs in various positions, where they had placed their cattle and grain. I immediately distributed my force into a number of small parties for the purpose of scouring the woods and discovering their hoards, in which I was tolerably successful; the Hos seem to have been taken by surprize from their not attempting any opposition to the loading of the bullocks I had with me with rice.

But after my return to the villages, they appeared in force on the opposite bank of a stream within 140 m of my encampment, began to fire arrows amongst the men and at the cavalry who wanted to water their horses. I immediately took out the troops and after a charge in which they lost 15 men and I had one cavalry and two horses wounded with battleaxes. They sought their safety in flight. I made several unsuccessful efforts through the medium of the *Bisi* of Jaintgarh during the rest of the day to get some of the inhabitants of the hamlet to come in to me, and at 11 o'clock p.m. the Hos made a feeble attempt to surprize my camp, wounding one of the sentries; finding the troops on the alert, they immediately retired.

The next morning little before day light, first destroying Balandia and its dependent hamlets, I commenced my return to camp. The road was almost entirely through a thick forest and strengthened in some parts by overhanging and (towards the road) inaccessible rocks, the Hos with great boldness availed themselves of those local advantages and hung on my flanks and rear; sometimes also appearing in the front until I came within five kilometres of your camp. Their numbers were very considerable and the quantity of arrows they discharged beyond my conception great. I arranged my party with the baggage and grain in the centre numerous flankers and a strong rear guard, of which two foot soldiers were killed, and of my whole party eight cavalry, seven foot soldiers and six horses wounded. Only one foot soldier, I am happy to state, dangerously.

The Hos must have suffered very severely, for they exposed themselves frequently to our fire; had any part of the country through which we passed admitted of the employment of cavalry we should have speedily got rid of the enemy; as it was they were enabled to plague us nearly the whole march.[46]

That foray of Maillard and its troubled aftermath was as far as Roughsedge was prepared to go. The military situation was muddled. Many villages had submitted, but often only to escape immediate destruction. Balandia was destroyed, but the spirit of its inhabitants was unbroken. The terrain was unfavourable to the Major. Moreover, the Hos were adapting their tactics. The frontal assault had given way to constant harassment through shooting arrows in wooded and rocky terrain, where the advantage was not with the Company troops. At the same time, it remained true that skirmishes slow down but rarely defeat an army. The Ho side too was vulnerable. It was vital for them to keep their villages intact and their retreats hidden. Roughsedge himself remained optimistic. He presented victory as within his grasp. If only he could have stayed ten days longer, Roughsedge sighed, he would have subdued all the Hos in the area, except those of the *pir* of Balandia.[47]

The fact is that he did not stay. Apart from the wounded, more than seventy of his men were so sick from the heat that they had to be carried on beds. Roughsedge called for the surgeon. But the heat was mounting. He wanted to leave Jaintgarh as soon as possible. But in a revealing aside Roughsedge noticed that Ghanshyam 'was more anxious than myself' to quit the place.[48] Therefore, he persuaded him to station some defence force in Jaintgarh. They agreed on 100 men from Sambalpur, to be paid by Ghanshyam. Roughsedge left Singhbhum for Sambalpur a few days after the burning of Balandia.[49]

The raja too left, leaving Babu Narayan Singh in charge. It did not help. Within five days, the Hos of Balandia attacked the fort. Narayan fled to Porahat, while Raghunath Bisi, the holder of the fort, fled with his family to Keonjhar. 'The few inhabitants of the place had time to carry off their property and no one was hurt - but the Hos set fire to, and destroyed the village.'[50] The village destroyed, he himself in Keonjhar, his military replacement on his way, Raghunath looked into an abyss.

But not all seemed lost. The capture of Jaintgarh was the starting point of hostilities between the 'loyal' and the 'refractory' Hos. Roughsedge was not precise on these. 'Many encounters took place with various success and mutual loss, but in the end the Loyalists proved victorious.'[51] That was written in May when it looked that things were going well for Ghanshyam. To top that, at the beginning of June, the 100 mercenaries arrived in Porahat.[52] A few days later, in mid-June, the 'loyal' Hos sent word through Raghunath Bisi, who apparently had returned, that if they would get fifty soldiers, they would 'undertake to take all the Hos of that quarter under his authority'.[53] Raghunath had not said whose authority was to be established, the raja's or his own. Roughsedge lost no time 'in communicating [to Ghanshyam] the good disposition' of the loyalist faction of the southern Hos.[54] However, Ghanshyam put the 100 men under Bahuran to use elsewhere in Hodisum.

Thus, Mata and his Balandia Hos were not subdued. They had merely suffered a setback. And they had a strategic hinterland. Their allies were the Hos of Thai *pir*, which was not touched in this campaign. From Thai *pir*, wrote Roughsedge a few weeks later, 'frequent attacks are made on travellers, and in one instance on the Post on the Captain Jacksons road'.[55] Evidently, Singhbhum was far from settled.

After Roughsedge recovered from fever in Sambalpur, he gave a lengthy description of his campaign and a short description of the Hos in his letter of 9 May 1820. He elaborated upon his strategic aims to check the raids of the Hos, to stop the depopulation of the border tracts, and to protect Captain Jackson's postal road. He proposed to extend the operations of the next season to the Kol *pirs* of Bamanghati, that is, the four easternmost *pirs* of the Kolhan. His special target would be Thai *pir*.

Governor General Lord Hastings's reply must have come cold as ice to his political agent. In a singularly short note, Secretary Metcalfe first ordered Roughsedge to put an end to his efforts to get the 'contested image', if this affair 'should not have been satisfactorily settled before the arrival of this letter [of 3 June 1820]'.[56] Worse, His Lordship, he wrote, was 'not satisfied of the necessity or expediency of your proceedings with regard to the Larka Kols without the previous sanction of government'.[57]

Roughsedge reacted as stung. He immediately—and for the second time—gave up on the statue of the Pauri Devi. However, he continued to beg 'with great deference to submit the following grounds of my assurance that I had the sanction of His Lordship in Council for affording aid to the raja of Singhbhum in the recovery of some portion of the authority possessed by his ancestors over the Larkas, and the prevention of further encroachment[s]'. Roughsedge referred to five previous letters written by him to the government during the last two years. In each of these, he had proposed to restore the raja's influence over the Hos. If the government saw that as an undesirable course, he 'should have been honored with an intimation to that effect'. What's more, he had tried to reach this objective 'by amicable means only, and had no intention to employ force if my [Roughsedge's] march were not opposed'. In addition, the weather had forced him to take the shortcut to Sambalpur through the Kolhan. Finally, the 'outrage' committed near Chaibasa caused 'the necessity of punishing so gross an insult to the British arms'. In short, Roughsedge 'had no choice but to adopt the most prompt and vigorous measures against the aggressors'.[58]

Roughsedge's defence was not successful. The governor general was 'not quite satisfied with the explanations'. He ordered Roughsedge to abstain from military and political actions not explicitly sanctioned by the government. To prevent misunderstanding, Roughsedge should submit 'distinct reports limited to specific objects', not 'scattered suggestions in divers[e] miscellaneous reports'.[59] In August 1818, when Roughsedge proposed that the Company should establish 'some control' over Singhbhum, it was understood that it was bound to lead to some involvement. But in 1820, when he invaded the Ho lands nearly as a matter of course, he had shown Calcutta that he was an unreconstructed forward defender. To his unpleasant surprise at the fag end of his career, Roughsedge was to find out that he had not grasped the post-Maratha environment of eastern India. But he had forced the hand of the East India Company.

The disagreements between Roughsedge and his superiors in Calcutta were not public knowledge. To the outside world, the Company was involved in Singhbhum. Therefore, it was imperative to evolve a strategy to make reality fit the perception. 'It has become necessary to deliberate on the course to be pursued towards that people [of the Hos], on which subject the Governor General in Council will be happy to receive your [Roughsedge's] opinions.'[60]

Roughsedge sent his answer on 20 June. He proposed first to weaken the power of the Hos and bring them under the surrounding states, then to establish a *cordon sanitaire* around the Hos by reinforcing the weak Porahat and placing Company troops at several places around the Kolhan as a backup force.[61]

He was most specific on the first part of his proposals. Just outside Singhbhum proper, it was necessary to curb, peacefully or by force, the Hos of 'Tall Poor' (Lalgarh or Thai *pir*), who threatened Jackson's Road. Inside the Singh area, Roughsedge was confident he could conciliate the Hos with the raja and the British government if he would be allowed to revisit Jaintgarh in the proper season. He estimated that there was not the least chance that the raja would get such a grip on the country that he could resort to unreasonable demands and high taxation. On the contrary, if the raja were not very conciliatory, he would soon lose the little authority he had acquired so recently. The East India Company should sanction the submissions of the villages already received, but not give a guarantee to the raja that he would always keep his position in these villages. The heads of the villages who had not yet come in should be invited to submit. His idea was to use proven pro-Porahat Hos to pressurise 'the more refractory and ill disposed'.

Finally, 'all who have or may come in should receive an assurance of the favour and protection of government, on the conditions of abstaining from the future indulgence of predatory habits, and [of] opening the roads in the respective divisions to the free and unmolested passage of travellers'. The very prospect had such a mitigating effect on the Major, that the Hos, who in May were still 'ferocious and sanguinary' savages, in June—even if they retained 'a wanton spirit of plunder'—were 'well provided with the comforts of life'.[62] Roughsedge was not the only one to think so.

Ghanshyam of Porahat treated his new position of lord of the Kolhan as a windfall. One can, as the Hos did, attribute this to the raja's greed. While greed there was, there also was reason in his rapacity. Roughsedge did not get his figures right. This, more than anything else, showed his weak grasp of the Singhbhum situation. Out of his Porahat income, Ghanshyam could not afford to pay the 100 soldiers Roughsedge had sent under the command of Bahuran Singh.[63] After ten months, the party had received in total Rs. 900, the equivalent of two months' salary.[64]

Something had to be done about the cash flow, and it had to be done without delay. As we have seen, Ghanshyam and Ghasi Singh of Chakradharpur each had a half-share in the Gumra pir.[65] For fifty years prior to Roughsedge's invasion, the inhabitants of Gumra had not been paying taxes, although Ghasi, with one or two servants, made 'occasional visits' to ask village heads for one rupee and some rice. After the campaign, Ghasi had gone to Gumra and stayed there for three months to collect a 'considerable sum'. Ghanshyam asked for his share. Some negotiations had followed, as Ghasi stated that he already had spent his money. They agreed that next year's collection would be wholly for Ghanshyam.[66] But Ghanshyam needed money now. He sent Bahuran with eighty soldiers to Chakradharpur to get 2,000 rupees.

The discussion between Bahuran and Ghasi, given here in Ghasi Singh's rendering, illustrates the wheeling and dealing that accompanied the financial and political bankruptcy of Singhbhum.[67] The Rs. 2,000, Bahuran explained, were to be raised from the revenue collected from Gumra. Ghasi Singh asked 'on what account?' The answer was that it should be from his account. Ghasi then pointed out that Ghanshyam 'had taken 42 villages out of the whole number of 120, and where was his share [in these 2,000 rupees]?'

The countermove of Ghanshyam was a full enquiry by his agent.[68] He ordered him to 'go to Gumra and make a strict enquiry, should you find any villages capable of paying fifty rupees from which Ghasi Singh has only taken five rupees, be sure you collect the difference, spare none of them, but collect from each according to its ability'.[69]

Meanwhile, in Chakradharpur, Ghasi could not raise more than Rs. 200. 'I had paid all I had collected, and was a poor man, where should I find two thousand Rupees?' Bahuran tried to make a deal. 'Very well, give me a bribe of fifty rupees and I will be merciful. I will just go for a few days through the villages of Gumra for if I do not I shall be accused of ingratitude to the raja.'[70] He took the bribe for which Ghasi had to get a loan, and started to collect revenue in Chakradharpur.

Ghasi continued in impotent rage: 'I never, Sir, paid any rent for Gumra, nor did any raja demand it.' He sent his brother Lalkant Singh to Ghanshyam Singh to present his case 'that I had paid the money and there was no necessity for his [troops] going [to] Gumra'.[71] Ghanshyam proposed then to 'divide the whole pir equally between me and yourself, and then the Subadar shall not go'. Even when pressed this hard, Lalkant did not give in. Roughsedge had given his brother 'possession of 120 villages of which you have taken forty, and now you want forty more. These I cannot give.'[72]

To put pressure on Ghasi, Bahuran kept him prisoner for a whole day.[73] Bahuran now proceeded in a systematic way. He took Ghasi with him into the Gumra *pir*. Bahuran had all the heads of the villages assembled and told them through interpreters that the revenue would be raised. Where 'they had paid 12 rupees to me [Ghasi] they would have to pay forty rupees, i.e. 30 rupees in cash, and 10 in rice [to Bahuran]'. For the last purpose Bahuran had a special large measure made, and in this way took 500 *seers*, possibly 477 kg[74] for each rupee. That was for the raja of Porahat. For himself 'he afterwards claimed one rupee, 28 kg of rice, 28 kg of *urad*, and a goat as a present from each village, and when he gave the heads turbans & cloths, he took a cow and two calves from each village for milk'.[75] This was not a big success. The rents were settled with only seventeen villages, to a total of Rs. 1,000, of which Rs. 300 went to Bahuran.[76] Bahuran had spent Rs. 300 worth of cloth for turbans and dresses.[77] And he was still Rs. 1,300 short.

Ghasi gave the village Kumhar Tola to a servant, Deo Needhee from Dhenkanal in Keonjhar. Higher taxes and foreigners lording over the land—this was neither the careful nor the conciliatory behaviour that Roughsedge had predicted just a few months earlier. The troops quickly grasped the spirit of the enterprise. In December 1820 and January 1821 they started to collect their salary *in natura*;[78] they took goats and chickens from the villagers. Ghasi Singh tried to make Bahuran stop this behaviour, but got abuses in reply.[79] The guards had grabbed the power.

The increased protein consumption of Bahuran's troops showed in ever greater bravado. Privates molested the daughter of the local leader Kuntu Pater of Pokharia. In one version, this happened when she was fetching water from a tank and she was 'forcibly dishonoured'.[80] Later, her father played the incident down, as Roughsedge wrote, 'evidently prepared with his lesson'.[81] 'My daughter was beating out rice in the house, three soldiers came, of whom two remained at the door and one going in laid his hand upon her bosom and asked her to allow him to assist her, she fled and he followed her for a short space . . . This is all that happened, and it only happened once.'[82]

At the time, Kuntu and his friends were not so coldblooded. He and his uncle Satera swore an oath 'on a tiger's skin, an arrow, some paddy and cow dung'. A meeting followed, in which the 'whole tribe' agreed that Ghasi Singh and Bahuran were taking 'all our money and grain so that we shall soon have nothing left'. They decided 'Let us get rid of them once and for all by attacking them and putting them to death.'[83] It was remarkable that just before this day Ghasi Singh seemed to have escaped from Bahuran's camp and hidden in Kuntu Pater's house. He then sent a Hindu cowherd into the camp to get his brother Lalkant out. On 29 or 30 January the local people, mainly Hos, surrounded Bahuran's camp on 350 m from the village of Pokharia.[84] Bahuran sent for help to the village of Dopai and to the Saraikela troops in Rajabasa. Half an hour after sunrise, when the envoys were a mere 200 m away, in the words of an eyewitness, 'The Hos began to beat their drums and sound their trumpets and in two parties from the south and the west, amounting to a thousand men, they approached the Subedar['s] encampment and bared their arrows.'[85]

The hard-pressed Bahuran decided to retreat towards Saraikela. He and his party were stopped near the village Cheri in Chiru *pir*. In a man-to-man combat, Bahuran and fourteen of his men were killed. The Hos caught Ghasi's brother Lalkant when he was running for his life. He was spared.[86] Four horsemen escaped to Saraikela.[87] The remainder of Bahuran's party, some fifty men under Ratan Singh, went to the fort of Chainpur.[88] In a no-risk gesture of goodwill, Bikram Singh of Saraikela went with his troops, but just up to the border. A relief party of fifty Hos from Ajodhya *pir* came too late to Cheri. These were probably under Singrai Tiu of Dopai, whom Roughsedge had met the year before.[89] Hos from Charai and Bantaria *pirs*, too, were reported to have 'remained faithful to the raja'.[90]

That did not diminish the immediate dangers. Bikram, who with guns on the roof of his palace in Saraikela, did not have much to fear from direct Ho attacks, wrote on 1 February. He had his information from the four mounted soldiers who, after their escape the previous day, had told him not to advance. They said that in the battle of Cheri Bahuran's men were 'all killed'. The Hos planned to attack Chainpur, Bikram wrote, and he had given orders to bring his relations and adherents from there to Saraikela.[91]

The northern Hos surrounded the mud fort of Chainpur. For seven days, the soldiers under Ratan and *mahapater* Bahadur Singh's own party of sixty were beleaguered.[92] On the eighth day, 6 February, the Ho side gathered in the nearby village of Cheerchamugga. Its village head, incidentally, was not a Ho, but a Mahto.[93] The collected force performed a ceremony.[94] The same morning they launched the attack on Chainpur from the western side, which was overgrown with jungle. Repulsed from that side, the Hos tried to enter the fort from the north.[95] Again repulsed, the Hos tried to flood the camp with water. The fierce battle lasted the whole day.[96] In the end, Commander Ratan Singh announced, 'My fort is gone. We can do no more.' He abandoned the fort, leaving all his cash, arms and ammunition. In this retreat, which was slow because the women and children fled with the soldiers, he lost fifteen men and had eight more wounded. When they reached the village of Barka Tappa in Chaitan Singh's area, they informed him and Bikram of Saraikela. But no one came from Chaitan Singh. Bikram sent one Padam Singh with some horses and goats.[97] Padam took the remnants of the garrison to Saraikela.

The mercenary force was looking at a military and a financial disaster. The Hos got hold of three horse-loads of brass pots, gold to the value of Rs. 100, and additional cash of Rs. 930.[98] The soldiers were a demoralised lot. They had escaped with nothing but the clothes on their backs. They were in a makeshift camp and ate the food handed out to them. They begged Roughsedge for some money to perform the last rites for their fallen colleagues and to buy some pots to cook.[99] With this stunning victory of the Hos, the barriers against their invasion of the Singh states—if they had such plans—seemed about to fall.

And down they came. In the capitals of the Singh states, panic broke out. Immediately after the sack of Chainpur, Roughsedge's favourite ruler, Chaitan Singh of Kharsawan, wrote him for immediate relief. He mentioned that as the advice and warnings of Ghasi Singh had not been heeded, the whole party of soldiers, except eight or nine men, had been killed. After that, the Hos had destroyed the fort at Chainpur and with it seven villages that belonged to the raja of Porahat. The peasants of the neighbourhood, including those of Chakradharpur, were all fleeing to the hills and had left their grain behind. The rumour was that the Hos had burned the fort of Chakradharpur. Chaitan's *pir* of Asantalia, just south of Kharsawan, was 'likewise deserted, Sir, from the violence of the Larkas', and continued: 'We shall be entirely ruined without your aid and presence.' Chaitan was able to give the reasoning of the Hos, who said that it was by Chaitan's advice that Ghanshyam Singh brought the Major to Singhbhum. 'We have no wish to quarrel with any other landlord, the rest are of our party.' Chaitan

54 | A Land of Their Own

had the right injured aristocratic touch: 'this is the language they use'. He continued in tears: 'If you wish to preserve me and the raja, pray grant us assistance.'[100]

Ghanshyam of Porahat's letter of 11 February made the picture of despair complete. Playing the fool, he stated, 'all at once troubles broke out'. Everybody had died in the battle at Cheri, even (he said) his man in Chakradharpur (Ghasi). After the fall of Chainpur, the inhabitants of the Chakradharpur area 'all quitted the country'. Ghanshyam warned Roughsedge of the grand design of the Ho attacks.

> The next object of the Hos was to attack me at my residence of Porahat, and I had only time to make my escape one day before that fixed for the assault. . . . For if I had waited their attack nothing could have saved myself and my family . . . and should they attack me here [in Anandpur], I have no road open to my flight.[101]

Here, too, tears flowed. 'I rely on your aid without which I must perish.' He had, he said, the courage to appeal to the good government of the British, as 'hitherto those who have depended on the British Government have benefited by its protection, and it is this, which encouraged me to hope for assistance'. The assistance had to be right for him, though. So, 'I sent to you Dharam Das Gosain who was in the action with . . . Bahuran Singh and can inform you of its details'.[102]

Dharam Das was good at his shady trade. Up to that point, Roughsedge felt that, as he had left the Hos 'peaceably disposed' the year before, 'gross misconduct in some quarters has led to the present disturbances'.[103] However, he was at a loss where to put that misconduct. Now, one week later, Dharam Das Gosain worked so well on Roughsedge, that the agent was taken in. He wrote that Gosain's narrative of 23 February was made 'with an intention of nothing but the truth'.[104] Whatever it was, it was not the whole truth, as Roughsedge was to admit elsewhere.[105] Dharam completely left out Ghanshyam's role in the events and blamed the destruction of Bahuran's force solely on the 'treacherous machinations' of Ghasi Singh.[106] It also was not anything but the truth. On Roughsedge's question to Dharam, 'Are you sure that you have never heard a report of the bad conduct of the soldiers in Gumra?' The answer was, quite absurdly, 'Quite sure, and I am convinced it would have been untrue.'[107]

The question of the safety of the post came up. On 12 February the responsible person in Bamanghati wrote that the post 'in hourly danger of being stopped' by, among others, the Balandia Hos.[108] One week later, Roughsedge found that 'no actual obstruction to the passage of the post has been offered on Capt. Jackson's Road'. He hoped that it was a false alarm, 'though such an occurrence would be far from extraordinary'.[109] The next day, 20 February, Roughsedge got another anxious letter about the safety of the post and the post runners, now on the more southern part of the route. Again there were no instances of actual obstruction of the post.[110] Nerves were tight.

While the mud of accusations, exaggerations and denials was flying to cover the tactical blunders of the Singh chiefs, the strategic effects of the successful Ho actions remained clearly visible. The *cordon sanitaire* around the Hos, which Roughsedge had built so hurriedly the year before, had collapsed.

Roughsedge immediately warned Calcutta that 'strong measures combined with conciliation after an impression has been made are absolutely necessary against this intractable tribe of ferocious savages, who inhabit a considerable extent of country within ten or twelve marches of the metropolis of British India. It is very clear that they can be subdued only by regular troops with horse, & no permanent effect could be obtained without the establishment of military posts in the heart of their districts for some years.'[111] First a major operation, a three-pronged attack from Sambalpur, Midnapur, and Cuttack; then a permanent garrison in the middle of the affected tract, was his solution.[112] There was a price tag attached. Due to recent downsizing, the 500 men needed for the last task could not be spared from the Ramgarh Battalion with its strength of 1,200 privates.[113] On 6 March, Roughsedge, who hated to campaign in the hot season, proposed a combined operation of the Midnapur and Ramgarh corps at the commencement of the winter season.[114]

Roughsedge did not have to wait long for strong opposition. Nathaniel Smith, Collector at Ramgarh and his long-time opponent, found the whole operation misguided. He did not see why the East India Company should conduct a major campaign to restore the fictional authority of the Singhbhum chiefs over the Hos.[115] At this point, the magistrate of the Jungle States, A. J. Colvin, who seemed to have been assigned the task of keeping an eye on Tamar, intervened on Roughsedge's side. His information was that the Tamar leader Kunta had participated in the battle of Chainpur, and that the Kols from Tamar just north of Singhbhum were preparing to go south to take part in the plunder.[116] Spread of the disturbances! It stressed the need to regain control of the situation. What was at stake now was not some small chiefs in some unpronounceable places, appearing in the sources as Chuckurdhurpoor, Cursuwa or Serie Kella, but the very strategy of containment.

Within a week, on 14 March 1821, the governor general declared himself in favour of a robust and immediate reply. 'The tranquillity of the country is not likely to be established on a firm basis,' he wrote, 'until such an impression shall be made by a military force upon the chiefs in their haunts, as shall effectually convince that savage race, that they can no longer expect to escape with impunity if they continue their habits of rapine and devastation'. He placed the whole operation in military hands, 'exclusively under the direction of the commanding officer of the troops, Lieutenant Colonel Richards'.[117] The idea was 'prompt and signal chastisement'.[118] Only after the resistance of the Hos had been crushed, will 'the civil functions of the governor general's agent . . . [again] come into operation in the settlement of the country and the adjustment of the boundaries and relations of the different chieftains'.[119] This was a significant development. The year before, Roughsedge had rushed his troops through this very territory to his beloved town of Sambalpur. He had been severely lectured for that. Roughsedge, in 1812 still seen as the most influential advisor of government on this part of the country,[120] now, nine years later, suffered his second major rebuff in a year.

Chapter 3

The Mouth of a Gun

...
*Plans for the invasion; the Second Kolhan Campaign;
the battle of the Khuntpani Gorge; the terms of the peace*
...

Roughsedge was instructed to provide Lieutenant Colonel Richards[1] with all available information on Singhbhum and the Hos. On 3 April 1821, he gave a lengthy sketch of Singhbhum and the Kolhan. It contained a neat summary of the history of the Singh attempts to recapture the Kolhan, and its political-military description covered practically the whole of Singhbhum. It gave estimates of the number of local fighters and the quality of their arms.[2]

In addition, Roughsedge drew up a plan to attack the Hos from four sides: Sambalpur, Cuttack, Midnapur and Bankura. He wanted a short campaign, not a lengthy military operation. He felt the pressure of time. Then there was his illness, which would certainly return with the heat and the rains. Roughsedge's nervousness and irritation that his task now was largely limited to advice translated itself in an unsolicited and extreme stand. He thought it likely that the people involved in the actions at Pokharia and Chainpur would flee to the hills. On 14 April he wrote to Calcutta.

> Their timely flight to the hills or other untoward circumstances, however, may deprive the troops in the short season before them, of any opportunity to bestow a signal chastisement, and yet with savages, after an unavailing trial of kindness and conciliation, terror alone can be expected to operate efficaciously & permanently; the interests of humanity ... would ultimately, I submit, be best served by the adoption of the most striking and impressive mode of punishing . . . . I reluctantly suggest, for the consideration of His Lordship in Council, whether it might not be expedient, if the principle of subjecting any Hos to capital punishment be considered justifiable, that those condemned to it or a portion of them should be blown from the mouth of a gun. This mode . . . appears to me calculated to make the deepest & most salutary impression in the minds of the Hos.[3]

This proposal aroused consternation in Calcutta. The governor general made it known that he found this punishment much too severe for a 'mere charge of insurrection'.[4]

Roughsedge was the agent at the South Western Frontier, though, and his political advice weighed heavily. He sketched a strategy to civilise the Hos after they had been subdued. Unlike in Chotanagpur, where immigrants had the upper hand, in Singhbhum, the Hindu groups feared the Hos so much that they courted their favour. He had little faith in the civilising capacities of the Hindu inhabitants of the 'valuable portion', that is, the Ghanshyam-controlled part, of Singhbhum. 'It is not in the nature of things that the raja or any other chief in Singhbhum will have it in his power for many years to molest or oppress the Larkas, they have been for more than half a century independent in reality of his and all other authority'. Again, the Hos did not understand Hindi or Odia and, as long as they would not master these languages, 'there can be little hope of improvement'.[5] Instead, Roughsedge banked on the military. Two companies of Hill Rangers in Saraikela and two companies of the Ramgarh Battalion in Chakradharpur would not only 'effectually protect the civilized and valuable portion of Singhbhum', but also have the mission to make the Hos 'acquainted with our customs and language'. Through 'encouragement & conciliation', the Hos should approximate that 'most useful class of men with whom they have one common origin, the Dhangar or Kols of Chotanagpur, of whom I believe thousands may at this moment be found exercising an honest industry in & near Calcutta and vast numbers are spread over the country wherever labour of more than ordinary severity renders their strength and assiduity desirable'.[6] Roughsedge had a harsh realism. His options for the Hos ranged from the mouth of the guns to hard labour as migrants.

He saw problems. The permanent deployment of troops was a departure from the policy of non-interference. Nevertheless, he pointed to its inevitability. The number of Hos was in the fifty thousand range. He sketched an open-ended threat by presenting the Ho people as 'rapidly increasing'. Moreover, he drew attention to the geographic position of Singhbhum, 'I mean its vicinity to the capital of British India.' Then there were their raids into Chotanagpur and Tamar to the North, and to the south into Keonjhar and Mayurbhanj. Jackson's Road was vulnerable. Lastly, he used the always-valid argument that an uncontained Kolhan would provide a safe haven for criminal elements from British territory. He concluded that perhaps it was 'worth while to make the sacrifice' to station troops in or near the Kolhan.[7] It turned out to be near rather than in the Kolhan. Evidently. To take over the policing of the Ho country was a bridge too far. The strategy decided upon was first to punish the Hos, then to contain them.

With Roughsedge's sketch of Singhbhum for Richards, Raghunath's star started to rise. Just a year before, in April 1820, Raghunath had been a refugee in Keonjhar. The turning points of Raghunath's luck were the battles of Chainpur and Cheri of early 1821. These removed the threat that Bahuran, Ratan and their mercenaries would rise as an alternative power in Singhbhum. On the other hand, the military reverse created the need for a second Kolhan campaign and, thus, for precise knowledge of the Ho country. Of course, Roughsedge already had made an extensive overview.[8] Raghunath Bisi could fill that in with some background. He had 'much information of [the] state of the country, disposition and habits of the Kols,' and, not unimportant, on 'the pitiable state of the raja'.[9] Payment was immediate. A few days before Roughsedge sent his extensive sketch of Singhbhum, he ordered the Ho leaders of the south-west of Bar *pir* and of Sant Bantaria to join him. Raghunath himself carried the order to the nearby Cuttack Detachment, for further delivery. It was a scoop. Nearly. The Hos of the neighbourhood had already joined the independents' camp.[10]

On both sides, preparations were going on. Roughsedge's strategy was to overawe the Hos in the shortest possible time. They were to be attacked from four sides: Sambalpur, Cuttack, Midnapur and Bankura.[11] The troops were got together without delay. The whole mobilisation took less than a month. The furthest off was the Body Guard of the governor general in Calcutta. At the end of March, it was ordered to march. Like Roughsedge, they were none too pleased, as a recently appointed officer wrote.

> We had to march upwards of 965 kilometres before we got to the point where the attack was to be made; and this was during the worst season of the year that men could be exposed [to] in tents. The thermometer stood any day in our tent at 43 and 44.5 [degrees], and on some days as high as 50; and when exposed to the sun at noon, it generally stood between 65 and 71.[12]

It is interesting to see how they perceived the aim of the campaign.

> To take the field . . . against a tribe of outrageous mountaineers, called Kooles (sic), who had made war against their peaceable neighbours, burnt their villages, murdered all their inhabitants, and plundered the whole of the country.[13]

The Hos, of course, had a different view of themselves. Still, the question here was to defend their villages, and if so, how. In the north, in Ajodhya, the Hos split. Three villages, at least two of which had already earlier opposed the attack on the soldiers at Pokharia, joined the British. On the other hand, nine 'refractory villages' were preparing to resist.[14] In the south, as we have seen, the Hos had got together. Here, too, preparations were going on.[15] Mata Pingua from Balandia, whose village had been burned the year before,[16] but who had not surrendered, again was a central leader of the resistance here. As a precaution against the invasion, as in the year before, the Hos had established hidden supply bases, ('*phoots*' or '*cooras*').[17] There they had large stocks of food, but also kept their families and property.

They had to oppose a force at least six times the size of Roughsedge's the year before. The newspaper *John Bull in the East* estimated that the Ramgarh Battalion together with the Body Guard, the 13th Native Infantry, the Hill Rangers and the Cuttack legion, there were 2,000 troops under the overall command of Colonel Richards.[18] The Ramgarh Battalion with 400 regulars, two six-pounders, and 100 irregular horse under Captain Thomas Frobisher came from the south, but as planned quickly went to the north of the theatre. Richards himself proceeded from Bamanghati in the east.[19] The Body Guard invaded from the north.[20]

The Second Kolhan Campaign started around 15 April 1821. Though it was successful for the Company's side, it had a rough start. On the second day, Captain Thornton of the Body Guard led 'a beautiful charge, and 'cut up' between 50 to 60 Hos, losing only two soldiers badly wounded, one servant dead. But the loss of their 'Native Doctor' by friendly fire suggested initial confusion'.[21] Still, they had the upper hand and the actions of the East India Company troops were particularly severe. As Richards wrote, 'Whenever resistance was met with, the villages were invariably burnt to the ground. . . . These villages were full of grain and well stocked with cattle.' On 17 April, after a few days of fighting, as many as fifteen villages were destroyed.[22] The army wanted to break all resistance before the Hos could regroup in the hills. They did not succeed.

> For three or four days after our arrival in their country they gave us battle on the plains; but finding themselves so dreadfully cut up, and being able to make no impression upon us, they betook themselves to the recesses of their highest mountains.[23]

But from there, there was no place to go. As Roughsedge observed, 'having been informed that the Larkas of ten villages of Ajodhya and Rajabasa, have collected with their families and grain in the gorge of a mountain near that village I have great hope that something important may be effected'.[24] Captain Frobisher gave a graphic description of his attack.

> I marched on the night of the 21st [April] at 8 P.M. with a detachment of 350 firelocks, two six pounders and 80 irregular horse to attack the *coora* near Khuntpani and the other refractory villages of Ajodhya. The distance being greater than was calculated upon and the road rendered difficult for near[ly] 6 kilometres by stockades of stones thrown up by the enemy, I did not reach Khuntpani till after sunrise nor the *coora* which was about three kilometres further before 7 o'clock.
>
> I found the Hos in number about 800 very strongly posted and stockaded within the gorge of a mountain, the only approach was through a defile about thirty-five or forty-five metres broad, the enemy occupied the summit of the hills on our flanks and in front and had likewise several breast works, they opposed our advance with a sharp fire of arrows but were quickly driven from their positions with a loss, which I estimate at about 80 men. Within the breast work were found [many thousand kilogrammes] of grain which being unable to carry away I caused to be destroyed.[25]

By now, 22 April, Ghanshyam of Porahat and Ghasi of Chakradharpur joined the fight in the north. First, they had merely asked for the return of the cattle. Roughsedge requested authorisation to order his own regular troops, who had supplemented their pay with loot, to return recovered cattle to these allies for a 'fair compensation' in money. The cattle and other plunder could then be used for the resettlement of the 'civilized inhabitants of Singhbhum'. Now, in addition, Ghanshyam and Ghasi showed themselves 'very anxious to be allowed to avail themselves of the opportunity to make reprisals'. The reason they gave was that their peasants had 'suffered severely by the depredations of the Larkas during the last three months', that is, from the time of Ratan's rout at Chainpur. Roughsedge authorised them to plunder Hodisum. The plunder was done by 'roving parties . . . in the mountainous and jungly parts' of Hodisum, going to places where regular troops would not go.[26] On 25 April, ten days after the beginning of the campaign, the resistance had taken to the hills.[27]

In the south too, the very speed of the Company army had unsettled the resistance. In villages and hiding places the Company's privates found fires still burning, the rice still warm.[28] On the Ho side, the cleavages of the year before—if they ever were gone—reappeared. The Hos of Bantaria and of the west of Jaintgarh (Bar) *pirs* joined the invasion forces of the Company. The Balandia Hos under Mata and those of the east and north-east of Jaintgarh opposed the Company troops.[29] In the centre and east of the Kolhan, resistance held out in Gumra. But most of its inhabitants had fled to the sparsely populated Saranda *pir* in the south-west,[30] the four Kol *pirs* of Bamanghati (Thai, Bharbharia, Lalgarh, and Anwla), to Rajabasa and even to Ajodhya *pir*.[31] That dispersal made the resistance even more vulnerable.

The Second Kolhan Campaign differed in important respects from the first. To start with, the Company's intelligence was much better. It had a much more systematic view of the people and the country, gathered from different, though still mostly non-Ho, sources. That made more precise planning possible. The Bengal Army's tactic of simultaneous invasions from different sides prevented the Hos from concentrating their forces. The invasion of Thai *pir* deprived them of an essential prerequisite of guerrilla warfare, a safe haven in the rear. By destroying the villages and the stocks of food on a large scale, the Company troops raised the stakes of the Hos for continuing the war. One thing had not changed on the Company side: their admiration of the bravery of the Hos.

> They betook themselves to the recesses of their highest mountains, where we were obliged to follow them, to hunt them down, and kill them like so many tigers, as they never would allow themselves to be taken prisoners, while they could keep hold of their bow-and-arrow and battle-axe.[32]

The Company troops were remarkably successful in attacking the fortified hideouts of the Hos. But it came at a price. The officer in Camp Sambalpur again drew attention to

> the very harassing nature of the expedition to everyone concerned. Out of the four medical men that commenced the campaign, only one survived the excessive fatigue they were obliged to undergo, so that the whole of the medical charge devolved upon him, [among others the care for] at one time upwards of 400 men sick in the camp.[33]

As we have seen, in its final days the campaign got more local involvement when Roughsedge allowed irregulars from the Porahat and the Chakradharpur side to join the plunder, mainly in the north. In the south, pro-government Hos from Bantaria and Bar joined the forces and proved to be good in discovering the hide-outs of the opposing side. The Ho resistance caved in.

On the 29th, Roughsedge and Richards issued a proclamation to the leaders in Gumra *pir*, 'which was framed to meet the level of comprehension' of the Hos, and 'simply stated' that the actions of the troops were the 'natural effect' of the Ho attacks on Bahuran and the Chainpur fort. 'From sentiment of commiseration', they gave the heads of the villages four days to appear in person to Gumra to submit 'to the British government', or to be treated without mercy. On Richards' insistence, Roughsedge had sent the proclamation also to the inhabitants of Thai, Bharbharia, Lalgarh, and Anwla.[34] These *pirs* were part of Bamanghati, hence under Mayurbhanj, and should have been superintended by the Commissioner in Cuttack.[35] The heads of the villages in Bantaria and Jaintgarh let it be known that they did not dare to come to Gumra, 'especially as they would have to pass through some of the villages belonging to . . . Kols with whom they were at variance'. They were directed to appear before Captain Macleod who campaigned in Jaintgarh.[36] His direct opponent, Mata of Balandia, got the special message that if he would not come, he would see 'the employment of our whole force for his destruction'.[37]

On 5 May Roughsedge could write to Richards that all the heads of Ho villages had submitted, except those of the Bharbharia, Lalgarh, and Anwla *pirs*. But he counted on their submission.[38] On 8 May he got the news that the villages of Anwla and Lalgarh *pirs* had submitted. On 9 May 1821 Lt. Col. Richards' force was broken up.[39] His final message showed his relief. He found 'infinite pleasure in expressing unqualified approbation of the conduct of the whole of the officers and men of every branch and department, who he has had the honor to command.' The campaign had been 'from the oppressive heat of the weather and the many natural obstacles that presented themselves . . . arduous in the extreme'.[40]

Roughsedge now held a meeting with the Ho leaders, which included those of Thai and Bharbharia *pirs*, to formalise the submission. It did not altogether go to plan; they were too accommodating. The new tax to be paid to the surrounding chiefs was projected at the rate of half a rupee per plough. But the Ho negotiators said they would 'cheerfully' pay a tax of one rupee per working plough.[41] He had to reason with them not to offer that rate—and again they were pleased. 'They expressed great satisfaction, when after consulting with some of the best informed men within my reach, I finally determined they should pay Eight annas'—half a rupee—'each plough for the next five years, and one rupee afterwards if the circumstances admitted of it'.[42]

To offer to pay more tax than was asked, as well as the rejection of that offer, was puzzling. Why would somebody offer to pay more tax, and why would the government turn down such an offer? Apparently, Roughsedge had left out here what the Hos had asked in return. We hear about that later, in Dalton's 1872 account. The Hos in the meeting 'earnestly prayed at this time to be taken under the direct management of the British Officers'.[43] But it was important to Roughsedge to keep the final outcome of this meeting equal to previous agreements with the Hindu chiefs and with the Hos who had submitted earlier. Roughsedge's assumption had been all along that he was restoring these chiefs to their power over all the Hos. The request of the Hos who submitted later to come directly under the British, and thus leave the Hindu chiefs out, struck at the fundaments of Roughsedge's new edifice. Dalton wrote, 'their wishes were not complied with'.[44] As Roughsedge explained to his superiors:

> I ought previously to have stated that the rightful sovereignty of the raja and babus of Singhbhum over the Hos of that district & of Niranjan Mahapater of Bamanghati over those of Thai Pir, is so strongly implanted in the minds of both parties that to have thrown any doubt over the question would have been taken by the former [the raja, babus and the *mahapater*] as an act of the most crying injustice, whilst it would only have tended to confuse and unsettle the Ho subjects.[45]

Roughsedge now explained to these mankis and mundas what their future relations with these chiefs and with the British Government would be.

The original text of the agreement between the East India Company and the village leaders of the Hos had been in English, but 'a translation of it, in the Kol language but in Odia character', was used to convey the message.[46] This made it probably the first piece of Ho language written on paper. The Hos could not read, so it was read to them.[47] Unfortunately, I could not trace the Ho language text, but we do have Roughsedge's English original. The terms were the following:

> First. We acknowledge ourselves to be subjects of the British Government, and engage to be loyal and obedient to its authority.

> Secondly. We agree our lawful chiefs and zemindars Eight annas for each working plough for the five years next ensuing, and afterwards one Rupee if our circumstances admit it.

> Thirdly. We engage to keep the roads through our Pergunnahs open and safe for all descriptions of travellers, and if robbery takes place, to deliver the Thi[e]ves to justice and account for the property stolen.

> Fourthly. We will allow persons of all castes to settle in our Villages, and afford them protection, and will also encourage our children to learn Orea or Hindoo language.

Lastly. If we should be oppressed by our chief or zemindar, we will not resort to arms for redress, but complain to the officers commanding the troops on our frontier or some other competent authority.[48]

Roughsedge mentioned that the heads of villages, 'affix[ed] their signatures to this engagement'.[49] That would have been remarkable for people who could not write. A more vivid description of the formal agreement ceremony was given by a witness. 'They acquiesced in the terms proposed for the regulation of their future behaviour, swearing, according to their custom, *on the tigers skin*, to abide faithfully by their agreement.'[50]

The immediate need of the East India Company was to secure the southern flank of the Kolhan. Richards placed a detachment of sixty firelocks and twenty horses under some commissioned and non-commissioned officers in Kathkaranjia.[51] This place was on Jackson's Road in Keonjhar. Richard's orders to the troops, too, were to 'hut themselves as soon as possible, to keep themselves informed of occurrences on the Kol frontier and to cultivate a good understanding with the heads of villages'. The commanding officer at Kathkaranjia received explicit instructions to rely upon Raghunath Bisi for his information. In return, he was to support Raghunath in anything short of offensive military action.[52] This gave Raghunath Bisi a crucial hold on the stream of information as well as a military backup.

There was a strategic reason for this arrangement. Hired for skills, not for attitude, Raghunath was the one in the south of the Kolhan who could deliver the required quiet border. Bisi and his villagers figured large in Roughsedge's scheme to change the ethnic composition of the area. In the agreement of submission of the village leaders of the Hos, he had expressly stipulated that the Hos would allow 'persons of all castes' to settle in their villages. This provision was made with Raghunath in mind. Roughsedge reinstated him in Jaintgarh[53] and provided him with some privates. It must have been then that Raghunath became the hereditary *divan* of Porahat.[54] As a fee for the management of the Jaintgarh *pir*, he was to receive Rs. 150 a year from the raja.[55] Raghunath's villagers had to rebuild their huts and prepare their lands before the rains started. In Raghunath's words: 'Sobur and Pohar, two villages of mine, were deserted. Major Roughsedge told me to cause them inhabited and gave me two hundred R[upee]s to that purpose. I had them inhabited.'[56] It did pay to move with the times.

To the east, on the Bamanghati side, immediate humanitarian relief was needed to stabilise the situation. Roughsedge lost no time. Already on 6 May, he drew attention to the ruinous losses of the Hos of Thai *pir*. They had suffered heavily during the campaign, even as, he acknowledged, they had 'little concern with the outrages which led to the invasion of their hitherto unsubdued district'. In a move to set them on their feet again, he proposed to give them small grants of money to buy bullocks and seed grain to tide over the next few months.[57] The same day, Richards agreed.[58]

On the northern flank of the containment arrangement, Roughsedge immediately assessed the political damage. He finalised his investigation of the attacks on Bahuran Singh's soldiers and the fort of Chainpur. Kuntu Pater was interrogated on 12 and 13 May 1821. Three days later, Ghasi Singh explained himself at length.[59] Back in Sambalpur, it took Roughsedge until August to recover and report. In his view, it was unlikely that Ghasi Singh had stirred 'so dangerous and unmanageable a machine as a body of armed Larkas'. He suggested the possibility that Ghasi had tricked Bahuran, who could only communicate with the Hos through Ghasi Singh's interpreters. In Roughsedge's view, the tax rise effected by Bahuran and Ghasi, and the insult to Kuntu Pater's daughter had caused the attack by the Hos. Roughsedge did not think that the care of the Hos to spare the lives of Ghasi Singh and his relatives implicated Ghasi in the Ho attacks. He attributed this to 'a remnant of the veneration for him as the descendant of their ancient rajas'.[60] Thus, to the north of the Kolhan, Ghasi Singh and the status quo just squeezed through.

As for the tribute, there was an imbalance in the treatment of Porahat on the one side and Saraikela and Kharsawan on the other side. The agreements between the East India Company and these three states, concluded at the beginning of 1820, had stipulated for each a yearly tribute of Rs. 101. But it turned out that this tribute was only collected from Porahat. This must have contributed to the long-standing enmity between Porahat and Saraikela, but it remained the practice till the rearrangement of the area in 1837.[61]

Chapter 4

A Champaign Country

...
*Roughsedge's observations; an exclusive people; creditable economy;
political divisions and cooperation; a land of villages*
...

Major Edward Roughsedge's despatches contained quite some remarks on the Hos. These were meant for use by the administration and the military, not for reflection or publication. Although Roughsedge's individual letters were quite systematic, neatly divided into paragraphs, the total body of his information was not. At those moments when he did not talk politics or taxes, he gave some information in the tradition, established in the late 1760s, that British officers of the East India Company reported 'the peculiar customs' of the people.[1] Roughsedge did not have the time, the inclination, nor the need to get more than basic and unsystematic information on these lands and peoples. The first information came from the Singhs. Until a few days before Roughsedge actually crossed the border river, he had not seen a single Ho, let alone had he listened to their side of the story. When he met them, his mind was already set upon forcing them under the rule of the Singh chiefs.

Roughsedge made his own observations on the Hos over very short periods of time, mostly in warlike situations, on days filled to the brim with his other duties. The First Kolhan Campaign of 1820 took Roughsedge twenty-three days, the Second Kolhan Campaign of 1821 and its legal aftermath lasted twenty-four days.[2] The major was mostly a good observer, though. It is on the more reflective side that we find him wanting. He saw what he needed, the general state of the land, the main political attitudes towards him and the Singh chiefs, the general exclusiveness of the Hos, their quite strong economy and, at closer view, a Hodisum divided into villages and *kilis* (clans).

He was ready to admit that his knowledge of the Hos was far from perfect. When, at the end of the Second Kolhan Campaign, Richards had asked him to take the task of settling the eastern *pirs* close to Bamanghati, he informed Calcutta that he 'rather would be relieved'. He cited as reasons 'the shortness of time before me, and their remote situation from the sphere of my public duties, together of my want of local knowledge of them'.[3]

At three moments in the last two years of his life, Roughsedge wrote down information on the land and the people of the Kolhan or Hodisum.

The first occasion was in his letter to the government, in the person of Metcalfe, on 9 May 1820. Roughsedge wrote it in Sambalpur about one month after the termination of his first campaign. This letter contained a detailed report of his actions. It briefly described the villages, economy, political system, marriage customs of the Hos, and their differences with the Mundas.

The second time Roughsedge paid extensive attention to the Hos was when he was preparing the Second Kolhan Campaign. He had orders from Calcutta to give full information 'regarding the force, position, military habits, and any other peculiar circumstances of the Kols', as well as geographical information.[4] He did his homework well. The extensive description of the Kolhan in his letter of 3 April 1821 greatly improved upon his letter of the year before.[5] Its core was, as we have seen, a detailed description of the *pirs* of Singhbhum and the Hodisum. The emphasis was on information useful for the military: number of villages, numbers of bowmen and matchlocks, political status of the *pirs*, and the disposition of the inhabitants towards the Singh chiefs.

Much of this was from third persons. His main informants were Bikram Singh of Saraikela, Ghanshyam Singh of Porahat and Raghunath Bisi of Jaintgarh. Together, they filled in Roughsedge's view on the relations of the Singhs with the Hos. When they spoke of Ho society itself, they did not give much information.

If there was a villain in the piece of the forced incorporation of Hodisum into the area under the overlordship of the East India Company, it was Raghunath Bisi. Evidence of a meeting between Roughsedge and Raghunath did not appear until April 1820, the end of the First Kolhan Campaign, when he and Ghanshyam Singh of Porahat reached Jaintgarh on the southern frontier of Singhbhum. While he was a constant source of friction with the Hos as well as with the raja of Porahat, Raghunath Bisi took care that his relations with the Company officers were good. Roughsedge's successor Gilbert described him in 1823 as 'particularly useful to the late Captain Roughsedge'.[6]

Roughsedge's notions of Ho society were formed early in the first campaign.[7] It was before he had seen much, let alone could have understood what he saw, so he was dependent on what the Singhs told him. He was aware that to rely on someone else's information made one dependent on his interpretation.[8]

He got information directly from Hos when he investigated the events that had led to the second campaign. He used these occasions also to obtain 'local information', like on the *kilis* of the Hos and on their trade with Saraikela. Even when hostilities were still going on, Roughsedge held interviews and interrogated people. Possibly on 21 April 1821, he spoke with Singrai, the Ho leader of Ajodhya *pir*. On the 27th and 28th of that month, Roughsedge interrogated some important people with knowledge of the attacks on Bahuran and Chainpur. After the cessation of hostilities, Kuntu Pater defended himself when he was interrogated on 13 May, and three days later Ghasi Singh made a long defensive speech.[9] On 7 August, Roughsedge wrote down his findings and added the verbatim reports of the interrogations.[10]

Roughsedge would have found it difficult to communicate with the Hos. The remark in his obituary that he had a thorough knowledge of Indian languages probably referred to Persian, the court language in northern India, and Urdu/Hindustani, the lingua franca of the army. Although he spent more than fifteen years in Munda-speaking areas, Roughsedge did not speak the language. During the First Kolhan Campaign, he mentioned that he had started to compile a 'copious vocabulary'. Of the language he could say no more than that it was 'merely oral; I have traced it to the hills of Palamau, and I believe [it] to have extended much further. It certainly is quite a distinct tongue from Hindi and Odia but will probably be easily traced to Sanskrit; . . . I will only add that it has a soft and pleasing sound when spoken.'[11] The list of words with its attempt at theory was a laudable effort for someone who was rushing through the tract at the head of his troops, but it could not have helped him much in speaking with the Hos. To compound his difficulties, 'not one in a hundred Larka' could speak Hindustani or Odia.

Roughsedge himself spoke with the Ho leaders through interpreters,[12] who were very few and had varying fluency in the Ho language. Some Tantis, weavers, lived in Ho villages and spoke Ho,[13] but either these people were not considered to be able to interpret, or Roughsedge just overlooked them. On his side of the border, so to speak, there were only four or five individuals who could speak some Ho.[14] Most were weavers. They stayed now on one side of the border, then on the other side to sell cloth. But they spoke only 'a little of the Larka language'.[15] There were some servants of Ghasi Singh, like Permee and Bullea, who could converse in Ho.[16] Roughsedge was not naive. He knew that interpreters could deceive him.[17]

Roughsedge did not attempt to speak to Ho women, even through translators. He was nearly completely silent about them. 'They don't marry until both sexes attain the age of puberty, and restrict themselves to one wife.'[18] An officer stationed close to Hodisum in 1822, stated that the Hos went nearly naked, 'except a small covering about the loins'.[19] Roughsedge did not even comment on the small dress of the women, as Colvin had done.[20] The women's sparse clothing was, however, very conspicuous to his soldiers, who were mostly from the higher castes of the northern plains. There, women of their social background led quite a secluded life and would appear in public only when fully dressed. As we have seen, Roughsedge recorded from hearsay the experiences of the only woman he mentioned. Soldiers had 'forcibly dishonoured' Mahadei, daughter of Kuntu Pater.[21] At least in Singhbhum, Roughsedge lived in a man's world.

On one occasion, Roughsedge's practical, military bent of mind made way for an emotional aside. For a man who was for such long periods without anybody whom he could consider his own class, a letter could serve as an emotional outlet. Even after 200 years, Roughsedge's surprise sounds fresh.

> The northernmost *pir* of Larka Kol named Ajodhya was separated from the civilized part of Singhbhum by a small river, the country on both sides being level and open: on crossing it the singular spectacle of a well cultivated champaign country studded with large villages, but inhabited by people who owned no laws, and were in a constant state of aggression and hostility with the rest of the world, presented itself.[22]

One notices, of course, the terms of the description: the Caesarean crossing of the river; the Tacitean opposition of civilisation to the savage;[23] the champaign country opposed to its lawless people. His observations clashed with his preconceived ideas.

> The mind is so accustomed to associate with the idea of predatory and lawless tribes their residence in the fastnesses and strongholds of woods and mountains, that it was with difficulty I could bring myself to believe that the smiling hamlets in view, contained inhabitants so ferocious and sanguinary as we found them to be.[24]

'As we found them to be'; in a masterly slide of time perspective, from the present into the future, the idea that had caused the campaign was brought to life by its effects.

Roughsedge could be stirred, but he was not shaken. In his view, the Hos were rebels. Roughsedge did acknowledge that for some fifty years the Hos had enjoyed 'perfect independence'.[25] Nonetheless, the major felt that this independence came from rebellion. He did not even try to understand them as politically separate from the neighbouring states. His entire career had prepared Roughsedge for this view. In his advice to his government, therefore, he had the Hos as his blank spot. He had no clue as to what moved the people of Hodisum. Admittedly, they were quite different people from the local chiefs.

While Roughsedge succeeded in imparting crucial geographical and military knowledge to Calcutta, he transmitted but a hazy image of the ethnic nature of his adversaries. His lack of knowledge stood out in his letter of 3 April 1821. Here Roughsedge distinguished merely between the 'civilized' parts of Singhbhum, mostly 'an open plain, inhabited by Brahmins and the usual cultivating classes of Hindus', and the villages of the 'Larkas'.[26]

The root of the problem was that like the other Bengal Army officers, Roughsedge followed the Hindustani custom in using the pejorative generic term 'Kols' to indicate the original peoples of Jharkhand. The same lack of distinction appeared with 'Larka Kols' in Singhbhum itself. Indeed, the Larka Kols in the centre of Singhbhum, the Kolhan, were Hos. Roughsedge, however, lumped these Larka Kols together with those in the north-west and north of Singhbhum. But the 'Kols' who lived in its Bandgaon area were Mundas, a people closely related but distinct from the Hos. To confuse things further, these north/north-west 'Larkas' were also seen as nearly identical to the Tamarians—they only wore fewer clothes.[27]

For Roughsedge, the perceived political boundaries of Singhbhum determined the ethnic denomination of its population. They were all 'Larka Kols'. If they were, in his words, 'independent' of the raja and other chiefs, they deserved the epithet 'refractory', otherwise, they were 'loyalist'.[28] Though many of the difficulties he encountered had an ethnic side, Roughsedge did not have much of an ethnographic map in mind. With this history of Roughsedge's knowledge of the Hos, in his letters we can expect very little of what we would now regard as anthropology.

The fierce exclusiveness of the Hos was standard in all Roughsedge's descriptions. Its prime objects were Saraikela, Kharsawan, Jaintgarh and Porahat, in that order. In the east of Hodisum, 'at this moment (1820) a party of a hundred armed men would refuse to go the direct road between

Bamanghati and Saraikela and all travellers make a circuit of 20 miles to the East to avoid these dreadful savages'. The next year, Roughsedge again stated that this road had 'for many years' been 'impassable for travellers and even bodies of armed men'. He attributed this to their fear of the inhabitants of the Thai *pir*.[29] The major well knew that this fear had its geography. The Hos of Bantaria *pir* gave passage to servants of Porahat. There was a modest regular commerce of traders who entered the Hodisum and, inversely, of Ho villagers who purchased goods in the Singh areas. Groups of Hos went to the two yearly markets in Saraikela.[30] In the Gumra *pir* in central Hodisum, Ghasi Singh could collect some revenue. Even the hatred of Brahmins was not absolute—at least on the Brahmins's side. Roughsedge observed that 'the favor and good graces of this usually . . . [contempted] tribe are courted by the Brahmin and other classes of Hindus who reside in the vicinity of their villages'.[31] Still, these contacts must have been rather limited as the fear of the Hos went deep. Ajodhya, 'though in the immediate vicinity of the civilized portion of Singhbhum, and perfectly open to attack had established an efficient independence, any attempt against which on the part of the raja or zamindars, the [Ho] inhabitants looked upon with great contempt'.[32]

To Roughsedge, the Hos, by virtue of not being controlled by the Company or their allies, were outside the reach of recognisable states, without civil society, and hence 'uncivilized'. Worse, they were 'a dreadful pest to the civilized part of Singhbhum'.[33] The terms in which Roughsedge expressed this idea can easily be misunderstood. In two places he used an animal simile.

The 'tiger's den' simile appeared in his description of the north and east of the Kolhan. This classic formulation of the independence of the Hos came in the oft-quoted sentence: 'A traveller would as soon think of entering into a tiger's den, as of traversing any part of Lurka Cole'.[34] It was a powerful image of Hodisum, expressing exclusion, fear, and admiration. These were not Roughsedge's words. The 'tiger's den' image came probably from Bikram Singh of Saraikela, where the border with Hodisum was practically closed.[35] Elsewhere, as we have seen, the Ho tiger was not as uniformly bloodthirsty as the Singhs wanted him to believe.

In Roughsedge's account of his first meeting with the Hos inside Hodisum, he himself used the 'wild buffalo' simile. On that occasion, as we have seen, five or six Hos wanted to go to sleep on the carpet in Roughsedge's tent, 'Such', Roughsedge wrote, 'is their savageness'. He went on to compare them to the Mundas and Oraons in Calcutta. The Hos were 'as much superior in size and form to the tame Dhangers, if I may use the expression, of Chotanagpur, though of common origin, as wild buffaloes are to the village herds'.[36] By mentioning the 'Danghers' (Oraons), Roughsedge brought the Hos as close to his Calcutta audience as he could. For some years, people from Chotanagpur had been coming to Calcutta to earn a living by hard work.[37]

The 'wild buffalo' remark, too, struck a chord. Two years before, in May 1818 Roughsedge was the host of a hunting party in the Mainpat, a largely deserted elevated tableland of Surguja.[38] The party discovered what they thought was a new bovine species, the Bos Gaurus. The spectacularly large animal (170–220 cm shoulder height) was living in 'wild and romantic retreats' of sal forests, quick to the attack, and hard to kill. It took Roughsedge sixteen to seventeen bullets. The Gaur, he was told, 'will not brook captivity; even if taken very young the mountain-calf droops and dies'. The expedition's account and its discovery were widely advertised by its participants and reached scientific journals in England and Germany. One of these sent Roughsedge's account to E. Desbassayns, the son of the governor general of the French possessions in India and possibly a participant in the hunting trip.[39] With this international angle, Roughsedge could count on Metcalfe, the recipient of the 'wild Buffalo' remark, to appreciate the reference. The expiatory phrase 'if I may use the expression' stressed the *double entendre* of this observation.

The dislike the Singhs had for the Hos, was reciprocated by them. In the cultural sphere, it was directed against Brahmins. In general, Roughsedge stated, the Hos were not at all in awe for Brahmins or cows.[40] We have seen that the Hos loathed Raghunath of Jaintgarh. Raghunath was probably a Brahmin.[41] The Hos laid waste a 'long line of Brahmin villages' to the immediate south-west of the Kolhan.[42] Roughsedge also heard that 'they make no scruple of putting to death any man of respectable caste who presumes to enter their territory, nor is there . . . a single Brahmin, Rajput or Muslim in any one of the numerous and well inhabited villages they possess'.[43]

Religion was not something that drew the Hos closer to their neighbours. Anyway, although Roughsedge was the son of a clergyman, he did not seem keen on other people's religion. His information on the subject is sparse indeed. His informants gave him 'very slight and confused' notions. The Hos 'consider[ed] the Sun to be a Deity and worship also an evil spirit'.[44] Others, too, understood little of Ho beliefs. In 1825, Andrew Stirling, secretary to the agent at Cuttack,[45] devoted two pages to the description of the 'Lurka-kol' in a long article on Orissa in the *Asiatick Researches*. Stirling described them as 'quite distinct . . . in language, features, manners, and religion from the Hindus of the plains'. His remarks on their religious system suggest an interview.

The Kols 'own none of the Hindu divinities'.

[What then, are their beliefs?]

They 'indeed seem scarcely to have any system of religious belief whatever'.

[Nothing? Don't they worship animals, or trees?]

'. . . but four things are held by them in high veneration, the Sahajna tree (*Hyperanthera Morunga*) [or the drumstick tree], paddy, oil expressed from the mustard seed, and the dog'. The leaves from the tree were used 'in all their contracts and negotiations', the oil to rub each other, 'which is considered to give solemnity to the proceeding'.

'The Kols', Stirling concluded in a mixture of admiration and denunciation, 'are a hardy and athletic race, black and ill favoured in their countenances, ignorant and savage to the last degree'.[46] This was rather vague. Stirling's was a description based on hearsay. But it gave more on Ho religion than Roughsedge had cared to see.

Roughsedge found the Hos lawless, but he was quite upbeat about their economy. In fact, he considered the Ho economy a promising starting point for their ultimate acceptance of 'their former chieftains', the Singhs.[47] Thus, he told Calcutta in an unusually pensive sentence that 'the absence of wants inseparable from a state of civilization usually . . . renders difficult the instruction of savages. But this obstacle does not exist with respect to the Larkas. . . . They are fond of comforts and luxuries, of which they enjoy a large proportion.' Apart from 'being particularly fond of flesh meats', the Hos 'constantly' made use of 'a fermented infusion of rice that is intoxicating'. In sum, they 'pass[ed] their time luxuriously'.[48]

The Hos were, wrote Roughsedge, 'good husbandmen and keep their lands in a highly creditable state of cultivation'.[49] This observation was corroborated in 1822 by a correspondent of the *John Bull in the East*, a Calcutta newspaper. He wrote that the Ho villages were sometimes large, the houses were built of wood and were 'kept very neat and clean'. Their economy was sound, 'cattle, sheep, goats, pigs and poultry in abundance, and their fields display the fruits of considerable skill and industry in agriculture'.[50] We know from later sources that water management was a problem for Ho agriculture, but Roughsedge did mention an embankment in the north of Hodisum, although it was breached when he came with his troops.[51]

There were skills the Hos did not have. Therefore, they allowed some weavers, cowherds and potters to reside in or near their villages. This did not diminish the Ho political supremacy. They held the members of the artisan castes 'under great subjection'.[52] Consequently, though the artisan castes were more or less part of the larger northern Indian cultures, their presence did not threaten the cultural hegemony of the Hos. The artisans used Ho as their language of commerce.[53] Moreover, they were few. Some twenty years later, non-Hos probably counted for not more than 12.5 per cent of the population.[54]

The local economy and that of the neighbouring states was so little geared to producing a surplus that when Richards placed garrisons around the Hodisum, he ordered them to take 'supplies for at least eight to six months'.[55] The external economic contacts of the Ho lands were of two kinds: raids and trade. Raids, many times for the capture of buffaloes, were important ingredients of Ho life. The extent and intensity of the raids confirmed this. Raids led to the destruction of thirty villages over Hodisum's southern borders.[56] The numbers of cattle taken could be considerable. As we have seen, Roughsedge mentioned 'a poor man' from whom 140 cattle were stolen on 15 March 1820. Eighty of these were eaten before the end of that month.[57] That suggested an extra-economic use. Indeed, we know from later sources that cattle figured prominently in the bride price. The number required for maidens of the better classes was, as Tickell stated twelve years later, twenty to fifty.[58]

Trade covered several products central to the Ho well-being. They made their own rice beer, but did not know how to distill something stronger, 'and their communication with the rest of Singhbhum is almost wholly confined to the purchase of spirits'.[59] That was an overstatement. There were other imports, such as cloth. While there were weavers living in the villages, some weavers from outside went into Hodisum to sell their produce.[60] Then there was the Ho demand for ornaments.

Cross-border trade movements covered quite some distance.[61] 'I', answered Baji Munda on a question of Roughsedge, 'sold the necessary quantity of grain to a Bhuiya named Sirdar who lives near Chakradharpur and came to my village to buy it'. This struck Roughsedge as rather improbable. 'The place you mention is very distant from your village, how could the Bhuiya penetrate so far into the Kolhan?' Not so difficult, Baji said, 'He is a sworn friend of mine and has been in the constant habit of bringing buffaloes [and] cash to my village, and exchanging them against grain', and added 'I have another Bhuiya friend Ghasi of Chochapoor to whom I sometimes sell grain.'

The Hos could also go the other way, as we can see in this interrogation of Baji.

-Where did the Hos purchase cloth, salt, and spirits?

At Saraikela, we used to go there ourselves and sometimes we went towards Chakradharpur.

-[Was there no marketplace] in all the Kolhan in which cloth, salt &ca, are sold?

None! We go to Saraikela to make our purchases at the annual fair on the 15th of Cartick,[62] we go there also on the festival of the God Hind. When the Banyas attend with necklaces and various other articles suitable to our wants, we go generally at the call of Sakut Comac of Saraikela.'

The trade was also a show of strength.

The village of Beekanto was our rendezvous and thence accompanied by him [Sakut Comac] the chief[s] armed with swords and battle axes and the common Kols [armed] with battle axes on their shoulders, used to go in large bodies to the fair at Saraikela.[63]

Commercial ties with the outside world did not make for economic integration in the region. Proof of this is that the value systems of the Hos and the outsiders diverged sharply. The difference in valuation appeared especially pronounced in the segment of top-end luxury goods. Daswati, a seventy-year-old Brahmin from Saraikela, said that Kundra Kumar from the Kolhan had bought the image of the Pauri Devi from a Ho for one bullock. In his turn, Kundra sold the image for four or five Rupees to Murburna. Once the image was outside the Ho orbit, its price rose steeply. Abhiram Singh of Saraikela offered the usufruct of five villages. But Muburna negotiated the post of *divan* in exchange for the image, 'the former divan Bedesee being discharged to make room for him'.[64]

Money was not vital to the Ho economy. The rupee indicated more a quantity of produce than a coin. Payment in kind made cheating easier. The measures used could be highly disadvantageous to the Hos.[65] Still, the volume of money present in the Kolhan was not wholly negligible. After the capture of Chainpur, the Hos recovered Rs. 930 cash, and Rs. 100 worth of gold,[66] most of it, we may presume, taken as revenue or rather plunder by Bahuran Singh. Evidently, coins and some bullion were kept as stock.

The sale of booty after Ratan's rout at Chainpur also showed how little the monetary economy had entered the villages. Two turbans fetched 15 *khandis* or 280 kg of paddy. A bullock and two rupees were good for two matchlocks. Unfortunately, we are not informed about the price of Bahuran's silver *hooka* or water pipe.[67] Roughsedge realised that the introduction of a monetary economy had to proceed slowly. The 1821 agreement of the Company officers with the heads of the villages was to pay eight *annas*, that was half a rupee, per plough to their chief for the first five years and afterwards one rupee, if circumstances would allow.[68] It was paid mainly in grain.[69]

At the start of the nineteenth century, the agrarian-based economy of Hodisum was fairly developed. To many, the economy delivered more than just subsistence. Still, most economic activities were restricted to the village and its immediate environment. Thus, inside of Hodisum, the economy was not a unifying force.

Neither was politics. When the Council in Calcutta reflected on the outcome of the First Kolhan Campaign, it dryly remarked, 'the effect of the above proceedings seems to have been to confirm the well disposed Kols in their submission to the legitimate authority of the raja of Singhbhum, whilst they by no means broke the spirit of the other party'.[70] Indeed, what Roughsedge encountered in the Hodisum was a population in which there were different political opinions, expressed in a political universe separate from that of the Singh states and of the East India Company.

During the First Kolhan Campaign, Roughsedge had difficulty to get a delegation from Ajodhya in the north, including Singrai Tiu of Dopai and at least one other village leader, speak to him.[71] Even on that occasion, the thoughts of the Ajodhya Hos were more directed towards differences with their fellow Hos than towards the army which was about to invade their country. They said 'it was chiefly owing to the threats of the southern Hos that they had thrown off their obedience to the raja'. Singrai was serious towards the British. When the invasion had just started, his Hos protected the soldier guard of a grain transport from attack by a large body of Hos.[72] On arrival in Rajabasa, Roughsedge received five or six village heads, who likewise warned him for the Hos on the road down south, who were preparing resistance.[73]

The Hos of Narsanda and Guntiya did meet him in battle. Again, not all the Hos in their neighbourhood participated in these actions. But the outrage caused by the high number of Ho casualties during the Narsanda massacres showed that even Hos who had already submitted to the Company troops harboured anti-British sentiments. However, their sympathy towards their Ho brethren was passive. This, together with the carnage wrought by the Company troops, quickly forced the north into submission, in the first instance to the East Indian Company, and then to Saraikela and Porahat.

In the south of Hodisum, too, the picture was not uniform. We have already seen how the Hos of Bantaria allowed passage to the servants of the raja of Porahat. They seemed to have used the invasion by Roughsedge's troops to try and settle an old score. Although for a long time they had not paid revenue nor professed obedience to the raja of Porahat, now they 'came into us very readily'. They had 'only one objection' to submission to the raja and relinquishment of their 'predatory habits'. The Bantaria Hos feared the Hos of the area north-east of Jaintgarh, the villages Balandia, Khairpal, and Gumuriya, as they had threatened to destroy the Hos who would ally themselves with the raja or to Roughsedge himself. That pointed to the same area to which the Ajodhya Hos had referred. The core of the resistance and of the feeling of independence here consisted of the Hos of Balandia.[74] Even though they burned the place, Roughsedge's troops did not succeed in submitting its inhabitants. As soon as Roughsedge left the Kolhan, the Balandia Hos in their turn attacked and set fire to the fort of Jaintgarh. Now the divisions among the Hos turned violent. The sack of Jaintgarh started a civil war in the south.[75] After 'many encounters' with 'various success and mutual loss', Roughsedge was informed that the 'loyalist' side had won. He took to this news as to a glass of whisky.[76]

Ghanshyam's perspective of the result of this first round of hostilities, we get in the political overviews made by Roughsedge on 15 April 1820 and his 1821 restatement sent to Richards.[77] Bahuran himself also gave his view on the situation on 5 November 1820.[78] Ghanshyam mentioned some twenty-six *pirs*. It was an inflated list. Kharsawan was independent of Porahat but he included it in his list as its leader was 'a well-wisher of raja'. Saraikela with its dependencies Dugni and Gora Singha were mentioned, but these also were not Porahat territory. Ghanshyam ruled Porahat itself (apart from 'the extremities'), Bandgaon, and Chakradharpur ('with exception of some Kol villages'). In Porahat's dependencies Anandpur, Kera, and Karaikela, nominal leaders were on the raja's side, but they had little control over the Hos and other 'Kols' living in their area. Through the zamindar of Chainpur, Ghanshyam had 'some influence' over the Hos here. In 'Jayantpur' he had only Jaintgarh, 'a ruined fort'.

The areas inside Hodisum where Ghanshyam did have influence or control were few. Roughsedge mentioned Asantalia, Ajodhya, Khuntpani (according to Bahuran, Khuntpani was 'conciliated and treat[ed] travellers well')[79] and Cherai in the north of Hodisum; in its west Jagannathpur (at least, the Hos here 'promise[d] to be obedient'). Ghasi of Chakradharpur was mentioned only as having a claim on Gumra, together with Ghanshyam himself. Still, here the area was 'in the hands of Kols for 50 years. No traveller passes through it'. Bahuran mentioned in his letter that the Jaintgarh and Barkela Hos had also promised to pay up. So the Hos 'loyal' to Ghanshyam came from three small *pirs* in the north and from the more substantial *pirs* of Chakradharpur and Jagannathpur in the west. These had come in during the campaign just concluded. Apparently, Ghanshyam had no worthwhile influence in the greater part of Hodisum.

The run-up to the Second Kolhan Campaign of 1821 saw the same basic division with important modifications. The 'refractory' centre and south were now joined by the east, consisting of the Kol *pirs* of Bamanghati. The campaign plan explicitly covered the eastern Thai *pir*, as that area served as a safe haven for the resistance around Balandia.[80]

The south-west of Hodisum was 'loyalist'; in the centre-south Bantaria was. Up north, the Hos of Charai remained with the raja. On the other hand, only three villages of Ajodhya *pir*, allocated to Saraikela, stayed out of the attack on Bahuran Singh and Chainpur. Roughsedge considered these as friendly villages but mentioned at least nine Ajodhya villages as 'refractory'.[81] These twelve might not have been all the villages of Ajodhya.[82]

There were political divisions among the Hos, but these did not fit in a simple scheme. One need not doubt the commitment of Mata and his Balandia Hos to ward off outside interference. In the north of Hodisum, however, the actions of the Hos were not always consistent with a simple pro-Company or pro-Singh stand. Ghanshyam's emissary Dharam Das Gosain said that when Bahuran was attacked at Chainpur, he had sent for help to Singrai of Dopai. Singrai came with some fifty men but, perhaps conveniently, too late, to help Bahuran. Bahuran retreated from Chainpur with disastrous consequences.[83] At that point, at Cheri, the Gumra Hos and the village chief of Chaibasa rescued Lalkant, the brother of Ghasi Singh of Chakradharpur.[84] The year before, most of these Hos had submitted only after fierce armed resistance. Surprisingly, Ghasi Singh himself was hidden in the house of Kuntu, the father of the girl whose unhappy fate had triggered the attack. Apparently, the

Hos appreciated the disagreements between Ghasi and Bahuran. Ghasi was escorted home by 100 Hos under Tandar, the munda of Asura. This was one of the villages that had taken part in the battle.[85] It appeared that there were more political flavours in Hodisum than just refractory and loyal.

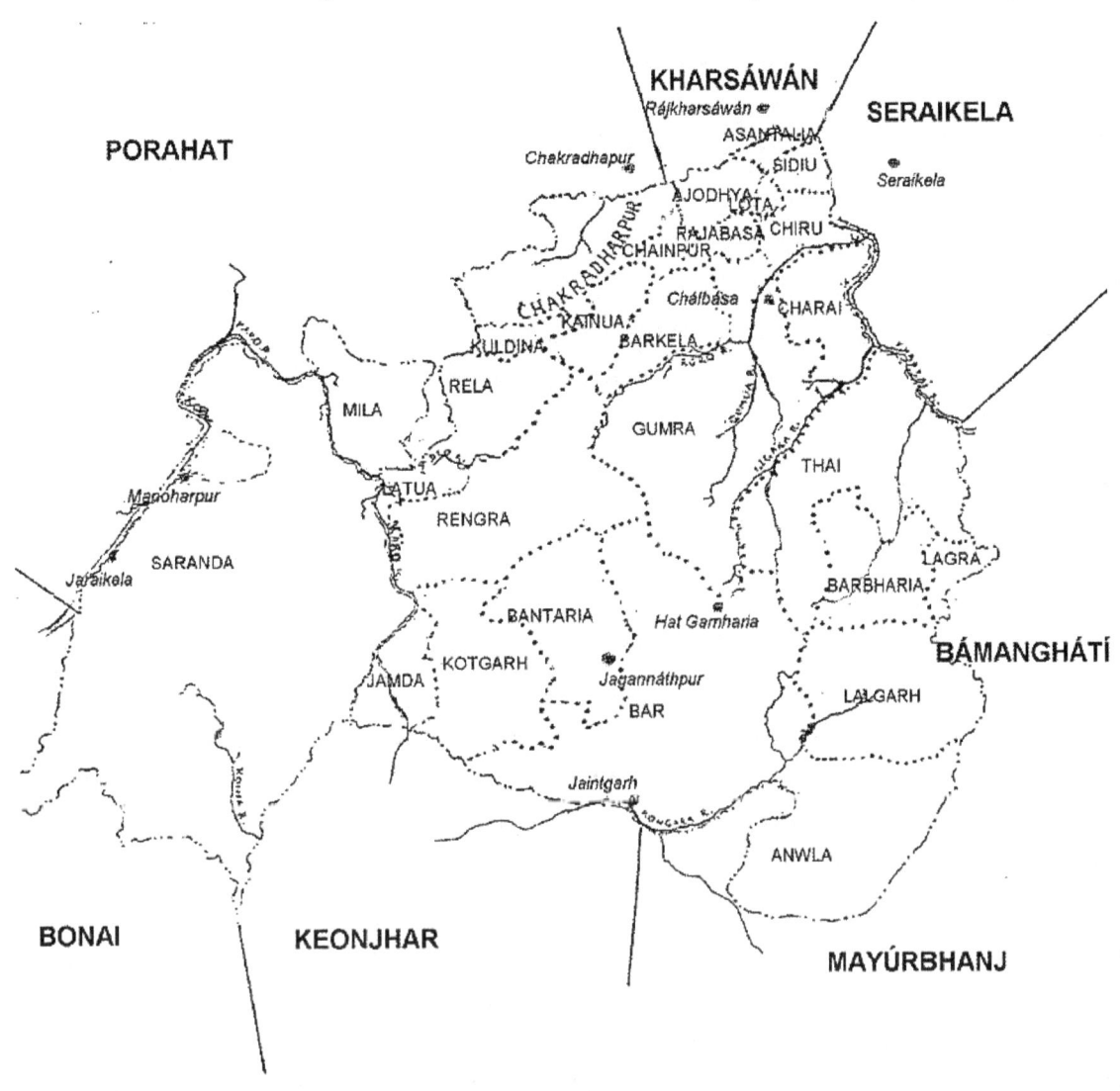

The *pirs* of Hodisum
Adapted from D. N. Majumdar, *A Tribe in Transition*, 1937.

Roughsedge approached these shades of opinion with a cool pragmatism. 'You will therefore treat them as friends', he wrote about his allies in Ajodhya to Frobisher on the eve of the Second Kolhan Campaign. And added, 'unless by their assembling in arms or making preparations to resist your detachment, they should compel you to act otherwise'.[86] Likewise, we saw pragmatism on the Ho side, especially when their villages were facing imminent destruction.

Ho politics was hard to grasp for Roughsedge. Much of the difficulty came from the type of information he got from Singhbhum. *Pirs* were the geographical units that Roughsedge, following Raghunath Bisi and Ghanshyam, mentioned. A *pir* was a definite grouping of villages, sometimes

75 | A Land of Their Own

small with the ideal number of twelve, sometimes very large, with the number of villages going up to 60, 120, and more.[87] Their names were widely used. *Pir* was the equivalent of *pargana*, outside the Kolhan a territorial unit with a political and military function. But with Ghanshyam, a *pir* inside Hodisum sounded like an area that could be taxed. It did not appear from Roughsedge's despatches that they had another function.

In no place in Roughsedge's extensive correspondence do we find an effective Ho political authority above the village level. Indeed, 'the influence of the personal character prevails there, as it does everywhere else, and some head men of villages regulate the motions of a dozen others, without having any recognised or established authority over them'.[88] To Roughsedge, Ho political life was based on the villages. Each of these had 'one or more hereditary head men called munda or manki, whom the rest obey more through prescription and attachment, I imagine, than fear, for no means of enforcing authority are apparent'.[89] Here, too, Roughsedge was not given to system building. He questioned Baji over his political role.

-For how many years have you been head of Guira?

I am hereditary head of that village . . .

-In the event of the commission of crime amongst you, who distributes justice?

Danco Buhera of Guira is one, and my younger brother Seidoo another who arbitrates or distributes of justice.[90]

We know—although Roughsedge did not report it—that the average village was small, with some 145 inhabitants.[91] These villages could have significantly different sizes and shapes. In the north of Hodisum there were compact villages, but in the south, even in 1872, 'the houses are so much scattered, that families may be almost said to live apart, or a village consists of a number of separate hamlets'.[92] That made the effective political unit even smaller.

Lack of institutions above the level of the village did not preclude cooperation between Hos of different villages. The clear example was the north of Hodisum at the time of the attacks on Bahuran's mercenaries. Hos from forty-two northern villages were in the force that inflicted the defeat on them. That was quite a number, but only a fraction of the total number of villages in this part of Hodisum.[93] True, Roughsedge had got inflated figures for the total number of villages in the area from Ghanshyam and Raghunath as after all these would be the basis of their projection of revenue. And the Ho witnesses in their turn would considerably play down the actual involvement of complete villages, as that could invite collective retribution. Even taking that into account, many villages had not joined collectively. The informants gave the names of some twenty-four local leaders. Again, that is many less than the forty-two villages implicated in the attack.[94] Village leaders could remain unnamed in the course of the interrogations, but judging from this, there seems to have been considerable scope for individuals to join the attack. Above all, it showed how limited was the authority of the much-touted mundas over their villagers.

That said, village leaders were important in the planning and commitment stages of the operation. The attack on Bahuran Singh was planned. According to Kuntu, who liked to downplay his own role, 'Doom Sirdar[, chief] of Bungoo Thon and Perdhar Sirdar of Gutilpee planned the attack the day before in the last mentioned village after they had concerted it, the Hos assembled and the battle took place.'[95] The planning even had a religious aspect. Before the attack on Chainpur a few days later, these men and three other leaders performed, what the translator called, a *puja* (religious ceremony). After the sack, they once more held a *puja*.[96] A planning session of one evening and two morale-boosting ceremonies did not amount to an elaborate or robust political or military structure. Roughsedge did not even look for it.

One could also look at Ho society as consisting of clans or *kilis*. At the end of the Second Kolhan Campaign, Roughsedge got an extensive list of the Ho *kilis* from the mouth of Keetee, a Ho leader from Thai *pir*. It contained no less than fifty-seven names.[97] This is the main place where Roughsedge hinted at other divisions than those that came from the Hos' attitude towards him, his troops and his allies. There were many more villages than clans. Roughsedge did not give information about the spread of *kilis* over the land and in the villages. He interviewed one Baji Munda twice, the second time exclusively to obtain 'local information'. Baji named four 'tribes' of the Larkas. He also told Roughsedge that there was a *pir* ('12 villages') of his Sundis, and that they married inside this *pir*.[98] Roughsedge was not aware that while marriage inside a *pir* was common, inside the *kili* it was out of the question. This particular group of villages was dominated by the Sundi *kili*.

When he questioned Baji, Roughsedge did get a glimpse of a political structure at the *kili* level—if that is what Baji meant.

-Who is the supreme head of the whole tribe of Sundis?

Doormoo of Guira is a man of property and respectability and they act under his influence.[99]

Could the *kili* have a political angle? It seems it could. We know from a slightly later source about the Pingua *kili*. The village of Balandia, the centre of resistance in the south, was mainly Pingua. Also, Suban, who died in 1822 after arrest by Raghunath Bisi, was of the Pingua *kili*. Much of the force that his sons brought together in 1830 to avenge him, came from this *kili* and it included Pinguas from other *pirs*, such as Lalgarh and Gumra.[100] Evidently, *kili* and *pir*, kinship group and canton, did not coincide.

Roughsedge missed something here. Part of the divisions he encountered in Hodisum was not political, but due to traditional enmity between clans. This showed in the fairly consistent pattern of resistance and non-resistance to the troops of the East India Company. The composition of the force of the sons of Suban threw light upon its motives. Whenever a Ho had received a serious injury or lost his life, this became a matter for the whole *kili*. The members of the *kili* would 'seldom allow a favourable opportunity of revenge to pass without taking advantage of it, however remote the period of injury may have been'.[101] There were more motives than the death of Suban. In 1821, Raghunath had directed a detachment of the Ramgarh Battalion against Balandia and the village got burned. Later, Raghunath was oppressing and overtaxing them. Still, evidently, it was the death of one of them that pushed many Pinguas, even from outside the area of Raghunath's control, to take part in the attack of 1830. It was a collective revenge. It also was an action against an outsider.

Inside the Hodisum, traditional enmity obviously had its limits. There was no evidence that Ho *kilis* or villages were constantly in a state of war with each other. The fact that the southern Hos could deliver a strong message to those of Ajodhya (do not pay taxes and keep the Singhs out) indicated that Ho society was a whole in which negotiations—and also ultimatums—could work. What we get from all this is something we would expect from politics anyway: inside Hodisum were different political opinions on how to deal with a clear and present danger of outside interference. Sometimes these swayed a whole village, sometimes a *kili*, sometimes only individuals. Roughsedge is silent about the political debates of the Hos, but could not ignore its outcomes. Neither could Ghanshyam. Ho politics showed a divided society, but a society nevertheless.

Roughsedge's emphasis on territorial authority at the expense of other ties had political consequences. There was no leader of the pack, no regular council in which the whole people gathered. The agreements of submission of May 1821 supposed a fragmented society. It was whole dealt with politically as it had been dealt with militarily, village by village. The obligation to pay taxes, especially to the Porahat raja, was based on the village being part of a *pir* that Porahat claimed. But taxes as such were not raised at *pir* level. Hodisum was treated as a collection of villages.

The lack of political structure of the Ho society as a whole had military consequences as well. To make the Hos behave as he wished, Roughsedge could not build upon the political structures of Ho society. 'The want of any authority beyond the precincts of their own villages amongst the Larka chiefs and the general indifference and apathy of their dispositions, form the grounds on which I should place little reliance on the efficacy of hostages to secure their future good conduct', wrote he.[102] The guarantors of the new arrangements were the Company troops around the Hodisum. For the Hos, Roughsedge wished that they could 'get rid of the recollection of their now long enjoyed independence and the feelings which spring from it'.[103]

That could be difficult, as was implicitly acknowledged at the other end of the political nexus, the Council in Calcutta. It saw the Hos as 'a race distinct from the great Hindu family both in manners, language, religion and appearance, inferior in some respects to the common inhabitants of the hills in point of civilization, but superior to them in courage and industry, and possessing large and flourishing villages with extensive tracts of well cultivated land'.[104] That should have been obvious. But politics had prevented a more all-round view of the Hos.[105] The views of the Singhs and Raghunath Bisi prevailed. These were political where they treated Ho society, and territorial where they treated the inhabitants. Roughsedge passed on these views to the outside together with his descriptions of ferocious Ho attacks. Only between 1830 and 1837 would the then agent on the South Western Frontier Thomas Wilkinson take a closer look at the Hos. For sixteen years, the 'smiling hamlets', which had struck Roughsedge when he first actually saw the land of the Hos, remained hidden behind the needs of their neighbours.

Chapter 5

The Return of the Pauri Devi

...
Roughsedge's death; Major Walter Raleigh Gilbert and the continuing affair of the Pauri Devi; the Hos chase the 'great man'
...

In June 1821, during or just after a tour through Boad, a dependency of Sambalpur,[1] Roughsedge got a fever and retired from the heat, which he was 'no longer able to bear'.[2] After an illness of over three months, he died on 13 January 1822, just eight months after his Second Kolhan Campaign, on the banks of a river close to Sambalpur. The officers of the Ramgarh Battalion erected a memorial for him in the Christian cemetery of his beloved town Sambalpur.[3] His obituary spoke of his humanity, and his 'utmost desire to avoid hostilities and spare blood'.[4] Not everybody agreed. More than fifty years later, old Hos would remember Roughsedge's first campaign as 'dreadfully severe'.[5]

In the dynastic sphere, the unfinished affair of the statue of the Pauri Devi demanded much attention of Roughsedge's successor. Major Walter Raleigh Gilbert (1785–1853) was the living link of Hodisum with the very foundation of the British Empire through his ancestor Humphrey Gilbert who took possession of Newfoundland in 1583.[6] On his first tour in Singhbhum, in 1823, he met Ajambar Singh, the son and successor of the recently deceased Bikram Singh of Saraikela. It seemed that Ajambar, along with his father's land, had inherited the hatred of his subjects and neighbours. Everything seemed quiet in Saraikela, but the Hos 'still entertain[ed] a lively recollection of the oppression and rapacity of his late father'. They refused to pay the revenue directly to Ajambar and instead delivered it to the officer of the Ramgarh Corps at Chakradharpur. 'So great is the aversion of the Kols to this family.'[7] Worse for Ajambar, the local Hos wanted to shore Porahat up against Saraikela. They asked the agent to restore the Pauri Devi image to Ghanshyam. Chaitan Singh of Kharsawan, who did not leave Gilbert's side during this tour, joined in this request.

On the next stage of Gilbert's tour, Raja Ghanshyam Singh met him at the boundary of his lands and, as Gilbert wrote, 'expressed great pleasure at seeing me'. A little lie would increase the impact of the meeting. Ghanshyam told him that this was the first time that he had ever come out of Porahat. But 'as in his interview with the late Political Agent he could not be prevailed on to sit down until he attained my promise to use my endeavour in getting the Devi restored to him'. Gilbert who saw the 'ruinous state' of Ghanshyam's country, and maybe was impressed by the political complications of the childless raja's blackmail to abdicate and to follow him to Hazaribagh, promised his 'every exertion'. He wrote to Ajambar in Saraikela, but got 'nothing but evasive answers'.[8]

That looked like a rerun of Roughsedge's attempts, but with different persons and in different circumstances. Gilbert, who apparently lived his forebear's motto '*Quid non*' ('Why not?', or rather 'Let's do it'), was not one to be trifled with. He asked the government for permission to act. Otherwise, the raja of Porahat would continue to have 'no regard whatever for himself, nor will he be held in any respect by the subjects of the country'. Inversing its position of a few years earlier, the government directed Gilbert to order Saraikela to restore the statue to the raja.[9] Ajambar again 'evaded compliance'. Now he defied the authority of Calcutta. The day before Christmas 1823, Secretary Swinton instructed Gilbert to use force if necessary. The colonel met Raja Ghanshyam at the border between Porahat and Saraikela. Together they marched to Saraikela. Apparently, Ajambar required some more heavy pressure. It took more than two months, until 8 March 1824, before a party of the Ramgarh Battalion entered Ajambar's house and 'without opposition was allowed to bring away the image'. 'On the following morning', wrote Gilbert with apparent emotion, 'a Brahmin attached to the corps and whom I had sent for that purpose brought the image to my tent and delivered it in my presence to Raja Ghanshyam Singh. . . . The raja and his household manifested the greatest joy and happiness.' The following day, Gilbert reprimanded Ajambar.[10] Calcutta had spoken; the case was closed, or so it seemed.

But in Singhbhum, the story went round that Ajambar had secretly prepared a number of spurious images, and that Ghanshyam received 'these fake images' (note the plural!). While Gilbert's Brahmin was searching for the statue, the wife of Ajambar sat with the real image tied around her neck at the brink of a large octagonal well,[11] 'ready to leap into the well for self-immolation' if the Saraikela fraud was found out. Further, it was said that after some time Ghanshyam discovered that he had been duped and threw away the image. A zamindar found it and installed it in his house. It was the Saraikela statue of the Pauri Devi that people considered powerful. Still, she would not be shown to the people. The whisper went that every night Pauri Devi rode the countryside on a white horse.[12] Whatever the reality content of this story, it showed a significant perception gap.

The Pauri Devi affair showed how little the East India Company intervention had changed in the Hindu part of Singhbhum. Saraikela continued to dominate the agenda. And apart from the cult of the Pauri Devi, impoverished Porahat had no policy towards the Hos to shore up its political gains. Thus, the early modern state announced its arrival in these marginal tracts less by a cultural rapprochement with the Hos than by attempts to push the exploitative ethnic frontier into their country. This was clear from events in Jaintgarh.

In Singhbhum proper, the special status of Jaintgarh's chief Raghunath Bisi made for centrifugal tendencies. He strengthened his local position by putting much more effort into his relations with the Company troops than in those with his superior the raja of Porahat. Even when Roughsedge lay dying in January 1822,[13] Jaintgarh and the other villages of Raghunath Bisi narrowly escaped an attack by the Hos. A Ho named Suban was accused of the murder of seven people and Raghunath sent him to Sambalpur where the political agent was. But Suban died 'of fever' on the road.[14] The Hos did not believe or care for the fever part of the story and Suban's Pingua *kili* called for revenge. The presence of the Company army detachment guarding Jackson's Road at nearby Kathkaranjia prevented the outbreak of hostilities.[15]

In 1823, the new political agent, W. R. Gilbert, reached Kathkaranjia. He found Raghunath Bisi waiting for him—and was impressed. The 'active intelligent man who keeps the officer commanding at that post informed of every occurrence that takes place amongst the Kols', immediately ingratiated himself with Gilbert. He did so by providing information, mainly recycled stuff from what earlier he had given to Roughsedge. Gilbert found among the inhabitants of the Kolhan all 'cheerfulness and willingness'. The Hos even wished the Company troops to stay, 'since they had nothing to fear so long as they remained amongst them'. Apart from soldiers, so little was needed. 'They were highly gratified with the attention I made it my study to pay them during my intercourse with them and they were quite delighted with the presents from government of the turbans, beads, and spirituous liquor.' Still, Gilbert knew that the Hos resented their submission to the neighbouring chiefs. However, he estimated that these could not oppress the Hos without his knowledge.[16] Evidently, the Hos did not consider him worthy of confidence. Raghunath passed himself off to Gilbert as 'heartily zealous in the cause of his master [the raja of Porahat] and well disposed to exert himself in promoting a good understanding between the raja and his subjects'. Therefore, Gilbert presented a horse to Raghunath in front of a gathering of Hos.[17]

Nothing of military consequence occurred in Porahat and Jaintgarh up to 1830.[18] But in the political field, there were quite some changes. In 1827 Ghanshyam Singh of Porahat died of cholera, still childless. His first cousin Achuta Singh succeeded him.[19] Gilbert presented the 'customary khellet' or dress of honour. Achuta was installed in the presence of a representative from Saraikela and of *Thakur* Chaitan Singh who had come from Kharsawan.[20] Agent Major Mackenzie made a new engagement with Achuta Singh, who was a minor, along the lines of the 1820 one, with an addition not to harbour 'thieves, murderers &ca.' He also had to promise to leave the management of his country to Ghasi Bisi and *Kunwar* Chakradhar Singh of Saraikela.[21] This was to prevent Krishna, favourite of the raja 'and a notoriously bad character', rising to power. Achuta strongly objected to the Company's favourites, and after some hesitation, Mackenzie allowed the new raja to appoint Krishna as his *divan*.[22]

Raghunath's 'hereditary' *divan*-ship had lasted about six years. The relation between the new raja and his ex-*divan* reached new depths. Raghunath, in Jaintgarh and safely away from Porahat, styled himself as independent, 'The [Porahat] raja is not the great man, I am the great man'.[23]

The Jaintgarh Hos could not agree with Raghunath's self-assessment. Bisi's business was to increase his capital by extra-economic means. He gave loans of a *pie*, about 450 grammes, of salt and demanded 37 kg of paddy after one year. In the case of failure to deliver, the principal plus interest went up to, in one case, six times that amount.[24] In another case, a Ho borrowed for a piece of cloth, and in return, Raghunath took a bullock or a cow from him. In addition to this usury, taxation under Raghunath was high and manifold. The land rent and the homage money (*salami*), both payable in rupees, were increased with a *pie* or 450 grammes of *ghee*. It was meant for the raja, but Raghunath kept the revenue for himself. In addition, he made people pay for his sentries and interpreters. He also committed outright robbery of pulse and fish.[25] That was dangerous in Jaintgarh, the more so as in 1826 the complaint of some Hos against the practices was not taken up, and their wish to be taken directly under the British Government was not granted.[26]

In August–September 1829, a group of Hos went to a hill, 3 km east of Jaintgarh, where they expected him to perform a religious offering. They found only his son there and went home.[27] The 'great man' only just escaped with his life. To get rid of Raghunath the Hos needed to do something more robust. On 5 February 1830, wrote Raghunath, the Hos of Anwla, Balandia, and four or five villages of Bamanghati (possibly he meant Lalgarh), all together about 400 to 500 people, were hatching plans to kill him and to destroy Jaintgarh.[28] As in Roughsedge's time, the Hos did not present one front. But the lines were differently drawn. Gumhuriya had been with Mata in 1821. Now its village head, possibly Ghunnoo, informed the Bisi. Raghunath called twelve soldiers to Jaintgarh and tried to enlist some of the Hos to his side. He sent out persons with the arrow, the traditional sign of the Hos to solicit participation in a war or raid. But his emissaries became afraid and returned after a few kilometres.[29]

The Hos plundered two of Raghunath's villages, Sobur and Pohar. These villages were deserted in 1820 and repopulated at Roughsedge's insistence after the campaign of 1821. They killed one man, wounded four more and took, still according to Raghunath, 400 cows and bullocks, 600 *maunds* (at smallest count about 550 kg) of rice and other grains, and all the property of the peasants there. On Raghunath's side, mass desertion followed. The inhabitants of all his villages and of Jaintgarh fled to Keonjhar. The soldiers remained in the fort, but the Hos gave them the message that they would burn the place in four or five days.

On 15 February 1830, some 1,500 Hos assembled under the leadership of Nakia Munda and Jumal Munda, sons of Suban, and, now Mata Pingua of Balandia re-appeared.[30] This last village, too, was mainly inhabited by members of the Pingua *kili*.[31] Raghunath had prior knowledge and fled to Keonjhar. An escort brought him to the detachment at Kathkaranjia. Jayantgarh weas destroyed. 'We have passed 20 or 25 generations amongst the Kols', wrote Raghunath Bisi on 20 February 1830, 'but hitherto they have never committed such excess'.[32] He complained, 'Myself and my family are only saved. All my property has been destroyed, not even a 1/4 seer (less than 250 grammes) of grain has been saved that my children may eat, nor have I the means of purchasing a yard of cloth.'[33]

Meanwhile, Raja Achuta Singh sent some 'respectable men', possibly under his *divan* Krishna, from Porahat into the Hodisum. He gave some of the Hos turbans and donated a buffalo to eat. Probably, the Hos saw it merely as a fit remuneration. After all, as they later stated, they had acted upon the written and verbal instructions of the raja of Porahat to drive Raghunath Bisi out of Jaintgarh.[34] Still, as far as the south of Hodisum was concerned, the Hos had regained their independence after an interruption of just nine years.

Naturally, acting Political Agent on the South Western Frontier Wilkinson suspected Raja Achuta Singh to have a hand in these developments. Wiser than Gilbert, Wilkinson also did not rule out misconduct by Raghunath towards the Hos. He sent a small party from his intelligence department to Porahat.[35] They ordered the raja to induce the Hos to come to his place and to state their grievances in the presence of Wilkinson's men. Moreover, Raghunath would be escorted to Porahat to be confronted with the Hos. Wilkinson's people would first take down the statements of both parties and then take Raghunath Bisi to Wilkinson's headquarters at Hazaribagh. They would invite the Ho village leaders to come with them, too. There was more to this than the eye could see, Wilkinson thought. He bypassed Raghunath and directed the officers commanding the nearby detachments to send interpreters into the Ho villages to find out whether or not they had been made to pay excess revenue.[36] But the Porahat raja obstructed the investigation. All of a sudden, witnesses were not able to appear. On the instigation of his *divan* Krishna,[37] the raja refused Wilkinson's men passage into the Kolhan to see for themselves. He insisted on explicit instructions from Wilkinson himself.[38]

All these delays must have angered Wilkinson, but it was important to him and his superiors to avoid stationing troops in Jaintgarh. This 'might lead to encounters, between the Kols and our troops and [Jaintgarh] is besides an unhealthy situation'.[39] On the other hand, there was the old fear that the disturbances might spread. Because, if Raghunath's authority was allowed to slip and the 'outrageous conduct' pass unpunished, other Ho leaders could take it as a precedent. During the events in Jaintgarh, there had already been much excitement in Lalgarh and Anwla *pirs*, where village leaders had stopped paying taxes.[40] If the deeper causes of the incidents were not clear to the East India Company's men, the oppressive behaviour by the very persons that they had put over the Hos was. The right remedies did not present themselves easily to Calcutta. The government wished to continue on a 'prudent and cautious course', and judged it 'sufficient for the present to address a suitable warning'. Wilkinson was to go personally to the area in the next cold season to start a full enquiry on the spot.[41]

Reflection: Another People's War

The position of the Singhbhum states was not a legacy of the strategic struggle of the East India Company with the Marathas. That poses the question of why their accession to the British sphere of influence became part of the political agenda. As we have seen, after the defeat of the Marathas there was no major strategic obstacle to accession to, or to put it inversely, to an extension of British influence. The opportunity was there, but what was the motive?

For Roughsedge, it was communications. In 1818, Captain James Nesbitt Jackson surveyed the area to establish a trajectory for a road from Midnapur to Nagpur.[1] Bikram Singh of Saraikela sent his *vakil* to assist him. Jackson came in for a shock when the *vakil* refused to guide him through the route from Bamanghati through the south of Hodisum, 'on the ground that the number of Hos rendered it impossible'. Both Captain Jackson and Roughsedge believed that Bikram was obstructing the survey.[2] Roughsedge wrote Calcutta in August that 'to establish some control' over Singhbhum was necessary to connect Cuttack to Benares and Sambalpur to Bengal.[3]

For Calcutta, it was quiet; the governor general was not interested in tribute. 'The exaction of tribute from the chiefs of Singhbhum forms no part of the views of His Lordship in Council.'[4] The main object of the Company's overlordship was to engage the chiefs of Singhbhum 'to prevent these districts from becoming . . . an injury of the public peace', for example by providing a safe haven for fugitive offenders from East India Company territory.[5]

But Ghanshyam was going for more. In return for coming under the Company, he wanted local pre-eminence: ritual by getting the statue of the Pauri Devi back in Porahat (lost around 1800); political by getting control over his nemesis Bikram of Saraikela (independent since 1720). And he wanted to get back control over the villages of the Hos (lost to his grandfather around in 1765).

Calcutta's communications to Roughsedge had been unclear. It had taken much of Roughsedge's persuasive powers to get permission to negotiate a treaty with the Singh states. Even then, the instructions to Roughsedge were brief. The strategic constraints were not well defined. He was to accept the states as he found them and not to interfere in family squabbles of the Singh dynasty. It was not necessary to re-establish the raja of Porahat 'in the possessions of his forefathers'.[6] The formulation was not explicit as to whether this rule extended to the relations of the raja with the Hos, or was restricted to Porahat's relations with the other Singh states. As we shall see, Roughsedge took the latter, restricted meaning. In the area of ritual prestige, he considered himself free to operate on the side of Porahat and get the return of the statue of the Pauri Devi. And within what he understood as the area of Porahat state itself, Roughsedge considered himself free to intervene against the Hos.

Apart from communications, a concern that played on an all-India scale, Roughsedge had two local strategic aims. He wanted to restore legality in the form of the prime place of the Porahat raja and to check the expansion of the Hos. To him it was clear from the very beginning,[7] that to achieve these objectives they should be combined in 'recovering [for Ghanshyam] some portion of the influence [over the Hos] which his ancestors had possessed'.[8] On the insistence of Calcutta, the question of the return of Pauri Devi was shelved in 1820. The Hos were subdued twice, the first time—much to the chagrin of Calcutta, as it saw no reason for military intervention—in 1820. The second time in 1821—now with support from Calcutta as the Hos had overrun a military outpost. Most Hos were forced to accept Ghanshyam as their overlord; some to do so with Bikram of Saraikela. A few years later, in 1824, Roughsedge's successor Gilbert quietly returned the Pauri Devi to Ghanshyam.

The good news was that Roughsedge's 1821 arrangements held longer than those following the First Kolhan Campaign had done. They held—with difficulty—until 1830 and attempts to revive them were abandoned seven years later. Because the bad news was that the ground realities did not remotely point to a stable situation.

In effect, what Roughsedge had done in Singhbhum was to fight what Edward Luttwak would call 'another people's war'.[9] Roughsedge had placed the Porahat raja over the Hos, a feat Ghanshyam could never have accomplished on his own. Thereby, Roughsedge had created an unstable situation, which had to be shored up by the presence nearby of the East India Company troops. Part of this shift of responsibility for the maintenance of the situation away from the one who was its first beneficiary came from the unclear architecture of the system of mutual advantages and obligations between the local powers and the Company. The political structure that Roughsedge established in the area was not an exclusively British construct. Its guiding ideas were, to borrow Roland Silva's apt phrase, of 'dual parentage'.[10]

When Roughsedge accepted the Singh states into the fold of the East India Company, he established a chain of command. From the Company's side, the chain of command worked from the level of the City of Palaces down to the door of the palaces of Saraikela and Porahat, but not further. In the eyes of the local rulers, the East India Company had established a sphere of influence. As they saw it, the representative of the dominant power, the political agent on the frontier, enclosed the power of the local chiefs and should come to the rescue of the palace itself when it was in need. In this respect, the new local arrangements looked more like the Indian than the Western feudal system.[11] The restitution of the Pauri Devi to Porahat fell in with the Indian way of meeting obligations. It did not entirely succeed. Playing it the local way, Saraikela had been able to counter Gilbert's interference by sowing doubts on the authenticity of the statue and, therefore, on the return of Porahat to ritual pre-eminence.

Anyway, it did not change the power relations on the ground. The East India Company had set up his chain of command with no territorial consequences for the feudal chiefs. The guideline that was implemented brought them in with the lands they actually controlled *vis à vis* each other, on the principle of '*uti possidetis*' (as you possess now). The strategic stalemate between Porahat and Saraikela, based on their roughly equal effective strength, continued. So did their weakness *vis à vis* the Hos.

In Singhbhum, therefore, the strategy of containment of the Hos by the local states was not sustainable in the long term. The reinforcement of the Singh states by the East India Company enabled them to bother the Hos. Both Roughsedge and Gilbert suspected so but calmed their unease with the idea that the local chiefs anyway were not powerful enough to oppress the Hos. But they did. They saw no other way to increase their income than to squeeze the population. The events around Jaintgarh and those earlier at Chainpur showed that British interference stopped far short of what the Singh states required to effectively control the Hos. These states could try and overawe individual villages, but if these villages united against them, the Singh chiefs stood no chance. They had to bank on the troops of the East India Company as their last resort. The ultimate military, and hence political, power had come to rest with the modern state that was spreading from Calcutta. At the other end of the power spectrum were not the local states, but the Hos. The Hos, not organised in a state and the losing party in Roughsedge's arrangement, were deeply divided on the advisability of adhering to or of ignoring these. In the end, they did both. For some Hos, the village peace was worth a goat a year, for others, peace meant keeping that goat. For some it was staying in their own village, for others it was augmenting their income by fighting for one of the neighbouring rajas—as long as it was not on Ho soil. The bottom line was, don't bother us.

Uti possidetis, or, as we would say now, the line of actual control, had been Calcutta's principle in regulating conflicting territorial and tax claims of the Singh states. Roughsedge had not applied this principle to the Hos. The arrangements of 1820–21 were based on information given by the Singh informants. This was elaborated but not put in question by Roughsedge's own findings on the Hos. The East India Company, like Roughsedge, did not know what moved them. The Company proceeded as if the Hos were subjects of the surrounding chiefs. But the Hos knew what to expect if they let the surrounding feudals in. That was a major, if largely unnoticed, snag. Soon, it would demand a major change of strategy.

Part II

A New Grand Strategy, 1831–1837

Chapter 6

The Genesis of Wilkinson's System

...
The Kol Insurrection of 1830-31; the 'force from Singhbhum'; debate on the causes; a non-regulation district; Thomas Wilkinson, a biography; the Wilkinson system
...

The deaths of Roughsedge and Raja Govind Nath Shah of Chotanagpur in 1822 presented a window of opportunity to the civil servants in the area to launch a full-scale attack on Chotanagpur's tributary status. Nathaniel Smith, Collector at Ramgarh and the late Roughsedge's arch-enemy, opposed recognition of Govind's successor, Jagannath Shah, as a tributary chief. Calcutta, however, did recognise Jagannath. Moreover, it decided once more against the introduction of the Bengal regulations in Chotanagpur. That move seems to have had no consequences, because in 1824 Calcutta turned down a request by Jagannath Shah to be exempted from the Bengal regulations. The Bengal regulations were introduced piecemeal. In the years up to 1831, first Smith and later S. T. Cuthbert introduced elements of these regulations.[1] This effort got the wind in its sails from the new raja's weak performance.[2]

The military line favoured one of their own in charge of a non-regulation system.[3] Cuthbert, a civilian who held the positions of judge, collector and magistrate at Ramgarh, was dead set against it. In a non-regulation system, he said, it would be the local zamindars who would run day-to-day administration at the local level. But in his experience, these zamindars were either weak in their head, outright fools, or mere minors. The use of the Bengal regulations, on the contrary, would have the effect of 'civilizing the people and ameliorating their condition'.[4]

The ground realities did not support this idea. Between the accession of Jagannath in 1822 and the Kol Insurrection of 1831, the events of 1790–1812 were repeated on a larger scale. An ever-larger part of the village product was diverted to the state or rather the state apparatus.[5] Of the 'seven obnoxious taxes', the tax on the local rice beer was especially resented by the original inhabitants. Rice beer (*hanria*) was a staple food of the households. It was brewed for local consumption and served as breakfast and party drink alike. The tax was introduced in 1822, abolished in 1826 and through a loophole, reintroduced in 1830.[6] The economic backbone of the social system of the original inhabitants was breaking.

The deterioration came mainly from a change of proprietorship from the original population to the family and retainers of the raja of Chotanagpur. About 75 per cent of the grants of land and villages was made to them.[7] Many retainers were foreigners, Hindus, Muslims and Sikhs, who became tax farmers of villages that the Chotanagpur raja gave them instead of paying them.[8] They had only a temporary stake in the land. Their interest was to collect the highest possible rents in the shortest possible period. They overruled the rights of existing office-holders in the villages. It happened that mankis were prevented from picking their own fruit trees or even to go fishing.[9] In addition, the 25 per cent of the land grants to immigrant peasants[10] created a new economic system in which the original population was marginal. The police, too, remained the preserve of recent immigrants to the area. The bottom line was that under Jagannath, there was no controlled police or justice.[11] That did not change when the raja, on his own request, was relieved of police management in February 1826.[12]

Indeed, the state had few good words for the original inhabitants, the great majority of the people living in its area. In 1808, Maharajah Govind Nath Shah described them as nothing but 'wild mountaineers and robbers ... incapable of understanding any order'. This was a persistent view. Years later, in 1832, his son, Jagannath Shah, represented them as 'in person resembl[ing] man, but in mind beasts'.[13] In the years before the uprising of 1831–32, the debt servitude of original inhabitants increased dramatically.[14] Taxes and immigration significantly contributed to the unpopularity of the Company, which people saw as upholding this system. But the loss of their land to the tax farmers was the most conspicuous part of it.

Agent Cuthbert saw the problem but did not press hard for a lasting solution.[15] In 1827, he noted the desperate situation of the original inhabitants with the unforgettable understatement that this peasantry, 'generally speaking, do not appear to enjoy a state of great comfort'. More concretely, he found their huts 'miserable' and their daily food 'of the poorest kind'.[16] The rule of the Chotanagpur raja amounted to 'such a system of feudalism giving rise and colour to every species of extortion and plunder, [that] it is not to be wondered at that the population of the province is so limited'.[17] Even so, Cuthbert did not go further than a recommendation to phase out the personal influence of the raja.[18] This ad hoc approach became obsolete with the Kol Insurrection.

Here we see a vast area, in which ethnicity, people, economic systems, cultures, and classes were divided by one and the same line. The original inhabitants were well aware of the ethnic character of the frontier and spoke of the Hindu and Muslim immigrants as *dikus*, foreigners.[19] Now, the frontier of colonisation reached Chotanagpur's outlying districts to the south, where the original inhabitants' society was intact. This, together with Bandgaon in the north of Singhbhum, was Munda area.

Inaction of Achuta Singh of Singhbhum was the immediate cause of the Kol Insurrection. In a short time, Bindrai, a manki from the Bandgaon area, was economically broken because a Hindu trader had used a loan to inflict usury, extortion, corruption, imprisonment and rape.[20] In the end, Bindrai and some friends complained to the Porahat raja's *divan*, Krishna,[21] who told them to 'do as we pleased, but [to] be careful not to involve Raja Achuta Singh in any difficulties by our conduct'. Help yourself! They did. He and some leaders from Singhbhum and Tamar came together in Lankah in Tamar and decided to act.[22]

The course of the Kol Insurrection through the Jharkhand plateau seemed a huge circle.[23] The disturbances started on 11 December 1831 in Sonapur, a little north of Singhbhum. A party from the Tamar villages Kochang and Kumang, probably under Dasai Manki, raided it. The raiders took 200 head of cattle from a Muslim tax farmer. A raid by 700 Kols, now including people from the northern parts of Singhbhum under Bindrai, his brother Singrai and Khandu Pater, followed. They plundered and burnt four nearby villages, held by two Sikhs. The two foreigners were wounded. The Mundas of Sonapur and Singhbhum now joined forces. About 1,000 of them made attacks on villages recently brought under Muslim tax farmers and killed one tax farmer. The bailiff of the Sherghati court, the court of the South Western Frontier Agency, went with some troops to Khunti. On 5 January, he offered the mankis of Sonapur the restoration of some villages. It was too late and too little. They replied that they would not leave a single tax farmer alive.[24] The insurrection had found its aim. The next move was an attack by 4,000 insurgents on Govindpur, the Sonapur capital. It fell on 12 January.

The insurrection swiftly spread to the whole of the Chotanagpur plateau with a general attack on the foreigners. Within two days, the number of insurgents grew to an estimated 14,000. To boost morale, the insurgents spread the rumour that the Larkas would come to join them.[25] Even at this stage, the 100–120 East India Company troops[26] under Wilkinson gained some successes. Some villages around Pithoria submitted. The troops repulsed an attack by 3,000 rebels on the town itself. By now, however, the insurrection had spread even to Chotanagpur's north-west corner.[27] By the end of January, the Mundas and Oraons had taken possession of the whole of Chotanagpur with the exception of the area around Wilkinson's stronghold Pithoria and two tracts in the south. They attacked the police, the tax farmers, and the other foreign people who had come to lord it over the villagers. The insurgents did not attack the houses of the traditional Hindu artisans. Neither did they seriously challenge the status of the traditional zamindars and rajas.

From the end of January 1832, reinforcements to the Company troops arrived. On 1 February, the government granted special powers to the Joint Commissioners, W. Dent and Thomas Wilkinson, to execute summary justice, with the proviso to do so only in emergencies.[28] On 4 February, Wilkinson applied for more mounted troops 'to make a very severe example'.[29] Given the vast disparity in military might and the extreme lack of communication between the two main sides in the conflict, this idea of 'very severe example' could lead to needless slaughter,[30] as well as narrow escapes[31] of the original population. By mid-February, the troops had restored the Company's power in the centre of Chotanagpur.

The Company troops started their final push into the south of Chotanagpur on 17 February. Three columns simultaneously swept the country in parallel lines as they moved from north to south.[32] The column fighting south and east of Khunti had a difficult time. In the end, the insurgents fled into the hills and the jungles; there was no place to go from there. The Company ordered the chiefs of Saraikela, Kera and Karaikela in Singhbhum to close off the insurgents' retreat. Then the troops destroyed their supplies and started to capture their families. The rains and the cold, too, told on the rebels. After several proclamations, the chiefs came in till the end of April 1832. The ones who had begun the Kol Insurrection were the ones to see its end.

Most of the attacks by the rebels had taken place in the heartland of the plateau, Chotanagpur proper. To give an indication of its size, the official number of victims of the uprising was put at 226 Hindus and 78 Muslims. The same official report found 4,086 houses destroyed, 17,058 cattle seized and 822,992 *maunds* of grain burnt. Jha, the foremost historian of the Kol Insurrection, added that the actual figures must have been higher.[33] There were, it seemed, no figures of the losses in life and property of the original population.

Hostilities started and ended in the estates in the south and east of Chotanagpur, farthest from the detachments of the Bengal army and in the area most recently drawn into the frontier society. The counteroffensive did not extend to the Hodisum; the furthest the troops went was Tamar and the village of Bamhani near Bandgaon.[34] But Singhbhum was involved; the passes were closed to the insurgents by Saraikela and Karaikela, and Chaitan Singh of Kharsawan was under suspicion of sheltering an insurgent manki and of hiding provisions of the insurgents for a bribe.[35] As we shall see, the final act was played in April 1833, when Bindrai and Sui, participants in the meeting in Lankah, gave themselves up and were handed over by Khandupater of Saraikela to Wilkinson, close to the town of Saraikela in Singhbhum.[36]

Who were these insurgents and what was the involvement of people from Singhbhum in the Kol Insurrection? When the Kol Insurrection broke out, the administration had very little precise knowledge of the inhabitants of Chotanagpur.[37] Eyewitness accounts of the disturbances of 1831–32, which appeared in newspapers, were hardly better. The first one, in June 1832, simply stated that there were 'Dhangas' and 'Coles or Kholes', joined by some 'Lurka-Coles'. That would amount to Oraons, Mundas and Hos, respectively. The Oraons were seen as 'a quiet, hard-working, simple race' and the Mundas as 'bold, sturdy and brave'.[38]

In August 1832, the Calcutta papers were full of news items on the operations against the insurgent Kols. One described the 'Dhanga Koles' as the people in Chotanagpur and the 'Lurka Coles' as the people in the neighbouring districts. Both these peoples were said to be alike in their 'readiness to have recourse to arms on the most trivial occasions.' In addition, they were 'wretchedly poor, being scarcely ever clothed' and their arms were 'of the rudest description'. The 'respectable class of them' was bound together by intermarriage, so that 'any injury . . . to one of them affects more or less remotely the whole body'. Of these, the Larka tribes were 'the most determined and warlike'.[39]

There was room for further confusion. At an early stage of the Kol Insurrection, a newspaper stated that these tribes were still known 'chiefly from the reports of Major Roughsedge, who stumbled upon them by accident'.[40] Let's leave aside the 'accident'. But, as we have seen, Roughsedge considered as Larkas both the Mundas living in the north of the Singh lands and the Hos living in Hodisum.[41] We are still left with largely undifferentiated Larka Kols.

Given this vague perception of ethnic boundaries, we should not take at face value the conventional wisdom that the Hos not only participated in the Kol Insurrection of 1831–32 but, indeed, that the 'force from Singhbhum' formed, as the officer-writer Edward Tuite Dalton remarked in 1872, 'the most formidable division of the rebel army'.[42]

First, was there a rebel army? Organisationally, not. Early in 1832, a Calcutta newspaper wrote that the Kol Insurrection was a series of 'simultaneous insurrections in various districts' on the South Western Frontier and that the participants 'were totally unconnected'. The correspondent mentioned that on two or three occasions, 'large bodies' of the Kols assembled.[43] This did not add up to a 'rebel army'. The Kol Insurrection was, as Jha rightly pointed out, 'nothing so grandiose . . . as a "national" rising to secure independence from the British. The enemy . . . was a more local and particular one.'[44] The similarity of the events in the different villages was the result of the same causes working in different localities rather than of a political programme.

In these series of smaller insurrections, only at the beginning and the end do we find a confirmed participation of Larkas from Singhbhum. At the beginning, as we have seen, one of the first and most famous leaders of the rebellion, Bindrai Manki, remarked to his colleagues of Sonapur and Tamar that they were of 'one caste and brethren'. That was not without foundation. But as far as Bindrai's remarks included Larkas, he meant those of the Bandgaon area. These, like Bindrai himself, belonged to the Munda people. Of the three more important leaders from the Singhbhum area, Bindrai and his brother Singrai were Mundas from Bandgaon and Khandu Pater was, judging from his name, a Bhuiya, and came from Saraikela.[45]

The Hos or rather the 'force from Singhbhum' did have an impact on the insurgents, as examples. This was recognised in Calcutta. The Vice President of the Calcutta Council Metcalfe stressed, 'their brethren the Singhbhum Kols, who are as free and independent as any people on the earth, acknowledging no governments, but that of their own village chiefs, for the most part paying revenue to no one, and scarcely acknowledging any allegiance to their nominal raja'.[46] Metcalfe could know; he was the addressee of Roughsedge's elaborate description of Singhbhum of 9 May 1820.[47] Now he made the realistic observation that since 1821 'the Singhbhum Kols [again] have been for the most part as independent as they were before'. This must have influenced their 'neighbours of the same tribe, those nearest partaking also of the same spirit'.[48]

Rumours of Larka support raised morale.[49] The Munda leaders further north used the Larka participation in this way.[50] The rank and file of the insurgents used the names of the Singhbhum Larka leaders as a war cry and reportedly, this caused many immigrants to flee.[51] If Hos did participate, they escaped being taken prisoner. A newspaper noted in the middle of February 1832 that 'none of the Kols hitherto taken were of the Larka tribes, the most determined and warlike.'[52] People called Larka Kols were sighted, but not in number. In March, Charles Metcalfe wrote that the 'Singhbhum people, that is the Larka Kols, are not seriously implicated, and I am glad of it'.[53]

While the Hos were called 'Larkas', not all who were called 'Larkas' were Hos. Of all the Larkas mentioned in the sources and in the overview of the trials,[54] not one came from Hodisum. The conclusion must be that the Singhbhum Larkas who took part in the Kol Insurrection were Mundas, mainly from the Bandgaon area. The bottom line is that there is no evidence of a significant participation of Hos in the Kol Insurrection of 1831–32.[55]

The insurgents were clear about their motives. 'We returned home, invited all the Kols our brethren and caste to assemble', said Bindrai. In Tamar, they held a meeting at which they gave an overview of the situation.

> The Pathans had taken our honour [of my wives] and the Singh our sisters and the Kuar [of Govindpur in Sonapur], Haranath Sahi, had forcibly deprived us of our estates of twelve villages [*pirs* or *parhas*], which he had given to the Singh. Our lives we considered of no value, and being of one caste and brethren, it was agreed upon that we should commence to cut, plunder, murder and eat. . . . We four should be answerable, . . . conceiving that [by] committing such outrages, our grievances would come to light . . . [and be noticed] if we had any master.[56]

But they could turn to no one. The Chotanagpur state was against them; the Singhbhum state had just told them to fend for themselves.

The same message of anger, despair and neglect came from Chotanagpur proper. This was clear from the incident at the village Tikoo. According to an eyewitness account, 'many hundreds' insurgents came to the Company army on 8 February 1832 'for the purpose (as they afterwards told me) of making submission, but we met them as enemies, and about sixty were killed'. On the third attempt, the correspondent looking through his glass saw 'two or three' walking before the others in his direction. 'It struck me in an instant', he continued, 'that they wanted to speak, and having picked up some words in their language, I bawled them out.' After they came close enough, he delivered to them a message of his commanding officer that if they would surrender, he would try to get mercy for them from the governor general. A few words were enough.

> The moment they heard the word 'Lord sahib' they threw down their arms in a minute, fell at my feet, hugged them, kissed them. They said they had no adawlut, no insaf, no feringee [Englishman] to speak to, and all they wanted was, that their complaints should reach the ears of government. . . . All they wanted was the Company's government.[57]

In the newspapers at least, there was a public debate in Calcutta on the causes of the events. The very fact of a public debate showed that a civil society was emerging in Company-held India. The press had considerably gained strength in the preceding decade. Although newspapers still had to wait for the press freedom that Charles Metcalfe was to bestow upon them in 1835, newspaper correspondents helped shape British Indian public perception.[58]

The *John Bull in the East* implicitly attacked the earlier agents in Chotanagpur by drawing the attention of the public to 'the intolerable cruelty of certain zamindars [and] their false representations'.[59] Indeed, as we have seen, their extreme views could turn very nasty. The raja of Silli, one of Chotanagpur's tributaries, asked the British officer Bowen for 'the total extermination of Kols in this quarter'.[60] This amounted to asking the East India Company to commit the genocide he himself did not have the power to execute. British public opinion rejected this explicitly. The *John Bull in the East* alleged that 'certain' zamindars created pretexts to call in Company troops 'to exterminate a race whom these cowards dread on account of their valour and conceive that they [the zamindars] are entitled to kill and slay like the wild beasts in the fields'.[61] The message of this news item was that the British were there to oppose these frontier state rulers in their tendency to genocide.[62]

94 | A Land of Their Own

Even the view that Kols were good-for-nothing was challenged. Chotanagpur was, in the eyes of another correspondent, 'the most fertile and best cultivated [district] that it has fallen my lot to see, . . . the cultivation extends to the very feet of the hills. Everyone here is astonished at the beauty and fertility of a country which we expected to find a perfect wilderness.'[63] Against such opinions, there was the law-and-order party. Here the rising acquired a socialist hue. The Kols were presented as harbouring 'a total disregard of the rights of property' and their rebellion as one 'of the populace against the higher classes'.[64]

In the corridors of power in Calcutta, too, the causes of the rebellion were dissected. A theory of a conspiracy by the raja of Chotanagpur was rejected.[65] In the view of W. Blunt, the tax rate was excessive and the nature of the taxation positively harmful. The raja, the landowners, the police and the revenue officers had shown 'most grievous' oppressive behaviour. He concentrated on the south of Chotanagpur, Sonapur, Tamar, Silli, Bundu and adjacent areas, where the mankis and mundas had lost their hereditary lands and positions only recently. Blunt called for reinstating them.[66]

Charles Metcalfe[67] agreed with Blunt's conclusions. He, too, drew attention to the 'excessive or undue illegal exactions' made by the raja, his feudatories and the police officers.[68] In fact, Metcalfe mentioned as oppressor everybody who represented the authority of the Chotanagpur state. He took an even more general view of the programme of the insurgents. In March, at the height of the Kol Insurrection, Metcalfe still showed surprise. It took him a few weeks to clear his thoughts on this subject.[69] In August 1832, Metcalfe stated in his minute that 'every inhabitant of the country that was not a Kol, was [to be] driven out or put to death; except the artisans whose workmanship they considered necessary for their own convenience.' The object, then, of the insurrection was

> the establishment of the independence of the Kols . . . . I do not mean that they seriously contemplated the probability of their subverting the British Empire in all quarters, alltho' their talking in the cups of taking Calcutta indicated that they had some wild ideas as beyond all rational bounds; but I have no doubt, however much they may have miscalculated, that they did intend to expel the British government from their own country, and establish their own independence.[70]

The Kol insurgents' examples were, as we have seen, 'their brethren the Singhbhum Kols, who are as free and independent as any people on the earth'.[71] But it was not only the people of Chotanagpur who liked freedom from foreign rule. The feeling of discontent in India, he wrote, was 'universal, not confined to particular places or classes, and owing not to any acts of our government, but to innate feelings, which no measures of our government can ever eradicate'.[72] However, the alleged general repugnance against the white foreigner did not make Metcalfe advocate 'any [general] course of measures of a harsh or vindictive character'.

> Our duty towards those committed to our care by Almighty Providence is happily the same whatever their feelings may be towards us. We are bound to cherish and protect them, to secure them from oppression and to give them good government. Excepting that we must adopt the precautions of keeping ourselves well prepared to put down rebellion wherever it may arise, our conduct towards them ought in every respect to be, what it would be, if they were heartily attached to our rule. Humanity, Duty, Policy and Common Sense unite in prescribing the same course.[73]

If you ever looked for a contemporary statement on the inevitability of paternalistic rule, here you have it.

By the time Metcalfe wrote these words, August 1832, the sentiment in Calcutta that the original inhabitants of Chotanagpur had been wronged had led to a more conciliatory policy on the ground. Now, Wilkinson implemented a 'soothing system', in which cessation of hostilities and subsequent surrender led to a pardon. Leaders such as Dasai Manki of Kochang and Sui Mandu of Bandgaon came in.[74] Immediately after the peace was restored, local police officers were suspended, so that they could not hinder 'a full investigation to any gri[e]vance [of] which they might have been authors'.[75] At least in Sonapur, Wilkinson started to restore mankis and mundas to their original positions. Other immediate, but more general, measures followed. The British authorities put an end to the spirit tax, the postal tax, poppy cultivation, and finally to debt slavery.[76] The judicial aftermath of the Kol Insurrection, too, saw a considerable mellowing of attitude. Although the maharaja of Chotanagpur insisted on heavy punishments, he did not get his way. The view that got the upper hand was that the existing laws in Chotanagpur were wholly inappropriate.[77] Capital sentences were suspended. In June 1833, a general amnesty followed.[78] These were immediate and ad hoc measures.

The problem was what to do with the state of Chotanagpur. Wilkinson made the nice distinction that Chotanagpur and its dependencies were 'more of tributaries than as subjects of ours'.[79] It was another way of saying that the East India Company did not have a grip on what went on there. When Calcutta considered a more permanent solution, it had to take wider considerations into account. The Charter of the East India Company was about to be renewed. To meet public and political criticism, the Court of Directors was moving towards a new mission of the British East India Company. In April 1833, it stated that it could have 'no other object, in undertaking to administer the territorial government for a further term, than the advancement of the happiness and prosperity of our native subjects'.[80] Desperate rebellions by poorly armed natives did not fit in with these sentiments. They were bad publicity.

The calls for a thorough revision of the system in Chotanagpur was part of a wide resistance inside the administration of the East India Company against the regulation system, the judicial, police and revenue rules of Bengal and Bihar.[81] In January 1832, Governor General Bentinck kept his options open. He quoted approvingly, 'Any fixed rule bearing upon people in such widely-different predicaments, and of different nations and tribes, must inevitably be futile.'[82] At this juncture, opposition to the Bengal regulations was well entrenched at the high end of the administration with the second highest, Metcalfe himself, at the apex.[83] In April 1832, Blunt noted in his minute that 'a serious error was committed in introducing our regulations into Chotanagpur, or in attempting to create revenue from taxes to be levied from subjects so uncivilised and so poor'.[84]

There were alternatives, consisting mainly of bypassing the local landlord as tax gatherer and assigning that role to the village. Elphinstone's 'village communities' in Bombay and the slightly earlier Munro's 'village republics' in the south had a communal responsibility for revenue and social order,[85] so had Metcalfe's 'village republics' in the Delhi area.[86] Now that Metcalfe was in Calcutta, his Delhi system got special weight. Concentrating power in a single officer at the spot, it made for a maximum of control with a minimum of means. Much depended on the personal qualities of his assistants, British officers, who were to personally oversee what went on in the villages.[87] It retained the spirit of the Bengal regulation system, but without its 'barbarous punishments' and 'technicalities and forms'.[88] All this made it a more accessible and cheaper system of justice. Its military simplicity became the norm for the administration of newly acquired territories.[89] Marginal areas and their often tribal population could get a special status.[90]

Underlying this was an increased readiness of the administration to sideline local chiefs and zamindars, and assume the responsibility themselves. In order to do this in Chotanagpur, it had to be first established that the area was unfit for the Bengal regulations. Here it helped that the Kol Insurrection had an obvious ethnic aspect. That reinforced the line of reasoning that the Bengal regulations did not agree with the character of Chotanagpur's population.[91] Metcalfe's secretary Major Sutherland wrote that the Kols required 'a peculiar form of government' along the line of comparable peoples like the Gonds and the Bhils. Like Blunt, he expressed the opinion that the system 'which we have latterly introduced [in Chotanagpur] does not seem to be suitable'.[92] This line was also taken by the Calcutta newspaper *Bengal Hurkaru,* in its call for 'a Mr Cleveland',[93] a reference to the British officer who in 1779–83 had pacified the hill tribes of the Daman-i-koh in present-day Santal Parganas.

On 16 November 1832, the Joint Commissioners Dent and Wilkinson sent in their extensive report on the Kol Insurrection. One of its purposes was to sketch the outlines of a future management of Chotanagpur.[94] Firstly, the administration should be entrusted to the raja and other traditional leaders. Secondly, British officers should closely supervise these leaders. These far-reaching recommendations led to dissenting notes, requests and suggestions. Interestingly, W. Dent himself wrote a note of dissent in which he opposed any significant future role for the raja.[95] On 3 June 1833, the die was cast in Calcutta. The raja part of the Joint Commissioners' report was not accepted, while, as we shall see, the village leaders' part was.

The government now asked the Joint Commissioners to draw up a comprehensive plan, with the extent and limits of the new jurisdiction, a suitable station for a European officer and for his assistants, and the means of controlling and supervising these assistants. They should consult the most important European officers and magistrates concerned. Importantly, the Joint Commissioners were asked to make 'a distinct draft of rules . . . as simple and concise as possible' covering the judicial, revenue and police affairs.[96]

The Agent on the South West Frontier Thomas Wilkinson was the central author of the new system. The government had turned to him for his personal opinion on Dent's note of dissent. When Wilkinson had to make the rules for the new set-up of Chotanagpur, W. Blunt advised him to take the rules for Arakan as his example.[97] So, after intensive consultations and manoeuvring, by the middle of December 1833, in the precise words of J. C. Jha, 'all preliminary consultations [had] . . . been completed and Capt. Wilkinson had emerged as the sole official head of the new administration. He was to set up a paternalist non-regulation system. . . . The swing of the pendulum away from the complex machinery and regulation of the [Bengal regulation] system was complete.'[98]

At the time, Wilkinson had considerable experience,[99] but not in what now would be called 'tribal affairs'. He was born on 15 March 1795 in the small, beautiful village of Crosby Ravensworth in Westmorland, England. His father was James Wilkinson, his mother Anne Eggleston. Thomas had a younger brother, James, who died in 1838.[100] Thomas became a cadet in the 9th Native Infantry. In the rainy season of 1813, he 'chummed' (shared lodgings) with John Hearsay of the prominent English and Indian Hearsay family. He joined the 6th Light Cavalry (presumably as a Cornet) in 1816. He distinguished himself in the Third Maratha War (1817–18). His old chum John Hearsay noted in the *Delhi Gazette* Wilkinson's role in leading troops into action during a difficult river crossing.[101] His father and mother died, respectively, in April and May 1820. Thomas Wilkinson served with the Nagpur Auxiliary Horse from 1819 until June 1830, when it was broken up; he received a donation of six months' pay. In the 1820s, Wilkinson worked under Elphinstone, a confirmed opponent of the regulation system.[102] He was noticed by Lord William Bentinck, who asked him on 3 April 1830 to officiate as Political Agent on the South West Frontier and as temporary commander of the Ramgarh Battalion.[103] During the military operations to quell the Kol Insurrection, he rose to become second in command on 8 February 1832. He was appointed Political Agent on the South West Frontier on 17 September 1832.[104]

Wilkinson did not exactly meet the press demand for a second Cleveland. But in the first stages of the Kol Insurrection, his exemplary punishments, although critically received, had been instrumental in restoring order to Chotanagpur. In the later stage, the way he had brought in the mankis and mundas of Sonapur and other areas to the south, had earned good press. After 1833 he, in his avatar of 'Alkinsum Sahib' or 'Al-Kishen Saheb',[105] made these mundas and mankis the actual owners of the village lands, which brought some initial relief.[106] Wilkinson probably did not have the immediate appeal with ordinary tribal people that August Cleveland had. But his relations with them, and that is especially their leaders, were good and lasting. In the early twentieth century, John Hoffman appreciated his behaviour after the Kol Rebellion.

> Captain Wilkinson stayed among them, learned their language, and, by granting pattas to mankis and mundas, and by his friendly disposition convinced them, that he would give them redress. I have myself still met people in the last decade of the 19th century, who spoke of him with that admiration, which their parents had instilled into them for *Alkinsun Saeob*.[107]

On this aspect of his person, and on that of Wilkinson as a boss, we have the view of his assistant Tickell. In 1840 he paid tribute to 'that truly wise and benevolent man'.[108]

Excellent was Wilkinson where it mattered even more. He was a consummate networker. Both Major Benson, private secretary to the governor general and Major Sutherland, private secretary to the vice president of the Council, Charles Metcalfe, were his personal friends.[109] In London, the Court of Directors was in raptures over the choice of Wilkinson. For them, he was by 'his personal character and his recent experience . . . eminently qualified' to be the first agent to the governor general of the newly formed non-regulation South West Frontier Agency.[110]

It was a bureaucratic necessity, of course, to put the South West Frontier Agency on non-regulation footing by a regulation, Regulation XIII of AD 1833.[111] It first stated that 'the present state of certain tracts of country, . . . the nature of the disturbances which recently prevailed . . . and the character of the inhabitants' rendered it 'expedient' to put together Chotanagpur, Palamau, Kharagdiha, most of Ramgarh, Kunda, part of the Jungle Mahals of Midnapur, and Dhalbhum. W. Dent had proposed the boundaries of the new area.[112] He had excluded some areas in the north of the plateau, where the non-Hindu population was small and where there had been no serious disturbances during the Kol Insurrection. The ethnic aspect of the insurrection largely determined the political boundaries of the new administration. Secondly, Regulation XIII placed this vast area under an officer to be denominated Agent to the Governor General. The agent was to take care of civil and criminal justice under special rules. In addition, he had to take on himself the superintendence of police, land revenue, customs, tax on alcoholic beverages, stamps, and all other local civil duties. The offices of magistrate, collector and judge were merged in the persons of the agent and his assistants. With Regulation XIII of 1833, the non-regulation system took effect in a large tract of land close to Calcutta.

On 13 January 1834, Wilkinson wrote to the government in Calcutta that he had divided his agency into three divisions: Manbhum, Lohardaga and Hazaribagh. Also, he forwarded his rules and letter of instructions to the assistants for approval.[113] He advertised the rules as 'best calculated for the people of the tracts placed under my charge'.[114] These special rules, to this day called Wilkinson's Rules, came in two sets, one for Civil Justice and one for Criminal Justice.[115] The enclosed letter to the assistant gave specific instructions on the establishment, its personnel, the annual tour, the village councils and the land question. They were of a thoroughly practical nature, sufficient to 'enable you to commence your work, but if there are any other points, on which you wish for further information, you must apply'.[116] They enable us to reconstruct fairly precisely what constituted the work of the assistants and are, therefore, prime documents for the history of the plateau, and as a few years later the Wilkinson system was applied to the Kolhan, for the history of Hodisum as well.[117]

Each assistant's first task was to find a central location in his district for his main station. His future residence should be within some nine km from there.[118] Of course, there should be a police station, a bungalow of two rooms with a veranda 3.5 m wide all around, the whole construction tiled or thatched.[119] But the success of Wilkinson's Rules and instructions depended on the efforts of the assistant; he was expected to be a workaholic.

> If you follow the course I have urged, you will have but little spare time. We must however recollect that we have not been selected for our situations for the purpose of working only a given number of hours according to rule, but to afford speedy and cheap justice to all who may appeal to us.[120]

In Wilkinson's hands-on approach, there was no time like the present.

Vital to the integrity of the system was the direct supervision of the staff. The assistant had to prevent the local personnel of the Court from making common cause among themselves and especially from acting as intermediaries between the plaintiffs, witnesses and the assistant.[121] All letters and reports were to be opened and read in the presence of the assistant. The personnel should not become too wise and readers should be changed frequently.[122] Moreover, the assistant was expected to encourage people to speak to him privately of the manner in which the personnel of his station had treated them.[123]

The great extent of the new agency, its bad communications, and the poverty of its inhabitants, together with their proven ability to break out in violent protest, called for a proactive approach. Instead of waiting in his office for cases to come to him, the assistant had to take justice to the people. Wilkinson wrote to his assistants that it was 'desirable that you should make an annual tour of your district with such part of your establishment as will enable you to conduct all the duties of your several offices'.[124] For this, he had asked the government in Calcutta to furnish his assistants with tents 'of the size of a captain's regulation tent and with carriage for the same when marching'.[125]

The instructions for the annual tour were in line with Wilkinson's penchant for micromanagement. These were precise and general at the same time. The assistant had to prepare an English and a Persian list of the names of all persons who since his last tour had been before the police or at his court. Then, he would proceed a convenient distance, halt for four or five days, and invite all the heads of surrounding estates and villages to meet him. The instructions to keep control of the incoming information were the same as those for the main station. So, 'when alone in your morning or evening walks or before breakfast when sitting in front of your tent or after dinner, [do] talk with [the village heads] freely, and encourage them to speak of the manner they had been treated' by the staff of his main station. As in the main station, at these conversations no personnel of the station, or even private servants were to be allowed. The assistant should speak with the heads of the estates and the villages about their own affairs and those of their neighbours. The object was 'in the course of one or two years [to] become intimately acquainted with the state of your district and condition of its inhabitants'.[126] The Kol Insurrection had taken the administration completely by surprise. That experience should not be repeated.[127]

Obviously, a yearly visit was not enough to establish law and order in the countryside. Wilkinson wanted to use the fashionable village republic to strengthen the assistant's work. He granted some autonomy to the village by setting up village councils with limited judicial power.[128] The village council consisted of three to five persons and was called *panchayat*, council of five. In principle, all villagers could be members. But in practice the assistants and the agent were to 'make their selection ... from amongst the persons most conversant with the matter at issue' or, better still, 'from amongst the most respectable and influential persons'. The rules implied the use of village councils to expedite justice in minor cases. The only grounds for appeal were corruption of the council or that the award would be 'contrary to the common law of the country or the rules enacted by the Governor General in Council'.[129] The aim was to make justice accessible.

The financial matters should be handled at the station itself.[130] But all complaints about balances, undue exactions or accounts could be received on plain paper and heard by the assistant. Any party that might feel so could appeal against the assistant's decision to the agent.[131] Having dealt with the finances, Wilkinson reverted to the judicial system.

Two English and two Bengali registers of the suits and cases were to be kept, 'prepared agreeably to the accompanying forms. . . . You should devote an hour a week in presence of parties or their agents to going over your registers . . . and issue such orders as will expedite them through your court.'[132] Justice had to be affordable, too. In this cash-starved district, the agent and his assistant were empowered to grant exemption from stamp duty and receive suits '*in forma pauperis*'.[133] Likewise, petitions, pleadings, settlements and the like did not need to be on the expensive stamped paper.[134] How much this contributed to simpler procedures can be gauged from the legalese of the earlier instructions. Up to then, complaints had to be submitted on the expensive 'Stampt Paper of the value specified in Number 8 of Schedule B Regulation X of 1829', and answers on 'Stampt Paper of the value specified in Number 9 of Schedule B Regulation X of 1829'.[135]

In criminal suits, the assistant had the power to pass sentences of imprisonment with or without hard labour for up to seven years.[136] The agent could revise all sentences passed by an assistant.[137] In civil suits, too, appeals could go from the courts of the native judges to those of the assistant, and from there to that of the agent.[138] There appeared some provisions for appeal against the verdict of the agent himself. He had to report heavy sentences, such as long imprisonment or death sentence, to Calcutta. These were subject to approval, modification or even reversal by the *Sadar Nizamat* court in Calcutta. In sum, the agent and his assistants had quite large powers, but certainly no *carte blanche*. Calcutta's court kept the last word.[139]

For all these attempts at making justice accessible to the local people, the new agent did not envisage a break in language policy. Hindustani in the Bihar part of the Agency and Bengali in the Bengal part were to remain the languages in court.[140] This measure was convenient for the administration, but very troublesome for the locals. Intricacies tend to get lost in translations. Add to that the general view of litigation as the continuance of aggressive exploitation by other means. The original inhabitants of Chotanagpur were on the defensive. Their huge disadvantages could not be balanced by an increased presence of a British officer. Here Wilkinson was more expedient than realistic.

Therefore, perhaps, Wilkinson covered the most important question, the land question, with a general rule. The Rules for the Civil Justice stipulated that

> No sale, transfer or mortgage of any landed property, on account of claims for rent, or on any other account shall be legal until the authority of the Governor General's agent, for such sale, transfer or mortgage, shall previously have been obtained.[141]

This was done with an official remark 'certifying on the back of the bond, that the sale, transfer or mortgage has been sanctioned'.[142] And there was little chance to get such a certificate.

> The Governor General's agent shall immediately have proclaimed, that in future his consent to the sale, transfer or mortgage of landed property belonging to . . . proprietors whose lands have been in their possession for generations will generally be withheld.[143]

This was an important check on the loss of those lands where the civil and religious functions of the villages were concentrated. It was part of a packet of measures to revitalise the administrative and the social structure of the village.[144] The land question was widely regarded as the root cause of the

Kol Insurrection in Chotanagpur. In 1839, Dr John Davidson would restate forcefully that nothing could ever reconcile the original inhabitants of Chotanagpur to the loss of their lands, and until they were protected in this sphere, 'we never can be sure of the peace of their country'.[145] As the century wore on, these proved to be prophetic words.

Chapter 7

Strategic Moves on the Ethnic Frontier

...
Non-interference if possible; Wilkinson's April 1833 meeting at Saraikela; the Bamanghati dispute; debate on the management of Bamanghati; the arena moves north; debate on the management of the Ho country; Wilkinson's letter of 22 August 1836; personal communication in Calcutta; the Third Kolhan Campaign
...

The actions of the Hos against Raghunath Bisi in 1830 did not look much different from the Kol Insurrection in Chotanagpur. However, their cause was different; so was their aftermath. In the Hodisum, oppression had reached the stage of extortion, but not, as in Chotanagpur, the stage of expropriation of the land. The chasing of Raghunath stopped extortion and interference in the nearby Ho villages. But even after the tax gatherer and exploiter stopped to show up, the area of the Hos did not become quieter. In Porahat territories in the north, unrest came from a general failure of the state. Elsewhere, even more seriously, much unrest was caused by quarrelling rajas and chiefs south and east of Hodisum. These put Hos on the battlefield as auxiliaries to their own armies. Precisely in these years, in which the discussions about the future system of the Chotanagpur area were in progress, developments in these states took an ugly turn. When the rulers wanted to restructure their states and get more power, their smaller fiefholders turned violent. The initial reaction of the Company was a shift of mood away from interference.

Immediately after the Kol Insurrection, Wilkinson went to Sambalpur, where the zamindars refused to obey the pro-British queen (and one-time favourite of Roughsedge) Mohan Kumari.[1] In March 1832, this episode prompted Wilkinson to share some thoughts with the Chief Secretary to Government George Swinton. In Wilkinson's view, the object in the states under his agency, where 'we cannot control effectually, or where we have no interest or object to do so', was to attach the local rulers and population to the British as a strategic reserve. As Wilkinson put it, 'that we may rely on their aid should a day arrive when we may stand in need of it'. The government could not gain this attachment by supporting an incompetent ruler against his subjects. If the Company kept troops in the state of such an oppressive ruler, the population would consider 'his acts however tyrannical . . . in a manner countenanced by us'. The ruler had, as we would say now, no moral hazard of government. Instead of having to live with the possibility that bad governance could cost him his power, the raja could continue to do as he pleased. He expected that if his subjects rebelled, Company forces would be his last resort. In Wilkinson's view, however, 'for internal government each chief must depend on his own forces, and on the support of his own subjects'.[2] Here, Wilkinson formulated the ultimate consequence of the 1818 change from a bipolar to a unipolar India. He advocated a return to the situation as it was 'before the Marathas became all-powerful in these parts'. That did not mean that the tributary states should be left alone entirely; they remained as client states. Wilkinson recommended that 'our detachments would be withdrawn; that the British government will hold itself answerable for the protection of each state from foreign aggression; whilst each will be held answerable for the peaceable conduct of its subjects towards its neighbours'.[3]

In these quarters, foreign aggression could come only from other relatively small states. To check this type of disturbance, a more concentrated military force would suffice. Instead of small detachments everywhere in the area, there should be one task force, the Ramgarh Battalion, increased to 1,000 men and 200 Irregular Horse. As Wilkinson perceptively remarked, the rapid deployment—in the parlance of the time the 'movable'—force[4] implied a more central positioning. This had the proviso that the climate there should not be bad for the health of the officers and their men. The government of Bengal agreed. It, too, found its army not large enough to provide 'a multiplicity of small detachments to be stationed on every spot where it may seem desirable to have troops'.[5] The detachments from Sambalpur, Singhbhum and Surguja could be withdrawn and this would significantly reduce the financial burden of the Company. The financial consequences for the states were yet to be thought through. The tribute, anyway trifling, might 'be continued at its present amount or simplified [?] or reduced, or altogether remitted'.[6] The government accepted Wilkinson's recommendation to increase the strength of the Ramgarh Battalion. But a move from Hazaribagh was not on the cards, as it was the only station for troops between Benares and Fort William.[7] Like Wilkinson, the Council viewed the health of the troops as a major military and political risk. At the highest level in India, Governor General Lord William Bentinck advised 'great caution' and solicited Wilkinson's opinion on 'the expediency of recruiting from the natives of that part of the country who can alone be accustomed to the climate'.[8] But even before the withdrawal of the troops was effected, Bentinck saw his fear materialise of 'a state of hostility between the opposing parties in any of these states'.[9]

One party was out of anybody's control. In late 1832, the cold season after the Kol Insurrection, some Larkas made raids from the north of Singhbhum into the neighbouring Sonapur and Chotanagpur. They lifted cattle and killed or wounded eight or nine individuals. None of these raiders was caught and Wilkinson could not say definitely from which part of Singhbhum they had come. But he had his suspicions. 'The name of Bindrai of Kutwa [in] Bandgaon has on each occasion been taken, and I fear with good reasons.'[10] The year before, Bindrai was one of the leaders of the Kol Insurrection. The raja of Singhbhum did not dare to apprehend him. Instead, he 'gave him 12 villages' and the title of manki.[11] This proved that Raja Achuta Singh and his liegemen had 'no means whatever of controlling the Kols within the territory'.[12]

Wilkinson's head interpreter, Nandu, witnessed in Porahat an assembly of a 1,000 'Kols', presumably both Mundas from Bandgaon and Hos. Bindrai and the other Kol leaders told the raja 'not to admit the gentlemen into his country, and if he did, they [the Kols] would plunder it'. The raja had to give in to this demand. Upping the stakes, Bindrai then threatened the *divan* with death 'if he brought the gentlemen into Singhbhum'.[13] At the end of the meeting, the leaders even told the raja not to send his people to their villages to collect rent. They would bring it themselves—if circumstances permitted. This 'Don't call us, we'll call you' made clear where the power laid. It also said much about the people at the meeting. Here, the action program of the Lankah meeting a few years earlier up north—'cut, murder, plunder and eat'—had morphed into a definite, but negatively formulated, programme of ethnic awareness—no Company troops, no police, no tax. In other words, leave us alone.

This independence had quite some defiance in it. Quite close to the garrison encampment at Chakradharpur, a manki murdered four of a family on suspicion of witchcraft.[14] A few hundred Kols celebrated this event, 'the deeds being considered by all meritorious'. Wilkinson asked the government for permission to bring troops into Bandgaon and force Bindrai to give 'such security for his future good behaviour as I may deem necessary' or, if he resisted, to attack him.[15]

In December, in a politically even more disruptive move, the Larkas of Kera and Porahat, possibly with assistance from Tamar and Kuchang, attacked Kharsawan and burned ten villages.[16] Wilkinson wrote:

> [Bindrai had] established a character as a daring leader, and has gained such ascendancy over the Kols of that [area] that they are ready to follow him on any plundering excursion, it may be his pleasure to undertake. The Sonapur mankis and mundas for the aid afforded them last year in the insurrection, will not oppose him, and there are many of their dependants, who would I fear join him in any plundering excursion into Nagpur.[17]

Wilkinson warned against a resurrection of the coalition of the Mundas of Sonapur and Tamar with their tribesmen of the Bandgaon and Kera *pirs* of Singhbhum. If Hos did take part in the cattle raids and the attack on Kharsawan, their participation did not appear to be massive or conspicuous enough to warrant a separate mention. Still, the overall situation in Singhbhum had considerably worsened. Now, there was not only Jaintgarh as trouble spot; the northern Singh states were added as points of concern. Raja Achuta Singh of Porahat stood in the middle, and directed the attention of the Larkas (Mundas and Hos) towards the outside.

At the same time, the government was engaged in the neighbouring Jungle Mahals of Midnapur, where it fought the guerrilla fighters of Ganga Narain.[18] It observed that their relations with Singhbhum 'seemed to be of a most unsatisfactory nature ... We derived no revenue and no advantage from the connection but we were called on to send troops into a most unhealthy country without any certain prospect of benefit from engaging in such operations.' The governor general invited Wilkinson to suggest a course of action to force Bindrai to behave himself in future, if necessary by military means.[19]

In his response of 12 January 1833, Wilkinson suspected the raja of Singhbhum to have a hand in the problems on his northern borders. Wilkinson had no doubt that Bindrai had given part of the plunder to the raja. Achuta had been openly anxious to subject Kharsawan and Saraikela. The raja, Wilkinson feared, wanted 'either to induce the government to send a force into Singhbhum to bring the Kols under his subjection' or to participate in their raids of the neighbouring states.[20] Against that wish stood that Kharsawan and Saraikela were vital to the regional militarily balance. These constituted 'a barrier to the incursions of the Kols of the interior of Singhbhum', the Hos, into the north. The legal position was less clear. An extensive overview of Roughsedge's negotiations with Singhbhum and the results of his 1820 and 1821 campaigns showed that the Company had 'no written engagement . . . by which we are bound to support' Chaitan Singh of Kharsawan.[21]

Calcutta reacted with apparent irritation to Wilkinson's assessment. It curtly reaffirmed that the East India Company was not bound to protect the Singhbhum chiefs against their subjects or each other. Achuta Singh, 'the nominal raja of Singhbhum', was 'bound to maintain good order amongst his nominal subjects and restrain them from exciting disturbance or committing aggression within our territory as [well as] that of the petty chiefs acknowledging our authority'. Wilkinson had to give both Achuta and the Hos the serious warning that, if the British were compelled to take military action, the Company would 'establish its own authority and retain possession of their country'. However, all parties must be told that 'we have no wish or intention to take possession of Singhbhum unless forced to do so'. It all boiled down to the government's position expressed at the end of January 1833 that experience showed that there was too much difficulty 'attending the seizure of such plunderers who have hills and jungles to hide in'. Calcutta preferred Bindrai to behave. It did not wish to have another hunt for Ganga Narain on its hands.[22]

A few weeks later, Kharsawan showed that it was useful. Ganga Narain had fled the Jungle Mahals to Singhbhum to invite the Larkas to join him. Before they committed themselves, they asked him to prove his ability by leading them in an attack on the fort of Kharsawan.[23] There, by a stroke of luck for *Thakur* Chaitan Singh, Ganga Narain was wounded by two arrows, after which Chaitan Singh's barber 'sprung on him and held him on the ground, while some of his friends cut his head off'.[24] The severed head of Ganga Narain was sent to Wilkinson.

Wilkinson took stock of the situation in the *pirs* of the Hodisum claimed by Achuta Singh. Was the claim recognised by the people? There were worrying facts. It appeared that Achuta controlled only the area from Porahat through Chakradharpur to Kera. Even so, he had little grip on the Hos living in that area, with the exception of those living around Porahat and Chainpur. Wilkinson thought that the quiet of Chakradharpur was the result of the East Indian Company troops stationed nearby. Ghasi Singh of Chakradharpur had influence in his part of Gumra, a 'ten Anna share', about 60 per cent. In the remaining area, the raja's part of the *pir*, Achuta commanded little respect. He was largely ignored in the *pirs* of the west and the north of the Hodisum, too, while Saranda and Jaintgarh were totally out of his control. So were Kera proper, under a zamindar who paid 'little or no difference' to the raja, Bandgaon, Karaikela and Kotgarh.[25]

At the beginning of April 1833, Wilkinson brought his troops into the Singhbhum area and camped at Saraikela. His programme here was to solve both the northern and the southern Singhbhum crises.

For this, he had ordered the main people to come, such as Raja Achuta of Singhbhum, *Thakur* Chaitan Singh of Kharsawan, the babu of Kera, as well as the mankis and mundas of the 'Cole peers' of Singhbhum. Probably, Kuntu Pater Manki, the father of Mahadei, was among those who were present. Apparently, Roughsedge had made up with him in 1821, as now Kuntu was on friendly terms with the agent.[26] The meeting was held under trees and lasted several days. At its high point, more than 300 people were present.[27] There were many problems to sort out. And this was the time. As promised, Achuta handed over Bindrai and some others to Wilkinson on 19 April. With this, one can say that the Kol Rebellion was brought to a conclusion.

When most of the mankis and mundas had arrived, Wilkinson opened with an ultimatum, the message he had received from Swinton at the end of January. It was an order to the raja of Singhbhum and 'several tribes' who have 'manifested a disposition to turbulence and plunder' to stop it, to return the plunder, and to hand over the main culprits, or their lands would be taken over. Their answer was they were prepared to do so. But they asked that the prisoners they would send in would not be permitted to return to Singhbhum, as they would avenge themselves on the persons who had apprehended them. In a development in another theatre, that of Mayurbhanj and Bamanghati, to which we shall come shortly, the leaders of the Thai and the Bar *pirs* returned 240 head of cattle and some brass pots to the *mahapater* of Bamanghati. The Hos of Singhbhum did the same with the northern Singhs and returned the more than seventy cattle, which they had carried off from Kharsawan and Dhalbhum.

Next, Wilkinson interrogated Kujri Manki, who had come in with the ruler of Kera (a minor) and his *divan* Jagu. The question was why the people from Kera had attacked the villages of Chaitan Singh's Kharsawan. Kujri declared under oath that Jagu had told him that Chaitan claimed his Jerrea *pir* in Kera and that he would then lose his village. Jagu had also told Kujri that he had 'nothing to apprehend from the Company's troops, as Ganga Narain Sing had effectively closed the ghats'. This accusation was made in front of all the Singhbhum chiefs and not less than 300 'Coles'. Wilkinson had to act and put Jagu in irons. That 'appeared to afford general satisfaction to . . . all present with the exception of the raja'. But Achuta was silenced by the fact that Jagu had confessed to the crime. Now, Kujri was reconciled to Chaitan on the promise that Kujri would restore all plunder. Jagu was put in irons to be sent to confinement in Hazaribagh.

Then, the border dispute between Kharsawan and Kera was solved. Two babus, one from each party, got the order 'to fix large stones at intervals along the disputed line'. The division of Gumra *pir* between Ghasi of Chakradharpur and Achuta of Porahat was assigned to a council consisting of members of the ruling families of Kharsawan and Saraikela. They arrived quickly at a settlement.[28]

Lastly, there was the problem of the attacks between Ramrai Manki and Achuta Singh. It appeared that Ramrai had fined some peasants of Achuta. In retaliation, Achuta had imprisoned some of Ramrai's men in Chakradharpur. But, according to Wilkinson, Ramrai had attacked Chakradharpur and made an attempt on the life of the *divan* Jagu on the instigation of Chakradhar of Saraikela. Achuta requested Wilkinson to remove Chakradhar from Singhbhum. Chakradhar was put under restriction to be sent to Hazaribagh, together with Jagu. Ramrai and Achuta were reconciled with each other.[29]

With these diplomatic successes, Wilkinson decided to economise on the military. 'The presence of a small detachment of troops in Singhbhum had not been productive of any good', and consequently, he withdrew them. The price for continued intelligence was the cost of 'an establishment [in Saraikela] . . . to enable me to obtain information of the proceedings of the Coles in Singhbhum, and the *pirs* of Bamanghati'. The estimated cost for the one writer and five interpreters was Rs. 440 per year.[30] Thus, Wilkinson gave out hopefully, 'it is the general opinion of the respectable portion of the inhabitants of Singhbhum that my visit . . . will lead to tranquillity for a few years, more particularly if Raja Achuta Singh does not again restore to office his *divan* Krishna whom he had discharged'.[31] In fact, it seemed an occasion for a new start, as both Jagu of Kera and Chakradhar of Saraikela were part of a general amnesty.[32]

The April 1833 meeting in Saraikela also made some progress on the southern front possible. Wilkinson had expressly ordered the mankis and mundas of Balandia and Jagannathpur to meet him in Saraikela. When they got the summons, they begged Raghunath Bisi, who was in Keonjhar, to 'accompany them and forget and forgive what had formerly taken place—he complied with their request and came with them'. At the questioning of Mata Munda of Balandia, Wilkinson heard that Raju Mahapater had assembled them and told that 'it was Raja Achuta Singh's wish and order that they should attack and drive the Bisi out of Jaint' in 1830. When questioned for the reason that this attack was so fierce, Mata answered that it was fuelled by 'a desire to be revenged on the Bisi for having formerly seized, and [taken] Jumal Munda's father towards Sambalpur who had died on the road'. Raju Mahapater stated in his turn that it was on 'instructions from the raja by one of his servants who had subsequently died'. So, the key witness having conveniently disappeared from the scene, raja Achuta 'denied ever having given orders'. 'The servant's death precluded the possibility of further investigation', stated Wilkinson. Something had to be done and 'I deemed it my duty to place Raju Mahapater in irons and confinement and with the sanction of Government I propose detaining him a state prisoner'.[33] So, Achuta came through rather unscathed. And it was clear that he and the Balandia Hos shared an opposition to Raghunath. Raghunath's position was compromised. At the meeting, the mankis and mundas of Balandia signed agreements to reinstate Raghunath Bisi in Jaintgarh and pay the annual tax of 8 *annas* per plough to him. Raghunath had to give 'a written engagement binding himself on no pretense whatever to collect more' from them. At the meeting that seemed to do, 'the mankis and mundas took the Bisi by the hand and the reconciliation was thus completed'.[34]

The April Saraikela meeting was as far as Wilkinson could go to bring the relations inside Singhbhum back to workable levels. It turned out a historical meeting. It was the last time Wilkinson tried to reach the Hos through the Singh feudals. It did not work. The definite return of the Bisi had to wait until 1837.[35] A more permanent outcome for the Hos had to wait for the solution of the much more serious crisis on the eastern frontier of the Kolhan, known as the Bamanghati dispute.

The Bamanghati dispute arose in 1818 when Raja Bikram Bhanj was restructuring his Mayurbhanj state. This implied a loss of land, revenue and status for the holder of his fief Bamanghati. For the East India Company, the dispute triggered three problems. To what end should the Company interfere in the relationship between the raja of Mayurbhanj and the *mahapater* of Bamanghati? Here, the South

Western Frontier Agent Wilkinson tended to support the status quo, the continuation of the *mahapater* in Bamanghati. The Commissioner of Cuttack, on the contrary, leant towards the Mayurbhanj side, where the ultimate aim was the removal of the *mahapater*. Where exactly would one place the administrative boundary between Orissa and Bihar? The problems straddled the boundary between the area under the Cuttack Commissioner to which Mayurbhanj belonged and the area under the governor general's agent on the South Western Frontier to which most Hos belonged. The question that came to demand most attention was, how could the Hos be kept in check? Used by both sides in the conflict as freebooters, they were out of control of either side. Would the Company continue with containment through the local rajas or would it actively engage in the area and pursue a grand strategy of pacification implemented by a British officer?

The tract Bamanghati was part of Mayurbhanj.[36] Since the thirteenth century, Bamanghati had been in the hands of the same family. At the end of the eighteenth century, the succession of Raja Damodar Bhanj of Mayurbhanj was not settled, with a relative from Keonjhar and his widow Sumitra Dei vying for the throne,[37] and Bamanghati annexed some villages belonging to Mayurbhanj. This fitted in with a more ambitious, but mostly unsuccessful expansion drive of its *mahapater* as, at about the same time, he was beaten when invading Hodisum. In this action, the *mahapater* 'lost so many men, that he has cautiously cultivated [the Hos'] good graces ever since', as Roughsedge had heard.[38] Thus, Bamanghati lost control of four *pirs*, Thai, Bharbharia, Anwla and Lalgarh, called the 'Kol *pirs*'. It still had a claim on these and, as will appear, had retained some influence. Around 1800, Kuchang, a northern outlier of Bamanghati, was annexed by Saraikela. Actually, this last loss happened with the connivance of the East India Company.

Kuchang came to the attention of the Company in 1768, when the raja of Ghatsila tried to bring this tract into its sphere of influence.[39] In 1770, the chief of Kuchang had raided Company territory.[40] A detachment under Captain Forbes sent against the raiders was surrounded, but relieved.[41] The Company toyed with the idea to annexe the country, but in 1773 they gave up the idea as it would encroach on the rights of the friendly raja of Mayurbhanj. Instead, he was pressed to bring the tract under Bamanghati. About 1800, Kuchang saw a rebellion under Jagarnath Bhuiya. The Company granted the tract to Abhiram Singh, then heir apparent of Saraikela, on condition that he would kill the chief, and pacify the tract. So it happened and Abhiram, the father of Bikram Singh, became the chief of Saraikela itself in 1803.[42]

Some years after these reverses for Bamanghati, the male dynastic continuity in Mayurbhanj was re-established. In 1813, Sumitra's successor Jamuna Dei, the second wife of Damodar and the daughter of Abhiram Singh of Saraikela, died.[43] Bikram Bhanj from the Keonjhar branch of the family, who already in 1800 had been pushed for this position, was now again brought in.[44] The new raja set out on a reorganisation course. He tried to regain control over the lands held by military service tenure holders, as their services were no longer needed. In 1818, Bikram was strong enough to summon the largest of these, Bamanghati's *Mahapater* Niranjan Das, to his capital Baripada and forced him to pay Rs. 700 a year as rent. The rent of the four Kol *pirs* was included in that sum.

Mayurbhanj state could still regard these as part of Bamanghati—control over these *pirs* was never officially relinquished—but in fact, these formed part of the Ho lands. This made for an unclear administrative architecture of the East India Company's overlordship here. When Roughsedge brought the Ho *pirs* under the neighbouring rajas in 1821, the ultimate oversight of these four *pirs* was entrusted to the South Western Frontier Agency, hence to Roughsedge. Roughsedge saw this as a temporary measure. Administrative logic demanded that the whole of Bamanghati as a dependency of Mayurbhanj fell under the Commissioner at Cuttack. Niranjan Das of Bamanghati took advantage of the situation in which his lands were under two British officers. It enabled him to consider himself, at least in all matters relating to the four 'Kol *pirs*', independent of Mayurbhanj. As far as the rest of his possessions was concerned, he refused to pay the increased rent that was part of Bikram's restructuring programme.

In May 1826, Niranjan died and his son Madhu Das succeeded him.[45] *Mahapater* Madhu Das was taken to Baripada and kept there for two months. Finally, he signed an agreement to pay Rs. 700 a year that his father had promised nine years previously. In the meantime, Bikram had sent his own agents into Bamanghati and into parts of the Kol *pirs* to collect the revenue for that year and the next. The Hos of Thai *pir* greatly resented this. In May 1827, the agent on the South Western Frontier Gilbert took the *mahapater* and the Mayurbhanj raja to his colleague in Cuttack to get them to negotiate. There, rent was fixed at Rs. 500 per annum.[46]

In 1829, the son and successor of Bikram, raja Jadunath Bhanj, placed himself under the Company.[47] From that moment on, the Bamanghati dispute took a turn for the worse. The 1827 agreement had not specified the number of the Bamanghati villages to be returned to Mayurbhanj. Now, Jadunath Bhanj planned to use force to take control over the major part of Bamanghati. There was room for this. During the disturbances in Jaintgarh in February 1830, the Hos of Lalgarh and Anwla *pirs* refused to pay the 1821 settlement rate of 8 *annas* per plough and wished to revert to a revenue of 1 or 2 rupees per village payable to the *mahapater*. After some haggling, in April, they agreed to pay the 8 *annas*.[48] We have seen that around this time, Hos from Anwla *pir* together with Hos from four to five villages of Bamanghati, joined the Pinguas of Balandia in the attack on Jaintgarh.[49] Apparently, like the Hos in Singhbhum, the Hos in these *pirs* of Bamanghati continued to be barely—if at all—controlled.

Jadunath Bhanj used the trusted tactic of sending discharged servants of his opponent—as well as three influential Santhals who a few years before had been banished from Bamanghati—into his adversary's area. In the name of the raja, they distributed turbans, buffaloes and cereals.[50] The delegation provided 'entertainments' (probably paid for rice beer for a dance feast); they promised tax freedom. To earn this, the Hos of the Kol *pirs* and the Bamanghati Santhals, a related people, had to attack the villages of Bamanghati proper. To grant tax exemption was no big deal for Mayurbhanj, since anyway it was not easy to gather taxes there. For the Hos, Jadunath's proposal had the additional advantage of plunder. This worked in Thai and Bharbharia *pirs*, where recently Madhu had taken a great number of cows above the rent and killed two people,[51] but not in Anwla and Lalgarh *pirs*, where the population continued to support the *mahapater*.[52] In November 1831, Bamanghati was attacked from Thai and Bharbharia *pirs*, while villages in Uparbagh in Mayurbhanj proper were attacked from Anwla and Lalgarh *pirs*.[53]

The situation needed to be calmed. A British officer best did this, but Wilkinson had to concentrate on the Kol Insurrection. Thus, on 30 November 1831 Wilkinson, at the time still only the officiating Political Agent on the South West Frontier, proposed to transfer the management of the four Kol *pirs* from his agency to the charge of George Stockwell, Commissioner of Cuttack and Superintendent of the Tributary Mahals of Orissa. The Judicial Department accepted this proposal and it went into effect on 5 December.[54] Now that the whole of Bamanghati as well as Mayurbhanj fell under Cuttack, there was space for a more robust type of negotiation.

Jadunath of Mayurbhanj got the order to stop military actions.[55] He and Madhu Das were summoned to Cuttack on 10 January 1832. Here, mere diplomatic pressure by the sole superpower was not enough to allay the deep running sentiments. For months, the raja and his *mahapater* could not be reconciled or made to agree at least to a practical settlement of their differences. These differences were huge. The raja demanded 305 villages as well as the rent of the four Kol *pirs*. Madhu Das offered 13 villages. Finally, on 11 March, Stockwell cut the wrangling short and announced his verdict. Firstly, the raja had the right to remove the *mahapater*, to let him continue in Bamanghati, or to impose any other arrangement. Secondly, this was a case of internal management, and as such the Calcutta Government had no wish to interfere. Lastly, Madhu Das 'as vassal must submit to and abide by the orders of his feudal chieftain'.[56] That meant a distinct defeat for Bamanghati. The same night, the *mahapater* fled.

Both sides in the conflict now took the military option; each side sought to bring Hos to its side to tilt the scale in its favour. The inhabitants of the four Kol *pirs* of Bamanghati were divided. As we have seen, the mainly Ho inhabitants of Thai and Bharbharia *pirs* were on the side of the raja of Mayurbhanj. Thirty of them sent a petition to the government in which they recognised Jadunath as their raja and complained of oppression—and overtaxation—by Madhu Dass.[57] The Hos were clearly freebooting. They did not attack each other's villages. Even outside the Kolhan, they rather colluded than collided. Two brothers of the Mayurbhanj raja, with a force of 500 men including Hos from the Thai and Bharbharia *pirs*, plundered Bamanghati. Dorawas and the *mahapater*'s troops fled. There was no mention of pro-Bamanghati Hos among them. When the raja's brothers left Bamanghati, the Hos of Thai and Bharbharia *pirs* stayed on. Adding to the troubles of the *mahapater* was that he learned that raja Jadunath had already collected an invasion force of 14,000 men to be joined by 6,000 more from his relative in Keonjhar. Madhu Das ordered the mountain passes to the south and east to be blocked. The British should not be antagonised, though, and he ordered that the postal service and the movements of Company troops were not to be disturbed. But on 3 April 1832 villages on the road from Midnapur to Sambalpur were plundered and burned by the *mahapater*'s men assisted by Hos from Lalgarh and Anwla. Some postal establishments on Jackson's road were reported destroyed.[58]

Once the disturbances had reached the postal road, something had to be done to bolster British overlordship over the area. Stockwell wanted to proceed in person with troops to Bamanghati, but Calcutta did not see the need for military action. As Calcutta, or rather Metcalfe, saw it, the Hos merely used the road to Sambalpur, where they daily met postal runners. But, he remarked, the insurgents did not molest them. Hence, they had 'no quarrel with our government but only with their superior the raja [of Mayurbhanj]'.[59] Jadunath Bhanj had to fend for himself. Still, Stockwell was sent to

Bamanghati to restore order by a show of force. In the meantime, Wilkinson pressed the *mahapater* and the Lalgarh Hos who were with him at the time to recover the packets that had been carried off. The postmaster general had written that one of these contained 'printed papers from the Lithographic Press', and the other medicines. After a few days, they found the packets in a village close to Jaintgarh. Wilkinson forwarded the packets unopened, and rewarded them with Rs. 100.[60]

The debate on the management of these tracts got heated. On 14 April 1832, Stockwell sent in proposals to restore permanent peace to the area.[61] He wrote, 'probably we ought to take the Kol districts under [our] own immediate management, dividing them into communities of several villages, and placing over them a man of energy through whom they should communicate directly with the agent'.[62] The manager should spend the revenue of the area on a military or police force recruited from the Hos themselves.[63]

On the ground, Stockwell moved towards Bamanghati, but the *mahapater*'s followers opposed him,[64] and he had to request reinforcements from Midnapur. This party, too, was attacked and Stockwell had to withdraw. He then asked for assistance from the troops on the southern Singhbhum frontier. Calcutta, extremely reluctant to start hostilities, asked Wilkinson to use his influence with the *mahapater* Madhu Das or with the Singhbhum chiefs. On 10 May 1832, Stockwell reached Bamanghati. A few days later, on 16 May, Wilkinson sent Calcutta an overview of the measures that he (Wilkinson) had taken before Stockwell had arrived: he had confirmed the rights of the *mahapater* and promised a full inquiry into the dispute on the condition of a cessation of all hostile activities.[65] In effect, Wilkinson had largely reversed Stockwell's verdict of over one month before, which had led to this fresh outbreak of hostilities.

That called for a countermove by Cuttack. On 17 May, Stockwell again proposed to bring the four Kol *pirs* under British administration or, alternatively, to give them to the six-year-old son of the *mahapater*.[66] As the new ruler over the Kol *pirs* would have to be placed under ward, the differences between Mayurbhanj and Bamanghati would have time to cool off. Calcutta refused to take over the four Kol *pirs*, citing the unhealthy climate as its pretext. The other idea, to invest the raja's son, was also rejected. It, too, would require the continuous presence of Company troops. Even worse for Stockwell, Calcutta announced that for an unspecified time, Bamanghati would be placed under Wilkinson and its rent would be paid to Mayurbhanj through Wilkinson. There would be no direct contact between Bamanghati and Mayurbhanj; communication between the two had to pass through Wilkinson and the commissioner at Cuttack. On this rebuff, Stockwell submitted his resignation. It was accepted on 12 June 1832.[67]

Stockwell's successor was Henry Ricketts.[68] He attempted to authorise the raja of Mayurbhanj to take the offensive against Bamanghati but was overruled.[69] In Bamanghati itself, the conflict grew in size and intensity. Both Mayurbhanj and Bamanghati incited 'Larkas' to fight a proxy war. Ricketts and Wilkinson were ordered to meet and summon the raja and the *mahapater*. So, they met at Narsinhgarh in Dhalbhum, four km south-east of Ghatsila. In this arrangement, on 1 April 1833, the two British administrators 'adjusted the differences' between the *mahapater* and the Mayurbhanj raja.[70] That was, of course, diplomat-speak for an imposition of terms.

There were weaknesses in this arrangement. At the local level, Calcutta had difficulty speaking with one tongue. Ricketts had proposed that the four Kol *pirs* should be declared independent of the surrounding chiefs and that the chiefs should stop collecting revenue from these.[71] But Wilkinson's status quo option won the day. The *mahapater* retained Bamanghati, including the four Kol *pirs*. He was to refer all matters concerning his contacts with Mayurbhanj to Ricketts and all his internal affairs to Wilkinson. The *mahapater* would get a written reconfirmation from the raja. Also, the Narsinhgarh adjustment promised a future without delivering for the present. Bamanghati proper could look towards paying a stiff increase in revenue, going up from Rs. 500 in 1833 to Rs. 800 in 1834, while in 1838, it would reach the final Rs. 3,000 mark.[72] This amount had to come from Bamanghati proper, as *Mahapater* Madhu Das had to promise the inhabitants of the four Kol *pirs* not to take more than the 8 *annas* per plough. From those *pirs*, the Mayurbhanj raja would receive a meagre Rs. 101 per year as tribute. The huge increase for the rest of Bamanghati was a problem. It was a future problem. In the short run, not much changed. But the greatest weakness was that the Bamanghati agreement was a settlement reached in a distant capital, not an arrangement implemented on the ground.

The sorely tried patience of the Company officials—and, I am afraid, of my readers—was tested even further.

In the cold and campaigning season of January 1834, again disturbances broke and now both the raja of Mayurbhanj and the *mahapater* asked for government intervention. This was declined. Ricketts remarked gleefully that 'the futile endeavours of Madhu Das Mahapater to levy rent and subject the Kols to his sway have, more than any intrigues of the raja, occasioned the existing restlessness amongst them, the plunder of nearly all his own territory and a large tract in Mayurbhanj'. He reiterated his opinion that the only chance for peace was to separate the Hos from both sides in the dispute.[73]

In a little over a year after the Narsinhgarh adjustment, things came to a head. Of these events, we have the report delivered on 13 June 1834 by Rup Singh, a government servant stationed at Bamanghati and a close observer.[74] Raja Jadunath's side plundered Bamanghati and Charai *pir* in the Kolhan and only the capital Bamanghati Garh was left untouched. Leaders of different ethnic groups, Tusa Sirdar, Kumlu Goala's son Chila Kol, the manki of Thai *pir* Dasa Bhumij and Bharbharia's Madhu Bhumij, went to Jadunath to offer part of the booty, consisting of a few cattle and some brass pots. In return, they got salt to the value of Rs. 4, and Rs. 100 in cash. The question as to whether the raja had instigated this specific attack or that it had been a spontaneous initiative of his local followers had now become irrelevant. By exchanging booty and presents, both sides had accepted responsibility for the action.

The question for the coalition was: where to go from here? The raja told his allies to convene all the mundas and mankis of Thai and Bharbharia *pir*. The power base of Madhu Das had to be destroyed. Its kernel was the group to which Madhu himself belonged, the Odia-speaking Gonds called Dorowas.[75] So, the raja ordered the Hos of Bharbharia and Thai to ethnic cleanse the whole of Bamanghati, except one village, Burda. They had to plunder 'so effectually that not a Dorawa . . .

should remain in the country'.[76] The problem of the Company troops was, according to the raja, non-existent. They were not in the area; besides, 'if you plunder Bamanghati you will be considered Marathas, and no one will be able to punish you; and I know the Sahibs will not attack you'. The raja also promised tax exemption. Some pressure, too, helped. During the general meeting in Bharbharia, Tusa Sirdar 'drew a sword and addressed the Larkas and told them that if they would not obey the raja's orders, the sword he had in his hand should destroy them—such he said were the raja's orders'. If, Tusa continued, the British troops came to attack the Hos, they could say that they were plundering on orders of the raja. The meeting was fittingly concluded with 'a feast of a buffalo and two goats'.[77]

The Bharbharia Hos sent arrows to the villages of Gumra, Charai, Barkela, Jerra, Jamda, Kotgarh and Thai, inviting them to come and assist in plundering Bamanghati. On this invitation, some 5,000–6,000 men, mainly Hos, assembled at Tusa's place at night. They burned a Dorawa village, killed its leader and several women, children and men, and carried off all the property they could find. As usual after a good fight, the talk was even better: 'if the sahibs[78] came to attack them, they would then plunder the raja's country as they were plundering now by the raja's orders'.[79] They declared their virtual independence by saying that 'the Hos would not now obey [the Mayurbhanj raja's orders] in their own pirs'. Rup Singh concluded that all Hos were now united, except those of Gumra, Kera, and Kharsawan.[80] Actually, more Hos abstained. Also missing from Tusa's invitation list were the important *pir* Bantaria and the pro-Bamanghati *pirs* of Lalgarh and Anwla.

The troubles got a more regional character. The Hos and other people on the Mayurbhanj side attacked Bamanghati fort on 22 June 1834. They were repelled when assistance for the defenders arrived from Saraikela.[81] There were some Santhals in this force. Now, not only Hos but also Santhals fought on both sides. In the last week of August 1834, a force of 1,000–1,200 Hos, Santhals, Kharias, Goalas and Bhumij took the Bamanghati fort. Madhu Das fled to Saraikela. The defeated troops of the Bamanghati *mahapater* were reinforced by the Hos of Lalgarh and Anwla; they made a stand and repulsed another attack by the raja's forces. The *mahapater*'s side captured a large number of guns and one elephant from the raja.[82] Madhu Das was still a force to be reckoned with. Moreover, he had strengthened his ties with Saraikela. A larger round of hostilities was imminent.

Now, the worry was in the Company's camp. When inciting the people of the Thai and Bhabharia *pirs* to attack Bamanghati, Jadunath of Mayurbhanj had outlined his next move. After they had subdued Bamanghati town for him, they were to attack Echa *pir* and, according to Rup Singh's report, 'having got possession of it, a stockade should be erected in Kita from whence Kuchang would be plundered'.[83] The problem, considered settled in 1800,[84] had been brought back to life in 1826 by Jadunath's father Bikram of Mayurbhanj when he asked Major Gilbert for the restoration of Kuchang. The next year, he had filed a case regarding Kuchang against Ajambar of Saraikela, but to no avail.[85] In 1834, a relation of the *kunwar* of Saraikela held the *pir*.[86] This part of Saraikela state did not belong to Singhbhum, neither was it Ho area, which made it easier for Mayurbhanj to employ Hos against it. The capture of Kuchang would strengthen Mayurbhanj, but at the expense of the strongest Singh state, Saraikela.

Porahat could easily join Mayurbhanj in this action. The raja of Porahat, Achuta Singh, was the declared adversary of the *kunwar* of Saraikela. He hoped to be able to use either the Company or the Hos to bring Saraikela and Kharsawan under his rule. Kuchang under Mayurbhanj and the rest of Saraikela under Porahat would mean a massive change in the Singhbhum area.

The problems of Bamanghati in the east and of the Singh states in the north and west were on the point of fusing. The result would be highly explosive. If they were launched in the proxy war between the parties, the Hos would fatally weaken Saraikela, but those of Thai and Bharbharia *pirs* would remain out of the control of Jadunath of Mayurbhanj. And there was no chance that Achuta of Porahat could muster the strength to control the Hos of the other *pirs*. One implication surfaced immediately: the informational nerve system of the Company, the postal service between Calcutta and Bombay, could be disrupted. Once more, as in 1821, the *cordon sanitaire* around the Hos was in a state of collapse.

From the middle of 1834 to November 1836 a three-cornered discussion took place between Ricketts, Wilkinson and Calcutta. Its subjects were the interstate disputes and the linchpin of the problems, the Hos. Wilkinson, the first responsible for the threatened Saraikela, realised that in a rapidly changing environment, repair of the *status quo ante* required a break with the methods of the past. Wilkinson's Singhbhum was di Lampedusa's Sicily. If the Agent wanted things to stay as they were, things would have to change.[87]

Immediately after Mayurbhanj's June 1834 attempt at Bamanghati Garh, Wilkinson wrote to Calcutta that the best solution would be an understanding between the raja of Mayurbhanj and the *mahapater* of Bamanghati. Together they stood a better chance of defending their states against the Hos. He feared, however, that the raja would not rest until he had taken complete possession of Bamanghati. After that, Mayurbhanj would go on to attack Saraikela. Even if the raja himself would not go on the attack, the Hos would continue their raids in several directions 'until they have been most severely punished'. Not one of the local chiefs was able to do this nor could they unite to do so. They had repeatedly broken their agreements with Wilkinson and with each other. His conclusion was that nothing short of sending a military force into the Kol *pirs* of both Singhbhum and Bamanghati would lead to a lasting solution. The Hos would not follow orders unless they were convinced 'that we both can and will punish them'. The military option was the only effective one against 'these restless freebooters'. They should be brought under 'complete subjection'.[88]

The government's answer was not as dismissive as before. It implicitly agreed that no lasting peace could be established in the area unless troops were permanently stationed there. However, that was 'an object if possible to avoid, on account of the unhealthiness of the country and the expense, as well as the probability that more extended operations would be required to check or control the wild inhabitants of the adjoining territories'. As long as the quarrel between the raja and the *mahapater* did not spill over into neighbouring areas, interference was not in the interest of the government. Still, and that must have encouraged Wilkinson, the government wanted him to see which—if any—obligations the Company had towards Saraikela in the Kuchang dispute.[89] The government wanted to establish a legal base for military intervention.

Wilkinson's reply came in October 1834, well after Bamanghati Garh had fallen to Mayurbhanj's auxiliaries. He drew attention to the fact that as early as 1818, the government had announced its intention to confirm the Singh chiefs in their actual possessions. This promise, with an explicit reference to Kuchang, was repeated to the *kunwar* of Saraikela in 1827 by Captain Gilbert and again in 1832 and 1834.[90] There could be no doubt of the Company's recognition of Saraikela's claim to Kuchang. Moreover, *Kunwar* Ajambar Singh had always been a good ally. In short, Wilkinson put forward the brief history of the Company's diplomatic presence in these tracts as an additional reason for military intervention.

In a letter a few months later, Henry Ricketts agreed with Wilkinson that as soon as Bamanghati was completely plundered, the Hos, that is, the Mayurbhanj party, would move on to Kuchang. Ricketts could not refrain from commenting on the main characters of the Mayurbhanj–Bamanghati dispute. He was harsh on Madhu Das, as his problems were due to 'his own obstinacy, perverseness and want of confidence in me'. On the contrary, Ricketts was mild on the raja of Mayurbhanj. 'Tho' it is impossible with our ideas of uprightness and honor not to regard with horror the means by which the raja has gained his ends, still, . . . the rude, uncivilized state of himself and his advisers, must be considered as some excuse for his conduct and the way in which he lost Bamanghati is not to be lost sight of.'[91] But Ricketts was sure that the raja would do no better than the *mahapater* in controlling the Hos. In fact, the Hos were stronger than each of these rulers was. Those Hos who now were fighting for the raja, last year had been fighting for the *mahapater* and 'and in all probability will only maintain their allegiance with the raja so long as he shows them the road to plunder'.[92]

The main problem, then, was 'how to dispose of the Kols'. Ricketts acknowledged Captain Wilkinson as the authority on the Hos, as Ricketts himself had met the Hos only on a few occasions. Ricketts understood the immediate employment of troops against the Hos as urged by Wilkinson in a perfectly one-dimensional way. Punish them, 'that is . . . destroy a considerable number and read the survivors a lesson which they will recollect for some time and be quiet'. However, that had been done before by Roughsedge, but now it seemed that 'their nature is precisely the same still, they are savage and cruel as ever'. At the same time, there were circumstances that rebelled against such Draconian measures. Ricketts noted that

> periodical attacks . . . without any attempt to cure or soften their love of violence and plunder and to keep up the recollection among them of the power of their teachers and the nature of the lesson read, appears but short sighted policy. . . . Moreover it is to be recollected that until these feuds commenced, . . . the Hos were comparatively speaking quiet. They have listened to the attractive inducement of wealth and plunder held out to them by the two litigants, and their alliance has been courted so urgently, it is not surprising such an uncivilized race should have yielded to the enticement, and gladly seized on the plunder pointed out to them. Cruel and savage as they are, they are not so deserving of punishment as those [chiefs] who knowing their barbarity; and [with] reckless wanton cruelly hesitated not to employ them.[93]

He saw several solutions. The first was old and obvious. It was to tell the rulers of the states bordering the Kol *pirs* that they had to pacify the Hos. The next one was new: use the financial stick. If these rulers failed to control the situation, they would be presented with a bill for half of the costs of the expeditionary force. Worse, a permanent force would be established in the Kol *pirs* and the local chiefs would be billed for half of its expenses. The last way out was to make reality regular. That meant to declare the Kol *pirs* independent of the surrounding chiefs; to stop for a few years the collection of revenue; to station an agent among them, invested with 'unlimited and uncontrolled authority' and to put under his command a force 'sufficient to afford protection against any sudden rising, and to enable him to punish immediately any act of cruelty and plunder'. Force might not even be necessary.

> If such agent would make himself acquainted with their language and while he ruled them at first with a rod of iron, endeavour by degrees to gain their confidence and win their affection, I think there would be a chance of reducing these savages to order and in some degree acclaiming them without resorting to the horrid process of a war of extermination.[94]

That would require an officer with a strong character. On the one hand, 'his task would be one of difficulty attended with some danger' but on the other hand, it was 'replete with interest and attraction. . . . [What was more, he would derive satisfaction from the thought that] any alteration must be for the better, by no possibility can they become more cruel, savage and lawless than they are.[95]

The government reacted coolly. Calcutta was not yet moving. Again, intervention with troops was 'an object if possible to avoid'. Still, the I-word was no longer unspeakable. Metcalfe, though 'anxious to avoid an interference', was 'aware that it may ultimately be difficult to do so'. The raja of Mayurbhanj would not get permission to take offensive action against Saraikela.[96] On 20 March 1835, a formal warning went out to the rajas of Singhbhum and Mayurbhanj that if they should launch an attack on any possession of the *kunwar* of Saraikela, 'either or both must be treated as a public enemy'.[97]

In June 1835, Wilkinson could still propose, 'if it be an object, not to take possession of Singhbhum' to strengthen the *cordon sanitaire* of Saraikela, Kharsawan, and Bamanghati. Wilkinson stressed that these states 'interpose between the Larkas of Singhbhum, and those [tracts] in our own immediate provinces which we are bound to protect'.[98] The government lost patience and reported to London: 'The principal cause . . . may be traced to the continuance of that spirit of rancorous enmity between the parties immediately concerned'.[99]

They were not very wrong in that. The raja of Mayurbhanj strengthened his position in this vital arena in a dynastic coup. He married his brother to the younger daughter of Chaitan Singh, Thakur of Kharsawan. Marriage was not a formal alliance, but it was second best. Chaitan asked Wilkinson to arrange that the Mayurbhanj party could pass through the Saraikela area. Ajambar of Saraikela answered Wilkinson that, if ordered, he would obey. But a passage of Mayurbanj troops would end in a quarrel and bloodshed, so high ran the feelings between the sides. So, the party from Mayurbhanj went through Chakradharpur.[100] This was perhaps not wholly unwelcome, as it was one of the strongholds of Mayurbhanj's Porahat allies.

On the ground, a proxy war of attrition was fought. Finally, in October 1835, the last village of the supporters of the *mahapater* in Bamanghati proper fell and the raja of Mayurbhanj made an attempt at Kuchang with the help of the Hos of Thai and Bharbharai *pirs*.[101] In a countermove, the inhabitants of Lalgarh and Anwla plundered villages in Bamanghati and Mayurbhanj.[102] Everything turned out as Wilkinson and Ricketts had predicted. Mayurbhanj's Jadunath had defeated Bamanghati and was now aiming at Kuchang. But the main result was that the Hos were at large.

In January 1836, Ricketts, reasoning haltingly along the official line of non-interference, proposed to strengthen the raja of Mayurbhanj on condition that he would recognise the *kunwar* of Saraikela's claim on Kuchang.[103] This went as far as to give the raja of Mayurbhanj the first chance to pacify the Hos and to arm him to that effect. He was to learn by return of post that Calcutta did not even wish to contemplate this prospect.[104] But Ricketts had warned that the alternative, a settlement of the dispute between Mayurbhanj and Saraikela, was not realistic. The raja regarded Wilkinson 'as his enemy—and believes him to be violently prejudiced in favor of Ajamber Singh and Madhu Das Mahapater'. Although Ricketts professed his firm belief that Wilkinson's motives were honourable, he considered it 'impossible that the raja should voluntarily submit the boundary dispute to Captn. Wilkinson's judgement'.[105]

At about the same time, November–December 1835, Wilkinson went to Saraikela. Here, he renewed his acquaintance with some friendly mankis and mundas of Singhbhum. These had apprehended some Hos from Charai and Rajabasa, who had plundered villages in Dhalbhum and Kuchang. They could not deliver Hos of Thai *pir*, who were on the side of the Mayurbhanj raja.[106] Just after that visit, on 2 February 1836, Raja Achuta Singh of Porahat died, leaving Arjun, a minor, as successor. The dowager queen, assisted by Arjun's uncle Jadunath Singh, superintended the Porahat state. She and Jadunath accused Chakradhar, the eldest son of Saraikela's Ajambar Singh, of having poisoned her late husband, presumably at a ceremony in Saraikela.[107] Wilkinson enquired into the matter and acquitted Chakradhar. But the rani objected to having him anywhere in Singhbhum. So, on 19 July, they agreed in front of Wilkinson that the queen and Jadunath would pay Chakradhar each year Rs. 100 on condition that he would not live inside Porahat state and its dependencies.[108] The Rs. 100 never came, but that was for the future.[109] At the moment, it was clear that for years to come, Porahat would not be a major player.

Meanwhile, the troubles in and around Bamanghati continued. To take the heat out of the conflict, Wilkinson removed Madhu Das Mahapater from Saraikela to Ranchi.[110] It did not work. Rattan Munni, a cousin of Madhu Das, who also had taken refuge in Saraikela, with 150–200 Hos and some Dorowas of Lalgarh *pir* made a counter-attack and plundered two villages in Bamanghati in April or May 1836. The protracted disputes had led to a permanent destabilisation of the area.[111]

Let's give a recap of the situation. Porahat was ruled by the widow of the raja and its effective ruler was her relation Jadunath (of Porahat). Both were keen on stirring up as much trouble with their traditional competitor Saraikela as they could. Mayurbhanj's Jadunath had taken possession of practically all of semi-independent Bamanghati and was planning to move on to truncate Saraikela, the Company's best ally in the area. Moreover, Saraikela and Kharsawan were essential to the East India Company. To the south of it were the Hos, freebooters for different local rulers, effectively doing as they pleased, dominating—and plundering—large areas in the region.

The first half of 1836 was the turning point in Wilkinson's thinking on Singhbhum. Having come around to military intervention, something more lasting presented itself to Wilkinson. His relative success with the Hos and Auckland's accession as governor general in Calcutta in March enabled him to formulate a grand strategy for the Singhbhum area. Wilkinson had not lost sight of the obligation of the main Singh states to maintain the status quo in the area. He also was convinced that these, as well as Mayurbhanj, failed to fulfil this strategic requirement. With their fighting, in which one side was bound to win, they threatened to upset the *cordon sanitaire* to the north and east of the Hos. After that would have fallen, they would be unable to control the Hos, unless they enabled them to get more plunder. The Hos might also be tempted to plunder on their own accord. But this plunder was in the British territory. A permanent destabilisation of the area was well possible. At the same time, his own efforts showed that a British officer on the spot could enforce the peace that Calcutta wanted.

The rethink resulted in his monumental letter of 22 August 1836 to the Bengal Government. The letter, written in Wilkinson's precise and clear style, has since been a major source of the early history of modern Singhbhum.[112] It gave the motive, the means and the opportunity for the forcible introduction of direct British rule into the land of the Hos.

Wilkinson started with the Company's obligations towards the Singh states. Here, due to the incomplete records of the South West Frontier Agency, he could not go too far back.[113] He did refer to the government's 1818 instruction that the Company wished the three Singh chiefs 'to be left in the secure enjoyment of their actual possessions, independent of each other, and owning the British Government a nominal tribute'. Agreements based on these principles were signed with Saraikela and Kharsawan in January 1820. A few weeks later, a similar agreement was reached with the raja of Porahat. The latter's request to get control over Saraikela and Kharsawan was turned down. But Roughsedge promised some assistance to him in regaining the image of the Pauri Devi and in stopping the raids of the Larkas. These verbal promises were not part of the unconditional acceptance of 'the protection of the British Government' by Porahat. Here, Wilkinson was careful to recall Metcalfe's part in the proceedings.

Then, he referred to the terms of the agreement between the Hos of Singhbhum and Bamanghati on one side and Roughsedge on the other side. These were: to acknowledge themselves to be subjects of the British Government; to pay the revenue of 8 *annas* (half a rupee) per plough; to give the right of safe passage to all travellers; to allow immigrants in their villages and even to teach their own children Odia and Hindi; and, lastly, to engage themselves when having grievances not to resort to arms, but to complain to officers of the Company troops stationed on the frontier. At the time,

Wilkinson concluded, these troops were intended not only as a check on the Hos but also to prevent the Hindu chiefs from 'making exactions from or otherwise oppressing them'.

Paras 22–37 of the letter contained Wilkinson's view on the struggle between the raja of Mayurbhanj and the *mahapater*. In it figured prominently the agreement of 1832, arranged by the commissioner of Cuttack and Wilkinson himself, in which the raja of Mayurbhanj confirmed the *mahapater* in his possessions, which put the capture of the *mahapater*'s last stronghold by the troops of the raja in a disadvantageous perspective. The consequence was, Wilkinson pointed out, a 'frequent' disruption of the post on the road between Calcutta and Bombay. 'It has never been satisfactorily established by what Kols, but I imagine some times by those of the two pirs under the influence of the mahapater, and some times by those under the influence of the raja'.[114] On two occasions, Hos from one of the parties in the disputes had attacked guards of the Ramgarh Battalion on the road between Bamanghati and Kathkaranjia.

In a quick aside, Wilkinson gave a view of internal affairs of the Hos. The belief in witchcraft and evil spirits amongst the Hos was universal and 'murders in consequence are very frequent. The murders are not confined as in other countries in India to the person supposed to be witch but all near relations of the supposed witch are sacrificed that none may remain to retaliate on the parties who committed the murders.'

The safety prospects, and that was the kernel of Wilkinson's argument, looked bad. The chiefs of Singhbhum and of Mayurbhanj could not even control the Hos of their own territory, 'although they can all command their services by holding out to them hopes of plunder'. They incited a people already prone to make raids. Until recently, Bamanghati and even now, Saraikela and Kharsawan functioned as a buffer between the Hos and the British territories. But, Wilkinson wrote, 'what I do apprehend, if affairs continue on their present footing' is that the southern Hos would continue to raid Gangpur, Bonai and parts of Sambalpur and Keonjhar. In the east, the Hos of Lalgarh and Anwla *pirs* would overrun parts of Mayurbhanj, ostensibly to support the *mahapater*. The victory of Mayurbhanj had effectively put an end to the buffer function of Bamanghati. The raja of Mayurbhanj could hold Bamanghati only as long as he could hold out the prospect of plunder to the Hos or allow them an uninterrupted passage into Dhalbhum. The pro-Mayurbhanj Thai, Bharbharia, and Balandia Hos, aided by some from other parts of Singhbhum, would raid villages in Dhalbhum. This was not all. The *kunwar* of Saraikela would have to overtax his strength to be constantly prepared against attacks from the south. Moreover, the postal service between Calcutta and Bombay, on the road close to the eastern and southern borders of the Ho area, 'will always be liable to interruption'. Lastly, something for the moralists, 'many murders will be annually committed on suspicion of witchcraft'.

Still, there was no immediate threat to the Company's possessions. So, Wilkinson sexed up the Ho menace. 'In a few years', he prophesied, 'we might expect to see [the Hos] located on our borders'. How did the barbarians reach the gates? In Wilkinson's analysis, 'the principle that every independent chief has a right to do that which seems fit to him' inside his own country, was to blame. This policy, wrote the agent, was not good when it hurt the interests of the government or of other allied small states.

The need of the day was a pre-emptive strike. In Wilkinson's words, it was 'the active interference of government for the reduction of the Kols to order, and the preservation of tranquillity in future'. He recommended a military campaign with as its initial function to make 'an example' in the *pirs* of Bharbharia, Anwla, Jaint, Balandia, and Rengra. In each of these, 'five or six villages ... belonging to the chiefs of greatest influence, should be attacked and destroyed, all the cattle & property plundered and the chiefs, if they did not fall in action, apprehended and kept in confinement'.[115] The same treatment should be given to one or two villages in each of the Charai, Gumra and Rajabasa *pirs*. Here, the mankis had remained loyal to Wilkinson, but their villagers had joined the Thai Hos. As we have seen on previous occasions, exemplary punishment was standard military fare.

Political measures had to follow. After the punishment had sunk in, pardon might be offered to the Hos of such *pirs* as had surrendered in their entirety. They would have to come to a meeting, in which 'they should be called on to make restitution of all cattle and other property (or an equivalent in cattle) which has been plundered from the neighbouring countries ... since the year 1830'.[116] The 'entirety' condition was important. Here we have the only instance before and after the establishment of the Kolhan Government Estate, in which *pirs* were mentioned as political units.

The imposition of peace assumed, Wilkinson came to the most difficult question, 'how to best provide for the future management of the Kols and the preservation of tranquillity after punishment has been inflicted'. Here again, he reasoned from the apparent inability of the rajas and other chiefs to control the Larkas. He implicitly rejected the usual British distant superintendence. If the local rajas and feudal chiefs thought they could count on the British military might, they would oppress their people so much that there would be constant insurrections 'which we should be obliged to suppress'. This, we might recall, had been Wilkinson's position all along. In 1832, it had led him to advocate a withdrawal of the Company troops to a central location from which they could be used as a rapid deployment force. Now, in 1836, the Bamanghati dispute had uncovered the weak spot of this strategy. To leave the centre stage to the local players might well surprise the sole superpower with the Hos as the new and less tractable star. Wilkinson had gone a long way.

Surprisingly, he halted at Ricketts' last stop. 'After well weighing the subject, the only plan which occurs to me, as likely to be attended with success, is to take the whole of the Kol pirs directly under our own management.' On the negative side, this would mean releasing the Hos from their nominal allegiance to the rajas of Singhbhum and Mayurbhanj, and also to the rulers of Saraikela, Kharsawan and the lesser members of their families. On the positive side, it meant 'to appoint an European officer to the charge of them'. This officer should have at his disposal a detachment of 500 muskets of the Ramgarh Battalion, a brigade of guns and 100 cavalry. He should station himself somewhere in the centre of Singhbhum, preferably 'in some eligible spot' in Gumra.[117]

The rest of Wilkinson's letter was a summary of his Chotanagpur system and an estimate of the costs of applying it to Hodisum. He emphasised that the success of this system depended on how it was put on track. Important was 'the personal character of the officer first appointed to the charge. He ought to possess good sound judgement, great firmness, patience, and tact in managing the natives & should be accessible at all hours.' This officer should administer all criminal and civil justice. In this, he was to make extensive use of the councils in the villages. Here, too, care should be taken to employ the best people available. The councils should consist of the mankis and mundas 'held in highest estimation' amongst the Hos. The appointment of the mundas of the villages should also chiefly depend on their popularity and influence. They should collect the rent from the Hos to the amount Roughsedge had imposed in 1821.

Wilkinson calculated that the costs of this arrangement would be 'little exceeding 20,000 Rupees which would in time decrease, if the country did not in short time pay it's own expenses'. To hold out the prospect of considerable expenses with no break-even point in sight was not in itself a very convincing sales effort. Peace was wonderful. It was needed. But at this moment of truth, peace turned out to be a constant drain on the exchequer. That was hardly a killer application of the new strategy. After all, the East India Company was an enterprise as well as a government, and had to count its pennies.

Wilkinson knew his audience. He threw in some intangibles he knew would go down well. He suggested introducing schools for 'the rising generation'. Finally, yet importantly, 'probably no finer field could be found in India for missionaries'.[118] In the reformist climate of the 1830s, evangelical influence on the affairs of the Company was strong.[119] Although the spread of Christianity was not the Company's policy, hints of its possibility in a place where conversion would stir no trouble were bound to strike a sympathetic cord. There was something for almost everybody in this letter.

The letter also showed Calcutta much more knowledge of the area than it had got ever before. Wilkinson showed here how valuable was his system of close personal oversight of a tract. However, there was another matter that first had to be solved. Wilkinson's elaborate letter was only part of getting his plan accepted. Ricketts was, he knew, bound to oppose him. All along, Ricketts' first choice had been to strengthen the raja of Mayurbhanj. Even when Ricketts had played with the idea of bringing the Kol *pirs* under direct British rule, it had never been his intention to have these removed from Cuttack's supervision. Still, this was the most logical thing to do. By far the greater part of the new Kolhan Government Estate would consist of land at present in the South Western Frontier Agency. Also, the expertise of working with the new system existed in the South Western Frontier Agency. The four Kol *pirs* of Bamanghati were best added to that agency. Now that Wilkinson had shown his hand, he did not look back.

Also in those days, the best approach to close a deal was a face-to-face meeting with the top executive. On 20 August 1836, two days before the final draft of the above letter, Wilkinson applied for 'a leave of absence for fifteen days for the purpose of visiting the Presidency [Calcutta] on duty'.[120] Wilkinson must have left immediately. Once there, undoubtedly he called on his friends, Major Sutherland, private secretary of Metcalfe—but Metcalfe had resigned on 5 August[121]—and Major Benson, who had been private secretary to the governor general up to the year before.[122] On 20 September, the main work in Calcutta done, he presented his bill for travelling charges to Calcutta on duty and back to Chotanagpur. The distance was 640 miles (over 1,000 km), at a travel allowance of half a rupee per mile, altogether Rs. 320.[123] The trip, especially the interview with the governor of

Bengal, had been a resounding success. After 'much personal communication' with Captain Wilkinson, the governor of Bengal felt the state of affairs to 'be a matter of reproach'.

> Within a distance of not 150 miles [240 kilometres] from Calcutta upon the line of road almost the most important in the empire, the country should yet be unknown and unexplored and stand as blank upon our maps as the least accessible parts of the interior of Assam. All we know of it is that from time to time bands of savages mostly armed with bows and arrows make predatory incursions from it upon our peaceful subjects and those of the countries dependent on us. . . . [As long] as this government is not exposed to foreign aggression, it seems to be our duty and our interest wherever it can be done without too much hazard of life and of expense to endeavour to gain strength by drawing within the pale of law and good order every country within our extensive frontier which like those of the Kols and the Konds not only for themselves set all government at defiance but by extending beyond their borders a feeling of insecurity and alarm check all industry and improvement in the neighbouring districts.[124]

With the victory of Wilkinson's strategy went the acceptance of his presentation of the country and the likely course of the campaign.

> The country of the Kols beyond the belt of jungle by which it is surrounded, is open, well [cultivated], & closely inhabited; there is no government but that of petty village chieftains. It is not likely that any active resistance will be made, and on the approach of any strong body of British troops in all probability the country will be deserted. The burning of one or two villages or the destruction in them of such crops or stores of grain as may be found, will, it may be expected, lead to the submission and to the exaction of such terms either of reparation or tranquillity in future as it may be thought right to insist upon. [In short, a] discretionary authority for these objects must be given to Captain Wilkinson'.[125]

The blank spot worried the governor. Hardly had Wilkinson left, as Mangles, secretary to the government of Bengal, sent him the 'Map of Singhbhoom & Adjacent Pergunnahs surveyed by Captn. Jackson in May 1821' and 'Map of Chota Nagpore and Singhbhoom surveyed by Ensign Tickell in July 1836'.[126]

The government agreed with the governor of Bengal; however, it added a proviso. The government expressed 'doubt whether the extreme measures of severity advocated by Captain Wilkinson were in the first instance absolutely necessary'.[127] In his turn, the governor of Bengal stipulated that such measures should be avoided from the moment that 'a general disposition to entire submission shall be manifested'.[128] The government, again, relying on 'the judgement, experience, and humanity of Captain Wilkinson, and being satisfied that the Right Honorable the Governor [of Bengal] will not authorize a recourse to any measure of severity that is avoidable' gave its sanction to the military plans.[129] The 320 miles back home must have sat easily on the governor general's agent.

The raja of Mayurbhanj, on the contrary, sped in great distress to the sympathetic ears of Ricketts. 'It is not surprising,' Ricketts wrote rather imprudently, '[because] all his difficulties and disasters have arisen from the countenance afforded by the authorities of Hazaribagh to his rebel vassal the mahapater of Bamanghati. And he now fears that . . . by means of Captain Wilkinson's representations he may be deprived of part of his territories [and] disgraced and ruined.' Ricketts forwarded these sentiments to Calcutta with implicit approval. He struck an apologetic note. 'It is difficult to explain this sort of feeling'—on the copy of the Board in London was written in lead pencil: 'It exists every where'—'but . . . the Mayurbhanj raja has said to me of Captain Wilkinson, "he may not desire to injure me but he must support those who are under his rule."' Ricketts asked permission to be personally present when the affairs of the tract would be settled finally.[130] He would have done better to remain silent. Calcutta indicated in a schoolmasterly fashion that

> the object of the present expedition into Singhbhum is neither to afford aid to one party or the other, but to put down & coerce to peaceable & inoffensive courses those whose acts of aggression upon territories belonging to the British government or under our protection, & attacks upon our communication with Bombay, have rendered the measures now about to be taken indispensable. The raja may rely upon being dealt with by government with all justice & reasonable consideration. In the meanwhile, it is his duty to attend upon Captain Wilkinson.[131]

Furthermore, the governor snapped, he would 'not admit the possibility of rivalry or partisanship in the two offices of Cuttack and Hazaribagh and such notions are at once to be set aside'.[132] Wilkinson had won the day.

On 22 August 1836, Wilkinson had given the outline of what was to be the Third Kolhan Campaign.[133] He proposed to employ the Ramgarh Battalion with two brigades of guns, and in addition two regular battalions of infantry and one more brigade of guns. One battalion and a brigade of guns were to enter Lalgarh and Anwla *pirs* from Bamanghati. The other brigade with guns and 100 Irregular Horse would proceed from Saraikela into the Thai and Bharbharia *pirs*. The extra brigade, again with guns and 100 horse, would attack Rengra *pir*. The expeditionary forces to Lalgarh and Thai could support each other, and the detachment that first had completed its work should afterwards enter Balandia and the Jaintgarh area. It would be even better if the two corps could enter Balandia and Jaint from different points at the same time. The plan aimed at maximum speed. The troops should not depend on the country for supplies, but should bring provisions for two months with them. The government agreed and placed the Ramgarh Battalion and the regiment at Bankura with two months' supplies at the disposal of Captain Wilkinson.[134]

At the beginning of November 1836, Wilkinson informed the rulers of Singhbhum and the Mayurbhanj raja of the objects of the campaign and warned against obstruction. Wilkinson received 'assurances of hearty co-operation' from Saraikela, Porahat, Kera, Karaikela, and Chainpur in Singhbhum, and from inside Hodisum messages had come from Jemadar Manki of Gumra, Dabru Manki of Cherai, and one Sarangi, in the sources rather obscurely referred to as 'Mankie of Bhunge'. Wilkinson had a good start. All these leaders, he wrote, had quite a following under the Hos. At the same time, it was his easiest part of the campaign. Wilkinson's allies had always been well disposed towards the British Government.[135]

Wilkinson reached Saraikela on 18 November and immediately sent for the friendly mankis of Gumra, Charai, Ajodhya and Asantalia *pirs*, who joined him on the 20 November. The next morning Wilkinson sent them with his interpreter Jungly to work on their countrymen in the Thai and Bharbharia *pirs*.[136] Thai *pír* was the first *pir* Wilkinson planned to enter. His message to the leaders was that when the troops would arrive at the border between Charai and Thai *pir*, they had to hand over 1,000 head of cattle, about the number they had carried off from Dhalbhum, and 30 named men who had been the leaders and advisors of the raids into the Company's and Saraikela's territories. The

Bharbharia Hos had to deliver up 500 head of cattle and 36 men. The leaders of both *pirs* were to engage themselves most solemnly to preserve the peace, to take no orders from the rajas or other chiefs, and to observe what rules government might prescribe for their future management. All this was in return for the promise that their villages would not be attacked.

When the heads of the Thai villages got the message the next day (distances inside Hodisum were not long), they asked the messengers a one-day respite to consult their Bharbharia allies. The next day, Wilkinson's Ho emissaries learned from some of their relations in the threatened *pirs* that people were assembling to kill them for having brought the Company's army into the country. In addition, they found that two servants of the Mayurbhanj raja, Herry and Muttra, did everything in their power to dissuade the inhabitants of the Thai and Bharbharia *pirs* from submitting to Wilkinson. So, Wilkinson's emissaries left, leaving their message in Thai *pir* with the request to make it known to the Hos of Bharbharia. In the meantime, the inhabitants of these *pirs* were already hiding their grain and cattle in the hills and jungle, 'which', Wilkinson wrote confidently, 'we shall have no difficulty in discovering'.[137] The campaign was on.[138]

Wilkinson had done his homework well. To get information, and to assure awards for the people who would help him to get the plunderers in, he had quite a war chest, 'an account of which, with what I may hereafter expend, I shall submit for the approbation and sanction of government'.[139] The bill amounted to Rs. 1,411 or the prospective taxation of well over 2,800 families.[140] To prepare his tactics, he had studied the records of Roughsedge's Kolhan campaigns. He knew that a detachment from 'the force under Col. Richards'[141] had been resisted even at a short distance from his own camp in 1821. His tactical answer to this possibility of guerrilla warfare was not to send out small detachments, 'as the least failure will have a bad effect'.[142]

It was Wilkinson's style to hit, and to hit hard at the very start, a nineteenth-century version of 'shock and awe'. On 3 December 1836, two companies under Captain Wilkinson and Captain Corfield, respectively, entered Thai *pir* from different sides. The actions were robust, with villages attacked, cattle taken and houses set on fire. As the army progressed, the heads of villages in Thai and Gumra *pirs* submitted and turned in some of the requested people. Even from Balandia and Jaintgarh villages, people came in to Wilkinson and promised to restore plundered cattle, a promise that he did not put much faith in.[143] Eight villages got an additional warning on 15 December. After two of these were destroyed, all eight submitted.

In Bharbharia *pir*, it took about two weeks to subdue the last two strongholds of resistance. On 29 December, Wilkinson arrived in Lalgarh *pir* and the day after, the four sirdars of the *pir* and 'heads of villages, some of whom had before been with me', came in and submitted. Here, he learned that 116 families of Dorowas, the group to which the *mahapater* belonged, refugees from Bamanghati, were in the Lalgarh and Anwla *pirs*. Wilkinson first attended to this problem, because he feared that if he left any Dorowas there, the Hos would get the idea that these were the cause of the arrests and would kill some. Wilkinson sent all the Dorowas to Saraikela and gave each family of refugees Rs. 2, 'of which I hope the Right Honourable the Governor of Bengal will approve'. With the flight of the Dorawas, the *mahapater* definitely lost his clout. Immediately after the Dorowas had reached his camp, Wilkinson without having to use force secured more than sixty Hos, 'many of whom are notorious plunderers, who were concerned in carrying off two [post bags] and attacking two detachments of troops at different periods'.[144]

He reached the centre of the last of Bamanghati's four Kol *pirs*, Majhgaon in Anwla *pir*, on 10 January 1837. Here, three of the four chiefs came in. The fourth was brought in by some mankis from the Singhbhum side. Wilkinson meant to keep him hostage 'until the most notorious of the plunderers, living in a manner under his protection, were brought to me, and until all the heads of villages had submitted'.[145] One more village was plundered, this time without loss of life. Now, the whole of Lalgarh and Anwla submitted. The village heads brought in 226 head of cattle. Here, altogether about 100 people, all except five people who were on Wilkinson's list, were taken into custody.[146]

The next stage brought Wilkinson to the Balandia part of Bar *pir*. On 23 January, most of its headmen submitted with the message that, as Wilkinson had feared, everybody whom he wanted had fled to the hills and jungles.[147] On the 26th troops under Captain Lawrence took some women, whose husbands he wanted, hostage. In retaliation, the Hos killed three of his camp followers, who were looting grain from a hideout that they had found abandoned. This setback was more than compensated in a search and comb operation by the troops of the Singhs and pro-Wilkinson Hos. They found—and looted—a large quantity of grain. The villagers now brought in some sixty wanted men. Finally, on 6 February, most villages of the Balandia area submitted. Only eight or ten men on Wilkinson's wanted list were still at large in that *pir*. Wilkinson took the headmen of the villages, to which they belonged, hostage.[148]

On 9 February, Wilkinson marched into Gamharia, took 16 prisoners and got 200 cattle. Four days later, he reached Jagannathpur. All the mundas of Bantaria *pir* placed themselves under the Company. As many of them had aided the Company's troops, that must have cost them little pain. The chiefs of Jamda *pir*, too, came in.[149]

As sickness had broken out among the troops, Wilkinson dismissed most of them. He kept 500 men of the Ramgarh Battalion, one brigade of guns, and a troop of the 5th Local Horse, and ordered the chiefs of Kotgarh and Rengra to meet him in Gumra or Chaibasa.[150] Now, Wilkinson concluded that all the chiefs of the villages in Jaintgarh and Bantaria 'have entered into solemn engagements of the same nature as the Kols of the Bamanghati pirs', and asked Calcutta for further instructions.[151] The successful outcome was no longer in doubt. On 28 February 1837, Wilkinson wrote that the Kotgarh, Jamda, 'Nottooa' (Latua?), Saranda, Rengra and 'all the Mankis & Mundas of the Singhbhum raja and his brethren' had followed.[152] The result was that the number of villages brought under the direct control of the government was 622, in an area of some sixty by hundred kilometres.

It was time for congratulations. Without having to wait for Wilkinson's final letter, the Secretary to the Government of Bengal R. D. Mangles wrote that

> the prompt and complete manner in which his views have been carried into execution, with so few casualties amongst the troops employed, with so small a sacrifice of life on the part of the tribes . . . & the modest

punishment inflicted . . . has afforded the Right Honourable the Governor of Bengal very great satisfaction. He considered this acknowledgement to be justly due to the ability & energy which you have displayed.[153]

London was duly informed, with the assurance that it was 'certain' that 'the British government alone would effectually ensure the peace of those wild frontier districts'.[154]

With this, it seems that the Ho lands were taken under direct East India Company rule as the Kolhan Government Estate. It seems, because there is no official rule or act pertaining to this fact. Possibly, there was no need for it. Regulation XIII of 1833, by which the agent on the South Western Frontier was made responsible for the new non-regulation district, had a provision that the governor general could annexe neighbouring parts to the new Agency and alter its borders.[155] The Kolhan Government Estate was not established by regulation or treaty. But established it was.

Chapter 8

The Arrival of the Assistant

...
The appointment of the assistant; a permanent army base at Chaibasa;
ethnic borders; the administrative architecture of the Kolhan Government Estate
...

Striking the iron while it was hot, Wilkinson pressed for the definite acceptance of his pacification strategy. After all,

> having excluded the raja and babus from all interference in the Kolhan, it devolves on the British Government to provide for its future management. . . . [So,] after the most mature deliberation, I see no other plan for adoption, but the one I suggested in the 55th & 56th paragraphs of my letter of the 22nd of August 1836, which would be likely to prove successful.[1]

Wilkinson again stressed that if there would be no 'functionary on the spot', the Kols, that is, the Hos and other inhabitants of Hodisum, would continue 'to settle their disputes in the same barbarous manner as hitherto, and murders will continue [to be] of frequent occurrence'. The officer was also necessary to prevent renewed interference by the surrounding rajas and babus. With the officer went the troops to sustain his authority. This would cost money. But eventually, the Hos would become more civilised and would make good the initial expenses by increased revenue. Importantly, there was a vantage point much nearer in the future. The government would be 'amply repaid for any expense . . . by having at its command a powerful people when compared with their neighbours through whom it could overawe . . . neighbouring zamindars who might venture to set Govt. at defiance'.[2]

To get the new Kolhan Government Estate up and running, Wilkinson personally announced the new arrangement to the Hos in March 1837. He took Lieutenant Samuel Richard Tickell with him. Wilkinson and Tickell organised three major *darbars* or official receptions in the Ho area. The first one was mainly attended by the Pingua Hos. Members of this *kili* had driven Raghunath from Jaintgarh. They covered the south of the Kolhan. The second one, for the middle part, was in Barkela, while the third at Saraikela covered the northern portion of the Kolhan. Wilkinson took care to make these festive and solemn occasions to mark the start of the new era. He explained the new arrangement and the end of interference by the rajas and Singh chiefs. He explained the return to the tax system as arranged by Roughsedge, half a rupee per plough. He rewarded old allies. All the village chiefs took a new oath of allegiance. A display and distribution of gifts such as rice beer, salt, sugar and scarlet cloth accompanied the function. The receptions ended with proper feasts.[3]

Importantly, many Hos had now seen Wilkinson's prospective assistant, Tickell. Prospective, as Wilkinson had no *carte blanche* in Calcutta. 'The arrangement', was the carefully worded message to Wilkinson, 'has been generally sanctioned by the supreme government'.[4] The problem was money, or the 'very small return which you [Wilkinson] calculate that territory will at present yield'. That, the governor felt, did not justify the immediate appointment of an officer here with the rank and salary of an assistant. Wilkinson had asked for an assistant's salary of Rs. 800 or 1,000 per month including his military allowance. It would come to a civilian expense of Rs. 500–700 per month.[5] Why not economise and for a start invest Lieutenant Tickell, 'who it is supposed will be left in command of the troops' with 'authority to discharge any political or civil functions which may necessarily devolve upon him as representing you [and] the British government'. So, Tickell was 'accordingly empowered to exercise these functions; [and] the Governor has been pleased to assign to him for that duty [a] civil allowance of Rs 200 per mensem'.[6] This was too mean. Wilkinson understood that if he wanted his man to work well, his man needed to eat well. Perhaps, he was as much pressed by his fear that making the political and civil powers additional to a military appointment could weaken his South Western Frontier system. So, he jumped on the godsend that the military line had pursued its own policy, and that 'Lieutenant Armstrong who has joined the Ramgarh Battalion as second in command, arrived in camp, on the 27th instant, to assume command of the troops in Singhbhum'. This blocked the road that Calcutta wanted to go. The question of the officer with the political and civil authority in the Kolhan was open again. Wilkinson could 'with great respect and diffidence . . . venture to suggest that Lieutenant Tickell, whose qualifications fit him for the situation, should be nominated to it, on a consolidated salary of 500 Rs per mensem'. He had already spoken with Tickell who had agreed to this salary. At the moment, he earned Rs. 248 a month. His Lordship had offered Rs. 200 as an allowance above Tickell's military salary. So, the difference was now a mere Rs. 52 per month, 'which I hope will not be considered excessive'. That was a slick move. There was, Wilkinson demonstrated, an advantage in having an officer 'who will not be liable to be changed, and who will be able to devote his whole time and attention to the management of the Hos (which will fully occupy his time)'.[7] Tickell's was a relatively modest salary. When Wilkinson became political agent in 1832, he drew Rs. 3,000 a month. His first assistants, J. R. Ouseley and P. Nicolson, got Rs. 1,000 a month. So did junior assistant and assistant surgeon Davidson on account of his 'superior abilities'.[8] From the proposals for management of the new government estate, which Wilkinson sent for approval to the government on 5 May 1837, it appeared that the appointment of Tickell was a foregone conclusion.[9] On 8 May, the army announced that 'The services of Lieutenant Samuel Richard Tickell, . . . are placed at the disposal of the Right Honorable the Governor of Bengal, for political and civil employment in the Kolhan, under Captain Wilkinson'.[10] Indeed, on 9 May followed the appointment of S. R. Tickell 'to be a Junior Assistant . . . on a consolidated salary of cos. Rs. 500 per Mensem, to be stationed in the Kolhan'.[11] The deliberations must have been quite secret. On 12 May, Thomas Simpson, who had been a junior assistant to Captain Wilkinson for over a year, sent his application for the job of an extra assistant for the Kol *pirs*. But Mangles had to inform him that 'Lieutenant S. R. Tickell had been appointed to the situation in the Kolhan, before your letter reached this office.'[12] Wilkinson had manoeuvred towards a complete victory. The man of his choice would supervise the introduction of his style of management of a territory just added to his charge.

On 5 May, Wilkinson wrote his precise instructions for the management of the Kolhan. Samuel Richard Tickell's appointment as Junior Assistant, a step into civilian administration, came in on 9 May 1837. Three days later, Wilkinson instructed Tickell to take charge of his new office. He received his instructions and a copy of the newly edited Criminal Rules on the next day, 13 May. The civil rules would follow later.[13] The Kolhan Government Estate was established on the go.

The peace was won by war, and most of the immediate measures Wilkinson proposed were related to the establishment of a sufficient force 'for the preservation of future tranquillity'. Initially, this force was set at the strength that he already had retained: 500 men of the Ramgarh Battalion, a brigade of guns and a troop of the 5th Local Horse. They should be stationed, if not in the Kolhan, 'which the medical officers are of opinion would be unhealthy', then in or near Saraikela. There was little time left. It was getting hotter every day, the rainy season was near and the troops still had to erect their shelters.[14] The Bengal government agreed with these proposals. On 28 February 1837, Wilkinson received the message that these 'would be this day laid, with His Lordship's recommendation, before the Supreme Government [of India]'. The secretary authorised Wilkinson to save time and to select a site for the cantonment, but only after he had made careful enquiries into its healthiness.[15]

On 13 March, the governor general elaborated what the secretary already had indicated. The troops were to be stationed 'in or near' Saraikela.[16] At this time, Wilkinson himself was looking for a place for the station of the assistant, the capital of the estate. It should be at the same time 'as centrical . . . as can be found' and 'affording a fair prospect of health to the troops'. This, he proposed, would be Chaibasa, which was 'in a perfectly open country, and on the banks of a stream of water'. The problem would be the site for a cantonment for the troops. 'There is a high spot sufficiently extensive for the force, close to the village of Kundubera about three miles'—five kilometres—'nearer to Gumlagarh than Chaibasa and which is within 600 yards'—550 metres—'of a stream of clear running water with a sandy bottom'. Water was a bit far, but a well could be sunk. The army surgeon, Dunbar, who was present when the choice fell on this site, had his doubts. The spot was quite near to the unhealthy jungle. Wilkinson thought this was not important, as the country was open to the north-east and west, allowing some breeze.[17] Saraikela was out of the picture. In Wilkinson's mind, the 'centrical place' of the Singhbhum area was Chaibasa.[18]

When Tickell arrived in Chaibasa, he was openly disappointed. The station had been 'selected hurriedly' and was 'situated on a barren gravelly plain, interspersed with brushwood and near piles of bare rocks'. The daytime heat was great, but the cool nights somewhat compensated for this, 'and the air [was] invigorating and exhilarating . . . owing probably to its particular dryness'. Nonetheless, not 2 km away, 'the country rises in undulating meadows, beautiful in appearance as an English park, and infinitely cooler than Chaibasa' (see Plate 5).[19] At the ugly spot, however, Wilkinson already had the troops and their horses 'comfortably hutted'.[20]

Shelter did not cover all the basic needs of the men. Wilkinson had foreseen this in his instructions. The troops and camp followers, as well as 'all Hindus and Mussulmans on your establishment', were warned to behave well with the women, as the Hos 'resent any criminal intercourse with their female relations, by any persons not of their own caste, by putting them to death'. Any complaint of the Hos of 'ill treatment of, or an attempt to seduce their women . . . should receive immediate attention and the offender be punished by fine'. If the offender were a soldier, Tickell was to ask the commander to deliver him up.[21] This must have been hard on the soldiers. The Ho girls were quite free and if they belonged to the 'lowest order', scantily dressed. There was no way out, as prostitution was 'quite unknown' among the Hos.[22] Camp life threatened to be drab.

As soon as the soldiers were there, wine and liquor sellers arrived. Without applying for permission, they started to trade, not only in Chaibasa but also elsewhere in the Kolhan. They even set up an illicit shop in the army cantonment. Tickell had to ask Wilkinson for instructions, could he issue licences, could he fine them, and if so, how much?[23] It was left to the assistant, and Tickell was also told that 'it rest exclusively with you' to grant 'licenses for the sale of intoxicating drugs including ganja and bhang'—both cannabis products—'in the military cantonment'. People without a license were not allowed to carry a quantity of cannabis 'greater than required for his consumption'. *Charas* (hashish) and some other drugs 'of a most noxious quality and highly prejudicial to health' were not to be sold at all.[24]

Wilkinson already had started to construct 'such public buildings as are considered necessary' in Chaibasa itself.[25] These occupied a large part of the village, as even fifteen years later, the number of houses was not more than 560, and the number of inhabitants in the bazaar and neighbourhood estimated at 2,300.[26] This has to be set off against the 500 troops stationed here in 1837. It is significant that one of the Ho names for Chaibasa is *Dongol*, given as 'encampment of many tents' or 'court complex'.[27] The construction programme was not easily accomplished with a local workforce that did not like or understand money. To get himself a 'temporary hut' built, William Dunbar, who constituted most of the medical establishment of the new capital, had to pay the labourers in rice, 'a commodity which at that time could not be very well afforded'; and that too after much bargaining.[28] Even if the Ho workers used little else but the axe, the multi-purpose attribute of Ho men, he was satisfied with their construction skills. The public buildings were constructed in the wattle and daub fashion reinforced with strong timbers. Dunbar observed that the buildings appeared strong and 'likely to stand for many years'.[29]

That was certainly true for the jail, a shed 36 × 3.6 m. The prison was a touchy subject. The Hos who had been taken prisoner or delivered up during the campaign had been brought to Kishenpur (an early name for Ranchi). Their mortality was very high. In June 1837, apparently in despair, they had attacked the guards. In the riot twenty-six Hos were shot, twelve wounded and four escaped.[30] When he wrote of the jail in Chaibasa, a note of apology crept into the agent's otherwise so confident letter.

'It is a much more comfortable building than the unfortunate people who will occupy it have ever had of their own, and will afford accommodation to as many prisoners, as you are likely to have.' It was a temporary building, too, to be completed before the rains. 'After the rains should another be required, I will obtain authority for constructing one, of a similar description on receiving timely intimation from you.'[31] We are favoured with a precise description. In 1854—so much for the temporary measure!—Henry Ricketts reported that the jail was 'an open mud shed, built in the shape of a square. Till lately there was no wall of any sort . . . . [The prisoners] remain there because they do not choose to run the risk of punishment for escaping. There is nothing to prevent any one from getting out, who has not made up his mind to remain inside. . . . It is built exactly on the plan in which native houses are for the most part erected.'[32] Native influences on the architecture of the jail did not contribute to its greater popularity. Wilkinson found that the whole idea of imprisonment held the greatest dread for the Hos. He spoke of 'the horror that this wild race have of being taken from their families into confinement'.[33]

To the modest prison belonged a guardroom of 9 × 3.5 m. It was not yet finished when Wilkinson wrote his instructions. The jail establishment would consist of one supervisor and eight armed guards. Tickell should try to get Hos to work in the jail, for 'when the Kols once get into the way of serving as jail guards, you may be able to raise such a body of Kols for police purposes, as well enable government to withdraw a portion of the Ramgarh Battalion, An object which they have ultimately in view, and which you should bear constantly in mind.'[34] In principle, there was room for the locals within the lower echelons of the staff.

At the time, the new administrative centre seemed like a quantum leap. But soon the buildings lost their shine. The assistant's quarters were, as Ricketts had the chance to remark seventeen years later, 'the worst I ever was in'. It consisted of 'one small confined and unwholesome room with a verandah, which is enclosed on one side for the writer and at the corners for treasury &c. There is no room for papers . . . . The presiding officer has no bench—seated at a little table surrounded with people, records, boxes and shelves, he has to sit for 7 or 8 hours per day in an atmosphere, which it is quite impossible any constitution should stand long.'[35] Tickell's own description of his living quarters was more generous. At least, the walls were thick. In 1841, some Hos brought a small pangolin, which Tickell kept for a week or so. When left at peace, it would walk freely in his room, but when he lifted Tickell's heavy bookstand, the animal was locked in a 'large room' and started to dig himself out through the wall, 'which was of sun-dried bricks and in about two minutes it had dug a hole large enough to cover itself', presumably 30–40 cm.[36] A thick wall made for coolness in the hot season, still, the air could be stuffy. We should not be surprised that Tickell was such an outdoor man.

The reasons for introducing the non-regulation system in 1833 in Chotanagpur had been 'the present state of certain tracts of country, . . . the nature of the disturbances . . . and the character of the inhabitants'.[37] The same reasons, differently worded, led to the institution of the Kolhan Government Estate four years later. The 'character of the inhabitants' was a way of expressing the ethnic consideration.

Initially, the area was defined in terms of 'inhabited villages which during the progress of the military operations, have been brought under the direct control of government . . . , scattered over a country from about 100 to 110 kilometres from north to south, and from 80 to 105 from east to west'.[38] Their number was not certain, for none of the Singh and Mayurbhanj chiefs had a list of villages or any other account of them. According to Wilkinson's own calculations, 387 villages were taken from Porahat, 51 from Saraikela, 3 from Kharsawan and 181 from Mayurbhanj. This totalled 622.[39] So, Tickell was ordered to 'lose no time' and copy Wilkinson's list 'into a book, prepared for the purpose, in the Devanagari and Persian characters, numbering the villages in each pir in a distinct series from one upwards, to the number of villages, there may be in each pir'. He had to report corrections to Wilkinson.[40] The old system was considered concluded inside the Kolhan when the Ho leaders entered into 'solemn engagements to obey the orders of the British government, and not those of the raja and other chiefs they have hitherto been under'.[41]

As the villages were the units that had submitted, it was surprising that in Wilkinson's instructions to Tickell, the Kolhan was mostly spoken about in terms of *pir*. In the contemporary military and political despatches, the only functions of the *pir* were to serve as a geographical indication or as an indication of an area claimed by neighbouring chiefs. The claims were now laid to rest anyway. That left the geographical function. In the instructions, the denomination of *pir* was changed into 'Cole Peer'. Wilkinson gave an extensive list. From Mayurbhanj/Bamanghati, four *pirs* were taken, from Porahat, sixteen *pirs* and from Saraikela, five *pirs* were transferred to the Kolhan Government Estate.[42]

The establishment of the Kolhan Government Estate meant an end to claims to the revenue of the Kolhan by the neighbouring chiefs and their dependants. They were compensated under various pretexts.[43] Wilkinson took Madhu Das Mahapater and some others, who he considered capable of creating disturbances in Bamanghati, to Saraikela.[44] Madhu was to be awarded 'a fair allowance' to support himself and his relations. This was to be paid by Mayurbhanj.[45] Wilkinson proposed Rs. 250 per month, a total of Rs. 3,000 a year. Ricketts' counterproposal was Rs. 1,200 per year. The government decided on the smaller amount. Wilkinson protested that this sum was insufficient. The end result was that the government grudgingly added 'a grant of Rs. 150 per mensem from the public funds, in addition to the sum of rupees 100 chargeable to the Mayurbhanj raja'. Captain Wilkinson was to use 'any proper opportunity for the reduction of the government grant'.[46] Arjun, the young raja of Porahat, was to be given a 'compassionate allowance' of Rs. 500 as compensation for his loss of revenue.[47] But the advisors of the Porahat raja 'dissuaded his acceptance'.[48] The main advisor was, as we have seen, Babu Jadunath.[49] A grant of Rs. 200 was awarded to Ghasi Singh of Chakradharpur. To prevent further claims in the area, it was 'distinctly explained to them, that the grants were made merely on account of their destitute condition, when compared with their ranks in society.'[50]

In 1837, Ajambar Singh of Saraikela died 'of illness brought on by exposure and fatigue in the Kol campaign, in the course of which he rendered important services'. Kind words, which showed Ajambar Singh's good relations with the East India Company. Ajambar was succeeded by his son Chakradhar Singh.[51] As Achuta of Porahat had died the year before, the two main Singhs of the pre-Kolhan Government Estate times were no more. The relative positions of these states towards each other had not changed. Saraikela was still strong, pro-British and led by the more experienced ruler,

Chakradhar. Porahat was still weak, now even left without the claims on Ho *pirs* that had made it appear larger than it was. It was ruled by the dowager queen and its minor raja Arjun's uncle Jadunath, and, as we shall see, these two obstructed British interference in its internal affairs.

From the outset, the assistant was seen as the policeman of the region. Chaibasa was in the first place a military outpost. In cases of hostilities between the raja of Mayurbhanj and Dhalbhum, Tickell was to 'at once proceed to the spot, with a detachment of at least 200 men, and half the horsemen in Singhbhum with a view to ascertain who are the aggressors, and arrest them, that full investigation may be made and the aggressing party brought to punishment.'[52] But disputes were not always of a military nature or between states only. Therefore, Wilkinson proposed two extensions of his assistant's jurisdiction.

The first extension was to give him powers to investigate and decide criminal and civil cases between people from his estates and inhabitants of Porahat, Saraikela, Kharsawan, Mayurbhanj and Keonjhar, 'whichever party may be aggrieved'. This was because 'justice is never done [by the chiefs of these estates], and the non investigation of complaints and withholding redress, may lead the aggrieved, more particularly the Kols, to take the law into their own hands'.[53] Ricketts easily accepted the first proposal.[54]

The other proposal by Wilkinson was to give the assistant power to investigate complaints brought forward by the subjects of the chiefs of Singhbhum and of Bamanghati 'against each other, and against their chief'. Again, the reasoning was that 'none of the zamindars will take the trouble to administer justice' and, secondly, that even if they would go through the motions, they would be tempted to oppress the inhabitants of their estate, as the Company troops were close by. Indeed, Mayurbhanj's Bamanghati was properly under Cuttack, 'but the distance is so great that I fear but a few [inhabitants] would take the trouble to go so far [to obtain justice]'.[55] Ricketts was 'entirely opposed' to this, as in practice, it would move the borders of the South West Frontier Agency at the expense of Cuttack. In his comments, he referred to the support Wilkinson had given to the *mahapater*: 'It is interference of this nature, out of and unconnected with the Kolhan, which originally . . . led to all the embarrassment which has been experienced in Bamanghati affairs and is not yet at an end.'[56] The government agreed with Ricketts' policy, though not necessarily with his reasoning. Calcutta found it 'desirable that the officers of government should abstain to the utmost possible extent from all intermeddling with such matters, having the chiefs and their subjects to arrange their own affairs according to their customs.'[57] Tickell was to concentrate on the Kolhan Government Estate.

The principles of an end to the direct influence exerted on the Hos by the surrounding rajas and other Hindu chiefs, and of a separate area for the Hos, were clear, but their application on the ground could lead to problems. A major one was where to fix the borders. The cold season of 1838–39 brought Tickell to the border between Bamanghati and the Kolhan, today the border between Jharkhand and Odisha. It was to be demarcated with a row of stones. The problem was where to draw the line on which these stones were to be put. So, Tickell asked Wilkinson for some guidance, whether I am to decide the question as a matter of boundary, without reference to the class of people who may be inhabiting the disputed tracts,

—Or whether (without being influenced by the existance (*sic*) of the old constituted boundaries separating the Kolhan from Bamanghati,) I am merely to draw a line of demarcation between the Santhal and Ho villages.[58]

If Tickell would keep the old borders, many Santhal villages would fall within the Kolhan Government Estate. The answer of Wilkinson was principled. He wrote that the inability of the rulers of Bamanghati and Porahat to control the Hos had been the cause of taking over the management of the Kolhan. Therefore, the boundary of the area under direct British administration should be 'fixed with reference to the class of people inhabiting villages on the borders' and run between the Ho villages and those inhabited by 'others than Coles'.[59]

A few weeks later, Tickell sounded relieved. Option one, not paying attention to the ethnicity of the actual inhabitants and establishing the border where it must have been historically, had caused him worry. A historical approach to the borderline was not suitable, if only because information on the extent of Mayurbhanj's claims or on 'the original founders of many of the bordering villages' could only be obtained from the people of the Mayurbhanj raja, 'the Koles knowing or caring nothing about the matter'.

I believe I would be acting according [to] your [Wilkinson's] views, were I to lay down as boundary between the raja's territory and the Kolehan, an arbitrary line, calculated to separate all such villages as are inhabited by Koles, from those inhabited by other classes, [while] relinquishing entirely to the raja [of Mayurbhanj] all the belt of jungle at present untouched (except in a few parts).[60]

The definition of what was a village was another problem, especially as some Ho hamlets were part of Santhal villages.[61] Here, Wilkinson was practical. The mixed villages, in which the majority consisted of Hos or other Kols, should remain in the Kol *pirs*. Mostly or wholly non-Ho villages cut off from Bamanghati by Ho villages should likewise be taken in the Kolhan.[62]

A more vexing question was the shifting frontier of cultivation. If Tickell would have been ordered to keep to the historical boundaries, not only would the Santhal villages have gone to the Kolhan, but 'I am given to understand that all the recently cultivated portions of the belt of jungle cleared by Santhal settlers, would also be annexed'.[63] Now that that option was out of the way, the problem was reversed and the clearings by the Hos were the problem. 'The want also of a defined boundary would preclude the Hos from felling and cultivating the intervening belt of jungles, which the Bamanghati Santhals claim as their own', wrote Tickell.[64] But in the last five or six years many Hos already had cleared and cultivated jungle over the former border (see Plate 7). If in the new set-up these tracts would come under Bamanghati/Mayurbhanj, they 'would have to relinquish the fruits of their labours in these jungles—of which they would have held undisputed possession, had not the intervention of Government restored confidence to the surrounding zamindars, who are now laying claims to these bordering neutral tracts'.[65]

Expulsion was not desirable, and Wilkinson found it a minor problem if some Hos would remain under Mayurbhanj. 'I have no objections to the Hos . . . paying taxes to the Mayurbhanj raja, if those patches by the boundary you are defining fall within Bamanghati, out of the Kolhan, [and] if the number of Ho Cultivators be not great. Whenever however the new clearings in the jungles made by the Hos adjoin the cultivation in the Ho villages, the land should be retained in the Kolhan.' Just to be sure, 'it will be as well to state that the boundary has been fixed subject to the approval of confirmation by the Agent'.[66]

The maintenance of order weighed heavily, too. Some Ho villages, 'which the raja declares he can himself control, and keep in order, under these circumstances and from their not forming any part of the four great Kol *pirs* of Bamanghati' remained under Mayurbhanj. For similar reasons, Wilkinson left a few villages with Abhai Singh, a junior member of the Singh family, who held the estate of Anandpur as a fief of the raja of Porahat.[67] In Manoharpur, Dasi Babu claimed the whole of Saranda, but it was found out that he never had effectually exercised possession over the Kol villages of the pir. . . . He was only allowed to retain Manoharpur'. Saranda became part of the Kolhan Government Estate.[68]

Ethnic considerations also shaped Wilkinson's policy towards the Dorowas. Before the campaign started, he had sent 116 Dorawa families to Saraikela. After the cessation of hostilities, there were also groups of Dorawa refugees in Singhbhum, Dhalbhum and Saraikela. These, Wilkinson feared, might attempt to go on plundering expeditions against peasants established on their former lands in Bamanghati. Hence, he directed the *kunwar* of Saraikela not to allow any more Dorowas to reside in his state. If any of the Dorowas of Saraikela would plunder in Bamanghati, the *kunwar* would be made 'answerable for them'. The raja of Dhalbhum got the order not to permit any Dorowas to reside west of Narsinhgarh, that is, west of the Subarnarekha river.[69] For the ethnic refugees from Bamanghati, peace did not mean a return to their homes. The primary strategic aim was not justice, but pacification.

All this did not make the Kolhan Government Estate an ethnically pure Ho area. One of the aims of the 1837 agreements had been the return of the Bhuiyas to Hodisum.[70] The Hos were by far the largest ethnic group in the Kolhan Government Estate, but there was a sizeable non-Ho population. Before censuses started to be held on a regular basis in 1872, population figures of the Kolhan were educated guesses at best. In 1821, Roughsedge had estimated the numbers of the Larkas at 'about fifty thousand and rapidly increasing'.[71] Tickell, who was the first to assess the revenue, estimated the whole population of the Kolhan to be 70,653, out of which the number of Hos would be about 62,000. He estimated the strength of the Hindu artisan castes at about one-seventh of the Hos, that is, 8,850.[72] During his intensive Survey and Settlement operations of 1913–18, however, Tuckey found a little over 9.5 per cent of 'old Diku holdings', holdings held by cultivators from castes and peoples other than Hos,[73] and by people who belonged to the Ho village community in a subordinate capacity.[74] We may then, tentatively, put the proportion of non-Hos in the Ho lands in 1837 at 12.5 per cent of the population.

The new administrative borders of the country were based upon ethnic differences. It should be stressed here that the new Kolhan Government Estate was not an ethnically defined entity, but a territorial administrative unit. That implied that Wilkinson's Rules, as well as the manki–munda system, applied to all the inhabitants of the Estate, not just to the Hos. The Rules and the system were two different things. Wilkinson's Rules covered the trials and punishments in civil and criminal cases. They did not establish the manki–munda system. That system was presupposed in Wilkinson's Rules even as the administration still had to officially nominate the mankis and mundas. The system would gradually cover the Kolhan Government Estate as individual mankis and mundas received their appointments.

'The Rules for Lieutt. Tickell's guidance in the administration of Civil Justice, I shall forward [to him] from Kishenpore', wrote Wilkinson on 5 May 1837.[75] Indeed, they came straight from the agent's files and were the same as those of 1834,[76] albeit 'with some trifling alterations'.[77] Most of these changes consisted of substituting mankis for rajas, zamindars and other Hindu chiefs in the text.[78] There were more changes. The issue of warrants or summons to accused, in 1834 still a formal affair with 'official seal' or 'as prescribed in the regulation Provinces', had become unwritten summons or simply apprehension by the manki or munda.[79] The use of Bengali for writing was done away with.[80] The threat of 'forfeiture of land in favour of some other member of the offender's family' in case of resistance to the court also disappeared.[81] The oath had diminished in importance. Unlike in Chotanagpur, in Kolhan, plaints and charges could be delivered and witnesses heard without demanding an oath, and this was left to the discretion of the assistant.[82] If administered, the oath would have to continue to be of a nature 'most binding on their consciences'.[83]

The agent made it clear that his rules were subject to change by himself. Also, these rules were not meant for the trial of criminal cases left from the period before the British takeover.[84] The application of the rules by the assistant was to be guided by a spirit of recognition of the fact that:

> the people in the Kol pirs have for so many years been so perfectly independent of all control that we cannot reasonably expect, at first, that they will promptly obey all orders. And although it will be necessary to see that whatever orders you give after mature deliberation are obeyed, it will be better to repeat your orders and point out the consequence of refusal, than in the first instance have recourse to force, to compel their observance.[85]

The exceptions here would be 'cases of theft, plunder, or other heinous offences' which would have to be immediately attended to.

Wilkinson conceived the administrative and judicial system from top to bottom and, characteristically, with no intermediate layers. There was a staff for the assistant. The staff stationed in Singhbhum, or rather Saraikela, in 1833, consisting of one writer and four bearers/interpreters, was now transferred to Tickell's office in Chaibasa. The new establishment was, Wilkinson wrote, 'ample', but 'probably less would not suffice'. The Persian writer, who was also able to write in Devanagari script, would head the office. He was, according to Wilkinson, 'a very useful servant. I have transferred him to your establishment on his former pay, as it would not be fair to reduce his salary.' Then there would be one English writer 'if procurable for 25 Rs'. If not, one Odia clerk, preferably also knowing Bengali, and one more servant would be appointed. The ten interpreters and bearers were important and they wore badges so that they could identify themselves when out of the station.[86] At their head would be one writer. The total wages for the fledgling administration came to Rs. 195. 5*an*.

10*p*. each month.[87] That was quite an increase from the expenses on the 1833 staff when wages amounted to Rs. 36. 10*an*. 8*p*. per month.[88] Some of these now came in with Tickell's appointment or were brought in later. We have already seen in 1834 in Chotanagpur that the agent did not put much faith in the reliability of the staff of his assistants.[89] Wilkinson's mind was focused on the assistant.

The cornerstone of Wilkinson's management philosophy was his man on the spot, who used his common sense, some general rules of justice and maximum accessibility in a pacifying and civilising mission. 'If there be no functionary on the spot to administer justice', Wilkinson wrote, 'the Hos will still continue to settle their disputes in the same barbarous manner as hitherto, and murders will continue of frequent occurrence, for on the most trifling occasions they have recourse to their bows & arrows.'[90]

The assistant had to communicate directly with the people. If that was not possible, he had to bypass his staff and use mankis or mundas. Wilkinson considered interpreters corrupt. His experience was 'how little are to be trusted, the interpreters we are obliged to employ, who, opportunity offering, . . . would either make exactions, or failing to obtain presents, from any persons to whom they might be sent to communicate orders, would . . . induce a belief that resistance to your authority was intended'.[91] If it really could not be avoided, Tickell could let an interpreter accompany a manki or a munda, when they carried a message, 'but when such is the case, his duty should only be to assure the person to whom the order was communicated, that it emanated from you'.[92] In this respect, Tickell was more than up to the mark. Soon, he could dispense with an interpreter when he talked with the Hos.[93] Most important was, Wilkinson wrote to his assistant, that

> You should at all times be accessible to the people under your charge, except at your hours for meals, and recreation, and take particular care not to transact business with them through the agency of any of your establishment . . . . Your patience and temper will be often tried, but I have every faith in your exercising both in the work for which you have been selected. [94]

Wilkinson could hardly have made a better choice and Tickell could work well under this 'truly wise and benevolent' boss. He found Wilkinson's Rules 'excellent arrangements', and characteristically added that these were 'so well seconded by the inherent good feelings of the people'.[95] As the Court of Directors in London put it, 'we may now look for the permanent maintenance of the public peace on that frontier, and for the eventual civilization of the rude tribes which occupy it'.[96] That required, as Tickell had stated, some cooperation of the people concerned.

The architecture of the Ho side of the new system rested on the mankis, the mundas and the councils. The use of the Ho word 'manki' instead of the non-tribal title 'zamindar' (landowner) indicated that in the Kolhan Government Estate, the government did not consider the local tax collector as the owner of the soil. This was a major difference between the rules for the more northern parts of the South Western Frontier Agency and those for the Kolhan.

The mankis formed the intermediate level. Each *pir* or, where it was seen as too large, each subdivision of the *pir* was placed under a manki. The instructions added that the assistant had to choose the manki, giving due consideration to the influence of the latter and 'with the general consent of the inhabitants of those villages over which he is placed'. The manki should find a deputy; the appointment of whom was subject to approval by the assistant.[97] Wilkinson gave Tickell a 'form of a sunnud [deed], prepared to be given to each manki in the Kolhan, [defining] the duties he has to perform'.[98] The content of the actual deeds followed this pattern.[99] The engagement contained the following points.[100] The manki had to preserve the public peace in the villages under him; see to the regular collection and punctual payment of the revenue; seize offenders against government and the peace of the country; report without delay the more serious offences within his division; apprehend these people; to settle all petty disputes in the villages in his charge; obey 'all lawful order' and not receive or obey 'any order verbal or written, of any raja or *zamindar*, or any of their subordinates which may be communicated . . . on any pretence whatever'.[101]

In each village, a munda, likewise chosen for his influence, was placed under the manki's superintendence. His installation was a formal affair, as he had to come in person before the manki and take 'an oath to obey and afford you [the manki] . . . every aid whenever required'. The munda had to report without delay 'all occurrences in his village' either to the manki himself or, if he were absent, his deputy.[102] In practice, the munda collected the rent and performed the functions of the manki in his village.[103] Little wonder that Wilkinson's instructions were mainly about the work of the munda.[104]

For their work, the mankis and mundas 'must each have allowed to them a portion of the gross assessment on the village, as a remuneration for their trouble in collecting the rent and attending to the police of their villages, probably about from one-sixth, to one-eighth, according to the produce of their villages'.[105] Eventually, the mundas got one-fifth and the mankis one-tenth of the revenue they collected. In March 1837, Tickell noticed that the amount of money the manki would keep was very small and suggested that he should get a piece of land for his work. Wilkinson answered in December that he did not agree. The avowed aim was to give the mankis and mundas a stake in the revenue collection so that they would prevent tax evasion.[106] Two years later, in March 1839, it appeared from a standard contract that the mundas got even less for their efforts—one-sixth of the net revenue.[107]

The rules for use of the village council or panchayat were nearly the same as those of the earlier 1834 rules for the South West Frontier Agency. These pertained to civil cases. In the instructions, some slight shifts in emphasis could be observed. In Chotanagpur, the council was to consist of three to five persons, 'the most conversant with the matter at issue'. In the Kolhan of 1837, Tickell was exhorted to select 'the most respected and most intelligent, amongst the Hos'.

In all the cases related to caste matters, the assistant should refer to the decision of the council of the caste.[108] With 'caste', Wilkinson probably meant here the *kili*. Wilkinson took pains to point out that there would be numerous cases on marriage. This was a consequence of the Ho custom of 'purchasing their wives for a number of cattle'. That, he wrote, led to complaints that the price had not been paid or, if it had, that the parents had not sent the bride to the prospective husband. The assistant should refer these cases to the councils.[109] As marriages were, as a rule, between people of different villages, disputes in this sphere would involve more villages and, of course, more *kilis*. Probably, for such cases, a special council could be convened. That was ambitious. The Hos were used to settle such questions without outside prompting. Even before marriage disputes could arise, the imposition of the new system led to mixed reactions.

Chapter 9

Poto Ho's Resistance

...
*Poto's alliance; the battle of Seringsia;
the hunt for the defeated; Wilkinson censored*
...

As soon as the hot and the rainy seasons of 1837 abated, and the raging cholera receded from the south of the Estate,[1] the task was to extend the reach of Wilkinson's system. It meant to go to the mundas and mankis, and to assess the lands for taxation. Wilkinson ordered his assistant to collect the rent at the same time, 'as the sum to be realized from each village will amount to very little and the share [of each peasant is a] mere trifle'.[2]

Tickell started in the north, where he reported difficulties with getting together the mundas of the villages bordering on Saraikela. Tickell suspected here the hand of Saraikela from which these villages had just been taken.[3]

In the *pirs* in the immediate neighbourhood of Chaibasa, things went more smoothly, and Tickell noted that here 'influence of our rule has already began to show itself'. Speaking of 'the good feelings of the people', Tickell was upbeat about the progress and wrote of 'his greatest satisfaction'. But he was talking about those places where people already were placed 'under the most moderate state of surveillance' and where there already had been some regular contact with 'their well advisers'. This was in the area stretching from a bit north of Chaibasa to as far south as Saranda, Jagannathpur, and into the north of Gumra *pir*.[4]

Elsewhere, the situation was 'not so favourable'. Tantis and 'some people from Porahat' had been active in the south-western Kotgarh and Jamda *pirs* arousing 'suspicion and terror' against the East India Company. On top of this came a disagreement between the manki Petamroo and his people and the *divan* of Porahat. Was the *pir* still part of the Porahat state or, as these Hos from Toonia *pir* wished, 'under the British Dominion'? They appealed to Tickell, but as usual, the decision was with Wilkinson.[5] It was part of Porahat.[6] Was the glass half full or was it half empty?

Amidst the boulders and jungles of the heartland of the south, people were organising resistance. On 21 October, Tickell reported that '[a] number of disaffected Koles, assembled together by some of the most notorious of those who escaped Capture last year, and composed in part of the prisoners released from Ranchi', assembled close to Balandia and were making well-stocked supply bases hidden in the jungle. He supposed that these troubles would encompass the greater part of Bar *pir*, especially the villages of Balandia and Gumuriya and some nearby villages, which had 'never been reduced to any order'.[7] Two days later, the picture became more clear and more threatening. As Raghunath Bisi wrote to Tickell, 'a considerable number of Koles have assembled in Bar Pir, headed by Poto'. They harassed the village of Toreeparre which did not want to take part in the movement. The crops were ravaged and the cattle driven off. Communication between the assistant and the mankis was cut off by surrounding their villages. It was revenge, too. They were after those people 'who were most active in seizing prisoners &ca' during the Third Kolhan Campaign, in Tickell's words to Wilkinson, 'your Circuit thro' the Kolehan last year'. The aim was to murder Raju, *mahapater* of Padampur[8] and the *mahapater* of Dulposee. And yes, again the target was Jaintgarh. From Gumuriya, there had been 'an ineffectual attempt to murder some of the inhabitants of Jaint—who are in consequence deserting & making their escape elsewhere'.[9]

Tickell was especially disappointed in the released prisoners. He wrote to Wilkinson, 'You will regret to hear that the Kols, whom you for the most humane reasons, freed from imprisonment at Kishenpore (Ranchi), no sooner effected their return to their homes, then they set indefatigably to work to collect accomplices and overthrowing the previous good order of the country—and it was an easy task for them among such a faithless savage race.'[10]

Not disappointments and moral denouncements, but intelligence was needed. It came one week later. Only in Bar *pir* and Aula *pir* the troubles were so serious as to require immediate action. The leaders there were Poto ('formerly' of the village Rajabasa just north of Jaintgarh), with Debi and Tope of the mainly Pingua village of Balandia (Wilkinson had not succeeded in apprehending them the year before), and further Jotong and Jonko of Pat Dumuria, Kochey and Pardhan of Darbila, Potel Gopari and Burrai (Bossa) of Parsa. They met at Pokam, 'a small village in the jungles at some distance to the south of Jaintgarh'. Altogether, there were twenty to twenty-five of them. As far as Tickell knew, they induced twenty-two villages to join.[11] Manguee Naik, a Bhuiya from Barbil in Keonjhar, gave the insurgents 'charms, medicines, &ca . . . to make them invulnerable'. He performed pujas 'and other antics' to ensure victory. From then onwards, Tickell harboured a grudge against 'that class of wretches, styled "sokas", ("goonees" or soothsayers) (who are but too common in and about the Kolehan) whenever they tempt these rude and simple people, into the purchasing of charms to render them invulnerable to shot or steel'.[12]

It was meant to be a formal union. Poto Ho sent around 'charmed arrows' to many villages to join. A day had been set for a grand puja with Manguee Naik, when Manguee was seized in Keonjhar for not paying taxes.[13] But many others did come. At the meeting in Balandia, Poto and his allies decided to occupy the Seringsia and Bhagalbila passes that separated the south from the north of the Hodisum. The programme was to kill all the *sahib log* (the Britishers and their troops) and expel all the outsiders, a measure obviously aimed at Jaintgarh in the first place. Further, they decided to go against the villages that were friendly to the new order.[14]

Against this union stood Tickell's informants. He mentioned Raju of Padampur (Pudmpur) and Bhim Deo (Beemdeo), *mahapater* of Jagannathpur, and several mankis and mundas of Bar *pir*. He also had information from 'travellers who have had occasion to pass through the haunts of the confederates'. This showed how far we are from the times when Roughsedge was almost solely dependent on Raghunath, an outsider in Jaintgarh who loathed the Hos—and was loathed by them. Tickell's sources stood much closer to the events and the people involved. Tickell promised Wilkinson that if other people made statements as well, he would take these down in Persian characters, which nearly amounted to a coded message, and pass them on to Wilkinson. Still, he was careful. He heard stories, but they were vague and unconfirmed, like 'that out of a party of 11 people bringing 32 heads of cattle for sale in the Detachment Bazar, 8 were recently murdered. The 3 survivors who escaped into a large village, are I understand on their way to me.' Another rumour was that a group of people from Keonjhar who came to sell salt had been murdered and plundered.[15] These were rumours. But these showed that Tickell's antennae were out, and that he was assessing his intelligence.

Still, Tickell was bitter, even against people who were not active in the resistance. He had expected more. He wrote, 'how much to blame have been the very best disposed of the friendly Koles in the peers in question, who have not made the slightest exertion to check this evil in the bud. And indeed at any time [they] suffered Poto & Burrai to range about their villages alone, altho' they well knew that a reward was upon their capture. It was in vain I used to represent daily to them, the mischief which would ensue, were not these people seized on the first opportunity.' It seemed that they were thoroughly intimidated. 'They were too alarmed at the prospect of retaliations from their relations to attempt anything against them. And have suffered themselves to be plundered and insulted with the utmost passiveness.'[16]

He saw no easy solution. British rule had not penetrated the countryside. One could not trust the mankis and mundas of the more distant parts of the Kolhan to keep order in their country before they saw the advantage of it. The heart of the matter was Balandia, 'in that immediate neighbourhood the people are thieves of such notorious a character and such long standing that ordinary precautions will not suffice to prevent them renewing their malpractices'.[17]

So, Tickell prepared to march into Bar *pir*. He first needed to pay the troops without delay and requested some funds. He had already spent Rs. 4,419. 13*an*. 5*p*. in October alone. There were arrears in the payment of the troops and the medical establishment.[18] On 12 November, Wilkinson arrived in Chaibasa. Now, there were assembled in and around the Kolhan 'the 31st Native Infantry, the Ramgarh Light Infantry, the 5th Local Horse, and a detachment of artillery, with four 6-pounders'.[19] Five days later, on 17 November, Wilkinson sent Captain Armstrong with 400 infantry, 60 cavalry and two guns, 200 auxiliaries from Saraikela, and Tickell with a few hundred Hos into Bar *pir*.[20]

Two days later, 19 November 1837, the Poto side ambushed the British column at Seringsia Ghat. The pass was at a strategic point close to a broad passage through the wooded hills that make up the division between the north and the south of Hodisum (see Plate 8). There were 'jungle & numerous ravines which bordered the road.'[21] A correspondent, apparently with the troops, gave an eyewitness account.

> The advance and rear guards had been strengthened, and all the baggage kept closed up to the rear of the column, in case of accidents, although we had not the remotest idea of an attack. The pass is a rocky ascent, winding through the hills, with jungle, rocks, and ravines on either side.

> By the time the column had got about half-way through, the advance guard (about thirty five metres ahead) picked up a bow-string and two arrows, crossed in the middle of the road (probably a challenge), and had scarcely gone ten paces further, when a flight of arrows came among them from the right, followed by screams like a heard of jackals. The arrows now fell as far as the horses, wounding several men.[22]

The ambush was well prepared (see Plate 9). The local account is that the Hos had spread seeds on the road to make the horses slip and had hung beehives by the roadside, which they activated by throwing stones. They shot with the *tonga: a:sar,* the powerful long-distance bow. The archer would have to use both hands and feet.[23] At Seringsia Ghat, there were not many spots from which the Hos could shoot from long distance. Still, the Hos

> had taken up capital positions. One man was killed, and five or six wounded; and a report reached us that three others died of their wounds at Khandband. After clearing the pass, we mustered our hands, and found that one subadar, one havildar, and thirteen sepoys were wounded, two severely, none dangerously. An arrow from a Cole bow will, at one hundred metres, do as much mischief as a bullet.[24]

Tickell's own account, written on the same day, was quite brief.

> The arrows fired were very numerous & the Koles kept their post, concealed behind rocks, trees &ca, with pertinacity & indeed did not show much inclination to retire until two or three rounds of grape had been fired at them. I do not believe any casualties occurred amongst them.[25]

On the British side, there were fourteen wounded (one person less than in the correspondent's report), of these, two severely.[26]

> And after clearing the top of the pass, the detachment reach[ed] this place without further molestation. The Hos being seen escaping to the right & left over the Commanding Hills.[27]

Captain Wilkinson ordered local reinforcements, both Hos and people from Kharsawan and some smaller places like Karaikela and Kera. He occupied Jagannathpur. His aim was Poto's village of Rajabasa, a few kilometres north of Jaintgarh. On the morning of 20 November, Gummo Manki of Dumriya, some twelve km north-east from Rajabasa, went with a large party to that village to capture Poto. Poto could not be found. Instead, the Dumriya Hos took some Rajabasa men prisoner. The next morning, they took a supply base near Rajabasa and plundered and burned the village itself. The next day, action swung back to the direction of the Seringsia pass, where six villagers of Tondanghatu, a village four km south of Jagannathpur, were captured. A party of 100 infantry, 50 cavalry and some Hos destroyed another supply base nearby.[28]

On hearing that a large party of 2,000 Hos had taken up position on a range of rocks in the jungle, Tickell proceeded. His troops consisted of 300 troops and the auxiliaries, 200 men from Saraikela, 40 from Chainpur and the rest Hos led by their own leaders.[29] They found nobody. The hamlets Ruia and Nizam Ruia were burnt on 24 November. Tickell allowed his auxiliaries to plunder the stocks concealed among the rocks. These were small stocks, hidden by people who were not well off: rice, maize, a few fowls and some mats. And the soldiers had cut the rice from five fields. From the tracks of men and bullocks, they saw that the party had retreated to the south.[30]

The troops now established a camp near Ruia. Over the next two weeks, the East India Company troops and their Singh and Ho allies burnt as many as six villages, carried off 600 cattle and captured large quantities of grain.[31] The attack on the hidden supply base near the village of Khandband on 1 December was a messy affair. Simpson's troops started to fire without orders and were 'not marching with sufficient promptitude' to the group of Hos and these could escape. Still, they killed one Ho, and a woman and a child were taken prisoner. A second Ho was killed by Tickell's Hos. The next morning, Lieutenant Simpson attacked another Ho supply and retreat base. Here, the Hos put up a defence. They harassed the approaching troops with arrows but could not make a stand when they retaliated.[32] Tickell, who forwarded Simpson's letter, was very pleased with the 'auxiliary Koles', who were 'very active in affording assistance'. When driving off cattle, they stood their ground against an attack and killed one Ho.[33] However, it would soon appear that not every Ho on the British side was giving such wholehearted support.

The Ramgarh Battalion, or rather Captain Armstrong, entered into the spirit of this warfare. On the 7th morning at 3 am, he set out with 200 men to capture another Ho base. At about 1.5 km from the place, Armstrong split his troops, sending 100 men with Lieutenant Simpson to the right and the other 100 men with himself taking the left. When Armstrong came near, he sent a *havildar* (sergeant) with a party of twenty to cut off the main escape route in a valley. They were ordered to move quietly and to hide behind trees and rocks. Armstrong followed a track till he heard shots from the valley. He quickly marched to the Ho base and arrived there at the same time as the *havildar*'s party.

Owing to the heavy jungle and rocks we had to descend, the Hos must have had notice of our approach, and had time to make good their retreat, which they did through the very dense jungle to the eastward. I heard the rush as of many men through the brushwood, but saw no one . . . . The havildar says that his men fired at about 28 men they saw in the base but they were a long way off.[34]

Simpson's detachment joined only half an hour later. They had been taken in a totally different direction. 'By dint of threats I made the guides take me to where the grain was concealed.' This spot was about 3.5 km to the south west.[35] The surprise had failed, the Hos disappeared as soon as the troops came near. But this happened in the very heartland of the resistance, and they lost whatever stock they had, while some of their women were captured. Resistance caved in. On 8 December, some eighty or ninety Hos were taken prisoner, including the leaders of the resistance, Poto and Deby. They had been tracked by Hos from the north and the west of Hodisum.[36]

Powers to try and sentence, even to pronounce the death sentence, had been given to Political Agent on the South Western Frontier Wilkinson in a government letter dated 5 December.[37] Wilkinson arrived in Tickell's camp in Jagannathpur on the evening of 18 December. The trial had to be postponed, though, as Wilkinson had fallen from his elephant. The trial started on 25 December and was concluded on the 31st December. The five leaders were sentenced to death and seventy-nine Hos were given various terms of imprisonment. Next day, Poto, Narra and Burrai were publicly hanged near Jagannathpur. A great number of Hos witnessed the hanging. Borah and Pandua were hanged the day after at a village near Seringsia Ghat. Here, many Hos of the northern *pirs* had gathered to see the public hanging. 'The examples', Wilkinson hoped, 'will be the means of preserving tranquillity for many years'.[38]

The main hostilities were over, but there remained some serious work to do. On 6 January, troops entered Anwla *pir*. The country appeared quiet; people prepared to pay the tax. They brought in 'the bad characters', Tickell wrote. It was a partial impression, though. There appeared 'few or no steps . . . taken' for the capture of Poto's followers. They had gone to the Mayurbhanj area and there Tickell could not operate. An appeal to the raja of Mayurbhanj had been without success and Tickell could find no 'proper, or trustworthy person in authority under him'. Tickell mentioned fifteen fugitives by name, who with their wives, children and property had gone off to the jungle of Bamanghati. He crossed three names off the list of Poto's followers, as they had been apprehended on 15 January, the day he sent his letter. Tickell asked for permission to do a mopping-up operation within three or four days.[39]

Two days later, however, a group of 500 Hos, who had scoured the jungle on the border with Bamanghati, returned to Tickell's camp. They only found very old traces of the remnants of the Poto party. Tickell wanted to withdraw from the border to tempt these people to return to the Kolhan, where they could be more easily captured. Therefore, he informed the commander of the detachment, Captain Armstrong, that there was no further need for the troops. He needed only a guard of 150, of which 50 could be used to escort the new prisoners, once they were captured. The party under Armstrong marched to headquarters on 18 January. The war was over. Apparently, fighting did not suit Tickell. The relief he felt showed in his easy flowing handwriting.[40]

In the capital where the events were reported, negative views on the Ho adversary had readily resurfaced. It is interesting to recall here the parting shot of the correspondent of the newspaper *The Englishman*, 13 February 1838.

> The Kols are an extremely indolent race, never working, except as much as is absolutely necessary to save them from starvation, and a prey to the most barbarous and absurd superstitions. They go about, women and men, almost in a state of nature: one yard of cloth would literally furnish *trousseaux* for a dozen Kol belles.[41]

In far-away London, the Board was not pleased, as well, and directed their misgivings at the governor general. This was caused by the heavy punishments as well as the fact that Wilkinson, who had been very much part of the events, had conducted the trial himself. 'It is satisfactory to learn that [the disturbances which broke out in parts of the Singhbhum country towards the end of 1837] were speedily suppressed,' wrote the Court of Directors to the Council in Calcutta on 12 March 1840. But 'the criminality of acts of violence and resistance to authority must be estimated according to the circumstances in which people are placed. ... The same strict rules of government and of judicature are not applicable to savage tribes as to men who [already] have been habituated ... to the protection and to the control of law.'[42]

That was a consideration which Wilkinson also had expressed in his instructions to Tickell. But the letter contained an unpleasant surprise.

[The Court is] compelled to state that we cannot approve the authority with which you invested Captain Wilkinson to bring the ringleaders in these disturbances to summary trial, and, at his discretion to inflict upon them the extreme penalty of death. ... We deeply regret that such acts of severity were deemed necessary; ... if unhappily any similar occasion should hereafter arrive, we desire that discretion of the same kind be not committed to an executive officer, who may have been actively engaged against the individuals under trial.[43]

The lack of distinction between the judiciary and executive power came easily to Wilkinson; it was a characteristic of his system. And then, there had been the heat of the hostilities. A cooling-off period due to illness had not been enough to stop him from setting a severe example. In any case, by the time the message from London had reached Calcutta and Singhbhum, it was 1840; Wilkinson had moved on and Tickell was on the point of doing so.

After the conclusion of hostilities on 17 January 1838, the rule over the Kolhan was in the hands of Samuel Richard Tickell. Now, he was his own man, or rather, Thomas Wilkinson's man.

Part III

The Establishment of the Estate, 1837–1842

Chapter 10

Post-Conflict Reconstruction

―⸺―

...
The costs of the Estate; a society in disarray; the ethnic borders of the estate; Tickell and the Manki-Munda system; the land market; a handful of copper coins; a school with six pupils; illnesses and witches; change of the guard in Ranchi
...

Samuel Richard Tickell could now devote his time to bringing the Kolhan Government Estate peace and to giving it shape. He was ordered not to press revenue collection, which to his chagrin remained a weak spot of his assistantship. Revenue collection was a major subject in his despatches to the East India Company. The Estate already had come at a cost. When the idea of annexation was accepted, the older idea of letting the local chiefs pay was quietly shelved. In the Kolhan, the bill was on the Company. The invasion itself by a force of 2,000 was a costly affair, which Wilkinson had not calculated. In addition, the final sheet of the Board's Collection on Wilkinson's Kolhan campaign showed expenses 'incidental to the operations in the Kol Country . . . sanctioned by Lord Auckland' at a total of Rs. 2,637. 12*an* 5*p*.[1]

When Wilkinson proposed to annexe most of the Hodisum, he made some projection of the costs of administering the Estate. He put it at Rs. 20,000, but the burden on the treasury would diminish as revenue would increase.[2] There were 622 villages in the Kolhan, but that was not reflected in the amount of taxes realised this far.

> As far as I have been able to learn, the amount annually realized from the Kolhan by the Singhbhum raja and his brethren the babus, has never in the aggregate exceeded 1500 rupees. I cannot however ascertain what the exact amount of collections has been, for no accounts of any description . . . have been kept by the raja, or any of the babus.[3]

Then, the aggregate revenue of the three Ho villages of Saraikela and that of the three villages of *Thakur* Chaitan Singh 'which are the most northern of those inhabited by Kols' could be another Rs. 550. 'If we state 2000 Rs. to have been the sum annually realized from all the Kol villages, which we have now taken under our own management, we shall not underestimate what they have yielded to those who have hitherto been nominally in possession.' Wilkinson could be frightfully precise. 'In addition to the above sum, the raja & babus received from some villages annually a goat and a small quantity of ghee, at the Dasahra, which were issued for Devi puja.'[4] This was projected to change in the medium term. To start with, the gap could be made less deep by adding the taxes from all those villages from which the chiefs never got revenue. On the other hand, a few villages, Chari and Charum, were given rent-free to Bhalbhadar Dandpal.[5] Wilkinson estimated that he could collect an additional Rs. 8,000 a year. That would make a tax income of Rs. 10,000 for the new government estate.

On the recurrent expenses side, the salaries for the assistant's establishment in Chaibasa was more than Rs. 2,340 per year. Tickell himself would earn Rs. 6,000. Add to that the costs of the 150 men of the Ramgarh Battalion, consisting of a brigade of guns and a troop of the 5th Local Horse. This was well over Wilkinson's revenue projection, as he himself was quick to acknowledge. 'This of course would fall short of the extra expense attending the arrangement, but the amount would be trifling in comparison to the advantages of preserving order and tranquillity in a country so near the seat of Govt. and immediately bordering on the productive provinces of Bengal and Orissa.'[6]

He had been wildly optimistic. The rent was Rs. 5,108 in 1837–38. Even when the military expenditure was not included, there was a gap of Rs. 3,232. In 1838–39, the revenue climbed to Rs. 5,633, an increase of Rs. 524 or 10.25 per cent.[7] It slowly moved up to Rs. 6,252 in 1840–41, still a gap of Rs. 2,088.[8] There was no profit in sight from the Kolhan Government Estate. Calcutta did not object. The total amount to be raised from the area, so pronounced a point in the policy discussion leading up to the change of grand strategy, did not appear to be an issue in its implementation phase. The Court of Directors regarded the deficit 'as a consideration of very inferior importance, if the new arrangements prove, in other respects, successful; and we desire that great care may be taken to afford no reasonable ground of dissatisfaction to the inhabitants by the introduction of imposts, or modes of levying them, to which they have been unaccustomed.'[9] Indeed, it was 'more the object at present to civilize the people and preserve tranquillity than collect high rents'.[10]

That tranquillity was urgently needed; the Kolhan was in disarray, and its people divided. Feuds between *kilis* demanded immediate attention. In themselves, feuds were much older than Wilkinson's Kolhan Campaign. Tickell described these as 'unhappy feuds . . . handed down through generations'.[11] They certainly had received a new impetus from recent events. Hos from the north and from the areas of Jagannathpur and Dumriya had been active with Tickell against the Hos under Poto Ho, roughly from the area between Balandia and Jaintgarh. Tickell knew that social calm rested on making sure that these first would not face retaliation from members of the *kilis* of the insurgents.[12] There also was an immediate need to calm emotions on the opposite side.

To tackle feuds was essential for social peace in general, too. Feuds did not have to wait for wartime conditions to flare up. They could easily be rekindled or reinforced by new grievances. Especially amongst the better-off Hos, marriages required cattle to be handed over to the father of the bride. Apart from this purpose and for using them for ploughing, the Hos did little with cattle. But the theft of cattle was endemic, and we have to surmise that it was one expression of traditional enmity. As Wilkinson had written to Tickell, cattle theft brought about immediate reprisals. The persons wronged 'accompanied by their brethren and friends' would 'immediately... repair to the village, in which the thief or thieves [live], raid [it], and drive off from thence cattle, without regard to whom they belonged; an attempt to make reprisals followed, and blood was not unfrequently shed.'[13] Tickell found that these feuds were 'owing rather to mistaken notions of honour, than to malignant feelings'. Whether he was smoothing a task that actually had been more difficult over, or whether Tickell stumbled upon a situation to which people themselves already wanted to put an end, he said it proved easy to end these feuds. He was surprised that 'through a little timely advice, quarrel *a l'outrance* of the oldest standing have been made up, and whole clans reconciled to each other'.[14] After all, they knew each other. Marriage had to be outside the clan.

The fighting of the last few years had wreaked havoc on individuals, as well. The case of Musammat Birang was the surviving example. She was accused of 'killing her daughter, by tying a rope round her neck' in December 1837. The daughter was six weeks old, Tickell explained.

> The circumstances of the case are, that the prisoner's husband [Gergenday] was taken prisoner, and sentenced to death; that his brother, named Kurry, offered to take the prisoner under his protection, on condition that she should kill her child, aged about one month and 15 days, she had by her husband [Kurry's brother]. To this she consented, and accordingly dashed the child on the ground, with an intention to kill it. On this Kurry said that it was not quite dead, and, twisting a rope, gave it into the prisoner's hand, telling her to tie it fast round the child's neck, and strangle it therewith. She did so in his presence, and thereby terminated its life.[15]

Kurry had tried to avoid punishment. He said that he did not push Musammat to kill her child, but 'only procured her the rope, agreeable to her desire; and as, previous to this, she oftentimes desired him to instruct her how to kill the child, he suggested the mode of strangling. Kurry stated that in his presence the child was killed and buried in the sand by the prisoner.' Kurry died in jail before the trial could be concluded. The witnesses 'declared they had not seen the actual perpetration of the murder, but that the prisoner confessed having killed the child herself'. So the whole case was now against the widow.

Tickell sentenced her to life in the Chaibasa prison. The confirmation by Captain Wilkinson said 'to suffer imprisonment for life in the criminal gaol, constructed for the Hos of Singhbhum.'[16] Her husband Gergenday had been sentenced to death after 'the late disturbances'.[17] Her new friend had died in jail when he was awaiting trial. She was only twenty-two years old and twice widow at the time she was convicted to spend the rest of her life in the Chaibasa prison.[18]

In the sphere of law and order, the manki-munda system would, it was hoped, shore up the new quiet. The system which Wilkinson had put on paper had to be uniform over the Kolhan. This was new. Mankis existed mainly in the border *pirs* of the Kolhan Government Estate, and Tickell himself extended the system to the interior. 'These border tracts had their chiefs or Mankis', he would write in February 1842, 'who were elected on paying a *salami* for the distinction by the zamindars and who used to present the amount of tax required. But in the interior, the Kolhan from the first presented, and indeed in a measure still presents, the anomaly of a people living together without an acknowledged head or ruler of any kind whatever'.[19]

Tickell mentioned the number of twenty-four and also of twenty-six *pirs*.[20] In 1867, the number of mankis in the Kolhan was 68 (and that of mundas was 710).[21] By the end of the nineteenth century, the Kolhan had seventy-three mankis for its twenty-six *pirs*.[22] That suggested, as Tuckey wrote eighty years after Tickell, that the position of the manki had been 'to some extent created and always carefully fostered by government'.[23] To some extent.

Tickell had a systematic mind. He noted, that 'the proportion of Mundas to their Mankis in several pirs, is very unequal . . . . Some of the mankis are placed over upward of 30 villages, & others over not more than 4 or 5.' He proposed that no manki should have less than twelve or more than twenty villages under his superintendence. In his view, except in one or two cases, this could be done by a different distribution of the villages in each *pir*, without having to create new mankis.[24] Wilkinson answered that he did not think it advisable to make any changes in the distribution of the villages amongst the mankis. After misconduct by a manki, a ceiling of twenty villages might be considered.[25] Thus, there remained a situation without a workable *pir* system, and the village was to be the effective administrative unit, albeit that they were in unequal groupings under a manki.[26]

The mankis were made responsible for the collection of revenue, but the actual work was done in the villages. The mundas could pay the rent directly to the assistant or through their mankis. Tickell was to give receipts for the rent collected and to explain the use of these to the mankis and mundas. Wilkinson would send the necessary forms soon after the Estate was established.[27] When they signed their engagements, the mundas of the villages were told that all Hos would have to pay taxes, at the rate already fixed by Roughsedge in 1821, half a rupee per plough, 'to which they with apparent cheerfulness agreed'.[28] A plough could be defined as a function of the quality of the soil, as the amount of land which would require from 75 to 95 kilogrammes of seed rice.[29] Or, one and a half year later, it could be 'as much land as may have required one plough for its cultivation'.[30]

Tickell tried hard to arrive at the correct number of ploughs. It was, Wilkinson conceded even before he had started, the 'most difficult part of your work'.

> Immediately the rains are over, you should assemble all the mankis and heads of villages of the several pirs . . . . [You should] in the first instance ascertain from them, the number of resident cultivators in each of their villages, and the number of ploughs that each cultivator employs in cultivating the lands of the village.[31]

If there was control, chances were high that he found evidence of tax evasion, a major irritant to the assistant. 'It will not be irrelevant . . . to mention that I find the Koles most stubbornly and troublesome in concealing the quantity of land they actually cultivate—and in many cases making use of the most barefaced deceptions in understating the ploughs in their own villages', wrote Tickell in November 1838. 'For this reason I have been obliged this year, to make use of my interpreters in assessing the villages'.[32]

Mundas did have an interest in the amount of realised revenue—they got part of it for their role in the collection[33]—but they also had to consider their standing in their village. Concealment for tax evasion was to some extent a collective act. Without the collaboration of the munda and the other villagers, individual people had no chance to hide the amount of land called 'a plough'. In 1840, Tickell stated that the revenue collected came to Rs. 6,500, hence 13,000 ploughs, and estimated concealment was at about 1/8th.³⁴ Apparently, he considered the amount of revenue, or rather the avoidance of evasion, as a prime indicator of his role in the application of the Wilkinson system to the Kolhan. At the end of 1838, the first year of peaceful tax collection, he noted with pride that his increased supervision—though still with the help of interpreters—had resulted in 'a surprising difference in the amount of the revenue from that of last year.'³⁵

To conceive a system and to actually make it work were two different things. After Seringsia, things came to a head at the old trouble-spot Jaintgarh where the ethnic border was inside the new estate. With Wilkinson's permission, Raghunath Bisi had returned to Jaintgarh. Raghunath got 'the care and management of that village, but I', Wilkinson wrote, 'consider it very undesirable to delegate any authority to him, over any village having Kol inhabitants'.³⁶ Here, once again, we meet Raghunath Bisi as the past master of the status quo ante. There were several deserted villages close to Jaintgarh, some of which were formerly occupied by Hindu *paiks* (tenure holders who paid no rents but rendered military service) and peasants. Most of these had fled the villages in 1830. With the introduction of British management, it was to be expected that they would return. The *paiks* got the message that from their return onwards, they must pay rents as peasants, as there was no more need for their military tenures. On the ground, it appeared that Hos had come to live in some of Raghunath Bisi's former villages. Raghunath now placed Goalas and Dorowas in these villages, and these people did not want to be put under a Ho munda or manki.

Tickell wrote on 21 November 1838 that Ghunnoo Manki of Gumuriya had lodged a complaint that Raghunath Bisi had taken two villages, Turli (Surroree) and Khuntiyapada (Kuntipada), from him and placed people in these. Tickell was uncertain. Raghunath had proceeded 'without any authority to that effect from me.'

> Altho' the Bisi has acted wrongly in tenanting deserted Villages without proper authority, yet I should feel averse to punishing him severely for so doing. His presence at Jaint affords so good an opportunity for the peopling that country with a race so much superior to the Hos. And more over, as he had reason to expect that the villages in question, to which the Hos have no right, will ultimately be brought under his charge.³⁷

Also, there was, again, the question of ethnic differences.

> There are several other villages, besides those in your list placed under Ghunnoo Manki, which are inhabited by Goalas and Bhuiyas and are considered agreeably to your Arrangement of 1837 as under Narra, and Bhishnoo mankis. These people from the very first have been most averse to placing themselves as peasants under Hos whom all Hindus (and not unjustly) look upon as an inferior race. And I must beg to express my conviction that unless these people are suffered to remain under the charge of respectable head men of their own classes, they will leave the Kolhan altogether, in preference of being under the authority of those, who are so far inferior to them in civilization.³⁸

These were extraordinarily negative sentiments about the Hos for Tickell, but he was triggered by a great chagrin. He had been cheated in the extent of land he could tax, and he did not get across when he wanted to assess the villages of the Hos here.³⁹ He even submitted a proposal which would, if accepted, blow up the idea of the Kolhan Government Estate as an area in which the Hos would run their own affairs in their villages.

I trust that these considerations will not only induce you to lose no time in procuring me the much wanted assistance of the Jaint Bisi as Tuhsildar [official in charge of the revenue] in his part of the Kolhan but that you will ultimately be of opinion that this duty should, in all other pirs, be carried on by some efficient person, whose proceedings would, of course, be checked by the presence of the mankis and mundas of villages themselves.[40]

The smooth talker Raghunath Bisi had done it again.

In his letter of 12 December 1838, Wilkinson put a stop to that. The Kolhan Government Estate was not meant for the local Hindu chiefs. Raghunath was compensated with land and the 'serdar'-ship, the equivalent of the manki-ship, over the villages inhabited by others than Hos. In the end, Raghunath was placed over thirteen villages. Ghunnoo, too, retained thirteen villages.[41] Really, Wilkinson exclaimed, 'we have seen enough of the jungle chiefs to learn, that whatever influence they gain over the Hos will be exercised for nothing but evil'.[42]

The revenue question shed some light on local agriculture. Not much, as Samuel Richard had little of an economist in him. What we get from both Wilkinson and him, are mere glimpses of the rural economy of the Kolhan Government Estate. In an economy in which little money was circulating, and where, moreover, the basic services of the state were financed with external funds, tax evasion benefitted the economy in the short term. It preserved the spending power of individual households. There the effect stopped. The Hos were not used to paying tax. Thus, evasion of tax did not so much increase liquidity, as prevent the little disposable income there was from flowing out of the agrarian sector. Even that income was not much used for investments. As Tickell noted, there was a cultural barrier against accumulation. 'The "levelling system" obtains so much among them, that there is no farmer or landholder in the country with capital sufficient' to build irrigation works.[43] The agricultural sector showed severe underinvestment.

Probably, there was also a severe shortage of available manpower. There was not a labour force that could be tapped. The Hos knew the idea of hired labour, though. They made a distinction between a *nalatannee*, 'hired labourer', who could also be a servant, *chittratannee*, and a *dassee*, 'fostered servant without wages'. They even had a word for 'beggar'.[44] Having words for occupations in the language, however, does not indicate how widespread these occupations are. In practice, they were rare and did not necessarily involve money. Even the troops and the assistant found it difficult 'to procure the commonest necessity or the simplest hired labour for money'.[45] Tickell mentioned one exception. When a woman was about to deliver a child, the husband would employ a widow as a midwife for a fee of eight *annas*.[46] This could well have been an isolated case or a practice restricted to the very richest Hos. They had words for the occupations taken up by people outside the Ho ethnicity, like blacksmith, potter, weaver and, of course, cowherd.[47]

The village was not the basic economic unit; the family was. The head of the family held the land, and his rights over it came close to private property. An indication for this was that in the Ho villages land was for sale. Wilkinson wrote that to ascertain the ownership of land would be very troublesome 'from the practice which has prevailed for generations of transferring small parcels of land by sale, or in pledge for loans. From the want of any written documents, for there are none in the country, it is difficult to decide, whether the lands have been sold on pledge.' The assistant should see to it that land already held for twelve years should generally be left undisturbed. This was an important restriction of legal memory[48] and indicated that a new regime had arrived. Land sale, Wilkinson found, was not limited to members of the same village. 'You must . . . ascertain the number of non-resident cultivators of the village lands, who reside in the other villages, as much land of villages is cultivated by men residing in other villages.'[49] These were remarks made in passing, tantalising allusions to a land market inside the Hodisum. It shows that at least in the more densely settled parts, the Ho economy was not one of mutually exclusive villages. In the new set-up of the Kolhan Government Estate, the village was a tax unit before an economic unit.

In addition to the land market, there was a lopsided market in moveable property. Cattle rearing was a separate branch of the economy, and, characteristically, it was not manned by Hos. The owners of the cattle would be Hos, but the actual work of tending to the cattle was outsourced to Goalas, Odia-speaking cowherds. In this, 'one man entrusts to another, a number of cattle to be taken care for, either cows, bullocks, buffaloes, goats, kids or pigs. The person having charge of them is entitled for his trouble, at the end of a given number of years, to one head of the cattle in a certain number, and for all the rest he must account to the owner.'[50] In practice, the owners used cattle only for ploughing, marriage contracts, and wedding parties. An explanation could be that the amount of meat of one cow or buffalo was too large for the daily needs of one family. And Hos did not drink milk.[51] So the Goalas kept the milk, made the ghee, and sold the cattle they were allowed to keep as a fee for their work. Here, there was a near immediate impact of the new order. As raids, which often had as their aim to steal cattle, were stopped, the regular herds remained as the most important source for cattle to be used as bride price. That caused a stricter supervision of the Goalas, who were seen as 'notorious cheats and robbers'.[52] The bride price was not the only use of cattle; it could provide some cash. 'Great quantities' of cattle and buffaloes were sold to Tamarians, knew Tickell, 'for the most trifling prices'.[53]

Tickell found that the private profit motive prevailed in the modest silkworm cultivation. The 'proprietors', wrote Tickell, preserved these parts of the jungles, called *asan* jungles, with great jealousy and care'.[54] This activity implicated an outside market, in which the cocoons could be sold, where they would be processed into *tasar* silk, and go on to enter the market for luxury goods. The trade in the Kolhan villages was done by Tamarians, who also traded in grain, and were loathed for their cheating and, in the countryside, for the stealing of cattle.[55] Their behaviour did little to make the profit motive respectable.

Local exchange was realised *in natura*: silk worms in exchange for necklaces, labour for livestock. Still, it was trade. Tickell had to start from a very low level. In 1837, the army surgeon William Dunbar, one of the first British inhabitants of Chaibasa, noted that the Hos had 'not the slightest idea of the use of money, all their simple transactions being carried upon the principle of barter'.[56] Barter did not make things cheap. As he complained, the Hos wanted to be paid in rice, which was expensive.[57] The Hos did not see much use for money. They were getting 'pretty well acquainted' with it, Tickell noticed, but 'hold copper coin in great disdain, seldom taking the trouble to count a large quantity, by reckoning it by the handful'.[58]

The initiative to establish a goods market had to come from the outside. 'When the rains are over', wrote Wilkinson in his instructions of 1837, Tickell's task was to induce traders to settle in the new town and to explore the possibilities to establish a weekly market. It had to be a real market, though, and Tickell was to see to it that 'no force or authority was used to make [the Hos] sell, for less than they were willing to take for their produce'. It was unclear what these products were, but Wilkinson hoped it would include enough grain for the troops.[59] He had hoped in vain. Even four years later, in 1841, everything for the military and the administration had to be imported from Hazaribagh and Bankura.[60] This need not surprise us. Even if the use of money had been more widespread, facilitating a livelier turnover on the market, the daily needs of more than 150 troops with their retainers, and also of the members of the assistant's establishment would have been way above the carrying capacity of Chaibasa's fledgling commercial establishment.

External trade, too, could be called limited at best. As we have seen, *tasar* cocoons and some cattle were exported. As in Roughsedge's time, there was some import of cloth, spirits, ornaments and salt.[61] Unlike Roughsedge, Tickell mentioned a regular Ho participation in the salt trade with the south and the east, bringing in widely varying quantities. Hos travelled 'all the way to Puri for the sake of purchasing salt', put it on bullocks and brought it back through Keonjhar, where they had to pay toll. The road through Bamanghati was better, but here the raja confiscated salt transported on a bullock, although for 'some douceur', loads of salt carried on the shoulder-yoke could pass here.[62]

The old road to Chotanagpur ran from Chakradharpur through Mailpir in Kera to Tamar. It was 'almost impassable during the rains'.[63] A new road between Chaibasa and Kishenpur (Ranchi) could boost trade and integration with the north of the South West Frontier Agency. It passed through the area which Tickell had surveyed a few years before. To build this road, Tickell proposed to make use of prisoners of Chaibasa jail and to ask local chiefs to provide guards.[64] The enumeration of these chiefs was a who's who of the north of Singhbhum: the *Thakur* of Kharsawa, Chakradhar Singh of Saraikela, Loknath Singh of Kera, Sonoo Kunda of Karaikela, Chait Chandra Mahapater of Chainpur, Kookurrum Singh of Bandgaon. For funds, 'the necessary measures will be taken to appropriate all sums realized on account of unclaimed property & fines, to the use of the roads, under the head of "Road Funds".' Samuel Richard Tickell would lose no time in setting the prisoners at work and in issuing orders to the neighbouring chiefs to furnish night guards.[65] Security arranged, the work could start, but the effect on the economy could, of course, not be immediate.

After three years, Tickell concluded that 'commerce has been scarcely at all introduced into the Kolhan; the people, among whom poverty is unknown, remain contented with the spoils of the chase, and the limited produce of their fields, which are only cultivated in sufficiency to meet present want.'[66] The Ho economy remained a largely closed system.

It is, therefore, not to be wondered that also the efforts to introduce cultural changes from outside ran up against a wall. Education had been an important add-on in Wilkinson's sale of the extension of his system to Calcutta. It was here that Wilkinson turned out to be most out of touch with the realities of Ho culture. The new school was to come 'under such instructions from the Committee of Education, as may appear best calculated to improve the condition of this wild people'.[67] The school was placed under the superintendence of the assistant and the commanding officer of the detachment in Singhbhum. Wilkinson had prepared the ground for this innovation. After exploratory talks with influential Hos, he had 'no doubt that many of them would send their children to any school which might be established, the more particularly'—we are in Hodisum—'if instructions was given free of expence'.[68] Calcutta eagerly supported the proposal 'as a means of relieving the rising generation of the Larka Kols from that gross ignorance to which you firstly attribute so much of the frolick and vicious habits of that people and their consequent misery'. It requested Wilkinson to put himself immediately in touch with the Committee of Public Instruction 'stating precisely the circumstances of the case, and the extent of your wishes. You will inform the committee that you have the Governor's authority for addressing them on the subject.'[69] This sounded a bit too eager. Indeed, the proposal did very well in London, where it was greeted with 'particular approbation'.[70]

The official enthusiasm on education was strengthened by the discussion on the medium of instruction in education, which had come to a head in 1835. In that year Thomas Babington Macaulay wrote his Education Minute, a powerful plea for instruction in the English medium. Its aim was to create an anglicised class of Indians that would stand between 'us and the millions whom we govern'. It did not cover the need of education for the masses.[71] But in the years leading to 1838, there was also a trickle-down theory, at the time called 'downward infiltration theory', in which educational reforms would eventually reach the 'rural vernacular schools'.[72]

What was the vernacular language in the Kolhan? It was Ho, of course, but no teacher could speak it. So in March 1838, Tickell proposed to teach the Hos in the school for the first one or two years in Odia, 'the common dialect of the Hindu portion of the population'. It would give the Hos 'the means of becoming familiarized with their more civilized neighbours'. After that, one could attempt to teach them the commercially and administratively more useful Hindi or English. The Hindus 'of the more respectable classes' understood this, and although they spoke Odia, they asked for education in English.[73] Instead of 'downward infiltration', there was upward climbing. Ambitions and plans apart, it was not working. As we shall see, in April 1839, there was one small school with one Odia teacher and six pupils.[74]

The limited effect of the developmental program can be seen in the sphere where at first it had seemed easiest to effect change, the health beliefs of the Hos. Part of the educational effort, Wilkinson had been careful to repeat, was to remove 'the dreadful prejudice' of witchcraft.[75] That was part of the health beliefs of the Hos. Luckily the Hos had 'nutritive food and drink' and 'built their villages in 'open airy positions'.[76] Still, illnesses were common occurrences. The Ho notions in this sphere led to economically unwise and juridically unacceptable behaviour. As Wilkinson wrote, the Hos believed that 'all their sickness proceed[ed] from three causes. First witchcraft, second the displeasure of their deotas or bongas, and third the spirit of someone who has died.' For the third cause, the spirit of a dead person, who was supposed to inflict the same disease as the one of he himself had died, the Hos saw, Wilkinson noted, no remedy. But when the illness was seen as caused by the *bonga* or ghost, they could try to appease the ghost by sacrifices, 'first of fowls, then goats, and if neither suffice, bullocks and buffaloes are offered'. This was a severe drain on the income. 'Much property is thus thrown away by those possessing it, and such as have no animals of the description above mentioned, frequently have recourse to theft to procure them.'[77]

Apart from costly, Ho notions of illness were socially destructive. According to Wilkinson, they saw witchcraft as its first cause.[78] Even 'the most intelligent' Hos were fully convinced that 'many individuals possess the power of destroying whom they please, from their knowledge of the art'.[79] The Hos knew only one way of definitely tackling witches. They killed them, not necessarily in anger, but always in fear, and often after proper preparation. There was quite a number of, as Tickell called them, 'wretches, styled "sokas", or soothsayers' in the Kolhan and on its borders. These soothsayers also denounced a person as a witch, 'dooming him to certain death'. That was a great irritant to Tickell who was convinced that the soothsayers stirred up trouble, 'for the Koles left to themselves are a people among whom crime is exceedingly rare'.[80] But the belief existed, and often the Hos did not need outsider witch finders to kill witches.[81] They reasoned that if the witch or wizard remained amongst them, their own destruction was certain. But if they got rid of the witch, they still had a chance to escape punishment.[82]

Wilkinson himself saw no other quick way to save the lives of the suspected witches than to order all the village heads to bring them to the assistant. He instructed Tickell to remove the suspected witch to another village, 'where the same prejudice does not exist against him'. Although Wilkinson stipulated that the suspected witch was allowed to take his moveable property with him, he acknowledged that deportation might appear to him or her 'unjust and harsh'. On the other hand, if Tickell would exercise 'the severest means', that is, the death penalty, to put an end to the killing of witches, it could easily lead to disturbances. But Tickell was to 'omit no opportunity of pointing out the wickedness and folly of the horrid practise they have hitherto pursued'. This instruction amounted to an admission of impotence. The measure of removing people accused of witchcraft would not remove the fear of witches from the others, Wilkinson admitted.[83]

He had some hope of destroying the 'baneful belief in witchcraft' by putting the problem back into the medical sphere. For this he established a hospital.[84] Tickell's task was to persuade the relations of the sick persons to bring them to the hospital where the military medical officer would attend to them. Wilkinson formed this plan after he had 'succeeded in getting many of the Hos to take our medicines from which they have derived such benefit, that applications are constantly made for it'.[85] He proposed Calcutta to give the medical officer Dunbar an extra allowance of Rs. 50 per month. The governor approved of this sum 'for the care of a hospital specially devoted to the reception and care of the Hos'.[86] Dunbar confirmed Wilkinson's observation that the Hos 'freely' took western medicines.[87] The practice seemed to have been first to try and appease the spirits. Only after the illness had taken a turn for the worse, people reported to the western-style doctor. That made for rather hopeless cases in the hospital. That, in its turn, meant bad publicity for the new medicine.

Within three years, writing from Nepal in 1840, Tickell sounded bitter on this subject, as 'the slight temporary reform that was effected among them, has altogether ceased'.[88] The Hos still held many 'private sacrifices' in their own houses to cure sickness. Apparently, the army surgeon had not become very popular. 'They never attempt resorting to medicine.' He added eloquently,

> In endeavouring to dissuade them from this dangerous folly, in which the father of a family, with unshaken bigotry sees his household swept away into the grave, and the whole of his livestock destroyed in vain effort to check the ravages of sickness, by sacrificing to the gods, we have as yet significantly failed.[89]

Illnesses caused fear, but epidemics struck terror. Tickell witnessed quite some, of cholera, fever, and smallpox, the last wrecking 'fearful havoc'.[90] On the 'first appearance of any epidemic, [the Hos] leave their houses and flee into the jungles, living apart from each other'.[91] This was, given the poor records of both their own and western medicine in stopping the spread of contagious diseases, quite a sensible approach. Wilkinson and Tickell saw it more as a sign of mistrust. Lapses in the new system of medicine did not help. When Tickell was preparing his article for publication, damaging news from his successor reached Ouseley that all the Hos refused to be vaccinated against smallpox, as in one village people had fallen ill after the vaccination.[92]

Wilkinson left in March 1839 to become the resident in Nagpur.[93] His departure was not a welcome change for Tickell. He had a good rapport with Wilkinson, whom, as we have seen, he considered a 'truly wise and benevolent' boss, and who guided him in the application of his 'excellent arrangements'.[94] There was a short interlude in which Dr John Davidson was in charge, 2 March–4 April 1839.[95] His successor was John Ralph Ouseley,[96] scion of the well-connected Ouseley family.[97] He did not have a great grasp of the realities of the original population. Within a year, Ouseley was gently lectured by Davidson, now his personal assistant, on his ideas about the original population of Chotanagpur.

> The Coles are by no means the extremely simple and easily imposed upon people that you appear to have been led to suppose. On the contrary they are in all that concerns their own small transactions, I should say an intelligent people, as much, if not more so than labouring class of any part of India, which I have visited.'[98]

So thought, much to the south, Tickell in the Kolhan Government Estate.

Chapter 11

Consolidation

...
The amnesty of 1839; failed attempts at cultural change; strained relations with Porahat; prevention of a sati; Tickell prepares to leave; Kathmandu interlude; return to the Kolhan; the seals of Porahat; the assistant explodes; the owls of Urkia
...

Inside the Kolhan, 1839–40 were years of consolidation. Tickell's efforts to establish good relations with the Hos and to speak their language paid off. He was known as 'Tikan Saheb'.[1] In this consolidation, the continued confinement of Hos in the local prison was a conspicuous negative point. Each year, the prisoners got one blanket and two pieces of cloth, a mat to sleep on. Twice a week at least, the jail building was fumigated. And as many times, the prisoners themselves were set to plaster the floor with cow dung.[2] Still, the mortality among the Ho prisoners was stated to be 'dreadful and depressing'. The medical officer attributed this to deep mental distress, together with changes in habits, occupation and diet. The Hos 'seem to entertain a horror of being imprisoned'.[3]

They got enough food, but it was not suited to their habits. Each prisoner was entitled to a daily ration of 700 gm of rice, 115 gm of *dal* (lentils), 5 gm of salt, and the same quantity of tobacco.[4] Each Sunday the prisoners got mutton, oil, and spices.[5] The 'ration system' was used for food; they just got the prescribed items and quantities of food. On Wilkinson's question, Tickell considered this 'very prejudicial to the health of the prisoners, as it deprives them of that mixed diet so essentially necessary to health.' He noted scurvy.[6] Early on, when he was discussing the establishment of the jail, Wilkinson already knew where the problem laid. 'You may also when any of the members of the family of a prisoner bring him *hanria* (rice beer) to drink, allow him to partake of it in moderation, as I am of opinion that for want of a beverage, which they have been accustomed to from infancy, many of the Singhbhum prisoners taken out of the Ho country have fallen sick.'[7] Tickell agreed, rice beer should have a central place in the diet, especially of the elderly Hos. 'The supply of it is at present precarious and dependent on the bounty of their friends.' The solution was to change to the 'money system'. If the prisoners had some money for food, they themselves could secure 'a moderate and steady supply of the article'. The experiences were good, 'the removal of the diseases before adverted to was mainly accomplished by the daily exhibition of a moderate quantity of the above liquor'.[8]

With the situation in the jail unsatisfactory and the Government Estate quiet, one could reconsider the sentences. London reminded the local administration in October 1838, that 'if the measures which have been taken should happily establish permanent tranquillity in the District, you may find it safe to liberate the prisoners in confinement on account of political disorder not likely to recur, an event which would offer particular gratification'.[9] In May 1839, Tickell wrote an extensive proposal to grant amnesty to most people who had been imprisoned for active resistance to the invasion. He did 'not think any apprehension may be entertained as to their future misconduct . . . . After the summary punishment inflicted on the ringleaders of that insurrection none are likely again to attempt the collecting of any number of these people, under the elusive idea of successfully resisting government.'[10] Out of the seventy-nine originally convicted, sixty-eight were still in prison. Tickell proposed to set free fifty-one prisoners serving terms of three to ten years, including three 'on account of their extreme youth, and of their having fallen in with & become connected with gangs . . . at a time when so large a tract of the Kolhan was in a state of excitement and of insurrection'.[11] Of these people to be set free, sixteen were serving sentences of five years, and twenty-seven of seven years.[12] But he proposed to keep seventeen in custody, who were sentenced on more charges than just rebellion, such as murder or highway robbery. These were people 'of a very different description from the above, and of general bad character'. Tickell feared local opposition to such a move, as 'the liberation of these might spread distrust & alarm among the peaceably disposed of the Hos, and disgust those who have suffered by them—in their property & the lives of their connections and friends'.[13] The move to set most prisoners free got a warm reception in London, 'We learn with much satisfaction that you authorise the release of all the Singhbhum Ho prisoners from whom no danger to the peace of the country was to be apprehended, and that subsequently . . . fifty one prisoners were set at liberty.'[14]

As Wilkinson had written, before the 'rising generation' of Hos had been educated, 'we cannot hope for that permanent improvement, which it is the object of government to promote'.[15] On 1 April 1839, Tickell indicated to Wilkinson's short-term successor, John Davidson, that as he was ordered to do so, he would try to get 'Kole boys' to go and study in Hooghly. But he considered it hopeless. Tickell could not understand how the Board could attribute to Wilkinson this idea of sending boys out of the Estate for education, 'as no one than him was better acquainted with the strong antipathy felt by the Koles, at any idea of leaving their own country, even for the shortest period'. Even offers of local education were hardly taken. After one and a half years, the Odia master had an attendance of only six boys, 'and this alone by feeding and clothing them myself' and with many 'other inducements to remain and receive education', Tickell wrote. The reason was 'the greatest distrust and alarm prevailing amongst the Kols in allowing their children to reside so much amongst Hindus (altho' in their own country!).' Tickell wanted to take notice of these 'superstitions, fears and ignorance'. To concentrate on establishing more schools now would obstruct all other attempts at improvement.[16] The next year, in 1840, there again was no schoolmaster.[17]

Under J. R. Ouseley, as under Wilkinson, formal education remained alien to the Hos. It took Ouseley till 1841 to get two teachers from the Shahabad district,[18] who started a school in which English and Hindi were taught.[19] It was a limited success, even though, as the parents were too poor to get their children to school, each boy—one did not speak of female education—got an allowance of half an *anna* to one *anna* per day.[20] So locally there was a conspicuous lack of results, but in Calcutta education was not negotiable. In 1845, just after Tickell had left Kolhan for good, the government turned down a proposal by Ouseley to remove the school to Puruliya. The number of pupils might be small (the highest figure came to sixty-one) but the governor general insisted that the assistant would make frequent visits to the school and 'encourage . . . especially the inhabitants of the hill country to send their children'. This was 'a most essential part of an officer's duty'.[21] It was a largely unsuccessful part. But as an imposed government programme it left in the archives a paper trail disproportionate to its impact.

An even more conspicuous failure was the attempt by Ouseley, and to some extent by Tickell himself, to introduce Christianity in the Kolhan. It was inspired by their own religious beliefs, as well as by their dislike of the Brahmins' influence on some Hos. Ouseley noted that the British occupation of the country of the Hos had introduced 'a crowd of Oriya Brahmins, who have not shown themselves before, and who were then endeavouring to make a mongrel kind of Hindu out of them'. That while in the Kolhan Government Estate 'the blessings of British rule were becoming more apparent daily, . . . the happiness of living in security appreciated.' Ouseley echoed Wilkinson, that a 'finer field for the Missionary never existed'. Because here, in the Kolhan, the people did not have castes, no 'recognised religion', would eat 'indiscriminately whatever was offered from the British table'. They were 'a bolder and finer race than most of the people of the country'.[22] One had to seize the opportunity. For this, Ouseley sought the help of the Bishop of Calcutta and wrote that 'Major Wilkinson's arrangements and conciliatory methods of ruling them as enforced by Lieut. Tickell' had given them a 'favourable opinion of the English in every way'.[23] Ouseley found the conversion to Christianity 'of the highest importance, far exceeding what could be done even with the expenses so cheerfully afforded to convert the population of some small and distant island in the Pacific Ocean'. The Christianisation of the Hos could be the start of 'the general conversion of India'. He received no reply.[24]

Ouseley's attempts to spread Christianity were not part of the Company's policy. The best-placed proponents of the non-regulation system, Munro, Elphinstone and Charles Metcalfe, moved against Christian missionaries where they thought their activities could stir up trouble with Hindus or Muslims.[25] Calcutta prescribed a cautious line of non-interference with Indian beliefs and practices, with the exception of extreme practices like infanticide and widow burning (*sati*). In the non-regulation system, Christian conversion was not even on the hidden agenda.

Religion did come up in private conversations, though. Tickell, with his direct access to the Hos, gave admonitions like 'Never steal', 'Do not do to others as you would that others would do to you. This is the great secret of well-doing'; 'Never take God's name in vain'. Tickell went much further than expounding some rules of behaviour and attempted a small sermon in the Ho language.

I speak for your good. I will not deceive you. Others have deceived you. Do not believe in false gods; there is but one God. My God is your God. What you say, he hears. Whatever you do, he sees. From his eyes, you cannot hide. In trouble, he will deliver you. In fear, he will preserve you. Without him, you will perish. With him fear nothing. Believe in him, and he will give you all things. He made you and can destroy you. Keep him in your hearts. Never forsake him. I leave you; but remember my words. Fare you well.[26]

This sermon showed a remarkable concern in a twenty-something officer, who spent his spare time hunting and collecting birds and beasts. 'My God is your God' was a striking illustration of the depth of Tickell's sympathy for the Hos.

While the relations with the Hos improved, and a potentially disruptive scheme like conversion floundered, the relations with Porahat continued to be strained. Ouseley commented upon the misrule of the estate of Singhbhum. Under the earlier rulers, the population here already had 'changed into a worthless set of inefficient cultivators; . . . Bhuiyas were the chief population.'[27] The state was nominally ruled by a minor of some ten years of age, Arjun Singh, and placed, perhaps as nominally, in charge of the political assistant of Singhbhum. The queen dowager and Arjun's uncle, Jadunath, who de facto ruled Porahat, wanted to increase its income. During the three years after the death of Achuta Singh, the relations of the palace with the subordinate chiefs of Chakradharpur, Kera, Bandgaon and Karaikela had been uneasy, and always these troubles had a financial aspect. Even from Porahat proper, general disgust was reported. Ouseley was 'surprised that the exactions of the Babu [Jadunath] have not caused a disturbance'. He attributed the quiet to the presence of troops in Chaibasa and the control by Tickell. Ouseley advised to strengthen that control and put Porahat under Tickell's direct superintendence, as it was 'the only remaining part of the Kol country not under our direct management'.[28] It would be an opportunity to prevent troubles between the Hos inside Porahat and the palace. 'The Coles [inside Porahat] do not feel that the raja has the power to enforce the payment of the revenue, consequently it is now more a matter of free will than compulsion if anything is paid. By the time the raja would be of age[, in 6 or 7 years, the] matter would I trust have been adjusted.'[29]

The palace, however, was doing its utmost to keep Tickell out of its affairs. He ran into trouble with the queen dowager over its financial management. Apparently, as soon as the ruling that the raja would be a ward was imminent, Jadunath and other babus had sent a party to collect rent from Bandgaon, 'altho' such a proceeding was quite unusual, probably with a view of securing as much ready money as possible before the estate was taken out of their hands'.[30] Around 20 October 1839, the Porahat palace sent one Mir Kumir Ud-din Hussain together with Jagdeet Mahtee to Calcutta. Hussein, 'having deluded the Rani and others into the belief that he would easily be able to reverse the orders of Govt. placing Porahat in the estate of wards, . . . extorted from her 600 Rs. for the purpose.'[31] Mir Kumir Ud-din Hussain's mission was not a success, but the relations with Porahat continued to be strained.

On 1 December 1839, Tickell gave the dowager queen notice that, as the young Arjun was a ward, 'all papers and documents relating to the income and expenditure of the zamindari were required, to be copied into my office'. Obstruction followed. Tickell 'having been refused access to the papers under various excuses for two days', gave notice to the *rani* that she had to give him access to the papers. Otherwise, 'I must adopt some other & harsher means of obtaining possession of them.' The threat did not have an effect, and 'at 10 o'clock I marched a small party of sepoys, into the court yard of her residence sending word that unless the papers were produced, I must enter the Underoon[?] myself & take them. They were then without further delay given up.' Tickell blamed these very uneasy relations on

> the ill designing babus who surround the Rani & the young raja, who wanted to keep the management of Porahat in their own hands. I need not describe to you the unwillingness I experience on all sides to give any information especially with reference to the sources and amount of revenue in the estate.[32]

The trouble in Kharsawan was of a more domestic nature. On 2 August 1839, Tickell warned Ouseley that Chaitan, the ruler of Kharsawan, was very ill, and the *rani* had announced that on his death she would become a *sati* (burn herself with her husband). Tickell had tried very much to talk her out of her plan. Ouseley sent another man to talk to her eldest son Opender Singh, and a letter to the *rani* explained 'how extremely displeasing such a conduct would be to the Government'. Besides, her husband 'might yet recover'. Two days later, Ouseley got a letter from Chaitan (but written by his son Opender). Chaitan announced subtly that he would die. He had suffered 'a long and violent illness'. He begged the government to bind themselves to let Opender succeed him, and that shares be given to his younger sons. The commitment was put to paper and was sent to Tickell on the eighth. The news came that the condition of the raja had slightly improved; the same day a letter came from Opinder in which he stated that his mother had no plans to become a *sati*. Therefore, he had taken care that Ouseley's letter would reach his mother. Some quiet? Not really.

The very next day, 10 August 1839, Masum Thakoor, 'the native doctor', wrote Ouseley that the illness was virulent. And yes, the *thakurani* contemplated *sati*. Ouseley sent Tickell, who was in Chaibasa, an express letter that he should go to Kharsawan with a secret letter to Opender. If Opender would, on the demise of his father, 'encourage . . . the concremation of his mother with the body', he would incur the 'certain displeasure of the Government'. The preparations for the ceremony even when his father was alive were 'highly improper'. Moreover, 'with God's will he might still recover'.[33]

But *sati* was in the air, or rather in the region. The sister of Chakradhar Singh of Saraikela had immolated herself with her husband, the demised raja of Keonjhar. Only the day before, Chaitan Singh's younger daughter, who was married to Chate Rai, the younger brother of the raja of Mayurbhanj, had performed *sati* in Baripada. Ouseley thought that the Kharsawan *rani* might not yet have received that news. In the meantime, without Ouseley's knowledge, 'all the usual preparations for Sati were made.' The local officers sent 'all the females' of Kharsawan to the *rani* to explain that the government would be very angry and, probably, that this would hurt the chances of her son Opender of succeeding his father.

Chaitan died on 11 August, and his widow prepared to mount the funeral pyre. The body of Chaitan was being carried to the pile, and the *rani* looked determined. The troops present occupied the two gates of the palace. At this tense moment, Samuel Richard Tickell arrived. He 'explained to her the injury her family would sustain from her loss.' Tickell promised to get her permission to live in Puri for the rest of her life. The *rani* 'took off her ornaments and fine dresses and consented to widowhood.'

Ouseley had reason to express his pleasure with Tickell. 'To Lieutt. Tickell's unwearing and humane attention I am indebted for success in preventing this Sati.'[34] This outcome was welcome to both the East India Company in Calcutta and the local Hos. The first was against *sati* as 'revolting to the human nature'.[35] The Hos wanted peace at night. *Satis* were not reborn, the Ghasis who lived among them said, 'but remain burning for ever in their pits, and come out at night, wandering about, still burning'.[36]

On 20 August, Ouseley got two letters from Opender. He expressed his thanks to Tickell and Ouseley for preventing his mother from performing *sati*. He lamented the loss of his father. He also requested his official appointment as the successor of his father the *Thakur* of Kharsawan. Ouseley wrote back that he could not give this appointment without authorisation by the government. On 24 August, Opender again asked for his appointment. Four days later, Ouseley wrote his account of the past few weeks to Calcutta and asked for the official appointment of Opender as the ruler of Kharsawan.

The problem in Calcutta was that his father Chaitan had not received a formal appointment letter. To write one now, 'would be unusual and might interfere with other people's rights or interest[s]', a sign that Calcutta was not sure of the ramifications of such an upgrade. So Opender received a letter in which he was thanked for his role in the prevention of the *sati*, and congratulated 'upon your succession to the estates and honours of your deceased father and to assure you of my personal regards'. The letter was diplomatic impression management, it specified nothing but the existing state of affairs in Saraikela, and it left out the role of Tickell, noting instead 'the praiseworthy conduct of yourself and the other members of the family in persuading your respected mother not to yield to the first impulse of affection which induced her to wish to sacrifice her life on the funeral pile of her deceased husband.'[37] But it was not the requested appointment letter.

The principle of the *rani* going to Puri was accepted, but the means, Rs. 1,200 to 1,500, were not present. Therefore, Tickell requested Ouseley on 4 January 1840 to ask Calcutta to give 'such a sum as he might consider as sufficient' as a 'mark of their approbation'.[38]

By now, at the beginning of 1840, Tickell made preparations for his departure. First, he tried to settle a question that must have vexed him for some years. There was no tent for him in which he could hold court. So, from May 1837 on, he had used 'my own private one'. Wilkinson had already recommended to Government to purchase a tent for the sum of Rs. 230 and now Tickell asked Ouseley for it.[39]

There was one more problem which he wanted to settle. On 24 March 1840, he wrote: 'Before leaving charge of the Kolehan, I should be sorry to omit calling it to your favourable notice the claims of Madhab Chandra Chowdry, my English writer, to an increase of salary.' He felt left behind when the salary of the *peshkar* (reader), who used to get the same salary as him, was raised. Mahdab Chandra had worked well, Tickell wrote, 'a good writer and excellent accountant'. He requested an increase to Rs. 40 per month, as Chowdry was 'very much deserving of such advancement'.[40]

Tickell must already have been busy packing when a last trick came from Porahat. Mir Kumir Ud-din Hussain had, according to Tickell, embezzled the more than Rs. 600 from the mother of Arjun. He had given a detailed list of expenses, for having translations done and for his trip to Calcutta. Tickell sent the list on with the words 'the whole is a fabrication'.[41] It was a fitting farewell from the Singhs.

On 11 May 1840, Tickell was appointed as assistant to and commander of the Escort of the Resident in Nepal Brian Houghton Hodgson.[42] Hodgson had invited him, and, it seems, he had done so rather urgently. The former assistant, Ensign Hastings Young, had died on the post, and Dr Christie, probably the army surgeon, was officiating as assistant for an extra Rs. 100 per month. Hodgson suggested Tickell as his new assistant, and he got the job on the same salary as he already had, Rs. 500 per month.[43] He was in office in the Kolhan until 27 May and left on the 1st of June 1840.[44] Soon, Tickell got stuck. He reached the Nepal frontier on 14 June, but could not proceed. That was unwelcome. For one thing, it was not safe to stay in Terai, the plains south of the foothills of the Himalaya. Here a particularly dangerous fever was endemic.[45] The other reason was financial. Tickell arrived in Kathmandu only on 9 July, and Calcutta got the confirmation twenty days later. As he was supposed to draw his salary from the moment he joined his new duty, this cost him more than a month's pay. Hodgson supported his request to the government for compensation for this 'great loss' due to 'causes . . . totally out of my control'. Hodgson mentioned Tickell's 'zeal and alacrity . . . in joining the Residency at this insalubrious season'.[46]

Calcutta had foreseen the weather. Even when Tickell got his appointment to Kathmandu, the secretary to the government wrote about the 'danger which a journey through the Terai at this season would involve, and had sanctioned his [Tickell's] remaining as an assistant to the agent South West Frontier till such time as he can proceed with safety to join you [the resident at Kathmandu]'.[47]

It was not only the hot season that had held Tickell up. Just a month before, a group of Gurkhas had occupied a tract of about 520 sq. km in the Terai, containing ninety-one villages and declared it a part of Nepal.[48] They had not yet withdrawn when Tickell set out, nor when he arrived at the Nepal border. The Nepal army vacated the tract only in July.[49] The immediate political background[50] was that the senior queen in Kathmandu persecuted her junior co-queen and tried to make the king abdicate. To build up her position, the senior queen headed the party in favour of war against the East India Company. Her aim was to become the regent of her son, crown prince Surendra. To build him up, she married him to two ladies simultaneously. The wedding took place on 5 May. On 21 June 1840, the Nepalese army in Kathmandu mutinied and moved to the Residency, 6,000 men against the escort of 100 that Tickell was supposed to come to command. The army was baying for the blood of the resident Brian Houghton Hodgson. When the Nepal raja and the senior queen pointed out to them that war would mean taking on an enemy which was much more powerful, they said: 'True the English Government is great, but care the wild dogs of Nepal how large is the herd they attack? They are sure to get their bellies filled. You want no money for making war, for the war shall support itself. We will plunder Lucknow and Patna. But first we must get rid of the Resident who sees and forestalls all.'[51] On the company's side, a military intervention against Nepal was not possible; its army was engaged in the Afghan War. Through cool-headedness and threats, Hodgson managed to stave off the attack.[52]

Tickell got through to him, although he got no pay for the period till he actually reached the Residency, as 'His Lordship in Council cannot feel himself justified in making an exception in Lt. Tickell's favour.'[53] Not surprising, given that the government had warned Tickell to proceed only when it was safe to do so.

The resident and his assistant were now confined to the Residency, a building in British style with a large compound in Kathmandu.[54] They were heavily provoked by 'insolent and faithless' Gurkhas.[55] This lasted until November when, partly due to manoeuvring by the British Resident, the anti-British faction headed by the queen was defeated.[56] In December 1840, Tickell finished here his 'Excerpts from the Letters of the Resident at Kathmandu to Government from 1830 to 1840'.[57] According to the Hodgson expert, Ramesh Dhungel, 'Without missing a single principal incident, it summarises the conspiratory politics and family rivalries [which] occurred in the court of Nepal, during the decade covered by the report.'[58] A more pro-British government came in power in Kathmandu in January 1841. The next month, the senior queen went on pilgrimage to Benares. She had not taken a visa, and Hodgson got orders to make her return, after which she started her intrigues again.

In the meantime, on 11 January 1841, Tickell got an appointment for Rajputana.[59] He never went there.[60] On 17 February, he got the same post, but now in Chotanagpur. Possibly that change came after Tickell was consulted on the complicated revenue affairs of Porahat.[61] Tickell requested postponement till 15 March 1841.[62] He left Kathmandu to become Assistant, a step higher than his earlier position of Junior Assistant, in . . . the Kolhan Government Estate.

In March 1841, Tickell travelled from a pleasantly cool Kathmandu into the hot season of Chaibasa. It was not a glorious homecoming. The problems he had left behind were still there or, at least in the view of Samuel Richard, had gone worse. Hardly had he settled in, when he had to send out troops to faraway Anandpur to enforce a decision made by his predecessor. On 6 February 1841, there had been a case of Ghasi Singh of Anandpur against Ramu Singh, the uncle and guardian of the *thakur* of Anandpur. (Apparently, Abhai Singh had died.) The result was that thirty-one villages were assigned to Ghasi by Tickell's precedessor. But Ramu had not been present when the case was heard, and, worse, he could not be found. It appeared that he had gone to the agent's court in Ranchi to appeal. So the implementation of the verdict was held in abeyance until 3 April 1841, when Tickell had just arrived in Chaibasa. The son of Ghasi, Prasad Singh presented him a petition to get the official possession of the villages. At that moment, nearly two months had passed since the verdict. Tickell issued a formal order to hand over the villages to Prasad. Ramu was summoned on 30 April. Two weeks later, on 12 May, Tickell noted that Ramu Singh had refused to obey this court order. He sent out a troop of horse under Captain Armstrong to fetch Ramu Singh and bring him to his court.[63] The detachment left on 21 May but found that Ramu had absconded. He was seized shortly afterwards, and was tried for 'Contempt of Court' on 4 June. Ramu was sentenced to a fine of Rs. 200, or imprisonment of two and a half months 'without iron or labor'. Moreover, he was not allowed to reside anywhere within Porahat. His accomplices were set free with a reprimand. To explain his leniency, Tickell referred to 'their extreme and barbarous ignorance of anything relating to the nature of a Court of Justice, and of their being a wild and jungly people brought up hitherto to acknowledge no authority same [save] that of their own zamindars.'[64]

It seemed that at least with his staff Samuel Richard started at the point where he had left. His English writer, Madhab Chandra Chowdry, was still waiting for his salary rise.[65] Now there were additional reasons for more pay. The workload had become heavier, as assistants had to communicate directly with the Revenue Department. So Tickell requested an increase by Rs. 10 a month. As somebody was leaving his establishment and his replacement was cheaper, the increase for the English writer was nearly budgetary neutral. Before, in 1837, Wilkinson had envisaged the starting salary to be Rs. 25 per month, so it probably meant an increase to Rs. 35 per month.

The jail came up again, that is, the health situation of the jail continued to cause worry. Cholera had broken out, introduced by people from Mayurbhanj, who lay dead or dying in the hospital, and caused 'much filth'. This happened in May–June 1841, at the peak of the hot season, and prisoners were especially at risk. Dr Chalmers, who was responsible for the health of prisoners, asked for a sweeper for the jail and the hospital. Tickell proposed to fill the vacancy as soon as possible for Rs. 4 per month.[66]

The relations between the administration in Chaibasa and the palace in Porahat, starting from an even lower point than where the assistant had left these, went on their bitter course downwards. Arjun was still not of age, of course, and communications with Porahat were nearly severed. On 13 April, within a few weeks of his arrival, already Tickell noted that he was moving in the dark. But 'the greatest inconvenience exists at present for want of any responsible person to be the channel of communication between me & the different chiefs of Porahat, to collect the revenue, to keep me informed of all that occurs within the estate and near the person of the minor raja—and to take the general management of Police duties.' Formerly these things were done by Manguee Patnaick and Opender Bissoï, who 'for want of any remuneration for the trouble, having for some time relinquished their employments . . . as . . . agents'. Thus, 'I am now kept in perfect ignorance . . . indeed since my return. . . . Matters proceed there as if the estate had never been in ward at all.' For everything, Tickell had to send an official letter to the raja 'in the same manner as when the estate was in his own management'. So, Tickell wanted to place two people on a small salary, Rs. 20 for the two. 'One of these I should recommend to be a man from some other part of India, as less likely to take part in its numerous intrigues which the residence at Porahat of Jadunath Singh, Chandra Deo, Rudra Singh and others, will doubtless give rise to.'[67]

Tickell was at a loss what to do with the state of Porahat. At the bottom of this laid the financial difficulties of the palace. The gross annual income of Porahat was Rs. 3,230; the expenditure 'required for the raja' Rs. 2,109.[68] It looked as if there was spare money, but possibly the income part of the balance sheet was a projection. One could not count on revenue from the Hos. The 'Kol *pirs*' of

Porahat proper did not contribute much or possibly nothing at all.[69] Irregular tax income contributed to a liquidity crunch.

Tickell's predecessor, who had taken up the assistantship when he was in Kathmandu, had done his part to get the Porahat finances afloat. Tickell had informed him before he left Kathmandu, in February 1841, that much land had been frittered away on Brahmins, militia, servants and handicraftsmen, 'who pay no rent, but render such services as may be required.'[70] The tenure holders of Anandpur, Kera, Chainpur, Bandgaon, and Karaikela now brought in a Rs. 458. 4*an*.[71] The Kols in Porahat proper, about two-thirds of the population and many of these Hos,[72] still brought very little revenue to Porahat, as they were assessed 'not according to the quantity of cultivation, but . . . at so much per village in respect to its size'. It was 'a nominal tribute'.[73] The raja and his family were 'really in distress for want of ready money'. Tickell asked for instructions, he had 'good reasons to suspect that illegal contributions are being levied thro'out Porahat to meet these exigencies'. About Jadunath, he preferred to say nothing, waiting for confirmation of the reports he heard about him, but 'matters will not proceed smoothly, until he and some others are again and finally removed from Porahat'.[74] The areas under Porahat did not produce enough. And with the duo in the palace, it was trouble all the way.

The *rani* and Jadunath needed the seals of Porahat to issue orders for extra taxes, so they were ordered to give these up. Again, they played it hard, and now sent Rudra Singh and Chandra Deo to Calcutta to appeal against the order from Chaibasa. Rudra returned from Calcutta with the petition, and written on its back was an order signed by the deputy secretary to the government. That looked like a fraud or corruption, but Tickell did not say so. He merely sent it back to Calcutta, presumably for verification. Rudra Singh was arrested in Porahat and brought in on 26 May.

> He was accompanied by Jadunath Singh the minor raja's uncle, and several others of the Porahat Babus. From Rudra Singh's deposition, and from Jadunath's voluntary confession there is no longer any doubt of the connivance of the latter & of the rani in the second attempt at appealing against the orders of Govt. Indeed, Jadunath Singh states having himself sent Rudra Singh & Chandra Deo for the purpose—with having supplied them with money (in all 400 Rupees). And leaves it pretty clearly to be understood that he will still continue this Course so long as he has the means and power.[75]

Tickell was determined to stamp out this behaviour. He asked for the arrest of Chandra Deo who still was in Calcutta, and even suggested at which places in that town he might stay. As there were some charges against him, Jadunath was kept under surveillance in Chaibasa.[76] The *rani* of Porahat 'most strenuously' refused to give up the seals, and when Tickell sent someone to fetch these from her, she threatened 'to destroy herself'. So Tickell had to ask for a letter from the agent himself, he 'felt rather at a loss' to deal with this 'most head strong and perverse woman'.[77]

Except for warding off outside interference, it is not clear what the *rani* and Jadunath really wanted. At no place in the sources can we find an indication of a program of state-building or of economic development for its less than 25,000 subjects.[78] It looked like a struggle to keep the palace itself going. Tickell got things a bit on track. Already the Porahat court had changed an irregular tax levy, twice a year and measured in handfuls of rice and salt, into a yearly levy of half a rupee per village. Tickell changed that into half a rupee per plough.[79] A few years later, in 1845, Arjun could start his rule with an annual income from rents of Rs. 6,004.[80]

To all these delaying tactics of the Singhs were added the tax evasions by the Hos. Tickell, as we have seen, considered his ability to prevent tax evasion as a measure of his success in dealing with the Hos. The next few letters, the last ones we get from Tickell on the Hos, were surprising. Something had gone wrong between the assistant and the people of Hodisum, now indicated not as 'Hos' but as 'Koles'. His letters of July 1841, four months after he came back, deserve to be quoted here quite extensively. 'The season having arrived for assessing the Kolehan for the year 1841/42', he asked whether he could double the rate of assessment to 1 rupee per plough.

> Although the amount of revenue to be derived from the Kolehan is not any object with Government, yet I am inclined to recommend the increase of the present nominal rent imposed on the Koles, as I think it is the only means of stirring into some slight degree of industry, one of the idlest races to be met perhaps in India.
>
> Large tracts of highly arable land remain in possession of the Koles from generation to generation, of which not about a third or a half, in many places is cultivated, but which they will allow no strangers or others to rent from them for any time, even with the express stipulation that when the owner of the soil has the means of sowing it, he is to retake the land into his possession.
>
> The small amount of revenue payable, makes the Kole indifferent to the nature & quantity of his crops, so as he has sufficient grown for the next years' food, with a small surplus for the succeeding crop. And in this manner tracts of land remain fallow and overrun by jungle, which might easily be reclaimed, if the owner had to pay a tax he must provide, in some way, against.
>
> It is notorious that the Koles are utterly indifferent to money, unless it can be procured without the least trouble. They sell nothing willingly, nor do any work from year's end to year's end, with the exception of sowing a little land for actual food for themselves. So that it is difficult to procure the commonest necessary, or the simplest hired labour for money. And the troops, as well as all other residents in the Civil & military station of Chaibasa, are obliged to depend for everything, on Hazaribagh, Bankura &ca. in the same manner as when the station was first established.
>
> I think making the Koles feel, a little, the <u>value</u> of money would ameliorate this.[81]

This was rage from rejection. Tickell had come back to a place he had loved less than one year before, as witness the pages of his Hodésum articles. Now he was exasperated.

A few weeks later, Tickell virtually admitted the breakdown of his communications with the Hos.

> I have the honour to have received your letter . . . and to state in reply that it would be impossible for me to say what would be the immediate effects of doubling the assessment of the Kolehan. Although I cannot but be of opinion that the ulterior results would be advantageous in promoting the civilization of these people. It is very possible that some uproar might be the consequence, but if this reason is, of itself sufficient to put a stop to the proposal referred to, the Koles must ever remain in the same condition as at present and that, instead of improving, is, I am inclined to think, retrograding, or at least relapsing into its former state.[82]

Samuel Richard Tickell had had it with the Hos, it seemed, and may the devil take the consequences. He did not even care to find out how the Hos would take this increase.

But the government did. That year 1841–42 saw a realised revenue of Rs. 6,252, an increase of Rs. 177 over the preceding year, or a mere 2.9 per cent.[83] Apparently, whatever the Hos knew about the value of their money, they were not ready to part with it. And Tickell got a rare dressing-down. As the Board of Control wrote to Calcutta in December 1842, reacting to an earlier despatch from Calcutta, 'We entirely approve of your having declined to accede to the proposals of Lieutenant Tickell for raising the rate of assessment by the Coles from half a Rupee to one Rupee per plough'. In effect, the reasons for this refusal were derived from the descriptions by Tickell himself: the people were too poor, they would not like to work more simply to be able to pay taxes, and the result would be discontent instead of 'a gradual introduction of settled habits',[84] and the taste for luxuries the market could offer them. The Court wrote:

> It is probable as stated by him [Tickell], that they are much more lightly taxed than some of their less barbarous neighbours but in their present state of wildness and ignorance of which his report affords the strongest evidence, our efforts should be directed rather towards the maintenance of peace and order and the gradual introduction of settled habits, and of a taste for the comforts and luxuries of civilized life than the increase of the revenue derived from them, and we cannot believe that the measure which he recommends would have had the effect which he anticipates, that of promoting a spirit of industry among a people whom he describes to be the most disinclined to labour of any in India, merely by rendering it necessary that they should cultivate more land for the purpose of paying the increased Government Revenue out of the profits, but that on the contrary, the attempt would be more likely to incite a degree of disaffection and resistance which it might be difficult to overcome.[85]

So that was the result of Samuel Richard's raging disappointment, the rambling sentences, the line under <u>value</u>. Emotions are not a good base for policy proposals. Tickell's idea to force the Hos into the market by higher taxes was shot down.

It had been a horrible hot season. You cannot step into the same river twice.

That winter, we do not hear any more about twilights enjoyed in the villages. His evenings in the assistant's bungalow were silent. 'The voice of the Oral [flying squirrel] . . . is a weak, low soft monotone quickly repeated—so low, in the same room you require to listen attentively to distinguish it.' Adding, perhaps wistfully, 'It is to the Koles, a sound ominous of domestic afflictions, and one of the signs they regard much in their marriage negotiations, so this pretty gentle creature gets a bad name . . . . Its nature is gentle and slothful.'[86]

Tickell spent his time in the jungle to collect—or shoot—animals at a furious pace. On 19 January 1842, he wrote to the Asiatic Society that Gomes, his taxidermist in Chaibasa, had got fever and would leave. Tickell asked the society for his pay, Rs. 168 1*an*. Tickell had spent a considerable amount, especially if set off against his income of Rs. 500 per month. He sent Gomes with a chest to the Asiatic Society.[87] It was opened with some awe. In it, the curator of the museum Edward Blyth found some twenty skins ranging from bats to an antelope, but more importantly 120 skins of birds belonging to eighty-one species, of which twenty-seven were new to the Society's collection. In addition, he could announce that Tickell had sent the prepared skin of a 'magnificent' Gaur, with a list of measurements taken directly from the animal. It would immediately be set up for exhibition. As Blyth added in a note when his monthly report was printed, that it had 'succeeded beyond expectations.'[88] In Chaibasa, Tickell did not expect much from more hunts. He had taken a new taxidermist, a Muslim, 'to preserve whatever I can pick up in my rambles'. Also technically, it was a try out: 'He gets now 5 Rs. a month, and has been promised more when he thoroughly knows his work; but in case of my not being successful in obtaining really valuable specimens, I shall not expect the Society to remunerate me for this expence, as it is a very trifling one.'[89] The gain was for the Asiatic Society's museum in Calcutta. In Chaibasa Tickell was cleaning his house.

Early in 1842, Tickell made his last annual tour to Saranda *pir*, the largest and least known of Hodisum's *pirs*. The *pir* had been brought to his special attention in July the year before, and Tickell had complained about 'the great difficulty I experienced in obtaining any knowledge of what occurred . . . and in investigating any complaints or cases originating in that place, owing to the distance to my court.' Moreover, in the whole place there was but one 'civilized man', Dasu Babu, who controlled the peasants and the 'Koles' living near him. So complaints against him were not likely.[90]

Not far from Saranda *pir*, he 'came upon a set of people . . . whose existence I only then for the first time ascertained'. They were 250–300 Bendkars, a people living in Keonjhar, in a small range of hills close to Jamda *pir* of the Kolhan. Tickell sent one of his party 'with money and fair speeches' to the Bendkars, and six of them came to his camp in Saranda *pir*, three men, an old woman and a boy and a girl, 'the two latter were pretty'. In general, they were 'tolerably fair, well-made and not devoid of intelligence'. Their housing consisted of 'mere hovels formed of branches, leaves and thatched with jungle grass'. They had some poultry, and got their food by 'grubbing in the jungle for roots, berries, hay, leaves of some species of trees'. They also had miserable crops of rice, *gora dhan* (coarse rice), gram, and maize.[91] Tickell questioned them 'minutely' on 'their manner, customs &c.' and found these similar to those of 'other Semi-Hindoo tribes', such as Bhumij, Bhuiyas and Santhals. However, their 'excessive seclusion' made them 'purely savage'. They did not even know the word 'saheb', the usual term for an Englishman. But from Tickell's information, their isolation was not absolute. They spoke both Ho and Odia, and were obliged to carry the baggage of Keonjhar's *divan* when he went on his annual visit to Puri. From these visits, some Bendkars knew the use of money. But normally, or rather occasionally, they went to the nearest villages to barter their modest produce for cloth. They had never seen a 'white face'. Everything was new to them, the tents, the horses, the elephants, the soldiers and the cavalry. Tickell found them 'pleasing in appearance, clean in person, and decorous in manner', perhaps also because his favourite trick had worked well. To their 'great astonishment and delight', Tickell gave 'the grand exhibition of a bird shot while flying past'.[92]

On 18 February 1842, for the last time, Tickell enjoyed the moonlit nights of the Hodisum jungle (see Plate 10). He noted the Cooing Hawk Owl

> perching on the summits of the highest trees, especially on the dead limbs of the Saul, which in places where clearings have been commenced, are ringed and burnt preparatory to felling by the settlers, with skeleton arms flung high over the surrounding jungle. On such elevated spot of a clear moonlit night, this bird perches, uttering its melancholy monotonous notes . . . repeated deliberately and softly with a mellow sweet intonation, and interrupted occasionally to make sallies into the air after large moths or beetles, . . . while

the forest seems to sleep in the moonlight, and no sounds reaches the ear, but the whispering rustle of leaves, stirred by the night air, some remote glade sends faintly back an answering cry; and thus the dialogue continues till signs of the coming morning appear.

In the cold season of 1842, when encamped at Urkia, in Saranda pir (Singhbhum) I often remained till after night fall, poling in a 'donga' or canoe along the Koël, for the chance of a shot at some one of the many animals that nightly drank its waters, and at such times the voice of this owl was the only sound that varied the ripple of the stream as from either shore they called to each other, like guardians of the sleeping woods.

It put him in a rare mood of contemplation.

These forests extend in unbroken solitude—save here and there where the wandering Santhals or Bhumijes have made a wretched little clearing—from the southerly parts of Singhbhum thro' Keonjhar & west of Sambalpur, the Gaur, the Urna, the Sambur, the Elephant, the Tiger, various species of deer, and packs of the wild dog find safe and unmolested shelter. Through such realm of shade and silence the Koël winds it's crystal waters, which here and there, hollowing out deep rocky pools, give shelter to huge alligators, and the banks during the mornings are enlivened by countless varieties of birds. These are indeed the dominions of nature; and the mind wonders that in the world so many centuries old, and tenanted by so many millions of restlessly exploring beings, there should be such vast tracts totally unknown![93]

It betrayed a deep sense of a world too big for one man. The river scene was a memory, too. Two years before, when he was preparing for Kathmandu, Tickell had described the Baitarani River, 'every wind of whose stream would be a subject for the artist's pencil, or the poet's pen, runs its crystal waters through . . . the vastness of canopying trees, and the luxuriance of wild vegetations'.[94] At that time, the beauties of nature and the sound of birds did not lead him on to musing about his place in this world, but to the more immediate urge to consider the 'poet's pen' he thought he did not have. Tickell had made up his mind. He had entered 'one uninterrupted sea of jungle, bounded to the N. and N.E. by the cultivated lands and villages of the Hos in Kotgarh and Bar pir', but, as he had to admit, 'whose limits in other directions have not been, nor probably ever will be, defined'.[95] He had gone as far as he could. It was over.[96]

There was nothing left but to pack. And to receive farewell gifts. In March, when Tickell was 'just about to leave' Hodisum for the second time, some Hos brought him a living pangolin, a *Manis crassicaudata*. It was caught on a hill 'at some distance from Chaibasa'. He had seen only two living specimens before. The young Lieutenant's meticulous scientific interest in this anteater must have caused considerable merriment to the onlookers, as its flesh was considered an aphrodisiac.[97] It was a farewell gift, and it struck the right chord. Tickell took it with him when he left. The poor animal was carried with his luggage and died 'after much protracted suffering . . . during the night of his fifth day'. He wrote a fond goodbye to it—in the shape of a scientific article, of course—when he arrived in Calcutta.[98]

...

Afterglow: A Complete History of Indian Birds

...

*Life after the Hodisum; the illustrated manuscript volumes;
Tickell as a painter and ornithologist; what about the 'Memoir'?*

From May 1842 until February 1843, Tickell spent his leave on the Cape in South Africa. He returned to the South West Frontier Agency as Junior Assistant in March 1843, perhaps just in time to say goodbye to his mother and her husband George King, who retired. We have a pictorial witness of his last stay in Chaibasa in one of Tickell's most puzzling paintings, the *Halcyon smyrnensis* or White-throated Kingfisher.[1] He had sighted the bird in Chaibasa on 2 April 1843. The painting itself was dated 25 February 1868. It showed the kingfisher sitting on a branch and overlooking a pool with lotuses and some ducks, with a steep bank. On a flat piece of land on the other shore, a few mud houses stood close together. Two women, each in a white sari and carrying a water-pot on her head, walk away from us. Next to the women is a man sitting, relieving himself. In the background, we see a Gothic or neo-Gothic church tower in the style of Canterbury cathedral. This picture was certainly composed; there was no church in Chaibasa. The stone structure contrasted with the simple buildings of the village. In November 1843, Tickell left for the second time, to become First Class Assistant in nearby Purulia, also known as Manbhum. The only living thing that reminded him of Hodisum was a parakeet, which was to stay with him till 1858. He honoured him with a painting made in 1869, four years into his retirement on the Channel Island of Jersey.

Before he took up his post in Manbhum, Tickell went to Darjeeling in November 1843. This we know from his paintings of birds which he had spotted and/or killed at the time in the area, and from his article 'Notes on a curious species of Tiger or Jaguar, killed near the Snowy Range, North of Darjeeling' which was published in the same year. From nothing more than the skin of an animal killed by others, he drew the animal in the following way. He took 'careful measurements, protracted on a scale', to give 'a tolerable approximation to true proportions and general aspect, and the markings of the skin are faithfully delineated, as well as the color of the fur carefully described'. In hindsight, we know it must have been a snow leopard. The lithograph of the drawing was shown on a meeting of the Society, where 'as the work of a native artist, its extreme fidelity was much admired'.[2]

So we know that he went to Darjeeling, a bit of what he did, but why did Tickell not go to Hodgson in Nepal? It was difficult to enter the Nepal kingdom and, anyway, Hodgson was preparing to leave his post. He had been sidelined by the governor general. He would depart from Kathmandu in December 1843 and went on to England in February the next year.[3] Tickell visited Calcutta, probably to say goodbye to Hodgson, in January, possibly February 1844. We have a description of Calcutta. Again, the birds were prominent as the vehicle of the mood of the officer, even on this visit to the centre of power, even at the farewell.

> As day breaks over the foggy, chilly street, the kites may be seen one by one lazily waking, and floating off into the air from their roosting places, on the roofs of the great houses in Chowrunghee, Govt. House place, Tank square, &ca. They seem there to be merely stretching themselves & looking about for the best foraging places . . . till the sun breaks up the fleecy pall that lays over the Maidan. Gentlemen and ladies return to shelter before the sun becomes disagreeable. The streets become thronged, the breakfast hour approaches. And the kites, punctual to that social meal, gather in numbers by every kitchen whence savoury odours are issuing. As the cook throws out refuse . . . down swoop the kites 'ere each morsel has well reached the ground and fly off, fighting for the prize in their claws.[4]

In July 1844, at the age of thirty-two, he married Maria Georgiana, the nineteen years old second daughter of John William Templer, in Bankura.[5] Tickell knew the family. They were stationed in Monghyr, a 170 km to the east of Patna, when Bishop Heber met the father in the 1820s.[6] Georgina's mother had died a few months before the wedding.[7] We see the new couple's living circumstances in one of Tickell's most optimistic paintings: a garden in bloom, some gardeners drawing water from the well, and as a sign of what his career could bring, a spacious bungalow in the background. Their first child, Maria Louise, was born in 1845 in Burdwan.[8]

Due to his heavy workload, Tickell was ordered to transfer, at least temporarily, the superintendence of the Dhalbhum estate to the assistant in Singhbhum in 1845.[9] As Ouseley foresaw at the time, it was not a temporary measure. Dhalbhum became part of the later Singhbhum District and now forms the district of East Singhbhum.

In 1847, Tickell left the Jharkhand area to pursue his career in Burma. He became assistant to the commissioner of Arakan. But Tickell went to Bhagalpur in March 1848, to stand in for Sherwill as revenue surveyor, and for the demarcation of the Daman-i-Koh. But he concentrated on his administrative duties and left the actual survey work to his assistants. That proved no success. He handed over in September.[10] In the same year, he might have visited Calcutta to see the prime minister of Nepal Jung Bahadur Rana who was on his way to England. He presented him with a painting of the conclusion of the Treaty of Sugauli in 1816. The painting was idealised, but the landscape was real; Tickell might well have sketched it when he was held up at Nepal's border in June 1840.[11]

Tickell returned to Arakan as Principal Assistant.[12] His eldest son Arthur Templer was born in 1850 and died 1852, just two years old. A bit surprisingly, from his paintings we find Tickell in March–June 1850 hunting birds and sketching landscapes in the Chotanagpur area, mostly in Hazaribagh, during what could have been a break from his Arakan duties. In a list of the birds of

Chotanagpur, Valentine Ball mentioned sixteen species discovered or claimed by Tickell.[13] That was Tickell's last known appearance in the area.

On 30 December 1852, just as the Second Anglo-Burmese War was drawing to a close, he was appointed principal assistant to the commissioner of the Tenasserim and Martaban Provinces; in 1855, he became commissioner of the same.[14] Here, in Moulmein, were born Morris, who lived only five months in 1853, and a still born child in 1854. Finally in 1855, Ada Elizabeth Tickell was born, who lived till 1947.[15] Three out of five children dead within ten years must have been an enormous strain on Tickell. From his own rare family sketches, admittedly not always the most convincing evidence, he was a family man. In 1856, Tickell went on a sick leave and in 1857–58 he was on fifteen months furlough without pay in England.[16] His youngest child, George Templer, was born on 28 August 1858 in Moulmein.[17]

After he left Hodisum, Tickell published ten more articles in the *Journal of the Asiatic Society of Bengal*, of which only three were on non-zoological subjects. Of these, his 1861 'Memoranda Relative to Three Andamanese', published in 1864, has some anthropological fame. This is also due to its exotic subjects. It is a fairly detailed and sympathetic description of three Andamanese in his care in the months May and June or July 1861. When they were handed to Tickell, they were in poor health and looked miserable, but cheered up, although one of them died. They never learned English and took everything in peacefully. They were overjoyed when they realised they were to be sent back home and when they were put on shore 'quickly vanished into the jungle!' Indeed, Tickell noted with great foresight,

> The experiment of civilizing these two, by weaning them from their wild habits and creating artificial wants . . . and thus form as it were the nucleus of increasing intercourse with a superior race, has certainly failed. . . . Indeed . . . , we may surmise that the colonization of the Andaman islands, when its spread begins to interfere with the aborigines, will tend rather to the extermination of the latter, than to any amelioration in their conditions.[18]

Tickell became Commissioner of Pegu in Burma in 1863. He retired at the rank of Lieutenant Colonel on 24 January 1865, sixteen days short of thirty-five years after he had come back to India.

At first, Tickell settled on the Channel Island of Jersey,[19] working at what must have been a great pace on his notes and paintings of birds, fishes and animals (see Plate 12). He had gathered material from the early 1830s on; most of it was from his Burmese period. He published many of these notes in *The Field, the Farm, the Garden: The Country Gentleman's Newspaper*. He signed the articles on game birds and wildfowl as 'Ornithognomon', and those on sport and natural history as 'Old Log'.[20]

In 1870, his eyes became inflamed during a fishing trip off the coast of Brittany. After 1871, he with his daughter Ada Elizabeth and his wife Georgiana moved to Cheltenham.[21] Tickell lost the sight in one eye first, and later in the other eye, too. In August 1873, when he wrote the binding instructions to one of his notebooks, he could still see. The last year of his life was of great suffering—and of clearing his affairs. He sold the Gainsborough painting of his grandfather Richard Tickell on 2 May 1874.[22] He donated six volumes of notes and drawings to the Zoological Society of London.[23] Samuel Richard Tickell died on 20 April 1875, as the twenty-year-old Ada who was present at the death registered with a daughter's concern, of 'exhaustion'.[24] He was sixty-four years old.

Tickell left behind a mass of papers and drawings. One year after his death, Arthur Walden was 'favoured by General Boyd and the Revd E. A. Tickell with an opportunity of examining all the original drawings and notes in their possession from which Colonel Tickell elaborated the more complete work under notice. They are bound up in two folio and three quarto volumes.'[25] Again two years later, Reverend Edward Arthur Tickell, Vicar of Ulrome,[26] came to the Zoological Society of London. He was bringing Samuel Richard Tickell's work to the place where they might be the most useful. He donated 'two folio and two quarto original illustrated manuscript volumes of the "Birds of India", by the late Colonel S. R. Tickell'.[27]

These donations were added to the earlier donation by order of Samuel Richard Tickell himself, of an illustrated manuscript work on the ornithology of India in seven small folio volumes, with 261 plates of birds (illustrating 276 species), descriptions of 448 species, and 5 plates containing illustrations of eggs of 42 species.[28] Some subjects required more than one physical volume. So now rests in the library of the Zoological Society a massive unpublished work of 2132 manuscript pages in fourteen volumes, of which eleven are on birds, one each on mammals, fishes and 'Reptiles, &ca', of British India. To date, these have been accessed only by the cognoscenti, mainly ornithologists.[29]

The volumes had grown out of an abandoned project with his friend Edward Blyth, Curator of the Indian Museum in Calcutta from 1841–62, to whom Tickell regularly had sent bird skins. The two had planned to do an illustrated work on Indian natural history together. But they fell out when Blyth published some of Tickell's findings first and named some of the species after himself.

The amount of work involved is astonishing, the more so, as we may suppose that the books were written after his retirement.

> The whole of the letter-press is most neatly written by hand. The characters of the orders, families, and genera Colonel Tickell adopts are given in detail; and each genus is illustrated by accurately drawn outlines showing, in most instances, the bill, feet, and wing-structure. These outlines are drawn with the very greatest care, and in each case to scale, and not by eye alone. Every species personally known to the author is figured . . . . It is a sad reflection that ill health prevented so much patient industry, so much unostentatious labour, so much artistic skill, so much enthusiasm in the good cause, so great a fidelity to nature, from being rewarded with that universal approbation publication would undoubtedly have secured.[30]

Tickell's manuscripts were based on many years of patient work on notes and drawings. As Walden noted, 'Being gifted with a ready pencil and a facile brush, Colonel Tickell, in most instances, made coloured drawings of the animals he secured; and in the course of time he had accumulated many drawings, together with copious notes relating to the species he had captured or observed.'[31] Some of his first efforts were lost, including several sketches. Tickell himself, a careful man who strove for completeness, mentioned it a few times: 'A drawing made of it at the time was lost by the sinking of my boat in the Ganges; and I have never met with the bird again.'[32] And again, 'the (by me supposed) young [bird] I lost my notes and drawing of; but a slight description was sent by me, in a "List of Birds collected in the Jungle Mahals," to the Journal of the Asiatic Society of Bengal in 1833'.[33]

How much Tickell wanted his work to be printed can be gauged from his precise instructions for the binding of the manuscripts on 17 August 1873. Sadly, the binding was not faultless. Walden noted that 'the subjects of the plates do not always belong to the subjects of the letterpress'.[34]

Tickell had intended his work to be a 'complete history of the Indian avifauna'.[35] He achieved a lot. There are 647 watercolour paintings in the volumes, and more are in the family's possession. He described 724 species of birds, accompanied by 501 colour paintings.[36] Of these, there are only about forty on birds and places of Chotanagpur, and twenty-two of these show village scenes in the background. No sightings made in Chotanagpur after 1850 are mentioned. In addition, scattered in the books are 100-odd vignettes. These are mostly snapshots of his immediate surroundings.

Tickell, as far as we know, never disclosed the source of his love of ornithology, nor did he mention his teacher or teachers of painting. In Nepal, he did paint, but unlike in his later work, the background of the birds is simple, just a branch or trunk with some leaves.[37] Add to that that Tickell became much more productive after he returned from his break of 1842–43 in South Africa and one might guess that he honed his painting skills there. Neither does Tickell explicitly indicate which painters had influenced him. One can point to some obvious examples which guided him in his efforts. On the British side, there were the illustrated bird books. One was by William Yarrell, *A History of British Birds*, serialised from 1837 to1841, and published in three volumes in 1843.[38] The second example was the two volumes by Thomas Bewick, with the same title *A History of British Birds*, and published in 1779–1804.[39] It is the last one that was closest to Tickell's in spirit and execution and he regularly referred to it. Tickell's paintings of birds had the advantage that they were in colour.[40]

On the Indian side, the influence on Tickell's painting came from Patna. Here, Charles D'Oyly and Christopher Webb Smith established 'The Behar Amateur Lithographic Press', and published, more for their pleasure, it seems, than for profit, two richly illustrated books on birds in India. The 1828 *Feathered Game of Hindostan* had twelve hand-coloured lithographed subjects with uncoloured backgrounds. The birds were drawn by Webb, and D'Oyly provided the landscapes. *Oriental Ornithology*, likewise with twelve hand-coloured lithographic plates appeared the next year. These works were certainly seen by Tickell when he visited his mother after his return from England in 1830. On that occasion, he might have met D'Oyly and Webb. If so, he must have seen their other works, like the *Birds of India*, with 295 watercolours and the companion volume with manuscript descriptions, *Notes on the Birds of India*. These were made between 1815 and 1830. Between 1829 and 1831, the pair made another 191 watercolours of birds.[41] The backgrounds made by D'Oyly vivid but have much less impact than Tickell's.

Tickell's birds, on the other hand, were rather stiff. His probable modus operandi was to shoot the birds, skin them, have them stuffed and then paint watercolours of the birds, which he put in settings taken from his sketches. So most of Tickell's birds were sitting still. Even then, Tickell got a very good press. Arthur Walden, who described the paintings held by the Zoological Society, remarked, 'many of the plates are works of art. It may be affirmed that nearly all are good, and that many are almost perfection.'[42]

> The attractiveness of the plates is moreover much enhanced by the backgrounds in which the figures are set. A knowledge of the haunts and habits of each species can almost be acquired by studying the accessories of each figure. Every plate is a highly finished landscape, true to nature, often enlivened by scenes from everyday life in India, either in the plains or in the jungle, in town or in cantonments.
>
> After the monotonous uniformity of the conventional backgrounds of illustrated English ornithological works, it is a relief and a pleasure to find every bird surrounded by real leaves, pecking at real flowers, or climbing real trees, or with real Indian buildings and Indian animals in the distance.[43]

In short, the few who had seen them recognised the manuscripts as 'Colonel Tickell's beautiful work'.[44]

Samuel Richard Tickell stood out in painting and sketching people in the countryside and villages. Tickell's paintings are the first pictorial representations of many areas of Jharkhand. We encounter a very observant Tickell. With great delicacy, he painted as his birds might have seen it, looking from high. We get to see the army marching into Chaibasa, the smoke of the clearings in the forests, and most of all people, often very small by distance, resting in the shade of huge trees, travelling over a country road.

It has to be noted that the actual paintings were made after Tickell's retirement, and hence years after he had witnessed the scenes. Many paintings were compositions of several drawings. Some scenes, like a small group of people chatting just outside Tickell's tent, reappeared several times. The church that Tickell put in Chaibasa certainly did not stand there. At least one vignette depicted a human sacrifice, a Meriah, a scene that was not witnessed by Tickell.

Tickell's vignettes were less elaborate than the more famous ones of Bewick.[45] Still, most of his more than 100 vignettes were very vivid, many were executed with sensitivity, and some with compassion.

> But as if his beautiful drawings were not a sufficient adornment to the work, Colonel Tickell has appended to most of the pages descriptive of the general small oval vignettes, done in Indian ink,
>
> ... scene after scene recalling to the Anglo-Indian at home memories of his Indian sojourn.[46]

In 1876, Walden remarked in his overview that Tickell belonged to 'that band of zoologists who, more than forty years ago, commenced in India the then much neglected study of natural history'.[47] Through his articles in the *Journal of the Asiatic Society* and in *The Ibis*, Tickell was in contact with all the major people interested in the birds of India. His main contacts were inside India. As we have seen, he frequently contributed specimens to the Museum of the Asiatic Society.[48] Its curator, Edward Blyth, corresponded with Charles Darwin, who was preparing his *The Origin of Species by Natural Selection,* and drew his attention to Tickell's work with a quote from Tickell's letter of 29 August 1855 on the Burmese otters, rabbits and geese.[49] Tickell corresponded with the ornithologist Allan Octavian Hume, who was to become one of the founders of the Indian National Congress in 1885.

Tickell was an ornithological pioneer, who added his name to seven birds—and at least one mammal.[50] The mammal is the Indian pygmy pipistrell (*Hesperoptenos Tickelli*). The birds are

Tickell's blue flycatcher (*Cyornis Tickelliae*), Tickell's thrush (*Turdus unicolor*), Tickell's flowerpecker (*Dicaeum erythrorhyncos T.*), Tickell's leaf warbler (*Phylloscopus affinis*), Tickell's hornbill (*Ptylomaemus Tickelli*), Tickell's brown or wreathed hornbill (*Anorrhinus Tickelli*), and the buff-breasted babbler (*Trichastoma* or *Pellorneum Tickelli*).

The meticulous precision and methodical dedication that made him Wilkinson's choice did not stand in Tickell's way of being a good writer. In the notes accompanying his paintings, he was, when he wanted, able to evoke scenery and people with astonishing vividness. Tickell was an English gentleman 'in the deep recesses of a strange country'.[51] His favourite pastime, sports, was in line with his interest in wildlife, the more intellectual break from his official work. The zoological manuscripts were an enormous work, which he concluded with a lead pencil remark: 'And thus end the lucubrations of five&thirty years!'

We are still missing a volume. In 1876, Arthur Walden had seen three notebooks. In 1877, Edward Tickell had brought two notebooks with drawings to the Zoological Society. There was another notebook extant. It had remained with Samuel Richard's daughter Ada Elisabeth. She probably brought it with her in 1881 when she married Benjamin Charles Scott, vice-consul in China at the time, in Strand, London.[52] The couple was back in England in 1911 and lived in Ealing with Ada's mother Georgiana and Ada's widowed sister, Mary Louisa Cooper.[53] Georgiana Tickell died in 1918; Mary Louisa in 1938; Ada continued to live in the same house. At the age of ninety-two, probably in the year that she died, she donated the small volume to the Natural History Museum. It was 15 May 1947, exactly three months from India's Independence.[54]

So that seemed to be it. Samuel Richard Tickell's magnum opus of twelve volumes lies buried in the archives; one small volume in the National History Museum in London, the other volumes, massive, handwritten and with original paintings, in the Zoological Society of London. Ornithologists remember him. Tickell was one of them. His 'Memoir on the Hodésum' with its descriptions of Ho society and culture did not fare particularly well.[55] In the late 1860s and in 1872, Edward Tuite Dalton used it, added significantly to it, and took over as the ethnologist of the Hos.[56] Tickell's hunting scene survived up to 1958 in P. C. Roy Chaudhury's Singhbhum Gazetteer as an 'amusing account'.[57] In post-Independence Ho historiography, Tickell's ethnographic contribution is mentioned only in passing.[58]

I was baffled. The 'Memoir on the Hodésum', the one article of the three treating the Hos that got some attention, was vivid and intimate, and at places even emotional.[59] It was written with great confidence. Something was missing. Were there no private papers, letters, notes left? With his descendants, I found some more paintings, and a few photographs from the period after his stay in the Hodisum, mainly of his wife and children. I spent endless evenings on the Internet trying to get anything from anywhere. But 'the door was always open'.[60] When I went back to Tickell's other articles in the very volume of the *Journal of the Asiatic Society of Bengal* in which the 'Memoir' was published, I was dumbfounded. Here, in the 'Grammar' and the 'Vocabulary', which I had glossed over, was page after page of verbatim recordings of his conversations in both Ho and English.[61] It appeared that Tickell had a lively contact with the Hos—and that they actually had told him a lot.

Part IV
Tickell's Hodésum Articles of 1840

Chapter 12

The Rude Forefathers

...
Family stories: to be young was very heaven;
Samuel Richard in London, Addiscombe and Patna;
the jungle of Dhalbhum
...

At first sight, Samuel Richard Tickell's family background, the more distant one of the late-eighteenth century of the theatre and music world of Bath and London and the closer one of the small British society of Patna in the 1810s, had little to prepare him to get along with the Hos. Or did it? Samuel Richard was born in Cuttack in 1811.[1] He was one generation removed from the Linley-Sheridan-Tickell clan iof the theatre world of Bath and London in the late eighteenth century. His father was Samuel Tickell (1785–1817).

When Samuel *père* was just two years old, his mother, the famous singer Mary Linley, died. He grew up in the family of his mother's equally famous sister Elizabeth Anne and his uncle Richard Brinsley Sheridan. When he was eight years old, his father, our Samuel Richard's grandfather, died. He became a cadet in 1800, and the next year, at the age of sixteen, Samuel arrived in India. Ten years later, he married Mary Morris.[2] In 1811, when his eldest Samuel Richard was born, Samuel was Adjutant. After Samuel Richard came Henry Porcher (1813), William Linley (1814) and Mary Rose (1815). Samuel took part in the Nepal War of 1814–15, and rose to become Captain. From 1815, when Samuel Richard was four years old, his father was stationed in Danapur close to Patna. His young brother, William Linley Tickell, died there in November, just eleven months old, and Henry Porcher in 1816. In 1817, Edward Lawrence was born.[3] Three and a half months later, in October 1817, his father Samuel Tickell died 'on the river' close to Ghazipur.[4] He died before he could pass on much to his son, Samuel Richard. He did leave behind a scrapbook filled with poems of family members, his own memorial poems including one on the occasion of his wedding anniversary, and a long poem in which Samuel transposed the story of the Good Samaritan to a setting on the road from Cuttack.[5] Samuel Richard was six years old when he was left with his mother, sister and brother.

The normal age for boys to go and get his education at home, in England that is, was about six or seven years old. This was also considered necessary to get a British accent, or even to learn to speak English properly, as small children tended to take the language of their nurse as their first language. So, sometime between 1817 and 1823, Samuel Richard set out from the bungalows of Danapur and the small English establishment of Patna[6] to go to London.

In England, he got the stories of his family by climbing the stairs of St. James' Palace where his aunt Elizabeth Anne Tickell (1781-1860) was living with Anne Boscawen (1745–1831), who at one time was engaged to his grandfather Richard Tickell. Another rich source of family lore was William Linley, who after two stints in India was living the life of a gentleman in London, deeply devoted to music, especially by Purcell and Handel.[7] As the last surviving member of the musical Linley family, he kept the most important paintings of his—and Samuel Richard's—family.[8] Together, they had a stream of stories and anecdotes about Samuel Richard's grandfather, the playwright Richard Tickell (1751–1793) and his bosom friend, the famous poet, theatre owner and radical parliamentarian Richard Brinsley Sheridan. These were tales of arranged marriage, dowry, pride, love, cover-ups and the ultimate adolescent rebellion, elopement.

The family bond between the two friends were the Linleys of Bath. In this Georgian period, Bath was one of the larger towns of England and rapidly expanding. It was second only to London as a centre of music, theatre, and painting. Thomas Linley the elder (1733–95) was a composer, a musician and the father of a musical family. His most gifted child was Thomas Linley the younger (1756–78), composer and violinist, known as the English Mozart. Like Wolfgang Amadeus Mozart, he was a child prodigy. In 1770, the two met in Italy and became friends. In 1778, Thomas drowned in a storm.[9] His compositions are still regularly performed. His sisters Elizabeth Anne (1754–92) and Mary (1758–87), both singers, were known as 'the fairies of Bath' and it is these we see on the 1772 Gainsborough painting 'The Linley Sisters'. Mary, the future grandmother of Samuel Richard Tickell, is seated and looks straight at the viewer.[10]

The standing fairy, Elizabeth Anne, was the prima donna of her father's concerts and had many suitors. Her parents arranged to marry the young girl off to an elderly but rich suitor, one Mr Long. She was sixteen at the time, and her husband-to-be was sixty. Elizabeth Anne wrote him a letter, however, in which she broke off the engagement, a move the other party understood. Her father, who did not know about the letter, threatened to persecute Long for breach of contract. Elizabeth became ill with worry, but Mr Long solved the question by settling 3,000 pounds on her, and by insisting that she kept his gifts of jewellery to the value of another 1,000 pounds.[11]

Elizabeth Anne, now with fortune added to beauty, continued to be much sought after. Among her suitors was a most insistent Major Mathews, according to the Victorian biographer Willing, 'a scoundrel and a married man'.[12] In Bath, he posed as a bachelor. When he did not get his way, he first threatened to take his own life; when that did not work, he threatened to spread slanders about her. Elizabeth did not dare to inform her parents. Instead, she confided in her lady friend, who persuaded her twenty-one-year-old brother—and secret admirer of Elizabeth—Richard Brinsley Sheridan to help

Elizabeth Anne to elope to France. The sister arranged a place to stay in France and a ship to get there. Sheridan and Elizabeth Anne Linley set off in March 1772. Her original plan was to enter a nunnery in France till she would come of age; at the time, Elizabeth was eighteen.

On arrival in France, Sheridan followed his heart—and used some persuasion. He insisted to Elizabeth that her reputation would be ruined if her elopement became known and persuaded her to marry him. Sheridan and Elizabeth secretly married in a little village near Calais. Her father, who had found out where they stayed, but did not know that they had married, persuaded them in an angry scene to return to England. After returning to their respective houses, the couple corresponded secretly.

The jilted suitor, Major Mathews, now published an article in which he denounced Sheridan as 'a liar and a treacherous scoundrel'.[13] Sheridan heard about this, immediately went to Mathews' house, where Mathews told him he was 'misrepresented'. That same evening Richard's brother showed him the copy of the Bath Chronicle with Mathews' article. Richard Brinsley rushed back, and they fought a duel, which Sheridan won. Although Mathews begged for his life, he denied the advantage, and Sheridan in his anger demanded a written apology and the sword of Mathews, which he broke into pieces. Later, while Elizabeth was away, performing in Oxford to the raptures of the public, Mathews challenged Sheridan to another duel. In the struggle both broke their swords, but in the wrestling that followed Mathews came out on top, and he was a heavy man. He stabbed Sheridan with his broken sword in the face and pierced his neck. Mathews drove off in the conviction that Sheridan was done for.[14] This 'made a considerable sensation at the time'.[15]

Betsy got the news, and although both families were not on speaking terms, she now 'claimed the right of a wife to tend her hurt husband, and so revealed the fact of the marriage in France'. Her father was now even more outraged. He denied the validity of the marriage and tried to marry his daughter off to one Sir Thomas Clarges. But his household was in disarray. Sheridan came to his door, asked him for permission to marry Elizabeth Anne, and offered him continued control over most of his daughter's money.[16] The father insisted that the first marriage be treated as invalid, as Elizabeth had been under age. Sheridan quickly finished his law studies, and one week later the pair remarried in England in April 1773.[17]

The Sheridans took a house, furnished it 'in the most costly style' and Richard Brinsley wrote plays.[18] His 1775 *The Rivals* was—in the second edition—a success. Together with his father-in-law, Thomas Linley the elder, who was performing at the Drury Lane Theatre Royal, Sheridan purchased the theatre in 1776. From Sheridan's side, it was largely on mortgage. Thomas Linley the younger played there as well.[19] In 1777, Sheridan directed *A School for Scandal*, widely regarded as his literary masterpiece, and a lasting success. Sheridan became the manager of the theatre and turned his attention more and more to politics.

His friend, Richard Tickell, (1751–93), was the grandson of the poet Thomas Tickell (1685–1740), the secretary to Joseph Addison.[20] Richard was born in Bath, in the same year as Richard Brinsley Sheridan. He entered the Middle Temple in 1768. In 1778, he presented a musical entertainment, *The Camp*, in the Drury Lane Theatre. Over the next five years, *The Camp* run fifty-seven times. Its subject was the Duke of Devonshire who led a militia to stop the invasion by France, which he believed imminent. Thomas Linley the elder provided some of the music. The text was by Richard Tickell and Sheridan.[21]

Around that time, Richard Tickell broke off his engagement with Anne Boscawen, who was six years his senior. He started a live-in relationship with the actress Miss Barnes,[22] with whom he had two children: Richard Barnes Tickell (1778?–94) and Zipporah (1779–1842). Also in 1778, Tickell wrote the hugely successful *Anticipation*, a booklet in which he pre-empted the arguments of the Opposition after the opening of the Parliament by imitating the style of the leading members of the House of Commons.

Richard Tickell and Richard Brinsley Sheridan were close friends. The relationship was cemented when Richard Tickell dropped Miss Barnes, and on 25 July 1780 married Sheridan's sister-in-law Mary Linley (1758–87). From this time, 1780, dates the portrait of Richard Tickell by Gainsborough. He painted it with evident sympathy for the sitter.[23] After *Anticipation*, Richard Tickell wrote an opera in three acts, *The Carnival of Venice*, which was produced in Drury Lane in 1781. Elizabeth Linley wrote some of the songs, Mary the music. *Anticipation* had got him some political friends, who secured him a commissionership in the stamp office in the same year.

Richard Tickell and Sheridan came to live close to each other. It came as close to an extended family as you can get; Richard Tickell's children called Sheridan's wife 'Mama-Aunt'.[24] 'Tickell spend much time with Sheridan, whom he clearly idolised. Tickell had more of vanity, and Sheridan more of pride. Tickell was perpetually gay and ambitious to shine in society; he was therefore always on the watch for some opportunity to make a brilliant sally, and often succeeded.' Mary had a tolerant attitude to her husband's behaviour. She felt that Tickell was merely following the footsteps of Sheridan of whom she was very fond.[25]

Sheridan 'delighted in practical jokes, and seems to have enjoyed a sheer piece of mischief, with all the gusto of a schoolboy. At this kind of sport, Tickell and Sheridan were often playfellows, and the tricks which they inflicted on each other were frequently attended with rather unpleasant consequences.' That did not matter much to them, the clever execution of the joke was more important than the pain it might inflict.[26]

Mary's death in 1787 was a heavy blow. Richard Tickell went into mourning for a year, and in private discussed plans to publicly announce that he would never remarry. He agreed that Elizabeth Anne Sheridan would look after his three children with Mary. They entered a radical political household.

Richard Brinsley Sheridan, who had entered parliament in 1780 as a friend of Charles James Fox, was counted 'among the best speakers of the house'. He used the weapon of ridicule to great effect. 'Like that of his great political rival, Pitt, his eloquence required the stimulus of the bottle. Port was his favourite wine.'[27] Sheridan opposed the war against the independence of America. He was active in the impeachment of Warren Hastings, a lengthy trial over the years 1788–94. Burke and Sheridan gave great speeches. When they described rapacious tax collectors and the torture of women's breasts, Mrs Sheridan was so overpowered that she swooned and had to be carried from the hall.[28] However, in the end, Hastings was acquitted. When the French Revolution started, Sheridan upheld the principle of non-intervention, as 'the French people should be allowed to settle their constitution and their affairs in their own way'. Likewise, Sheridan opposed the union of the English and Irish parliaments.[29] He also was a strong supporter of an uncensored press.[30] The management of the Royal Theatre in Drury Lane was the financial mainstay of the household. In 1791, the Theatre Royal in Drury Lane was demolished and the construction of a new theatre began.

Richard, meanwhile remarried in 1788 with Sarah Ley, who was eighteen years old. They moved to Hampton Court, where he had lived with his first wife. As was perhaps to be expected, Sarah was not popular with his old friends, who saw her as beautiful, empty and a spendthrift. Clouds were gathering above Richard Tickell. Elizabeth Anne, who took care of Tickell's children with her sister Mary, died in 1792.[31] Richard's father, John Tickell, died in April 1793.[32] Richard was in great financial distress. He became depressed and jumped from the window, others say from the parapet, of his apartments at Hampton Court. Sara Ley brought the news of his suicide together with Richard's children—who apparently had been taken back after his remarriage—immediately to Sheridan. He took Richard's children in and saw to it that his friend's demise was proclaimed an accidental death.[33]

The Theatre Royal reopened on a grander scale in 1794, still under the management of Richard Brinsley Sheridan. Sheridan remarried in 1795, with Esther Jane Ogle. They lived, a mutual friend remembered, 'most splendidly' and kept company 'with some of the most eminent characters in the high world'.[34] His Theatre Royal burned down in 1809. On the occasion Sheridan was seen watching the fire with a glass of wine in his hand, remarking 'A man may surely be allowed to take a glass of wine by his own fireside.' Financially broken, he withdrew from its management in 1811.[35] After his death in 1816, he was gratefully remembered and buried in Westminster Abbey with great pomp and circumstance.[36]

Within a few years of Richard Tickell's death in 1793, all his children would be out in the big wide world. His eldest with Miss Barnes, Richard Barnes Tickell, was already in Canada, where he became a clerk in 1792, got a licence to practice law in 1794 and became the aide to Gen. Simcoe, lieutenant-governor of Upper Canada.[37] In 1795, Richard Barnes Tickell drowned in a snowstorm on the Niagara River.[38]

In 1795, the younger Zipporah, who lived with Anne Boscawen, married with Ebenezer Roebuck in London when she was sixteen years old. Five years later, they went to Madras, leaving three children in the care of Miss Barnes. In 1807, Zipporah returned to England with her youngest children who were born in Madras. After she arrived, her husband died in India. Soon, she remarried, with John Simpson, 'guided', as her son later wrote, 'more by passion than by prudence'. In 1815 they went to Canada, taking Zipporah's children with Roebuck and her mother Miss Barnes with her. Miss Barnes died sometime between 1815 and 1819. On 9 February 1842, Zipporah died in Coteau-du-Lac, Canada.[39]

Elizabeth Anne, Richard Tickell's eldest child with Mary Linley, was the namesake and favourite of 'mama-aunt' Elizabeth.[40] She was adopted by the playwright Sophia Lee.[41] Lee had high hopes for

Betty's career on the stage, but she never was a success. In fact, she was seen as rather dull. Sophia Lee died in 1824. By that time, Betty had long succeeded Zipporah in the household of Richard's former fiancee, Miss Anne Boscawen.[42] She aways lived off other people. William Linley remembered her in his testament.[43]

Richard Brinsley, the second child, was the namesake of Sheridan. He died in 1805 on the frigate Phoebe off the coast of Sardinia, an event that later was transformed into death at Trafalgar.[44]

The youngest, Samuel Tickell, Samuel Richard's father, born in 1775, was the namesake of his uncle Samuel Linley, who died in 1778 as a midshipman.[45] Samuel Tickell became a cadet in 1800 and arrived in India in October 1801, where, as we have seen, he died in 1817.

This left Elizabeth Anne Tickell, William Linley and Anne Boscawen to pass on the family lore to the young Samuel Richard. Anne Boscawen was described by a lady visitor as 'niched in the old court garret with a most fantastical little balcony, and terrace full of plants, flowers, and foreign birds'. She was 'full of old court news, and of the King's going to throw down her apartments;—could talk of nothing else, and of her waylaying the King on his departure for Ireland'.[46] Two elderly ladies with foreign birds, hardly an exciting environment for a young boy fresh from the banks of the Ganges, but one could meet people there. The household was well connected with the Court, where Anne Boscawen worked.[47]

These were stories from another age, from the fast years leading up to the French Revolution, when 'it was bliss to be alive'.[48] British society had moved on since the Napoleonic wars. By the 1820s, it was more restrained and given to respectability.[49] Later in the nineteenth and early twentieth century, we find attempts to cover the stories up, to make Richard Tickell more Victorian and to edit Miss Barnes and even Zipporah out of the story.[50] That was not yet the case in the 1820s. Zipporah's fifth son, John Arthur Roebuck, was a regular visitor to Elizabeth's and Anne Boscawen's apartment after he arrived in London from Canada in 1824.[51] He was also known to William Linley. Zipporah Roebuck, née Barnes Tickell, had stayed in Madras in the first years of the nineteenth century, at the same time as William Linley. He had seen John Arthur as a baby.[52]

Samuel Richard got a private education, a bit surprisingly in France, where he stayed with Revd W. Jukes. Tickell himself described the subjects as 'partly classical—French and arithmetic'. It is possible, that in this period Samuel Richard visited Switzerland. In his 'Memoir', Samuel Richard referred to the 'shining white teeth' of the Ho girls, which reminded him of 'Swiss peasant girls'.[53] Still, the observation might have been a literary allusion, for example, to Lord Byron's Swiss tour.[54] Likewise, we cannot exclude a visit to Italy. In the same 'Memoir', Tickell referred to the originally classical Greek statue of the Apollo Belvedere, the extant copy of which was in Rome. It also was possible that Tickell had seen the plaster cast in the house of Sir John Soane.[55] When he went to London in immediate preparation for further education, he stayed with Robert Markland Barnard of Colney. Markland Barnard was a friend of Anne Boscawen, and—at least in 1813—Master of the very prestigious Mercers Company of London.[56] With him, Tickell read 'Caesar's commentaries & various parts of Arithmetic'.[57]

On 30 May 1827, sixteen-years-old Tickell petitioned to become a cadet for 'the Artillery & Engineering Seminary' of the East India Company at Addiscombe. To enter, he had to show a good knowledge of arithmetic, a good handwriting, and be competent in English and Latin.[58] Samuel Richard became a cadet in 1828. Sureties for him were given by William Linley and by Robert Markland Barnard.[59] Perhaps one should not read too much into it, but his application did not go entirely smoothly. William Linley excused himself that he could not be present when Samuel Richard had to appear in person accompanied by him and Markland Barnard. In his application of a week later, filled in by Samuel Richard in a childlike handwriting, he stated 'My father is dead, & my mother on her voyage to England from India'.[60] The following two years at Addiscombe were devoted to 'mathematics, fortifications, military drawing, surveying and civil (or landscape) drawing'.[61] Samuel Richard started out from England to India in June 1829.[62]

Apart from Latin, mathematics and his courses at Addiscombe, what was the intellectual baggage that Samuel Richard took with him on the ship to the country of his birth? We do not have a list of the books which he took to India. We can guess these from his earliest articles, with the proviso that the last of these articles is from 1840, a full ten years after his arrival in India. He need not have brought all these books with him. Additional books could be purchased in Calcutta, or ordered from England. From his first article, we get that Samuel Richard before or just after he came to India, read the zoologists and ornithologists John Gould, Thomas Pennant, John Latham, Thomas Bewick and Georges Cuvier.[63] In his 1840 'Memoir' he quoted Shakespeare, Sir Walter Scott and Thomas Gray.[64] By then, he had 'a heavy bookstand, containing four large shelves filled with books (a weight which I do not think two stout men [could] have lifted off the ground)'.[65]

Samuel Richard Tickell arrived in India on 9 February 1830. The early stages of his career are not entirely clear. Hodson mentioned that he became ensign on 12 June 1829, in effect from November 1829.[66] The first date was before he left England, the other must have been at the start of the voyage to India. On 22 April 1830, he entered the 68th Native Infantry (NI). But on 31 May 1830, news arrived in India that the promotions on arrivals of military personnel were cancelled by general orders of 13 January, a few weeks before Samuel Richard's arrival.[67] Also, there was the recently instituted qualifying examination to pass.[68] We find Tickell again on 3 September, now in the 72nd NI and probably still a cadet.

It was a rough start, and in this period Samuel Richard must have made a visit to his mother in Patna. It was not the family he had left behind. After the demise of his father, Samuel Richard's mother had waited a few years and remarried in March 1822, with George King, of the Civil Establishment, and surgeon in Patna.[69] The next year, Samuel Richards's half-brother George Abel King was born. On 10 July 1824, another half-brother, Charles, was born. Not one month later, George Abel died, 'aged 1 year, 5 months, and 9 days'—the pain shines through in this precision—and Charles was baptised in August.[70] These were very taxing times, and Samuel had at best been a very distant witness to them. Of the original family, Mary Rose was fifteen, and Edward Lawrence thirteen. It is likely that they were in England for education, possibly brought there by his mother. We will hear about Mary Rose later.

Patna had progressed. Emma Roberts visited the place in 1824. 'The civilians', she wrote, 'have now established themselves at Bankipore, a convenient spot by the river's side, a short distance beyond the suburbs. The houses of the numerous civil servants of the Company who belong to the Behar district, are built in the style of those of Calcutta, and are chiefly *pukkah* [made of bricks]; many are very stately edifices, having broad terraces overlooking the Ganges, and being surrounded with luxuriant plantations.'[71] As Patna-Bankipur-Danapur was on the banks of the river Ganga, it caught every visitor 'up the country'. Among these was the rather shallow Emily Eden, the sister of Governor General Lord Auckland, in 1837. She wrote an extensive account of her travels with her brother and devoted space to Patna. If you get tired of her interminable dance parties and professions that she did not understand Hindustani, well, it was the 1830s and the neighbourhood of Patna and one could not be choosy about the people one met. One should keep in mind the small scale of the English establishments. Emily Eden, who as the sister and travel companion of Governor-General Auckland could get anybody to her parties, was very pleased with seventy-four people, who had come from as far as a hundred kilometres.[72] Of course, you could get a more clerical view in Bishop Heber's account of his visit to Patna in 1824.[73] Apart from the often insufficiently equipped and staffed churches and low turnout of the flock, Heber noted the rather lively scenery of the towns he passed. Patna was 'a very great, and from the water at some little distance, a very striking city, being full of large buildings, with remains of old walls and towers, and bastions projecting into the river, with the advantage of a high rocky shore, and considerable irregularity and elevation of the ground behind it. On a nearer approach, we find, indeed, many of the houses whose verandahs and terraces are striking objects at a distance, to be ruinous.' Then came a stretch with 'scattered cottages and bungalows, interspersed with trees, till some more large and handsome buildings appear about three miles [five kilometres] further. This is Bankipur, where are the Company's opium warehouses, courts of justice, &c, &c, and where most of their civil servants live.'[74] The Hebers stayed 'very pleasantly on a high bank above the river' at the residence of Opium Agent, later Commercial Resident, Sir Charles D'Oyly.

Charles D'Oyly was the very centre of the intellectual, cultural and social life of Patna.[75] Surrounding him were people we already know or will come to know better. His sister-in-law was married to Walter Raleigh Gilbert, who just at that time came out on the side of the Porahat raja in the Pauri Devi case.[76] D'Oyly's wife was a lifelong friend of Brian Houghton Hodgson, then doing the work of a Resident in Nepal.[77] D'Oyly had established the 'United Patna and Gaya Society' or 'Bihar School of Athens', for the promotion of Arts and Sciences and 'for the circulation of fun and merriment of all descriptions'.[78] It could be that Indians also took part. D'Oyly painted a riotous, but probably invented, party, in which we see a free intermingling of English men and women with Indian men—the only Indian women are the dancing girls.[79] His house was even used for weddings. One of the young couples, at whose wedding in the summer of 1824 George and Mary King, recovering from the shocks of birth and death in quick succession, might have been present, was Christopher Webb Smith, the judge at Ghazipur, with Anne Jesse Mackenzie.[80] In the late 1820s, Sir Charles D'Oyly and Christopher Webb Smith established 'The Bihar Amateur Lithographic Press'. It was meant to print and popularise their two books on birds.[81] The publication house was short-lived—it was said that it ran only two years. But the impression its books made on Samuel Richard Tickell was to last a lifetime.

Tickell's military career picked up very slowly. Hodson noted Samuel Richard's first appointment as 'acting Ensign' on 12 March 1832 and added 'after two years in India'. That leaves the impression that at that time, Tickell only got the job, but not the rank. In 1832, Tickell was still—or rather again—cadet, now with the 31st NI (Native Infantry). From 23 December 1832 to 22 February 1933, he was with the 22nd NI and took part in 'operations against the Kols and Chuars'.[82] That was Ganga Narain's or the Bhumij Revolt in the Jungle Mahals of Midnapur and in Dhalbhum. At his own request, he went back to the 31st NI.[83]

His tour of duty in these troubled tracts triggered Samuel Richard's first published article, the 1833 'List of Birds, collected in the jungles of Borabhum and Dholbhum' in the *Journal of the Asiatic Society of Bengal*.[84] The list contained sixty birds. Twelve of these were killed by Tickell, apparently for description and to get specimens to the Asiatic Society.

The descriptions were formal, gave the length, colours, some habits, and the place where the bird was spotted. Ornithology was very much a work in progress, and Tickell knew he was walking on untrodden ground. At the end of his article, he recalled that many birds of the Himalayas were described by the efforts of 'one or two gentlemen',[85] but that to its south much was still to be done. This applied also to other animals. The gaur was already discovered (by Roughsedge, whom Tickell did not name). One might, Tickell speculated, confirm a sighting of a hippopotamus in the Bhil country, or even, as he himself glimpsed in the woods near the Subarnarekha, of an animal that could be an orang-utan.[86]

The 'List of Birds' contained remarks on sounds, the countryside and the people of the jungle and hills. Tickell had a good ear. His numerous descriptions of sounds were clear. To enhance the impression, Tickell sometimes added the feelings the sounds evoked. The voice of the jungle horned owl was 'hoarse and hollow, and connected with the gloomy scene and hour in which it is heard, the repulsive laugh in which it occasionally rents its notes *"Haw, Haw, Ho!"* cannot fail to strike a fanciful listener with unpleasant associations'. We sit with him when he observed that the brown owl is 'completely nocturnal, and in a moonlit night, its incessant cries are heard to a great distance, resembling strongly those of a strangling cat'.[87] The Shahmour Warbler's song was

> equal in compass, power, depth and modulation to that of the Nightingale. . . . And in unison with the surrounding scenery, in which nature seems to have lavished every fantastic invention of beauty, the effect produced on the mind and ear can alone be appreciated by those who have witnessed the magnificence of a tropical forest.[88]

He was vivid on the settings. He mentioned 'the wild and lovely scenes' of the blossoming cotton tree.[89] Tickell infused his landscapes with feelings. He noticed that the Malabar Hornbills 'are never met with in the high rocky lands, nor in the barren tracts of sal jungle, but abound in the rich meadows composing the valley of the Subarnarekha, where the country in many parts has the appearance of a well-cultured English park'. Compare this to the Trogon Duvaucelli, who 'frequents the thickest jungle at the bottom of ravines and dried rocky nalas [river beds], . . . those abodes of everlasting shade, where the meridian sun barely penetrates, overhanging arches of vegetation, and which are inhabited by undisturbed flocks of bats, owls, and night-jars'. These regions are

> rendered in parts uninhabitable . . . from the influence of pestiferous exhalations, issuing more or less throughout the year from abysses, overgrown by rank vegetation, where the light of the day seldom enters, and the cadaverous weeds, fixed in a stagnant atmosphere, never wave in refreshing breeze.[90]

Samuel Richard took himself—and us—away from the scenes of wild skirmishes, burning villages, and desperate shots of grape at unseen enemies in deep foliage. At this time and place, there were no people in his writings he considered worth more than passing attention as 'the half-humanized denizens of the jungles'.[91] Tickell's jungle could be tough, stifling and often gloomy. But it had scenes and moments of rare beauty (see Plate 6). When we sit in the bright moonlight of Jharkhand, listening to the distant owls' cat's cries, we are just with Samuel Richard, a man pondering, perhaps, the meaning of 'home'.

In February 1833, his career picked up, at last.[92] The government recalled the order to hold promotions. In 1835–36, we see Samuel Richard as a proper ensign in the Ramgarh Light Infantry on survey work in the 'Kol country', that is, the South West Frontier Agency. His work resulted in two maps. One was a plan of the army cantonments of Doranda, close to the 'station of Kishenpoor', now Ranchi. Kishenpur derived its name from Agent to the Governor-General on the South Western Frontier Thomas Wilkinson. The other one was a proper map of parts of Chotanagpur and of Singhbhum with some roads leading towards Hazaribagh and Bankura.[93] Thomas Wilkinson took to the young ensign. He had good reasons to. Tickell was cultured, systematic, not afraid to go alone in the jungle, and he was born in the country. Now things went fast. On 4 August 1836, Tickell became Lieutenant.[94] As we have seen, on 22 August, Wilkinson sketched his plans to take over the Ho lands and left for Calcutta.[95] On 30 August, Tickell was transferred, now permanently, to do duty with the Ramgarh Light Infantry;[96] the same day he asked for and got a leave of absence till 1 October.[97] He became a member of the Asiatic Society of Bengal.[98] After Tickell's leave, Wilkinson kept him by his side. Samuel Richard got an additional assignment at Rs. 100 per month to survey the area during the operations.[99] On 3 December, the Third Kolhan Campaign started and it ended on 28 February 1837. The next month, the hostilities over, Tickell was with Thomas Wilkinson when he explained the new order to the Hos. He got his appointment as Junior Assistant in the Kolhan on 9 May 1837. The twenty-five year old started on the 12th of May.

Chapter 13

The Hodésum Articles

...

Cold Kathmandu; 'Grammatical construction of the Ho language' and 'Vocabulary of the Ho Language'; 'Memoir on the Hodésum'; conjectural history; the great hunt; green retreats around unpicturesque villages; agriculture 'to meet present wants'; a small and difficult market; kilis and social relations; food and drink; dances; myths, rituals and songs; a witch in my dream; 'Eyá, goikiddäing'; the Ho character

...

Wilkinson's order to his assistant was not so much to get revenue in, but to get close to the people, to get to know them well enough to prevent more violent outbreaks. Tickell went much further. We are quite well informed about his life and work among the Hos, at least when we compare it with a Raghunath or even a Roughsedge. There are important gaps. There is no known stock of his private papers left, all the more regrettable as there must have been many. Tickell was an avid note taker.

The bulk of Samuel Richard Tickell's writings on the Hos consisted of one large article, 'Memoir on the Hodésum (improperly called the Kolehan)', published in 1840 in two instalments in the *Journal of the Asiatic Society of Bengal*. In the same year, it was followed by the eleven pages of the 'Grammatical Construction of the Ho Language', to which was added the 'Vocabulary of the Ho Language'. The series concluded with a short postscript published in 1841 on a minor point of local archaeology.[1] In addition, there were the despatches Tickell wrote to the agent of the governor general on the South Western Frontier. And, importantly, there were scattered, but sometimes quite elaborate remarks in his manuscript books and published articles on zoological subjects.[2] To take the expression 'view' more literally, there are several paintings and drawings by his hand on Hodisum and the Hos.

The Hodésum articles, the backbone of his descriptions, constituted a body of work that was both formal and emotional. Tickell related a range of experiences from administration through religion to fun. Above all, his descriptions were vivid. One can imagine one's self sitting with Tickell and listening to his dialogues. Thus, Tickell left us Ho sentences like 'You sing a song, and he will play the flute, all the girls will dance' and 'Go quietly, and peep over the wall, see what he is doing.'[3] He wrote his articles after 'three years of constant intercourse' with the Hos, which might 'perhaps have induced me to pass lightly over faults to which they are but too liable'. All the European residents of Chaibasa, he assured us, shared this tendency.[4] These were cheery general remarks. But when we try to reconstitute Tickell's moods and motives, we shall see that he does not easily open up.

The 'Vocabulary' and 'Grammatical construction', and the bulk of the 'Memoir' were written before Samuel Richard left the Kolhan Government Estate for Nepal, that is before 1 June 1840. Samuel Richard reached the Nepal border on 14 June, but was, much to his chagrin, held up there until 9 July. Immediately afterwards, in July or August, the first instalment of the 'Memoir' was published in number 103 of the *Journal of the Asiatic Society of Bengal*. The second instalment together with the 'Grammatical construction' and the 'Vocabulary' was published in number 104, which appeared in or just after December 1840. So it is probable that Tickell revised the first part of his 'Memoir' before leaving the Kolhan, and the second part while waiting on the Nepal border or just after his arrival in Nepal. There he added the last few pages.[5]

Nepal meant Kathmandu, where Tickell, with the army escort he commanded, was, as we have seen, holed up in the Residency. Resident Brian Houghton Hodgson was the elder of the two. He was forty-one when Tickell came in at the age of twenty-nine. They had a lot in common, the collection of animals and especially birds, and some ethnographic interest. Hodgson's interests went much further than Tickell's. Hodgson collected an astonishing number of Sanskrit, especially Buddhist, manuscripts, and went deep into the Buddhist religion. Hodgson's resources, too, were much larger than Tickell's. He had architectural drawings of temples made with the help of a forerunner of the camera, the *camera lucida*, 'a device which allows an accurate tracing to be made of a building and a complex view, whose image is projected through a lens on a sheet of paper'.[6] The same or a like device was used by the two local artists Hodgson employed to paint the birds and animals in his collection.[7] Hodgson himself was not much of a painter. All this was quite far from the do-it-yourself approach of his younger assistant. Hodgson's far greater resources produced more, but not necessarily better results. It is likely that Tickell taught some techniques to Raj Man Singh, Hodgson's drawer and painter, and had some influence on their style, as Tickell's birds and their settings were more lifelike.[8]

Hodgson had already made his mark in ethnographic accounts when Tickell arrived.[9] He had written three articles on ethnological subjects, one on Nepali languages, one on military tribes and the last one on the Newars, treating mostly their mythical history.[10] In ethnological matters, no influence of Hodgson on Tickell can be traced. Tickell's manuscript was at least in draft ready when he arrived at the Residency, and one cannot readily imagine him not showing it to his senior. It is sure they discussed—and not always agreed—on its main points. After Tickell had left, Hodgson got the offprint of Tickell's linguistic work on the Hos.[11]

The resident and his assistant met in a mixture of family affairs, money matters, and, possibly, professional ethnological rivalry. Samuel Richard Tickell's sister Mary Rose Tickell was the widow of Brian Houghton Hodgson's favourite brother.

William Edward John Hodgson[12] was born in 1805. He came to India in 1823 and took part in the capture of Bharatpur in January 1827. After that, he fell ill and spent most of the next two years with his brother in Kathmandu. William spent another year in Kathmandu in 1831.[13] In 1833, Brian got the post of Resident with a huge increase in income. That was welcome as the family back home, too, depended heavily on him, and he still had to save for his pension. William again had a breakdown in health in 1834 and Brian wanted to send him to the Cape to recover. The plan was that on his return he would command the Escort in Kathmandu, the post that Tickell was to fill later.[14] But William got married in Danapur in 1835 with Mary Rose Tickell, the sister of Samuel Richard. She was twenty years, Lieutenant William Edward John Hodgson twenty-nine years of age. The idea now was to get them both to Kathmandu. This plan was unlikely to succeed as English women were not allowed in Nepal. Still, it was a prospect on which Brian, who felt lonely in Kathmandu, had set high hopes.[15] In the meantime, Brian's financial situation started to improve. By 1837, he had paid off his debts and started to save. In 1838, William and Mary Rose had a child, but it died soon after birth. William died a few months later in the army town of Mhow.[16] The heartbroken Mary Rose put up a tablet to the memory of her man 'Let me die the death of the righteous, and let my last end be like his.'[17]

William left behind a considerable debt of British Pounds 1,000, at the time, Rs. 10,000. It had to be repaid by his surviving elder brother. In addition, Brian had to send the young widow to England, which set him back another Rs. 1,000.[18] That amounted to his full salary for more than three months.[19] On 1 January 1840, just before Samuel Richard started preparations to go to Kathmandu, Mary Rose remarried, with Thomas Lumisden Strange, son of the first Chief Justice of the Supreme Court at Madras.[20] Their first child, a daughter, was born in 1841 in Switzerland. That did not indicate straitened circumstances, though it could point to her suffering a weak health.[21] All this while Brian H. Hodgson was trying hard to save, as his time in Nepal would be up in 1843.[22] As he wrote to his father, 'I must calculate every sou beforehand.... I am but in weakly health, and shall retire as soon as my time is out.'[23] That was not a good situation to enter with the loss of more than one month of pay. We now understand Tickell's—and Brian Houghton Hodgson's—request for payment for the time lost on the Nepal border.[24]

W. W. Hunter's hagiography of Hodgson, written in 1896, was curiously silent on Tickell. All Hunter had to say about him was, that he prepared the *Memorandum on Nepal*. He even got his initials wrong. It looked as if Hodgson did not mention Tickell during his frequent conversations with Hunter, and that Hunter only knew about Tickell in Kathmandu from his handwritten report.[25] Hodgson left India early 1844 and it is quite possible that Tickell was one of the guests at his farewells. They never met again. Hodgson returned to India to live in Darjeeling from 1845–58, thirteen years, in which Tickell was not too far off in Burma. There seemed to be other reasons than busy schedules for this systematic silence.

The two, probably, just did not agree with each other.[26] Unlike Hodgson, whose constitution was weak, who delighted in studies of manuscripts, and who was following high-caste Nepali customs, Tickell was strong and an outdoor man. He must have chafed at his confinement to the residency compound. The birds he painted in Kathmandu were not, as was to become his hallmark, placed in a landscape, but were close-ups, on the bark of a tree, or surrounded by a few leaves.[27] Life here was in huge contrast to his life in Hodisum, where he was not adverse to a nightly hunt for a tiger, shot birds from the sky to impress the Hos, while composing a grammar of their unwritten language.

In Tickell's articles, the words 'Hos', 'Hodésum', 'the Ho language' appeared for the first time. In his earlier despatches, Tickell still had spoken about the 'Coles' or the 'Koles'. In 1840 Tickell was the first to call the estimated 60,000 people 'Hos', the name they used for themselves.[28] He found the foreign appellation of 'the Kolehan' 'improper', substituting 'Hodésum' for it. Apparently, the appellations 'Hos' and 'Hodésum' came to him in the course of his study of the language. In the 'Grammatical construction', 'Ho' is translated as 'Kole'; in the 'Vocabulary' 'Ho' appeared as the translation of the lemma 'a Lurka Kole'.[29] In the 'Memoir', the word 'Hos' appeared from the eleventh page onwards.[30] After he came back from Kathmandu in 1841, Tickell reverted to 'Koles' in his despatches, but at that time he was disappointed in the Hos. In his 1842 article on the Bendkars, published two years after the Hodésum article, the 'Kolehan' reappeared, but the Bendkar's use of the 'Ho' language was noted. In another article the same year, Tickell used the expression 'Larka Kols'.[31] Fortunately, one of the effects of the Hodésum articles was that the name of 'Larkas' was on the way out and that of 'Hos' stuck.

The words 'Ho' and 'Hodésum' and especially where, as in the title of his main article, that last word was coupled with the correction 'improperly called Kolehan', established the Lieutenant as a linguistic insider. His was a bit for respectability. 'I have had 50 copies of the Grammatical construction, Vocabulary, and Dialogues of the Ho language struck off, and shall be happy to distribute them (gratis) to parties desiring to have them', was his note to the 'Grammatical construction'.[32] It worked. In the proceedings of the Asiatic Society of 1841, there were two requests, one by a civilian in Jabalpur and one from a Captain in Assam, to have copies of the articles for comparison with the language of the Gonds and of the Garos, respectively.[33] The 'Vocabulary' also found its way to Hodgson in Kathmandu.[34] Tickell broke new ground. This was the first ever grammar and published wordlist of a Munda language.

In 1838, Tickell started to speak some Ho. In December, we saw him still relying on interpreters. So it was 1839 when he began to master the Ho language and to write the grammar. Then how did Tickell learn the language? Part of it in court sessions, of course. He had whole interrogations translated. But that was the smaller part of his knowledge of the language. Wilkinson's order was to speak to the people without an interpreter. So we can imagine Tickell taking down notes directly when conversing with the people. We should not imagine a one-to-one teacher situation here. In those days, people were hardly ever alone.[35] So we imagine him taking his lessons sitting with a small company in the compound of a house of a munda or a manki, 'substantial and capacious, built so as to enclose a square'.[36]

As people working with pre-Independence sources in Indian archives know, the British in general were very bad in recognising and in taking down sounds of other languages. Here, Tickell was helped by his musical ear. He was so good in distinguishing sounds that even in 2010, one student of Ho residing inside Hodisum found his wordlist very useful.[37] Tickell found the sounds of the Ho language 'exceedingly pure and liquid . . . and may well be rendered by the English alphabet, or still better the French one, as that admits of the slight nasal inflection which prevails in many words in the Ho dialect'. But, indeed 'in some words the inflections of the vowels are inconceivably complex and mellifluous'.[38] Anyway, the language was pleasing to his ears.

> The general euphony or cadence of the language is sprightly and cheerful; if the subject be of complaining nature it subsides into a strange chaunt, the sentences being linked together by such see-saw sounds, as "na-do na-do enete na-do".[39]

He first learned unconnected words and small sentences.[40] His 'Vocabulary', twenty-eight double column pages with words, expressions and complete dialogues in Ho with English translations, contained 1,650 words and small sentences. These would cover approximately 75–80 per cent of the Ho he heard.[41] And when learning a language by speaking it and hearing it all day, one grasps more than one really knows. Tickell could get meaning from body language and from other sentences which he understood. '*Umma kajee do ka'ing etoitanna*' is rendered as 'I do not understand you',[42] but literally it was 'Your language, I do not know'. With this level of understanding, Tickell could easily manage daily life, but he was still capable of making painful mistakes. In addition, in conversation and in court he would likely miss some important words and be dependent on an interpreter for these.

Tickell arranged his wordlist in eighteen groups, but the first one only contained the word 'God'. Most of the sentences came in the thirty-four dialogues. He devoted seven pages to coherent groups of sentences under such headings as 'Dialogues', 'Out of doors—Shooting &c..', 'Weather, &c', 'With a Prisoner, &c.', covering negotiations, quarrels, interrogations, confessions of guilt and even a full-blown sermon.[43] These form invaluable material both on the Hos and on Tickell's relation to them.

Here, sometimes, grandfather Richard came back. Samuel Richard Tickell's dialogues had a theatrical quality. They sounded lively and had non sequiturs.

—Where do you come from?

From Ramila, which is in Keonjhar.

. . .

—What business have you come on?

Some dispute about land.

—Where is your house?

In Ramila, I tell you.

—*Okomanna te um hooilena?*

Ramila te eeng hooilena: Kenjree re Ramila.

. . .

—*Chikan kajee reum hoojooèna.*

Otea epesèr minna.

—Umma oado okorea?

Ramila re, metamtannying.[44]

Insight in the grammar did not come easy. 'The speakers themselves are unable to give the least information on the construction of what they are saying.'[45] However, 'the system on which they are founded may be detected in due time by patient comparisons of them'.[46] Then came a qualitative jump in the understanding: 'With this difficulty [of establishing a general grammar] once mastered, it is inconceivable with what ease the most (apparently) complex and difficult languages become familiar.'[47]

To become familiar with the language was quite a feat, but Tickell found it hard to transmit its feeling. 'The language of their songs', he writes, 'is poetical and pleasing; it would not however bear translation. Ideas which in the English idiom would be dull and stupid, and words which would be common place, in the smooth mellifluous accents of their dialect sound interesting, and often beautiful.'[48] In the end, Tickell only gave the burial song. He promised more songs, but as the 'Vocabulary' had 'grown more voluminous that I had anticipated', he left these out.[49] Apart from difficulties in translating words and sentences, or of conveying the poetical quality of a song, there was the basic problem of conversion of what one side said into meaning to the other side. Obviously, some of the questions were understood but just did not make sense.

—What is your father's name?

He is dead.

—Yes, but did you not call him by some name when alive?

We called him Harree, but I tell you he is dead, Sir!

—*Aappoo'm do chikan noomoo?*

Goien aï!

—*Ea, mendo aïo jeedakaure kache'pe noomootadaï?*

Harree'le metaa: goienaï, gomke! Metam! [50]

On the positive side was that the speaker was not afraid to make clear that it did not make sense. '*Metam!* I told you/Mark my word!'

The 'Memoir on the Hodésum' appeared in two instalments. It offered Tickell's observations of important aspects of Ho society and culture. Also, he gave ample space to information that the people gave him in their own language. Thus, he gave voice to what in the beginning of his article still was 'this wild and aboriginal race' and at the end of it had become 'a light-hearted and good-natured race'.[51]

The publisher, the Asiatic Society, highlighted the 'Memoir' as an 'ample and able statistical account of Hodésum'.[52] That did not make it a schematic exercise. Tickell's view on the Hos was comprehensive and quite, but not rigidly, structured. The first part treated history, geography and ended abruptly with his archaeological discoveries. The second instalment started with Ho people and society, interrupted the account with the great hunt, and went on with religion, economy and the Ho character. There were obvious omissions. Conspicuously absent were the feelings of the Hos about their loss of independence. The opening moves of the pacification strategy such as the long wavering over its introduction and the immediate reaction to it in the Poto resistance of 1837 were dismissed in a sentence. The tribulations of introducing a basic modern state in the area, such as court cases and collection of taxes, too, had but a marginal place in the 'Memoir', though they had been very much present in Tickell's despatches.

As additions and sometimes as correctives to Tickell's observations, I will make use of the account by Dunbar, who was the army surgeon during the last Kolhan Campaign and among the first inhabitants of the cantonment of Chaibasa. That account was published in 1861 but was obviously taken from a manuscript made in these first years of the Kolhan Government Estate.[53]

Tickell wrote the first thirty-six pages of the 'Memoir', as well as the sentences and examples of his Ho grammar, from notes jotted down when and where he got the information. This material stood closer to his actual experiences. Tickell indicated precisely where the part 'verbatim from their lips' ended, from which point he had to 'conclude the theme from memory'.[54] He used his memory to make general remarks on the 'crafty' Hindus, on the Ho *kili* and the Ho food and trade. Some very complimentary remarks on the beauty, gentle behaviour and love of truth of the Hos also figured in this part. In these last five of the forty-one pages of the Hodésum article emerged some of the most firmly set ideas of Tickell.

Tickell gave a conjectural history of 'this wild and aboriginal race'.[55] This history was the first one recorded on the spot and used such different sources as the Porahat raja's records, stories of the Oraons and early British despatches. It did not mention the Hos themselves as a source of information for this early period. Method-wise, this can be seen as a weakness. On the other hand, more than thirty years later Dalton had to state that the Hos had little more to say on their early history than that they were related to the Mundas and came from the Chotanagpur area.[56] A methodical strong point was that Tickell did not attempt to find primeval social institutions of the Hos. He attributed the beginnings of the *pir* system to the neighbouring chiefs and placed these close to the modern period. Tickell's sense of history was practical. History explained the present distribution of peoples over this tract. It also explained the contemporary political status of the area.

From the distribution of small colonies of people 'speaking the same, or nearly the same dialect as the Hos, or Larka Kols of Singhbhum' Tickell found that the 'main stock' probably lived in an area approximating the present state of Chattisgarh. As relatively few Munda speakers lived there in historic times, this statement seemed mainly to rest on his observation that the regions had 'never been explored, and are wrapped in the greatest obscurity'. More north, as Tickell heard it, the Oraons were pushed out of their former homes by Hindus, who in their turn might have been under pressure from Muslim conquerors. They settled peacefully among the Mundas in Chotanagpur. Then, the Oraons fell under the influence of a Brahmin, who 'trumped up a story' about a foundling, who was to be king over the tracts. This was the first of the Nagbanshis. In their turn, these brought in the Hindus with their 'tyranny and extortions'. But the Mundas revolted. After a long struggle, they were confined to the jungles in the south and east of Chotanagpur. Many Mundas migrated to the jungles south and west of Porahat, but 'a great proportion traversing the hills and forests . . . passed out eastward into the open tract now called Singhbhum and the Kolhan'. These were the Hos.[57]

This view hardly seems tenable. The immigration of Hindus and others from the Ganges plains into the Chotanagpur plateau took serious form only in the second half of the seventeenth century, well within the purview of the, admittedly scarce, local chronicles. However, they are silent about a mass emigration. In any event, Tickell found that these Hos were now 'separated entirely' from the Mundas of eastern Chotanagpur, although some names of clans could be found in both.[58] The following last part of this account of the early history of these tracts, as we have seen, was corroborated in the 1910s by the settlement officer Tuckey.[59] It has become standard.

Bhuiyas, Tickell continued, possessed the country and gave the Hos permission to form settlements, first in the woods and later in the central open tracts. The next rulers of the country were the Sarawaks (Saraks), said to be Bengali Brahmins. They were expelled by the Bhuiyas. Other people passed through these lands on their way from Patna and Benares to Puri, 'but their dread of the Hos deterred all thoughts of settling'. When a party of Marwaris took up residence as guests in the house of a Bhuiya *mahapater*, they reproached the Bhuiyas for 'living on terms of equality with a people who were Mlechis, or unbelievers, and as fugitives from another country, should be considered as subservient to them'. Thus, they made the Bhuiyas their allies. The struggle, 'the details of which are handed down disguised with much fable in the traditions of the Oriya Brahmins' and were preserved 'in the Madela, or records of the Porahat family', took a surprising turn when the Marwaris allied themselves with the Hos and defeated the Bhuiyas. The Marwaris took 'Porahat and the rich open plains to the northward, now called Singhbhum'. The Hos withdrew to occupy 'the remaining tract of open land, . . . the Hodésum'.[60]

Apart from stories, there were ruins, but when Tickell stumbled by accident on extensive archaeological remains, he simply did not have the tools to explain what he had discovered.[61] The first instalment of the 'Memoir' ended with a fairly detailed description of the ruins of Kesnagarh, Benisagar, and Khiching in or near the Lalgarh and Anwla *pirs*.[62] He could only state that, as there were no records on them, they must have been from a time before the first known Bhuiya of the country. From the size of the trees on the ruins, he estimated that these ruins were deserted about 200 years before his time.[63] That would put them at 1640, probably a serious miscalculation, as in the Singhbhum chronicle there is nothing about a destruction of Benisagar—and Khiching—in the seventeenth century.[64] It could well date from the invasion of Feroz Shah Tughlaq, Sultan of Delhi, in 1360.[65] Tickell confessed his ignorance of this type of Indian antiquities in no uncertain words. The ruins did wake up the romantic in him, and here, once again, his descriptions, not so much his thoughts, captivate us.

> Thickets and briars matting over richly carved ghauts [bathing places] and temples; old avenues and plantations whose symmetry can now scarcely be detected amidst overwhelming jungle, offer a vivid picture of what these deserted tracts once were; and the mind instinctively pictures to itself a once opulent and

prosperous people, whose forgotten dust rests perhaps within the funereal shades of these ancient forests, as their fates and fortunes, alike unknown, lie buried in the elapsed vastness of time![66]

Tickell's Hindu informants from Bamanghati and Mayurbhanj and even their Brahmin attendants recognised only the most common modern Hindu gods. They and the local Hos did not dare to touch the statues, so Tickell had three of these dug out from the red soil by some Oraons ('Nagpoor Dhangars') in his party, and took these with him.[67] In a letter one year later, Tickell changed his original contention that the Sarawaks (Saraks) were Bengali Brahmins; now he thought it more likely that they were Jains.[68] This letter was spurred by a private letter to him by his erstwhile mentor Wilkinson—and this is the last time we know about a contact between the two. Probably it was in this letter to the Asiatic Society that Tickell enclosed some sketches of idols.[69]

To continue with Tickell's historical overview, after 'five or six generations' of rule, the Marwaris, or the Singh family, split into the Anandpur, Saraikela and Kera branches, while Bandgaon, Karaikela, Chainpur and Kharsawan remained service tenures of Porahat, though later Kharsawan became 'in a manner hereditary and independent'.[70] Here, Tickell was not very precise. Early on, Kharsawan had become independent, but from Saraikela, at one split removed from Porahat.

Coming to the years leading up to the establishment of the Kolhan Government Estate, Tickell neatly summarised the situation. Most Singhbhum states and fiefs had bad relations with their neighbour: Anandpur with Gangpur, Porahat with Sonapur in Chotanagpur, Kera with Tamar and Chotanagpur, and Saraikela had a quarrel with Mayurbhanj over Kuchang. All of these used Hos as freebooters. Some of these chiefs 'induced [the Hos] to pay rent' and some money at the occasion of Hindu festivals, for their freebooting.[71] In Tickell's view, the actions of the Hos in these disturbances were 'chiefly, if not entirely' instigated by the Hindu *zamindars*, 'to wreak their own malice on their neighbours'.[72] The *mahapater* of Lalgarh (actually of Bamanghati which had a claim on Lalgarh) and the Mayurbhanj raja broke in an open quarrel in 1831–12. This resulted in the plunder of the Jungle Mahals and the interruption of the post. Thus, the government 'was at length obliged to interfere'. In 1836-37 'effectual measures were taken to prevent disturbances of the kind, by taking the Hos under our immediate control'.[73] This very fast history provided his readers with some background to the political set-up of the area.

The fact that Tickell had gained access to the records and history of the Hindus in Singhbhum, that is Porahat,[74] did not, as we have seen, translate into sympathy for the Singhs, Bhuiyas, or, for that matter, Hindus in general. In the 'Memoir', too, it was a source of concern for Tickell that his Hodisum was threatened by, in his words, 'crafty people' who had 'lure[d]' his Hos, especially those near the boundaries, 'into following their ceremonies, rites, festivals, and prejudices'. He did not like the Hos to become 'as subservient to Brahmins as any Hindus would be'.[75] Part of the charm of the Hos was that they were 'totally distinct from the Hindus'.[76] Here, Tickell restated in emotional terms the strategic *raison d'être* of the Kolhan Government Estate—and his job. He wanted the Hos to remain on the other side of the ethnic frontier and to preserve 'so striking a contrast to the mass of people in Hindustan'.[77] It also showed how far the Indian plains were from the Hodésum. Tickell exclaimed with relief, 'no squabbling, no abuse or high words, . . . none of the vile traits of common Hindustani life'.[78]

This dislike of the local Brahmins and sympathy for the Hos makes Tickell look like somebody with strong sympathies and antipathies and less a social mixer. In fact, in Singhbhum he was a rather easy-going socialite. There were redeeming features to his constant handling of obstruction and quarrels by Raja Arjun's very emotional mother, by the scheming Jadunath, by the local bullies Raghunath Bisi of Jaintgarh and Chakradhar Singh of Saraikela. The 'Memoir' contained a very nice and lengthy description of a great hunting party for all the major peoples of the region.

> But the grand meeting is in May, about the 'Cheyt Prub', when people of all sects and classes repair to the hills north of Singhbhum. The preliminaries of the 'Hankwa' are arranged by ambassadors and emissaries from Singhbhum, the Kolhan, and the Jungle Mehals, and vast multitudes draw in from every quarter . . . . On the given day, these crowds, extended in lines, draw towards a common centre, sweeping the Jankiburu hills and other ranges which reach from Chotanagpur to the Subarnarekha river, separating Tamar from Singhbhum; as the lines approach each other, the slaughter commences. The uproar is difficult to describe, and the scene the wildest imagination can picture.

> Those deep secluded valleys, those barely pervious dells, the huge solitary hill tops, buried in one vast sheet of pathless jungle, which except on this annual occasion are never visited by any man, now swarm with countless hordes. In front of them animals pass and repass, bewildered by opposing hosts. The huge gaurs rouse from their noon-day retreats, and stalk with stately steps along the hill side, till infuriated by the increasing din, they rush through the forest, heedless of rock or ravine, and rending the branches in their ponderous flight—the wild buffaloes thunder across, brandishing their immense horns, stamping and wheeling round their young ones . . . . The fairy like 'Orey,' or small red deer, with noiseless feet comes skimming over the tangled underwood, skipping in wild starts to the right and the left, and sorely bewildering a host of thakurs, rajas, and their body guard, who perched upon scaffolds in vain try to bring their lengthy matchlocks to bear; with snort and puff a 'sounder' of pigs scurry through.

> The redoubled uproar from without, draws the attention of something which has excited the beaters. The reeds and grass are seen to wave, as if some bulky form were sliding through them, and at length, loath to leave the haunts which had concealed him so long, out comes the tiger, with a lumping, stealthy trot, crouching to the earth, with ears quivering and turning to catch every sound. He has soon passed into leafy depths, from which his hollow growl may be occasionally heard.

> And last of all, as the peacocks begin to mount into the air, and the jungle fowl with noisy cackle take wing, a loud sonorous grunt or shoot ushers in the sturdy old 'Bhaloo,' who forced from the friendly shelter of rocks, comes bundling over the ground, and shaking his sides in a heavy gallop, oft stopping, wheeling around, and threatening his enemies.

> The report of matchlocks; the 'click' of arrows striking against trees; the shouts of the multitude; the roars, screams and groans of the animals; the piping of flutes; the beating of drums; the braying of trumpets; reach their climax and the multitude composed of all classes and sorts, meet near the raja's scaffold to compare notes of the sport. . . . Mid great shouting and gabbling the parties claim and carry off their several heads of game, or wrangle for the arrows sticking in the carcasses and elsewhere about.[79]

Here, Tickell was on top of his job as assistant. He showcased his knowledge of the local groups: the 'ever dancing and singing' Santhals, the 'wild' Kharias, the Kurmis, Tantis, Sundis, Goalas,

Bhumij 'with sonorous "dammas" or kettle drums', the Nagpur Mundas, 'with huge ornaments stuck through their ears', the southern Kols, and 'the far comer from Saranda with their chain earrings and monstrous turbans', Bhuiyas 'with their long bows ornamented with horse tails', and the *paiks* of the rajas, 'dressed out in all colours', and 'lastly' the rajas, *thakurs*, and other chiefs 'with guns of Delhi manufacture, prodigious swords, or an occasional "Angrezee bundook" [English shotgun], the gift of some sahib long passed from the scene, seldom fired, but kept for show in a venerable clothing of rust'. The Hos, 'simple and unpretending, but with the heaviest game bags' had the pride of place.[80]

> All then repair to the banks of the nearest streams, where they form their temporary camps; fires are lighted, the game is cut up, bundles of provisions unpacked, and for a mile or upwards along the wooden vista, the clear bright water reflects innumerable groups, which on either bank are cooking, eating, drinking, sleeping, laughing, or dancing. Such is the faint description of a scene in which I have often mingled, and look back to with much regret; *'Tis merry, 'tis merry in good green wood'*.[81]

Indeed, the land of the Hos appealed to Tickell 'in whom a passion for field sports joined a love for the beauties of nature'.[82] He started the description in Gazetteer style, only warming up when he described the countryside. In this first part of the 'Memoir', Tickell used words like 'Kolehan' and 'Koles'. It must have been written quite early, before he hit on 'Hodésum' and 'Hos'.

'The Kolehan as now constituted comprehends a tract of open undulating country, averaging from ninety km in length north and south, from sixty to ninety km in breath.' He noted the distinction between the settled north, 'exceedingly populous, but in many parts stony and barren', and the southern part, 'rich in soil, beautiful in appearance; but an absence of inhabitants gives it an air of desolation'. The western part was 'situated among hills and vast jungles, containing a few fertile valleys', while the inhabitants of the far south Saranda was 'one mass of mountains, clothed in forests, where the miserable inhabitants, few and solitary, can scarce struggle for mastery with the tiger'.[83] He noted streams of great beauty, but useless as waterways, with some waterfalls on the border of the area. The hills were not very high, not more than 300 m, but with 'profound valleys, which give the hills, from that side, an appearance of great magnitude'. There were different ranges of hills and mountains with their types of stones—and even with gold in some streams, 'but the Koles do not know how to collect it', though the Hindus there knew.[84]

His description of the jungle with its flora and game was extensive,[85] though Tickell himself found it far from exhaustive. 'But to enumerate all the beautiful flowers which enrich these green retreats— the fruits and roots, to every one of which the natives attach some specific virtue or harm; the inexhaustible variety of plants, shrubs and fungi, ferns, creepers &c. which clothe in all varieties of fantastic imagery the shady dells; or the cool banks of foliage-canopied streams, would be a task far exceeding my powers, or the limits of this memoir.'[86]

He remarked that the animals were 'not nearly so abundant as in better watered jungles, besides which the Hos and Odias are inveterate hunters, and their attacks on game of all kinds are pursued on an exterminating scale'. In the west of the country, elephants were unknown. The gaur and the wild buffalo were very numerous, as were several types of deer, but not the rare antelope. There were many jackals and two races of wild dog, whose 'ferocity, speed, and cunning, have gained them a superstitious veneration among the Koles'. There were many tigers and leopards, and bears 'infest almost every clump of rock throughout the plain'.[87] The bear was the animal to shoot on the hunt.

> A large male or dog bear is a powerful, and at times dangerous animal. . . . The skull of the bear is almost as large as that of a tiger. . . . The voice of the bear is loud and deep; when irritated he sends out abrupt startling roars, putting to flight sometimes the best shikarree [hunting] elephants, who are not moved at the hollow, guttural sounds of a roused tiger; when wounded it whines and groans in a most lamentable manner, and the voice has then a strong human expression. It is only during rage or pain, that bears are ever heard. . . . Very deep jungles of tall forest trees and heavy grass, or large hills, they do not appear to frequent so commonly, probably from fear of tigers, who will destroy and devour them. . . . They appear bewildered by the shouting and drumming of the beaters, and only bent on urging on their headlong course. . . . The head is the most vulnerable part, and a single ball striking between the eyes at the root of the muzzle is of more effect than volleys poured into the carcase.[88]

We even get a dialogue on a bear hunt.

-Come along, come along, let's go a hunting. Let's all come along. Let's go to Dugra hill. There are plenty of bears there, and peafowl, and chicquera deer. Do you all scour the hill. We will stop the ghats.

There's a bear coming, sir. Dubro has shot him in the back with an arrow. This way, this way, he is crossing over, he is hit! He has tumbled in the ravine. It is a she-bear; there are two cubs. . . .

-Don't kill the bear's cubs, I will rear them.[89]

Of all the birds, Tickell mentioned only the partridge by name in the 'Memoir'. 'Birds of all kinds are scarce and wild, especially those fit for food, [again] on account of the keenness with which the Koles pursue, trap, haw, and shoot them.' This in contrast to the 'deep, moist woods', which afforded so many varieties that 'an enumeration would be useless'. Well, he did try in the 'Vocabulary', and they amounted to more than eighty.[90] For insects, 'an 'entomologist would find an exhaustless field of research and discovery in the jungles of this country'.[91] He found the Kolhan 'peculiarly prolific in snakes of all varieties'.[92]

That included the local monster of Loch Ness, the 'Garra Bing', 'a monstrous species of snake, . . . infesting rivers swollen by torrents, which destroys both men and cattle, should they venture in.' Tickell mentioned it, 'as the opinion is so general, but it is probable that the sudden and mysterious deaths which occur in these mountain torrents, are occasioned by what seamen call the "under tow" and "back water", caused by the violent passage of water over rocks and deep holes.'[93]

Importantly, in the cold season, the climate was 'truly luxurious' and had—a quote from Shakespeare's Hamlet—'"a nipping and an eager air" without fogs or mists'.[94] It could be quite cold, 'it froze last night; there was frost on the ground this morning.'[95] Hamlet might not be the most carefree reference one can imagine, but Tickell was again at his descriptive best when he depicted the rains with a painter's eye, 'these are not accompanied by the gloomy sky and unceasing torrents which fall in the plains of India, the landscape is pleasingly chequered by passing showers, and the tender foliage of the forests glistens alternately with golden breaks of sunshine, or mellowed shades of green.'[96]

In the general setting of these vast forests, but close to the villages, Tickell established his most relaxed contacts with the Hos. Sports was a good way to enter the countryside—and at that time all of the Hodisum was countryside.

> The Hos are keen sportsmen, I have frequently, returning home with an empty bag, met parties of them with provoking bundles of dead quail in their hands. On these occasions they would laugh heartily at the success of their system over mine [with Manton's and Purdeys, and Westley Richard's guns], but generally end by offering me half of their spoils. My retaliation used to be in snipe (Khets). These birds, they confessed, their hawks could not overtake, and a successful right and left shot would restore the credit of the 'Boondookoo' [gun-man].[97]

This manly competition could disturb the quiet atmosphere in the villages, as appeared when Tickell used his gun to show off. 'At the first break of dawn,' he had seen the flying foxes settling for the day in their tree in the centre of the village.

> The usual noise of a village . . . do not appear to disturb them, or to cause further stir than a production of two or three heads from their mantles . . . . The report of a gun causes dreadful commotion; they rise in clouds from the trees, and continue circling round and round[, only to settle again in the tree after much] shrieking, cackling'.[98]

The first thing that strikes the reader of Tickell's Hodésum articles is that the assistant liked to be there, and that the Hos returned the good feelings, even when he occasionally caused a disturbance.

The villages were hardly ever built close to the rivers, 'where the vastness of canopying trees, and the luxuriance of wild vegetation, show the richness of soil; while seven to eight km inland, the country is populous and well cultivated.' The villages were not large, and quite far apart. They were 'in general unpicturesque, owing to their building on high barren spots, where the trees attain no size'. But Tickell found it sensible, 'the open, barren spots they select are more healthy than those selected for beauty would be'.[99] The layout of the villages was 'very irregular'.

> Each house being separated and hedged in by itself, with its own little plot for planting maize, til, or tobacco; a street for suggers [carts], generally runs through the village, and in the centre, an open space of turf, shaded by one or two tamarind trees, contains the slabs of stone under which 'the rude forefathers of the hamlet sleep'. On these stones the people assemble daily to talk or lounge, when there is no work to do in the fields.[100]

If a Ho would be worth three or four ploughs, he lived 'in a very comfortable manner'. As we have seen, the houses of the rich, the mundas and mankis, were 'substantial and spacious, built as to enclose a square', its principal building, plastered with mud and cow dung, had a veranda 'supported on carved wooden pillars, and covered with an excellent thatched roof'. It was divided into a sleeping room, an eating room, and storage. Opposite the main house, there would be a simpler one for 'servants, travellers, or guests'. Its flanks were joined by byres, a granary, and often a pigsty. In the middle would be a pigeon house.[101] Pigeon rearing was a peculiarity of all Hos, rich or poor.[102]

Given that agriculture was the main economic activity in the Hodisum, Tickell had surprisingly little to say about it. The ploughing was done by buffaloes, and as we have seen, a pair of buffaloes, 'a plough' was the unit of taxation. These were not used to their full potential. The rice fields of the Hos were only cultivated 'to meet their present want'.[103] Still, they grew plenty of fruits and succulents, 'jingee, khukra, cucumber, pumpkin, maize, and baugun', and planted trees: castor oil trees, jackfruit trees. The Saraks had left behind mango trees, 'but few now remain'. The Hos liked the tamarind, 'which is met in every village, and grows in great luxuriance'.[104] Even so, Tickell summed it up with 'they are bad husbandmen'. Dunbar would agree, but also gave additional information. He noted that

> Cultivation and agriculture appear to be at the lowest ebb in the Kolhan. Scarcely anything but *dhan* is raised, and the fields in which it is sown are so small, so ill-formed, and to all appearance so badly attended to, that abundant crops are, I suspect, of rare occurrence. . . . Some few of the inhabitants cultivate an inferior kind of cotton plant, and a few weavers prepare the scanty clothing worn by either sex. In some Cole villages a little sugar-cane is grown, and some tobacco (*sookool*), an article highly prized, in the shape of raw green cheroots.[105]

In the hills, the Hos cultivated on less permanent fields. From his wording, Tickell found that a marginal practice. He mentioned 'nomad tribes' of the Hos.[106] Every three years they moved on, clearing a new part of the forest. According to Tickell, they grew an inferior rice (dhan) in the uplands. On the new clearings the soil would be fertile, especially the first year.[107] The hillsides, too, could sustain cultivation, and the Hos planted these 'up to their summits' with a variety of crops, including cotton and tobacco.[108]

Even in the more settled agriculture, investment was not to be seen. The Hos made no 'tanks and bunds to meet the exigencies of the dry season'. At the root of that, Tickell saw a lack of capital, as the 'levelling system' worked so much, that nobody had sufficient capital to do such works. Worse, the old tanks, left behind by the Sarawaks, 'have all been destroyed by the Hos, who let out the water for the sake of sowing the rich mud at the bottom; or have allowed them, through superstitious motives to fill up from neglect'.[109] Dunbar, too, noticed that. 'The Hos', he wrote, 'have not yet learned the simple art of digging tanks . . . . The very few diminutive tanks seen were in the vicinity of villages partly inhabited by Hindus, and these contained a miserable supply of foul and ill-tasted water.'[110] Paradoxically, the Hos resorted to a more labour-intensive way of watering their crops. Their country was undulating, said Tickell, and for irrigation of their fields they choked up the small streams with soil brought from the upland. This was 'a process of infinite toil'.[111]

Tickell did not describe the men farming. He rather saw them hunting. The Ho men wore 'very little clothing', just a narrow piece of cloth, called 'Botoe'. They wore earrings and 'small beads or plaited necklaces and bracelets; most of them also wear charms against snakes, tigers, or diseases, tied around their necks. These the Hindus in the neighbourhood make a profitable trade of, in selling to them.' The men were 'fine powerful fellows', and, as we saw, 'eminently handsome, with figures like the Apollo Belvedere'.[112] The women did the work in the fields. These, especially when belonging to 'the lowest order', went about 'in a disgusting state of nudity wearing nothing but a miserably insufficient rag around the loins'. But 'their breasts and necks are loaded with immense bundles of bead necklaces, of which they are extravagantly fond'.[113] To this, we might add Dunbar's observation that the women wore 'a profusion of coloured beads suspended from their necks, and have their ears pierced with a number of small brass rings'.[114] The 'Vocabulary' added brass bracelets on the upper arm, a nose ring, toe rings, finger rings.[115] All these had to be procured. In the jungles, never far off the villages, some Hos grew 'vast quantities of Tasar worms', these jungles were preserved 'with great jealousy and care', a good indication both of the instinct for private property, and the stimulant of trade, because the cocoons were sold to visiting bead merchants, who 'bartered them in return for necklaces'.[116]

But the market was in Chaibasa, the market that Tickell was to stimulate and Dunbar had found so small. In the Hodésum articles, Tickell had little to say about Hos selling things. Rice production was for home consumption. The Hos had cattle but needed it for the bride price. They had sheep, goats and poultry, but from these they only parted 'with difficulty, as they require them for their sacrifices, &ca.' We regret that he was not more specific here. The difficulty showed in the bargaining for a goat.

—What is the price of this goat?

Two rupees.

—You ask a very dear price.

No; it is a large goat.

—I will give you only one rupee.

No, I won't take it.

Here Tickell learned fast and while keeping to the price—the Hos were inflexible once they had taken a position—he concentrated on the condition of the merchandise.

—How many fowls will you sell for a rupee?

Twenty fowls for a rupee.

—Well, but give me good fat ones.[117]

The assistant did not always have to go to the market. There was a push factor operating as well. Tickell was foreign and had money. But, apparently, the seller sometimes did not have a clue what he wanted.

Hello Sir; will you buy this monkey?

—Why; what do I want with a young monkey?

Oh, there was a Sahib here, used to buy them, once. That is why I asked you.

—I want none of your wild beasts, but bring me fowls, goats, cows, eggs, rice, straw, wood.[118]

Counting of money was done in a peculiar way. The Hos did not care for small quantities. The Hos reckoned it by the handful, 'to the unfeigned astonishment of our Hindoo servants, who would squabble for the tenth part of a cowree (shell).'[119] Still, the Hos had a decimal-vigesimal[120] system of counting: up to ten, then up to twenty in the style of ten plus one, etc., going through thirty, thirty plus one, etc. and finally arriving at forty (two times twenty). After that, they would continue in the same way till the next multiple of twenty. In this way you would say 98 as '(4 times 20) plus 10 plus 8': *oopoonhissee gel eerilia*.[121] Which, by the way, is the same in the French *quatre-vingt-dix-huit*. For a rupee, half a rupee (eight *annas*) and quarter rupee (four *annas*), they had separate words: *taka, adelee,* and *sikkee*.[122] The trouble with the assessment of half a rupee per plough indicated that the Hos well were aware of the value of money, their own money.

Though Tickell could—and did—relate to the people under his charge, he was not an insider to their families. The Hos had many words for relationships, but Tickell had not made a proper study of them. So these terms did not enter the 'Vocabulary', nor did the names of their 'clans' or *kilis*.[123] Here, the 'Memoir' is curious. In the fighting before and just after the takeover of the Kolhan groups belonging to different *kilis* had clashed, and as we have seen, Tickell made or decreed peace between them.[124] As he was prone to attribute wrongs to Brahmins, he attributed this social division into *kilis* to the influence of 'the curse of caste'. He must have felt that something was wrong in this observation—in the choice of marriage partners, the exogamous *kili* was just the opposite from the endogamous caste. Therefore, Tickell added that 'its follies are strangely mixed up with the distinction of relationship'. There were just 'a great number' of these clans, and Tickell could never find out who founded them or how they got their names. The rules were that a man could not marry into his *kili* 'as it is looked upon as a kind of brotherhood'.

Tickell's encounters with the *kilis* had been quite political, but when discussing the *kili* in the 'Memoir', he concentrated on co-dining. The rules, as Tickell gave them, restricted social mixing with members of other *kilis*. A Ho could not even eat with a member of another *kili*.[125] With non-Hos, they were even more particular. All Hos, it seemed, gave up preparing food when the shadow of a person from a different *kili* or a non-Ho fell on it. They believed that such a shadow polluted the food because a shadow contained 'the essence or soul of a man'.[126] However, this restriction did not seem to extend to the table of the visiting agent J. R. Ouseley, from which they would eat 'indiscriminately whatever was offered'.[127] There seemed to have been ways out of this strict rule. Thus, Hos did not take water from an earthen pot that might have been touched by people from 'other classes', but Tickell could offer Hos drinks in his wine glasses.[128] But that, probably, was in Chaibasa.

The Ho cuisine was varied, but not rich. The Hos ate beef ('all but the border and half Hinduised ones', Tickell added), mutton, goat, fowl, hare, deer and fish. The poor ate pig. Bears, monkeys, snakes and other wild animals were not Ho food.[129] The list of meats and the talk about sports suggested the hunt as a major source of protein for the Hos. It was not the sole source. The Hos had 'vast numbers of cattle', but turned these over to the Goalas for herding. Cattle were used as payment for brides,[130] and that was a step towards consumption. The slaughter of a buffalo marked a big occasion, as the neighbouring chiefs so well understood when they wanted to enlist the Hos on their side. Cow or buffalo meat was not for ordinary occasions. Unless one was poor, and the animal already dead. The 'lowest classes' would even eat 'bullocks that have died, from disease, or in the fields, even though far advanced in decomposition, and will devour stale eggs, half-putrid fish &c. &c.' This corroborated by Dunbar, 'much of what we consider carrion [is] eagerly sort for and devoured'.[131] These 'filthy habits', Tickell soothed us, were 'confined to the very lowest and poorest of people'.[132]

Important for the joy of Ho existence was *ili* or rice beer, (nowadays called *diang*), which was 'both meat and drink to them'. There was also a spirit *arkee* (a name the experienced amateur recognises as arrack), a strong drink distilled from the *mahua* berry by some Hindus.[133] But *ili* was —and is—the national Ho drink. Tickell gave the recipe. 'It consists of rice and water boiled and mashed together, and then left for three days, with a piece of "Rannoo" (a bitter root) to aid the process'. When Hos went hunting, it often sustained them for two or three days.[134] Rice beer was essential, too, for social life. 'It was thought', Tickell observed, 'a sign of enmity to stop even at the door-way without [getting] a 'stirrup cup' of Eely'.[135] It was also a part of all festivals and rites.

Tickell was mild on their drinking habits. The Hos, he noted, 'seldom drink to a disgusting excess and quarrels from intoxication are not of common occurrence'.[136] Against this enthusiastic evidence, we have the sobering observation of the army surgeon. 'They are greatly addicted to drunkenness; all, from the manki to the poorest villager, drink their intoxicating liquids on every occasion, and it is no uncommon thing to see a whole village in a state of brutal intoxication.' The doctor sighed, 'It has frequently been remarked with wonder what an enormous quantity a Cole can drink without apparently being in the least affected.'[137] This again supports Tickell on the effects of the drink, but perhaps not in a way he would have liked.

The village was the stage of social life. It was from here, from the heart of Ho society, that some of Tickell's best memories came.

> On calm summer evenings [the Hos] are fond of assembling at their doors to listen to the flute, the girls sing in concert, the younger ones go through the quiet, demure dance of the country, and papa and mama sit aloof looking approvingly on, and solacing themselves with a little 'Eely' [rice beer]; while twilight lingers their happy laughing voices, or the wild humming melody of their songs is heard . . . . The language of their songs is poetical and pleasing . . . . The men and musicians are generally in the centre of a large circle composed of women locked with their arms around each other . . . . All step with the greatest exactness in the tune, and the effect is most singular and pleasing.[138]

This showed rural contentment on a summer evening in a way that every British reader could understand.

More people would come together during the four Ho festivals, as Tickell wrote, 'little more than singing, dancing, and immoderate drink, besides offering up a goat or two, or a few fowls'. These festivals were held in each village separately and in different villages the same festival could be two or three months apart. 'The villages do not unite in these merry makings, but go through their ceremonies at separate times, and at their own sacred groves.'[139] During the most important festival, Mag (*mage*), 'the men and women occasionally put on grotesque finery, and their songs and dances are wild and pretty'. On that carnivalesque occasion, the 'Koles' (note the change from 'Hos'!) 'abandon their usual decent behaviour to women, and both sexes go tramping through and about their villages, chanting the most odious filthy recitative, in which the youngest who can lisp are allowed to join'.[140] Other festivals were the 'Bah Purub' (*ba porob*, flower feast in February or March), 'Batta Oolee' (*batauli*, the feast for protection of the paddy when it starts to flower)[141] held in June–July, and 'Namagom' (*nama gom*, new wheat), 'before eating the newly cut crops of the year'.[142] So, the festivals followed the agricultural cycle.

The Ho dances were, in an echo of Darcy's remark on Elizabeth Bennett in *Pride and Prejudice*, some of the prettiest sights Tickell had ever seen.

> The men and musicians are generally in the centre of a large circle composed of women, locked with their arms around each other; the circle is headed by the eldest matrons, and brought up by the smallest girls, a space being left between, they *chassez* [sic] backwards and forwards, keeping exact time, and going slowly around the men in the centre. Sometimes another large circle of men forms outside them, but all step with the greatest exactness in the tune, and the effect is most singular and pleasing. The 'Magh Purub' dance, when they go scampering through the villages four or six abreast, and in close column, is very like our 'Galoppe' and when the performers are well dressed, I have seldom seen anything prettier.[143]

Because these 'young women and girls of the better class—are well, and at times handsomely dressed, with a tasteful proportion of ornaments'.

> [They were] without the stupid shyness and false modesty thought proper among Hindu women; they are becoming and decorous in their manners, most pleasing in their looks, and doubly engaging from the frank and confiding simplicity which true innocence alone gives. Some few are very pretty.... Their open, happy countenances, snowy white teeth and robust, upright figures, remind one of Swiss peasant girls.[144]

He could not have made this remark without having individuals in mind.

We are at the dance, watching. Why not join the party? Tickell found the Ho drink *eely* 'not badly flavoured, and use would make it, I should think, just as palatable as our common small beer'. Everybody liked it, especially after some food. As we have seen, Ho men would also drink from Tickell's wineglasses,[145] and that was an instance of manly exchange. When they became slightly jolly, Tickell could ask in his best Ho for a song, some flute play and for some dances by the girls. Tickell could preach, but he loved some relaxation.

Tickell was the archetype of the 'undubashed' officer, who could talk with the people without the help of an interpreter.[146] But, as we have seen, with translating poetry he got weak in his knees. He felt stronger when he translated Ho stories and ceremonies taken 'verbatim from their lips',[147] and here he was particularly painstaking. In 'The Kole History of the Creation of the World', which he knew was bound to create much interest, he gave the circumstances and methods of the recording. It 'was communicated to me by some of the mankis orally, and copied almost verbatim.' Moreover, he did not edit out an obvious flattery to his own person, when the mankis placed the English as the elder brothers to the Hos themselves.[148]

The ceremonies and rites followed mainly the life cycle with the couple as the starting point: marriage, childbirth, name giving, followed by an extensive description of funeral rites, and a long list of gods and spirits. To find out whether a party was agreeable to marriage, go-betweens were used, 'four or six respectable men'. The omens were as important as the negotiations; both had to be right. Tickell added a long list of omens and their meanings. A major question to be covered was the bride price, to be paid by the father of the bridegroom. 'This is generally twenty, thirty, forty, or fifty head of cattle, according to the old gentlemen's means; sometimes when the requisite number of cattle cannot be paid, rupees, goats, sheep, or dhan [rice], are given to make up the number. For every thirty head of cattle, one plough of bullocks and a buffalo, also a few brass pots, &ca. are given over and above the bargain.'[149] The bride price was extremely high. It was quite costly to be a respectable Ho.

Not all Hos had four ploughs or were mankis telling stories about creation with the good grace to, no matter how tenuously, include the British guest in it. In his discussion of marriage Tickell left out the inexpensive short cut of the accomplished fact, a route which, according to Dunbar, most Hos took.

> When a youth has fixed his affections on a female, generally the inhabitant of some neighbouring village, she is waylaid and carried off to his house by himself and his friends. So soon as information of this reaches the parents of the girl, they proceed to the village of the ravisher, not, however, in general, with any hostile purpose. Interviews take place between the friends on either side, and at length matters are brought to a final settlement; the new husband paying to the father of his spouse a certain number of cows, goats, or buffaloes, according to his means, or the beauty and comeliness of his bride. After this a scene of feasting and intoxication generally follows, in which women and children as well as men participate.[150]

At the other end of life, death, came the grief of parting. Tickell gave a song, sung after the burning of the body (and before the burial of the bones). He called it the ceremony of the calling of the departed. The object was to induce the spirit of the departed to return to the house and to announce his return by a sign such as some ashes left on the floor, some disturbance of the rice, some drops of water on the ground. It was sung at the burial ground, 'in a plaintive wild strain'.[151]

K'alleeng erankedmia

K'alleeng enkakedmia

Hoojoorooamén

Booqité 'leengposakeamia assooladmia

Essoodinmidté leeng tykena

Miadoaré leen tykena;

Na da alum bageea!

Gama needa ko

Rabang rabang poio dinko dâra

Nendre do alum honorbýa.

Atarked jang japarré alum tingoona;

Hoojoo rooámen

Hesa soobaré umdo ka tý dýa

Gama hoojooredo

Rabang hoioré

sarjum do Boogité ka doimiai.

Oáté hoojoomèn

Umnangenté oa do boogikidallé! Alleeng do

Moonooite heating metanna, alleeng dóleeng minna,

Umnangente mandeeleeng doikia,

dahleeng-doikia;

Hoojoomén oatehoojoomén

Dooïrimén alleeng tar!

We have never scolded you,

Never wronged you;

Come to us back.

We have ever loved and cherished you,

And have lived long together

Under the same roof;

Desert it not now!

The rainy nights

And the cold blowing days, are coming on;

Do not wander here.

Do not stand by the burned ashes;

Come to us again!

You cannot find shelter under the peepul.

When the rain comes down,

The saul [tree] will not shield you from the cold bitter wind.

Come to your home!

It is swept for you, and clean; and we

Are there who loved you ever;

And there is rice put for you

and water.

Come home, come home.

Come to us again!

The mankis gave Tickell—perhaps, as Edward Tuite Dalton thought, because he prompted them[152] —an account of their beliefs in rebirth. When people died they went to Sing Bonga 'who asks them how they have lived, and judges them'.

The wicked he whips with thorny bushes, and sometimes buries them in great heaps of human ordure, and after a while sends them back to be born in this world as dogs, cats, bullocks, lizards. &c. The good man he

212 | A Land of Their Own

sends back to be born a still greater and better man than he lived before, and all that he had given away in charity, Sing Bonga shows him heaped up in heaven, and restores it to him.[153]

A list of spirits or *bongas*, who were extensively worshipped in cases of illness, had the interesting remark that the Hos had 'no notion of a devil or any evil spirit, their opinion being that he only who created, is able to destroy or torment either here or hereafter'.[154] Probably Tickell meant here only that there was no equivalent of the Christian Devil. If we were to take him literally, he would here directly contradict Wilkinson's observation that the Hos believed that sickness could come from 'the displeasure of their deotas or bongas'.[155] In fact, the Hos made many private sacrifices in their own houses. Nothing could shake their faith 'in the one resource of offering sacrifices to the god who is supposed to be chastising them' with bad luck or illness.[156]

Outside Chaibasa, outside of the direct influence of the new administration, witches were killed. Tickell touched on the subject at the end of his direct observations. Behind 'any misfortune' stood a witch, and these were discovered by 'certain signs, or by the divination of some augurer'. In the cases of illness, the discovery was 'most frequently ... [made] by the declaration of the patient himself'. He saw the witch in his dreams, 'standing on him, and sacrificing to the gods, to procure his dissolution'. If somebody was singled out, he was slain openly or murdered in the night. There was only one way out for the accused: the ordeal consisting of putting her or his hand into boiling oil, or water, or stand on red hot iron, 'or he was tied up in a sack and thrown into the water, with the option of floating on the top, if he could'. Tickell was of the opinion that there was 'the inflexible integrity of the Koles in speaking truth'. So the accusation of practising witchcraft must have come from a real dream.

> Being taught from his infancy to attribute every misfortune to preternatural agency, it is not to be wondered at, that when in his turn afflicted, his apprehensions rest upon some one, with regard to whom a previous quarrel, or other cause of ill-will, suggests the fear of retaliation, and these thoughts, long nourished while waking, would naturally embody themselves in sleep in some dreadful dream, which at once substantiates all the suspicions of the sufferer![157]

In an effort, perhaps, to dilute the impact of the offence by making it more common, Tickell found not so many diviners among the 'Koles'—he avoided the word 'Hos' here, too—as among the Hindus of the region. He assured his readers that 'the dreadful effects of this belief [in witchcraft] ... have now, through fear of our laws, almost wholly ceased'.[158] That was way too optimistic, but Tickell did not see many crimes.

He noted the absence of such behaviour as 'lying, deceit and dishonesty'.[159] He was overdoing here. There is, of course, a Ho word for 'lie', and Tickell even gave the translation of an admonition not to lie: '*Labbakajee do káï bogeea*/Lying is not proper'. Lying did even make him lose his temper, when he suggested to a wavering witness. '*Umdo saree ka jee do ka oodoobtanna*', literally 'you our main point [we talk about] do not show' or, in English idiom, 'you are beating around the bush'—which, obviously, is not the same thing as lying. But Tickell made it, 'you do not speak the truth'.[160]

He had some bad experience with evasion of taxes. Still, he had a favourable opinion of the Hos. 'Fervently it is to be trusted, alas, the hope may be Utopian, that the introduction of our Courts of

Justice, in checking the lawless tendency of the Koles, may not destroy those virtues which are inherent in a primitive state of society.' This he contrasted, once again with the 'duplicity and bad propensities' of the Hindus.[161] His Christian sermon, given at the very end of the 'Vocabulary', can also be understood as an attempt to give the Hos the whole package, so to speak, of British influence.

The Hos did not have a carefree life. Outside the village was the jungle. Hunting there could be dangerous. 'Did you kill your son Kapur? *Umdo amma hon Kapore goikeea chee?*', Tickell asked a man who delivered himself up to him. Out of it came the first ever Ho story to appear in print, '*Eyá, goikiddáïng*. Yes, I killed him.' It was 1837–38, a night in the woods of Ooisooia in Hodisum. His son Kapur was starving.

> *Eyá, goikiddáïng. Rengé' leeng gojotanna. Jometeá do ján jeta do k'aïng emaï dya. Rákiddaï, eean medre nelkidaï. Pe do ka týkidda, entenado otéré geetee enáï. En beer ré getee enaï, ondo k'aï tingoo rooý dya. Needa hendiènte, koola o rátanna aioomadáïng. Enkoola do jeedakanre habmiaï torá, eeng bagee endredo, mente adakiddaïng, kóa! Entenádo. Goikedmiaïng! Enté do hooang ré eeng topotadýa. Beer jeeloo do kako jomaï, menté. Maïté eeng seniena, jan pé o bannoá, essoo eeng hassooièna. Ondo nádo en beer ré bolokedté, iewaïng tannaï, adakidaïng. Enté nado eeng goyenaïng. Mendo nádo dimsee aï kewaing tana. Setta ré, singee ré, needa ré kewawing tannaï, Appooing, appooing, hey appooing! Enté k'aïng jómdya, k'aïng pýtee dya, k'aïng landa dya, jeed do k'aïng jeed dya, ná do! Mar, fansee emáïng mén, mar, buddee té goikeeing mén, gomké enté chabiena nee gé!*

> Yes, I killed him. He cried, and looked in my face. I had nothing to give him to eat. He was weak, and laid down on the ground. He laid down in the jungle and could not rise again. Night was coming on, and I heard the tiger roaring. And I thought 'he would seize you, my poor boy, if I left you'. And so I killed you! I then buried him in a ravine, lest the wild beast devour him. I went away slowly, for I was weak and ill. And when I had got further into the forest, I thought I heard him call. And then I fainted away. But now he calls me every day. In the morning, and noon, and night I hear him call: 'Father, oh Father!' I cannot eat, I cannot work, I cannot laugh, I can live no more! So hang me, Sir; kill me quick, and this wretchedness is over![162]

Of all the dangers lurking outside the village, the tiger was foremost—and he could not be satisfied with a chicken or two. The Hos had several ways of killing a tiger. They knew a tiger trap, *koola ranatang*, 'made like a huge rat trap'.[163] Another way was to lay down a carcass in the evening, sit up all night in a tree, wait till the tiger would come in the morning and shoot him. To kill a tiger after he had eaten one of the villagers was an urgent need.

> Throughout Central India, many firmly believe that the spirit of the last person killed by a tiger, rides upon his head, & guides him to the next victim, who thus relieves the first. Such a superstition served of course to enhance the terror and horror amongst the survivors in a lone village, where a tiger has carried off one or two of its few inhabitants.[164]

The tiger was a threat which Tickell's hunting skills could meet.

> Amongst a simple and superstitious people, so often victims to his restless power, it is no wonder that the tiger should be vested with supernatural attributes. The Koles look upon him as an instrument of the Almighty to punish evildoers. They swear by him and many even do not take his name in vain. They avoid this by calling him by some Hindoo name & title.

When in Singhbhum, I frequently went after these animals & was always staunchly supported by my Ho friends. Their desire to destroy a common enemy, & their superstitious dread of him were often amusingly blended. As we approached any spot where a tiger was supposed to be, the Manki, or headman of the village sliding up to me, would indicate the place by a cautious inclination of the head. And whisper that 'Raja Chakradhar Singh' was probably taking his rest there that morning: that he & some of his people would go to his 'durbar' [court] 'to see if he was visible, and that he would place me so that I might be able to take my slam.' All this, of course, I gravely assented to. To have said in so many words that the tiger was there—that he and his man would go & beat him towards me, & that he would put me so that I could have a shot would have been sacrilege!¹⁶⁵

With this, the Hos returned the old compliment of the Singhs that they were peopling a 'tigers den'.

The 'Memoir' ended with a short summary of the Ho character, and was probably written in Kathmandu, 'having left them and their country.'¹⁶⁶ The Hos loved truth, were honest, obliging and of a happy-go-lucky disposition. They had killed witches but did not murder to gain or to rob. The Hos were hospitable. It was custom to offer rice beer to somebody who dropped in. 'On the whole', Tickell said, they were 'a lighthearted and good-natured race, irascible, though quickly appeased.' They could not stand 'harsh words suddenly spoken'. With women it went even further 'the mere hearing of a few words of reproach will induce them to commit suicide'. This could happen with both sexes, though. 'The mere bantering a lad on his predilection for any girl, has led to self-destruction.' That is all Tickell had on bantering and joking with the Hos. He did not mention it even in his village evening scene, though he heard laughing.¹⁶⁷ He gave the word for 'jest', though, and even for 'ridicule'.¹⁶⁸ The Hos could be contented; they could riotously celebrate; but in Tickell's accounts they did not make fun. This—and his lack of family terms—showed that to quite some extent Samuel Richard remained an outsider to Ho daily life. It seems he had a problem. Grandfather Richard Tickell's bag of practical jokes could turn out drastically wrong here, as they did not understand 'jokes of an injurious nature'.¹⁶⁹

These remarks were immediately followed by those on their faults, consuming meat and fish in an 'advanced' state of 'decomposition', their 'indolence and dirt'. Often, the poorer people were 'very filthy' and, except in the warm season,'seldom touch[ed] water', Tickell knew.¹⁷⁰ But earlier, in the 'Vocabulary', there had been a dialogue suggesting that bathing and washing clothes were common.

—It has been very hot today. I want to bathe.

We all bathe here, under the tree. Don't go in there, somebody has been washing clothes.¹⁷¹

True, in the 'Memoir', Tickell did not go all the way. In three succeeding—and concluding—sentences, he limited the faults first to the 'poorer people', then to the 'lowest classes', and finally to 'the very lowest and poorest' of the Hos. Still, to place this criticism at the very end, just after the convivial '"stirrup" cup" of Eely', was a curious way to balance his positive account. Did Brian Houghton Hodgson suggest this to Tickell or was it a flash of clarity? At the very end of the 'Memoir', Samuel Richard Tickell was faltering. Something was not going well when he wrote these words in Kathmandu.

...

Reflection: That Tickell Woman

...

The Hodésum articles was not all of Tickell's views on the Hos. In his official letters, he heavily criticised them as tax evaders. The subject, like other issues of administration, was not treated in his Hodésum articles. These showed another side of Tickell's first straight run in his career in a lonely spot. In his daily working life, of course, he was the local upholder of law and order for the East India Company. The greater discretionary powers and the merger of offices of the non-regulation Wilkinson system gave the opportunity to people like him to run an administration single-handedly. The frontier of governance brought forward the lone frontier man of Anglo-Indian literature.[1] In this genre, the modern state, western culture and decency were contained in a single Britisher among the natives. He was an individual because there were few people of his own kind around. Later in the century, in the epoch we call Victorian, it would demand the stiff upper lip. Now, earlier in the century, chances were that the lone frontier man fitted in a romantic trend. That suited Tickell more. That he liked the Hos, did not in itself make Tickell a romantic, though.

In his writings *Weltschmerz*, the contemplation of the world as a painful place, was absent. Part of this was the result of the grand strategy applied to the Hos. To be assistant among them, meant to be part of an ongoing affair. Tickell was not staying with the remnants of a tribe, as in James Fenimore Cooper's *The Last of the Mohicans*.[2] British imperialism in India did not see the genocide and mass replacements that accompanied the expansion of the USA.[3] Contemplation of loss came in when Samuel Richard described the ruins of Benisagar. There, as well as when he was alone in the jungle on the eve of departure, he could be carried away with feelings and musings which we can recognise as belonging to the Romantic era.

Also, Tickell did not feel out of place. India easily was his home. After all, he was born in Cuttack, not far from the Kolhan, and raised in Danapur. When he came back from England, he would not have remembered his Odia, but certainly picked up his Hindustani fast. Even with the Hos, who spoke none of these languages, he felt at home after a few months and had learned the language. In itself, knowledge of a local language, then like now often a *conditio sine qua non* of employment in an overseas branch office, does not guarantee sympathy or even understanding; while inversely sympathy and understanding between expat and local do not absolutely need a command of the local language.

But learning a language remains a good way to establish a close rapport with the people speaking it. In the Hodésum articles, Samuel Richard was part of the social events he described. There is no self-consciousness of the look-at-me-among-this-people type that would have made the Ho more exotic and the author more exceptional. Tickell's 'Memoir' evokes a sense of belonging and its tone is remarkably upbeat.

When writing a large piece, especially when it is charged with emotions, the author hears 'past and future in one stroke of the temple bell'.[4] By choosing instances from the high culture of Europe, Tickell drew his readers closer to his subject. But also to himself; he used some of his early experiences in his 'Memoir'. He likened the Ho men to the Apollo Belvedere statue of which he probably saw a copy in London, and his comparison of Ho girls to Swiss peasant girls could be a reference to the family acquaintance Byron.[5] Tickell entered a quote from Shakespeare's Hamlet to describe Hodisum's 'a nipping and an eager air'.[6]

Tickell's connection with the Romantic movement showed in his literary allusions. For Tickell, connecting with literature often was connecting with his family background. His great hunt of the Hos and other peoples of the Singhbhum area was a 'scene the wildest imagination can picture', and he concluded it with a Sir Walter Scott quotation, 'Tis merry, tis merry in good green wood'.[7] Scott had contacts with the Tickell family. In the first decades of the eighteenth century, Samuel Richards great-great grandfather the poet—and secretary of Addison—Thomas Tickell had exchanged letters in 'an intimate and friendly intercourse' with Jonathan Swift. Scott, who was a Swift buff, had been given access to this correspondence by Major Thomas Tickell, the elder brother of Samuel Richard's grandfather Richard and, naturally, 'the representative of the poet'.[8] The Major's son, again a Richard, had served in India. The Major's grandson, Samuel Richard's near namesake Lieutenant Richard Samuel Tickell, was two years older than his relation, and like him, born and serving in India. Richard Samuel and Samuel Richard Tickell might well have met in 1835 when Richard Samuel was with the Ramgarh Light Infantry 'for the performance of a special duty'.[9] Samuel Richard could be in a mud house in Chaibasa, but he remained very much a Tickell.

Samuel Richard's family background also showed in his approach to village life. Since his grandfather's days, his branch of the Tickells was not a landed family. For his description of the Ho village, he used an image and a line from Thomas Gray's popular poem 'Elegy Written in a Country Churchyard'. Under the shade of some tamarind trees in the centre of the Ho village were the burial stones under which 'the rude forefathers of the hamlet sleep' (see Plate 11). With this poem, Tickell went to 1751, when much of the English countryside of smallholders with its local dialects, customs and beliefs was still intact. Gray's 'Elegy' showed an undisturbed peasantry going about their life. For Tickell, village life was to be savoured in a more direct way than for the Cambridge *literatus* Gray.[10]

In Tickell's view as an administrator, the Ho village should certainly bring in more taxes. Still, to change it was not on the agenda. Innovation and investment, prominent features of English agriculture in the last decades of the eighteenth and the first decades of the nineteenth century, were far from his thoughts. Tickell loved animal life, but farm animals could not hold his attention. Instead, as we have seen, he waxed eloquent on his pastime hunting. In this, he tuned in well with the Hos, but they felt more than him the stark necessity of depending on the jungle for meat. At the end of the day, when Samuel Richard Tickell returned to his small library and his caged parakeet, he was a city bird.

Still, we have this striking difference between the admiring 'Memoir' and the bitter tone of Tickell's despatches after he returned from Kathmandu. In his 'Memoir', Samuel Richard Tickell realised with regret that he had left the Hos.[11] He liked them. He could speak with them. He had individuals in mind, even where he wrote of the people in general.

How did the Hodésum articles fit into Tickell's personal life? Tickell was worried, as the final remarks of the 'Memoir', written as a general roundup and without the help of his notes, showed. With Hos, husbands and wives treated each other well and 'the modesty of the females [was] proverbial'.[12] They had this sensitivity, even about jokes. If Tickell had a Ho sweetheart, they had words before he left. About what? Possibly about cleanliness or, more probably, about indolence, the two vices he mentioned before finishing his article.

Samuel Richard Tickell finished his 'Memoir' while staying with Brian Houghton Hodgson. Hodgson was pinching pennies, and Tickell was in his moral debt for what Hodgson had done for his sister Mary Rose. On top of that, Tickell arrived with a flat purse, having lost one and a half month's pay to join his assignment in Kathmandu.

They soon had a quarrel. Hodgson had just arrived at the notion that as far as they were not Aryan, the people south of the Himalayas were all of a dark race, which he called Tamulian. Apparently, Tickell, thinking about his beautiful Ho girls, opposed him. That rankled. Hodgson returned to the question twice after his retirement. In 1847, after he had returned from England and lived in Darjeeling, he wrote that 'among the Kols I have seen *many* Orauns and Mundas nearly black, whereas the Larkas or Hos (says Tickell) are as pale, and handsome too, as the highest caste Hindu?'[13] Still, having seen no Hos, Hodgson could not disprove Tickell's remark. He diminished it by calling it 'a confined observation' of just one group'.[14] He returned to it years later. The question now was whether the Hos 'differed essentially in type from the neighbouring races'. 'I will now add a few words as to my brother-in-law Tickell's [mistake]. Last season Capt. Ogilvie, Tickell's successor, in the charge of the very district wherein the latter studied the Ho physical and lingual characteristics, came to Darjiling. I questioned him regarding the alleged fairness and beauty of the Ho'. Hodgson produced 'four no doubt unusually fair, well made, and well-featured Oraon and Munda men . . . . Capt. Ogilvie's answer was distinct, that the men before him were nearly or quite as fair and as handsome as the Ho of Singhbum and not either in feature in feature or in form essentially distinguishable from the Ho'.[15] Thus, after a full sixteen years, Hodgson felt he had proved his point on the Hos against Tickell.[16]

In Kathmandu, Tickell, denied his due with the ethnological article he had brought with him and in which he had poured so much emotion, was confined to the—albeit spacious—Residency and its compound. He could not get along with Hodgson and as it was a small community and Brian Houghton was heading it, it meant that Tickell felt lonely.

Hodgson was not alone. In the compound lived a small community of Muslim washermen of the Rajaka section of the caste of Dhobis. In 1833, one of these, Mehr-un-Nissa Begum, probably a widow, had become the live-in partner of his former brother-in-law's brother. To the outside world, Hodgson never mentioned her by name, but he did recognise his two children by her, Henry, born in 1835 and Sarah, during the period 1835–37.[17]

Could it be done? must have been one of the questions Tickell was struggling with. He saw the live-in relationship and the children of Brian. But that was in Kathmandu and Brian Houghton Hodgson was the Resident. There and in that position this, albeit discreetly, could be done without hurting one's career. Not in Bengal, not anymore, and not by a Junior Assistant on the way up in his career. There is evidence of wavering. He changed his plan to go to Rajputana. He got the same post of Assistant, but now for Chotanagpur and starting the 17th of February, but within five days he requested a postponement till 15 March 1841, for 'very urgent private matters'.[18]

In London, Samuel Richard had heard the stories about his dashing grandfather, the playwright Richard Tickell, about his grandmother's sister Elisabeth Anne Linley, the fairy from Bath. Behind the parapet of St. James' Palace, he had heard about the actress Miss Barnes from his aunt, from his grandfather's jilted fiancée and from her own grandson. She once had been the live-in lover of grandfather Richard Tickell and, like Mehr-un-Nissa with Brian Houghton Hodgson, mother to two of his children.

Was the outcome of Tickell's life in Hodisum one of a Greek drama in which fixed characters clash, or one of a Shakespearean Hamlet, who would make choices with memories and a character pushing him in different directions?[19] In his childhood India, he had gone through the deaths of his father and of his small brother, through witnessing his mother facing the necessity to carry on and start a new family, through the severance of his intimate ties by leaving for education in Belait. As a young adult, he had to handle the return to his people who to a large extent had become strangers. His was a life loaded with painful adjustments and secret rejections.

He was going on thirty, and conscious about his limitations. Tickell felt inadequate to translate Ho songs, poetry, and their ideas which, he feared, lost their originality in his translation. As time went on, he felt more at ease with painting than with writing. Tickell could not in words do justice to 'the beautiful flowers which enrich these green retreats', or even enumerate them fully, 'it would exceed my powers, or the limits of this memoir'. Part of these beauties were 'the cool banks of foliage canopied streams'. The river, the 'beautiful Baitarani', placed him for the choice how to express himself, 'every wind of whose stream would be subject for the artist's pencil, or the poet's pen'.[20] Tickell was no poet, but he did paint the beauty of the jungle. Actually, in the period he was collecting his material for the 'Memoir', Tickell had little spare time to enjoy the jungle at leisure. Unfortunately, close to the villages, 'birds of all kinds are scarce and wild, especially those fit for food, on account of the keenness with which the Koles pursue, trap, hawk, and shoot them.'[21] We have seen him come back from an unsuccessful hunt close to a village.[22] He was so taken up with his work and the Hos, that he felt that he had to limit his passion for collecting birds. 'The deep moist woods afford immense varieties to the ornithologist, an enumeration of which would be useless.'[23]

That was a loss, but at the time Tickell did not seem to mind it much. He engaged with the Hos. The 'Memoir' was not an emotional diary. Still, emotions shone through many pages. Tickell was much at ease with the men and the women of the Hos, the village evenings and the dances. He did not like the habit of the poorer Hos of eating carrion, and their lack of personal hygiene. But he confessed his 'partiality' for the Hos, and for 'the virtue inherent in a primitive state of society'.[24] He liked the sound of the Ho language but was silent about the Ho music itself. He did approve of the village songs and of dances. One should not overlook that Tickell elevated one Ho dance to the Gallope of English society. In the carnival atmosphere of Mage with its 'odiously filthy recitative', he had remembered London.[25]

Tickell had a bit of a conservationist in him, at the very least in his notion of decency. He disliked the Hindus of the neighbourhood, who had given him plenty of trouble with their dynastic squabbling and deceit. He dreaded the effects of civilisation such as lying—but he clearly meant the Indian civilisation he knew.[26]

We see Tickell wavering in Kathmandu, but we do not see a final choice. Even if the wheels of fate did not drive him towards a final decision as in a Greek drama, Tickell had to confront his memories. Hamlet went to the castle rampart and saw his father's ghost. Samuel Richard Tickell on the roof of the Residency looked at the mountains of Nepal on one side and the road to Hindustan on the other side, and faced his grandfather's ghost.

The balance of this primitive belonging and his wish to move on with his life and career was tipped on his return to the Kolhan in 1841. As an administrator, Samuel Richard Tickell was disappointed. As soon as he came back in Hodisum, he got caught up in troubles with the chiefs of the neighbourhood. With the Hos, too, he found that there had been no material progress and he even saw the danger of relapse. The tax evasion in Hodisum—always a sore point and one he had avoided in his 'Memoir'—made him lose patience. Tickell wished, in the end, the Hos to be more like himself. But, as his last despatches from Hodisum showed, communication broke down.

Part of this came from his time perspective. The non-regulation system was linked up with Utilitarianism. It had a radical streak, as Utilitarianism carried the idea 'of some sudden sweeping transformation of Indian society . . . [in which] India would be propelled at a bound from feudal darkness into the modern world. This sort of attitude', Stokes remarks, 'could only flourish in an age brought up to believe in sudden conversion.'[27] Tickell, too, had no idea how long and how crooked the road of culture change could be. The exposure of the Hos to the new system had been a few years only. And, in spite of its innovations, the immediate results for Ho society had been conservative. In Hodisum, the preconditions of a rapid change or 'sudden conversion' were not present. Tickell could learn Ho, the Hos saw no reason to learn English—or for that matter even Hindi or Odia. The arrival of the modern state had not brought about a cultural revolution in Hodisum. That was a disappointment for the Christian and the Utilitarian in Tickell. It came on top of a serious disappointment in the personal sphere.

For the Bendkars, he had shot a bird. For the Hos, Tickell climbed a tree. 'English sportsmen'—but not me, meant Tickell —

> are not so successful . . . as their patience seldom admits of sitting up [a tree] till daybreak, which is the time for the tiger to make his meal. It is exceedingly difficult of a night, even in bright moonlight to take aim, the sight of the gun being so indistinct or invisible. . . . The best plan is that adopted by natives as depicted. . . . A bright cherâgh or oil lamp lighted is put into a common pot in the side of which a hole is made, and the pot is so placed that the light falls full on the carcase, while the gunner is seated in darkness. It is said that the tiger so far from being deterred by the light, comes more readily to the carcase when so temptingly brought into view.[28]

Tickell departed for a long leave at the Cape. He returned to another part of the South Western Frontier Agency. In private life, he went on to marry and start a family. Eventually, his career brought him to Burma. He would continue to spend his free time in the jungle, shooting birds.

From church records, we have the names of his wife and children, but in Tickell's own Hodésum writings we hardly ever get concrete persons with names. The only Ho individual who comes alive is the unnamed 'Ho prisoner' who had killed his son Kapur in the woods. He was hidden in the appendices. And with all his compliments to the girls of Hodisum, Samuel Richard did not name of any of them. Still, Tickell showed the world the human face of the Hos. By putting them, their language, their beliefs, customs and their land in the Hodésum articles with a glowing tribute to their character, Tickell wrote the people of the Hos into the worldwide community under their own name and—as yet—collective identity.

...

Conclusion: A People in Their Own Land

...

In the history of the Hos, an overwhelmingly agricultural people on the ethnic frontier, land and identity went together. Both were contested. The history of these parts is tied up with state and ethnic formation, and this was expressed in often violent exchanges over land, taxes and administration. Thus, from the official papers of the first four decades of the nineteenth century, the history of the Hos appears as a political history. At first glance, the Hos looked like a bunch with law and order and revenue problems with the surrounding states. Surprisingly, when we study the records closely, it was the other way round. Not so much the Hos, but the local rajas and chiefs had law and order and revenue problems. These stopped to be relevant to the Hos, after 1837, when their land was transformed into the Kolhan Government Estate. British supervision showed. Large- and small-scale violence went down; some central administration took root. Life in the estate went on much as before. Soon, the public image of the Hos took a decisive turn for the better.

The ethnic frontier with the Odia-speaking areas long determined the political and social architecture of Singhbhum. State formation started here in the fourth century and got a more firm form in the ninth century with the buildings of Khiching and Benisagar at the southern border of the present-day West Singhbhum District. According to its founding myth, Singhbhum proper was set up around 1205, when the local Bhuiyas invited one Darpa Singh to rule over the area. The Singhbhum chronicle, most of which was written in 1643, informed us obliquely of ethnic shifts in the area. In the thirteenth century, the main population were the Odia-speaking Bhuiyas. Saraks, who probably were Jains, also were important here and remained so till about 1600 CE. The Hos were latecomers to the area, at least in the south. The chronicle mentioned speakers of Munda, 'Kols', as recent arrivals here in the thirteenth century. In roughly the same area, it first noticed 'Hos' as settlers in the 1590s. Largely unnoticed by the chronicle, there were Munda speakers in the north of present-day West Singhbhum, where they were the original inhabitants.

At the end of the sixteenth century, Raja Man Singh and his Mughal troops brought a new format of legitimation of the rajas' rule into the Odisha area. Within a few decades, the Singhs presented, or reinvented, themselves as Rajputs. Singhbhum reached its greatest extent in the second half of the seventeenth century under the rajas Chhatrapati and Kala Arjun Singh. They erected a modest state structure based on a militarily backed *pir* (cantonment) system. The state was intrinsically weak and depended on the strength of its ruler. Around 1720, the Singh family split and so did their realm. When the minor branch of the Singhs in Saraikela went its own way, the power of the major branch in Porahat crumbled. This process was completed by the middle of the eighteenth century, in no small measure because the Munda speakers of the east and south of Singhbhum established their independence. Thereby they confirmed their existence as a new people, the Hos. From the first modern description of them in 1767, we get that they made raids on their neighbours for cattle, while with rare exceptions they stopped outsiders from entering their country. The Hos were the main power of the area.

In 1819, the year after the East Indian Company had become the sole superpower, it started negotiations with Raja Ghanshyam Singh of Porahat. These were quite difficult. For placing himself under the British, Ghanshyam demanded the Company's assistance to re-establish the pre-1720 situation as he understood it. The East India Company declined to interfere in the relations between the Singh states, or to re-establish Ghanshyam's ritual pre-eminence by returning to him the Pauri Devi, the dynastic deity. In the end, Roughsedge, the political agent on the South Western Frontier, agreed to bring most Hos under Ghanshyam. In 1821, he succeeded, although it had taken two heavily fought campaigns. The Ho reaction to the East India Company was divided. Singrai of Dopai in the north sided with Roughsedge, but Mata of Balandia in the centre resisted the new arrangements.

At the conclusion of the hostilities, the Hos got a rough deal. The ethnic frontier started to move into Hodisum. Raghunath Bisi of Jaintgarh, nominally subservient to Porahat, wanted to become independent and, worse for the Hos, he squeezed the local population. In 1830, the local Hos chased him. The new agent, Wilkinson, suspected the hand of Porahat. Elsewhere in Singhbhum, too, the frontier state was faring hardly better. The rulers did not have a program of public works to make their rule attractive. To their subjects, they offered but their need for cash to meet the requirements of their families and retainers. The Hos, too, who did not feel like they were subjects, were supposed to pay these taxes. They did so irregularly, and often not at all. The Hos did not need the Singhs; the Singhs needed them.

The East India Company was not involved in these post-1821 developments, in which the Singh chiefs were too weak to rule but strong enough to provoke the Hos. In Chotanagpur, just north of the Ho country, the Kol Insurrection of 1831–32 showed Calcutta that the frontier of ethnic colonisation by people from the Ganges plains had to be superseded by an administrative frontier of good governance by the British themselves. That change of grand strategy was accomplished by Agent Thomas Wilkinson. Its starting point was the realisation that the rules and regulations as applied to the peoples of the Gangetic plains were incompatible with the needs of the original inhabitants of the Chotanagpur plateau. Especially in the centre and south, these formed the vast majority of the population. Wilkinson drew up sets of simple rules for civil and criminal cases to ensure accessible and affordable justice to them. To blunt the edge of the ethnic differences with recent immigrants, the sale of land to outsiders was—in principle—stopped. Wilkinson's non-regulation system of 1833–34 meant increased supervision by a British officer together with more autonomy at the grass-roots level of the inhabitants. The frontier went into its imperialist phase.

Within a few years, Wilkinson extended his system to the country of the Hos. Here, the immediate cause was the failure of the local states to reconstruct themselves without upsetting the Company's strategic security arrangements with regard to the Hos. In the 1820s and 1830s, Jadunath Bhanj, raja of Mayurbhanj on the southern and eastern borders of Hodisum, pressurised his Bamanghati fief holder Madhu Das over the amount of revenue. Their violent and persistent disagreements set into motion developments they could not control. They enlisted eastern Hos to fight for them on Bamanghati or Mayurbhanj territory. But even the raja of Mayurbhanj, the strongest party, was told to stay out of the Ho villages. Mayurbhanj came out victorious over Bamanghati. At that junction, Achuta Singh of Singhbhum saw an opportunity for expansion. He prepared to join hands with Mayurbhanj in an attack on Saraikela. But in British eyes, Saraikela was needed to prevent the Hos from disturbing the Company territories to their north and east. In 1837, after lengthy deliberations, the East India Company stopped further connections between the local chiefs and the Hos. In a short but brutal campaign, Hodisum was brought under direct British rule. Now, again, the Hos were divided about the East India Company. On Wilkinson's side were many Hos from the north of Hodisum and the area Gumra near Chaibasa. He encountered the heaviest resistance in the east, centre and south of Hodisum: the Thai, Bharbharia, Balandia, and Bar *pirs*. The new British area was called the Kolhan Government Estate

The rationale behind the Estate was that the Hos were very distinct from the Hindu rulers and peoples in the area, and whatever contacts they had with the rulers were detrimental to the public peace in a wider area. That made it unwise to keep them in the same administrative set-up. The Ho and their Hindu neighbours lived in different worlds. Contacts were few. Hardly any outsider spoke Ho; the Hos themselves did not speak other languages. Some songs showed Hindu influence. Hindu influences could also be seen in 1821, in some pujas—which the Hos held together with the Bhuiyas on the eve of battles—and in 1837, in some practices promoted by border Brahmins and other religious practitioners—such as holding a puja before or wearing bullet proof amulets during battle. Also, there were the witch finders, often people from outside. Many of these outside influences were bound up with disruptions of normal life, war and illness.

Apart from paying some taxes sometimes and from going on plundering expeditions as auxiliaries of the local chiefs in the period 1831–37, Hos had few ties with the outside world. They did not use money and this kept trade to a minimum. There were two yearly festivals with a market in Saraikela, and an annual hunt on the northern border with Tamar, but these events took place outside of Hodisum. A handful of outsiders, mainly weavers, went on trading trips inside the area. Ethnic differences were shored up by economic isolation. With it went mutual negative stereotypes.

Up to and including the Poto Ho resistance, the opinions these people had of each other, at least as they appear in the sources and statements, were negative. The local feudal chiefs told the British—first the new power in the area, later its sole superpower—what they thought it needed to know to further the interests and aims of their palaces. The Singh rulers feared and loathed the Hos. In 1767, the Hos were 'banditti'; in 1820, they were 'tigers'; most of the other times, they were pigs, 'Kols'.

The East India Company officers found that, if given a chance, these chiefs would oppress the local population, which would lead to disturbances they could not control. Moreover, their relations with each other were more often than not driven by ancient claims and 'rancorous enmity'. So they would appeal to the East India Company for help, as in 1818, 1820, 1823 and 1830. Such appeals often gave rise to great irritation.

All this time the Hos looked upon the Singh raja of Porahat 'with great contempt'. The same was their view of Raghunath Bisi in Jaintgarh. They feared and loathed Ajambar and his son Chakradhar of Saraikela as the embodiment of tigerish wickedness.

On the British side, about which we have the most information, we see the appreciation of the Hos going up and down with their compliance. For Roughsedge in 1820–21, the Hos were of two kinds. The loyal ones were 'manly', with strong, independent behaviour like 'wild buffaloes', the Hos that opposed him were a 'dreadful pest'. After Roughsedge, in the mid-1830s when the area was in permanent turmoil, the judicial secretary to the Bengal Government condensed the official knowledge of the Hos as 'bands of savages mostly armed with bows and arrows [who] make predatory incursions . . . upon our peaceful subjects'.

Thus, the attitude of the Singhs towards the Hos went from the fear of never getting the revenue, through greed to get it all, to feeling side-lined by losing it all; and that of the British went from aggression, through stand-offishness to, ultimately, partiality. These attitudes were politically expedient, but also were bound up with their self-images—the Singhs as rulers wronged by their subjects and the British as the reluctant, but successful, bringers of order.

On the opinion of the Hos about the British, there is little. The Narsanda massacres of 1820 had made a deep impression. The Hos remembered Roughsedge as 'dreadfully severe' in battle. At least in rhetoric, to 'keep the sahib out' was as important as to keep the Singhs out.

The constant in the story, and what they themselves felt most deeply, is the aversion of the Ho people to outside interference in their village life. The Hos lived in a world largely turned upon itself. When the strong East India Company army started to act, their internal divisions became acute. The Hos confronted outside interference in different ways. These point to intensive discussions leading to flexible responses. When Roughsedge was preparing his invasion of the Kolhan in 1820, Hos from the south warned those close to the northern border that they had to oppose interference by the Porahat raja and the Saraikela *kunwar*. To mention this might have been a diplomatic move of northern village leaders to stave off punishment by Roughsedge's troops. It certainly indicated a practice of dialogue among the Hos, involving many villages. This is also suggested by the events from the next year, 1821, when Bahuran's mercenaries started to plunder villages and raped Mahadei, the daughter of a village head. People from the northern area formed a formal alliance to chase them from their Pokharia camp and to capture their Chainpur fort. The political dialogue could extend over a wide area. In 1822 and 1830, Hos of the Pingua *kili* got together against Raghunath both to oppose his economic exploitation and to revenge the death of their prominent leader Suban. They came from different places as far as Balandia, but they all belonged to Suban's Pingua *kili*. This alliance showed itself stable. It was reactivated after the institution of the Kolhan Government Estate, when within a few months Poto, a leader from Rajabasa, used Balandia as his base to attack the Company troops. By now, also, there was a more entrenched opinion favouring cooperation with the British. Possibly, some of this support came from opposition to traditional rivals. Gummo of Dumriya even travelled twelve kilometres of bad roads to burn Poto's Rajabasa. In the last days of 1837, Poto and his Hos were beaten in the battle of Seringsia.

When the British stepped in to take over the Ho lands, they did not 'divide to rule'. There already was a clear distinction between the Hos and their Hindu neighbours. Though some Hos lived in villages which continued to be under the local chiefs, the administrative borders of the Kolhan Government Estate mainly followed the Ho ethnic border. The Estate re-affirmed, not created, the separate Ho social and cultural space.

That showed in the work of its first assistant, Samuel Richard Tickell. When he arrived in the new capital Chaibasa, Ho society was in disarray and its economy heavily affected by the fighting. Moreover, a large part of the population in the south of the new estate continued to oppose the new system. Again, Balandia was at the centre of the resistance, now under the leadership of Poto Ho. It was crushed at the end of 1837 in the battle of Seringsia. Over the next two years the new assistant, who liked to be in the area, was engaged in setting up the Wilkinson system. In 1840, disappointed in the impact of his reforms on government finance and local culture, Tickell departed for Kathmandu. On his return the next year, he again found that the Hos were not interested in paying taxes or changing their habits. In 1842, Tickell left to ultimately pursue his career in Burma.

Tickell surveyed their fields; the Hos did not like that. They were, however, sensitive to power, and, indeed, sensitive to a friendly approach. It is clear that at the personal level they liked the assistant, and that Tickell liked them. Still, there were times the administrator won out in Tickell. He, too, would call them 'savage', when the Hos resisted actively as under Poto in 1837, or afterwards passively as with their concealment of taxable lands. Even when, with occasional unflattering opinions of the Hos, he hinted towards enforcement, Calcutta would have none of it. Tickell found the Hos defending their interests. The archives contain echoes of tough negotiations on political and revenue issues.

Most of his experiences were different. In accordance with his brief to get to know the Hos, he did not see them only during negotiations in shadowed mango orchards and trials in stuffy courtrooms. Obviously, the best occasions to meet were hunting trips and the evenings with storytelling, drinks, songs and dances. So, many of his experiences, as they found their way in the Hodésum articles, did not come from the political part of his work, but from being there.

Much depended here on Tickell's personality. Samuel Richard Tickell had a family background which both prepared him for life with Hos and made continuation about impossible. From his dashing but impoverished socialite grandfather Richard Tickell he had inherited a feeling for theatre, which helped him to accept the unexpected from people, and his musical ear helped him to reproduce the sounds of the Ho language. When Tickell made an effort to talk, the Hos returned the compliment.

They told him the myths and stories that were important to Ho life. Tickell wrote down theatrical, sometimes very vivid dialogues and he observed the village dances—and girls—with a keen eye. He participated much in Ho society but did not go native, become part of it. In the end, the cultured officer had to consider his personal relations with them, and his future career in the administration. He left Hodisum and went back to his old passion ornithology. He became quite a painter of birds and their natural habitats.

In his small series of ethnographic and linguistic Hodésum articles, Tickell passed on much, but certainly not all, of what the Hos told him. He presented a sympathetic and vivid portrait of the Hos, their land, society and culture. To Tickell, the Hos had mostly good qualities: light-hearted, hospitable, and beautiful. Communication was not without its pitfalls, though. Hos could be touchy to the point of being suicidal. The Hos, although indolent and dirty, were engaging. In Tickell's accounts, one senses the rapport between him and the people he described, a mutual sympathy with which we in the twenty-first century of fusion are more at ease than with the cold distance which we have come to expect from local administrators and from academics studying Ho culture and society.

By 1820, there were about 65,000 Hos, of which some 50,000 were outside of the area controlled by the local Hindu rajas and chiefs. Twenty years later, that number had increased by, possibly, some 20 per cent. The Hos continued to expand their arable area. In 1820, Roughsedge mentioned mostly woods and rocks, except for the 'champaign country' to the north and south of Chaibasa. In the decades leading to the establishment of the Kolhan Government Estate, they cleared much jungle in the centre and the east of Hodisum. There had been richer and poorer Hos ever since observers entered the country. But nearly every Ho household owned the land it worked, and the Hos were egalitarian in spirit. Even the short-tempered Roughsedge admitted that the Hos lived in 'smiling hamlets', something for which the Singhs had not prepared him.

Tickell filled in this picture with many a detail. Life could be cruel. Villages were surrounded by jungle where the tiger roamed. Epidemics, attributed to malignant spirits and witchcraft, wrought havoc on society. But central was the social life of the village, often peaceful with the soft evening light falling on the flat burial stones, the bowl of *diang* for the parents and the communal singing and dancing by the boys and girls.

Still, we are little informed about the internal organisation of Ho society. It had far outgrown the *pir* system of the Singh rajas of the seventeenth and early eighteenth centuries. From the mid-eighteenth century on, a *pir* was a geographical indication of an area on which the Singhs had largely ignored claims on revenue. The names of these *pirs* were taken over by the East India Company. The Hos, apparently, did not care much for the formal territorial arrangement that was implied in the *pir*. This expressed politically that the social and cultural distances between the Hos and the surrounding peoples, never small, had been increasing.

Ho society was divided into clans or *kilis*. The social distance between clans was expressed by not sharing food. This seemed much less so when it came to drinking rice beer. Tickell mentioned the custom of offering it to friends and visitors. It was also drunk at evenings, and in social gatherings in the compounds of the houses. The *kili* was not a self-contained unit. Marriage had to be out of the *kili*. An obvious way to meet possible partners was to go to one of the feasts in another village; the Hos liked to party. The outer limit of the marriage circle would, of course, be the ethnic boundary of the Ho people. We have seen that strive between *kilis* was a factor in the Kolhan Campaigns. More direct evidence of some *kili* organisation was the action of the Pingua *kili* against Raghunath in 1829-1830. Poto's resistance of 1837 had a large component of Pinguas as well, but the solemn conclusion of his alliances points to the heavy involvement of others. The fighting had left much bad blood, and one of the first things Tickell did, was to effect a conciliation between traditionally opposing *kilis*.

Except for these feuds inside, and the cattle raids in- and outside Hodisum, which were stopped, Ho life went on much as before. The difference was the British supervision. After 1837, though the Hodisum was part of British India, the Kolhan Government Estate continued to shield Ho agriculture from competition by outsiders. Consequently, there was little investment in productivity. In a stifled, largely self-sufficient economy—and one in which there were many claims on the small incomes—the accumulation of capital was slow. In the few years between 1837 and 1842, the modest government investments in roads, too, had only a marginal impact. The main social development was the regulation of, and thereby the boost to, the manki–munda system. The mankis and mundas had to see that crime committed inside their villages was reported to the court in Chaibasa. Their role as tax-gatherers for the state brought them some part of the revenue. Tax evasion was not rigidly investigated and the lack of reports on witch killings taken at face value. This live-and-let-live policy with its lack of immediate confrontations showed. Despite his misgivings about their industry, Samuel Richard Tickell gave the Hos a glowing testimonial as a people. From their side, the Hos accepted the Kolhan Government Estate and the Wilkinson system in so far as these enabled them to do what they wanted, to live a fairly egalitarian life without foreign encumbrances.

The Kolhan Government Estate was the land around which the Ho identity evolved. Its effects are still felt today. The new system that Tickell implemented also meant that the Hos, while exercising much autonomy, were now part of a much wider and more modern administrative system. Potentially, this made external contacts easier for them. As Tickell realised in the hot season of 1841, to engage successfully with the modern world, the Hos still had quite some distance to cover. The establishment of the Kolhan Government Estate was not the end of the road for the Hos of Hodisum. But they had a place to start from; they had their land.

Appendix: Impact of Tickell's articles

Tickell wrote his 'Memoir on the Hodésum' for the public, ethnologists, for example. In Tickell's time, ethnology as such was not yet organised. Individual ethnologists, mainly interested in what we now call physical, linguistic and religious anthropology, were scattered in far-off towns such as Paris and London. Thus, Tickell was an ethnographer without the support of an ethnographic community. But he was not a *bourgeois gentilhomme* who spoke prose without knowing it. He had local publications as sources of insights and methods. After Andrew Stirling's article on Orissa (Odisha) in 1822, there appeared in the *Asiatick Researches* more contributions on marginal tracts and their population.[1] Tickell's treatment of the Hos stood out, as it was much more vivid. For thirty-two years, his description of the Hodisum, and his grammar and list of words, remained the authoritative source on the Hos and their language. The appearance of Dalton's *The Descriptive Ethnology of Bengal* in 1872 marked the end of this period.

We are looking at peculiar documents. Tickell's 'little partiality in their favour' gave these, especially the 'Memoir', an intensity that lifted it way above the earlier accounts by Roughsedge and Wilkinson, and even the efforts by Dalton thirty-two years later. The image of the Hos that the Hodésum articles presented, had a dual parentage. Its core came from intensive contacts between the author and his subjects. This gave these articles a worthy place in the Indian ethnographic sphere. For the Hos, and unknown to them, Tickell's Hodésum articles were epoch-making. For the first time, the Hos and their language appeared in print, the ultimate worldwide medium of his day.

As we have seen, Hodgson gave a frosty reception to Tickell, and probably also to his manuscript 'Memoir', in 1840. In articles in 1847 and again in 1856, Hodgson made clear that he doubted Tickell's remarks about the racial characteristic of the Hos, moreover, he largely ignored Tickell's linguistic work.[2] Tickell made an early appearance in the *Calcutta Review* of 1856, where he was quoted on the burial customs of the Hos.[3]

For the more general ethnological public, it was important that Tickell's Hodésum figured prominently in Latham's description of the Kols in his *Descriptive Ethnology of Asia, Africa and Europe*, published in 1859.[4] In this book, Latham used (with acknowledgements) Tickell's article on the Bendkars. However, he had more regard for Captain Macpherson's paper on the Khonds than for

Tickell's 'Memoir'.[5] Nevertheless, Latham considered the Ho 'the best known of all the Kols; not, however, because they have been visited by the greatest number of Europeans, but because they have been made the subject of a valuable monograph by Lieutenant Tickell'.[6] Making use of a small paragraph of the 'Memoir', Latham presented the Hos as 'locomotive agriculturists'. By far the most space in Latham's description was taken up by condensations of Tickell's 'Marriage Ceremonies', 'Signs and Omens', 'Funeral Rites', and a selection from his 'Gods and Spirits'. Latham's whole piece was incredibly dull and dry, but literal quotations from a Ho funeral song and Tickell's 'Kole History of the Creation of the World' infused a little life.

In the 1860s and 1870s, Tickell's fame reached Germany. The geologist Emil Stöhr, who had come to Singhbhum from Germany with his assistant Schenk 'to fix upon the spots where mines are to be established',[7] wrote an account on 'Die Singhbhum-Abteilung der Provinz der Südwest-Grenze von Bengalen'. A large part of this account was based on Tickell's 'Memoir' with some additions from other sources and his own observations.[8]

Edward Tuite Dalton knew the Hodésum articles, and he relied much on the 'Memoir' in his various descriptions of the Hos, respectively in his 1866 article on 'The "Kols" of Chota Nagpore,[9] in 1868 in the text accompanying a photograph in the *People of India*[10] and in 1872 quite extensively in his monumental *Descriptive Ethnology of Bengal*.[11]

Spencer selected some of his quotations from Tickell's 'Memoir' in his *Descriptive Sociology* of 1876.[12] In 1880, Valentine Ball he mentioned Tickell as a source for the early history of Singhbhum in his *Jungle Life*.[13] Likewise, Tickell was mentioned as a source in Balfour's *Cyclopedia of India* in 1885.[14] As a titbit on funeral ceremonies, Tickell was reborn in 1892 on page 123 of the second issue of *North Indian Notes and Queries*.[15] Hoffmann used Tickell in the lemma on the Hos in his monumental *Encyclopaedia Mundarica*, published piecemeal from 1930 onwards.[16] Finally, Tickell's 'Memoir' figured as the zero line in D. N. Majumdar's *A Tribe in Transition* (1937), the first academic anthropological monograph on the Hos, and its 1950 successor volume, *The Affairs of a Tribe*.[17]

Tickell's archaeological descriptions, mainly about Benisagar and Kesnagar, did not raise much dust. In 1874, Beglar called it 'not always reliable', but it seems he had more a change remark on Udaipur in mind.[18] In 1983, Joshi was more complimentary, Tickell's work belonged to a small number of 'valuable works of reference'.[19]

In post-Independence Ho historiography, Tickell's ethnographic contribution was mentioned in passing by S. Sen Gupta and A. K. Sen, both in 2011. In 2014, his 'Vocabulary' was used by P. Sen.[20] In 2012, it seems, the 'Memoir' was published by a small publisher in Kolkata.[21]

Tickell had quite some impact on official writings. Risley's Singhbhum volume of the *Statistical Account of Bengal* contained three extensive quotes.[22] His descriptions also inspired O'Malley's *District Gazetteer* of Singhbhum of 1910.[23] A remark by Tickell on the introduction of the manki system was used in Tuckey's settlement report of 1920.[24] His presence continued to be felt in P. C.

Roy Chaudhury's 1958 *District Gazetteer* of Singhbhum. It is not clear here how much of the influence came directly from Tickell's work, or indirectly through Dalton. But Roy Chaudhuri quoted the hunting scene in full as 'Colonel Tickell's amusing account'.[25]

Tickell figured for a long time as a prime source in linguistic remarks. In 1854, Max Muller mentioned Tickell and wrote about 'a most interesting memoir published by Lieutenant Tickell'. Apparently, he had also read Tickell's linguistic work.[26] In 1860, Mason mentioned Tickell's researches as adding proof to his theory that the Mon or Talaing of Burma were linguistically related to the Mundas. He found that Tickell's memoir 'affords the most complete view of the people and their language, that has as yet been made public'.[27] Probably on the recommendation of E. T. Dalton, the 'Grammar' was reprinted in 1866.[28] This reprint was used by Friedrich Müller in his *Allgemeine Ethnographie* published in 1879.[29] Meanwhile, in 1873, Jellinghaus, a German missionary in Ranchi, mentioned that the Munda and Larka languages had received little attention from Europeans, with the exception of '*eines sehr kürzen Aufsatzes über Volk und Sprache der Larka Kolh vom Mr. Pickel in den Journal der Asiatic Society 1840*' (a very short article on the people and language of the Larka Kol by Mr. Pickell). Without difficulty, we recognise in Herr Pickel our Lieutenant Samuel Richard Tickell.[30] In 1904, Sten Konow, who wrote part of Grierson's *Linguistic Survey of India*, mentioned 'the well-known Colonel Tickell' while refuting Hahn's view that the Munda languages belonged to the Dravidian group.[31] Today, too, Samuel Richard Tickell's name is recognised as a pioneer of Munda linguistics, even by an authority like J.B.F. Kuiper.[32]

Bibliography

Archives

The Athenaeum Library, Liverpool

Elizabeth Roughsedge-Wareing, 'Biographical note', no date.

Bihar State Archives, Patna (BSA)

Singhbhum Old Correspondence (SOC), volumes 118, 122, 123.

British Library, Oriental and India Office Collection, London (OIOC),
http://www.nationalarchives.gov.uk

Board's Collections (BC): 3403; 5707; 7,008; 7,411; 10,611; 14,293; 14,294; 14,295; 18,889; 20,327; 21,438; 21,439; 21,872; 21,873; 58,533, 58,890, 58,896; 58,897; 58,901; 58,902; 58,903; 58,904; 58,906, 66,544; 66,545; 66,546; 66,561; 69,239.

Bengal Political Consultations, 1821, 1830.

Cadet papers.

Foreign Department, Political Consultations; Despatches, 1843, 1846.

'Hodgson Papers, Inventory of Hodgson's private papers at the British Library', MSS EUR Hodgson/25 Ethnography and languages 1830s–1850s.

Home Miscellaneous, vols. 724, 754, 769, 781, 787, 925.

India and Bengal Despatches, 1837, 1838, 1844.

India Office Family History Search (website), http//indiafamily.bl.uk.

Darwin Correspondence Project (website), http://www.darwinproject.ac.uk

National Archives of India, New Delhi (NAI)

Foreign Department, Political Consultation, 1830, 1832.

Foreign Department, Secret. 6 August 1832.

Foreign Department, 1830–1899, entries on anthropometry; Chota Nagpur; Keonjhar; Kharsawan; Mohurbhunj; Native States; Ouseley; Seraikella; Singhbhoom; South West Frontier Agency; Tributary Mehals.

Natural History Museum, London
'Original water-colour drawings and illustrated MS relating to Indian Birds', forming one of a set of volumes from which the illustrated MS work by Tickell on Mammals, &c. of India, in the Library of the Zoological Society of London was elaborated, [abt. 1870].

West Bengal State Archives, Kolkata (WBSA)
Judicial (Criminal) Proceedings, Lower Provinces, 1828, 1838.

Zoological Society of London, London
'The Zoological Works of Samuel Richard Tickell', illustrated manuscript work in 14 volumes, [1865–73].

Books and articles

'Account of the Kholes or Coles', *The Asiatic Journal and Monthly Register for British and Foreign India, China, and Australasia*, n.s., 8 (May–August 1832): 264–66.

Acharya, Paramananda. 'A Note of the "Bhum" Countries in India'. *Indian Culture* 12, no. 2 (1945): 37–46.

Adiga, Aravind. *The White Tiger*. London: Atlantic Books, 2008.

'A History of British Birds (1843)'. *Wikipedia* (website). Accessed 15 December 2013. https://en.wikipedia.org.

Ahuja, Ravi. '"Captain Kittoe's Road". Early Colonialism and the Politics of Road Construction in Peripheral Orissa'. In *Periphery and Centre, Studies in Orissan History, Religion and Anthropology*, edited by Georg Pfeffer, 293–318. Delhi: Manohar, 2007.

Aitchison, C. V. *A Collection of Treaties, Engagements, and Sanads Relating to India and Neighbouring Countries:Containing the Treaties, etc., Relating to the Bengal Presidency, Assam, Burma and the Eastern Archipelago, Revised and continued Up to the present time by the Authority of the Foreign Department*. Vol. 1. Calcutta: Office of the Superintendent of Government Printing, India, 1892.

Aitchison, C. V. *A Collection of Treaties, Engagements, and Sanads Relating to India and Neighbouring Countries*. Vol. 2. Calcutta: Government of India, Central Publication Branch, 1930.

Allen, Charles. *The Prisoner of Kathmandu: Brian Hodgson in Nepal 1820–43*. London: Haus, 2015.

———, ed. *Plain Tales from the Raj: Images of British India in the Twentieth Century*, edited in association with Michael Mason; Introduction by Philip Mason. London: Futura, 1976.

Alliston, April. 'Introduction'. In Sophia Lee, *The Recess; or, A Tale of Other Times*, edited by April Alliston. Lexington: University Press of Kentucky, 2000.

Amin, A. H. 'Technical and Tactical Superiority of the Enfield Rifle over the Brown Bess'. Book review of *The Sepoy Rebellion of 1857–59, An Analysis*. *Defence Journal* (May 2001). Accessed 13 July 2011. http://www.defencejournal.com/2001/may/sepoy.htm. 'The Arian Race', *Calcutta Review* 26 (1856): 474–548.

Arbuthnot, Alexander J. 'Ricketts, Sir Henry (1802–1886)'. *Dictionary of National Biography*, 1148–49. Vol. 16. 1921–22. Reprint, London: Oxford University Press, 1963–64.

Areeparampil, Mathew. 'Migration of the Hos to Singhbhum'. In *Singhbhum, some historical gleanings*, edited by Asoka Kumar Sen. Chaibasa: Department of History, Tata College, 1986.

———. 'A Bibliography of the Ho Tribe and Singhbhum'. Chaibasa: Tribal Research and Training Centre, 1991. Typed. Unpublished.

———. S*truggle for Swaraj: A History of Adivasi Movements in Jharkhand (from the Earliest Times to the Present Day.* Lupungutu: Tribal Research and Training Centre (TRTC), 2002.

Armstrong, Frederick H. *Handbook of Upper Canadian Chronology*. Revised edition. Toronto and London: Dundurn Press, 1985.

Asher, Frederick M. *The Art of Eastern India, 300–800*. Minneapolis: The University of Minneapolis Press, 1980.

Auber, Peter. *Rise and Progress of the British Power in India*. By Peter Auber, M.R.A.S., late Secretary to the Honourable the Court of Directors of the East-India Company. 2 vols. London: Wm. H. Allen, 1837.

'Austroasiatic Languages', *Wikipedia* (website). Accessed 25 March 2015. https://en.wikipedia.org.

Baker, D. E. U. *Colonialism in an Indian Hinterland, The Central Provinces, 1820–1920*. Delhi: Oxford University Press, 1993.

Balfour, E. 'Kol'. In *The Cyclopaedia of India and of Eastern and Southern Asia: Commercial, Industrial, and Scientific, Products of the Mineral, Vegetable and Animal Kingdoms, Useful Arts and Manufactures*. Vol. 2, H-Nysa, 3rd edition, 584–92. London: Bernard Quaritch, 1885.

Ball, Valentine. 'Notes on Some Stone Implements Found in the District of Singbhoom by Captain Beeching'. *Proceedings of the Asiatic Society of Bengal* (January–December 1868): 177.

———. 'On the Ancient Copper Miners of Singhbhum'. *Journal of the Asiatic Society of Bengal* 38 (1869): 171–75.

———. 'Stone Monuments in the District of Singhbhum—Chota Nagpur'. *The Indian Antiquary* 1 (1872): 291–92.

———. 'On the Avifauna of the Chutia (Chota) Nagpur Division, S.W. Frontier of Bengal'. *Stray Feathers: Journal of Ornithology for India and its Dependencies* 2 (1874): 355–439.

———. *Jungle Life in India; or, The Journeys and Journals of an Indian Geologist*. London: Thos. De la Rue, 1880. Also reprinted as *Tribal and Peasant Life in Nineteenth Century India*. New Delhi: Usha, 1985.

Banerjee, Mangobinda. *An Historical Outline of Pre-British Chotanagpur (From earliest times to 1765)*. Ranchi: Educational Publishers, 1989.

Banerji, R. D. 'Rajput Origins in Orissa'. Appendix VI to *History of Orissa, From the Earliest Time to the British Period*. Vol. 2, edited by R. D. Banerji, R. Chatterjee, M. C. Das, 421–36. Calcutta, R. Chatterjee/Prabasi Press. 1931.

Banton, Michael. 'The Classification of Races in Europe and North America, 1700–1850'. *International Social Science Journal* 39, no. 1 (February 1987): 45–60.

Bara, Joseph, 'Tribal Education, the Colonial State and Christian Missionaries: Chhotanagpur, 1839–1870', in *Education and the Disprivileged: Nineteenth and Twentieth Century India,* edited by Sabyasachi Bhattacharya (Hyderabad: Orient Longman, 2002), 123-52.

———. 'Seeds of Mistrust, Tribal and Colonial Perspectives on Education in Chhotanagpur, 1834—c. 1850'. *History of Education* 34, no. 6 (2005): 617–37.

Basu, Analabha, Neeta Sarkar-Roy, and Partha P. Majumder. 'Genomic Reconstruction of the History of Extant

Populations of India Reveals Five Distinct Ancestral Components and a Complex Structure'. *Proceedings of the National Academy of Sciences of the United States of America* 113, no. 6 (February 9, 2016), 1594–1599. Published online before print (January 25, 2016). Accessed 26 January 2016. http://www.pnas.org/content/113/6/1594.full.

Basu, Analabha, Namita Mukherjee, Sangita Roy, Sanghamitra Sengupta, Sanat Banerjee, Madan Chakraborty, Badal Dey, Monami Roy, Bidyut Roy, Nitai P. Bhattacharyya, Susantha Roychoudhury, and Partha P. Majumder. 'Ethnic India: A Genomic View, With Special Reference to Peopling and Structure.' *Genome Research* 13 (2003): 2277–2290. *Genome Research* (website). Accessed 26 January 2016. http://www.ncbi.nlm.nih.gov/pmc/articles/PMC403703/.

Basu, K. K. 'The History of Singhbhum 1821–1836'. *Journal of the Bihar Research Society* 42 (1956): 283–98.

——. 'Early Administration of the Kol Peers in Singhbhum and Bamanghati'. *Journal of the Bihar Research Society* 42 (1956): 357–76.

——. 'Tour-Diary of J. R. Ouseley'. *The Orissa Historical Research Journal* 5 (1956): 166–78.

——. 'Larka Kols of Singhbhum'. *Journal of the Bihar Research Society* 43 (1957): 74–79.

Bailey, Frederick George. *Caste and the Economic Frontier: A Village in Highland Orissa.* Second impression. Manchester: Manchester University Press, 1959.

Bayley, A. R. 'A Note on Sheridan'. *Notes and Queries* 11-X, no. 239 (1914): 61–63.

Bayly, Christopher Alan. *Imperial Meridian: The British Empire and the World, 1780–1830.* Studies in Modern History. London and New York: Longman, 1989.

——, ed. *The Raj, India and the British, 1600–1947.* London: National Portrait Gallery Publications, 1990.

Beeching, Captain. 'Notes on Some Stone Implements in the District of Singhboom by Captain Beeching'. Communicated by V. Ball, Esq., *Proceedings of the Asiatic Society of Bengal* (January–December 1868): 177.

Beglar, Joseph D. *Report of Tours in the South-Eastern Provinces in 1874–75 and 1875–76.* Calcutta: Office of the Superintendent of Government Printing, 1882. Reprint, Varanasi: Indological Book House, 1970.

Bell, Julian. 'England's Great Neglected Artist'. Review of *The Art of Thomas Bewick* by Diana Donald, *New York Review of Books* 62, no. 16 (22 October–4 November 2015): 12–16.

'Bhat'. *Wikipedia* (website). Accessed 18 December 2013. https://en.wikipedia.org.

Bhattarcharya, Sudhubushan. *Studies in Comparative Munda Linguistics.* Simla: Indian Institute of Advanced Study, 1975.

Black, Clementine. *The Linleys of Bath.* London: Martin Secker, 1911. Accessed 31 December 2010. http://www.archive.org/stream/linleysofbath00blacuoft/linleysofbath00blacuoft_djvu.txt.

Blench, Roger. 'Reconstructing Austroasiatic Prehistory'. 2014, 1–13. Accessed 5 March 2015. http://www.academia.edu/5165573/Reconstructing_Austroasiatic_prehistory.

'Blowing from a gun, The Mughal tradition'. *Wikipedia* (website). Accessed 13 September 2015. https://en.wikipedia.org.

Blyth, Edward. *Catalogue of the Birds in the Museum Asiatic Society.* Calcutta: J. Thomas, 1849.

——. 'Blyth to Darwin [22 September 1855]'. University of Cambridge, *Darwin Correspondence Project* (website). Letter 1755. Accessed 24 October 2010. http://www.darwinproject.ac.uk/entry-1755.

Boddington, Reginald Steward. *Genealogical Memoranda Relating to the Sparks and Tickell Families*. London: privately printed, 1877.

Boivin, Nicole. L., Melinda A. Zeder, Dorian Q. Fuller, Alison Crowther, Greger Larson, John M. Erlandson, Tim Denham, and Michael D. Petraglia, 'Ecological Consequences of Human Niche Construction: Examining Long-term Anthropogenic Shaping of Global Species Distributions', *Proceedings of the National Academy of Sciences of the United States of America* 113, no. 23 (7 June 2016): 6388-6396 . Published online before print June 7, 2016. Accessed 7 June 2016. http://www.pnas.org/content/113/23/6388.full.

Bongard-Levin, G. M. 'The Origin of the Mundas'. In *Studies in Ancient India and Central Asia.* Vol. 7 of Soviet Indology Series of Indian Studies: Past and Present, Debiprasad Chattopadhyaya (ed.), 1–20. Calcutta: R. K. Maitra, 1971). Article first published 1957.

Bose, Nirmal Kumar. 'The Hindu Method of Tribal Absorption'. In Nirmal Kumar Bose, *Culture and Society in India*, 204–15. Bombay: Asia Publishing House, 1967. Article first published 1941.

Bosu Mullick, Sanjay. 'Gender Relations and Witches among the Indigenous Communities of Jharkhand, India'. In *Gender Relations in Forest Societies in Asia: Patriarchy at Odds*, edited by Govind Kelkar, Dev Nathan and Pierre Walter, 119–46. New Delhi: Sage, 2003.

Bouton, J. W. *The Havemeyer Library: Catalogue of the Extensive and Valuable Library* (Formed by a well-known collector who has devoted many years and a large expenditure of money in its formation, Comprising an unusual assemblage of fine art and illustrated works, unique extra illustrated copies, @ standard authors in all departments of literature, Now offered for sale at the very reasonable prices affixed by J.W. Bouton, 1125 Broadway, New York). New York: Printed for the publisher, 1889.

Bowles, W. L. 'Linley, Wm, esq.'. *The Annual Biography and Obituary* 20 (1836): 434–35.

Bradley-Birt, F. B. *Chota Nagpur: A Little Known Province of the Empire*, 2nd ed., enlarged and rev. London: Smith, Elder, 1910.

Breman, Jan C. 'Civilisatie en racisme, Een staat van terreur, Kongo rond de eeuwwisseling' [Civilization and racism: A state of terror, Congo around 1900]. In *Kolonialisme, racisme en cultuurpolitiek*, edited by Jan Breman and others. Special issue, *De Gids* 154, no. 5–6 (1991): 448–93.

Briggs, Asa. *The Age of Improvement, 1783–1867*. 1959. Published with corrections and revised Note on Books, 9th impression. London and New York: Longman, 1991.

The British Critic: Quarterly Theological Review and Ecclesiastical Record. Unsigned review of '*Narrative of a Journey through the Upper Provinces of India, from Calcutta to Bombay, 1824—1825* by Reginald Heber'. Vol. 4 (London, 1828): 200–28. *Google Books* (website). Accessed 6 January 2011. http://books.google.nl/books.

Brooks, Isabelline. 'Colour Prejudice and William Yarrel'. 2004. *Ibooknet* (website). Accessed 1 March 2011, http://www.ibooknet.co.uk/archive/news_april04.htm.

Brother Anthony of Taizé, 'The Tickell Family'. *An Sonjae* (website). Accessed 10 July 2009. http://hompi.sogang.ac.kr/anthony/GrigsbyTickell.htm.

'Brown Bess'. *Wikipedia* (website). Accessed 13 July 2011. https://en.wikipedia.org.

Bruinesse, Martinus van. 'Agha, Shaikh and State: On the Social and Political Organization of Kurdistan'. PhD thesis, Utrecht, 1978.

Burns, Thomas S. *Rome and the Barbarians, 100 B.C.–A.D. 400*. Baltimore and London: The Johns Hopkins

University Press, 2003.

Burrows, Lionel B. *The Grammar of the Ho Language*. Calcutta: Catholic Orphan Press, 1915. Reprinted as *The Grammer of the Ho Language: An Eastern Himalayan Dialect*. New Delhi: Cosmo Publications, 1980.

Campbell, James M., ed. *Khandesh District*. Gazetteer of The Bombay Presidency 12. Bombay: Government Central Press, 1880. Reprinted 1985 by J. M. Torgal, Bombay: Gazetteers Department, Government of Maharashtra.

Chanda, Ramaprasad. 'Note on the Ancient Monuments of Mayurbhanj'. *Journal of the Bihar and Orissa Research Society* 13, part 2 (1927): 131–36.

Cardew, F. G. *A Sketch of the Services of the Bengal Native Army to the Year 1895*. Calcutta: Office of the Superintendent of Government Printing, 1903.

—— [Carnogan, Janet C.]. *Centennial, St. Mark's Church, Niagara, 1792-1892*. Toronto: James Bain, 1892.

Carson, Penelope. 'An Imperial Dilemma: The Propagation of Christianity in Early Colonial India'. *The Journal of Imperial and Commonwealth History* 18, no. 2 (1990): 169–90.

Chaubey, Gyaneshwer, Mait Metspalu, Ying Choi, Reedik Mägi, Irene Gallego Romero, Pedro Soares, Mannis van Oven, Doron M. Behar, Siiri Rootsi, Georgi Hudjashov, Chandana Basu Mallick, Monika Karmin, Mari Nelis, Jüri Parik, Alla Goverdhana Reddy, Ene Metspalu, George van Driem, Yali Xue, Chris Tyler-Smith, Kumarasamy Thangaraj, Lalji Singh, Maido Remm, Martin B. Richards, Marta Mirazon Lahr, Manfred Kayser, Richard Villems and Toomas Kivisild. 'Population Genetic Structure in Indian Austroasiatic Speakers: The Role of Landscape Barriers and Sex-specific Admixture'. *Molecular Biology and Evolution* 28 (2011): 1013–24. Accessed 28 February 2015. http://mbe.oxfordjournals.org/content/28/2/1013.full.

Chaudhuri, Binay Bushan. *Peasant History of Late Pre-colonial and Colonial India*. Vol. 8, Part 2 of *Project of History of Indian Science, Philosophy, and Culture*, edited by D. P. Chattpodhyaya. Delhi: Centre for Studies in Civilizations, 2008.

Chaudhuri, Nirad C. *Thy Hand, Great Anarch!: India, 1921–1952*. Chatto and Windus, 1987. Paperback edition, London: The Hogarth Press, 1990.

Chaudhuri, Sashi Bhusan. *Civil Disturbances During the British Rule in India (1765–1857)*. Calcutta: The World Press, 1955.

Chaudhuri, Sibadas, Comp. *Index to the Publications of the Asiatic Society, 1788–1953*. Volume 1, Parts 1 and 2. Calcutta: The Asiatic Society, 1956.

Choudhury, Sadananda. 'The British Salt Revenue Policy in Orissa'. *The Orissa Historical Research Journal* 16, no. 1 (1975): 57–61.

'Christopher Webb Smith (1793–1871) and Sir Charles William D'Oyly', sale 6807, 24 September 2003. *Christie's* (website). Accessed 19 December 2010. www.Christies.com.

Chakrabarti, Dilip. 'The Idea of Diffusion as an Explanatory Model'. Chapter 2 of *Theoretical Issues in Indian Archaeology*. New Delhi: Munshiram Manoharlal, 1988.

'Civil Appointments &c.', in 'Asiatic Intelligence, Calcutta', *The Asiatic Journal and Monthly Register for British and Foreign India, China, and Australasia*, n.s., 24 (September-December 1837): 96.

Clark, Grahame, 'The Invasion Hypothesis in British Archaeology' *Antiquity* 40 (1966): 172–89.

Cobden-Ramsay, L. E. B. *Feudatory States of Orissa*. Bengal Gazetteers. Calcutta: Bengal Secretariat Book Depôt, 1910. Reprint, Calcutta: Firma KLM, 1982.

Cocker, Mark and Carol Inskipp. *A Himalayan Ornithologist: The life and work of Brian Houghton Hodgson.* Oxford, New York, Tokyo: Oxford University Press, 1988.

Cohn, Bernard S. 'Representing Authority in Victorian India'. In *The Invention of Tradition*, edited by Eric Hobsbawn and Terence Rancer, 165–209. Cambridge: Cambridge University Press. 1983.

———. *An Anthropologist Among the Historians and Other Essays*. Delhi: Oxford University Press, 1987.

'Cole Insurrection', *The Asiatic Journal and Monthly Register for British and Foreign India, China, and Australasia*, n.s., 26 (May–August 1838): 19–20.

Coleman, Charles. *The Mythology of the Hindus: with Notices of Various Mountain and Island Tribes Including the Two Peninsulas of India and the Neighbouring Islands; and Appendix Comprising the Minor Avatars and the Mythological and Religious Terms &&c. of the Hindus, with Plates Illustrative of the Principal Hindu Deities; &c.*. London: Parbury, Allen, 1832. Reprint, Delhi: Asian Educational Services, 1995.

'Commonplace-book, Verse Compiled by Members of the Tickell Family, in England and India'. British Library Manuscript, add. MS 59656, circa 1787–1816.

Cooper, James Fenimore. *The Last of the Mohicans.* 1826. Republished in Penguin Popular Classics. Harmondsworth: Penguin Books, 1994.

Corbridge, Stuart Edward. 'Ousting Singbonga: The Struggle for India's Jharkhand'. In *Dalit Movements and the Meanings of Labour in India*, edited by Peter Robb, 121–50. Oxford: Oxford University Press, 1999.

Council of the Zoological Society of London. *Report of the Council of the Zoological Society of London, the Year 1877: Read at the Annual General Meeting, April 29th, 1878.* London: Taylor and Francis, 1878. On *Internet Archive* (website). Accessed 20 February 2011. http://ia700404.us.archive.org/27/items/annualreportzool78zool/annualreportzool78zool.pdf.

Craven, J. A. *Final Report on the Settlement of the Kolhan Government Estate in District Singhbhum.* Calcutta: Bengal Secretariat Press, 1898.

Craven, Mary. 'Elizabeth Linley, Afterwards Mrs. Sheridan'. In *Famous Beauties of Two Reigns, Being an Account of Some Fair Women of Stuart and Georgian Times* (With a Chapter on Fashion in Femininity by Martin Hume), 171–93. London: E. Nash, 1906.

Cruikshank, Ernest Alexander. *The Correspondence of Lieut. Governor John Graves Simcoe: With Allied Documents.* Collected and edited by Brigadier-General E. A. Cruikshank, for the Ontario Historical Society. Vol. 3, 1794–1795. Toronto: Ontario Historical Society, 1925.

Crooke, William. *An Introduction to Popular Religion and Folklore of Northern India.* Allahabad: Government Press North Western Provinces and Oudh, 1894; repr., New Delhi: Asian Educational Services, 1994.

Cunningham, Alexander. 'Vikrama-Samvat'. In *Book of Indian Eras, With Tables for Calculation of Indian Dates*, 47–50. Calcutta: Thacker, Spink, 1883.

Cuvier, Georges. 'B. Gaurus (the Gaur)'. In *The Animal Kingdom, Arranged in Conformity with Its Organization, with Additional Descriptions of all the Species Hitherto Named, and of Many not before Noticed*, edited by Edward Griffiths and others. Vol. 5: 373–74. London: G. B. Whittaker, 1827.

Dalrymple, William. *White Mughals: Love & Betrayal in Eighteenth-century India.* London: Flamingo, 2003.

———. 'Plain Tales from British India'. *The New York Review of Books* 54, no. 7 (April 26, 2007): 47–50.

Dalton, Edward Tuite. 'The "Kols" of Chota Nagpore'. Special Number on Indian Ethnology 1866, *Journal of the Asiatic Society of Bengal* 35, part 2 (1867): 153–98.

Dalton, Edward Tuite. 'The "Kols" of Chota Nagpore'. *Transactions of the Ethnological Society of London*, n.s., 6 (1868): 1–41.

———. 'The Coles of Chota Nagpore'; 'The Ho Tribe, Otherwise Called the Lurka or Fighting Coles of Singbhoom'; 'Cole Christians, The Mission in Chota Nagpore'. Texts accompanying plates in *The People of India: A Series of Photographic Illustrations, with the Descriptive Letterpress, of the Races and Tribes of Hindustan*, edited by John Forbes Watson and John William Kaye. Originally prepared under the authority of the Government of India, and reproduced by order of the Secretary of State for India in Council. Vol. 1. London: India Museum, 1868.

———. *Descriptive Ethnology of Bengal.* Illustrated by Lithograph Portraits copied from Photographs. Calcutta: Office of the Superintendent of Government Printing, 1872. Also reprinted as *Tribal History of Eastern India*. New Delhi: Cosmo, 1978.

———. 'Rude Stone Monuments in Chutia Nagpur and Other Places'. *Journal of the Asiatic Society of Bengal* 42 (1873): 112–9.

Damodaran, Vinita. 'Colonial Construction of the "Tribe" in India: the Case of Chotanagpur'. *The Indian Historical Review* 33, no. 1 (January 2006): 44–76.

Das, Binod S. *Changing Profile of the Frontier Bengal (1751–1833)*. Delhi: Mittal, 1984.

Das Gupta, Sanjukta. *Adivasis and the Raj: Socio-economic Transition of the Hos, 1820–1932*. Critical Thinking in South Asian History. New Delhi: Orient BlackSwan, 2011.

Dass, Dayal. *Charles Metcalfe and British Administration in India*. New Delhi: Criterion Publications, 1988.

Datta, Ann and Carol Inskipp. 'Zoology . . . Amuses Me Much'. In *The Origins of Himalayan Studies: Brian Houghton Hodgson in Nepal and Darjeeling, 1820–1858*, edited by David Waterhouse, 134–53. Abingdon: RoutledgeCurzon. 1st Indian reprint 2005.

Datta, Kali Kinkar, ed. *Unrest against British Rule in Bihar, 1831–1859*. Prepared in the State Central Records Office, Political Department, Bihar, Patna. Patna: Superintendent Secretariat Press, Bihar, Patna, 1957.

Davies, C. Collin. *An Historical Atlas of the Indian Peninsula*. 1959. Reprint, 2nd edition. London: Oxford University Press, 1972.

'Deaths'. In *Allen's Indian Mail and Register of Intelligence for British and Foreign India, China, and All Parts of the East* 3:172. London: W. H. Allen, 1845.

Deeney, John. *Ho Grammar and Vocabulary*. Chaibasa: Xavier Ho Publications, 1975.

———. *Ho-English Dictionary*. Chaibasa: Xavier Ho Publications, 1978.

———. 'Comparison of the Munda and the Ho Languages'. In *The Munda World: Hoffmann Commemoration Volume*, edited by P. Ponette, 44–52. Ranchi: Catholic Press, 1978.

Depree, G. C. *Geographical and Statistical Report: On that Portion of the Chotanagpore Division which Has Come under the Operation of the Topographical Survey Department*, By Captain G. C. Depree, in charge No. 4, Topographical Party, and Ex-Officio Assistant Commissioner, Cuttack and Chota Nagpore (Continued from the Report on Chota Nagpore), Dated Office No. 4, Topographical Party, Chotanagpore Division Survey. Dorundah 1st October 1868), (1868), 23–46.

Deshpande, Arvind M. *John Briggs in Maharashtra: A study of District Administration under Early British Rule*. Delhi: Mittal, 1987.

Desika Char, S. V., ed. *Readings in the Constitutional History of India, 1757–1947*. Delhi: Oxford University Press, 1983.

Devi, Ritambari. *Indian Mutiny: 1857 in Bihar*. Delhi: Orient Publications, 1989.

Dhungel, Ramesh K. *Brian H. Hodgson and his Nepali and Himalayan Manuscripts, at the British Library (Eur Mss Hodgson) (1/10/2007), At the Royal Asiatic Society (26/11/2007), SOAS, University of London and CNASS, TU, February 2008*. Forthcoming.

'The Disturbed Districts'. *The Asiatic Journal and Monthly Register for British and Foreign India, China, and Australasia*, n.s., 8 (May–August 1832): 144–45.

Dodwell, Edward; Miles, James Samuel (compilers and editors). *Alphabetical List of the Officers of the Bengal Army: With the Dates of their Respective Promotion, Retirement, Resignation, or Death , Whether in India or in Europe, From the Year 1760 to the Year 1834 Inclusive, Corrected to September 30, 1837*. London: Longman, Orme, Brown, [1838].

Dumont, Louis. 'The "Village Community" from Munro to Maine'. Chapter 6 of *Religion, Politics and History in India: Collected Papers in Indian Sociology*, 112–32. Le monde d'outre-mer passé et present, Première serie - Etudes 34. Paris/The Hague: Mouton, 1970.

Dunbar, William. 'Some Observations on the Manners, Customs and Religious Opinions of the Lurka Coles'. *Journal of the Royal Asiatic Society of Great Britain and Ireland*, 1st ser., 18 (1861): 370–77.

Duncan, David. *Asiatic Races*. Compiled and abstracted by Prof. David Duncan, in *Descriptive Sociology; or, Groups of Sociological Facts*, edited by Herbert Spencer; compiled and abstracted by David Duncan, Richard Scheppig, James Collier, Division I, Part 3-A. London and Edinburgh: Williams and Norgate, 1876.

E. 'The Nepaul War'. No. 7 of 'Sketches of the Later History of British India'. *The Asiatic Journal and Monthly Register for British and Foreign India, China, and Australasia*, n.s., 21 (September–December 1836): 116-30.

Eden, Emily. *Up the Country: Letters Written to Her Sister from the Upper Provinces of India*. 1866. Reprinted from the 1930 edition by Edward Thompson, with a new introduction by Elizabeth Claridge and notes by Edward Thompson. London: Virago, 1984.

The Editor of the Royal Military Calendar. 'The Late Major Edward Roughsedge'. *The East India Military Calendar: Containing the Services of General and Field Officers of the Indian Army* 3:227–29. London: Kingsbury, Parbury and Allen, 1826.

'Elizabeth and Mary Linley'. *Dulwich Picture Gallery* (website). Accessed 11 September 2015. http://www.dulwichpicturegallery.org.uk/explore-the-collection/301-350/elizabeth-and-mary-linley/.

Elwin, Verrier. 'The Kol Insurrection'. *Man in India* 25, no. 4, Rebellion Number, (1945): 258–60.

'Emma, Lady Hamilton'. *Wikipedia* (website). Accessed 1 January 2011. https://en.wikipedia.org.

Ernst, Waltraud. *Mad Tales from the Raj: The European Insane in British India, 1800–1858*. London and New York: Routledge, 1991.

'Extract of a Letter from an Officer, dated Camp Sumbhulpoor, July 24th, 1821'. In 'Monthly Register, Foreign Intelligence', *The Scots' Magazine and Edinburgh Miscellany*, n.s., 89, part 1 (1822): 123.

'Extract of a Letter from an Officer, dated Camp Sumbhulpoor, July 24th, 1821'. In *The Gentleman's Magazine and Historical Chronicle* 92, part 1 (January to June 1822): 76–77.

'The family Book of the princes of Beerbhoom, A Persian MS Obtained from the Rajah's Dilapidated Palace'. In *The Annals of Rural Bengal.* Vol. 1, *The Ethnical Frontier of Lower Bengal with the Ancient Principalities of Beerbhoom and Bishenpore*, 447–49. London: Smith, Elder & Co, 1868. Reprint Delhi: Cosmo Publications, 1975.

Ferguson, Niall. *Empire: How Britain Made the Modern World.* London: Allen Lane, The Penguin Press, 2003.

Firminger, Walter Kelly, ed. *Bengal District Records, Midnapur.* Vol. 1, *1763–1767* (published 1914). Vol. 2, *1768–1770* (published 1915). Calcutta: Bengal Secretariat Press, 1911.

———. 'The Ceded Lands'. In 'Historical Introduction to the Bengal Portion of "The Fifth Report"', in Walter Kelly Firminger (ed.), *The Fifth Report from the Select Committee of the House of Commons on the Affairs of the East India Company, Dated 18th July, 1812, Edited with Notes and Introduction by the Ven. Walter Kelly Firminger,* vol. 1, *Introduction and Text of Report* (Calcutta: R. Cambray, 1917), cxiii–cxix.

Fisher, Michael H. 'Indirect Rule in the British Empire: The Foundations of the Residency System in India (1764–1858)'. *Modern Asian Studies* 18 (1984): 393–428.

Forbes, Charles James Forbes Smith. 'On the Connexion of the Móns of Pegu with the Koles of Central India'. *Journal of the Royal Asiatic Society of Great Britain and Ireland* 10 (1878): 234–43.

Fuchs, Stephen. 'The Origin of the Mundas'. In *The Munda World: Hoffmann Commemoration Volume*, edited by P. Ponette, 68–80. Ranchi: Catholic Press, 1978.

Gardew, F. C., Comp. *A Sketch of the Services of the Bengal Native Army: To the Year 1895*, compiled in the office of the Adjutant General in India. Calcutta: Office of the Superintendent of Government Printing, 1903. 'The Georgian Era'. *The Mirror of Literature, Amusement, and Instruction: Containing Original Essays; Historical Narratives, Biographical Memoirs, Sketches of Society, Topographical Descriptions, Novels and Tales, Anecdotes, Select Extracts from New and Expensive Works, The Spirit of the Public Journals, Discoveries in the Arts and Sciences, Useful Domestic Hints, etc. etc. etc.*, vol. 19, no. 535 (February 25, 1832): 122–24; no. 536 (March 3, 1832): 137–39.

Ghadei, Balabhadra. 'Orissa in the Great Revolt of 1857'. *Orissa Review* (August 2008): 10–13. Accessed 14 August 2011. http://www.orissa.gov.in/e-magazine/Orissareview/2008/August-2008/engpdf/or-august-2008.pdf.

Ghosh, Abhik. 'Prehistory of the Chotanagpur Region, India, Part 1: Making Sense of the Stratigraphy'. *The Internet Journal of Biological Anthropology* 1, no. 2 (2008). 17 pp. Accessed 12 April 2011. http://ispub.com/IJBA/1/2/12571.

———. 'Prehistory of the Chotanagpur Region, Part 2: Proposed Stages, Paleaolithic and the Mesolithic'. *The Internet Journal of Biological Anthropology* 2, no. 1 (2008). 37 pp. Accessed 10 August 2010. http://ispub.com/IJBA/2/1/9185.

———. 'Prehistory of the Chotanagpur Region, Part 3: The Neolithic Problem and the Chalcolithic'. *The Internet Journal of Biological Anthropology* 2, no. 2 (2009). 18 pp. Accessed 12 April 2011. http://ispub.com/IJBA/2/2/11792.

———. 'Prehistory of the Chotanagpur Region, Part 4: Ethnoarchaeology, Rock Art, Iron and the Asuras'. *The Internet Journal of Biological Anthropology* 3, no. 1 (2009). 20 pp. Accessed 12 April 2011. http://ispub.com/IJBA/3/1/5134.

———. 'Prehistory of the Chotanagpur Region, Part 5: State Formation and General Conclusions'. *The Internet Journal of Biological Anthropology* 3, no. 2 (2009). 30 pp. Accessed 12 April 2011.

http://ispub.com/IJBA/3/2/6874

Ghosh, Suresh Chandra. *The Social Condition of the British Community in Bengal, 1757–1800*. Leiden: E. J. Brill, 1970.

Ghosha, Pratapachandra. 'Notes on, and Translation of, Two Copper-plate Inscriptions from Bamanghati'. *Journal of the Asiatic Society of Bengal* 40 (1871): 161–69.

Gole, Susan. *A Series of Early Printed Maps of India in Facsimile*. New Delhi: Jayaprints, 1980.

———. *India Within the Ganges*. New Delhi: Jayaprints, 1983.

Gordon, Stuart. *Marathas, Marauders and State Formation in Eighteenth-Century India*. Delhi, Calcutta, Chennai, Mumbai: Oxford University Press, 1994.

Gosnell, Chris. 'The Sheridan Family'. *Ocotillo Road: The Internet Home of Chris Gosnell and Family* (website). Accessed 14 August 2015. http://ocotilloroad.com/geneal/sheridan1.html.

Gray, Thomas. 'Thomas Gray to Horace Wadpole'. 1748. In *Works*, edited by Edmund Grosse, 2:219. 1895. *Spencer and the Tradition: English Poetry 1579-1830* (website). Accessed 20 February 2011, http://spenserians.cath.vt.edu/CommentRecord.php?action=GET&cmmtid=1793.

Gray, Thomas. 'Elegy written in a Country Church Yard' [1751]. *RPO: Representative Poetry Online* (website). Accessed 23 November 2011. http://rpo.library.utoronto.ca/poem/882.html.

———. 'Elegy Written in a Country Churchyard' (1751), Commentary on *The Thomas Gray Archive: A Collaborative Digital Collection* (website). Accessed 11 September 2012. http://www.thomasgray.org/cgi-bin/display.cgi?text=elcc.

Greenberger, Allen J. *The British Image of India: A Study in the Literature of Imperialism, 1880–1960*. London: Oxford University Press, 1969.

Grewal, Bikram. 'Samuel Tickell (1811–1875)'. In 'Birdmen of India: The Pioneers', *Birds of India* (website). Accessed 26 February 2011. http://www.kolkatabirds.com/birdmenpioneers.htm.

Grierson, George Abraham, ed. and comp. *Linguistic Survey of India*. 11 volumes (20 parts). Calcutta: Government of India, Central Publications Branch, 1904–28.

Grignard, Andrew F. 'The Oraons and Mundas, From the Time of Their Settlement in India'. *Anthropos* 4 (1909): 1–19.

Guha, Ranajit. *Elementary Aspects of Peasant Insurgency in Colonial India*. Delhi: Oxford University Press, 1983.

Hahn, Ferdinand. *Kurukh Grammar*. Calcutta: Bengal Secretariat Press, 1900. Also 2nd ed. Calcutta: Bengal Secretariat Press, 1908. Reprinted as *Grammar of the Kurukh Language*. Delhi: Mittal, [1985].

———. 'Dravidian and Kolarian Place Names in Mirzapur, Shahabad and Gaya'. *Journal of the Asiatic Society of Bengal* 72 (1903): 91–93.

Haldar, Rakhal Das. 'An Abstract of the Annals of the Nagbansi Raj Family of Chota Nagpur'. *Man in India* 8, no. 4 (1928): 259–93.

Hamilton, Walter. *The East-India Gazetteer: Containing Particular Descriptions of the Empires, Kingdoms, Principalities, Provinces, Cities, Towns, Districts, Fortresses, Harbours, Rivers, Lakes &c. of Hindostan, and the Adjacent Countries, India Beyond the Ganges, and the Eastern Archipelago; Together with Sketches of the Manners, Customs, Institutions, Agriculture, Commerce, Manufactures, Revenues,*

Population, Castes, Religion, History, &c. of their Various Inhabitants. 2 vols., 2nd ed. London: Wm. H. Allen, 1828.

Haque, M. A. 'Route of Firuz Shah's Invasion of Orissa in 1360 A.D.'. *The Orissa Historical Research Journal* 15, nos. 3 and 4 (1967): 62–68.

Hardwicke, T. 'On the Bos Gour of India'. *The Zoological Journal* 3 (January 1827–April 1828): 231–33.

Hasrat, Bikrama Jit. *History of Nepal: As Told by its Own and Contemporary Chroniclers.* Hoshiapur: V. V. Research Institute Press, 1970.

Heber, Reginald. *Narrative of a Journey Through the Upper Provinces of India, From Calcutta to Bombay, 1824–1825 (with Notes upon Ceylon), An account of a Journey to Madras and the Southern Provinces, 1826, and Letters Written in India by the late Right Rev. Reginald Heber, D. D., Lord Bishop of Calcutta,* edited by Amelia Heber. 2 vols. London: John Murray, 1828.

Heesterman, J. C. 'Power and Authority in Indian Tradition'. In *Tradition and Politics in South Asia,* edited by R. J. Moore, 60-85. New Delhi: Vikas, 1979.

———. *The Inner Conflict of Tradition: Essays in Indian Ritual, Kingship, and Society.* Delhi: Oxford University Press, 1985.

Highfill, Philip H., Kalman A. Burnim, and Edward A. Langhans. 'Barnes, Miss'. In *Biographical Dictionary Of Actors, Actresses, Musicians, Dancers, Managers, and other Stage Personnel in London, 1660–1800.* Vol. 1 (Abaco to Belsille), 293-94. Carbondale and Edwardsville: Southern Illinois University Press, 1973.

'Histories of the Tete-à-Tete annexed; or Memoirs of Anticipator, and the Barn-door Fowl (nos 31, 32.)'. *The Town and Country Magazine; or Universal Repository of Knowledge, Instruction and Entertainment* 18 (London: printed for A. H. Junior, Fleet Street, November 1786): 569-70.

Hobsbawn, Eric J. *Bandits.* 1969. Republished, Harmondsworth: Penguin Books, 1972.

Hodgson, Brian Houghton. *Essay the First, On the Kocch, Bódo and Dhimal Tribes.* In three parts. Calcutta: J. Thomas, Baptist Mission Press, 1847.

———. 'The Aborigines of Central India'. *Journal of the Asiatic Society of Bengal* 17, part 2 (1848): 550–58.

———. 'Aborigines of the Nilgiris, with Remarks on their Affinities'. *Journal of the Asiatic Society of Bengal* 25 (1856): 498–522.

Hodson, V. C. P. *Historical Records of the Governor-Generals's Body Guard.* London: W. Thacker / Calcutta: Thacker, Spink, 1910.

———. *List of the Officers of the Bengal Army, 1758–1834: Alphabetically Arranged and Annotated with Biographical and Genealogical Notes.* 4 vols. London: Phillimore, 1927–47.

Hoffmann, Johann. *Mundari Grammar.* Calcutta: Bengal Secretariat Press, 1903.

Hoffmann, John and Arthur van Emelen. *Encyclopaedia Mundarica.* Vols. 1–13. Patna: Superintendent, Government Printing, Bihar and Orissa, 1930–50.

Hoffman[n], John. *The World of the Mundas.* 2 vols. New Delhi: Critical Quest, 2005.

Holmes à Court (website). Search Name Index. Last updated 21 August 2010. Accessed 11 August 2011. http://holmesacourt.org/namesearch.php?q=Tickell.

Hume, Allen Octavian and E. W. Oates. *The Nests and Eggs of Indian Birds,* edited by E. W. Oates. Vol. 1, 2nd edition. London: R. H. Porter, 1889–90.

Hunter, William Wilson. *The Annals of Rural Bengal*. Vol. 1, *The Ethnical Frontier of Lower Bengal with the Ancient Principalities of Beerbhoom and Bishenpore*. London: Smith, Elder & Co, 1868. Reprint, Delhi: Cosmo Publications, 1975.

———*A Comparative Dictionary of the Languages of India and High Asia: with a Dissertation, Based on the Hodgson Lists, Official Records, and MSS*. London: Trübner and Co, 1868. Reprint, New Delhi: Oriental, 1976.

———. 'Notes on the Services of B. H. Hodgson, Esq., F. R. S., F. R. A. S., Corr. Member of the Institute of France, Chevalier of the Legion of Honour, and Late British Minister at the Court of Nepal, Collected by a Friend' (Pseudonym of W. W. Hunter). Unpublished, 1883.

———. 'Singhbhum'. In *The Imperial Gazetteer of India*. Vol. 12, 2nd ed., 529–41. London: Trübner, 1887.

———. *Life of Brian Houghton Hodgson*. London: John Murray, 1896. Reprint, New Delhi, Madras: Asian Educational Services, 1991.

———. *A Brief History of the Indian Peoples*, edited by W. H. Hutton. 23rd ed. (1st ed., 1882). Oxford: At the Clarendon Press, 1903.

'Hunterian Transliteration'. *Wikipedia* (website). Accessed 24 May 2012. https://en.wikipedia.org.

Innes, Jane Alicia. 'Big Boileau Chart'. *Burning Violin* (website). Accessed 17 February 2011. http://burningviolin.org/family/WebCards/ps06/ps06_491.htm.

'Insurrection at Chota Nagpore'. *The Asiatic Journal and Monthly Register for British and Foreign India, China, and Australasia*, n.s., 8 (May–August 1832): 131–32.

Jackson, James Nesbitt. 'Map of the Part of the District of Singhbhoom and Adjacent Pergunnahs Occupied by and Subject to the Incursions of the Koles'. Compiled and Partially Surveyed by J. N. Jackson, Captain, DA:QM.G. (Deputy Adjutant and Quartermaster General), May 1821.

'Jagabandhu Patnaik'. *Wikipedia* (website). Accessed 13 July 2011. https://en.wikipedia.org.

'Jane Austen's Pemberly'. *Orchard Gate Books* (website). Accessed 8 January 2011. http://www.orchard-gate.com/pemberly.htm.

Jellinghaus, Th. 'Kurze Beschreibung der Sprache der Munda Kohls in Chota Nagpore besonders nach ihren den Volksstamm charakterisierenden Eigenthümlichkeiten' [Short Description of the Language of the Munda Coles in Chota Nagpore Especially of the Typical Characteristics of the Tribe]. *Zeitschrift für Ethnologie: Organ der Berliner Gesellschaft für Anthropologie, Ethnologie und Urgeschichte* 5 (1873): 170–79.

Jha, Aditya Prasad. 'Nature and Scope of Chota Nagpur Commissioner's Pre-1859 Records'. *The Indian Archives* 15 (1957): 15–26.

Jha, Jagdish Chandra. 'British Contact with Singhbhum, 1821–1831'. *Journal of the Bihar Research Society* 47 (1961): 124–28.

———. 'Ganga Narain the Hero of the Bhumij Revolt of 1832–33'. *Journal of Historical Research* 5, no. 1 (1962): 25–31.

———. 'Early British Contacts with Singhbhum'. *Patna University Journal* 18, no. 1 (1963): 148–56.

———. 'History of Land-Revenue of Chota-Nagpur in the First Half of the 19th Century'. *Journal of the Bihar Research Society* 50 (1964): 105–13.

———. *The Kol Insurrection of Chota Nagpur*. Calcutta: Thacker, Spink, 1964.

———. 'Nature of the Bhumij Revolt of 1832–33'. *Journal of Historical Research* 8, no. 2 (1966): 5–9.

———. *The Bhumij Revolt (1832–33): Ganga Narain's Hangama or Turmoil*. Delhi: Munshiram Manoharlal, 1967.

———. 'The British Occupation of Kolhan (Singhbhum) 1836–37'. *Journal of Indian History* 45, no. 135 (1967): 799–806.

———. 'Singhbhum under the South-West Frontier Agency, 1837–54'. *Journal of the Bihar Research Society* 55 (1969): 151–57.

———. Book review of *The Ho Tribe of Singhbhum* by C.P. Singh. *Journal of the Bihar Research Society* 62 (1978 [reprint mentioned 1976]): 301–2.

———. *The Tribal Revolt of Chotanagpur (1831–1832)*. 2nd rev. and enlarged ed. of *The Kol Insurrection of Chota Nagpur*, 1964. Patna: Kashi Prasad Jayaswal Research Institute, 1987.

———. 'Historiography of Tribal Movements in Bihar'. In *Peasant Struggles in Bihar, 1831–1992: Spontaneity to Organisation*, edited by Kaushal Kishore Sharma, Prabhaker Prasad Singh, Ranjan Kumar, 13–22. Patna, Delhi: Centre for Peasant Studies, 1994.

———. 'Nature of Tribal Uprisings of Chotanagpur, The Kol and Bhumij Revolts, 1831–1833'. In *Peasant Struggles in Bihar, 1831–1992: Spontaneity to Organisation*, edited by Kaushal Kishore Sharma, Prabhaker Prasad Singh, Ranjan Kumar, 37–47. Patna, Delhi: Centre for Peasant Studies, 1994.

Johnson, Samuel. 'Thomas Tickell'. *The Lives of the Most Eminent English Poets: With Critical Observations on Their Works, 1779–1781*, edited by Samuel Johnson, 79-82. *The Literature Network* (website). Accessed 10 September 2009, www.online-literature.com/samuel-johnson/3223.

'John William Templer, 23 Nov 1794–26 Mar 1873'. *The Templer Family from Somerset, Devon and Dorset* (website). Accessed 28 April 2016. http://my.rootsmagic.com/templerfamilycouk/individual.html#601

Jones, Stephen. 'Richard Tickell'. In *Biographia Dramatica; or, A Companion to the Playhouse*. 1812. Reproduced in 'Spenser and the Tradition, 1713–1714' on *English Poetry 1579–1830* (website). Accessed 3 May 2012.

http://spenserians.cath.vt.edu/BiographyRecord.php?action=GET&bioid=34612.

Joshi, Arjun. 'The Origin of the Bhanjas of Khijingakotta'. *The Orissa Historical Research Journal* 16, nos 1 and 2 (1967): 41–53.

———. 'Sculptural Art of Khijjingakótta'. *The Orissa Historical Research Journal* 23, nos 1–4 (1978): 33–58.

———. *History & Culture of Khijjingakotta under the Bhanjas*. Delhi: Vikas, 1983.

Joshi, Harihar Raj. 'Brian Houghton Hodgson—The Unsung Story'. In *The Origins of Himalayan Studies: Brian Houghton Hodgson in Nepal and Darjeeling, 1820–1858*, edited by David Waterhouse, 39–48. Abingdon: RoutledgeCurzon. First Indian reprint 2005.

Kaye, John William. *The Administration of the East India Company: A History of Indian Progress*. London: Richard Bentley, 1853.

Kennedy, Paul. 'Grand Strategy in War and Peace, Toward a Broader Definition'. In *Grand Strategies in War and Peace*, edited by Paul Kennedy, 1–7. New Haven and London: Yale University Press, 1991.

Kejariwal, Om Prakash. *The Asiatic Society of Bengal and the Discovery of India's Past*. Delhi: Oxford University Press, 1988.

Khan, Razib. 'Sons of the Conquerors: The Story of India?', in 'Gene Expression', blog on *Discover, Science for the Curious* (website), October 28, 2010, accessed 9 May 2016, http://blogs.discovermagazine.com/gnxp/2010/10/sons-of-the-conquerers-the-story-of-india/#.VzBODr6M6jr .

———'Tibeto-Burmans in Bengal, and Indians in ancient Malaya'. On Gene Expression (website), accessed 30 August 2018, https://www.gnxp.com/WordPress/2018/08/29/tibeto-burmans-in-bengal-and-indians-in-ancient-malaya/.

'The Kholes'. *The Asiatic Journal and Monthly Register for British and Foreign India, China, and Australasia*, n.s., 8 (May–August 1832): 186–68.

'The Kholes'. *The Asiatic Journal and Monthly Register for British and Foreign India, China, and Australasia*, n.s., 25 (January–April 1838): 136.

Knight, Charles. 'B. Gaurus, the Gour or Gaur'. In *The English Cyclopaedia: A New Dictionary of Universal Knowledge*, compiled and conducted by Charles Knight, 626–27. London: Bradbury and Evans, 1854.

Kolff, Dirk H. A. *Naukar, Rajput and Sepoy: The Ethnohistory of the Military Labour Market in Hindustan, 1450–1850*. University of Cambridge Oriental Publications, no. 43. Cambridge: Cambridge University Press, 1990.

'Kols—Funeral Ceremonies'. *North Indian Notes and Queries: A Monthly Periodical* 2, no. 7 (1892): 123.

Konow, Sten. 'Mundás and Dravidas'. *The Indian Antiquary* 33 (1904): 121.

———, ed. *Munda and Dravidian Languages*, edited and compiled by George Abraham Grierson. Vol. 4 of *Linguistic Survey of India*. Calcutta: Superintendent of Government Printing, 1906.

Kopf, David. *British Orientalism and the Bengal Renaissance: The Dynamics of Indian Modernization, 1773–1835*. Berkeley and Los Angeles: University of California Press, 1969.

Kuiper, F. B. J. *Proto-Munda Words in Sanskrit*. Verhandeling der Koninklijke Nederlandsche Akademie van Wetenschappen, afd. Letterkunde, Nieuwe Reeks, deel 51, no. 3. Amsterdam: N. V. Noord-Hollandsche Uitgevers Maatschappij, 1948.

Kujur, Francisca. *Raja Arjun Singh of Porahat (1829 A.D.–1890 A.D.)*. Allahabad: K. K. Publications, 2007.

Kulke, Hermann. 'Kshatriyaization and Social Change: A Study in Orissa Setting'. In *Aspects of Changing India: Studies in Honour of Prof. G. S. Ghurye*, edited by S. Devadas Pillai, 398–409. Bombay: Popular Prakashan (also published in Sonderdrucke der Mitglieder 177, Heidelberg: Südasien-Institut der Universität Heidelberg), 1976.

———. 'Early State Formation and Royal Legitimation in Tribal Areas of Eastern India'. In *Aspects of Tribal Life in South Asia I: Strategy and Survival. Proceedings of an International Seminar Held in Berne 1977*, edited by Rupert R. Moser and Mohan K. Gautam, 29–37. Berne: The University of Berne, Institute of Ethnology, 1978.

———. *Jagannatha-Kult und Gajapati-Königtum: Ein Beitrag zur Geschichte religiöser Legitimation Hinduistischer Herrscher* [Jagannatha Cult and the Kingdom of Gajapati: A Contribution to the History of Religious Legitimation of Hindu Rulers]. Wiesbaden: Franz Steiner Verlag, 1979.

———. 'King Anangabhima III, The Veritable Founder of the Gajapati Kingship and of the Jagannath Trinity at Puri'. *Journal of the Royal Asiatic Society of Great Britain and Ireland* 113 (1981): 26–39.

———. 'Die Frühmittelalterlichen Regionalreiche: Ihre Struktur und Rolle im Prozess Staatlicher Entwicklung

Indiens' [The Early Mediaeval Regional States: Their Structure and Role in the Process of the Development of the State in India]. In *Regionale Tradition in Südasien*, edited by Hermann Kulke und Dietmar Rothermund, 77–114. Wiesbaden: Franz Steiner Verlag, 1985.

———. 'Periodization of Pre-modern Historical Processes in India and Europe, Some Reflections'. *The Indian History Review* 19, no. 1–2 (1992–93): 21–36.

Kumar, Purushottam. 'Chota Nagpur as the South-Western Frontier Agency (1834–1854)'. *Journal of Historical Research* 6, no. 1 (1963): 31–37.

———. 'The Ramgarh Battalion and its Relationship with the Civil Administration of Chotanagpur, 1795–1854'. *Journal of Historical Research* 8, no. 2 (1966): 27–45.

———. *History and Administration of Tribal Chotanagpur (Jharkhand)*. Delhi, Lucknow: Atma Ram and Sons, 1994.

Kumar, Vikrant, Arimanda N. S. Reddy, Jagedeesh P. Babu, Tipirisetti N. Rao, Banrida T. Langstieh, Kumarasamy Thangaraj, Alla G. Reddy, Lalji Singh and Battini M. Reddy. 'Y-chromosome Evidence Suggests a Common Paternal Heritage of Austro-Asiatic Populations'. *BMC Evolutionary Biology* 7, no. 1 (2007): 47 ff. Accessed 28 February 2015. http://www.biomedcentral.com/1471-2148/7/47 .

Laeequddin, Mohammed. *Census of Mayurbhanj State, 1931*. Vol. 1, *Report*. Published under the Authority of the State. Calcutta: Caledonian, 1937.

Lampedusa, Giuseppe Tomasi di. *Il Gattopardo* [The Leopard]. New York: Pantheon 1958 (English translation, 1991).

Latham, Robert Gordon. *A Descriptive Ethnology*. 2 vols. London: John van Voorst, 1859. Reprinted as *Tribes and Races: A Descriptive Ethnology of Asia, Africa & Europe*. Delhi: Cultural Publishing House, 1983.

———. *Ethnology of India*. London: John van Voorst, 1859.

Leach, E. R. *Political Systems of Highland Burma: A study of Kachin Social Structure*. London School of Economics Monographs on Social Anthropology, no. 44. London: The University of London, The Athlone Press, 1954. Reprint, 1970.

Lewis, W. H. 'Orissa Division', in 'Preparation of Record of Old Inscriptions in Christian Burial Grounds'. *List of Old Inscriptions in Christian Burial Grounds in the Province of Bihar and Orissa*. Patna: n. p., 1926.

Li Shang-Yin. 'Written on the Monastery Wall'. In *Poems of the Late T'ang*, translated by A. C. Graham. Harmondsworth: Penguin, 1968, 161.

'List of the Members of the Royal Asiatic Society of Great Britain and Ireland'. *Journal of the Royal Asiatic Society of Great Britain and Ireland* 17 (1860): 12.

'List of Subscribers'. *Calcutta Journal of Natural History and Miscellany of the Arts and Sciences in India* 2 (1842).

Long, James. 'The Kols, The Insurrection of 1832; and the Land Tenure Act of 1869'. *Calcutta Review* 50 [title page mentions 49], (1869): 108–58.

———. *Selections from Unpublished Records of Government for the years 1748 to 1767 Inclusive: Relating Mainly to the Social Condition of Bengal, With a Map of Calcutta in 1784*. Calcutta: Office of the Superintendent of Government Printing, 1869. Reprint with a Foreword, Notes and a Bio-Bibliographical Sketch of J. Long, edited by Mahadevaprasad Saha, Calcutta: Firma K. L. Mukhopadhayay, 1973.

Lostly, J. P. 'The Architectural Monuments of Buddhism: Hodgson and the Buddhist Architecture of the Kathmandu Valley. In *The Origins of Himalayan Studies: Brian Houghton Hodgson in Nepal and*

Darjeeling, 1820–1858, edited by David Waterhouse, 77–110. Abingdon: RoutledgeCurzon. First Indian reprint 2005.

Low, G. Carmichael, Douglas Dewar, T. H. Newman, G. A. Levett-Yeats. 'A Classification of the Original Watercolour Paintings of Birds of India by B. H. Hodgson, S. R. Tickell, and C. F. Sharpe in the Library of the Zoological Society of London'. *Proceedings of the Zoological Society of London* 100, no. 3 (1930): 549–625.

'Lurkas' *(Extract from a Private Letter)*. *The Asiatic Journal and Monthly Register for British India and Its Dependencies* 10 (July-December 1820): 609.

Luttwak, Edward N. *The Grand Strategy of the Roman Empire: From the First Century A.D. to the Third*. Baltimore and London: The Johns Hopkins University Press, 1976. Paperback ed., 1981.

———. 'Give War a Chance'. *Foreign Affairs* 78, no. 4 (July–August 1999): 37–44.

'Linley (Thomas)'. In John Gorton, *A General Biographic Dictionary:A New Edition Continued to the Year 1833*. Three volumes. Vol. 2, n.p. London: Wittaker, 1833.

MacLean, Kenneth. *Agrarian Age: A Background for Wordsworth*. New Haven Connecticut: Yale University Press, 1950. Reprint, Hamden Connecticut: Archon Books, 1970.

MacPherson, T. S. *Final Report on the Operations for the Preparation of a Record of Rights in Pargana Porahat,District Singhbhum, 1905–1907*. Calcutta: The Bengal Secretariat Book Depôt, 1908.

Mahapatra, L. K. 'Ex-Princely States of Orissa, Mayurbhanj, Keonjhar and Bonai'. In *Tribal Polities and State Systems in Pre-Colonial Eastern and North Eastern India*, edited by Surajit Sinha, 1–50. Calcutta, New Delhi: K. P. Bagchi, 1987.

Mahapatra, Sita Kant. 'The Insider Diku: Boundary Rules and Marginal Man in Santal Society'. *Man in India* 56, no. 1 (1976): 37–49.

Mahto, S. *Hundred Years of Christian Missions in Chotanagpur Since 1845*. Ranchi: The Chotanagpur Christian Publishing House, 1971.

'Major Edward Roughsedge'. *The Asiatic Journal and Monthly Register for British India and Its Dependencies* 14 (July–December 1822): 232–33.

Majumdar, Dhirendra Nath. 'The Traditional Origin of the Hos: Together with a Brief Description of the Chief Bongas (or Gods) of the Hos'. *Journal of the Asiatic Society of Bengal*, n.s., 20 (1924, published 1925): 193–97.

———. *A Tribe in Transition: A Study in Culture Pattern*. Calcutta: Longmans, Green, 1937.

———. *The Affairs of a Tribe: A Study in Tribal Dynamics*. Lucknow: Ethnographic and Folk Culture Society, 1950.

Mao Tse-Tung. 'Where Do Correct Ideas Come From?', 1963. Published in Mao Tse-Tung, *Four Essays on Philosophy*, 134–36. Peking: Foreign Languages Press, 1968.

'Marriages'. *The Annual Register; or, A View of the History, Politics, and Literature of the Year 1829*, vol. 28 (1830): 199.

Marshman, John Clark. 'Limitation of Time for the Cognizance of Suits'. Addendum to *Guide to the Civil Law of the Presidency of Fort William: Containing all the Unrepealed Regulations, Acts, Constructions and Circular Orders of Government, to which is Prefixed An Epitome of Every Act and Rule*, paras 16–24 (Serampore: Serampore Press, 1842): 524–30.

Martin, Montgomery. *The History, Antiquities, Topography, and Statistics of Eastern India: Comprising the Districts of Behar, Shahabad, Bhagalpoor, Gorukhpoor, Dinajepoor, Puraniya, Rungpoor, and Assam, in Relation to their Geology, Mineralogy, Botany, Agriculture, Commerce, Manufactures, Fine Arts, Population, Religion, Education, Statistics, etc., Surveyed under the Orders of the Supreme Government, and Collated from the Original Documents at the E.I. House, with the Permission of the Honourable Court of Directors by Montgomery Martin, Author of the "History of the British Colonies," etc.*. 3 vols. London: Wm. H. Allen, 1837.

'Mary Rose Tickell', 2007. *Lyons Family Tree Guide* (website). Accessed 5 February 2010. http://lyons.familytreeguide.com/getperson.php?personID=I2342.

Marx, Karl. *Notes on Indian History: (664–1858)* [after 1870]. Moscow: Progress, 1986.

Masani, Zareer. *Macaulay: Britain's Liberal Imperialist*. London: The Bodley Head, 2013.

Mason, Francis. 'The Talaing Language'. *Journal of the American Oriental Society* 4 (1854): 279–88.

Mason, Philip. *A Matter of Honour: An Account of the Indian army, Its Officers and Men*. London: Jonathan Cape, 1974.

Masica, Colin P. 'Aryan and Non-Aryan Elements in North Indian Agriculture'. *Aryan and Non-Aryan in India*, edited by Madhav M. Deshpande and Peter Edwin Hook, 55–151. Ann Arbor: Center for South Asian and Southeast Asian Studies, The University of Michigan, 1979.

'Maund'. *Wikipedia* (website). Accessed 07 December 2014. https://en.wikipedia.org.

'Mayurbhanj (Princely State), Present ruler, predecessors and short history'. *Rootsweb* (website). Accessed 14 May 2011. http://freepages.genealogy.rootsweb.ancestry.com/~royalty/ips/m/mayurbhanj.html.

Mearns, Barbara and Richard, 'Samuel Richard Tickell (1811–1875)'. In *Biographies for Birdwatchers: The Lives of Those Commemorated in the Western Palearctic Bird Names*, 381–83. London, 1988.

'Memorial stone in St James Church, Piccadilly, by Elizabeth Anne Tickell, dau of Richard Tickell'. *Find a Grave* (website). Accessed 13 August 2015. http://www.findagrave.com.

Miles, Jack. *God, A Biography*. New York: Vintage Books, 1996.

'Military Appointments, &c.' *The Calcutta Monthly Journal* 30 (May 1837, published 28th June 1837): 60–64. Reprinted in *Calcutta Monthly and General Register of Occurrences, Throughout the British Dominions in the East: Forming an Epitome of the Indian Press for the Year 1837,* 3rd series, vol. 3 (Calcutta: Samuel Smith, 1838).

'Military Appointments, Promotions, &c.' *The Asiatic Journal and Monthly Register for British and Foreign India, China, and Australasia*, n.s., 12 (September–December 1833): 110–12.

'Military Appointments, Promotions, &ca.'. *The Asiatic Journal and Monthly Register for British and Foreign India, China, and Australasia*, n.s., 13 (January–April 1834): 200–202.

'Military Appointments, Promotions, &c..', *The Asiatic Journal and Monthly Register for British and Foreign India, China, and Australasia*, n.s., 22 (January–April 1837): 56-57, 128–29.

'Miscellaneous'. In *The Quarterly Oriental Magazine, Review and Register* 2 (Calcutta: Thacker, 1824): lix, lxiv.

Mishra, B. 'History'. *Keonjhar* (website). Accessed 12 December 2002. http://www.keonjhar.com.

Misra, K. K. *Social Structure and Change among the Ho of Orissa*. Delhi: Gian, 1987.

Mishra, Sushila. *History of the Freedom Movement in Chota Nagpur (1885–1947)*. Patna: Kashi Prasad Jayaswal Research Institute, 1990.

Mitra, K. P. 'Defence of the Frontier of Bihar and Orissa against Maratha and Pindari Incursions (1800–1819)'. *Bengal, Past and Present* 60 (1941): 49–57.

———. 'Insurrection of the Coles in Chotanagpur'. *Bengal, Past and Present* 61 (1942): 72–88.

Mohapatra, Ramesh Prasad. *Jaina Monuments of Orissa*. Delhi: D. K. Publishers, 1984.

Moore, Thomas. *Memoirs of the Life of the Right Honourable Richard Brinsley Sheridan*. 2 vols. London: Longman, Reese, Orme, Brown, and Green, 1826.

Moore, Thomas. *Letters and Journals of Lord Byron: with Notices of his Life*. 2 vols. London, 1830–1831. *Lord Byron and His Times* (website). Accessed 2 January 2012. http://lordbyron.org/monograph.php?doc=ThMoore.1830&select=AD1813.13#AD1813.13-2.

Morgan, Lady (Sydney). *Lady Morgan's Memoirs: Autobiography, Diaries and Correspondence*. 2 vols, 2nd ed., rev., London: Wm. H. Allen, 1863. *Lord Byron and his Times* (website). Accessed 8 January 2012. http://lordbyron.org.

Morley, John C., 'Robert Hankinson Roughsedge'. In 'Monumental Inscriptions from the Churchyard of St. Nicholas, Liverpool'. *Miscellanea Genealogica(l) et Heraldica*, n.s., 4, (1884): 434.

Mukherjee, Prabhat. 'The Commissioners of Orissa I, Sir Henry Ricketts'. *The Orissa Historical Research Journal* 11, no. 2 (1962): 106–13.

Müller, Friedrich. *Allgemeine Ethnographie* [General Ethnography]. Zweite, umgearbeitete und bedeutend vermehrte Auflage [2nd, revised and considerably augmented edition], [1st edition was 1873.] Wien: Alfred Hölder,

1879.

Müller, Friedrich Max. 'The Last Results of the Researches Respecting the Non-Iranian and Non-Semitic Languages of Asia and Europe, or the Turanian Family of Language (letter of Professor Max Muller to Chevalier Bunsen, on the classification of the Turanian languages). In *Outlines of the Philosophy of Universal History: Applied to Language and Religion*, edited by Christian Charles Josias Bunsen.

1:263–519. London: Longman, Brown, Green and Longmans, 1854. *Internet Archive* (website). Accessed 8 June 2014.

https://archive.org/stream/outlinesphiloso01bunsgoog/outlinesphiloso01bunsgoog_djvu.txt.

Bosu Mullick, Samar. 'The Cradle of the Munda: Birth of a New Branch of Austroasiatic', in *Journal of Adivasi and Indigenous Studies (JAIS):* 10, no. 1, (February 2020): 14-25.

Munda, Ram Dayal. 'Cultural Elements in Ho Songs'. In *Bihar in Folklore Study an Anthology*, guest editors, L. P. Vidhyarthi and G. Chaubey, 171–79. Calcutta: Indian Publications, 1971.

'Munda languages'. *Wikipedia* (website). Accessed 25 March 2015. https://en.wikipedia.org.

Murray, E. F. O. 'The Ancient Workers of Western Dhalbhum'. *Journal of the Asiatic Society of Bengal*, 3rd ser. 6, no. 2 (1940): 79–104.

Nation, Paul and Robert Waring. 'Vocabulary size, Text Coverage and Word Lists' [1997]. *Université catholique de Louvain* (website). Accessed 23 March 2011. http://www.fltr.ucl.ac.be/fltr/germ/etan/bibs/vocab/cup.html.

'Necrology no II, Mr. Henry Wesley Voysey. *Asiatic Monthly Miscellany* 19 (January–June 1825): 262–63.

Nieboer, Herman Jeremias. *Slavery as an Industrial System: Ethnological Researches*. 2nd rev. ed. 's Gravenhage: Nijhoff, 1910.

'Obituary [Anne Boscawen Gowland, dau. of Robert Markland]'. *The Gentleman's Magazine and Historical Chronicle* 103, part 2 (July to December 1833), (London: Sylvanus Urban, 1833): 94.

O'Malley, Lewis Sidney Steward. *Singhbhum, Saraikela and Kharsawan*. Bengal District Gazetteers, Calcutta: The Bengal Secretariat Book Depôt, 1910.

O'Malley, Lewis Sidney Steward. *History of Bengal, Bihar and Orissa under British Rule*. Calcutta: The Bengal Secretariat Book Depôt, 1925.

O'Malley, Lewis Sidney Steward. *The Indian Civil Service, 1601–1930*. London: John Murray, 1931. Reprint, London: Frank Cass, 1965.

'The Ornithological Library of Richard Howard'. Lot 175 of Sothebys, auction 28, Smith (Christopher Webb) and Sir Charles D'Oyly, *The feathered Game of Hindostan*, April 1999. *Sotheby's* (website). Accessed 19 December 2010. www.sothebys.com.

Oppenheimer, Stephen. *The Origins of the British*. London: Robinson, 2007.

Pallottino, Massimo. *The Etruscans*. Rev. and enlarged ed, based on the 6th Italian ed. (1st Italian edition 1942), translated by J. Cremona and edited by David Ridgway, 1973. Harmondsworth: Penguin Books, 1978.

Panda, Deepak. 'Government Cemetery at Sambalpur Have Many Belongs to Europeans'. *Deepak Panda Blog*, 6 August 2014. Accessed 30 March 2016. http://sambalpurhistory.blogspot.nl.

———. 'Anglo-Indians Buried at Sambalpur, Odisha, India at the Government Cemetery'. *Deepak Panda Blog*. 1 September 2015. Accessed 30 March 2016. http://sambalpurhistory.blogspot.nl/.

Panigrahi, Devendra N. *Charles Metcalfe in India: Ideas and Administration, 1806–1835*. New Delhi: Munshiram Manoharlal, 1968.

Panigrahi, K. C. 'The Archaeological Remains at Benisagar in the Singbhum District of Bihar'. *Journal of the Bihar Research Society* 42 (1956): 1–11.

Parlby, Samuel. 'Late Major Roughsedge'. In *The British Indian Military Repository* 1 (Calcutta: Church Mission Press, 1822): 330–33.

Patnaik, Jagannath. *Feudatory States of Orissa (1803–1857)*. 2 vols. Allahabad: Vohra, 1988.

Patra, K. M. *Orissa under the East India Company*. New Delhi: Munshiram Mahoharlal, 1971.

Paty, Chittaranjan Kumar. *History of Seraikella and Kharsawan States*. New Delhi: Classical Publishing Company, 2002.

Pearse, Hugh. *The Hearsays: Five Generations of an Anglo-Indian Family*. London: William Blackwood and Sons, 1905.

Pearson, J. T. 'Memorandum on the Gaur and Gayal'. *Journal of the Asiatic Society of Bengal* 6, part 1 (1837): 225–30.

Peers, Douglas M. '"The Habitual Nobility of Being": British Officers and the Social Construction of the Bengal Army in the Early Nineteenth Century'. *Modern Asian Studies* 25, no. 3 (1991): 545–69.

Penner, Peter. 'James Thomason's Role in Vernacular Education'. Chapter 6 of *The Patronage Bureaucracy in North India: The Robert M. Bird and James Thomason School, 1820–1870*, 141–69. Delhi: Chanakya Publications, 1981.

Philip. C. L. 'Confidential History of Seraikella State, Completed to 1927 by C. L. Philip'. Typescript. Chaibasa: Tribal Research and Training Centre, 1927.

Philips, Cyril H., ed. *The Correspondence of Lord William Cavendish Bentinck, Governor-General of India, 1832–1835*, edited and with an introduction by C. H. Philips. 2 vols. Oxford: Oxford University Press, 1977.

Phillimore, R. H., ed. (1968). *Historical Records of the Survey of India. Volume V. 1844 to 1861*. Dehra Dun: Survey of India.

'Postscript to Asian Intelligence'. *The Asiatic Journal and Monthly Register for British and Foreign India, China, and Australasia*, n.s., 8 (May–August 1832): 120.

Pradhan, R. K. 'Ho'. *Adibasi*, 1963–64, no. 3 (Bhubaneshwar: Tribal Research Bureau, Orissa, 1964), 167–70.

Prakash, Gyan. *Bonded Histories: Genealogies of Labor Servitude in Colonial India*. South Asian Studies 44. Cambridge: Cambridge University Press, 1990.

Prasad, A. K. *The Bhils of Khandesh: Under the British East India Company (1818–1858)*. Delhi: Konark, 1991.

Prasad, S. N. *Catalogue of the Historical Maps of the Survey of India (1700–1900)*. New Delhi: The National Archives of India, 1975.

'Proceedings of the Asiatic Society, Wednesday Evening, the 5th October, 1836'. *Journal of the Asiatic Society of Bengal* 5 (1836): 587–99.

Prusty, R. P. 'Study of Microlith Industry in Orissa'. *The Orissa Historical Research Journal* 24, 25 and 26 (1980): 133–46.

Rae, William Fraser. 'Tickell, Richard'. In *Dictionary of National Biography, 1885–1900*, vol. 56. Republished as 'Tickell, Richard (DNB00)'. *Wikisource* (website). Accessed 7 September 2009. https://en.wikisource.org/wiki/Tickell,_Richard_%28DNB00%29.

Rahn, Urs. 'Modern Pangolins'. In *Grzimek's Encyclopedia of Mammals*, edited by Sybil P. Parker, vol. 2: 630–41. New York: McGraw-Hall, 1990.

Rau, Felix and Paul Sidwell, "The Munda Maritime Hypothesis", in *Journal of the Southeast Asian Linguistic Society JSEALS* 12, no. 2, (2019): 35-57.

Raut, L. N. 'The State of Mayurbhanj During the Years of Maratha Supremacy in Orissa'. *The Orissa Historical Research Journal* 28, nos. 1 and 2 (1982): 88–107.

Raynor, Caroline. 'Roughsedge'. In *St Thomas' Church, Park Lane, Liverpool, Archaeological Watching Brief Report*, 25–26. Oxford: Oxford Archaeology North, 2010.

Records Department. *India Acts*. Vol. 1. Calcutta: William Thacker and Co, 1834–40.

Records Department. 'A.D. 1833 Regulation XIII'. *Bengal Regulations, Revenue and Judicial 1826–34*.

Renfrew, Colin. *Archaeology and Language: The Puzzle of Indo-European Origins*. Harmondsworth: Penguin Books, 1989.

——, e.a. 'Archaeology and Language: The Puzzle of Indo-European Origins by Colin Renfrew, A CA Book Review'. *Current Anthropology* 29 (1988): 437–68.

Rennell, James. *The Provinces of Bengal Situated on the West of the Hoogly River with the Maharatta Frontier*. Inscribed to Harry Verelst Esqr. by his obliged humble servant J. Rennell, 1774. Map reproduced in Jagdish Chandra Jha. *The Bhumij Revolt*, 198. Delhi: Munshiram Manoharlal, 1967.

Rennell, James. *A Bengal Atlas: Containing Maps of the Theatre of War and Commerce of that Side of Hindoostan, Compiled from the Original Surveys; and Published by Order of the Honourable the Court of Directors for the Affairs of the East India Company by James Renell, Late Major of Engineers, and Surveyor General in Bengal*, 1781.

———. 'A General View of the Principal Roads and Divisions of Hindoostan, 1792'. In *Memoir of a Map of Hindoostan or the Moghul Empire with an Introduction, Illustrative of the Geography and Present Divisions of that Country and A Map of the Countries Situated Between the Heads of the Indian Rivers, and the Caspian Sea, also, A Supplementary Map, Containing the Improved Geography of the Provinces Contiguous to the Heads of the Indus, to which is added, An Appendix, Containing an Account of the Ganges and Burrampater Rivers*. 3rd ed. London, 1793, 315. Also reprint, Calcutta: Editions Indian, 1976, 365.

'Review of Eastern News'. *The Asiatic Journal and Monthly Register for British and Foreign India, China, and Australasia*, n.s., 26 (May–August 1838): 3–4.

'Richard Sheridan'. *Spartacus Schoolnet* (website). Accessed 17 May 2008. www.spartacus.schoolnet.co.uk/PRsheridan.htm.

'Richard Tickell ca 1780'. Part of Lot 8: Thomas Gainsborough R. A. 1727–1788. Sotheby. 27 November 2003. *Sotheby's* (website). Accessed 10 January 2010. www.Artfact.com.

Riccio, Maria Eugenia, José Manuel Nunes, Melissa Rahal, Barbara Kervaire, Jean-Marie Tiercy, and Alicia Sanchez-Mazas, 'The Austroasiatic Munda Population from India and Its Enigmatic Origin: A HLA Diversity Study', *Human Biology* 83, no. 3 (June 2011): 405-35. On *BioOne* (website). Accessed 22 May 2016. doi: http://dx.doi.org/10.3378/027.083.0306

Ricketts, Henry. 'Report on the District of Singhbhoom'. *Selections from the Records of the Bengal Government*. Vol. 16, 61–115. Calcutta: Military Orphan Press, 1857.

Risley, Herbert Hope. *Districts of Hazaribagh and Lohardaga*. Vol. 16 of *A Statistical Account of Bengal*, edited by W. W. Hunter. London: Trübner, 1877. Reprint, New Delhi: Concept, 1976.

———. *Singbhum District, Tributary States of Chutia Nagpur, and Manbhum*. Vol. 17 of *A Statistical Account of Bengal*, edited by W. W. Hunter. London: Trübner, 1877. Reprint, Delhi: Concept, 1976.

———. *Tribes and Castes of Bengal: Ethnographic Glossary*. 2 vols. Calcutta: Bengal Secretariat Press, 1891–92. Reprint, Calcutta: Firma Mukhopadhyay, 1981.

Roberts, Emma. Chapter 7 [Patna] of *Scenes and Characteristics of Hindostan, with Sketches of Anglo-Indian Society*. London 1835. Republished in *Carey's Library of Choice Literature: Containing The Best Works of the Day, in Biography, History, Travels, Novels, Poetry, &ca. &ca*. 1 (Philadelphia, 1836): 165-69.

Robertson, John George. 'Richard Brinsley Sheridan (1751–1816)'. *Encyclopaedia Britannica*, 11th ed., vol. 4, 845–47. Cambridge: Cambridge University Press, 1911. *Theatrehistory.com* (website). Accessed 12 July 2009. www.theatrehistory.com/irish/sheridan001.html.

Robertson, Herbert. 'Clonegald Churchyard'. *Journal of the Memorials of the Dead* 6 (1904-05-1906): 198-99. On *County Carlow, Clonegald, Journal of the Memorials of the Dead* (website). Accessed 1 March 2011. http://home.people.net.au/~ousie/county_carlow_memorials_of_the_dead_JPMD_Clonegald.htm.

Roebuck, John Arthur. 'Autobiography'. In *Life and Letters of John Arthur Roebuck, P.O., Q.C., M.P., with Chapters of Autobiography*, edited by Robert Eadon Leader. London, New York: Edward Arnold, 1897.

'Roebuck Coat of Arms / Roebuck Family Crest'. *Coat of Arms Store & Family Crests Gifts* (website). Accessed July 2009. http://www.4crests.com/roebuck-coat-of-arms.html.

Roy, B. K. 'British Conquest of Ho-Desum'. *Journal of Historical Research* 3, no. 1 (1960): 25–31.

———. 'Kuchang in Singhbhum Politics During 1768–1773'. *Journal of Historical Research* 4, no. 2 (1962): 5–10.

———. 'Kol Movement of 1832 in Tori Parganah (Palamau District)'. *Journal of Historical Research* 5, no. 1 (1962): 32–35.

———. 'Singhbhum: As Known to the East India Company till February 1768'. *Journal of Historical Research* 8, no. 2 (1966): 1–4.

———. 'An Official Account of the Outbreak and Suppression of the Kol Insurrection During January, 1832'. *Journal of Historical Research* 9, no. 2 (1967): 34–39.

———. 'An Account of the Actions Taken by the East India Company's Government to Deal with the Situation Arising in Chotanagpur During the Month of January, 1832'. *Journal of Historical Research* 10, no. 2 (1968): 48–52.

———. 'Captain Roughsedge and the Reorganisation of Police System in Chotanagpur (Ranchi District) During 1809'. *Journal of Historical Research* 12, no. 1 (1969): 109–13.

Roy, Sarat Chandra. 'A Note on some Remains of the Ancient Asuras in the Ranchi District'. *Journal of the Bihar and Orissa Research Society* 1, part 2, (1915): 229–53.

———. 'Relics of the Copper Age found in Chota Nagpur'. *Journal of the Bihar and Orissa Research Society* 2, part 4, (1916): 481–84.

———. *The Mundas and Their Country*. Calcutta, 1912. Reprint, London: Asia Publishing House, 1970.

———. 'Distribution and Nature of Asur Sites in Chota Nagpur'. *Journal of the Bihar and Orissa Research Society* 6 (1920): 393–423.

———. 'Ethnographical Investigation in Official Records'. *Journal of the Bihar and Orissa Research Society* 7, part 4 (1921): 1–34.

———. 'Ethnographical Investigation in Official Records'. *Journal of the Bihar and Orissa Research Society* 25 (1935): 231–50.

———. Review of '*A Tribe in Transition. A St udy in Culture Pattern* by D. N. Majumdar'. *Man in India* 18, no. 1 (1938): 71–76. [unsigned review]

———. 'A Historical Document'. *Man in India* 51, no. 3 (1971): 191–207.

Roy Chaudhury, P. C. 'A Forgotten Agrarian Disturbance in Chotanagpur'. *Bengal, Past and Present* 75 (1956):60–65.

———. *Singhbhum*. Bihar District Gazetteers. Patna: Superintendent Secretariat Press, 1958.

———. *Singhbhum Old Records*. Patna: Superintendent Secretariat Press, 1958.

———. *Temples and Legends of Bihar*. Bhavan's Book University 127. Chaupatty, Bombay: Bharatiya Vidya Bhavan, 1965.

Sa, Fidelis de. *Crisis in Chota Nagpur: With Special Reference to The Judicial Conflict between Jesuit Missionaries and British Government Officials, November 1889–March 1890*. Bangalore: A Redemptorist Publication, 1975.

Sahu, Murali. *The Kolhan Under British Rule*. Jamshedpur: Sushanta Kumar Sahu, 1985.

——. 'Some Old Records Concerning Singhbhum', cyclostyled copy in the Tribal Research and Training Centre, Bara Guira, n. pl, n.d.

Saint-Hilaire, Geoffry. 'Notice sur une nouvelle espèce de boeuf, nommé Gaour par les Indiens, &ca.' [Note on a New Species of Bovines, Named Gaour by the Indians, &ca.] In vol 9 of *Mémoires du Museum d'Histoire naturelle,* par les professeurs de cet établissement, ouvrage orné de gravures [by the professors of that establishment, work illustrated with gravures], 71–75. Paris, 1822.

——. 'v. Geoffroy St. Hilaire'. *Isis von Oken*, Erster Band, Heft 1/6 [vol. 1, no. 1/6], 1823, 384–86.

'Samuel Linley', *Wikipedia* (website). Accessed 13 July 2009. https://en.wikipedia.org.

'Samuel R. Tickell, Biography'. *India Office Family History Search* (website). Accessed 5 January 2011. http://indiafamily.bl.uk.

'Sati Regulation XVII, A. D. 1829 of the Bengal Code: 4 December 1829'. *Women in World History* (website). Accessed 15 February 2011. http://chnm.gmu.edu/wwh/p/103.html.

Sawaiyan, A. K. *Kolhan, The land of the Hos*. Gutusai, Chaibasa: Ekta Prakashan, n.d. [published after 1979].

Schwerin, Detlef. *Von Armut zu Elend, Kolonialherrschaft und Agrarverfassung in Chota Nagpur, 1858–1918* [From Poverty to Misery: Colonial rule and Agrarian law in Chota Napur, 1858–1918]. Wiesbaden: Steiner, 1977.

Scott, Walter. 'The Tale of Alice Brand'. 1810. On *Tam Lin Balladry* (website). Accessed 11 September 2015. http://tam-lin.org/stories/Alice_Brand.html.

Scott, Walter. 'The Life of Jonathan Swift D.D.'. In Walter Scott, *The Complete Works of Sir Walter Scott, with a Biography and his Last Additions and Illustrations*. In 7 vols. Vol. 6, 1–90. New York: Conner and Cooke, 1833.

Scott, Walter, 'Scott to Matthew Weld Hartstongue, 22 December 1811'. In *The Letters of Sir Walter Scott*, edited by Herbert J. C. Grierson. In 12 vols. Vol. 3, p. 43. London: Constable, 1932–37. On *The letters of Sir Walter Scott* (website). Accessed 13 October 2012. http://www.walterscott.lib.ed.ac.uk/etexts/etexts/letters.html.

Sen, Asoka Kumar. 'Writing Local History and the District Record Room'. *Proceedings of the Indian Historical Records Commission,* 58th Session, 2003, 81–89.

——. 'Tribe-Peasant Continuum, The Dynamics of Ho Identity'. In *Changing Tribal Life: A Socio-philosophical Perspective*, edited by S. Gopal, 299–309. Delhi: Concept, 2006.

——. 'Collective Memory and Reconstruction of Ho History'. *Indian Folklore Research Journal* 5, no. 8 (2008): 87–103.

——. 'Gleaning Historical Materials from a Myth: A Study of the Kole History of Creation of the World'. *Indian Folklife* 28 (2008): 12–16.

——. 'Redefining Archaeology and the Ethno-history of Pre-Colonial Singhbhum'. *Indian Folklore Research Journal*, no. 10 (2010): 100–118.

——. *Representing Tribe: The Ho of Singhbhum under Colonial Rule*. New Delhi: Concept, 2011.

——. *From Village Elder to British Judge, Custom, Customary Law and Tribal Society*. New Delhi: Orient BlackSwan, 2012.

———. 'Assertion of Political Identity: The Ho Adivasis of Singhbhum 1770-1859'. *Journal of Adivasi and Indigenous Studies* 1, no. 1 (2014): 18-32.

———. 'Reconstructing Adivasi Village History: Problems and Possibilities'. *Journal of Adivasi and Indigenous Studies* 2, no 2 (August 2015): 16–37.

———, ed. *Singhbhum: Some Historical Gleanings*. Chaibasa: Department of History, Tata College, 1986.

Sen, Dharani and Uma Chaturvedi. 'Further Finds of Stone Axes in Singhbhum'. *Man in India* 35 (1955): 305–15.

Sen, D., G. S. Ray and A. K. Ghosh. 'Palaeoliths from Manbhum and Singhbhum'. *Man in India* 42 (1962): 10–18.

Sen, Padmaja. 'The Culture of the Present: An Understanding of the Adivasi Aesthetics. *Journal of Adivasi and Indigenous Studies* 1, no. 1 (2014): 32-42.

'Seraikella, Princely State'. *Indian Rajputs* (website). Accessed 10 May 2016. http://www.indianrajputs.com/view/seraikella.

'Short Account of the Lurkacoles'. *John Bull in the East*. Reprinted in *The Asiatic Journal and Monthly Register for British India and Its Dependencies* 13 (January–June 1822): 136–37.

Sidwell, Paul. 2018. 'Austroasiatic Studies: state of the art in 2018'. Presentation at the Graduate Institute of Linguistics, National Tsing Hua University, Taiwan, May 22, 2018.

Sifton, J. D. *Final Report on the Survey and Settlement of the Manoharpur Estate in Singhbhum*. Bankipore: The Bihar and Orissa Secretariat Book Depot, 1914.

Singh, C. P. 'The Martyrs of Singhbhum'. *Journal of the Bihar Research Society* 57 (1971): 149–53.

———. 'A Brief Survey of the Economic Condition of Singhbhum During the Initial Years of the British Administration'. Silver Jubilee Number, *Journal of Historical Research* 19, no. 1 (1976): 50–54.

———. *The Ho Tribe of Singhbhum*. New Delhi: Classical Publications, 1978.

Singh, Kumar Suresh. *The Dust-Storm and the Hanging Mist: A Study of Birsa Munda and His Movement in Chhotanagpur (1874–1901)*. Calcutta: Firma K. L. Mukhopadhyay, 1966.

———. 'State-Formation in Tribal Society: Some Preliminary Observations'. *Journal of the Indian Anthropological Society* 6 (1971): 161–81.

———. *Birsa Munda and His Movement, 1874–1901: A Study of a Millenarian Movement in Chotanagpur*. 2nd ed. of *The Dust-Storm and the Hanging Mist: A Study of Birsa Munda and His Movement in Chhotanagpur (1874–1901)*. Calcutta: Oxford University Press, 1983.

———. 'Medieval Tribal Bihar'. In *The Comprehensive History of Bihar*, vol. 2, part 1, 225–89. Patna: Kashi Prasad Jayaswal Research Institute, 1983.

———. *Tribal Society in India: An Anthropo-historical Perspective*. New New Delhi: Manohar Publications, 1985.

Singh, Madan Paul. *Indian Army Under the East India Company*. New Delhi: Sterling, 1976.

Singh, S. N. 'A Short History of Jails in Chotanagpur During the Early British Rule'. *Journal of Historical Research* 4, no. 2 (Republic Day 1962): 35–39.

———. 'Some Important Dates in the Modern Administrative History of Chotanagpur'. *Journal of Historical Research* 5, no. 2 (1963): 24–28.

Singh Deo, Tikayet Nrupendra Narayan. *Singhbhum, Seraikella and Kharswan Through the Ages*. No place, no publisher, 1954.

Sinha, S. C., Jyoti Sen, and Sudhir Panchbhai. 'The Concept of Diku among the Tribes of Chota Nagpur'. *Man in India* 49, no. 2 (1969): 121–38.

Sinha, Surajit. 'State Formation and Rajput Myth in Tribal Central India'. *Man in India* 42, no. 1 (1962): 35–80.

———. 'Vaisnava Influence on a Tribal Culture'. In *Krishna: Myths, Rites, and Attitudes*, edited by Milton Singer, 64–89. Honolulu: East-West Center, 1966.

Sinha, Surendra Prasad. 'Disquiet and Depredation in Chota Nagpur (1795–1800 A.D.)'. *Bulletin of the Bihar Tribal Research Institute* 5 (1963): 143–61.

———. 'Thakur Bholanath Sahy of Tamar (1795–1800)—The First Freedom Fighter of Chotanagpur'. *Journal of Historical Research* 6, no. 2 (1964): 43–48.

Sinha, Vishwa Nath Prasad. *Chota Nagpur Plateau: A Study in Settlement Geography*. New Delhi: K. B. Publications, 1976.

'Sir C. Metcalfe'. *The Asiatic Journal and Monthly Register for British and Foreign India, China, and Australasia*, n.s., 26 (May–August 1838): 16–19.

Sircar, Sailendra Nath. *Khiching (Ancient Khijjinga); or, A Lost Chapter of Orissa*. Calcutta: Hirendra Nath Sircara, [1939].

Sita Ram. *From Sepoy to Subedar, Being the Life and Adventures of Subedar Sita Ram, a Native Officer of the Bengal Army*, written and related by Himself, translated and first published by Lieutenant-Colonel Norgate, Bengal Staff Corps at Lahore, 1873. Paperback edition by James Lunt. London: Macmillan, 1980.

Skrine, Francis Henry. *Life of Sir William Wilson Hunter, K.C.S.I., LL.D.: A Vice-President of the Royal Asiatic Society, etc.* London: Longmans, Green, and Co, 1901.

[Smyth, William]. *Memoir of Mr. Sheridan*. Leeds: J. Cross, 1840.

Spear, Percival. *The Nabobs: A Study in the Social Life of the English in Eighteenth Century India*. Calcutta, Allahabad, Bombay, Delhi: Rupa, 1991 (first published in 1963).

———. *A History of India*, vol. 2. 1965. Reprinted with Epilogue, Harmondsworth: Penguin Books, 1970.

———. 'The British and the Indian State to 1830'. In *Tradition and Politics in South Asia*, edited by R. J. Moore, 151–71. New Delhi: Vikas, 1979.

Sprenger, A. 'Notice of a Ruin in Singhbhum'. *Journal of the Asiatic Society of Bengal* 20 (1851): 283–84.

Spry, Henry. *Modern India: With Illustrations on the Resources and Capabilities of Hindustan*. Vol. 1. London: Whittaker, 1837.

Stein, Burton. *Thomas Munro: The Origins of the Colonial State and His Vision of Empire*. Delhi: Oxford University Press, 1989.

Stirling, Andrew. 'An Account, Geographical, Statistical and Historical of Orissa Proper, or Cuttack'. *Asiatick Researches: Comprising History and Antiquities, the Arts, Sciences, and Literature of Asia.* 15 (1825): 163–338. [Reprinted as Asiatic Researches, New Delhi: Cosmo Publications 1979–80]

Stöhr, Emil. 'Die Singhbhum-Abteilung der Provinz der Südwest-Grenze von Bengalen'. *Petermann's Mittheilungen über wichtige neue Erforschungen auf dem Gesammtgebiete der Geographie*, 7. Band, Heft VI [The Singhbhum District of the South Western Frontier Province of Bengal, Petermann's

Announcements on Important New Research in the Whole Field of Geography, vol 7, part 6] (1861): 219–26.

Stokes, Eric. *The English Utilitarians and India*. Oxford: Clarendon Press, 1959. Indian paperback edition, Delhi: Oxford University Press, 1989.

Strange, Mike. 'Buckinghamshire—Strange and derivates'. *Your Total Event* (website). Accessed 21 March 2011. http://www.yourtotalevent.com/people/STRANGEinBuckinghamshire.htm.

Streumer, Paul. 'The Historical Roots of the Kolhan Movement'. In *Nationalism, Ethnicity and Political Development, South Asian Perspectives*, edited by Diethelm Weidemann, 5–23. New Delhi: Manohar, 1991.

Streumer, Paul. 'De moderne staat en haar kleine volken' [The Modern State and its Small Peoples]. In *Adivasi: Het andere India*, edited by Frits Cowan, 74–83. Amsterdam: Koninklijk Instituut voor de Tropen/Tropenmuseum, 1992.

——. Review of *Mad Tales from the Raj: The European Insane in British India* by Waltraut Ernst. *Medische Antropologie* 5, no. 2 (1993): 321–24.

——. 'Changes and Chances in a Long View: The Ho People of West Singhbhum and the Challenges of Rapid Economic Growth'. In *Social Exclusion and Adverse Inclusion, Development and Deprivation of Adivasis in India*, edited by Dev Nathan and Virginius Xaxa, 261–71. New Delhi: Oxford University Press India, 2012.

——. 'A Seventeenth Century Ideology: The Singhbhum Chronicle on Rajputs and Tribals'. *Journal of Adivasi and Indigenous Studies* 2, no 2 (August 2015): 1–15.

'Surguja District'. *Wikipedia* (website). Accessed 3 August 2010. https://en.wikipedia.org.

Tapper, Richard. 'Anthropologists, Historians, and Tribespeople on Tribe and State Formation in the Middle East'. In *Tribes and State Formation in the Middle East*, edited by Philip S. Khoury and Joseph Kostiner, 48–73. Berkeley: University of California Press, 1990.

Tätte, Kai, Luca Pagani, Ajai K. Pathak, Sulev Köks, Binh Ho Duy, Xuan Dung Ho, Gazi Nurun Nahar Sultana, Mohd Istiaq Shariff, Md Asaduzzaman, Doron M. Behar, Yarin Hadid, Richard Villems, Gyaneshwar Chaubey, Toomas Kivisid, and Mait Metspalu, 'The Genetic Legacy of Continental Scale Admixture in Indian Austroasiatic Speakers", *Scientific Reports* 9 (2019): 1-9.

Taylor, George Rogers, ed. *The Turner Thesis: Concerning the Role of the Frontier in American History*. Problems in American Civilization, Readings selected by the Department of American Studies, Amherst College. Boston: D. C. Heath, 1949.

Taylor, James Henry. *Final Report on the Survey and Settlement Operations in the Porahat Estate, District Singhbhum, 1900–1903*. Calcutta: Bengal Secretariat Press, 1904.

——. *Pir Notes: Prepared during the Settlement of the Porahat and Subordinate Estates, District Singhbhum, 1900–1903*. Calcutta: Bengal Secretariat Press, 1904.

Thapar, Romila. *A History of India*, vol. 1. Harmondsworth: Penguin books, 1966.

——. 'The Perennial Arians'. *The Thatched Patio* 5, no. 6 (1992): 24–31.

'The Collections'. *Sir John Soane's Museum* (website). Accessed 10 January 2010. www.soane.org/collections.html. 'Thomas Tickell'. *Wikipedia* (website). Accessed 17 May 2008. https://en.wikipedia.org.

Thompson, John Beswarick. 'John Simpson'. *Dictionary Canadian Biography Online* 10 (1871–80) (website). Accessed 10 July 2009. http://www.biographi.ca/009004-119.01-e.php?&id_nbr=5267.

Tickell Family. n.pl., n.d. Book in the private papers of descendants of Richard Tickell.

'Tickell'. *Family Search, International Genealogical Index* (website). Accessed 17 May 2008. http://familysearch.org.

Tickell, Samuel Richard. 'List of Birds Collected in the Jungles of Barabhum and Dholbhum'. *Journal of the Asiatic Society of Bengal* 2, part 2 (1833): 569–83.

———. '*Memoir on the Hodésum* (Improperly Called *Kolehan*)'. *Journal of the Asiatic Society of Bengal* 9, part 2 (1840): 694–710, 783–808.

———. 'Grammatical Construction of the Ho Language'. *Journal of the Asiatic Society of Bengal* 9, part 2 (1840): 997–1007.

———. 'Vocabulary of the Ho Language'. *Journal of the Asiatic Society of Bengal* 9, part 2 (1840): 1063–90.

———. 'Supplementary Note to the Memoir on the Hodésum, vol. ix, pp.649 and 783'. *Journal of the Asiatic Society of Bengal* 10 (1841): 30.

———. 'Remarks on the Characters and Habits of Ursus Labiatus, with a figure, Plate VII'. *Calcutta Journal of Natural History and Miscellany of the Arts and Sciences in India* 1 (1841): 199–207.

———. 'Remarks on the Moschus Memina'. *Calcutta Journal of Natural History and Miscellany of the Arts and Sciences in India* 1 (1841): 420–22.

———. 'On the Orál, or Singhbhoom Flying Squirrel, Pteromys Orál'. *Calcutta Journal of Natural History and Miscellany of the Arts and Sciences in India* 2 (1841): 401–8.

———. 'Notes on the Bendkar, a People of Keonjur'. *Journal of the Asiatic Society of Bengal* 11 (1842): 205–7.

———. 'Manis Crassicaudata., (Auct), M. Pentadactyla (Ibid.), Short-tailed or thick-tailed Manis–In Hindustan, generally called "Bujjerkeet" –Orissa, "Bujjer-Kapta" and "Surooj Mookhee"–By the Lurka Koles, "Armoo"'. *Journal of the Asiatic Society of Bengal* 11 (1842): 221–30.

———. 'Notes on a Curious Species of Tiger or Jaguar, Killed Near the Snowy Range, North of Darjeeling'. *Journal of the Asiatic Society of Bengal* 12, part 2 (1843): 814–16.

———. 'Remarks on Pteropus Edulis, Geoffrey', *Calcutta Journal of Natural History and Miscellany of the Arts and Sciences in India* 3 (1843): 29–36.

———. 'On the Oology of India—A Description of the Eggs, also Nests, of several Birds of the Plains of India, Collected Chiefly During 1845–46'. *Journal of the Asiatic Society of Bengal* 17 (1848): 297–305.

———. 'Notes on the Heuma, or "Shendoos" A Tribe Inhabiting the Hills North of Arakan'. *Journal of the Asiatic Society of Bengal* 21 (1852): 207–11.

———. 'Description of a New Species of Horn-bill'. *Journal of the Asiatic Society of Bengal* 24 (1855): 285–87.

———. 'Order Chelonia'. *Journal of the Asiatic Society of Bengal* 31 (1862): 367–70.

———. 'Memoranda Relative to Three Andamanese in the Charge of Major Tickell, when Deputy Commissioner of Amherst, Tenasserim, in 1861'. *Journal of the Asiatic Society of Bengal* 33 (1864): 162–73.

———. 'Language of the Kolarian Aborigines;—Grammatical Construction of the Ho language'. Special number on Indian Ethnology 1866, *Journal of the Asiatic Society of Bengal* 35, part 2 (1867): 268–78.

——. 'Excerpts from the Letters of the Resident at Kathmandu to Government from 1830 to 1840'. Manuscript, OIOC, 1840.

——. 'The Zoological Works of Samuel Richard Tickell'. Illustrated manuscript work in 14 volumes. London: Zoological Society of London, 1865–73.

——. 'Original Water-colour Drawings and Illustrated MS Relating to Indian Birds'. Forming one of a set of volumes from which the illustrated MS work by Tickell on Mammals, &c. of India, in the Library of the Zoological Society of London was elaborated, London, Natural History Museum, [abt. 1870].

'Time immemorial'. *Wikipedia* (website). Accessed 20 November 2014. https://en.wikipedia.org.

Tooley, Ronald Vere. *A Dictionary of Mapmakers, Including Cartographers, Geographers, Publishers, Engravers,etc. from the Earliest Times to 1900*. Part 6 of Hutchinson to Kruse, *Map Collector's Series* 8, no. 78. London: Map Collectors' Circle, 1971.

'Trail of Tears'. *Wikipedia* (website). Accessed 23 April 2013. https://en.wikipedia.org.

Traill, George William. 'Statistical Report on the Bhotia Mehals of Kamaon'. *Asiatick Researches: Comprising History and Antiquities, the Arts, Sciences, and Literature of Asia* 17 (1832): 1–50.

Tripathi, Sila. 'Seafaring Archaeology of the East Coast of India and Southeast Asia during the Early Historical Period', *Ancient Asia,* 8, no 7 (2017): 1-22., spec. pp. 15, 18.

Trivedi, R., Sanghamitra Sahoo, Anamika Singh, G. Hima Bundu, Jheelam Banerjee, Manuj Tandon, Sonali Gaikwad, Revathi Rajkumar, T. Sitalaximi, Richa Ashma, G. B. N. Chainy and V. K. Kashyap. 'Genetic Imprints of Pleistocene Origin of Indian Populations: A Comprehensive Phylogeographic Sketch of Indian Y-Chromosomes'. *International Journal of Human Genetics* 8, 1–2 (2008): 97–118.

Tuckey, A. D. *Final Report on the Resettlement of the Kolhan Government Estate in the District of Singhbhum, 1913–1918*. Patna: Superintendent, Government Printing, Bihar and Orissa, 1920.

Union of British Ornithologists. 'Colonel S. R. Tickell'. Jubilee Supplement, *The Ibis: Quarterly Journal of Ornithology*, 9th ser., 2 (1908): 289–290. *Internet Archive* (website), accessed 6 October 2009, http//www.archive.org/stream/ibias29brit_djvu.txt.

Upadhyay, V. S. 'Studies on Pre-Historic Archaeology in Bihar'. Special Number on 25 Years of Anthropology in Bihar: Silver Jubilee Volume, *Journal of Social Research* 21, no. 2 (1978): 168–73.

Van Driem, George, 'Austroasiatic Phylogeny and the Austroasiatic Homeland in Light of Recent Population Genetic Studies', *Mon-Khmer Studies*, 37 (2007): 1-14.

Van Troy, Joseph. 'The Pre-Historic Context of the Coming of the Mundas to the Ranchi Plateau: A review'. *Sevartham: Indian Culture in a Christian Context* 15 (1990): 27–41.

——. 'Prehistory and Early History of Chotanagpur'. In *Cultural Chota Nagpur: Unity in Diversity*, edited by Sanjay Bosu Mullick, 23–41. Published for William Carey Study and Research Centre. New Delhi: Uppal, 1991.

Vasu, Nagendranath. *The Archaeological Survey of Mayurabhanja*. Calcutta: published by the Mayurabhanja State, 1911.

Verardo, Barbara. 'Rebels and Devotees of Jharkhand: Social, Religious and Political Transformations among the Adivasis of Northern India'. PhD thesis, London School of Economics and Political Science, 2003.

'Vigesimal'. *Wikipedia* (website). accessed 19 November 2015. https://en.wikipedia.org.

Virottam, Balmukund. *The Nagabanshis and the Cheros*. New Delhi: Munshiram Manoharlal, 1972.

———. 'The Singh Rulers of Medieval Singhbhum'. Silver Jubilee Number, *Journal of Historical Research* 19, no. 1 (1976): 70–74.

Walden, Arthur. 'Notes on the late Colonel Tickell's manuscript Work entitled "Illustrations of Indian Ornithology"'. *The Ibis: Quarterly Journal of Ornithology*, series 3, vol. 6 (July 1876): 336–57. *Internet Archive* (website). Accessed 24 February 2011. http://www.archive.org/details/ibis63brit.

Waterhouse, David. 'Brian Hodgson—A Biographical Sketch'. In *The Origins of Himalayan Studies: Brian Houghton Hodgson in Nepal and Darjeeling, 1820–1858*, edited by David Waterhouse, 1–24. Abingdon: RoutledgeCurzon. First Indian reprint, 2005.

———, ed. *The Origins of Himalayan Studies: Brian Houghton Hodgson in Nepal and Darjeeling, 1820–1858*. Abingdon: RoutledgeCurzon. First Indian reprint, 2005.

Watson, John Forbes and John William Kaye, eds. *The People of India: A Series of Photographic Illustrations, with the Descriptive Letterpress, of the Races and Tribes of Hindustan, Originally Prepared under the Authority of the Government of India, and Reproduced by Order of the Secretary of State for India in Council*. Vol. 1. London: India Museum, 1868.

'Webb-Smith Collection'. *University of Cambridge*, Department of Zoology, Special Collections (website). Accessed 19 December 2010. www.zoo.cam.ac.uk/library/webbsmith.hml.

Wenskus, Reinhard. *Stammesbildung und Stammesverfassung: Das Werden der Frühmittelalterlichen Gentes* [Formation and Constitution of Tribes: The Emergence of the Early Mediaeval Clans]. Köln: Böhlau, 1961.

Whelpton, John. *Kings, Soldiers and Priests: Nepalese Politics and the Rise of Jang Bahadur Rana, 1830–1857*. Delhi: Manohar, 1991.

Whelpton, John. 'The Political Role of Brian Hodgson'. In *The Origins of Himalayan Studies: Brian Houghton Hodgson in Nepal and Darjeeling, 1820–1858*, edited by David Waterhouse, 25–48. Abingdon: RoutledgeCurzon. First Indian reprint, 2005.

Wild, Antony. *The East India Company: Trade and Conquest from 1600*. New York: The Lyons Press, 2000.

Wilkinson, Theon. *Two Monsoons: The Life and Death of Europeans in India*, 2nd ed. (1st ed., 1976). London: Duckworth, 1987

Wilkinson, Thomas. 'Wilkinson's Rules'. Appendix VI to N. N. Sinha and S. K. Chattopadhyay, *Commentaries on Chotanagpur Tenancy Act 1908: With Rules, Notifications and Other Allied Laws, Amended with Act no. 45 of 1982 and Bihar Finance Act no. 58 of 1982*, 425–30. Allahabad: Rajal, 1985.

'Wilkinson'. On *Westmorland Papers* (website). 2004–2011. Accessed 1 December 2011. http://www.northofthesands.org.uk/westmoreland/parish/12/crosby_ravensworth. .

'William Ouseley'. *Wikipedia* (website). Accessed 7 February 2011. https://en.wikipedia.org.

'William Gore Ouseley'. *Wikipedia* (website). Accessed 7 February 2011. https://en.wikipedia.org.

'William Linley'. *Wikipedia* (website). Accessed 13 July 2009. https://en.wikipedia.org.

'William Marsh Cooper, China Consular Service'. In 'The British Consuls in South Formosa', *The Takao Club* (website). Accessed 12 January 1014. http://takaoclub.com/britishconsuls/william_marsh_cooper.htm.

Willing, Thomson. 'Mrs. Sheridan, portrait by Sir Joshua Reynolds'. In *Some Old Time Beauties: After portraits by the English masters, with Embellishment and Comment by Thomson Willing*, edited by Thomson Willing, 37–50. Boston: Joseph Knight, 1895.

Wilson, H. H. *A Glossary of Judicial and Revenue Terms and of Useful Words Occurring in Official Documents Relating to the Administration of the Government of British India, From the Arabic, Persian, Hindustani, Sanskrit, Hindi, Bengali, Uriya, Marathi, Guzarathi, Telugu, Karnataka, Tamil, Malayalam, and Other Languages, Compiled and Published under the Authority of the Honorable the Court of Directors of the East-India Company*. London: Wm. H. Allen, 1855.

Wilson, Ben. *Decency and Disorder: The Age of Cant, 1789–1837*. London: Faber and Faber, 2008.

Witzel, Michael. 'Regionale und Ueberregionale Faktoren in der Entwicklung Vedischer Brahmanengruppen im Mittelalter' [Regional and Supra-regional Factors in the Development of Groups of Vedic Brahmins in the Middle Ages]. In *Regionale Tradition in Südasien*, edited by Hermann Kulke and Dietmar Rothermund, 37–76. Wiesbaden: Franz Steiner Verlag, 1985.

Woolf, Leonard. *Diaries in Ceylon, 1908–1911: Records of a Colonial Administrator, Being the Official Diaries Maintained by Leonard Woolf while Assistant Government Agent of the Hambantota District, Ceylon,* Edited and with a preface by Leonard Woolf, and, *Stories from the East: Three Short Stories on Ceylon, by Leonard Woolf, 1908–1911*. Reprint by *The Ceylon Historical Journal* 9, nos 1–4 (July 1959–April 1960). 2nd edition. Dehiwala: Tisara Press, 1983.

Woolf, Virginia. *A Room of One's Own*. 1928. Republished, Harmondsworth: Penguin, 1967.

Wood, Patrick. 'Thomas Linley, Mozart's Boyhood Rival'. *Early Music America* 15, no. 1 (Spring 2009): 34–37.

Wordsworth, William. 'French Revolution as it Appeared to Enthusiasts at His Commencement'. In *The Complete Poetical Works*. London: Macmillan, 1888. On Bartleby.com, (website) 1999. Accessed 16 May 2016. www.bartleby.com/145/.

Xaxa, Virginius. *State, Society, and Tribes: Issues in Post-Colonial India*. Delhi: Dorling Kindersley, licensees of Pearson Longman, 2008.

———. '"Tribes", Tradition and State'. *The Newsletter*, Spring 2010: 18. Leiden: International Institute for Asian Studies.

Yorke, Michael. 'Decisions and Analogy: Political Structure and Discourse among the Ho Tribals of India'. PhD thesis, University of London, 1976.

Yule, Henry and A. C. Burnell. *Hobson-Jobson: A Glossary of Colloquial Anglo-Indian Words and Phrases, And of Kindred terms, Etymological, Historical, Geographical and Discursive*. 2nd ed. by William Crooke. London: John Murray, 1903. Reprint, London and New York: Routledge and Kegan Paul, 1985.

Yule, Paul. *Metalwork of the Bronze Age in India*. Prähistorische Bronzefunde. Abteilung XX—Band 8. [Prehistoric Bronze Finds, Part 20, vol. 8] München: C. H. Beck'sche Verlagsbuchhandlung, 1985.

Zide, Arlene R. K. and Norman H. Zide. 'Proto-Munda Cultural Vocabulary: Evidence for Early Agriculture'. In *Austroasiatic Studies*, edited by Philip K. Jenner, Laurence C. Thompson, Stanley Starosta, part 2:1295–1334. Honolulu: The University Press of Hawaii, 1976.

Zide, Norman H., ed. *Studies in Comparative Austroasiatic Linguistics*. Indo-Iranian Monographs. The Hague: Mouton, 1966.

Zide, Norman and Ram Dayal Munda. 'Descriptive Dialogue Songs in Mundari'. In *Anthropology and Archaeology:Essays in Commemoration of Verrier Elwin, 1902–64*, edited by M. C. Pradhan, R. D. Singh, P. K. Misra, D. B. Sastry, 272–83. Oxford: Oxford University Press, 1969.

Zide, Norman and Ram Dayal Munda. 'Structural Influence of Bengali Vaisnava Songs on Traditional Mundari Songs'. *Journal of Social Research* 13, no. 1 (1970): 36–48.

Zoological Society of London. 'Proceedings of the Scientific Meetings of the Zoological Society of London for the Year 1874'. London. 1875. *Internet Archive* (website). Accessed 14 November 2010. http://www.archiveorg/stream/proceedingsofgen74zool/proceedingsofgen74zool_djvu.txt.

Notes

Abbreviations in the notes

AJMR	*The Asiatic Journal and Monthly Register for British India and Its Dependencies* (January 1816–December 1829), vols. 1–28; *The Asiatic Journal and Monthly Register for British and Foreign India, China, and Australasia*, New Series (January 1830–April 1843), vols. 1–40 and *The Asiatic Journal and Monthly Miscellany* (May 1843–April 1845), vols. 1–4.
AR	*Asiatick Researches: Comprising History and Antiquities, the Arts, Sciences, and Literature of Asia*. Reprinted 1979–80 as *Asiatic Researches*, New Delhi: Cosmo Publications.
BC	Board's Collections. London: British Library, Oriental and India Office Collection (OIOC).
BPP	*Bengal, Past and Present.*
BSA	Bihar State Archives, Patna.
IJBA	*The Internet Journal of Biological Anthropology.*
JAIS	*Journal of Adivasi and Indigenous Studies*
JASB	*Journal of the Asiatic Society of Bengal.*
JBORS	*Journal of the Bihar and Orissa Research Society.*
JBRS	*Journal of the Bihar Research Society.*
JHR	*Journal of Historical Research.*
JRASGBI	*Journal of the Royal Asiatic Society of Great Britain and Ireland.*
MII	*Man in India.*
NAI	National Archives of India, New Delhi.
OHRJ	*The Orissa Historical Research Journal.*
OIOC	Oriental and India Office Collection, British Library, London.
PASB	*Proceedings of the Asiatic Society of Bengal.*
SOC	Singhbhum Old Correspondence. Bihar State Archives, Patna.
WBSA	West Bengal State Archives, Kolkata.
WCIV	Rules for Civil Justice: attached to Wilkinson to C. Macsween, 13 January 1834 (London: OIOC), BC 58,892.
WCRIM	Rules for Criminal Justice: attached to Wilkinson to C. Macsween, 13 January 1834 (London: OIOC), BC 58,892.
WINS	Wilkinson to Ensign P. Nicolson, 7 January 1834, Extract from Fort William Judicial Consultation, 17 February 1834 (London: OIOC), BC 58, 892.
WP	*Wikipedia* (website), https://en.wikipedia.org.
WR	Rules for Civil Justice for the Kolhan, enclosure in Wilkinson to Mangles, 5 May 1837 (London: OIOC), BC 69,239.

Prologue: The Independence of the Hos

[1] Samuel Richard Tickell, 'Memoir on the Hodésum (Improperly Called Kolehan)', *JASB* 9, part 2 (1840): 706–9.
The plate on this page is a view from the western side of the Kutaitundi Temple, Khiching. Taken from Mohammed Laeequddin, *Census of Mayurbhanj State: 1931*, vol. 1, *Report,* published under the Authority of the State (Calcutta: Caledonian, 1937).
[2] C. P. Singh found for Singhbhum that 'source materials for writing the history . . . prior to the grant of the Dewani to the British E.I.C. . . . were almost non existent'. See C. P. Singh, *The Ho Tribe of Singhbhum* (New Delhi: Classical Publications, 1978), 25. The sigh that there are 'virtually no records available for reconstructing the history of Singhbhum before 1765' can be readily understood. See Jagdish Chandra Jha, review of *The Ho Tribe of Singhbhum* by C. P. Singh, *JBRS* 62 (1978; repr. mentioned 1976): 302.
[3] John Hoffmann and Arthur van Emelen, *Encyclopaedia Mundarica,* 13 vols., vol. 6, (Patna, Bihar and Orissa: Superintendent, Government Printing, 1930–50): 1814–15. 'Ho' from the Munda 'Horo', hence with a long 'o'.
[4] The great similarity between the Mundas and the Hos was noticed practically immediately after British entered the Ho land. See Roughsedge to Metcalfe, 9 May 1820 (London: OIOC), BC 21,438. See also Tickell, 'Memoir', 803; Edward Tuite Dalton, *Descriptive Ethnology of Bengal*, Illustrated by Lithograph Portraits copied from Photographs (Calcutta: Office of the Superintendent of Government Printing, 1872; repr., *Tribal History of Eastern India* [New Delhi: Cosmo], 1978): 178.
Father Hoffmann considered the Hos and the Kumpat Mundas ('ordinary Mundas') as the same tribe. See Hoffmann and Van Emelen, *Encyclopaedia Mundarica*, vol. 6: 1769; vol. 9: 2881. Elsewhere Hoffman considered the Hos and the Hasada Mundas of the Khunti area of Ranchi district as 'one and the same people'. See Hoffmann and Arthur van Emelen, *Encyclopaedia Mundarica* 6: 1825–26. Surprisingly, the other early twentieth century expert on the Mundas, S. C. Roy, was silent on this question in his extensive *The Mundas and Their Country*. Most linguists stressed the similarity. See Sten Konow ed., *Munda and Dravidian Languages*, vol. 4 of *Linguistic Survey of India*, ed. and comp. George Abraham Grierson (Calcutta: Superintendent of Government Printing, 1906): 8, 21, 118; Lionel B. Burrows, *The Grammar of the Ho Language* (Calcutta: Catholic Orphan Press, 1915; repr., *The Grammer of the Ho Language: An Eastern Himalayan Dialect* [New Delhi: Cosmo, 1980]): 1. Tickell, who in 1840 wrote the first grammar of a Munda language, was the first one to see a 'marked' difference between the languages of the Ho and the Mundas. John Deeney saw significant 'divergence between the two languages in grammar and considerably more divergence in vocabulary'. See John Deeney, *Ho Grammar and Vocabulary* (Chaibasa: Xavier Ho Publications, 1975): vii–viii; John Deeney, *Ho-English Dictionary* (Chaibasa: Xavier Ho Publications, 1978): iv; John Deeney, 'Comparison of the Munda and the Ho Languages', in *The Munda World: Hoffmann Commemoration Volume*, edited by P. Ponette (Ranchi: Catholic Press, 1978): 44–52.
[5] There is quite some literature on Munda languages and their relations to each other. The most widely accepted conclusions are very briefly summarised in 'Munda languages', *WP*, accessed 25 March 2015.
[6] In 1854, the American missionary Francis Mason related the Ho language to the South-east Asian Talaing (Mon) on the basis of S. R. Tickell's Ho grammar. See Francis Mason, 'The Talaing Language', *Journal of the American Oriental Society* 4 (1854): 282.
Mon belongs to the Mon-Khmer group of languages, later called Austroasiatic. See 'Austroasiatic languages', *WP*, accessed 25 March 2015.
[7] Blench, Roger. 'Reconstructing Austroasiatic Prehistory', (2014): 1–13, esp p. 4. Accessed 5 March 2015. http://www.academia.edu/5165573/Reconstructing_Austroasiatic_prehistory.
Also: Kai Tätte, Luca Pagani, Ajai K. Pathak, a.o., 'The Genetic Legacy of Continental Scale Admixture in Indian Austroasiatic Speakers', *Scientific Reports* 9 (2019): 1-9, esp. p. 5.
[8] Maria Eugenia Riccio, José Manuel Nunes, Melissa Rahal, a.o., 'The Austroasiatic Munda Population from India and Its Enigmatic Origin: A HLA Diversity Study', *Human Biology* 83, no 3 (2011): 405-35, on *BioOne* (website), accessed 22 May 2016, doi: http://dx.doi.org/10.3378/027.083.0306.
[9] Kai Tätte, Luca Pagani, Ajai K. Pathak, a.o. 'The Genetic Legacy of Continental Scale Admixture in Indian Austroasiatic Speakers', 5.
[10] Sila Tripathi, "Seafaring Archaeology of the East Coast of India and Southeast Asia during the Early Historical Period", *Ancient Asia*, 8, no 7 (2017): 1-22, espec. pp. 15, 18.
[11] Paul Sidwell, 2018. 'Austroasiatic Studies: state of the art in 2018'. Presentation at the Graduate Institute of Linguistics, National Tsing Hua University, Taiwan, May 22, 2018.
Felix Rau and Paul Sidwell, 'The Munda Maritime Hypothesis', in *Journal of the Southeast Asian Linguistic Ssociety JSEALS* 12, no. 2, (2019): 35-57.
[12] Samar Bosu Mullick, 'The Cradle of the Munda: Birth of a New Branch of Austroasiatic', in *Journal of Adivasi and*

Indigenous Studies (JAIS), 10, no. 1, (February 2020): 14-25.

[13] Khan, Razib. 'The maturation of the South Asian genetic landscape', March 31, 2018. On Gene Expression (website), accessed 2 April 2018, https://www.gnxp.com/WordPress/2018/03/31/the-maturation-of-the-south-asian-genetic-landscape/.

[14] Gyaneshwer Chaubey a.o., 'Population Genetic Structure in Indian Austroasiatic Speakers: the Role of Landscape Barriers and Sex-specific Admixture', in *Molecular Biology and Evolution* (2011): 1013–24, esp. 1022. accessed 28 February 2015, http://mbe.oxfordjournals.org/content/28/2/1013.full.

[15] There is small component (4%) in the genetic build-up of Bengalis (Khan, Razib, 'Tibeto-Burmans in Bengal, and Indians in ancient Malaya'. On Gene Expression (website), accessed 30 August 2018, https://www.gnxp.com/WordPress/2018/08/29/tibeto-burmans-in-bengal-and-indians-in-ancient-malaya/) . But migration of Munda speakers into Bengal took place well after 1800.

[16] George Van Driem, 'Austroasiatic Phylogeny and the Austroasiatic Homeland in Light of Recent Population Genetic studies', *Mon-Khmer Studies*, 37 (2007): 7.

[17] That does not mean that Ho women are from India and half of the Ho men are from SE Asia. Genetic inheritance implies much more than just DNA. Every Ho (and other Munda speaker) has both Ancient Ancestral South Indian and SE Asian ancestry.

[18] Gyaneshwer Chaubey, Mait Metspalu, Ying Choi, a.o. 'Population Genetic Structure in Indian Austroasiatic Speakers: the Role of Landscape Barriers and Sex-specific Admixture', *Molecular Biology and Evolution* (2011): 1013–24, accessed 28 February 2015, http://mbe.oxfordjournals.org/content/28/2/1013.full).

[19] There are longstanding problems to determine what was the part of the Austroasiatics, to which the Mundas and the Hos belong, in the peopling of India, and which role played the South-east Asian connection in their genesis. The theories from the pre-DNA era rested on linguistic, ethnological and archaeological insights arranged in models of diffusion of the major groups. In these the Munda speakers were seen either as early, perhaps the first, migrants coming from the west, or as invaders coming in later from South-east Asia. There is a useful summary by Dilip Chakrabarty. (Dilip Chakrabarti, 'The Idea of Diffusion as an Explanatory Model', chapter 2 of *Theoretical Issues in India Archaeology* (New Delhi: Munshiram Manoharlal, 1988): 28–33.)

DNA research is a powerful line of enquiry, and at some point in the presentations, its results are coupled with this earlier linguistic or ethnographic evidence. (Archaeological evidence is not much used here.) DNA research not only reconfirmed the place of the Austroasiatic group as a major actor in the peopling of India, but also clarified how the Indian branch of this group came into existence.

In 2003, Basu e.a. saw the Austroasiatics as the earliest settlers of India, and pointed to the 'underlying unity of the female lineages' in the country. They saw a double event: the ancestors of the Austroasiatics would have entered India from the west, but later some Austroasiatics entered from the north-east. (Analabhu Basu, Namita Mukherjee, Sangita Roy, a.o., 'Ethnic India: A Genomic View, With Special Reference to Peopling and Structure', *Genome Research* 13 (2003): 2277, 2281.)

Again, in 2016, they added the ASI (Ancient South Indians) to the earliest inhabitants of India. (Analabha Basu, Neeta Sarkar-Roy, and Partha P. Majumder, 'Genomic Reconstruction of the History of Extant Populations of India Reveals Five Distinct Ancestral Components and a Complex Structure', *Proceedings of the National Academy of Sciences of the United States of America* 113, no. 6 (February 9, 2016): 1594–1599, published online before print (January 25, 2016), accessed 26 January 2016, http://www.pnas.org/content/113/6/1594.full.)

For the male part, the evidence points to a South-east Asian connection, as demonstrated by Kumar a.o., 2007. Here, they assumed an Indian origin for this common link between Indian and South-east Asian Austroasiatic males. (Vikrant Kumar, Arimanda N. S. Reddy, Jagedeesh P. Babu, a.o., 'Y-chromosome Evidence Suggests a Common Paternal Heritage of Austro-Asiatic Populations', *BMC Evolutionary Biology* 7, no. 1 (2007): 47, accessed 28 February 2015, http://www.biomedcentral.com/1471-2148/7/47.)

In 2008, the Indian origin of the South-east Asian Austroasiatic group, was strongly refuted by Trivedi a.o. Their article also gave a more detailed insight in the genesis of the Indian Austroasiatic population. They concluded that 'these tribes probably experienced a major demographic event, such as a common founder effect followed by a bottleneck that greatly reduced the Y-chromosome diversity in the Austro-Asiatic tribes of eastern India'. Thus their arrival of in India would have been 'a single event . . . a major male-mediated migration into India', encountering the 'original settlers of the subcontinent' who would be people akin to those now living in south India. In sum, Trivedi e.a. suggested 'a common Pleistocene origin of Indian populations, which was subsequently followed by migrations of Austro-Asiatic speaking tribal males from SE Asia.' (R. Trivedi, Sanghamitra Sahoo, Anamika Singh, a.o., 'Genetic Imprints of Pleistocene Origin of Indian Populations: A Comprehensive Phylogeographic Sketch of Indian Y-Chromosomes', *International Journal of Human Genetics* 8, 1–2 (2008): 114–18.)

Admixture would tally well what we know of areas more comprehensively covered by DNA research. It appears that in many areas of Asia-Europe, immigration even when accompanied by major economic or political changes did not make more than a significant dent (15–30%) in the existing DNA pool. A well-studied example is the population of Great Britain. 'The most important message of my genetic story is that three-quarters of British ancestors arrived long before the first farmers', wrote Oppenheimer in 2007. (Stephen Oppenheimer, *The Origins of the British* (London: Robinson, 2007): 470.)

So who were earlier, the Dravidians (ASI), the Austroasiatics, or possibly some unnamed others (as expressed in 'female lineages')? The methodical question is how to link DNA material—or for that matter any material remains—to present-day linguistic groups. That problem is compounded when we go to the Pleistocene, ending some 8,000–9,000 BCE, in which even primeval forms of such languages did not yet exist or at best were in the process of formation. Basu's relative unity at the female side of India's population does not absolutely need a linguistic tack, but indicates a wide substratum underlying most of the present-day Indian linguistic groups and tribes. The Austroasiatics would have come in and mixed locally with that substratum—as did others. Which is exactly what Razib Khan argues in 2010. 'It seems that mtDNA lineages unite South Asians, while the Y lineages separate them ... Men on the move have reshaped the genetics and culture of South Asia, but the mtDNA still point to an ancient Eurasian group with distant but stronger affinities to the east than the west.' He 'very tentatively' placed the arrival of the Mundas sometime between 8,000 and 2,000/1,000 BCE. That is some time window. (Razib Khan, 'Sons of the Conquerors: The Story of India?', in 'Gene Expression', blog on *Discover, Science for the Curious* (website), October 28, 2010, accessed 9 May 2016, http://blogs.discovermagazine.com/gnxp/2010/10/sons-of-the-conquerers-the-story-of-india/#.VzBODr6M6jr).

The most comprehensive overview seems to be Chaubey e.a. 2011, They placed the earliest Austroasiatics in South-east Asia. Their contribution to the gene pool of Mundas in India was not indicated with a date, but they did give the magnitude. It would have been about 25% and exclusively male. (Gyaneshwer Chaubey, Mait Metspalu, Ying Choi, a.o. 'Population Genetic Structure in Indian Austroasiatic Speakers: the Role of Landscape Barriers and Sex-specific Admixture', *Molecular Biology and Evolution* (2011): 1013–24, accessed 28 February 2015, http://mbe.oxfordjournals.org/content/28/2/1013.full).

The South-east Asian male contribution to the genes of the Munda peoples of India seems well established, but its possible date still very vague.

[20] Paul Sidwell, personal communication, June 2018.

[21] Kai Tätte, Luca Pagani, Ajai K. Pathak, a.o., 'The Genetic Legacy of Continental Scale Admixture in Indian Austroasiatic Speakers", 1-9.

[22] For the speculative migration of the Munda speakers, see Andrew F. Grignard, 'The Oraons and Mundas: From the Time of Their Settlement in India', *Anthropos* 4, no. 1 (1909): 11–14; Sarat Chandra Roy, *The Mundas and Their Country* (Calcutta, 1912; repr., London: Asia Publishing House, 1970): 9, 10–13, 20–61, 67–70; Stephen Fuchs, 'The Origin of the Mundas', in *The Munda World: Hoffmann Commemoration Volume* edited by P. Ponette (Ranchi: The Catholic Press, 1978): 68–80.

The western detour seems unlikely. From the small number of Austroasiatic (or Proto-Munda) words in Sanskrit, Burrow concludes that these languages 'were situated only in eastern India'. Quote from Burrow's 1968 *Collected Papers on Dravidian Linguistics*, p. 328, in Colin P. Masica, 'Aryan and Non-Aryan Elements in North Indian Agriculture', *Aryan and Non-Aryan in India,* edited by Madhav M. Deshpande and Peter Edwin Hook (Ann Arbor: Center for South Asian and Southeast Asian Studies, The University of Michigan, 1979): 138–39.

Before we can rest this question, it is fair to point to Bongard-Levin (1957). He connected the ancestors of the Mundas to the Copper Hoard culture of north west India in the centuries before the 11th century BCE. However, this is a circular argument, as he treats as axiomatic the idea that before the Aryans came, Mundas or Proto Mundas formed the population of the upper Gangetic Basin, and from that connected the Copper Hoard culture to them. See G. M. Bongard-Levin, 'The Origin of the Mundas' (1957, repr. in *Studies in Ancient India and Central Asia*, vol. 7 of *Soviet Indology Series* of *Indian Studies: Past and Present*, edited by Debiprasad Chattopadhyaya, Calcutta: R. K. Maitra, 1971): 15.

[23] Joseph Van Troy, 'The Pre-Historic Context of the Coming of the Mundas to the Ranchi Plateau, A review', *Sevartham: Indian Culture in a Christian Context* 15 (1990): 37. Or even 200 years later, at the end of the fourth century BCE. See Joseph Van Troy, 'Prehistory and Early History of Chotanagpur', in Sanjay Bosu Mullick (ed.), *Cultural Chota Nagpur: Unity in diversity*, published for William Carey Study and Research Centre (New Delhi: Uppal, 1991), 36–7.

See also Romila Thapar, *A History of India*, vol. 1 (Harmondsworth: Penguin books, 1966), 50–57.

[24] Rev. Hahn poured over the maps of the area, and found that 'only a few names of villages, rivers and hills which seem to be of Kolarian and Dravidian origin'. See Ferdinand Hahn, 'Dravidian and Kolarian place names in Mirzapur, Shahabad and Gaya', *JASB* 72 (1903): 91-93. Names of rivers and hills do, however, often indicate who were the first settlers in an area.

[25] Arlene R. K. Zide and Norman H. Zide, 'Proto-Munda Cultural Vocabulary, Evidence for Early Agriculture', in Philip K. Jenner, Laurence C. Thompson, Stanley Starosta eds., *Austroasiatic Studies*, part 2: 1295–1324 (Honolulu: The University Press of Hawaii, 1976).

We have the evidence of Kuiper that the Sanskrit word for 'plough' comes from Proto-Munda. See F. B. J. Kuiper, *Proto-Munda Words in Sanskrit*, Verhandeling der Koninklijke Nederlandsche Akademie van Wetenschappen, afd. Letterkunde, Nieuwe Reeks, deel 51, no. 3 (Amsterdam, N. V. Noord-Hollandsche Uitgevers Maatschappij, 1948).

[26] To explain differences between the northern and southern groups of Munda languages, Zide and Zide considered two possibilities. The first was that the North and South Munda groups of languages may not both have derived from a 'single proto-language' and had 'a partly independent history'. The second being that the North Munda group had sometime shifted

their 'ecological habitat'. Arlene R. K. Zide and Norman H. Zide, 'Proto-Munda Cultural Vocabulary', 1331. That second possibility would tally with Van Troy's idea that (Proto) North Munda speakers came to Chotanagpur from the eastern Ganges valley.

[27] The earliest remains of mankind on the Chotanagpur plateau have received little attention to date, although the first finds date from the 1860s. In 1868, Beeching described the discovery of stone implements in the Chaibasa and Chakradharpur areas. See [Beeching, Captain], 'Notes on Some Stone Implements in the District of Singhboom by Captain Beeching', communicated by V. Ball, Esq., *PASB*, January–December 1868, 177; Roy, *The Mundas and Their Country*, 10. In 1874, Ball got 'a remarkably fine stone adze' from the Superintendent of Police in Chaibasa. See Valentine Ball, *Jungle Life in India; or, The Journeys and Journals of an Indian Geologist* (London: Thos. De la Rue, 1880; repr., *Tribal and Peasant Life in Nineteenth Century India* [New Delhi: Usha, 1985]), 136, 140, 472–75, 675–83. For further finds in Singhbhum, see Dharani Sen and Uma Chaturvedi, 'Further Finds of Stone Axes in Singhbhum', *MII* 35 (1955): 305–15; D. Sen, G. S. Ray and A. K. Ghosh, 'Palaeoliths from Manbhum and Singhbhum', *MII* 42 (1962): 10–18.

For overviews, see for Bihar, V. S. Upadhyay, 'Studies on Pre-Historic Archaeology in Bihar', Special Number on Twenty Five Years of Anthropology in Bihar: Silver Jubilee Volume, *Journal of Social Research* 21, no. 2 (1978): 168–73;

for the Odisha part, R. P. Prusty, 'Study of Microlith Industry in Orissa', *OHRJ* 24, 25 and 26 (1980): 133–46;

and for the Chotanagpur area,

Abhik Ghosh, 'Prehistory of the Chotanagpur Region, part 2: Proposed Stages, Paleaolithic and the Mesolithic', *IJBA* 2, no. 1 (2008), 37 pp., accessed 10 August 2010, http://ispub.com/IJBA/2/1/9185;

Abhik Ghosh, 'Prehistory of the Chotanagpur Region, part 3: The Neolithic Problem and the Chalcolithic', *IJBA* 2, no. 2 (2009), 18 pp., accessed 12 April 2011, http://ispub.com/IJBA/2/2/11792;

Abhik Ghosh, 'Prehistory of the Chotanagpur Region, part 4: Ethnoarchaeology, Rock Art, Iron and the Asuras', *IJBA* 3, no. 1 (2009), 20 pp., accessed 12 April 2011, http://ispub.com/IJBA/3/1/5134;

And his conclusions in Abhik Ghosh, 'Prehistory of the Chotanagpur Region, part 5: State Formation and General Conclusions', *IJBA* 3, no. 2 (2009), 30 pp., accessed 12 April 2011, http://ispub.com/IJBA/3/2/6874.

[28] Joseph Van Troy, 'Prehistory and Early History of Chotanagpur', in Mullick ed., *Cultural Chota Nagpur*, 24.

[29] Subhashis Das, *Megaliths of India* (website), accessed 11 November 2011, http://www.megalithindia.in/; Sasandiris and Birdiris of Jharkhand (blog), accessed 11 November 2011, http://megalithsofjharkhand.blogspot.com/

Subhashis Das, *Indianmegaliths* (website), accessed 11 November 2011, http://indianmegaliths.wordpress.com/.

The one attempt of dating a burial site by E. T. Dalton was quite vague, ranging from 200 to 2,000 years old. See Edward Tuite Dalton, 'Rude Stone Monuments in Chutia Nagpur and Other Places', *JASB* 42 (1873): 116.

[30] One can assume that the area of the Munda speakers expanded in a way akin to the 'wave of advance' of early agriculturists in Europe. Colin Renfrew, who took the idea from Ammerman and Cavalli-Sforza, puts that rate on 18 km for each generation, taken at 25 years. See Colin Renfrew, *Archaeology and Language: The Puzzle of Indo-European Origins* (Harmondsworth: Penguin Books, 1989), 128–30. A useful discussion of this and other ideas put forward by Renfrew can be found in Colin Renfrew, e.a., 'Archaeology and Language: The Puzzle of Indo-European Origins by Colin Renfrew, A CA Book Review', *Current Anthropology* 29 (1988): 437–68.

[31] Both the Late Pleistocene global colonisation and the Neolithic spread of agriculture after 9,700 BCE caused major changes in the the local ecosystems around the world. See Nicole. L. Boivin, Melinda A. Zeder, Dorian Q. Fuller, Alison Crowther, Greger Larson, John M. Erlandson, Tim Denham, and Michael D. Petraglia,'Ecological Consequences of Human Niche Construction: Examining Long-term Anthropogenic Shaping of Global Species Distributions', *Proceedings of the National Academy of Sciences of the United States of America* 113, no. 23 (7 June 2016): 6388-6396, published online before print June 7, 2016, accessed 7 June 2016, http://www.pnas.org/content/113/23/6388.full.

[32] He attributed the disappearance of the iron industry of the Asuras of the Khunti area to the arrival of the Mundas. See Van Troy, 'Pre-Historic Context', 37; Van Troy, 'Prehistory and Early History of Chotanagpur', 32. This, of course, looks like a restatement of the Asura myth of the Mundas, of which S. C. Roy gave an extensive version. See Roy, 'The Legend of Lutkum Haram and Lutkum Buria', appendix 2 to *The Mundas*, 336–50. Roy did some archaeological research into sites and graves associated with the Asurs, some of which were just north of Singhbhum, but could not reach any firm conclusion. They represented 'three or at least two different stages of culture, namely, first a Neolithic culture, next a Copper Age culture and after that, or partly overlapping that, an early Iron Age culture.' See Sarat Chandra Roy, 'Distribution and Nature of Asur Sites in Chota Nagpur', *JBORS* 6 (1920): 397. See also Sarat Chandra Roy, 'A Note on some Remains of the Ancient Asuras in the Ranchi District', *JBORS* 1, part 2, (1915): 229–53; and also his 'Relics of the Copper Age found in Chota Nagpur', *JBORS* 2, part 4, (1916): 481–84.

Probably Abhik Ghosh was right when he stated that these remains were 'mostly within the early historic period', and, a bit more precise, 'the late centuries B.C. and the early centuries A.D.' See Abhik Ghosh, 'Prehistory of the Chotanagpur Region, Part 4: Ethnoarchaeology, Rock Art, Iron and the Asuras'.

[33] In a tantalisingly bare statement: 'From the Ho folksongs, it appears that they [the Hos] have migrated from Chotanagpur, where they were one with the Mundas.' See Ram Dayal Munda, 'Cultural Elements in Ho Songs', in *Bihar in Folklore Study:*

An Anthology, guest eds. L. P. Vidhyarthi and G. Chaubey (Calcutta: Indian Publications, 1971), 175. The Nagbansi rajas of Chotanagpur are not mentioned in the songs. From this, Roy concluded that the Hos must have left before that time. See Roy, *The Mundas and Their Country*, 30–61, 71.

[34] Well, thirty-four of his 124 Ho *kilis*, actually. See Deeney, *Ho Grammar*, 111–18.

[35] Van Troy, 'Prehistory and Early History of Chotanagpur', 40–41. Although not free from migrationism, Van Troy rejected the idea of a mass movement of Mundas down the South Koel valley. See Van Troy, 'Prehistory and Early History of Chotanagpur', 34.

[36] Presumably the Oraons which were with him when he discovered Benisagar. See Tickell, 'Memoir', 707.

[37] In the 'Memoir', Tickell called them 'Bangalee Brahmins'. Tickell, 'Memoir', 696. Later, he followed the lead of Wilkinson and called them 'Jains'. See Samuel Richard Tickell, 'Supplementary Note to the Memoir on the Hodésum, vol. ix, pp. 649 and 783', *JASB* 10 (1841): 30.

[38] Tickell, 'Memoir', 696–97. The quote is on page 697.

[39] Dalton, *Descriptive Ethnology of Bengal*, 178.

[40] A. D. Tuckey, *Final Report on the Resettlement of the Kolhan Government Estate in the District of Singhbhum, 1913–1918* (Patna, Bihar and Orissa: Superintendent, Government Printing, 1920), 17.

[41] Asoka Kumar Sen, 'Writing Local History and the District Record Room', *Proceedings of the Indian Historical Records Commission,* 58th session (2003), 98, paraphrasing Tuckey's Khuntkatti Papers. See also Asoka Kumar Sen, 'Reconstructing Adivasi Village History: Problems and Possibilities', *JAIS* 2, no 2 (August 2015): 16–37.

Oral history often served a present need and focused on the narrator's own people at exclusion of others, as Tuckey found in the 1910s. See Tuckey, *Final Report*, 21.

[42] See Tuckey, *Final Report,* 19–21. See on this and other limitations—and possibilities—of using local lore, Asoka Kumar Sen, 'Reconstructing Adivasi Village History: Problems and Possibilities', *JAIS* 2, no 2 (August 2015): 16–37.

[43] This point of the use of a genealogy only a few generations deep, to maintain correct relations among neighbours came to me when I reread Leach on the Kachin of Burma. See E. R. Leach, *Political Systems of Highland Burma: A study of Kachin Social Structure*, London School of Economics Monographs on Social Anthropology 44 (London: The University of London, The Athlone Press, 1954; repr., 1970), 126–29.

For the rights to the land, or to a position in local society like Manki or Munda, a memory has to stretch back only as far as to the 'time immemorial', that is, to the beginning of the legal fact—or fiction.

[44] Exceptions were the Hos in Saranda, who claimed to have come from the West. But there Tuckey found that all villages were previously occupied either by Hindus or by Hos belonging to other than the present clans. See Tuckey, *Final Report,* 18. Apparently, in the preceding decades their self-awareness had changed significantly. Forty years before Tuckey, Dalton found that the Hos of Saranda he visited had no ideas about coming from another area. See Dalton, 'Rude Stone Monuments', 114.

[45] Tuckey, *Final Report*, 18.

[46] Mathew Areeparampil, 'Migration of the Hos to Singhbhum', in *Singhbhum, Some Historical Gleanings*, ed. Asoka Kumar Sen (Chaibasa: Department of History, Tata College, 1986), 16.

As Wenskus, following Hans Krabe, pointed out, names of geographic features, such as mountains and rivers are quite resistant to changes of language in an area. They could well indicate the language of the original occupants. See Reinhard Wenskus, *Stammesbildung und Stammesverfassung: Das Werden der Frühmittelalterlichen Gentes* (Formation and Constitution of Tribes: The Emergence of the Early Mediaeval Clans) (Köln: Böhlau, 1961), 163–65. I am grateful to Professor Marcel van der Linden, who drew my attention to this book.

[47] Tuckey, *Final Report*, 18. In the east, he mentioned parts of Thai, Bharbharia and Lagra. The more recently settled parts of the south were Anwla *Pir* and an adjoining strip in Lalgarh *Pir*, the south of Bar *Pir*, Kotgarh and Jamda *Pirs*, and the west of Bantaria *Pir*.

[48] Tuckey, *Final Report,* 19.

[49] T. S. MacPherson, *Final Report on the Operations for the Preparation of a Record of Rights in Pargana Porahat, District Singhbhum, 1905–1907* (Calcutta: The Bengal Secretariat Book Depôt, 1908), 46.

[50] We can only guess at the situation in West Singhbhum and adjacent tracts before the Gupta Empire, the fourth to the sixth century AD. An exhaustive inventory of bronze-age metalwork in India did not draw definite chronological conclusions for the Chotanagpur plateau. See Paul Yule, *Metalwork of the Bronze Age in India*, Prähistorische Bronzefunde Abteilung XX - Band 8 [Pre-historic Bronze Finds, Part 20, vol. 8] (München: C. H. Beck'sche Verlagsbuchhandlung, 1985). The copper hoards were dated by Van Troy after 1100 BC. See Van Troy, 'Prehistory and Early History of Chotanagpur', 30. A single find of Roman coins, discovered in or near Bamanghati in the 1860s or 1870s, sheds but little light on the first centuries AD. See Joseph D. Beglar, *Report of Tours in the South-Eastern Provinces in 1874–75 and 1875–76* (Calcutta: Office of the Superintendent of Government Printing, 1882; repr., Varanasi: Indological Book House, 1970), 72–73; Arjun Joshi, *History & Culture of Khijjingakotta Under the Bhanjas* (Delhi: Vikas, 1983), 14, 30. Asoka Kumar Sen, as before him Markham Kittoe in Beglar's report, contends that it indicates a trade route. See Sen, 'Redefining Archaeology and the Ethno-history of Pre-Colonial Singhbhum', *Indian Folklore Research Journal* 10 (2010): 102. However, it is a single find of high value and would rather

have served as a hoard than as capital for trade. These isolated finds do not add up.

[51] On Khiching itself a small but interesting body of literature has come into existence. Tickell, 'Memoir', 708–09; Beglar, *Report of Tours in the South-Eastern Provinces*, 74–77; Ramaprasad Chanda, 'Note on the Ancient Monuments of Mayurbhanj', *JBORS* 13, part 2 (1927): 131–36; Sailendra Nath Sircar, *Khiching (Ancient Khijjinga); or, A Lost Chapter of Orissa* (Calcutta: Hirendra Nath Sircara, 1939?); Arjun Joshi, 'The Origin of the Bhanjas of Khijingakótta', *OHRJ* 16, nos. 1 and 2 (1967): 41–53; Arjun Joshi, 'Sculptural Art of Khijjingakótta', *OHRJ* 23, nos. 1 to 4 (1978): 33–58; Arjun Joshi, *History & Culture of Khijjingakotta*.

[52] Beglar, *Report of Tours in the South-Eastern Provinces*, 70. See also K. C. Panigrahi, 'The Archaeological Remains at Benisagar in the Singbhum District of Bihar', *JBRS* 42 (1956): 1–11.

[53] 'Gupta Seal Points to Ancient Varsity Relic', *Telegraph*, 17 October 2003, accessed 1 July 2009, http://www.telegraphindia.com/1031017/asp/ranchi/story_2469957.asp;
'History Hub in Land of Promise—ASI Takes Note of West Singhbhum Village with Long and Probably Illustrious Past', *Telegraph*, 1 December 2005, accessed 15 April 2011,
http://www.telegraphindia.com/1051201/asp/jharkhand/story_5539141.asp;
'ASI Finds Temple Relics in Jharkhand', *Times of India*, 15 January 2008, accessed 1 July 2009, http://timesofindia.indiatimes.com/India/ASI_finds_temple_relics_in_Jharkhand/articleshow/2700878.cms;
'A Khajuraho-like Temple in Jharkhand?' *Rediff*, 25 April 2008, accessed 1 July 2009, http://ia.rediff.com (link broken).

[54] A stone inscription at Asunput from the fourth or fifth century indicated a Bhanja dynasty. See L. K. Mahapatra, 'Ex-Princely States of Orissa: Mayurbhanj, Keonjhar and Bonai', in *Tribal Polities and State Systems in Pre-Colonial Eastern and North Eastern India*, ed. by Surajit Sinha (Calcutta, New Delhi: K. P. Bagchi, 1987), 44.

[55] See for the modest view Paramananda Acharya, 'A Note of the "Bhum" Countries in India', *Indian Culture* 12, no. 2 (1945): 41. For more optimalist assessment see Mahapatra, 'Ex-Princely States of Orissa', 44.

[56] P. C. Roy Chaudhury, *Singhbhum*, Bihar District Gazetteers (Patna, Bihar: Superintendent Secretariat Press 1958), 67.

[57] Frederick M. Asher, *The Art of Eastern India, 300–800* (Minneapolis: The University of Minneapolis Press, 1980), 60.

[58] Panigrahi, 'The Archaeological Remains at Benisagar', 10.

[59] Joshi, *History & Culture of Khijjingakotta*, 39.

[60] 750 (Vikramaditya) Sambat. See Tikayet Nrupendra Narayan Singh Deo, *Singhbhum, Seraikella and Kharswan Through the Ages* (no place, no publisher, 1954), 18. Following Cunningham, I take the start of the Vikrama-Samvat at 57 BCE, as did Singh Deo. See Alexander Cunningham, 'Vikrama-Samvat', in *Book of Indian Eras, With Tables for Calculation of Indian Dates* (Calcutta, Thacker, Spink, 1883), 47.

[61] Mahapatra, 'Ex-Princely States of Orissa', 44. This area was part of the Khiching *mandala* or group of states.

[62] Joshi gives the eighth century AD as a tentative date. See Joshi, 'The Origin of the Bhanjas of Khijjingakótta', 41–53, esp. 50. Elsewhere, he tends to assign these copper plates to the eleventh century. See Joshi, *History & Culture of Khijjingakotta*, 42–43. See also Pratapachandra Ghosha, 'Notes on, and Translation of, Two Copper-plate Inscriptions from Bamanghati', *JASB* 40 (1871): 162.

[63] At this time, the Bhanjas were probably feudatories of the Bhauma kings, who ruled from the Ganges to Ganjam. See Joshi, *History & Culture of Khijjingakotta*, 55.

[64] Panigrahi gave the eighth century. See Panigrahi, 'The Archaeological Remains at Benisagar', 10–11. Asher opted for the seventh century. See Asher, *The Art of Eastern India*, 59–60.

[65] Joshi, *History & Culture of Khijjingakotta*, 27.

[66] At least up to 1110. See Joshi, 'Sculptural Art of Khijjingakótta', 34. The people of Khichingakotta ate meat. See Joshi, *History & Culture of Khijjingakotta*, 92.

[67] Joshi, *History & Culture of Khijjingakotta*, 1, 85–86. See also Michael Witzel, 'Regionale und Ueberregionale Faktoren in der Entwicklung Vedischer Brahmanengruppen im Mittelalter' [Regional and Supra-Regional Factors in the Development of Groups of Vedic Brahmins in the Middle Ages], in *Regionale Tradition in Südasien*, eds. Hermann Kulke and Dietmar Rothermund (Wiesbaden: Franz Steiner Verlag, 1985), 61; Hermann Kulke, 'Die Frühmittelalterlichen Regionalreiche, Ihre Struktur und Rolle im Prozess Staatlicher Entwicklung Indiens' [The Early Mediaeval Regional States: Their structure and Role in the Process of the Development of the State in India], in *Regionale Tradition in Südasien*, eds. Hermann Kulke und Dietmar Rothermund (Wiesbaden: Franz Steiner Verlag, 1985), 89–90.

[68] Lewis Sidney Steward O'Malley, *Singhbhum, Saraikela and Kharsawan*, Bengal District Gazetteers (Calcutta: The Bengal Secretariat Book Depôt, 1910), 208. In this he followed Tickell. See Tickell, 'Memoir', 706–7. Beglar visited Keshnagar, did some hasty excavations without finding even a brick. In Keshnagar only undatable remnants of a mud fort were found. See Beglar, *Report of Tours in the South-Eastern Provinces*, 71. More recently, Panigrahi found that Benisagar could have been a 'proselytizing centre' of Shaivas, particularly the Pashupata sect. See Panigrahi, 'The Archaeological Remains at Benisagar', 10–11. On the other hand, R. P. Mohapatra called Benisagar 'a stronghold of Jaina activities' and described several Jaina images preserved in the nearby Khiching museum. See Ramesh Prasad Mohapatra, *Jaina Monuments of Orissa* (Delhi: D. K. Publishers, 1984), 115–17.

[69] Hermann Kulke, *Jagannatha-Kult und Gajapati-Königtum: Ein Beitrag zur Geschichte religiöser Legitimation Hinduistischer Herrscher* [Jagannatha Cult and the Kingdom of Gajapati: A Contribution to the History of Religious Legitimation of Hindu Rulers] (Wiesbaden: Franz Steiner Verlag, 1979), 224, 226.

[70] Dalton, *Descriptive Ethnology of Bengal*, 139–50; Herbert Hope Risley, *Tribes and Castes of Bengal, Ethnographic Glossary*, vol. 1 (Calcutta: Bengal Secretariat Press, 1891–92; repr., Calcutta: Firma Mukhopadhyay 1981), 108–16.

[71] Thakurani is '[a] goddess, a lady, a mistress, the wife of a spiritual preceptor, the wife of a Rajput chief, and the like'. See H. H. Wilson, *A Glossary*, 517.

[72] Kulke, *Jagannatha-Kult und Gajapati-Königtum*, 224; see also Hermann Kulke, 'Early State Formation and Royal Legitimation in Tribal Areas of Eastern India', in *Aspects of Tribal Life in South Asia I: Strategy and Survival, Proceedings of an International Seminar Held in Berne 1977*, edited by Rupert R. Moser and Mohan K. Gautam (Berne: The University of Berne, Institute of Ethnology, 1978), 33.

[73] Joshi, *History & Culture of Khijjingakotta*, 7–8. Chamunda is a form of Durga. Khichingeshvari's temple stood in Khiching's Thakurani compound.

[74] Kulke, *Jagannatha-Kult und Gajapati-Königtum*, 227.
The temple of Hara was rebuilt in the 1920s or 1930s as the Khichingeshvari temple. See Joshi, *History & Culture of Khijjingkotta*, 35, 109–10; Laeequddin, *Census of Mayurbhanj State*, 16.

[75] Singh Deo, *Singhbhum, Seraikella and Kharswan Through the Ages*, 24.

[76] Mahapatra, 'Ex-Princely States of Orissa', 44.

[77] In a series of highly illuminating studies, Hermann Kulke has thrown light on the way in which between the sixth and the thirteenth century Hindu rajas in the Hindu-tribal frontier area legitimised their rule over their tribal subjects. See Hermann Kulke, 'Kshatriyaization and Social Change, A Study in Orissa Setting', in *Aspects of Changing India: Studies in Honour of Prof. G. S. Ghurye*, ed. by S. Devadas Pillai (Bombay: Popular Prakashan; also published in Sonderdrucke der Mitglieder 177, Heidelberg: Südasien-Institut der Universität Heidelberg, 1976), 404. See also Hermann Kulke, 'King Anangabhima III, The Veritable Founder of the Gajapati Kingship and of the Jagannath Trinity at Puri', *JRASGBI* 113 (1981): 26–39; Kulke, 'Early State Formation and Royal Legitimation', 35–36. For Keonjhar and Bonai, see Dalton, *Descriptive Ethnology of Bengal*, 147.

[78] In Tickell's 1840 Hodésum article, the Dom raja was connected with Keshnagarh, near Benisagar. He was told that it was the seat of a raja of the 'Raj Dom tribe who killed a cow, and wrapped a Brahmin in the hide, which tightening as it dried, squeezed him to death'. A big fire from heaven destroyed the raja 'with all its people, houses and riches'. Only one Tanti escaped, 'warned by the bullock he was ploughing with'. Tickell's informants here were Brahmins, possibly the 'mookhtur' of the Mayurbhanj raja and the 'Burkoonur' (*bara kunwar*) of Rorwan and 'several of their Brahmin attendants'. He saw only 'the remains of a square brick fort, well ditched round'. See Tickell, 'Memoir', 706–7. The story is also mentioned by O'Malley. See O'Malley, *Singhbhum*, 217. Apart from this story there is nothing to suggest a prominent role of the Doms in this, or any other, period in Singhbhum.
Beglar visited the place in 1874–75, but found nothing and, to make matters worse, his servants were 'threatened with violence for attempting to procure labour even at exorbitant rates'. To cap it all, he found the people 'extremely disinclined to give any information'. Possibly he meant here the inhabitants of Keshnagar who were not 'Kol'; earlier, he was treated fairly enough by the Hos of Benisagar. See Beglar, *Report of Tours in the South-Eastern Provinces*, 71.

[79] Singh Deo, *Singhbhum, Seraikella and Kharswan Through the Ages*, 18–19.

[80] [J. A. Craven], *Final Report on the Settlement of the Kolhan Government Estate in District Singhbhum* (Calcutta: Bengal Secretariat Press, 1898), 25.
On Valentine Ball's authority, Dalton connected the Sarawaks or Jains with the copper mines to the east of the Kolhan. See Dalton, *Descriptive Ethnology of Bengal*, 178–79. This seems a circular argument. Ball had referred to an earlier version of Dalton—probably Edward Tuite Dalton, 'The "Kols" of Chota Nagpore', Special Number on Indian Ethnology 1866, *JASB* 35, part 2 (1867): 153–98—as the basis of his statement and then put questions to the local people about the mines of Dhalbhum. He got a clear answer only when he mentioned the Saraks. See Ball, *Jungle Life in India*, 167–68. Apparently, he did not mean to indicate the builders of Benisagar. Ball dated the mines to the eleventh century. See Valentine Ball, 'On the Ancient Copper Miners of Singhbhum', *JASB* 38 (1869): 171–75. The story of the Jains or Saraks as the workers of the ancient copper mines was taken up by Risley. See Risley, *Tribes and Castes of Bengal*, vol. 2, 236–37.

[81] In Bar *pir* 13, in Aula 7, in Lalgarh 4, in Saranda 4 and 4 together in Kotgarh, Gumra and Bantaria. See Sen, 'Redefining Archaeology', 107. Tuckey did the survey in 1913–14. See Tuckey, *Final Report*, 27.

[82] One route from Jaintgarh to Chaibasa and, more east, one from south of Benisagar to Manbhum, where there were fourteenth- and fifteenth-century temples of the Saraks. See Tuckey, *Final Report*, 18.

[83] Tuckey, *Final Report*, 9.

[84] On Chainpur, see MacPherson, *Final Report on the Operations*, 244–46. Karaikela was noted in 1820 by Roughsedge. See Roughsedge to Metcalfe, 9 May 1820 (London: OIOC), BC 21,438.

[85] In Saranda (16), Jamda (4), Kotgarh (2), Latua (1) and Rela (1). See Sen, 'Redefining Archaeology', 105.

[86] 'The military force on which the raja chiefly depended were Bhuiyas; his titulary deity, the Pawri Devi, was a Bhuiya divinity,

corresponding with the Thakurani Mai of the Keonjhur Bhuiyas'. See Dalton, *Descriptive Ethnology of Bengal*, 179.
In the beginning of the twentieth century, the Pauri Devi had shrines in Jagannathpur and Jaintgarh in the Kolhan and temples in Porahat and Saraikela, while at some fourteen other places in Singhbhum she was worshipped in a more simple fashion. See O'Malley, *Singhbhum*, 213–15.

[87] Singh Deo, *Singhbhum, Seraikella and Kharswan Through the Ages*, 20–21, 26.

[88] G. C. Depree, *Geographical and Statistical Report, on that Portion of the Chotanagpore Division which Has Come Under the Operation of the Topographical Survey Department* (1868), by Captain G. C. Depree, in charge No. 4, Topographical Party, and Ex-Officio Assistant Commissioner, Cuttack and Chota Nagpore (Continued from the Report on Chota Nagpore), Dated Office No. 4, Topographical Party, Chotanagpore Division Survey. Dorundah 1 October 1868, p. 44.
S. Das Gupta stated that the fort at Porahat was also known as Chakradharpur. See Sanjukta Das Gupta, *Adivasis and the Raj, Socio-economic Transition of the Hos, 1820–1932*, Critical Thinking in South Asian History (New Delhi: Orient BlackSwan, 2011), 68. But Chakradharpur is on the plains at some 25 km distance from Porahat.

[89] Singh Deo, *Singhbhum, Seraikella and Kharswan Through the Ages*, 12–42.

[90] The *Vamsa* was not clear about differences between 'Kols', 'Larka Kols' and 'Hos'.

[91] This provenance from the west was not mentioned by Tuckey.

[92] The periodization of history is tricky. I use 'modern' in the same way as it is done for European/North American history. It started sometime in the sixteenth or seventeenth century when new administrative and economic models developed. For the preceding stage, which was in India very different from that in Europe, I have used the term medieval, because of its situation in time between the classical age (ending in India around the fourth century CE), and the modern age. In this I am strengthened by Hermann Kulke. See Hermann Kulke, 'Periodization of Pre-modern Historical Processes in India and Europe, Some Reflections', *The Indian History Review* 19, no. 1–2 (1992–1993): 21–36.

[93] Herman Jeremias Nieboer, *Slavery as an Industrial System: Ethnological Researches*, 2nd rev. ed. ('s-Gravenhage: Nijhoff, 1910).

[94] Singh Deo, *Singhbhum, Seraikella and Kharswan Through the Ages*, 25.

[95] Singh Deo, *Singhbhum, Seraikella and Kharswan Through the Ages*, 26–31.

[96] Singh Deo, *Singhbhum, Seraikella and Kharswan Through the Ages*, 34.

[97] Acharya, 'A Note of the "Bhum" Countries', 48; M. A. Haque, 'Route of Firuz Shah's Invasion of Orissa in 1360 A.D.', *OHRJ* 15, nos. 3 and 4 (1967): 6; L. N. Raut, 'The State of Mayurbhanj During the Years of Maratha Supremacy in Orissa', *OHRJ* 28, nos. 1 and 2 (1982): 88–89.

[98] Joshi puts the division of the kingdom sometime before 1100. See Joshi, *History & Culture of Khijjingakotta*, 40. The genealogy of the Keonjhar Bhanjas gave Adi Bhanj as their first raja. On the insistence of the Bhuiyas, he would have split Keonjhar off from Mayurbhanj in 1398. A somewhat suspicious source, as in 1870 this genealogy was known to 'only two people'. See Keonjhar, Annual Administrative Report, 1869–70, in Captain J. Johnstone to Superintendent Tributary Mehals, Cuttack, 1 April 1870, NAI: Foreign, Political, October 1871, proc. 271, 6–7. In the late 1860s, the Bhuiyas claimed that they had installed the younger branch of the Bhanja family on the throne at the beginning of the eighteenth century. See L. E. B. Cobden-Ramsay, *Feudatory States of Orissa*, Bengal Gazetteers (Calcutta: Bengal Secretariat Book Depôt, 1910; reprint Calcutta: Firma KLM, 1982), 214. B. Mishra placed the split much earlier, in 1128 and gave Jyotibhanj as the name as the first ruler of Keonjhar, where his brother in Mayurbhanj was Adibhanj. See B. Mishra, 'History', Keonjhar (website), accessed 12 December 2002, www.keonjhar.com/history.

[99] In Keonjhar, the Bhuiyas had the right of investiture of the new king. See Dalton, *Descriptive Ethnology of Bengal*, 144–47. In Mayurbhanj, the rajas invited Brahmins from the north and settled them in forty-two villages around the central hills of the kingdom to the east of Khiching. A copper plate even mentioned the gift of four villages in Uttarakhanda, possibly the area around Porahat. See Joshi, *History & Culture of Khijjingakotta*, 11, and map on third page following page 160. It remained imperative for the Bhanja rajas of both states to be on good terms with the Bhuiyas. The implications of this for Mayurbhanj, Keonjhar and Bonai, were pointed out by L. K. Mahapatra See Mahapatra, 'Ex-Princely States of Orissa', 23.

[100] Nagendranath Vasu, *The Archaeological Survey of Mayurabhanja* (Calcutta: published by the Mayurabhanja State 1911), 5. See also Joshi, *History & Culture of Khijjingakotta*, 66. It is possible that this change of name took place earlier and indicated a merger of the Bhanja areas with the kingdom of the Mayurs sometime in the thirteenth or fourteenth century. See Acharya, 'A Note of the "Bhum" Countries', 41. Later, its capital was transferred to Baripada. See Laeequddin, *Census of Mayurbhanj State*, 16. The date of the shift east is given as 'the sixteenth century, according to tradition' by Laeequddin. See Laeequddin, *Census of Mayurbhanj State*, 16.

[101] Singh Deo, *Singhbhum, Seraikella and Kharswan Through the Ages*, 35.

[102] Singh Deo, *Singhbhum, Seraikella and Kharswan Through the Ages*, 28.

[103] Jagannath Patnaik, *Feudatory States of Orissa (1803–1857)*, vol. 1 (Allahabad: Vohra, 1988), 43.

[104] This was the fifth uprising of the Bhuiyas—and the first in which other peoples joined them. See Singh Deo, *Singhbhum, Seraikella and Kharswan Through the Ages*, 26–37.

[105] Detlef Schwerin gave 1591. See Detlef Schwerin, *Von Armut zu Elend: Kolonialherrschaft und Agrarverfassung in Chota Nagpur, 1858–1918* [From Poverty to Misery: Colonial Rule and Agrarian Law in Chota Napur, 1858–1918] (Wiesbaden: Steiner, 1977), 402.

J. Patnaik mentioned the year 1592. See Patnaik, *Feudatory States of Orissa*, 43. K. S. Singh gave '1591–2 A. D. or thereabout'. See Kumar Suresh Singh, 'Medieval Tribal Bihar', in *The Comprehensive History of Bihar*, eds. Syed Hasan Askari and Qeyamuddin Ahmed (Patna: Kashi Prasad Jayaswal Research Institute, 1983), vol. 2, part 1, 257.

[106] Patnaik, *Feudatory States of Orissa*, 48.

[107] Patnaik, *Feudatory States of Orissa*, 43–48.

[108] The archaeologist Joshi found that the areas then under Mayurbhanj rule stretched from Tamar and Midnapur town in the north to the river Baitarani in the south, and from the sea in the east to the western border of Singhbhum. See Joshi, *History & Culture of Khijjingakotta*, 26–27.

[109] Andrew Stirling, 'An Account, Geographical, Statistical and Historical of Orissa Proper, or Cuttack', *AR* 15 (1825; repr., 1979-80): 227–35. Stirling added to Singhbhum: 'Now an Independent Estate'.

[110] Singh Deo, *Singhbhum, Seraikella and Kharswan Through the Ages*, 36.

[111] Singh Deo, *Singhbhum, Seraikella and Kharswan Through the Ages*, 36.

[112] Singh Deo, *Singhbhum, Seraikella and Kharswan Through the Ages*, 29, 36–37. A mere mention in Dalton, *Descriptive Ethnology of Bengal*, 179.

[113] Mahapatra, 'Ex-Princely States of Orissa', 23–24.

[114] Singh Deo, *Singhbhum, Seraikella and Kharswan Through the Ages*, 37.

[115] In 1868, Depree noticed that 'the fruit is small and the trees receive no care'. See Depree, *Geographical and Statistical Report*, 27.

[116] Sen, 'Redefining Archaeology', 107.

[117] Singh Deo, *Singhbhum, Seraikella and Kharswan Through the Ages*, 37.

[118] Singh Deo, *Singhbhum, Seraikella and Kharswan Through the Ages*, 29.

[119] Singh Deo, *Singhbhum, Seraikella and Kharswan Through the Ages*, 29. 'Bharandia' and 'Dukri (Singhbhum)' in the original. Balandia is in the centre of Hodisum; Dukri is in the settled valley of Mailpir, and about 15 km. to the north of Chakradharpur as the crow flies.

[120] Singh Deo, *Singhbhum, Seraikella and Kharswan Through the Ages*, 29–30, 37–38.

[121] Tickell, 'Memoir', 697.

[122] Singh Deo, *Singhbhum, Seraikella and Kharswan Through the Ages*, 14.

[123] Singh Deo, *Singhbhum, Seraikella and Kharswan Through the Ages*, 14.

[124] The right to rule was given in two dreams, one at the end of the seventh century from the Pauri Devi and the second at the beginning of the thirteenth century from Rama himself. See Singh Deo, *Singhbhum, Seraikella and Kharswan Through the Ages*, 14–16, 16–19.

[125] First in the time of the Mahabharata, with the grant of the title of Rathor, a division of the Rajputs, to the ancestor of the first Singh raja. Rajputhood was reaffirmed at the beginning of the second Singh dynasty, around 1205, when the founder Darpa Singh came from Marwar to Odisha, and ended up as raja of Singhbhum. Singh Deo, *Singhbhum, Seraikella and Kharswan Through the Ages*, 15, 16–20.

[126] Banerji could find no other explanation 'for this craze for Rajput origin' than 'the preponderance of the Rajputs as warriors and mercenaries in the 17th century, when under the Mughals they spread their fame'. See R. D. Banerji, 'Rajput Origins in Orissa', Appendix VI to R. D. Banerji, R. Chatterjee and M. C. Das, *History of Orissa: From the Earliest Time to the British Period*, vol. 2 (Calcutta; R. Chatterjee/Prabasi Press, 1931), 421, 428–29, 435–36.

The Mayurbhanj Bhanjas, too, changed their local Kshatriya genealogy into one going back to the Rajputs. See Kulke, 'Kshatriyaization and Social Change', 404, note 24. It was done quite drastically, pushing the Rajput story to the sixth century. See Cobden-Ramsay, *Feudatory States of Orissa*, 239.

In a similar process, the Ujjainiya Rajputs emerged from the Chero tribe in Bhojpur, a little north of Chotanagpur, in the early fourteenth century. See Dirk H. A. Kolff, *Naukar, Rajput and Sepoy: The Ethnohistory of the Military Labour Market in Hindustan, 1450–1850*, University of Cambridge Oriental Publications 43 (Cambridge: Cambridge University Press, 1990), 59, 184.

[127] Kulke, *Jagannatha-Kult und Gajapati-Königtum*, 227. Another purpose of the Rajput myth in the Vamsa Prabha Lekhana could be to pass over a possible emergence of the Singh Rajputs from the ranks of the Bhuiyas. In his 1872 *Descriptive Ethnology of Bengal*, Dalton ridiculed the Rajput claim of the Singhs and their neighbours. See Dalton, *Descriptive Ethnology of Bengal*, 140. He acknowledged, however, that they were accepted as such by other 'noble families'. See Dalton, *Descriptive Ethnology of Bengal*, 179.

[128] Chotanagpur's political history was quite different from that of Singhbhum. Here the Mughals actually invaded the country in 1585, and its ruler, probably Madhu Karan, participated in Man Singh's expedition to Orissa. His successor Durjan Sahi threw off his allegiance to the Mughals sometime after 1599. In 1615, the Mughal army invaded Chotanagpur, (called Kokrah

by the Mughals) arrested Durjan. He was kept prisoner in Delhi for twelve years, released and sent back in 1627. On his return he set himself up as shah, changed his name in Durjan Sahi, shifted his capital and built a new palace using Moghul style elements. He ruled till 1639 or 1640. See Bulmukund Virottam, *The Nagbanshis and the Cheros*, Delhi: Munshira Manoharlal, 1972, 5-14; Sarat Chandra Roy, *The Mundas and Their Country*, 82-85.

[129] That was implied in the invitation to the Singhs to rule over the Bhuiyas in the Benusagar area. The relation was also mythically restated, in the story of how Pauri Devi came to Singhbhum, was hidden by the Bhuiyas, let herself be found and worshipped by the Singh raja. Singh Deo, *Singhbhum, Seraikella and Kharswan Through the Ages*, 20–21.

[130] Paul Streumer, 'A Seventeenth Century Ideology: The Singhbhum Chronicle on Rajputs and Tribals', *JAIS* 2, no 2 (August 2015): 1–15.

[131] Singh Deo, *Singhbhum, Seraikella and Kharswan Through the Ages*, 19.

[132] Laeequddin, *Census of Mayurbhanj State*, 17; Patnaik, *Feudatory States of Orissa*, 51.

[133] Singh Deo, *Singhbhum, Seraikella and Kharswan Through the Ages*, 38–39.

[134] *Nayak*s were leaders of soldiers, *paiks* just soldiers, here probably Bhuiyas, as these terms were never used for 'Kols' or Hos.

[135] Even in 1820, to maintain a detachment of 100 mercenaries was too heavy a burden for the Singh state. See Wilkinson to Swinton, 12 January 1833 (London: OIOC), BC 58,904.

[136] Singh Deo, *Singhbhum, Seraikella and Kharswan Through the Ages*, 38–39.

[137] There is one possible exception. 'Jamda' means 'an arbour or shelter of branches and leaves'. See Deeney, *Ho-English Dictionary*, 158. But against that stands the remark by Tuckey on the village from which Jamda got its name, 'Jamda which was called after a Bhuiya clan of that name'. See Tuckey, *Final Report*, 20.

[138] Singh Deo, *Singhbhum, Seraikella and Kharswan Through the Ages*, 39.

[139] His name was Madhab Pratap Singh, 'the second son' of Kala Arjun Singh, according to O'Malley. See O'Malley, *Singhbhum*, 206, 221. Without naming him, he was the younger son of Kala Arjun Singh in MacPherson, see MacPherson, *Final Report on the Operations*, 169; Roy Chaudhury, *Singhbhum*, 442. S. Das Gupta followed Roy Chaudhuri, see Das Gupta, *Adivasis and the Raj*, 70.
Against that stands the lone but important voice of Taylor who, still without naming him, indicated the first ruler of Anandpur as 'the second son of Raja Chattrapati Singh Deo, and youngest brother of the Raja Kala Arjun Singh Deo', James Henry Taylor, *Pir Notes Prepared During the Settlement of the Porahat and Subordinate Estates, District Singhbhum, 1900–1903* (Calcutta: Bengal Secretariat Press, 1904), 34. The source was used but in this case not followed by O'Malley.

[140] Singh Deo, *Singhbhum, Seraikella and Kharswan Through the Ages*, 29.

[141] Asoka Kumar Sen, 'Collective Memory and Reconstruction of Ho History', *Indian Folklore Research Journal* 5, no. 8 (December 2008): 100.

[142] Probably, because there is uncertainty about the date. Johnstone gave 1716 as the date of the destruction of Chamakpur ('Chummuckpore') in his Keonjhar Annual Administrative Report, 1869–70. See Captain J. Johnstone to Superintendent Tributary Mehals, Cuttack, 1 April 1870, NAI, Foreign, Political, October 1871, proc. 271, 5–6. Such a late date is hardly possible. By that time Singhbhum was on the verge of a split, and its politics centred on its north.

[143] O'Malley, *Singhbhum*, 216; Roy Chaudhury, *Singhbhum*, 433. Johnstone believed that Chamakpur was conquered by the Keonjhar rajas. See Keonjhar Annual Administrative Report, 1869–70, 5–6.

[144] Wilkinson to Tickell, enclosure in Wilkinson to Mangles, 5 May 1837, para 34 (London: OIOC), BC 69,239.

[145] Singh Deo, *Singhbhum, Seraikella and Kharswan Through the Ages*, 38.

[146] O'Malley, *Singhbhum*, 216.

[147] Virottam discussed the difficulties of the exact dates of Ram Shah. See Virottam, *The Nagabanshis and the Cheros*, 15, 41. Raja in the original.

[148] Rakhal Das Haldar, 'An Abstract of the Annals of the Nagbansi Raj Family of Chota Nagpur', *MII* 8, no. 4 (1928): 279–80. According to the Annals, Jagannath changed the name of the place from Jaintgarh to Porahat.

[149] Latin expression for 'Till here and no further'.

[150] 'Enceinte' is given by Singh Deo. See Singh Deo, *Singhbhum, Seraikella and Kharswan Through the Ages*, 39. It is a rectification of Davies' 1854 'anciente' as the description of the state of the queen of the late 'Poorsuttam Sing'. See Davies to J. Allen, [1854], (Patna, BSA), SOC. O'Malley mentioned that it was Chhatrapati who died 'leaving his wife enceinte'. See O'Malley, *Singhbhum*, 221–22. His child Arjun Singh II was nicknamed 'Kala', which Singh Deo gave as 'deaf' and O'Malley as 'black'. See O'Malley, *Singhbhum*, 222; Singh Deo, *Singhbhum, Seraikella and Kharswan Through the Ages*, 39. Apparently, as Singh Deo pointed out, O'Malley had taken Arjun Singh II 'Kala', for Arjun Singh III, who was a posthumous child. See Singh Deo, *Singhbhum, Seraikella and Kharswan Through the Ages*, 40. Davies mentioned that Bikram Singh was granted 'Seraikela, Asunthulia & Rajabassa peers, with the title of Koomaur, with permission to exercise unrestricted authority therein'. See Davies to J. Allen, no date, probably 1854, (Patna, BSA), SOC.

[151] Singh Deo, *Singhbhum, Seraikella and Kharswan Through the Ages*, 38–39.

[152] O'Malley, *Singhbhum*, 229. There is no disagreement on the way Saraikela state came into existence, but here there is about the date. Paty gave it as 1620. See Chittaranjan Kumar Paty, *History of Seraikella and Kharswan States* (New Delhi: Classical Publishing Company, 2002), 10–11. So did the website *Indian Rajputs*. 'Seraikella, Princely State', *Indian Rajputs* (website), accessed 10 May 2016, http://www.indianrajputs.com/view/seraikella.This is unlikely. Paty mentioned that Bikram was the son either of Purushottam or Jagannath; the website *Indian Rajputs* that he was the son of Jagannath. Both possible fathers ruled well after 1620. Moreover, when the *Vamsa* was rewritten in 1643, it did not mention the split. If it had occurred so recently, it would certainly have noted it.

[153] His other uncle, Ajamber, got Kera as a rent-free maintenance grant. Kala Arjun's father, Purushottam, did not appear in the short history of Kera in Taylor's *Pir Notes*. Here Bikram and Ajamber were sons of Jagannath Singh III. See Taylor, *Pir Notes*, 21.

[154] Roy Chaudhury, *Singhbhum*, 250.

[155] Singh Deo, *Singhbhum, Seraikella and Kharswan Through the Ages*, 29. Balandia was the seat of a Ho of the Pingua *kili* who was one of Arjun Sing II Kala's 'sirdars' in the 1660s or 1670s. See Sen, 'Collective Memory and Reconstruction of Ho History', 100.

[156] Tuckey, *Final Report*, 9.

[157] Tuckey, *Final Report*, 13. See also MacPherson, *Final Report on the Operations*, 108.

[158] In 1741, the Marathas had invaded Odisha from the west, while the Alivardi Khan and his Afghans came from the north into Mayurbhanj. See Patnaik, *Feudatory States of Orissa*, 54–55.

[159] Percival Spear, *The Nabobs: A Study in the Social Life of the English in Eighteenth Century India* (1963; republished, Calcutta, Allahabad, Bombay, Delhi: Rupa, 1991), xix.

[160] The *Vamsa* mentioned a family relationship with the rajas of Bonai, who were of the same clan as the Singh Rajputs, See Singh Deo, *Singhbhum, Seraikella and Kharswan Through the Ages*, 17–18. In 1590, we saw a group of Hos carrying the dowry of a (Chota) Nagpur princess to Singhbhum. For marital relations of the house of Singhbhum with Panchete, see W. Hunter to Board, 26 September 1798, in Jagdish Chandra Jha, *The Bhumij Revolt (1832–33): Ganga Narain's Hangama or Turmoil* (Delhi: Munshiram Manoharlal, 1967), 50. Letters by and to Singhbhum rulers, preserved in the Saraikela archives, showed 'ties of closest relationship and constant correspondence' with the rulers of Mayurbhanj, Keonjhar, Bonai, Bamra, Gangpur, Dhalbhum, Bakala, and Sambalpur. See Singh Deo, *Singhbhum, Seraikella and Kharswan Through the Ages*, 32. Precisely because they indicate successes in the negotiations, matrimonial alliances between dynasties were not indications of weakness. Thus, we find in the local external relations of the Singhs no indication that they were out of peer esteem between 1720 and 1770. On the contrary, the dynastic and trade links with Sambalpur pointed to a high, if somewhat stale, regional standing. In 1767, Raja Jagannath IV was 'by marriage a distant relation to the Sumbulpore raja', with whose district there was a 'constant correspondence'. See Vansittart to Verelst, 13 December 1767, in Walter Kelly Firminger ed., *Bengal District Records: Midnapur, 1763-1767*, vol. 1 (Calcutta: Bengal Secretariat Press, 1914), 279. The power of Porahat must have been weakened much nearer to home.

[161] Dripnath was to have a long career as the 'grandfather of the present raja' of Chotanagpur. In 1820, he is first mentioned as 'the grandfather of the present Zemindar of Chota Nagpore'. See Roughsedge to Metcalfe, 9 May 1820 (London: OIOC), BC 21,438. He reappears in 1872 as 'Dripnath Sahi, the grandfather of the present Rajah of Chutia Nagpur' in Dalton, *Descriptive Ethnology of Bengal*, 180. Through the good offices of Herbert Hope Risley, in 1877 the raja was still alive in a quote. See Herbert Hope Risley, *Singbhum District, Tributary States of Chutia Nagpur, and Manbhum*, vol. 17 of *A Statistical Account of Bengal*, ser. ed. W. W. Hunter (London: Trübner, 1877, reprint Delhi: Concept, 1976), 108. This remained so until 1887. See William Wilson Hunter, 'Singhbhum', in vol. 12 of *The Imperial Gazetteer of India*, 2nd ed. (London: Trübner, 1887), 532. Of course, the 'present raja' Govind Nath Shah did not rule from 1806 till 1887, but he did so from 1806 to July 1822. See Virottam, *The Nagabanshis and the Cheros*, 188, 205.

[162] Virottam, *The Nagabanshis and the Cheros*, 51-52, 96, 144–45.

[163] Gangpur's raja was Dripnath Saha's nephew. The sister of the raja of Keonjhar was his wife; his eldest son was married to the eldest daughter of the raja of Sambalpur. See Virottam, *The Nagabanshis and the Cheros*, 143.

[164] Roughsedge to Metcalfe, 9 May 1820 (London: OIOC), BC 21,438.

[165] At about the same time, the Marathas forced the raja of Keonjhar to contribute 20,000 troops to the Maratha army. See Patnaik, *Feudatory States of Orissa*, 64.

[166] Roughsedge to Metcalfe, 9 May 1820 (London: OIOC), BC 21,438.

[167] Roughsedge to Metcalfe, 9 May 1820 (London: OIOC), BC 21,438. Dalton mistakenly attributed the second attack to Raja Jagannath Sahi of Chotanagpur in 1770. See Dalton, *Descriptive Ethnology of Bengal*, 180.

[168] The steep ascent was mentioned by Dalton. See Dalton, *Descriptive Ethnology of Bengal*, 180. That suggests the Tebo Ghat on the present-day Chaibasa-Ranchi road.

[169] Roughsedge to Metcalfe, 9 May 1820 (London: OIOC), BC 21,438.

[170] Vansittart to Verelst, 6 February 1768, in Walter Kelly Firminger ed., *Bengal District Records: Midnapur, 1768-1770*, vol. 2 (Calcutta: Bengal Secretariat Press, 1915), 303.

[171] Laeequddin, *Census of Mayurbhanj State*, 17–19; Raut, 'The State of Mayurbhanj', 92–93; Patnaik, *Feudatory States of Orissa*, 54–70.

[172] Raut, 'The State of Mayurbhanj', 94. Morattas in the original.

[173] In 1760, the Company received from Mir Kassim the control over the Midnapur District. For the troubled history of Midnapur during the first years of Company rule, see Walter Kelly Firminger, 'The Ceded Lands', in 'Historical Introduction to the Bengal Portion of "The Fifth Report" to Walter Kelly Firminger (ed.), *The Fifth Report from the Select Committee of the House of Commons on the Affairs of the East India Company, Dated 18th July, 1812, Edited with Notes and Introduction by the Ven. Walter Kelly Firminger*, vol. 1, *Introduction and Text of Report* (Calcutta: R. Cambray, 1917), cxxiii–cxxxi.
Midnapur was nominally a feudatory revenue-payer to the East India Company and the British representative there, the Resident, was the actual ruler. For the institution of Resident for the East India Company, see Michael H. Fisher, 'Indirect Rule in the British Empire, The Foundations of the Residency System in India (1764–1858)', *Modern Asian Studies* 18 (1984): 393–428.

[174] James Henry Taylor, *Final Report on the Survey and Settlement Operations in the Porahat Estate, District Singhbhum, 1900–1903* (Calcutta: Bengal Secretariat Press, 1904), 1.

[175] John Ferguson (died 1773), became ensign in 1765, and lieutenant in 1767. In 1769 he 'resigned owing to ill health in order to go home. Sailed on the *Vansittart* from England in May 1773 with the intention of returning to his duty in India. Whilst the fleet was detained at the Cape in Sept., he became involved in a dispute with a Capt. Ro(a)che, who stabbed him in a so-called duel. Roche tried to escape into the country, but was caught and racked on the wheel. According to a later account . . . he was twice honourably acquitted of murder'. See V. C. P. Hodson, *List of the Officers of the Bengal Army, 1758-1834: Alphabetically Arranged and Annotated with Biographical and Genealogical Notes*, vol. 2 (London: Phillimore, 1928), 173.

[176] For this episode, I mainly follow Jha, *The Bhumij Revolt*, 3–5. See also: O'Malley, *Singhbhum*, 27–28; the same text in Roy Chaudhury, *Singhbhum*, 73–74.

[177] J. Fergusson to G. Vansittart, 4 June 1767, in Firminger, *Bengal District Records: Midnapur* 1: 200. O'Malley, *Singhbhum*, 32. Representative for Vakil in the original.

[178] Vansittart to Verelst, 13 December 1767, in Firminger, *Bengal District Records: Midnapur* 1: 279. Sowenauth Sing in the original.
B. K. Roy gives Seonath Sing. See B. K. Roy, 'Singhbhum: As Known to the East India Company till February 1768', *JHR* 8, no. 2 (1966): 1.

[179] 'Dacoits or robbers, called "banditti" in the early records'. See Lewis Sidney Steward O'Malley, *The Indian Civil Service, 1601–1930* (London: John Murray, 1931; repr., London: Frank Cass, 1965), 29. When the East India Company gradually established effective rule in Bengal and Bihar, unruly local landowners and rajas were called banditti. See William Wilson Hunter, *The Annals of Rural Bengal*, vol. 1, *The Ethnical Frontier of Lower Bengal with the Ancient Principalities of Beerbhoom and Bishenpore*, (London: Smith, Elder, 1868; repr., Delhi: Cosmo, 1975), 69–87.
'These zemindars are mere freebooters who plunder their neighbours and one another and . . . their tenants are banditti whom they chiefly employ in these outrages'. See Baber to Warren Hastings, 6 February 1773, quoted in Jha, *The Bhumij Revolt*, 12–13. O'Malley indicated 1778 for this last quotation. See Lewis Sidney Steward O'Malley, *History of Bengal, Bihar and Orissa Under British Rule* (Calcutta: The Bengal Secretariat Book Depôt, 1925), 683.
Here, as in the other references, 'banditti' should not be equated with Hobsbawn's 'social bandits'. This phenomenon, he stressed, belonged to a society moving away from organisation along lines of kinship towards 'agrarian capitalism'. See Eric J. Hobsbawn, *Bandits* (1969, republished Harmondsworth: Penguin Books, 1972), 18–21.

[180] Vansittart to Verelst, 13 December 1767, in Firminger, *Bengal District Records: Midnapur* 1: 279. Patcomb, Nagpore, Gongpore, Moratta, Coongur, Mohrbunge, Burraboom, Gatseila, pergunnahs, Coles, Sumbulpore, Singboom, Moguls in the original. Coss in the original. The numbers are respectively '40 and 50', '8 or 10' and '90'. The local coss of the Kolhan is stated to be the distance which a man can walk before a fresh-picked branch will wither in his hand'. See Risley, *Singbhum District*, 86. In Bengal, the standard coss was about two miles. See Henry Yule and A. C. Burnell, *Hobson-Jobson: A Glossary of Colloquial Anglo-Indian Words and Phrases, and of Kindred Terms*, Etymological, Historical, Geographical and Discursive, 2nd ed. Preface by William Crooke (London: John Murray, 1903; repr., London and New York: Routledge and Kegan Paul, 1985), 261–62.
I have taken one coss as two miles, approximately 3.2 km.

[181] Vansittart to Verelst, 13 December 1767, in Firminger, *Bengal District Records: Midnapur* 1: 279.

[182] O'Malley, *Singhbhum*, 32. Same text in Roy Chaudhury, *Singhbhum*, 79.

[183] Taylor, *Final Report Survey and Settlement Porahat*, 2.

[184] Verelst to Vansittart, 15 March 1768, in Firminger, *Bengal District Records: Midnapur* 2, no. 303. Morattas in the original.

[185] Patnaik, *Feudatory States of Orissa*, 80.

[186] C. Morgan to Vansittart, 8 July 1768, quoted in Jha, *The Bhumij Revolt*, 6.
Added to this was the problem of getting food. 'For God's sake send me a supply of fowls by the return of the post for I have nothing to eat'. See Roy Chaudhury, *Singhbhum*, 75. Daks in the original.

[187] Jha, *The Bhumij Revolt*, 8.
[188] Described in Vansittart to Verelst on 3 August 1768. See Laeequddin, *Census of Mayurbhanj State*, 19.
[189] Colin Renfrew, e.a., 'Archaeology and Language: The Puzzle of Indo-European Origins by Colin Renfrew, A CA Book Review', *Current Anthropology* 29 (1988): 438. For the invasion hypothesis see Grahame Clark, 'The Invasion Hypothesis in British Archaeology' *Antiquity* 40 (1966): 172–89; Romila Thapar, 'The Perennial Arians', *The Thatched Patio* 5, no. 6 (1992): 28.
[190] Richard Tapper, 'Anthropologists, Historians, and Tribespeople on Tribe and State Formation in the Middle East', in Philip S. Khoury and Joseph Kostiner eds., *Tribes and State Formation in the Middle East* (Berkeley: University of California Press, 1990), 51.This reads like an elaboration of Maarten van Bruinesse's seminal statement that Kurdish tribes 'do not simply represent a stage of evolution preceding the state but are, in several ways, creations of surrounding states'. See Maarten Martinus van Bruinesse, 'Agha, Shaikh and State: On the Social and Political Organization of Kurdistan' (PhD thesis, Utrecht, 1978), 148–49.
[191] John Deeney, 'Ho compared to the Hasada and Naguri dialects of Munda', a section of 'Comparison of the Munda and the Ho Languages', *The Munda World: Hoffmann Commemoration Volume*, edited by P. Ponette, (Ranchi: Catholic Press, 1978), 50-52, quote from p. 51. Still, Fr. John Deeney was convinced that the two dialects of Munda were closer to each other than to Ho.
[192] 'Nobody asks where "the Italians" or "the French" came from originally; it is the formation of the Italian and French nations we study.' See Massimo Pallottino, *The Etruscans*, 1st Italian edition 1942, revised and enlarged edition based on the sixth Italian edition, trans. J. Cremona, ed. David Ridgway 1973 (Harmondsworth: Penguin Books, 1978), 78–79.
[193] Roughsedge to Ch. Metcalfe, 9 May 1820 (London: OIOC), BC 21,438; Metcalfe's Minute, NAI, Foreign Department, Secret, 6 August 1832, procs. 8–11.
[194] '"Laraka", the fighters, a common name for the Hos'. See Dalton, 'The "Kols" of Chota Nagpore', 166. 'Larái' means 'a fight, battle; to fight'. See Deeney, *Ho-English Dictionary*, 207. To be called 'Larka Kols' was fine by the Hos, see Hoffmann and van Emelen, *Encyclopaedia Mundarica* 6: 1764. Obviously 'larka' is a loan word, as one would expect from an adjective to 'Kol'. Hindi knows 'larna', 'to fight', 'to quarrel', and from that 'laráí ka', 'warlike' or 'martial', while Urdu has 'laráku', 'quarrelsome'. 'Laráku' still has the long 'á', which is dropped in 'larka'. It could be that initially the Singhs would call the Hos '(violently) quarrelsome', but that the Hos took the meaning as derived from battle, therefore 'martial', and that this became the general usage.
[195] Such a process is called a 'tribal breakout'. As Chris Bayly has noticed, tribal breakouts took place at the precise moment when these ethnic units acquired a leadership bent on establishing a state. See Christopher Alan Bayly, *Imperial Meridian: The British Empire and the World, 1780–1830*, Studies in Modern History (London and New York: Longman, 1989), 37.
[196] Which, unfortunately, was what Surajit Sinha thought. See Surajit Sinha, 'State Formation and Rajput Myth in Tribal Central India', *MII* 42, no. 1 (1962): 35–37. Sinha concluded his survey of other states in Central India with a perceptive remark. 'Whether a particular state is primarily an internal growth or the creation of an adventurous Rajput or pseudo-Rajput lineage, the final forms of the political structure . . . look more or less alike in essential features, namely, a feudalistic superstructure on a tribal base'. See Sinha, 'State Formation and Rajput Myth', 71. The manki of Barbharia *pir*, which was his example here, was appointed or recognised by the raja of Mayurbhanj—or earlier by the mahapater of Bamanghati. For a 'feudal superstructure' it is not enough to have claims. The feudals should exercise state power over people. Precisely that was lacking inside Hodisum.
[197] Roughsedge to Metcalfe, 9 May 1820 (London: OIOC), BC 21,438.
[198] Roughsedge to Metcalfe, 9 May 1820 (London: OIOC), BC 21,438.
[199] Roughsedge to Richards, 3 April 1821 (London: OIOC), Bengal Political 24 April 1821. Roughsedge to Metcalfe, 9 May 1820 (London: OIOC), BC 21,438.
[200] 'Second examination of Bajee Moond of Garia in Goomlah 28th April 1821 for the Purpose of Obtaining Local Information', appendix to: Roughsedge to Swinton, 7 August 1821 (London: OIOC), BC 21,439.
[201] The Vaishnavite reformer Chaitanya is said to have passed through Chotanagpur in the sixteenth century (Roy, *The Mundas and Their Country*, 97–98; Singh, 'Medieval Tribal Bihar', 257–58. Vaishnavite Bhakti influences dating from the seventeenth century have been traced in Munda and Ho songs. See Norman Zide and Ram Dayal Munda, 'Structural Influence of Bengali Vaisnava Songs on Traditional Mundari Songs', *Journal of Social Research* 13, no. 1 (1970): 39. These influences could have come from two sides. From the east, from Bengal, as the influence of Vaishnavism on the religion of the Bhumij would suggest. See Surajit Sinha, 'Vaisnava Influence on a Tribal Culture', in *Krishna, Myths, Rites, and Attitudes*, ed. Milton Singer [Honolulu: East-West Center, 1966], 64–89. Or it could have come from the south-west, the Chhattishgarh (Nagpur) side. See K.S. Singh, 'Medieval Tribal Bihar', 257.
In the Vaishnavite elements of tribal songs, we hear a splendid example of Bose's 'Hindu method of tribal absorption'. See Nirmal Kumar Bose, 'The Hindu Method of Tribal Absorption' (1941; repr., *Culture and Society in India* [Bombay: Asia Publishing House, 1967]), 204–15. (Except, of course, that we have here the tribal method of Hindu absorption.)

[202] J. C. Heesterman, *The Inner Conflict of Tradition: Essays in Indian Ritual, Kingship, and Society* (Delhi: Oxford University Press, 1985), 167.
[203] Roughsedge to Metcalfe, 9 May 1820 (London: OIOC), BC 21,438.

Part I: Another People's War, 1818–1830

Chapter I: Difficult Negotiations

[1] Roughsedge to Metcalfe, 9 May 1820 (London: OIOC), BC 21,438.
[2] Francis Buchanan to Thomas Brown, 13 September 1807 (London: OIOC), BC 5,707. See also Spear, *The Nabobs*, 85–87.
[3] Gilbert to Swinton, 14 June 1823 (London: OIOC), Bengal Political Consultations, 27 June 1823.
[4] 'Kunwar, vernacular corruption of Kumar, and Kumari . . . a youth, a prince, a princess'. See H. H. Wilson, *A Glossary*, 303. 'Thakur, Thakoor, H. &c . . . An idol, a deity: any individual entitled to reverence or respect, whence it is generally applied to persons of rank and authority in different parts of India, as a lord, a chief, a master, a spiritual guide, the Bhat or genealogist, the head of a tribe, the head of a village, and the like'. See H. H. Wilson, *A Glossary*, 517.
[5] The words 'British Government' are from the original.
'The Kooar of Kharsawan was not given any written engagement or a perwannah'. See Wilkinson to Swinton, 12 January 1833 (London: OIOC), BC 58,904. Here, Wilkinson seemed to have suffered from his incomplete files. Roughsedge did give the Kharsawan chief 'a Perwannah confirmatory of his existing possession agreeably to a schedule delivered into me, and certified to be correct by the Rajah, with the exception of the Northern Boundary of his Estate, which is contested with the Zemindars of Tamar'. See Roughsedge to Metcalfe, 9 May 1820 (London: OIOC), BC 21,438.
[6] These guidelines were formulated in August 1818. See Wilkinson to Mangles, 22 August 1836 (London: OIOC), BC 66,546.
[7] Government to Roughsedge, 29 August 1818, quoted in Jagdish Chandra Jha, 'Early British Contacts with Singhbhum', *Patna University Journal* 18, no. 1 (1963): 149–50.
[8] Adams to Roughsedge, 29 August 1818, cited in Wilkinson to Macsween, 29 October 1834 (London: OIOC), BC 66,544.
[9] Wilkinson to Swinton, 12 January 1833 (London: OIOC), BC 58,904.
[10] Resume of Major Roughsedge's Letter of 2 February 1820, in Wilkinson to Swinton, 12 January 1833 (London: OIOC), BC 58,904. 'Lurka Coles' in the original.
[11] Major Roughsedge's Letter of 2 February 1820, cited in Wilkinson to Swinton, 12 January 1833 (London: OIOC), BC 58,904
[12] Roughsedge, Pergunnahs of Singbhoom, compiled from information by Gunshyam Sing and from other sources, 15 April 1820 (London: OIOC), BC 21,439. See also the table but wrongly sourced to a letter from Ghanshyam to Roughsedge, in Das Gupta, *Adivasis and the Raj*, 85–88.
[13] Roughsedge to Richards, 3 April 1821 (London: OIOC), BC 21,439. Unless otherwise indicated, the quotes in these descriptions are from this source.
[14] Wilkinson to Mangles, 22 August 1836 (London: OIOC)BC 66,546.
[15] On the map prepared by Rennell for Orme in 1778, 'Singboom' is merely mentioned. Reproduced in Susan Gole, *India Within the Ganges* (New Delhi: Jayaprints, 1983), 198. On the Actual Survey, first published in 1776, and its last contemporary reprint 1794, 'Singboom' lost its places and some mountains, but the neighbouring 'Tomaar' (Tamar) got a better treatment. Again, on the map 'General View of the Principal Roads, etc.', published in Rennell's Memoir of 1793, Singhbhum was indicated by some unclear boundaries. However, its name did not appear on his maps.
See also: James Rennell, *The Provinces of Bengal Situated on the West of the Hoogly River with the Maharatta Frontier, Inscribed to Harry Verelst Esqr. by His Obliged Humble Servant J. Rennell* (1774), reproduced in J. C. Jha, *The Bhumij Revolt*, 198;
James Rennell, *A Bengal Atlas: Containing Maps of the Theatre of War and Commerce of that Side of Hindoostan*, compiled from the Original Surveys and published by the Order of the Honourable the Court of Directors for the Affairs of the East India Company by James Renell, Late Major of Engineers and Surveyor General in Bengal, 1781;
James Rennell, 'A General View of the Principal Roads and Divisions of Hindoostan, 1792', in *Memoir of a Map of Hindoostan or the Moghul Empire with an Introduction, Illustrative of the Geography and Present Divisions of that Country and A Map of the Countries Situated Between the Heads of the Indian Rivers, and the Caspian Sea, also, A Supplementary Map, Containing the Improved Geography of the Provinces Contiguous to the Heads of the Indus, to which is added, An Appendix, Containing an Account of the Ganges and Burrampater Rivers* (Calcutta: Editions Indian, 1976; repr., 3rd ed. of the original print, London, 1793, 315), 365.
For a complete overview of Rennell's printed maps see the invaluable Susan Gole, *India Within the Ganges*, 186–96, especially Maps 3.1, 11.2 and 12.1.

Renell's maps were not nearly enough, as became evident during the preparations for the Second Kolhan Campaign in 1821. Roughsedge had nothing better to offer to Lieutenant Colonel William Richards, who would head the next invasion of Hodisum, than a map by Arrowsmith, on which he could not find Jaintgarh, Anandpur and not even Porahat. See Roughsedge to Richards, 9 April 1821 (London: OIOC), BC 21,439. This map was probably the one published by Aaron Arrowsmith in 1816 on which material unmarked on the earlier maps by Rennell was incorporated. It improved only marginally on Singhbhum, adding a north-south road leading to a fort Singboom as capital.

Possibly this came from the survey of the country south of Chotanagpur state by Carmichael Smyth and, after 1813, Captain Raper. Roughsedge had endorsed this survey. A deeper knowledge of the country and especially of the 300 passes leading into the countries south of Ramgarh would help to ward off the inroads of the Pindaris. See Sashi Bhusan Chaudhuri, *History of the Gazetteers of India* (Delhi: Ministry of Education, Government of India: the Manager of Publications, [date shows 1964] 1965), 34–35.

The general result of these unsatisfactory maps was that Roughsedge had to prepare a verbal sketch of the area. See Roughsedge to Richards, 5 April, 7 April and 9 April 1821 (London: OIOC), BC 21,439. As William, later Sir William, Richards was the son of the William Richards who assisted Rennell in his survey work, he might have had some idea of the region which he was about to subdue. See 'Richards, Sir William' and 'Richards, William' in Hodson, *List of the Officers of the Bengal Army*, 640–41.

[16] Ronald Vere Tooley, *A Dictionary of Mapmakers, Including Cartographers, Geographers, Publishers, Engravers, etc. from the Earliest Times to 1900*, part 6 of *Map Collectors' Series* 8, no. 78 (London: Map Collectors' Circle, 1971), 268.

[17] Roughsedge to Metcalfe, 9 May 1820 (London: OIOC), BC 21,438. In 1820–21, the safety of Captain Jackson's Road would be an important consideration for Roughsedge to operate against the Hos. Roughsedge to Metcalfe, 3 June 1820 (London: OIOC), BC 21,438.

Ahuja, rather unsurprisingly, pointed out that the road followed 'the course of a long established pathway'. He attributed the name 'Jackson's road' to the view that Jackson 'was seen as pioneer of civilization'. See Ravi Ahuja, '"Captain Kittoe's Road", Early Colonialism and the Politics of Road Construction in Peripheral Orissa', in *Periphery and Centre: Studies in Orissan History, Religion and Anthropology*, ed. Georg Pfeffer (Delhi: Manohar, 2007), 298–99. He did not quote, and I did not find, contemporary evidence for this last statement.

[18] James Nesbitt Jackson, 'Map of the Part of the District of Singhbhoom and Adjacent Pergunnahs Occupied by and Subject to the Incursions of the Koles, Compiled and Partially Surveyed by J. N. Jackson, Captain, DA:QM.G (Deputy Adjutant and Quartermaster General), May 1821'.

On the map, Ajodhya *pir* (canton) and Saraikela were merely indicated. More details were given for the *pirs* of Rajabasa, Gumra, Thai and Lagra. In the south, we are given Aonlapeer, Lahlgurh, Burndea, Jyantgurh, Satbantrahrah, Surnda (Anwla, Lalgarh, Barndia, Jaintgarh, Bantaria and Saranda), all blank but with one or two villages. The west of the Kolhan ('Colhauns'), except for Porahat, was left blank.

See also S. N. Prasad, *Catalogue of the Historical Maps of the Survey of India (1700–1900)* (New Delhi: The National Archives of India, 1975), 147, entry no. F.56/912.

[19] Roughsedge did not refer to the 1767 Pitamber Singh/Vansittart description in his overviews of the history of Singhbhum. In fact, even Dalton did not know about these. See Dalton, *Descriptive Ethnology of Bengal*, 179. The letters, of course, were in the Midnapur files. The administrative division of the area had its impact on the range and, hence, on the understanding of its history.

Roughsedge also missed that in 1793 the East India Company had made the chiefs of Saraikela and Kharsawan agree not to give shelter to fugitives from British territory. See O'Malley, *Singhbhum*, 230; Jha, *The Bhumij Revolt*, 14.

[20] Roughsedge to Major G. H. Fagan, 4 April 1808 (London: OIOC), BC 7,411. Singboom, Lurka Pere in the original.

[21] Roughsedge to Edmonstone, 30 May 1809, quoted in Roughsedge to Adam, 12 May, 1818. Referred to in C. P. Singh, *The Ho Tribe of Singhbhum*, 62. It is possible that Roughsedge gave this information to support a request by the raja of Porahat to bring his country under the British Government. 'Possible', because C. P. Singh is the only source for this 1809 request. See C. P. Singh, *The Ho Tribe of Singhbhum*, 62, and notes 13 and 14. In his later overviews, which unlike this source were included in the Board's Collections, Roughsedge himself did not mention it.

[22] Kumar, *History and Administration of Tribal Chotanagpur*, 101.

[23] Roughsedge to Major G. H. Fagan, 4 April 1808 (London: OIOC), BC 7,411. Singboom, Lurka Pere in the original.

[24] Dalton, *Descriptive Ethnology of Bengal*, 180.

[25] Roughsedge to Richards, 3 April 1821 (London: OIOC), BC 21,439. Charai was given as 'the southern part of Cherie' Gumla as Goomla. Taeepeer for Thai *pir*.

[26] Roughsedge to Metcalfe, 9 May 1820 (London: OIOC), BC 21,438.

[27] Roughsedge to Metcalfe, 9 May 1820 (London: OIOC), BC 21,438.

[28] Roughsedge to Metcalfe, 9 May 1820 (London: OIOC), BC 21,438.

[29] Edward Tuite Dalton, 'The "Kols" of Chota Nagpore', 165–66. This is the only place where this action has been mentioned.

[30] Roughsedge to Metcalfe, 9 May 1820 (London: OIOC), BC 21,438.

[31] Roughsedge to Metcalfe, 9 May 1820 (London: OIOC), BC 21,438. Lurkas, Jyuntgur in the original.
[32] Roughsedge to Metcalfe, 9 May 1820 (London: OIOC), BC 21,438.
[33] Roughsedge to Richards, 3 April 1821 (London: OIOC), BC 21,439.
[34] Roughsedge to Metcalfe, 9 May 1820 (London: OIOC), BC 21,438.
[35] Roughsedge to Richards, 3 April 1821 (London: OIOC), BC 21,439.
[36] Roughsedge to Richards, 3 April 1821 (London: OIOC), BC 21,439. Cohers, Lurkas, in the original.
[37] Roughsedge to Richards, 3 April 1821 (London: OIOC), BC 21,439.
[38] O'Malley, *Singhbhum*, 247–48.
[39] 'Bahadur, H. &c . . . A hero, a warrior: under the Mohammadan government, a title of honour given to the nobles of the Court, usually associated with some others, as Khan-bahadur, Raja-bahadur'. See H. H. Wilson, *A Glossary*, 570.
[40] Singh Deo, *Singhbhum, Seraikella and Kharswan Through the Ages*, 54–56. Raja Abhiram Singh, Zaminder, Pargana Singhbhum in the original. See also Roy Chaudhury, *Singhbhum*, 79.
[41] Roughsedge to Lt. Col. Paton, 25 February 1808 (London: OIOC), BC 7,411. Davies to Allen, no date, (Patna: BSA), SOC, vol. IV, 1855–1856. See also Singh Deo, *Singhbhum, Seraikella and Kharswan Through the Ages*, 57–59.
[42] Roughsedge to Metcalfe, 9 May 1820 (London: OIOC), BC 21,438. Opiom in the original. It must have been Abhiram as Bikram was not even fourty at that time. The confusion does not end here. P. Kumar mistakenly made these remarks refer to Ghanshyam. See Purushottam Kumar, *History and Administration of Tribal Chotanagpur (Jharkhand)* (Delhi, Lucknow: Atma Ram and Sons, 1994), 103.
[43] Roughsedge to Richards, 3 April 1821 (London: OIOC), BC 21,439. Singboom in the original.
[44] Roughsedge to Metcalfe, 9 May 1820 (London: OIOC), BC 21,438. See also Kumar, *History and Administration of Tribal Chotanagpur*, 112.
[45] Roughsedge to Richards, 3 April 1821 (London: OIOC), BC 21,439.
[46] Gilbert to Swinton, 28 October 1827, 'Papers concerning Sarguja, Sambalpur and Singhbum 1818—1830' (London: OIOC), H/724.
It is possible that Ghanshyam directly succeeded Harihar. Both Harihar and Raghubar were not in the list of succession in Singh Deo, *Singhbhum, Seraikella and Kharswan Through the Ages*, 30.
[47] Roughsedge to Richards, 3 April 1821 (London: OIOC), BC 21,439. Wilkinson, n.d., but between September 1832–August 1834, 'List of Zemindars and Their Estates and of Pergunnahs Under the Koss Management of the Rajah of Singbhoom' (London: OIOC), BC 58,534.
[48] Note in margin to 'Translation of an Urzee from Ruttun Sing Jemedar of a company of Burkundauzes employed in Singboom dated the 13th of May and received the 23rd of July [Bangala] 1821', in Roughsedge to Swinton, 17 February 1821 (London: OIOC), BC 21,438. Later, Wilkinson stated that the raja had a share of 6 annas (37.5 per cent) and Ghasi Singh of 10 annas (62.5 per cent). See Wilkinson, 'List of Zemindars', BC 58,534, September 1832–August 1834.
[49] Roughsedge to Swinton, 7 August 1821, Bengal Political Consultations, 15 September 1821 (London: OIOC), BC 21,439. Goomlah in the original.
[50] '10 seers' in the original. In 1877, a *seer* in the Kolhan was about 955 grammes. See Risley, *Singbhum District*), 85. Wilson concurred: 'SER, commonly, but incorrectly, SEER . . ., a measure of weight, . . . generally reckoned in Bengal at eighty tolas, or Sicca weight, or as one-fortieth of a man or maund . . .The standard Ser was = avoirdupois weight 2 lb. 0 oz. 13.863 dr.'. See H. H. Wilson, *A Glossary*, 474.
[51] 'Ghassee Singh's Defense, 16th May 1821', in Roughsedge to Swinton, 7 August 1821 (London: OIOC), BC 21,439.
[52] Wilkinson, 'List of Zemindars', BC 58,534, September 1832–August 1834.
[53] Roughsedge to Richards, 3 April 1821 (London: OIOC), BC 21,439.
[54] Governor General's Agent to Lieutenant S. K. (*sic*) Tickell, 12 December 1838, in Roy Chaudhury, *Singhbhum Old Records*, 15. Coles in the original.
[55] 'Bisi, Bisee, Uriya . . . A fiscal division of the country, a province or district paying revenue under the Hindu Government of Orissa . . . Bissoï . . . Uriya. The chief of a district in Orissa, collecting the Government revenue, and exercising police and judicial authority'. See H. H. Wilson, *A Glossary*, 90.
[56] Translation of a letter from Ruggonauth Bussee to the Political Agent, 20 February 1830 (London: OIOC), Bengal Political Consultations, 28 May 1830.
[57] It was granted by Raja Harihar Singh. See Governor General's Agent to Lieutenant S. K. (*sic*) Tickell, 12 December 1838, in Roy Chaudhury, *Singhbhum Old Records*, 14.
[58] Roughsedge to Metcalfe, 9 May 1820 (London: OIOC), BC 21,438. Bramins, Killedar in the original. That Raghunath was the unnamed Brahmin follows from a letter he wrote in 1830. See Murali Sahu, *The Kolhan Under British Rule* (Jamshedpur: Sushanta Kumar Sahu, 1985), 45, note 2.
[59] Roughsedge to Metcalfe, 9 May 1820 (London: OIOC), BC 21,438.
[60] O'Malley called these khorposh, or maintenance grants. See O'Malley, *Singhbhum*, 225. T. S. MacPherson used the expression of 'fiefs or subordinate grants involving military service'. See MacPherson, *Final Report on the Operations*, 18.

61 In 1821, Roughsedge mentioned Chainpur, a little inside the Hodisum, as 'a mud fort belonging to rajah Gansham Sing at Chinepoor'. See Roughsedge to Swinton, 17 February 1821 (London: OIOC), BC 21,438. Chainpur was 'a service grant of a few villages held by . . . a tenure-holder, whose family had already settled in Porahat previous to the advent of the Singhs'. See James H. Taylor, *Final Report on the Survey and Settlement Operations in the Porahat Estate, District Singhbhum, 1900–1903* (Calcutta: Bengal Secretariat Press, 1904), 2.

62 Roughsedge to Metcalfe, 9 May 1820 (London: OIOC), BC 21,438. Roughsedge wrote his name as Obei Sing.

63 Roughsedge to Richards, 3 April 1821 (London: OIOC), BC 21,439. Frequest, Greak, Banie, in the original.

64 Roughsedge to Richards, 3 April 1821 (London: OIOC), BC 21,439. Pergunnahs, Rajah in the original.

65 Roughsedge to Metcalfe, 9 May 1820 (London: OIOC), BC 21,438.

66 Roughsedge to Metcalfe, 16 February 1820 (London: OIOC), BC 21,438.

67 Gilbert to Swinton, 1 October 1827, 'Papers Concerning Surguja, Sambalpur and Singhbum 1818–1830' (London: OIOC), H/724.

68 Gilbert to Swinton, 4 June 1823 (London: OIOC), Bengal, Political Consultations, 27 June 1823.

69 According to Roy Chaudhury, in the second half of the sixteenth and the first half of the seventeenth century, the rajas of Porahat had switched to a form of Buddhism. Conversion to Buddhism in the sixteenth century in Orissa is very improbable. According to Roy Chaudhury, the raja had also thrown away the image. An old woman sold the image to the *divan* of Saraikela, who gave it as a toy to his daughter. That night, both raja Abhiram and his *divan* dreamed that the Pauri Devi demanded to be installed in the temple inside the palace. So happened, and the power of Saraikela increased. This placed the coming of the idol to Saraikela around, or a little before 1800. See P. C. Roy Chaudhury, *Temples and Legends of Bihar*, Series: Bhavan's Book University 127 (Bombay: Bharatiya Vidya Bhavan, 1965), 17–21.

70 Bengal Political Consultation 39, 3 June 1820 (London: OIOC), BC 21,438.

71 Wilkinson to Mangles, 22 August 1936 (London: OIOC), BC 66,546.

72 'Translation of an Arzee from Rajah Gunsham Sing, zamindar of Singboom dated and received the 24th Faughun or 23 February 1820' (London: OIOC), BC 21,438. Rajah, Debee, Pooja, Abiram Sing, Bickram Sing, Baboo, brought, Rajah, in the original. I have give 'May-June 1790' for 'In the month of jyte 1177', as the year 1177 must be a copying error.

73 'Translation of Bickram Sing's reply received 28th February [1820]' (London: OIOC), BC 21,438. Rajah, Debee, Banscutta, Poorahaut, Ranee, Sing, Seriekela, Powrie Debee, in the original. Bikram forgot here Kala Arjun, which makes his second Arjun actually the third.

74 In 1823, the 'Kols' attributed the growing power of the chief of Saraikela to the possession of the 'Pooreea Dehee', which was stolen from Porahat by 'Ibrahim Singh'. See W. R. Gilbert to Swinton, 14 June 1823 (London: OIOC), Bengal Political Consultations, 27 June 1823.

75 Professor D. Kolff drew my attention to the multiples of 12, for which I thank him.

76 The first reliable figures we get are from the census of 1872. See Risley, *Singbhum District*, 34. Starting with the Census figures of the Hos, and lowering the total population's numbers proportionally to those of Roughsedge's 50,000 Hos, we arrive at a total inhabitants count of the area of around 110,000.
The whole area would have had 65,000 Hos. Not all lived outside the chiefs' states, but it appeared that even inside those states many Hos were outside of their control. If we assume that the proportion of 'Kols' in each state did not change, and that 80 per cent of these would have been Hos, we come, very roughly to Hos in Saraikela 5,000, in Kharsawan some 3,000, and in Porahat 7,000 Hos. These are the upper limits. The Hodisum proper would then have a population of 57,000 people, of which 50,000 were Hos.

77 Edward Roughsedge was named after his grandfather. His father Robert Hankinson Roughsedge lived from 1771–1829 and was married to Elizabeth War(e)ing. See John C. Morley, 'Robert Hankinson Roughsedge', in '*Monumental Inscriptions from the Churchyard of St. Nicholas, Liverpool*', vol. 4 of *Miscellanea Genealogica(l) et Heraldica*, n.s., (1884): 433–34.
Apart from his numerous official letters, there are few sources on the life and person of Major Edward Roughsedge (1774–1822). His Cadet papers contained a one-page general statement by Benshaw, Rector (London: OIOC), Cadet Papers, L/Mil/9/107/671). He was, of course, mentioned in the *List of the Officers of the Bengal Army*. See Hodson, *List of the Officers of the Bengal Army*, vol. 3, 700–701. See also Edward Dodwell, James Samuel Miles (compilers and editors), *Alphabetical List of the Officers of the Bengal Army: With the Dates of Their Respective Promotion, Retirement, Resignation, or Death, Whether in India or in Europe, From the Year 1760 to the Year 1834 Inclusive, Corrected to September 30, 1837* (London: Longman, Orme, Brown, [1838]), 220-21. See also his obituaries: 'Major Edward Roughsedge', *AJMR* 14, (July–December 1822): 232–33 and nearly the same text in: The Editor of the Royal Military Calendar, 'The Late Major Edward Roughsedge', *The East India Military Calendar: Containing the Services of General and Field Officers of the Indian Army* 3 (London: Kingsbury, Parbury, and Allen, 1826): 227–29; and Samuel Parlby, 'Late Major Roughsedge', in *The British Indian Military Repository* 1 (Calcutta: Church Mission Press, 1822): 330–33.

78 Caroline Raynor, 'Roughsedge', in *St Thomas' Church, Park Lane, Liverpool, Archaeological Watching Brief Report* (Oxford: Oxford Archaeology North, 2010), 26.

79 The biographical note has been preserved in the library of The Athenaeum Club, of which Robert Hankinson Roughsedge

was one of the founding members. See Elizabeth Roughsedge-Wareing, 'Biographical Note' (no date), ref. LRO/Hf352 CEN 1/17/2. I am grateful to Ms Joan Hanford of The Athenaeum Club Library for forwarding a copy of the Biographical Note. See also Raynor, 'Roughsedge', 25.

[80] For a short biography of Roughsedge, see Hodson, *List of the Officers of the Bengal Army*, vol. 3, 700–01.

[81] On the social background of the Indian Civil Servants in this period, see the still useful Lewis Sidney Steward O'Malley, *The Indian Civil Service, 1601–1930* (London: John Murray, 1931; repr., London: Frank Cass, 1965). See also Bernard S. Cohn, *An Anthropologist Among the Historians and Other Essays* (Delhi: Oxford University Press, 1987), 500–53.

[82] This fate was common. Between 1796 and 1820, only 201 officers succeeded in retiring to Europe on a pension, while 1,243 died or were killed in action. See Philip Mason, *A Matter of Honour: An Account of the Indian army, Its Officers and Men* (London: Jonathan Cape, 1974), 174.

[83] Surendra Prasad Sinha, 'Disquiet and Depredation in Chota Nagpur (1795–1800 A.D.)', *Bulletin of the Bihar Tribal Research Institute* 5 (1963): 156–60. A shorter version of the same in Surendra Prasad Sinha, 'Thakur Bholanath Sahy of Tamar (1795–1800), The First Freedom Fighter of Chotanagpur', *JHR* 6, no. 2 (1964): 47.

[84] Hodson, *List of the Officers of the Bengal Army*, vol. 3, 700. Roughsedge is mentioned in E., 'The Nepaul War', no 7 of 'Sketches of the Later History of British India', *AJMR* n.s., 21 (September–December 1836): 123.

[85] Edward Dodwell, James Samuel Miles (compilers and editors), *Alphabetical List of the Officers of the Bengal Army*, 220-21.

[86] Kumar, *History and Administration of Tribal Chotanagpur*, 16–19.

[87] Mao Tse-Tung, ed., 'Where Do Correct Ideas Come From? 1963', in *Four Essays on Philosophy* (Peking: Foreign Languages Press, 1968), 134.

[88] Roughsedge to Lt. Col. John Paton, 25 February 1808; Roughsedge to Major G. H. Fagan, 4 April 1808 (London: OIOC), BC 7,411.

[89] 'Major Edward Roughsedge', 233.

[90] Spear, *The Nabobs*, 87.

[91] Below the rank of Major, marriage was uncommon in the Bengal Army, but till the 1820s and 1830s it was fairly common especially for senior officers to take to 'concubinage of long standing' with Indian women. See Mason, *A Matter of Honour*, 176. This could lead to a fascinating mix of British and Eurasians in one family. Splendid example was of course, the Hearsays. See Hugh Pearse, *The Hearsays: Five Generations of an Anglo-Indian Family* (London: William Blackwood and Sons, 1905). Charles Metcalfe was married to an Indian (Jat) lady. See Devendra N. Panigrahi, *Charles Metcalfe in India: Ideas and Administration, 1806–1835* (New Delhi: Munshiram Manoharlal, 1968), 22.
For a detailed account of one such marriage, see William Dalrymple, *White Mughals: Love & Betrayal in Eighteenth-Century India* (London: Flamingo, 2003).

[92] Douglas M. Peers, '"The Habitual Nobility of Being": British Officers and the Social Construction of the Bengal Army in the Early Nineteenth Century', *Modern Asian Studies* 25, no. 3 (1991): 549. See also: Mason, *A Matter of Honour*, 97. Eighty per cent were Brahmins and Rajputs, and ten per cent Muslims from Awadh, Bihar and Rohilkhand, that is, from North India. This composition was a leftover from the late-eighteenth century, when indigenous armies were disbanded and the Bengal Army grew in size. Once this composition was established, it continued itself, as the army largely replenished its number by soldiers bringing in relatives and people from their own village and background. Sepoy Sita Ram was taken to the army by his uncle. See Sita Ram, *From Sepoy to Subedar: Being the Life and Adventures of Subedar Sita Ram, a Native Officer of the Bengal Army*, written and related by Himself, translated and first published by Lieutenant-Colonel Norgate, Bengal Staff Corps at Lahore, 1873, paperback edition by James Lunt [London: Macmillan, 1980]), 2–4. Apart from this explicit instruction to Indian men and officers, there were also recruiting parties sent out, mainly staffed by native officers, who also would employ people from their own background. See Mason, *A Matter of Honour*, 166; Madan Paul Singh, *Indian Army Under the East India Company* (New Delhi: Sterling, 1976), 147–48. One result was that other groups in North India were left out of this high-caste army. See Dirk H. A. Kolff, *Naukar, Rajput and Sepoy: The Ethnohistory of the Military Labour Market in Hindustan, 1450–1850*, University of Cambridge Oriental Publications, 43 (Cambridge: Cambridge University Press, 1990), 183–87. Another result of this quite homogeneous composition was that in the Bengal Army 'the victory of caste was complete'. See Mason, *A Matter of Honour*, 125.

[93] Roughsedge to Blunt, 16 August 1807; Roughsedge to John Patton, 8 February and 25 February 1808 (London: OIOC), BC 7004.

[94] Roughsedge to Metcalfe, 9 May 1820 (London: OIOC), BC 21,439.

[95] M. H. Hallet and T. S. Macpherson, *Ranchi*, Bihar District Gazetteers, 1917, quoted in Verrier Elwin, 'The Kol Insurrection', *MII* 25, no. 4 (Rebellion Number, 1945): 258–60. But Singh Deo indicated 1818. See Singh Deo, *Singhbhum, Seraikella and Kharswan Through the Ages*, 58–59. S. N. Singh erroneously gave 'South Bihar' instead of 'Southwestern Frontier'. See S. N. Singh, 'Some Important Dates in the Modern Administrative History of Chotanagpur', *JHR* 5, no. 2 (1963): 25. There is a contemporary precedent for this, though. At one locus in 1821, Roughsedge is mentioned as 'Political Agent to Government

96 Fergusson's 1767 expedition to the west of Midnapur, which we have seen in the Prologue, and the acquisition of Chotanagpur in 1771, which we shall treat shortly, pushed the Company's power deep into the mountainous and jungle areas south of the Bihar and west of the Bengal plains, and reached areas claimed by the Mahrattas.

97 The Marathas had defeated the British in 1779 in western India. By the 1790s, Calcutta looked at two incompatible strategic goals. Coexistence of the East India Company and the Marathas was no longer a viable long-term option. Still, in the short and medium term, the Company wanted peace and trade. See Percival Spear, *A History of India*, vol. 2 (1965; repr., with Epilogue, Harmondsworth: Penguin Books, 1970), 90.

98 The freebooting Pindaries were 'mounted marauders and plunderers . . . originally nothing more than a body of irregular horse allowed to attach themselves to the Mohammadan armies, employed especially in collecting forage, and permitted, in lieu of pay, to plunder'. See Wilson, *A Glossary*, 414. In 1812, they could still threaten the Ganges valley. Five years later, in 1817, they were stopped on their way to Chotanagpur and retreated to Sambalpur. See Balmukund Virottam, *The Nagabanshis and the Cheros* (New Delhi: Munshiram Manoharlal, 1972), 177. In the same year, Calcutta decided to put an end to the menace. In 1819, their last resistance was broken. See D. E. U. Baker, *Colonialism in an Indian Hinterland: The Central Provinces, 1820–1920* (Delhi: Oxford University Press, 1993), 40, 48.

99 The frontier concept I derive from the Turner thesis of 1893, which summarised important aspects of white society when and where it clashed with the original inhabitants of North America. The frontier in present-day Jharkhand and Odisha was between the Biharis and the Odias on one side and the original population on the other. It is important here to realise that the frontier was not a line, but rather a broad strip of land, in which encounters between bearers of mutually exclusive cultures took place. For a comprehensive discussion, see George Rogers Taylor (ed.), *The Turner Thesis: Concerning the Role of the Frontier in American History*, series Problems in American Civilization, Readings selected by the Department of American Studies, Amherst College (Boston: D. C. Heath, 1949).

For eastern India, the frontier concept was used by F. G. Bailey. See Frederick George Bailey, *Caste and the Economic Frontier: A Village in Highland Orissa*, 2nd impression (Manchester: Manchester University Press, 1959). Surprisingly, Bailey took the concept only indirectly from Turner. His settlers and traders' frontier came from W. K. Hancock, *Survey of British Commonwealth Affairs*, vol. 2, *Problems of Economic Policy, 1918–1938*, part 1 (London, etc.: Oxford University Press, 1940). Bayley's frontier concept was taken up by Jha. See Jagdish Chander Jha, *The Bhumij Revolt*, 111.

100 Gyan Prakash, *Bonded Histories: Genealogies of Labor Servitude in Colonial India*, South Asian Studies 44 (Cambridge: Cambridge University Press, 1990), 58–76, especially 72. Gyan Prakash did not, however, use the frontier concept.

101 Virottam, *The Nagabanshis and the Cheros*, 3–4.

102 Virottam, *The Nagabanshis and the Cheros*, 8–12. Although one can debate on the extent of efficient Mughal control, it is hard to agree here with Prakash that the rulers of Chotanagpur never were under the Mughals. See Prakash, *Bonded Histories*, 65–66, note 63.

103 Smith stated in 1823 that the rajas 'for the last two generations' had 'adopted the religion of the Rajpoots'. See Jagdish Chandra Jha, *The Tribal Revolt of Chotanagpur (1831–1832)*, 2nd rev. and enlarged ed. of *The Kol Insurrection of Chota Nagpur*, 1964 (Patna: Kashi Prasad Jayaswal Research Institute, 1987), 33, note 4.

104 The oldest proof is from 1667. See Hoffmann and Van Emelen, *Encyclopaedia Mundarica* 2: 512.

105 Sarat Chandra Roy, 'Ethnographical Investigation in Official Records', *JBORS* 7 (1921): 6; Virottam, *The Nagabanshis and the Cheros*, 51.

106 In 1771, Dripnath Sahi, the Nagbanshi chief of Chotanagpur, appeared before Captain Camac in Palamau and 'after exchange of turbans with [him], duly acknowledged himself a vassal of that great power, gave as tribute Rs. 3,000 and agreed to do service against the Mahrattas'. See Virottam, *The Nagabanshis and the Cheros*, 98.

E. T. Dalton thought that this event took place in 1772. See Dalton, *Descriptive Ethnology of Bengal*, 170. The same year is given by P. Kumar. He, in a rather careless way, makes the turban 'ablaze with diamonds', 5. Sarat Chandra Roy did not mention the turban. See Roy, *The Mundas and Their Country*, 102–04.

107 Minute, April 1832 by Thomason, Deputy Secretary to Government, quoted in Roy, *The Mundas and Their Country*, 42.

108 Dalton, *Descriptive Ethnology of Bengal*, 170. Herbert Hope Risley, *Districts of Hazaribagh and Lohardaga*, in vol. 16 of *A Statistical Account of Bengal*, ser. ed. W. W. Hunter, (London: Trübner, 1877; repr., New Delhi: Concept, 1976), 19, quoted in Jha, *The Tribal Revolt of Chotanagpur*, 44.

109 There was an invasion by the Marathas in 1772, See Virottam, *The Nagabanshis and the Cheros*, 136–38. On the irregular payment of revenue, see Roy, *The Mundas and Their Country*, 104; Virottam, *The Nagabanshis and the Cheros*, 139–42.

110 John William Kaye, *The Administration of the East India Company: A History of Indian Progress* (London: Richard Bentley, 1853), 91–92. In Bengal, the Company was not the sovereign but merely the holder of the *divani* of Bengal for the Delhi Mughals. The government of Bengal could not promulgate laws. It called these regulations.

111 In 1773, Palamau, Ramgarh and Chotanagpur were transferred from the charge of the Patna Council to the more central one of the Presidency of Bengal itself. The administration and revenue collection was made the express charge of the zamindars.

See Jha, *The Tribal Revolt of Chotanagpur*, 11. In 1774, the pendulum swung towards the British territory option or, more exactly, to the system in use in Bengal proper. The Calcutta Council decided to entrust the collection work to a civil officer for the reason that the command of a military force was quite different from the task of collecting the revenue. See Virottam, *The Nagabanshis and the Cheros*, 142. It did not work. No wonder, as in 1778, the revenue was fixed by a man so out of touch with this hilly jungle country that he thought it was a well-populated, cultivated plain. See Jha, *The Tribal Revolt of Chotanagpur*, 44.

In 1780, the District of Ramgarh was created. See Singh, 'Some Important Dates', 25. It was placed under a civilian who combined the functions of judge, magistrate and collector. However, Chotanagpur proper was but a 'nominal part of this district'. See Roy, *The Mundas and Their Country*, 105.

The swing now went into the direction of tributary status. In 1789, the government decided that the Bengal regulations would never be applied to Chotanagpur. See Jha, *The Tribal Revolt of Chotanagpur*, 46; Kumar, *History and Administration of Tribal Chotanagpur*, 22. A separate Chotanagpur settlement was promulgated for 10 years, a relatively short period. See Virottam, *The Nagabanshis and the Cheros*, 176–77, 190 and Dalton, *Descriptive Ethnology of Bengal*, 170. The Raja increased the taxes, but continued not to pay the stipulated revenue to his overlord the East India Company. See K. P. Mitra, 'Defence of the Frontier of Bihar and Orissa Against Maratha and Pindari Incursions (1800–1819)', *BPP* 60 (1941): 56–57; Patnaik, *Feudatory States of Orissa*, 118. In 1798 W. Hunter proposed to sell Chotanagpur to a tax farmer. The Board of Revenue, however, opposed this. See Virottam, *The Nagabanshis and the Cheros*, 155.

Virottam consistently mentioned W. W. Hunter, prolific writer and historian in the latter half of the nineteenth century, where it should be W. Hunter, collector of Ramgarh, at the end of the eighteenth century. See Virottam, *The Nagabanshis and the Cheros*, 148–51, 153–5. For information on the real W. Hunter, see Om Prakash Kejariwal, *The Asiatic Society of Bengal and the Discovery of India's Past* (Delhi: Oxford University Press, 1988), 85–86.

[112] Kumar, *History and Administration of Tribal Chotanagpur*, 11–12, 16. The 1795 date is convincing. On unclear grounds, S. N. Singh gives 1773 as the beginning of the Ramgarh Battalion. See Singh, 'Some Important Dates', 25.

A good assessment of the troubled strategic relationship between the Ramgarh Battalion and the civil administration in Chotanagpur in Roughsedge's time can be found in Kumar, *History and Administration of Tribal Chotanagpur*.

[113] In 1803, the Civil Line and the Military Line were made equally responsible for the maintenance of law and order. It was more a political than a practical move.

[114] We owe this important observation to Purushottam Kumar. See Kumar, *History and Administration of Tribal Chotanagpur*, 13.

[115] Virottam, *The Nagabanshis and the Cheros*, 158–59.

[116] Kumar, *History and Administration of Tribal Chotanagpur*, 13.

[117] Roughsedge to Magistrate of Ramgarh, 5 May 1809, cited in B. K. Roy 'Captain Roughsedge and the Reorganisation of Police System in Chotanagpur (Ranchi District) During 1809', *JHR* 12, no. 1 (1969): 110–11. See also Kumar, *History and Administration of Tribal Chotanagpur*, 14–15.

[118] He was of the view that the new police would consist of local men, better adapted to local conditions than hired strangers (Roughsedge to Magistrate of Ramgarh, 5 May 1809, quoted in Roy, 'Captain Roughsedge and the Reorganisation of Police System in Chotanagpur', 110–11). It was to be placed directly under the raja. Roughsedge realised that the behaviour of local landowners vested with police power had mostly not proven satisfactory. See Jha, *The Tribal Revolt of Chotanagpur*, 55; Kumar, *History and Administration of Tribal Chotanagpur*, 14–15.

[119] Jha, *The Tribal Revolt of Chotanagpur*, 58, note 1.

[120] Jha, *The Tribal Revolt of Chotanagpur*, 58, note 1. The immediate object of the annual tour was to avoid the permanent stationing of a European officer in Chotanagpur.

[121] Roy, *The Mundas and Their Country*, 106; Dalton, *Descriptive Ethnology of Bengal*, 170; Virottam, *The Nagabanshis and the Cheros*, 161.

[122] Kumar, *History and Administration of Tribal Chotanagpur*, 18.

[123] Kumar, *History and Administration of Tribal Chotanagpur*, 22.

[124] S. T. Cuthbert, 1827, in Roy, 'Ethnographical Investigation' (1921): 17.

[125] Kumar, *History and Administration of Tribal Chotanagpur*, 16, 22.

[126] Patnaik, *Feudatory States of Orissa*, 104–6.

[127] Patnaik, *Feudatory States of Orissa*, 113.

[128] Political Letter to Bengal, 14 September 1808 (London: OIOC), BC 7,004.

[129] 'Marquis of Hastings on the Company assuming the role of Protector over the whole country, 1 December 1815'. See S. V. Desika Char, ed., *Readings in the Constitutional History of India: 1757–1947* (Delhi: Oxford University Press, 1983), 195–97.

[130] The inspiration to use this term came from the excellent Edward N. Luttwak, *The Grand Strategy of the Roman Empire: From the First Century A.D. to the Third*, 1976, paperback edition (Baltimore and London: The Johns Hopkins University Press, 1981). A grand strategy is a set of policies, in which a nation co-ordinates military and non-military elements to further its long-term interest in relation to other nations. This set of policies is 'strategic', because it aims at establishing a lasting

situation. It is 'grand' because it is directed simultaneously at various aspects of society and culture. See Paul Kennedy, 'Grand Strategy in War and Peace, Toward a Broader Definition', in *Grand Strategies in War and Peace*, ed. Paul Kennedy (New Haven and London: Yale University Press, 1991), 5.

[131] Christopher Alan Bayly, *Imperial Meridian: The British Empire and the World, 1780–1830*, Studies in Modern History (London and New York: Longman, 1989), 60, 106.

[132] Patnaik, *Feudatory States of Orissa*, 140.

[133] Mitra, 'Defence of the Frontier of Bihar and Orissa', 56–57; Patnaik, *Feudatory States of Orissa*, 118.

[134] In modern historiography, P. Kumar attributed this attitude to the sexual favours that Roughsedge allegedly received. I have to discuss this allegation, as it pertains to a central idea of this book that strategic considerations and sexual attraction could go hand in hand. In Kumar's view, after Roughsedge became political agent in 1819, he became inflated with success. He allegedly ruled like a king in Sambalpur with 'princely chicanery, women, French wine'. Kumar stated that Roughsedge kept a luxurious harem. In it was also Mohan Kumari, the wife of the ruler of Sambalpur. Though as his work progressed, Kumar repeated and embellished his statements on Roughsedge's libido, he did not give a single source for this view. See Kumar, *History and Administration of Tribal Chotanagpur*, 18, 20, 81, 152–53, 155.

[135] The experienced jungle traveller Ball found its climate 'very pleasant'. See Ball, *Jungle Life in India*, 515.

[136] Dalton, *Descriptive Ethnology of Bengal*, 179–80.

[137] Ruddell to Bickram Sing, 1819. See Singh Deo, *Singhbhum, Seraikella and Kharswan Through the Ages*, 59.

[138] Roughsedge to Metcalfe, 20 June 1820 (London: OIOC), BC 21,438.

[139] Roughsedge to Metcalfe, 3 February 1820 (London: OIOC), BC 21,438.

[140] Wilkinson to Mangles, 22 August 1836 (London: OIOC), BC 66,564.

[141] Roughsedge to Metcalfe, 25 June 1819, referred to in Roughsedge to Metcalfe, 20 June 1820 (London: OIOC), BC 21,438. 'Lurkas' in the original.

[142] Roughsedge to Metcalfe, 16 January 1820 (London: OIOC), BC 21,438.

[143] Roughsedge to Metcalfe, 16 January 1820 (London: OIOC), BC 21,438. Wakeel Narrain Sing in the original.

[144] Roughsedge to Metcalfe, 16 January 1820 (London: OIOC) BC 21,438.

[145] Tamar was one of the six parganas subordinate to the Chotanagpur raja. This subordination did not extend much beyond paying the revenue, and the right of the raja of Chotanagpur to receive Rs. 1,000 for the investiture of his subordinate chief by giving him the *tilak*. See S. T. Cuthbert, Magistrate at Ramgarh, 21 April 1827, in Roy, 'Ethnographical Investigation' (1921): 6–7; see also Roy, *The Mundas and Their Country*, 110–12.

[146] To find the culprit, they performed an arrow shooting test, which pointed to one Treebhooban Manki. He escaped, but the Tamarians murdered one of his sons, and burned his house and village. That triggered a jacquerie against the alien rent farmers. See Roy, *The Mundas and Their Country*, 113.

These rent farmers had settled in the area in the last four decades. Roughsedge's first thought was that the Tamarians had suffered from 'some gross act of oppression committed by Govind Shahi towards some chief of the insurgents', paraphrased in Virottam, *The Nagabanshis and the Cheros*, 178–79. See also the more detailed account in Dalton, *Descriptive Ethnology of Bengal*, 170–71.

[147] The government sent the magistrate of the Tributary States, A. J. Colvin, to Tamar to investigate. In his report Colvin expressed thoughts about handling these border populations, which within fifteen years would be generally accepted in Calcutta. Better, he said, it would have been not to extend to this tract the Bengal regulations, which were 'not well adapted to the character of the greater portion of the inhabitants'. Colvin asked for 'the permanent residence of a joint magistrate with the special powers of register (registrar), in the centre of the district. [He] should invariably make a tour through the district for the purpose of receiving complaints and redressing grievances both civil & criminal on the spot . . . In all such cases he should be guided by the plain dictates of equity alone.'

But Colvin knew that an increased military commitment was not on the strategic agenda. His alternative proposal was to put Tamar on the same footing as the Orissa Tributary States. See A. J. Colvin to W. B. Bayley, Chief Secretary to Government, 10 April 1821 (London: OIOC), BC 21,872. Pergunnah in the original. Both proposals got no follow-up.

[148] Wilkinson to Mangles, 22 August 1836 (London: OIOC), BC 66,546.

[149] Adams to Roughsedge, 29 August 1818, cited in Wilkinson to Macsween, 29 October 1834 (London: OIOC), BC 66,544.

[150] Roughsedge to Metcalfe, 16 February 1820 (London: OIOC), BC 21,438. Wakeel Narrain Sing in the original.

[151] Roughsedge to ?, 27 September 1819 (London: OIOC), BC, vol. 787. Rajah in the original.

[152] Roughsedge to Metcalfe, 16 February 1820 (London: OIOC), BC 21,438.

[153] In November, Roughsedge sent some troops, but now it appeared that the whole of Tamar was in insurrection against Govind Shah. See Virottam, *The Nagabanshis and the Cheros*, 182–85. Roughsedge's military reinforcements arrived in December and he himself set out for Tamar.

[154] 'Translation of a letter from Rajah Gunsham Sing, Zemindar of Singboom', attached to: Roughsedge to Metcalfe, 16 February 1820 (London: OIOC), BC 21,438.

[155] Many files had been lost even early in the nineteenth century. In 1834, the 'greatest number of the Native Records whilst

Major Roughsedge was Agent, were not in the Office'. See Wilkinson to Macsween, 29 October 1834 (London: OIOC), BC 66,544.

[156] Roughsedge to Metcalfe, 9 May 1820 (London: OIOC), BC 21,438.

[157] Roughsedge to Metcalfe, 3 February 1820 (London: OIOC), BC 21,438. Lurkas in the original. There was a slightly different version of Ghanshyam's demands, in which Ghanshyam indicated that he wanted more than just authority and an idol from the other Singh states. He had demanded direct control over certain areas, 'of which he had been forcibly deprived' by Saraikela and Kharsawan. As far as the Hos were concerned, he wanted more than checks on their raids. He had asked Roughsedge to help him in 'reducing to subjection the Lurka Coles, who were in possession of by far the greatest portion of his country'. See Wilkinson to Mangles, 22 August 1836 (London: OIOC), BC 66,546. This letter was written by Wilkinson to establish his case for taking the Ho lands under East India Company rule.

[158] Resume of Major Roughsedge's Letter of 2 February 1820, in Wilkinson to Swinton, 12 January 1833 (London: OIOC), BC 58,904. Tribute for Peshkush in the original.
See also: 'Translation of a Kuboolyut taken from Rajah Ghunsham Sing Deo of Porahat, in Singbhoom, dated 1 February 1820', in C. V. Aitchison, *A Collection of Treaties, Engagements, and Sanads Relating to India and Neighbouring Countries: Containing the Treaties, etc., Relating to the Bengal Presidency, Assam, Burma and the Eastern Archipelago*, vol. 1, Revised and continued Up to the present time by the Authority of the Foreign Department (Calcutta: Office of the Superintendent of Government Printing, India, 1892), 144.

[159] 'Translation of the Pottah given to Rajah Ghunsham Sing Deo of Porahat, in Singbhoom, dated 1st February 1820', in Aitchison, *A Collection of Treaties,* 145.

[160] Wilkinson to Mangles, 22 August 1836 (London: OIOC), BC 66,546. Here the wording was not entirely clear. One could also read this passage in such a way that the trip of Roughsedge and the raja of Porahat took place in March.

[161] Jagdish Chandra Jha, 'British Contact with Singhbhum, 1821–1831', *JBRS* 47 (1961): 125.

[162] Roughsedge to Metcalfe, 9 May 1820 (London: OIOC), BC 21,438. Bramin, Rajpoot, Mussulman, Lurka Cole, Baminghatee, Seraikela, 20 miles in the original.

[163] Roughsedge to Metcalfe, 21 March 1820, (London: OIOC), BC 21,438. This is from Fr Mathew's copy in the Tribal Research and Training Centre, Guira. He mistakenly gave 21 May as the date. By that time, Roughsedge was already in Sambalpur. Rajah, zemindars, Singboom in the original. See also O'Malley, *Singhbhum*, 33.

[164] For Singrai Tiu being present at that occasion, there is an interpolation by Roughsedge in the 'Narrative of Durrum Das Gossein in the service of the Zemindar of Singboom written down on this 24 of February 1821', appendix to Roughsedge to Swinton, 25 February 1821 (London: OIOC), BC 21,438. For the name of the village see Roughsedge to Captain Frobisher, 21 April 1821 (London: OIOC), BC 21,439.

[165] Roughsedge to Metcalfe, 9 May 1820 (London: OIOC), BC 21,438.

[166] Roughsedge to Metcalfe, 9 May 1820 (London: OIOC), BC 21,438. Rajah, Singboom in the original.

[167] Roughsedge to Metcalfe, 9 May 1820 (London: OIOC), BC 21,438. Rajah, Coles in the original.

[168] 'Narrative of Durrum Das Gossein in the service of the Zemindar of Singboom written down on this 24 of February 1821', in Roughsedge to Swinton, 25 February 1821 (London: OIOC), BC 21,438.

[169] Through the good offices of the chief of Saraikela, Rudan was arrested in July 1820. See Virottam, *The Nagabanshis and the Cheros*, 185; Jha, *The Tribal Revolt of Chotanagpur*, 58–59.

[170] Roughsedge to Metcalfe, 9 May 1820 (London: OIOC), BC 21,438.

[171] Roughsedge to Metcalfe, 20 June 1820 (London: OIOC), BC 21,438.

Chapter 2: Attack and Counterattack

[1] Roughsedge mentioned 22 March. See Roughsedge to Metcalfe, 9 May 1820 (London: OIOC), BC 21,438. Both C. P. Singh and M. Sahu, however, mentioned 18 March as the day Roughsedge entered the Kolhan. Sahu quoted Roughsedge to Nicol, 31 March 1820 in the Bihar State Archives. See Sahu, *The Kolhan Under British Rule*, 21, 28. C. P. Singh quoted the same letter in the National Archives of India. See C. P. Singh, *The Ho Tribe of Singhbhum*, 67, 88.

[2] Roughsedge to Metcalfe, 9 May 1820 (London: OIOC), BC 21,438. This observation is a strong illustration of the adage 'beauty is in the eyes of the beholder'. Or did the country change considerably in the next few decades? See this description by William Durbar of what he saw during the 1837 campaign: 'Advancing from Kirsawa, you cross the Sunjay river, always a beautiful stream, . . . beyond is the Colehan. The change in appearance of the land is now very striking: scanty patches of cultivation here and there meet the eye—all else is barren rocky waste, or a bushy jungle'. See William Dunbar, 'Some Observations on the Manners, Customs and Religious Opinions of the Lurka Coles', *JRASGBI* 1st ser., 18 (1861): 376.

[3] Roughsedge to Metcalfe, 20 June 1820 (London: OIOC), BC 21,438.

[4] Roughsedge to Metcalfe, 9 May 1820 (London: OIOC), BC 21,438. Preceeding, Coles, Raja Bassa, Goomha, Pergunnah in the original.

⁵ Kumar, *History and Administration of Tribal Chotanagpur*, 105.
⁶ Roughsedge to Metcalfe, 9 May 1820 (London: OIOC), BC 21,438. Adjauden, rajah in the original.
⁷ Roughsedge to James Nicol, Adjutant General, 31 March 1820 (London: OIOC), BC 21,438.
⁸ Roughsedge to Metcalfe, 9 May 1820 (London: OIOC); Home Miscellaneous, vol. 724, 1818–1830: Papers Referring to Sarguja, Sambalpur and Singhbum from 26 May 1818 to 12 May 1830.
⁹ Roughsedge to Metcalfe, 9 May 1820 (London: OIOC), BC 21,438. 'Raccutts' in Fr. Mathew Areemparampil's copy in the Tribal Research and Training Centre, Guira.
¹⁰ Roughsedge to Metcalfe, 9 May 1820 (London: OIOC), BC 21,438.
¹¹ That started the actual hostilities of the First Kolhan Campaign. Kumar's contention that this started a see-saw tribal warfare that lasted till 1837 is not correct. See Kumar, *History and Administration of Tribal Chotanagpur*, 105.
¹² 'Extract from a Private Letter', *AJMR* 10 (July-December 1820): 609. C. P. Singh misrepresented this episode, suggesting that after the attack Maillard 'wantonly killed an innocent grass-cutter'. See C. P. Singh, *The Ho Tribe of Singhbhum*, 68. Of course, it was the Hos that ('wantonly' if you want) killed a grass-cutter ('innocent' if you want) of the Ramgarh Battalion. See also: Sahu, *The Kolhan Under British Rule*, 23–24.
¹³ Roughsedge to James Nicol, Adjutant General, 31 March (London: OIOC), BC 21,438.
On John Peter Maillard, see Hodson, *List of the Officers of the Bengal Army*, vol. 4 (London: Phillimore, 1946), 573. Dalton called the officer Maitland. See Dalton, *Descriptive Ethnology of Bengal*, 181. So did, following him, O'Malley in *Singhbhum*, 33-34.
¹⁴ Roughsedge to James Nicol, Adjutant General, 31 March (London: OIOC), BC 21,438.
¹⁵ 'Extract from a Private Letter', 609. Lurkas, sewars in the original.
See also The Editor of the Royal Military Calendar, 'The Late Major Edward Roughsedge', *The East India Military Calendar: Containing the Services of General and Field Officers of the Indian Army* 3 (London: Kingsbury, Parbury, and Allen, 1826): 229.
¹⁶ Roughsedge to James Nicol, Adjutant General, 31 March (London: OIOC), BC 21,438. Lurkas, Battle axe in the original.
¹⁷ 'Extract from a Private Letter', 609. Lurkas in the original. See also The Editor of the Royal Military Calendar, 'The Late Major Edward Roughsedge', *The East India Military Calendar: Containing the Services of General and Field Officers of the Indian Army* 3 (London: Kingsbury, Parbury, and Allen, 1826): 229.
¹⁸ Roughsedge to Nicol, 31 March 1820 (London: OIOC), BC 21,438. Lurkas, battle axe in the original..
¹⁹ Roughsedge to Metcalfe, 9 May 1820 (London: OIOC), BC 21,438. Roughsedge greatly appreciated this, and also the personal bravery of Ajambar, his 'great manliness and bravery he showed in perilous circumstances while his uncle and some others were wounded'. See Roughsedge to Ajambar Sing, 13 April 1820, in C. L. Philip, 'Confidential History of Seraikella State: Completed to 1927 by C. L. Philip', typescript, (Chaibasa, Tribal Research and Training Centre, 1927), 6.
²⁰ Roughsedge to James Nicol, Adjutant General, 31 March 1820 (London: OIOC), BC 21,438. 'intentions' in Mathew Areeparampil's copy in the Tribal Research and Training Centre, Guira.
²¹ Roughsedge to James Nicol, Adjutant General, 31 March 1820 (London: OIOC), BC 21,438. Duphayee in the original.
²² Roughsedge to James Nicol, Adjutant General, 31 March 1820 (London: OIOC), BC 21,438. Gootea Suhar in the original.
²³ Roughsedge to James Nicol, Adjutant General, 31 March 1820 (London: OIOC), BC 21,438.
²⁴ 'Extract from a Private Letter', 609. Lurkas in the original.
²⁵ Roughsedge to James Nicol, Adjutant General, 31 March 1820 (London: OIOC), BC 21,438. Lurkas in the original. See 'Extract from a Private Letter', 609.
There is no evidence for Kumar's contention that women were raped at that occasion. See Kumar, *History and Administration of Tribal Chotanagpur*, 107.
²⁶ 'Short Account of the Lurkacoles', *John Bull in the East*, repr., *AJMR* 13, (January–June 1822): 136–37. Lurkacole in the original.
I am grateful to Fr. Mathew Areeparampil of the Tribal Research and Training Centre, then in Lupungutu near Chaibasa, who drew my attention to this source.
²⁷ The information about the feet is from Mathew Areeparampil, *Struggle for Swaraj: A History of Adivasi Movements in Jharkhand from the Earliest Times to the Present Day* (Lupungutu: Tribal Research and Training Centre (TRTC), 2002), 123–24. Fr. Mathew stated that the range of the long distance bow would be one mile, but I prefer the insight of the officer, who mentioned 200 yards.
²⁸ 'Short Account of the Lurkacoles', 137. Cropt in the original.
²⁹ Roughsedge to James Nicol, Adjutant General, 31 March 1820 (London: OIOC), BC 21,438.
³⁰ 'Brown Bess', *WP*, accessed 13 July 2011.
³¹ A. H. Amin, 'Technical and Tactical Superiority of the Enfield Rifle over the Brown Bess', in review of *The Sepoy Rebellion of 1857–59, An analysis*, in *Defence Journal*, May (2001), accessed 13 July 2011, http://www.defencejournal.com/2001/may/sepoy.htm.
³² 'Brown Bess'

33 Singh, *Indian Army Under the East India Company*, 144.
34 'Short Account of the Lurkacoles', 136–37.
35 Roughsedge to Nicol, 31 March 1820 (London: OIOC), BC 21,438.
36 They described them to Dalton as 'dreadfully severe'. See Dalton, 'The "Kols" of Chota Nagpore', 166.
37 'Extract from a Private Letter', 609. Lurkas in the original.
38 Roughsedge to Metcalfe, 9 May 1820 (London: OIOC), BC 21,439.
39 Roughsedge to James Nicol, Adjutant General, 31 March 1820 (London: OIOC), BC 21,438. Lurkas in the original. See also 'Extract from a Private Letter', 609.
40 Roughsedge to Metcalfe, 9 May 1820 (London: OIOC), BC 21,439.
In the flush of victory, Roughsedge called it 'their humble submission'. See Roughsedge to James Nicol, Adjutant General, 31 March 1820 (London: OIOC), BC 21,438.
41 Spear, *The Nabobs*, 85–86.
42 Roughsedge to Metcalfe, 9 May 1820 (London: OIOC), BC 21,439. Coles, Rajah in the orginal.
43 Roughsedge to Metcalfe, 9 May 1820 (London: OIOC), BC 21,439.
44 Roughsedge to Metcalfe, 9 May 1820 (London: OIOC), BC 21,439.
45 The name Mata (Matta in the original) appears in Roughsedge to Swinton, 7 August 1821 (London: OIOC), BC 21,439.
46 Maillard to Roughsedge, 9 April 1820 (London: OIOC), BC 21,438. Burndea, Coles, Coorehs, 150 yards, Pady, Nullah, Sowars, Besai of Gynt Gur, Sepoyhees, three miles, Sowars, sepoyhees, Sepoyhee, Colesin the original. Dalton added the detail that Maillard (he called him Maitland) himself 'narrowly escaped death in a personal conflict with a Larka'. See Dalton, *Descriptive Ethnology of Bengal*, 181.
47 Roughsedge to Metcalfe, 9 May 1820 (London: OIOC), BC 21,439.
48 Roughsedge to Metcalfe, 9 May 1820 (London: OIOC), BC 21,439.
49 Deliberately vague date, as Roughsedge is not specific here. I go by the date of Maillard's report to Roughsedge, assuming that both wanted to clear the paperwork before they set off. See Maillard to Roughsedge, 9 April 1820 (London: OIOC), BC 21,438.
50 Roughsedge to Metcalfe, 9 May 1820 (London: OIOC), BC 21,438. Coles in the original.
51 Roughsedge to Metcalfe, 9 May 1820 (London: OIOC), BC 21,438.
52 And not in Jaintgarh as Sahu thought. See Sahu, *The Kolhan Under British Rule*, 27.
53 Roughsedge to Metcalfe, 20 June 1820 (London: OIOC), BC 21,438. Lurkas in the original.
54 Roughsedge to Metcalfe, 20 June 1820 (London: OIOC), BC 21,438.
55 Roughsedge to Metcalfe, 20 June 1820 (London: OIOC), BC 21,438. Dawk in the original.
56 Metcalfe to Roughsedge, 3 June 1820 (London: OIOC), BC 21,438.
57 Metcalfe to Roughsedge, 3 June 1820 (London: OIOC), BC 21,438. Lurka Coles in the original.
58 Roughsedge to Metcalfe, 20 June 1820 (London: OIOC), BC 21,438. Rajah of Singboom, Lurkas in the original.
59 Metcalfe to Roughsedge, 15 July 1820 (London: OIOC), BC 21,438.
60 Metcalfe to Roughsedge, 3 June 1820 (London: OIOC), BC 21,438. Lurka Coles in the original.
61 Roughsedge to Metcalfe, 20 June 1820 (London: OIOC), BC 21,438.
62 Roughsedge to Metcalfe, 20 June 1820 (London: OIOC), BC 21,438. Lurkas, Rajah's in the original. Divisions for Talooks in the original.
63 Wilkinson to Swinton, 12 January 1833 (London: OIOC), BC 58,904. Previously, Bahuran Singh was in Maratha service. See A. J. Colvin to W. B. Bayley, 9 March 1821 (London: OIOC), BC 21,873.
64 Kumar, *History and Administration of Tribal Chotanagpur*, 114.
65 Note in margin to 'Translation of an Urzee from Ruttun Sing Jemedar of a Company of Burkundauzes employed in Singboom dated the 13th of May and received the 23rd of July 1821', in Roughsedge to Swinton, 17 February 1821 (London: OIOC), BC 21,438.
66 Roughsedge to Swinton, 7 August 1821 (London: OIOC), BC 21,439.
67 Roughsedge to Swinton, 7 August 1821 (London: OIOC), BC 21,439. Ghassee Sing, Goomla in the original.
68 Roughsedge to Swinton, 7 August 1821 (London: OIOC), BC 21,439. Mooctar in the orginal.
'Mooktear, s. Properly Hind. from Ar. mukhtar, chosen, but corruptly mukhtyar. An authorised agent; an attorney.' See Yule and Burnell, *Hobson-Jobson*, 589.
69 Roughsedge to Swinton, 7 August 1821 (London: OIOC), BC 21,439. Goomla in the original.
70 Roughsedge to Swinton, 7 August 1821 (London: OIOC), BC 21,439. Goomla, Rajah in the original.
71 Malgoozaree, Goomla, Rajah, Gumla in the original.
'Mal-guz.ari, corruptly, Malgoozarry, H . . . revenue assessment; the payment of revenue: also the person or land subject to such payment. See Wilson, *A Glossary*, 323.
72 'Ghassee Singh's defense, 16th May 1821', in Roughsedge to Swinton, 7 August 1821 (London: OIOC), BC 21,439. Pergunnah in the original.

73 Roughsedge to Swinton, 7 August 1821 (London: OIOC), BC 21,439.
74 Five hundred *seers* would be 477 kg. See Risley, *Singbhum District*), 85; H. H. Wilson, *A Glossary*, 474. This would give an idea, but the *seer* was fluctuating widely.
75 'Ghassee Singh's defense, 16th May 1821', appendix to Roughsedge to Swinton, 7 August 1821 (London: OIOC), BC 21,439. Ooreed, Nuzzer in the original. The text gives '1 cundee'. In a note, a 'cundee' or *khandi* is given as about 30 *seers*. That would make it about 28 kg. Normally, a *khandi* would be 20 *seers*, a little less than 19 kg.
76 'Translation of an arzee from Rukun (Ratan) Sing Jemedar of a Company of Burkundazess in Singhbhum dated the 13th of May and received the 13th of July 1821', appendix to Roughsedge to Swinton, 17 February 1821 (London: OIOC), Bengal Political Consultations, 10 March 1821.
77 'Translation of an arzee from Rukun (Ruttun) Sing Jemedar of a Company of Burkundazess in Singhbhum dated the 13th of May and received the 13th of July 1821', appendix to Roughsedge to Swinton, 17 February 1821 (London: OIOC), Bengal Political Consultations, 10 March 1821.
78 Kumar, *History and Administration of Tribal Chotanagpur*, 114.
79 'Translation of a letter from Chytan Sing Tacoor, 5th February 1821', added to A. J. Colvin to W. B. Bayley, 8 February 1821 (London: OIOC), BC 21,873.
80 'Information given by the Coles of Seemea and Haroha, 27th April 1821'; 'Examination of Singrai the faithful Lurka Sirdar of Adjandea', appendices to Roughsedge to Swinton 7 August 1821 (London: OIOC), BC 21,439.
J. C. Jha mistook her for the daughter of Ghasi Singh who, in his turn, was made into 'the village headman'. See Jha, 'Early British Contacts with Singhbhum', 151.
81 Roughsedge to Swinton, 7 August 1821 (London: OIOC), BC 21,439.
82 'Information given by the Coles of Seemea and Haroha, 27th April 1821'; 'Examination of Singrai the faithful Lurka Sirdar of Adjandea'; 'Examination of Coondoo Pater a Sirdar of Cooreea, 13 May 1821'; appendices to Roughsedge to Swinton 7 August 1821 (London: OIOC), BC 21,439. Soldiers for 'Burkundazes' in the original.
83 'Examination of Coondoo Pater a Sirdar of Cooreea, 13 May 1821', appendix to Roughsedge to Swinton 7 August 1821 (London: OIOC), BC 21,439.
84 The interpreters, spreading more alarm, mentioned that the Hos under Mata of Balandia were at a distance of about 5 km and intended to attack at night, a message Bahuran did not believe. When the attack started he blamed Ghasi Singh for it. See 'Translation of an arzee from Rukun (Ratan) Sing Jemedar of a Company of Burkundazess in Singhbhum dated the 13th of May and received the 13th of July 1821', appendix to Roughsedge to Swinton, 17 February 1821 (London: OIOC), Bengal Political Consultations, 10 March 1821.
85 'Narrative of Durrum Das Gossein in the service of the Zemindar of Singboom written down on this 24th of February 1821', appendix to Roughsedge to Swinton, 25 February 1821 (London: OIOC), BC 21,438. Coles in the original. Murali Sahu gave 1,500 men. See Sahu, *The Kolhan Under British Rule*, 32. So did P. Kumar. See Kumar, *History and Administration of Tribal Chotanagpur*, 114. The date is arrived at by counting back from the sack of Chainpur on 6 February 1821. Subedar was at the time the highest rank for an Indian in the Bengal Army, taken as just below the British commissioned officers.
86 'Examination of Coondo Pater a Sirdar of Cooreea, 13 May 1821', appendix to Roughsedge to Swinton, 7 August 1821 (London: OIOC), BC 21,439.
87 C. P. Singh, *The Ho Tribe of Singhbhum*, 75.
88 Kumar, *History and Administration of Tribal Chotanagpur*, 114.
89 'Narrative of Durrum Das Gossein in the service of the Zemindar of Singboom written down on this 24th of February 1821', appendix to Roughsedge to Swinton, 25 February 1821 (London: OIOC), BC 21,438.
90 'Narrative of Durrum Das Gossein in the service of the Zemindar of Singboom written down on this 24th of February 1821', appendix to Roughsedge to Swinton, 25 February 1821 (London: OIOC), BC 21,438. Rajah in the original. See also Roughsedge to Richards, 5 May 1821 (London: OIOC), BC 21,439.
91 'Translation of a petition from Bikram Sing zumeendar of Singbhoom dated 22 Mugh 1227 B.S.', appendix to Colvin to Bayley, 8 February 1821 (London: OIOC), BC 21,873. Sowars in the original.
92 Kumar, *History and Administration of Tribal Chotanagpur*, 115; Sahu, *The Kolhan Under British Rule*, 33.
93 Mahto is the name of a Hindu caste. Another name of the village was Cheroha Niyea.
94 'Second Examination of Bajee Moond, 28 April 1821', appendix to Roughsedge to Swinton, 7 August 1821 (London: OIOC), BC 21,439. The translator called it a puja.
95 C. P. Singh, *The Ho Tribe of Singhbhum*, 76.
96 K. K. Basu gave the 6th. See K. K. Basu, 'Larka Kols of Singhbhum', *JBRS* 43 (1957): 78. This does not tally with Chaitan Singh's letter of 5 February 1821. See 'Translation of a letter from Chytan Sing Tacoor dated the 27th of May Bungala or 5th February and received 16th February 1821', appendix to Roughsedge to Swinton, 17 February 1821 (London: OIOC), BC 21,438). I presume a copyist's error and take Chaitan's letter to have been written on 15 February 1821.
97 Kumar, *History and Administration of Tribal Chotanagpur*, 115–16.
98 Basu, 'Larka Kols of Singhbhum', 78. P. Kumar gave their losses as follows: the Police colours; three loads of brass pots,

seven *sawars* (swords), gold to the value of Rs.500, silver to the value of Rs. 600, and in cash Rs. 930. See Kumar, *History and Administration of Tribal Chotanagpur*, 116.

[99] 'Translation of an arzee from Rukun (Ratan) Sing Jemedar of a Company of Burkundazees in Singboom dated the 13th of May and received the 13th of July 1821', appendix to Roughsedge to Mr Secretary Swinton, 17 February 1821 (London: OIOC), BC 21,438.

[100] 'Translation of a letter from Chytan Sing Tacoor dated the 27th of May Bungala or 5th February and received 16th February 1821', appendix to Roughsedge to Mr Secretary Swinton, 17 February 1821 (London: OIOC), BC 21,438. Lurkas, Zemindar in the original.

[101] 'Translation of a letter from Rajah Gansham Sing dated 25th of May Insillee or 11th of February and received the 21st of February 1821', appendix to Roughsedge to Swinton, 25 February 1821 (London: OIOC), BC 21,438. Lurkas, Poorahaut in the original.

[102] 'Translation of a letter from Rajah Gansham Sing dated 25th of May Insillee or 11th of February and received the 21st of February 1821', appendix to Roughsedge to Swinton, 25 February 1821 (London: OIOC), BC 21,438. Durrum Dass Gossain, Bohorum Sing in the original.

[103] Roughsedge to Swinton, 17 February 1821 (London: OIOC), BC 21,438.

[104] Roughsedge to Swinton, 7 August 1821 (London: OIOC), BC 21,439.

[105] 'Narrative Of Durrum Das Gosein in the service of the Zemindar of Singboom written down on this 24th of February 1821', appendix to Roughsedge to Swinton, 25 February 1821 (London: OIOC), BC 21,438. Although he generally was convincing to Roughsedge, on 24 February Dharam Singh went too far when he accused Bikram Singh of Saraikela of instigating the attack of the Hos on Chainpur. See Roughsedge to Richards, 3 April 1821 (London: OIOC), Bengal Political Consultations, 24 April 1821.

[106] Wilkinson to Mangles, 22 August 1836 (London: OIOC), BC 66,546.

[107] 'Narrative Of Durrum Das Gossein in the service of the Zemindar of Singboom written down on this 24th of February 1821', appendix to Roughsedge to Swinton, 25 February 1821 (London: OIOC), BC 21,438. Burkundauzees, Goomla in the original.

[108] 'Translation of a letter from The Dawk Writer at Bammunghattee in Mohurbung to Major Roughsedge dated 12th February 1821', Appendix to Roughsedge to Swinton, 17 February 1821 (London: OIOC), BC 21,438.

[109] Roughsedge to Swinton, 17 February 1821 (London: OIOC), BC 21,438.

[110] Roughsedge to Switon, 1 March 1821 (London: OIOC), BC 21,438.

[111] Roughsedge to Swinton, 17 February 1821 (London: OIOC), BC 21,438.

[112] Roughsedge to Swinton 6 March 1821, quoted in Kumar, *History and Administration of Tribal Chotanagpur*, 119–20.

[113] Roughsedge to Swinton, 17 February 1821 (London: OIOC), BC 21,438.

[114] Sahu, *The Kolhan Under British Rule*, 35.

[115] Kumar, *History and Administration of Tribal Chotanagpur*, 21, 121–22, 125.

[116] Kunta 'had sent an arrow from Village to Village through the Pergunnahs of Tamar, Boondoo, Barinda, and Patcoom with a message purporting that those who were inclined to side with him should forward it to the next Village, but that those who on the contrary intended to oppose him, should break the arrow in which case they might be expected to be shortly attacked by him'. However, the last piece of information was that Kunta wanted these people to stay and plunder Tamar. See A. J. Colvin to W. B. Bayley, 9 March 1821 (London: OIOC), BC 21,873. This contradicted the earlier information about Singhbhum being a target of the raids. Moreover, the importance of this information was belittled, 'only one [person in Tamar having] heard anything about the arrow'. See Virottam, *The Nagabanshis and the Cheros*, 186. Still, it again drew attention to the importance of having states strong enough to stop the spread of disturbances. Roughsedge wrote back that the government had decided to effectively reduce the Kols of Singhbhum. Later that year, Kunta was arrested in Dhalbhum. He was convicted and died in prison. See Virottam, *The Nagabanshis and the Cheros*, 185, 187.

[117] Nicol to Swinton, 17 March 1821 (London: OIOC), BC 21,873. Sirkars in the original.

[118] Nicol to Richards, 22 March 1821 (London: OIOC), BC 21,438.

[119] Nicol to Swinton, 17 March 1821 (London: OIOC), BC 21,873.

[120] Board to Government, 30 October 1812, quoted in Jha, *The Tribal Revolt of Chotanagpur*, 16.

Chapter 3: The Mouth of a Gun

[1] William Richards, the later Sir William, was four years junior to Roughsedge and had since his return—'arrival' in the *List of Officers*—to India in 1794 set upon a splendid military career. He married twice, the first time to a 'natural dau[ghter] of Andrew Wilson Hearsay . . . by an Indian lady'. The second time in Agra in 1830, to Henrietta Herd 'aged 18, spinster' and 'a native lady of the Jat tribe'. After the First Kolhan Campaign, we find (now) Colonel William Richards fighting in the First Burmese War. He expelled the Burmese from Assam, and occupied Rangpur and Sylhet before marching into Burma proper

and storming the Arakan Heights in March 1825. He left Burma due to ill health, became Commander of the Agra Fort in 1826, and was Commissioner and Agent on the Agra and Mathura Frontier from 1828—1833. In 1833, he joined the general Staff in Nainital and commanded the Dinapore Division. He retired in 1838 and died in 1861, having 'resided continuously in India for 67 years'. See Hodson, *List of the Officers of the Bengal Army,* vol. 3, 641–42. Sir William was related to more than thirty officers of the Bengal Army.

[2] Roughsedge to Richards, 3 April 1821 (London: OIOC) Bengal Political Consultations, 24 April 1821.

[3] Roughsedge to Swinton, 14 April 1821 (London: OIOC), Bengal Political Consultations, 12 May 1821.

[4] Roughsedge to Swinton, 14 April 1821; Swinton to Roughsedge, 12 May 1821 (London: OIOC), BC 21,438. Hos for Lurkas in the original.

The punishment of blowing from a gun dated from Mughal times. See 'Blowing from a gun, The Mughal tradition', *WP*, accessed 13 September 2015, https://en.wikipedia.org/wiki/Blowing_from_a_gun#The_Mughal_tradition.

Sixty years before Roughsedge it was introduced by the Board, as the previous method of capital punishment by whipping to death, 'does not sufficiently contribute to deterring criminals, as the example is not sufficiently public'. See Proceedings, November 17, 1760, in James Long, *Selections from Unpublished Records of Government for the years 1748 to 1767 Inclusive: Relating Mainly to the Social Condition of Bengal, With a Map of Calcutta in 1784* (Calcutta, Office of the Superintendent of Government Printing, 1869; reprint with a Foreword, Notes and a Bio-Bibliographical Sketch of J. Long, ed. Mahadevaprasad Saha (Calcutta: Firma K. L. Mukhopadhayay, 1973), letter 479. In 1764 then, Major Munro blew the leaders of a sepoy uprising in Patna from the guns. See Karl Marx, *Notes on Indian History (664–1858),* [after 1870], (Moscow: Progress, 1986), 69.

As the answer of the governor general to Roughsedge showed, by 1818, it was not government policy to blow insurgents from the mouth of a gun, as K. K. Basu seemed to imply. See K. K. Basu, 'Larka Kols of Singhbhum', *JBRS* 43 (1957): 78. In the 1990s, this misjudgement found its way to Corbridge. See Stuart Edward Corbridge, 'Ousting Singbonga: The Struggle for India's Jharkhand', in *Dalit Movements and the Meanings of Labour in India,* ed. Peter Robb (Oxford: Oxford University Press, 1999), 128.

[5] Roughsedge to Swinton, 14 April 1821 (London: OIOC), BC 21,438.

[6] Roughsedge to Swinton, 14 April 1821 (London: OIOC), BC 21,438. Rajah, Zameendar, Singboom, Lurkas, Bramin, Hindoos, Singboom, Coles, Bangher, Chota Nagpore in the original.

[7] Roughsedge to Swinton, 14 April 1821 (London: OIOC), BC 21,438.

[8] Roughsedge, Pergunnahs of Singbhoom, compiled from information by Gunshyam Sing and from other sources, 15 April 1820 (London: OIOC), BC 21,439. See also the table, wrongly sourced to a letter from Ghanshyam to Roughsedge, in Das Gupta, *Adivasis and the Raj,* 85–88.

[9] W. R. Gilbert to Swinton, 14 June 1823 (London: OIOC), Bengal Political Consultations, 27 June 1823. Kolas, Rajah in the original.

[10] Roughsedge to Richards, 3 April 1821 (London: OIOC), Bengal Political Consultations, 24 April 1821.

[11] Roughsedge to Swinton, 14 April 1821 (London: OIOC), Bengal Political Consultations, 12 May 1821.

[12] 'Extract of a Letter from an Officer, dated Camp Sumbhulpoor, July 24th, 1821', in 'Monthly Register, Foreign Intelligence', *The Scots' Magazine and Edinburgh Miscellany,* n.s., 89, part 1 (1822): 123. 600 miles in the original. Temperatures in Fahrenheit given as 110, 112, 122 and 'between 150 and 160' in the original.

[13] 'Extract of a Letter from an Officer', *The Scots' Magazine and Edinburgh Miscellany,* 123. See also 'Extract of a Letter from an Officer, dated Camp Sumbhulpoor, July 24th, 1821' in *The Gentleman's Magazine: and Historical Chronicle* 92, part 1 (January–June 1822): 76–77.

[14] Roughsedge to Captain Frobisher, 21 April 1821 (London: OIOC). BC 21,439. Refractory Villages in the orginal.

[15] Roughsedge to Richards, 3 April 1821 (London: OIOC), Bengal Political Consultations, 24 April 1821.

[16] Maillard to Roughsedge, 9 April 1820 (London: OIOC), BC 21,438.

[17] 'Coorah is a depot in which the Coles collect their families, grain & property'. See Richards to Nichol, 26 April 1821, London: OIOC), BC 21,439. The word cannot be found in Deeney's Dictionary. 'Phoot' is not a Ho word; the aspirated p ('ph') is a foreign import. Deeney gives only *phutbol* (football). See John Deeney, *Ho-English Dictionary* (Chaibasa: Xavier Ho Publications, 1978), 266.

[18] 'Short Account of the Lurkacoles', 137.

The officer in Sambalpur thought the number was 5,000. 'Extract of a Letter from an Officer', *The Scots' Magazine and Edinburgh Miscellany,* 123.

[19] C. P. Singh, *The Ho Tribe of Singhbhum,* 79.

[20] V. C. P. Hodson, *Historical Records of the Governor-Generals's Body Guard* (London: W. Thacker / Calcutta: Thacker, Spink, 1910), 87.

[21] Hodson, *Historical Records of the Governor-Generals's Body Guard,* 89. His son, 'studying medicine under his father, was taken on as a subordinate Medical officer in the Body Guard'. See Hodson, *Historical Records of the Governor-Generals's Body Guard,* 89.

[22] Richards to Nicol, 17 April 1821 (London: OIOC), BC 21,439.

[23] 'Extract of a Letter from an Officer', *The Scots' Magazine and Edinburgh Miscellany*, 123.
[24] Roughsedge to Richards, 22 April 1821 (London: OIOC), BC 21,439. Lurkas, Adjondea, Raja Bassa in the original.
[25] Thomas Frobisher to Richards, 23 April 1821 (London: OIOC), BC 21,439. Coothpan, Adjoundea, Lurkas, Cootpan, two coss, one coss, Coothpan, forty or fifty yards, 'some thousand maunds' in the original. One *maund* varied much according to the location. The *maund*'s usual weight in Bengal was 37.255 kilogrammes. In 1838, it would be set slightly higher at 82.28 lbs. av., that is, approximately 37.32 kilogrammes. See Yule and Burnell, *Hobson-Jobson*, 563–65. See also 'Maund', *WP*, accessed 7 December 2014.
[26] Roughsedge to Richards, 22 April 1821 (London: OIOC), BC 21,439. Lurkas in the original. See also Roughsedge to Swinton, 30 April 1821 (London: OIOC), BC 21,439.
[27] Richards to Nicol, 25 April 1821 (London: OIOC), BC 21,439.
[28] A. Macleod to Richards, 17 April 1821 (London: OIOC), BC 21,439.
[29] Roughsedge to Swinton, 30 April 1821 (London: OIOC), BC 21,439. Mala in the original.
[30] C. P. Singh, *The Ho Tribe of Singhbhum*, 81.
[31] Roughsedge to Swinton, 30 April 1821; Roughsedge to Richards, 5 May 1821 (London: OIOC), BC 21,439.
[32] 'Extract of a Letter from an Officer', *The Scots' Magazine and Edinburgh Miscellany*, 123.
[33] 'Extract of a Letter from an Officer', *The Scots' Magazine and Edinburgh Miscellany*, 123.
[34] Roughsedge to Swinton, 30 April 1821 (London: OIOC), BC 21,439.
[35] Swinton to Roughsedge, 12 May 1821 (London: OIOC), BC 21,439.
[36] Richards to Nichol, 3 May 1821 (London: OIOC), BC 21,439. Coles in the original.
[37] Roughsedge to Swinton, 30 April 1821 (London: OIOC), BC 21,439. Mala in the original.
[38] Roughsedge to Richards, 5 May 1821 (London: OIOC), BC 21,439.
According to Virottam a similar insurrection took place in Chotanagpur. In early April 1821 'Kols of Chota Nagpur' started to loot, and attacked a body of troops. At the end of April the insurgents were driven to the hills. Then, on Roughsedge's recommendation hostilities were suspended. The 'rebel leaders' submitted in middle of May 1821. 'Thus peace was restored in Chota Nagpur which remained undisturbed till the outbreak of the Kol Insurrection in 1831'. If this were true, there were two identical problems and sequences of events in the same year, one with the Mundas of Chotanagpur, one with the Hos in Singhbhum. Virottam had the right quotations but placed them wrongly on the map! See Virottam, *The Nagabanshis and the Cheros*, 188, notes 80–84. The proof that his 'Kols of Chota Nagpur' actually were the Hos of Singhbhum is to be found in his note 82. The letter referred to here, Roughsedge to Richards, April 29, 1821, treated only Singhbhum.
[39] Wilkinson to Mangles, 22 August 1836 (London: OIOC), BC 66,546.
[40] Richards to Mc.Leod, 7 May 1821 (London: OIOC), BC 21,439.
[41] Kumar, *History and Administration of Tribal Chotanagpur*, 126.
[42] Roughsedge to Swinton, 8 May 1821, in 'Papers concerning Sarguja, Sambalpur and Singhbum, 1818–1830' (London: OIOC), H/724.
[43] Dalton, *Descriptive Ethnology of Bengal*, 182. This wish was repeated in 1826, after the agreed period of five years, as appears from the none-too-precise compilation of Dalton's information, appearing in the *People of India*. 'In 1826, in consequence of the intermediate good behaviour of the Lurkas, the restriction limiting the assessment to eight annas was renewed for a further period of five years. It was noticed at this time that the Lurkas evinced a perfect willingness to be guided and ruled by British officers, and the utmost repugnance to the authority arrogated over them by the Singbhoom chiefs.' See Edward Tuite Dalton, 'The Ho Tribe: Otherwise Called the Lurka or Fighting Coles of Singbhoom', text accompanying plates in *The People of India: A Series of Photographic Illustrations, with the Descriptive Letterpress, of the Races and Tribes of Hindustan, Originally Prepared under the Authority of the Government of India, and Reproduced by Order of the Secretary of State for India in Council*, edited by John Forbes Watson and John William Kaye, vol. 1 (London: India Museum, 1868), [no pagination].
In 1826, it added to the effect of two consecutive bad harvests caused by a drought. As Assistant Gilbert wrote, 'the former assessment could not without endangering disquiet and disturbances be augmented'. He kept it at eight annas per plough, to which all parties agreed. 'Even this trifle these poor people have been incapable of realizing in cash, and it was paid in Kind i.e. goat and rice.' See Gilbert to Swinton, 18 August 1826, 'Papers concerning Sarguja, Sambalpur and Singhbum 1818–1830', (London: OIOC), H/724.
Quite possibly, Dalton had access to more papers than just this letter, or he might have telescoped events of 1821 and 1826.
[44] Dalton, *Descriptive Ethnology of Bengal*, 182.
[45] Roughsedge to Swinton, 8 May 1821, in 'Papers concerning Sarguja, Sambalpur and Singhbum, 1818–1830' (London: OIOC), H/724. Rajah, baboos, Singbhoom, Lurkas, Narindum, Bamanghattee, Taeepeer, Lurka in the original. Sanjukta Das Gupta mistakenly extended this feeling of 'crying injustice' to the Hos as well. See Das Gupta, *Adivasis and the Raj*, 98.
[46] Richards to Mc.Leod, 7 May 1821 (London: OIOC), BC 21,439. Cole, Oreeah in the original.
[47] Kumar, *History and Administration of Tribal Chotanagpur*, 126.
[48] Roughsedge to Swinton, 8 May 1821, in 'Papers concerning Sarguja, Sambalpur and Singhbum, 1818–1830' (London:

OIOC), H/724. See also 'No LII, Agreement of the Lurka Coles in 1821', in Aitchison, *A Collection of Treaties*,148. A resume in Wilkinson to Swinton, 12 January 1833 (London: OIOC), BC 58,904.

[49] Roughsedge to Swinton, 8 May 1821, in 'Papers concerning Sarguja, Sambalpur and Singhbum, 1818–1830' (London: OIOC), H/724.

[50] 'Short Account of the Lurkacoles', 137. Cursive as in the orginal.

[51] Richards to Roughsedge, 6 May 1821 (London: OIOC), BC 21,439. The exact place of Kathkarinjia is not clear. There is a Kathkaranjia on the border of Sundargarh and Simdega districts, but it is rather far from the south of the Kolhan. There is a small town Karanjia in Mayurbhanj, some 5 km south-east of Khiching, and about 15 km south of Captain Jackson's road. A detachment close to the second place seems to make most sense.

[52] Richards to Mc.Leod, 7 May 1821 (London: OIOC), BC 21,439. Cole in the original.

[53] According to Jha, Roughsedge rewarded Raghunath Bisi 'for his services to the troops' with 'Chainpur jagir' on 8 May 1821. See Jha, 'Early British Contacts with Singhbhum', 156. Chainpur was under Ghasi Sing of Chakradarpur. Jha's statement is also surprising, as a few days after that date Roughsedge was to interrogate witnesses and also Ghasi Singh. The case was not yet decided. Obviously, Jaintgarh was the reward.

[54] Wilkinson to Swinton: 26 December 1832 (London: OIOC), BC 58,902.

[55] Wilkinson to A. Sterling, 12 May 1830. See Sahu, *The Kolhan Under British Rule*, 40–41.

[56] 'Translation of a Letter from Ruggonauth Busee Brahmin of Jyntgurh of Singboom dated the 8th and received the 18th February 1830 to the Political Agent South Western Frontier' (London: OIOC), Bengal Political Consultations, 28 May 1830.

[57] Richards to Roughsedge, 6 May 1821 (London: OIOC), BC 21,439. District for Pergunnah in the original.

[58] Richards to Roughsedge, 6 May 1821 (London: OIOC), BC 21,439.

[59] Roughsedge to Swinton, 25 February 1821; Roughsedge to Frobisher, 21 April 1821; Roughsedge to Swinton, 7 August 1821 (London: OIOC), BC 21,438.

[60] Roughsedge to Swinton, 7 August 1821 (London: OIOC), BC 21,439. Lurkas, Rajahs in the original.

[61] Depree, *Geographical and Statistical Report*, 29, 44.

Chapter 4: A Champaign Country

[1] This habit was instituted at a meeting of the 'President and Select Committee' on 16 August 1769. See William Wilson Hunter, *The Annals of Rural Bengal*, 9. See also John William Kaye, *The Administration of the East India Company: A History of Indian Progress* (London: Richard Bentley, 1853), 163–65.

[2] In 1820, Roughsedge was in the Ho area from 18 March till (probably) 9 April. See Roughsedge to Metcalfe, 9 May 1820 (London: OIOC), BC 21,438. In 1821, he entered Ho area on 23 April. See Roughsedge to Frobisher, 21 April 1821; Frobisher to Richards, 22 April 1821 (London: OIOC), BC 21,439. The hostilities were terminated on 30 April. The last interrogation took place on 16 May 1821, probably in Chakradharpur. See Roughsedge to Swinton, 7 August 1821 (London: OIOC), BC 66,546.

[3] Roughsedge to Swinton, 30 April 1821 (London: OIOC), BC 21,439.

[4] Swinton to Roughsedge, 24 March 1821, in C. P. Singh, *The Ho Tribe of Singhbhum*, 79). Coles in the original.

[5] Roughsedge to Richards, 3 April 1821 (London: OIOC), Bengal Political Consultations, 24 April 1821. A short resume was published by K. K. Basu. See K. K. Basu, 'The History of Singhbhum 1821–1836', *JBRS* 42 (1956): 285–88. Unfortunately, he did not give references for his extensive direct quotes.

[6] W. R. Gilbert to Swinton, 14 June 1823 (London: OIOC), Bengal Political Consultations, 27 June 1823. Rajah in the orginal.

[7] Roughsedge to Metcalfe, 9 May 1820 (London: OIOC), BC 21,438.

[8] Roughsedge to Swinton, 7 August 1821 (London: OIOC), BC 21,439.

[9] Roughsedge to Swinton, 25 February 1821; Roughsedge to Frobisher, 21 April 1821; Roughsedge to Swinton, 7 August 1821 (London: OIOC), BC 21,438.

[10] Roughsedge to Swinton, 7 August 1821 (London: OIOC), BC 21,439.

[11] Roughsedge to Metcalfe, 9 May 1820 (London: OIOC), BC 21,438. Palamou, Hindee, Oreea, Sanscrit in the original.

[12] Roughsedge to Metcalfe, 20 June 1820 (London: OIOC), BC 21,438.

[13] Roughsedge to Metcalfe, 9 May 1820 (London: OIOC), BC 21,438.

[14] Roughsedge to Swinton, 14 April 1821 (London: OIOC), Bengal Political Consultations, 12 May 1821; Roughsedge to Metcalfe, 9 May 1820 (London: OIOC), BC 21,438. Lurka in the original.
This makes improbable Das Gupta's statement that there were 'a large number of dobhasias or interpreters'. See Das Gupta, *Adivasis and the Raj*, 78. Elsewhere, she gives a short overview. See Das Gupta, *Adivasis and the Raj*, 54. In it figure one Goala, twice a small number of 'people belonging to the Tanti community' and one individual Tanti as interpreters, beside reproducing a general statement that Tantis could act as interpreters and messengers. This broadly tallies with Roughsedge's 'four or five'.

[15] 'Translation of an Urzee from Ruttun Sing Jemadar of a Company of Burkundauzees employed in Singboom dated the 13th of May and received the 23rd of July 1820' (London: OIOC), BC 21,438. Lurka in the original.

[16] Roughsedge to Swinton, 7 August 1821 (London: OIOC), Bengal Political Consultations, 15 September 1821.

[17] Roughsedge to Richards, 3 April 1821 (London: OIOC), Bengal Political Consultations, 24 April 1821.

[18] Roughsedge to Metcalfe, 9 May 1820 (London: OIOC), BC 21,438.

[19] 'Short Account of the Lurkacoles', *John Bull in the East*, repr., *AJMR* 13, (January–June 1822): 136–37.

[20] A. J. Colvin to W. B. Bayley, 10 April 1821 (London: OIOC), BC 21,872.

[21] 'Information Given by the Coles of Seemea and Haroha, 27th April 1821'; 'Examination of Singrai the Faithful Lurka Sirdar of Adjandea', appendices to: Roughsedge to Swinton 7 August 1821 (London: OIOC), BC 21,439.

[22] Roughsedge to Metcalfe, 9 May 1820 (London: OIOC), BC 21,438. Lurka Cole, Adjaudent, Singboom in the manuscript. Pir for Talook in the manuscript.

[23] On the literary devices used by Caesar and Tacitus in their descriptions of peoples outside the Roman Empire, see Thomas S. Burns, *Rome and the Barbarians, 100 B.C.–A.D. 400* (Baltimore and London: The Johns Hopkins University Press, 2003), 121–22, 180–82.

[24] Roughsedge to Metcalfe, 9 May 1820 (London: OIOC), BC 21,438.

[25] Roughsedge to Metcalfe, 9 May 1820 (London: OIOC), BC. 21,438.

[26] Roughsedge to Richards, 3 April 1821 (London: OIOC), BC 21,439. Bramins, Hindoos, Lurkas in the original.

[27] 'They intermarry and the woman adopts the custom of the tribe she becomes connected with, either by the use or rejection of clothes'. See A. J. Colvin to W. B. Bayley, 10 April 1821 (London: OIOC), BC 21,872.

[28] Roughsedge to Metcalfe, 9 May 1820 (London: OIOC), BC 21,438.

[29] Roughsedge to Metcalfe, 9 May 1820 (London: OIOC), BC 21,438. Baminghatee, Seraikela in the original. 20 miles is about 35 km.
Roughsedge to Richards, 3 April 1821 (London: OIOC), Bengal Political Consultations, 24 April 1821.

[30] 'Second examination of Bajee Moond of Garia in Goomlah 28th April 1821 for the purpose of obtaining local information', appendix to: Roughsedge to Swinton, 7 August 1821 (London: OIOC), BC 21,439.

[31] Roughsedge to Swinton, 14 April 1821 (London: OIOC), Bengal, Political Consultations, 12 May 1821. Bramin, Hindoos in the original.

[32] Roughsedge to Metcalfe, 9 May 1820 (London: OIOC), BC 21,438. Singboom , Rajah, Zemindars in the original.

[33] Roughsedge to Metcalfe, 9 May 1820 (London: OIOC), BC 21,438. Singboom in the original.

[34] Roughsedge to Metcalfe, 9 May 1820 (London, OIOC), BC 21,438. In the early years of the twentieth century, Bradley-Birt tried—in vain—to improve on this: 'It was the Tibet of Chota Nagpore'. See F. B. Bradley-Birt, *Chota Nagpur: A Little Known Province of the Empire*, 2nd rev. enl. ed. (London: Smith, Elder, 1910), 87.

[35] A. K. Sen took the simile 'tiger's den' as an example of 'how British ethnographer-administrators formed judgments that determined the content of colonial ethnography'. Well, Roughsedge got it from a local feudal chief. And Roughsedge had very little of an ethnographer. Sen also stated that the First Kolhan Campaign took 'almost two months'. It was about twenty-three days. And that in this campaign 'the English ... had met their match'. I skip comment on that. Moreover, that last idea would have prompted 'the General' to make his 'tiger's den' statement. Roughsedge was Major. And this statement was from before the campaign had even started. See Asoka Kumar Sen, *Representing Tribe: The Ho of Singhbhum under Colonial Rule* (New Delhi: Concept, 2011), 52, 54, 55.

[36] Roughsedge to Metcalfe, 9 May 1820 (London: OIOC), BC 21,438. Chota Nagpore in the original.

[37] Blunt to Metcalfe, 14 April 1832, Metcalfe's Minute, NAI: Foreign Department, Secret, 8 August 1832, procs. 8–11.

[38] 'The high-lands of Surguja district have peculiar 'pat formations'—highlands with small tablelands.' One of these is the Mainpat. See 'Surguja District', *WP*, accessed 3 August 2010.
The Mainpat would not remain well preserved. 'Formerly the Mainpat was a magnificent hunting field, especially noted for its herds of antelope and Gaur. The late Maharaja of Sirguja strictly preserved it, but on his death it fell into the hands of his widow, a very money-loving old lady, who allowed it to become one of the great grazing tracts, ... the wild animals have in consequence witdrawn from it.' See Dalton, *Descriptive Ethnology of Bengal,* 223.

[39] Geoffry Saint-Hilaire, 'Notice sur une nouvelle espèce de boeuf, nommé Gaour par les Indiens, &ca.' [Note on a New Species of Bovines, Named Gaour by the Indians, &ca.], in vol 9 of *Mémoires du Museum d'Histoire naturelle,* par les professeurs de cet établissement, ouvrage orné de gravures [by the professors of that establishment, work illustrated with gravures], (Paris, 1822), 71–75.
See also Geoffry Saint-Hilaire, 'v. Geoffroy St. Hilaire', *Isis* von Oken, Erster Band, Heft 1/6, (1823): 384–86; 'Necrology no II, Mr Henry Wesley Voysey', *Asiatic Monthly Miscellany* 19 (January–June 1825): 262–63; T. Hardwicke, 'On the Bos Gour of India', *The Zoological Journal* 3 (January 1827–April 1828): 231–33.
The note by Roughsedge on the Gaur was discussed in 1837 by Assistant Surgeon J. T. Pearson, Curator of the Museum of the Asiatic Society. See J. T. Pearson, 'Memorandum on the Gaur and Gayal', *JASB* 6 (1837): 225–28. Sibadas Chaudhuri

erroneously gave volume 5 (1836) as the locus of this memorandum. See Sibadas Chaudhuri (Comp.), *Index to the Publications of the Asiatic Society, 1788–1953*, vol. 1, part 1 (Calcutta: The Asiatic Society, 1956), 229.

See also the discussion of the discovery in Charles Knight, 'B. Gaurus, the Gour or Gaur', in Charles Knight (comp.), *The English Cyclopaedia, A New Dictionary of Universal Knowledge* (London: Bradbury and Evans, 1854), 626–27.

The quotation is from Georges Cuvier, 'B. Gaurus (the Gaur)', in Georges Cuvier, *The Animal Kingdom: Arranged in Conformity with its Organization, with Additional Descriptions of all the Species Hitherto Named, and of Many not Before Noticed*, ed. Edward Griffiths, F.L.S., A.S. &ca., and others, vol. 5 (London; G. B. Whittaker, 1827), 373–74. On page 399 of volume 4 the name 'Bos Gaurus' is attributed to Hamilton Smith.

[40] Roughsedge to Metcalfe, 9 May 1820 (London: OIOC), BC 21,438.

[41] Roughsedge to Metcalfe, 9 May 1820 (London: OIOC), BC 21,438. Bramins, Killedar in the original.

[42] Dalton, 'The "Kols" of Chota Nagpore', 165. Bramin in the original.

[43] Roughsedge to Metcalfe, 9 May 1820 (London: OIOC), BC 21,438. Bramin, Rajpoot, Mussulman in the original.

[44] Roughsedge to Metcalfe, 9 May 1820 (London: OIOC), BC 21,438.

[45] Sadananda Choudhury, 'The British Salt Revenue Policy in Orissa', *OHRJ* 16, no. 1 (1975): 58.

[46] Andrew Stirling, 'An Account, Geographical, Statistical and Historical of Orissa Proper, or Cuttack', *AR* 15 (1825; repr., 1979–80): 202–5. The part on the 'Coles' is on page numbers 202–3. On the article as a whole, see Om Prakash Kejariwal, *The Asiatic Society of Bengal and the Discovery of India's Past* (Delhi, etc.: Oxford University Press, 1988), 139–40.

Stirling knew Sanskrit and would become the Persian Secretary to Government and Deputy Secretary in the Secret and Political Department. See Theon Wilkinson, *Two Monsoons: The Life and Death of Europeans in India*, (1st ed., 1976; 2nd ed. London: Duckworth, 1987), 71–72. Stirling's remarks on the purity of the spoken language of Odisha showed that he was a good listener. For his lengthy article he took information from the local rajas, from the epic poem of Orissa, the Kanji Kaveri Pothi, and he mentioned that 'every temple of importance has its legend or Sthan Puran, every almanack maker his Panji, and Bansabali, composed in the local tongue'. See Andrew Stirling, 'An Account, Geographical, Statistical and Historical of Orissa Proper, or Cuttack', *AR* 15 (1825; repr., 1979–80): 207. The bulk of Andrew Stirling's article was devoted to the physical features of the country, the population and its customs and a partly mythical history of the Orissa tracts. With its use of Persian language sources, and his sensible attempts at explaining the historical origin and the contemporary workings of military, dynastic and political dependence, Stirling's account was a breakthrough in the study of early modern history of Odisha.

[47] Roughsedge to Swinton, 14 April 1821 (London: OIOC), Bengal, Political Consultations 12 May 1821.

[48] Roughsedge to Swinton, 14 April 1821 (London: OIOC), Bengal, Political Consultations 12 May 1821. Lurkas in the original.

[49] Roughsedge to Swinton, 14 April 1821 (London: OIOC), Bengal, Political Consultations 12 May 1821. Lurkas in the original.

[50] 'Short Account of the Lurkacoles'. From the detailed description of the weapons of the Hos and the space devoted to the campaign of 1821, the author was an officer of one of the invading Company detachments. On the other hand, the observation that they considered themselves 'of the same caste with (Saheb Log) the English' suggested a more peaceful intercourse. Quite likely, the author was stationed in one of the four encampments around the Kolhan after the campaign.

[51] Roughsedge to Metcalfe, 9 May 1820 (London: OIOC), BC 21,438.

[52] Roughsedge to Metcalfe, 9 May 1820 (London: OIOC), BC 21,438.

[53] Roughsedge to Metcalfe, 9 May 1820 (London: OIOC), BC 21,438.

[54] In 1838, Tickell, who was the first to make an assessment of the revenue, neglected to take a census. Afterwards Tickell estimated the number of members of Hindu artisan castes at about one-seventh of the total population. See Tickell, 'Memoir', 700. In his intensive Survey and Settlement operations of 1913 to 1918, Tuckey found a little over 9.5 per cent of 'old Diku holdings', that is, holdings held by 'cultivating castes and tribes other than Hos, such as Gowallas, Bhuiyas and Gods, or else people of castes who belonged to the Ho village community in a subordinate capacity, the Kamars, Magadha Gowalas, Kumhars and Tantis'. See Tuckey, *Final Report*, 24–25. Taking a middle ground, we tentatively put the number of non-Hos in the Ho lands in 1821 at not more than 12.5 per cent of the population.

[55] Roughsedge to Nicol, 25 April 1821 (London: OIOC), BC 21,439.

[56] Roughsedge to Metcalfe, 9 May 1820 (London: OIOC), BC 21,438. These were not Ho villages destroyed in interclan fighting among the Hos, as Das Gupta seemed to think. See Das Gupta, *Adivasis and the Raj*, 35.

[57] Roughsedge to Metcalfe, 9 May 1820 (London: OIOC), BC 21,438.

[58] 'twenty, thirty forty, or fifty head of cattle'. See Tickell, 'Memoir', 789). Dalton mentioned forty. See Dalton, 'The "Kols" of Chota Nagpore', 178. The number became 'forty to fifty' in 1872. See Dalton, *Descriptive Ethnology of Bengal*, 192.

[59] Roughsedge to Metcalfe, 9 May 1820 (London: OIOC), BC 21,438. Singboom in the original.

[60] Roughsedge to Swinton, 17 February 1821 (London: OIOC), BC 21,438. They spoke a little Ho, and could and did act as interpreters and informants.

[61] In this and in the next two quotations there are in the original: Booya, Chuckurdepore, Lurka Cole, Sereikela, Buneas, Bangees (tangis), Coles, Gassee.

[62] Probably the Kartik Purnima (full moon) in November.

[63] 'Second examination of Bajee Moond of Garia in Goomlah 28th April 1821 for the purpose of obtaining local information', appendix to: Roughsedge to Swinton, 7 August 1821 (London: OIOC), BC 21,439. Italics added. The manuscript gives Bangees, an obvious copying error for Tangees (battle axes). Booya, Sereikela, Chuckurderpore, Buneas, in the original. I have left out Q and A before sentences and substituted – for Q.

[64] 'Abstract of the Evidence of the Cause of the Poora-Dihee: Rajahs Evidence', appendix to: Roughsedge to Metcalfe, 9 May 1820 (London: OIOC), BC 21,438. Dewan in the original.

[65] 'Ghassee Singh's defense, 16th May 1821', appendix to: Roughsedge to Swinton, 7 August 1821 (London: OIOC), BC 21,439.

[66] K. K. Basu, 'Larka Kols of Singhbhum', *JBRS* 43 (1957): 78.

[67] 'Examination of Jakree Sirdar of Keera Gote an Intelligent Man of Some Influence 12 May 1821', appendix to: Roughsedge to Swinton, 7 August 1821 (London: OIOC), BC 21,439.

[68] Wilkinson to Swinton, 12 January 1833 (London: OIOC), BC 58,904.

[69] One instance was the village of Garia in Gumra *pir*. See 'Second examination of Bajee Moond of Garia in Goomlah 28th April 1821 for the purpose of obtaining local information', appendix to: Roughsedge to Swinton, 7 August 1821 (London: OIOC), BC 21,439.

[70] Political Letter Bengal, 9 May 1823 (London: OIOC), BC 21,438. Coles, Raja of Singboom in the original.

[71] Roughsedge to Metcalfe, 9 May 1820 (London: OIOC), BC 21,438.

[72] Roughsedge to Metcalfe, 9 May 1820 (London: OIOC), BC 21,438.

[73] Roughsedge to Metcalfe, 9 May 1820 (London: OIOC), BC 21,438. Coles in the original.

[74] Roughsedge to Metcalfe, 9 May 1820 (London: OIOC), BC 21,438.

[75] Roughsedge to Metcalfe, 9 May 1820 (London: OIOC), BC 21,438.

[76] Roughsedge to Metcalfe, 20 June 1820 (London: OIOC), BC 21,438. Fifty years after him, Dalton saw it as a struggle mostly between the Hos of the northern *pirs* against those of the south. See Dalton, *Descriptive Ethnology of Bengal*, 181–82.

[77] Roughsedge, 'Pergunnahs of Singbhoom, compiled from information by Gunshyam Sing and from other sources', 15 April 1820 (London: OIOC), BC 21,439. See also the table, wrongly sourced to a letter from Ghanshyam to Roughsedge, in Das Gupta, *Adivasis and the Raj*, 85–88.

[78] 'Translation of a letter from Boherun Singh, Subedar, employed in Singboom, dated the 2nd and received the 15th of Cartick', enclosure to Roughsedge to Metcalfe, 14 November 1820 (London: OIOC), BC 21,438.

[79] 'Translation of a letter from Boherun Singh, Subedar, employed in Singboom, dated the 2nd and received the 15th of Cartick', enclosure to Roughsedge to Metcalfe, 14 November 1820 (London: OIOC), BC 21,438.

[80] Roughsedge to Metcalfe, 9 May 1820 (London: OIOC), BC 21,438.

[81] Roughsedge to Frobisher, 21 April 1821 (London: OIOC), BC 21,439.

[82] Roughsedge himself had given the number of villages in Ajodhya as twelve, but that could be an explicatory translation of '*pir*'. See Roughsedge to Richards, 3 April 1821 (London: OIOC), BC 21,439. When Tuckey made his list of villages in the 1910s, Ajodhya had thirty-two villages, all but one of them founded by Hos. See Tuckey, *Final Report*, 19.

[83] 'Narrative Of Durrum Das Gossein in the Service of the Zemindar of Singboom Written Down on this 24th of February 1821', appendix to: Roughsedge to Swinton, 25 February 1821 (London: OIOC), BC 21,438. Duppia in the original.

[84] 'Translation of a letter from Rajah Gansham Sing dated 25th of May Insillee or 11th of February and received the 21st of February 1821'; 'Narrative Of Durrum Das Gossein in the service of the Zemindar of Singboom Written Down on this 24th of February 1821', appendices to: Roughsedge to Swinton, 25 February 1821 (London: OIOC), BC 21,438. 'Examination of Jakree Sirdar of Keera Gote an intelligent man of some influence, 12th May 1821', appendix to: Roughsedge to Swinton; 7 August 1821 (London: OIOC), BC 21,439.

[85] 'Examination of Coondoo Pater a Sirdar of Coorea 13th May 1821', appendix to: Roughsedge to Swinton, 7 August 1821 (London: OIOC), BC 21,439. Assora in the text.

[86] Roughsedge to Frobisher, 21 April 1821 (London: OIOC), BC 21,439.

[87] Roughsedge to Richards, 3 April 1821 (London: OIOC), BC 21,439.

[88] Roughsedge to Metcalfe, 9 May 1820 (London: OIOC), BC 21,438.

[89] Roughsedge to Metcalfe, 9 May 1820 (London: OIOC), BC 21,438. Moondha, Mankee in the original. Indeed, in his scattered references we find at least one village Dulkee with two mundas: Pack Koe and Matta. 'Second examination of Bajee Moond of Garia in Goomlah 28th April 1821 for the purpose of obtaining local information'; 'Examination of Jakree Sirdar of Keera Gote an Intelligent Man of Some Influence 12th May 1821', appendices to: Roughsedge to Swinton, 7 August 1821 (London: OIOC), BC 21,439.

[90] 'Second examination of Bajee Moond of Garia in Goomlah 28th April 1821 for the purpose of obtaining local information', appendix to: Roughsedge to Swinton, 7 August 1821 (London: OIOC), BC 21,439. Goera in the original. I have left out Q and A before sentences and substituted – for Q.

[91] In 1836, the estimate of people living in the Kolhan was 90,000, of which about 60,000 were Hos. These 90,000 lived in 620 villages. See Dalton, *Descriptive Ethnology of Bengal*, 182. That made about 145 inhabitants per village.

[92] Dalton, *Descriptive Ethnology of Bengal*, 190.

[93] Roughsedge to Richards, 3 April 1821 (London: OIOC), BC 21,439. Ghanshyam Singh of Porahat blamed the Hos of Gumra and Balandia (Barandiya) for the battle of Pokharia and the sack of Chainpur. Together these areas comprised at least 112 villages.

[94] 'Information given by the Coles of Seemea and Haroha taken on the 27th of April 1821'; 'Declaration of Beja Moonda and the five other Coles of Goera'; 'Examination of Jakree Sirdar of Keera Gote an Intelligent Man of Some Influence 12th May 1821', appendices to: Roughsedge to Swinton; 7 August 1821 (London: OIOC), BC 21,439.

[95] 'Examination of Coondoo Pater a Sirdar of Cooreea 13th May 1821', appendix to: Roughsedge to Swinton; 7 August 1821 (London: OIOC), BC 21,439. Coles in the original.

[96] 'Second examination of Bajee Moond of Garia in Goomlah 28th April 1821 for the purpose of obtaining local information', appendix to: Roughsedge to Swinton; 7 August 1821 (London: OIOC), BC 21,439.

[97] 'List of the Tribes into which the Lurkas of Singboom and Mohurbunge are divided taken from the statement of Keetee a Lurka Sirdar of Taeepeer', Bengal, Political Department, 15 September 1821 (London: OIOC), BC 21,439.

[98] 'Second examination of Bajee Moond of Garia in Goomlah 28th April 1821 for the purpose of obtaining local information', appendix to: Roughsedge to Swinton; 7 August 1821 (London: OIOC), BC 21,439. Saories in the orginal.

[99] 'Second examination of Bajee Moond of Garia in Goomlah 28th April 1821 for the purpose of obtaining local information', appendix to: Roughsedge to Swinton, 7 August 1821 (London: OIOC), BC 21,439. Soorees, Goera in the original. I have left out Q and A before sentences and substituted – for Q.

[100] C. P. Singh, *The Ho Tribe of Singhbhum*, 93–94. Suban also appeared in the sources under the name of Sooltan.

[101] Wilkinson to Swinton, July 24, 1830, quoted in C. P. Singh, *The Ho Tribe of Singhbhum*, 93.

[102] Roughsedge to Swinton, 14 April 1821 (London: OIOC), Bengal, Political Consultations, 12 May 1821. Lurkar Sirdars in the original.

[103] Roughsedge to Swinton, 14 April 1821 (London: OIOC), Bengal, Political Consultations 12 May 1821.

[104] Political Letter Bengal 9 May 1823 (London: OIOC), BC 21,438. Hindoo in the original.

[105] To see society, the mind has to remove the political smokescreen obscuring its view. This is as true for Europe after the French Revolution as for the India after Plassey. For India, see Percival Spear, 'The British and the Indian State to 1830', in *Tradition and Politics in South Asia*, ed. R. J. Moore (New Delhi: Vikas, 1979), 162.

Chapter 5: The Return of the Pauri Devi

[1] Dalton, *Descriptive Ethnology of Bengal*, 285, footnote.

[2] Quoted in Kumar, *History and Administration of Tribal Chotanagpur*, 128.

[3] Lewis, W. H. 'Orissa Division', in 'Preparation of Record of Old Inscriptions in Christian Burial Grounds', *List of Old Inscriptions in Christian Burial Grounds in the Province of Bihar and Orissa* (Patna: no publisher, 1926), 12, 15. We owe to the local historian Deepak Panda a few pictures of the memorial. He mentioned that Roughedge was cremated at Sambalpur. See Deepak Panda, 'Government Cemetery at Sambalpur Have Many Belongs to Europeans', *Deepak Panda Blog*, 6 August 2014; 'Anglo-Indians Buried at Sambalpur, Odisha, India at the Government Cemetery', *Deepak Panda Blog*, 1 September 2015, both accessed 30 March 2016, http://sambalpurhistory.blogspot.nl/.

[4] 'Major Edward Roughsedge', 233.

[5] Dalton, 'The "Kols" of Chota Nagpore', 166.

[6] Walter Raleigh Gilbert was the fifth in line from Humphrey Gilbert.

Humphrey Gilbert, after a career in Ireland, suggested in 1567 to Queen Elizabeth I that England should start settlements in America to challenge Spain and Portugal. In 1583, he took possession of Newfoundland for England by cutting a piece of turf. Newfoundland was the first British possession overseas, and Gilbert had thereby started the British Empire. See 'Humphrey Gilbert', *WP*, accessed 4 December 2010.

Humphrey's son Raleigh Gilbert was the second in command of the Popham colony, an unsuccessful colonial settlement in Maine, founded in 1607, a few months after the Pilgrim fathers from Leiden in Holland had started Jamestown, the first permanent settlement of the British in America. See 'Popham Colony', *WP*, accessed 4 December 2010.

Humphrey Gilbert's younger half-brother was Sir Walter Raleigh. In 1595 and 1616, Raleigh was in eastern Venezuela and Guyana looking for El Dorado. On the second expedition he attacked a Spanish outpost. For this Raleigh was beheaded at Whitehall in 1618. See 'Walter Raleigh', *WP*, accessed 30 March 2010. Walter Raleigh Gilbert was named after him.

Walter Raleigh Gilbert would play a prominent part in the First and the Second Anglo-Sikh wars. He was the one who, after the defeat of the Sikhs in the Gujarat battle of 1849, chased the Sikh army till Sher Singh and Chatar Singh surrendered their swords to him near Rawalpindi. Walter Raleigh Gilbert became baronet in 1850 and lieutenant-general in November 1851. A memorial obelisk to him was erected on Bodmin Beacon. See 'Sir Walter Gilbert, 1st Baronet', *WP*, accessed 4 December 2010.

[7] Gilbert to Swinton, 14 June 1823. (London, OIOC), Bengal Political Consultations, 27 June 1823.

[8] Gilbert to Swinton, 14 June 1823 (London: OIOC), Bengal Political Consultations, 27 June 1823.

[9] Wilkinson to Mangles, 22 August 1836 (London: OIOC), BC 66,546.

[10] Gilbert to Swinton, 27 April 1824 (London: OIOC), Bengal Political Consultations, 27 June 1823. Rajah Gunsham Sing in the original.

P. Kumar has here 'a party of Brahmins' getting the image. See Kumar, *History and Administration of Tribal Chotanagpur*, 129.

[11] Nice detail, but the well still exists and is round.

[12] Chaudhury, *Temples and Legends*, 20–21. Much obliged as we are to Roy Chaudhury for this delightful story, I am sorry to note that he mistakenly attributed the action to Bikram Singh instead of to his son Ajambar Singh.

[13] And not in 1821, as Sahu wrote. See Sahu, *The Kolhan Under British Rule*, 40–41.

[14] Wilkinson to Mangles, 22 August 1836 (London: OIOC), BC 66,546.

[15] And not the person of Roughsedge, as C. P. Singh would have it. See C. P. Singh, *The Ho Tribe of Singhbhum*, 92. Roughsedge died on 22 January 1822.

[16] Gilbert to Swinton, 14 June 1823 (London: OIOC), Bengal Political Consultations, 27 June 1823.

[17] Gilbert to Swinton, 14 June 1823 (London: OIOC), Bengal Political Consultations, 27 June 1823. Rajah in the original.

[18] Wilkinson to Mangles, 22 August 1836 (London: OIOC), BC 66,546.

[19] Achete and, sometimes, Achoot in the contemporary English language sources. Gajraj, the third son of Jagannath Gajarat was still alive, but he, 'being an infirm old man (nearly seventy years old)', agreed with the wish of Ghanshyam that not he, but his son would be the new raja. On his deathbed Ghanshyam named Achuta as his successor. See Gilbert to Swinton, 1 October 1827, 'Papers concerning Surguja, Sambalpur and Singhbum 1818–1830' (London: OIOC), H/724.

[20] Gilbert to Swinton, 28 October 1827, Papers concerning Sarguja, Sambalpur and Singhbum 1818-1830 (London: OIOC), H/724.

[21] Wilkinson to Swinton, 12 January 1833 (London: OIOC), BC 58,904. Chakradhar Sing was the son of Ajambar Singh of Saraikela.

[22] Wilkinson to Swinton, 12 January 1833 (London: OIOC), BC 58,904.

[23] Sahu, *The Kolhan Under British Rule*, 42. Rajah in the original.

[24] C. P. Singh, *The Ho Tribe of Singhbhum*, 94. Singh gave 1 *pie* = half *a seer*. Raghunath asked 2 *kundees* of paddy for principal and interest of one year. A *kundee* was 20 *seers* or half a *maund*. A *seer* in the Kolhan was about 955 grammes. See Risley, *Singbhum District*, 85- 86. See also H. H. Wilson, *A Glossary*, 474. That makes the principal plus interest 40 *seers* or 37 kg of paddy . In case of failure of the harvest, the principal plus interest went up to 12 *kundees* of paddy, a stunning 240 kg of paddy for an loan of about 0.5 kg of salt.

[25] Wilkinson to Sterling (Stirling), May 12, 1830, paraphrased in C. P. Singh, *The Ho Tribe of Singhbhum*, 94. See also Sahu, *The Kolhan Under British Rule*, 41.

[26] See Dalton, 'The Ho Tribe: Otherwise Called the Lurka or Fighting Coles of Singbhoom'.

[27] C. P. Singh, *The Ho Tribe of Singhbhum*, 95.

[28] 'Translation of a Letter from Ruggonauth Busee Brahmin of Jyntgurh of Singboom dated the 8th and received the 18th February 1830 to the P.l Agent SW Frontier', enclosed in Wilkinson to A. Sterling (Stirling), 12 May 1830 (London: OIOC), Bengal Political Consultations, 28 May 1830. Booreea, Coles in the original.

C. P. Singh added two villages of Gumra. See C. P. Singh, *The Ho Tribe of Singhbhum*, 94.

[29] 'Statement of Lackuie Sooree and Kuldar Sooree', enclosed in Wilkinson to A. Sterling (Stirling), 12 May 1830 (London: OIOC), Bengal Political Consultations, 28 May 1830.

[30] Areeparampil, *Struggle for Swaraj*, 90–91.

[31] In 1836, Wilkinson mentioned 'Mahta Moonda of Burndea' (Mata) together with 'Toomal Moonda' (Jumal) as the leaders. See Wilkinson to Mangles, 22 August 1836 (London: OIOC). BC 66,546.

[32] 'Translation of a Letter from Ruggonauth Bussee to the Pol. Agent dated 20 Febr. 1830'. Appendix to Wilkinson to A. Sterling (Stirling), 12 May 1830 (London: OIOC), Bengal Political Consultations, 28 May 1830. Coles in the original.

[33] Raghunath Bisee to Political Agent, 26 February 1830, quoted in Sahu, *The Kolhan Under British Rule*, 43.

[34] C. P. Singh, *The Ho Tribe of Singhbhum*, 96–97.

[35] 'A Mufussee and his men of the intelligence Dept.' Wilkinson to A. Sterling (Stirling), 12 May 1830 (London: OIOC), Bengal Political Consultations, 28 May 1830.

[36] Wilkinson to A. Sterling (Stirling), 12 May 1830 (London: OIOC), Bengal Political Consultations, 28 May 1830.

[37] According to Wilkinson, who greatly disliked him, Krishna practically ruled Porahat. See C. P. Singh, *The Ho Tribe of Singhbhum*, 96–97.

[38] C. P. Singh, *The Ho Tribe of Singhbhum*, 96.
[39] Wilkinson to A. Sterling (Stirling 12 May 1830 (London: OIOC), Bengal Political Consultations, 28 May 1830. Coles in the original.
[40] Wilkinson to A. Sterling (Stirling), 12 May 1830 (London: OIOC), Bengal Political Consultations, 28 May 1830.
[41] Swinton to Wilkinson, 28 May 1830 (London: OIOC), Bengal Political Consultations, 28 May 1830.

Reflection: Another People's War

[1] Tooley, *A Dictionary of Mapmakers*, 268.
[2] A view Roughsedge later recognised as wrong. See Roughsedge to Metcalfe, 9 May 1820 (London: OIOC), BC 21,438. Lurkas in the original.
[3] Roughsedge to Adams, 12 August 1818, paraphrased in Sahu, *The Kolhan Under British Rule*, 19.
[4] Government to Roughsedge, 29 August 1818, quoted in Jha, 'Early British Contacts with Singhbhum', 149–50.
[5] Wilkinson to Swinton, 12 January 1833 (London: OIOC), BC 58,904.
[6] Adams to Roughsedge, 29 August 1818, cited in Wilkinson to Macsween, 29 October 1834 (London: OIOC), BC 66,544.
[7] In 'early 1819', Roughsedge included military reconnaissance in his instructions to Rudell; in June 1819, he arrived at the conclusion that in the next cold season Ghanshyam Singh should be helped to 'reduce the rapidly increasing power of the Lurkas'. See Roughsedge to Metcalfe, 20 June 1820 (London: OIOC), BC 21,438.
[8] Roughsedge to Metcalfe, 9 May 1820 (London: OIOC), BC 21,438.
[9] Edward N. Luttwak, 'Give War a Chance', *Foreign Affairs* 78, no. 4 (July–August 1999): 37–44.
[10] The idea of 'dual parentage' I owe to Dr Roland Silva of the Central Cultural Fund of Sri Lanka. He and Ir. Ashley DeVos coined the phrase in the early 1980s while addressing an ICOMOS conference on the buildings of the Dutch colonial period in Sri Lanka (Dr Roland Silva, personal communication).
[11] Heesterman stressed the 'dispersed' nature of authority, 'enclosed in the network of personal relations'. According to him, in the Indian context, authority could only come from 'the renunciatory sphere'. Of course, with power, the situation was different, as he was well aware. See J. C. Heesterman, 'Power and Authority in Indian Tradition', in *Tradition and Politics in South Asia*, ed. R. J. Moore (New Delhi: Vikas, 1979), 75, 81, 85).
For the encompassing nature of (political) power in India, I drew my inspiration from Cohn. See Bernard S. Cohn, 'Representing Authority in Victorian India', in *The Invention of Tradition*, eds. Eric Hobsbawn and Terence Rancer (Cambridge: Cambridge University Press. 1983), 165–209.

Part II: A New Grand Strategy, 1831–1837

Chapter 6: The Genesis of Wilkinson's System

[1] Kumar, *History and Administration of Tribal Chotanagpur*, 23–25.
[2] Virottam, *The Nagabanshis and the Cheros*, 188.
[3] Kumar, *History and Administration of Tribal Chotanagpur*, 23–25.
[4] Quoted from Cuthbert's report in Kumar, *History and Administration of Tribal Chotanagpur*, 28.
[5] Binay Bushan Chaudhuri, *Peasant History of Late Pre-colonial and Colonial India*, vol. 8, part 2 of *Project of History of Indian Science, Philosophy, and Culture*, general ed. D. P. Chattpodhyaya (Delhi: Centre for Studies in Civilizations, 2008), 725.
[6] Jha, *The Tribal Revolt of Chotanagpur*, 63, 173–74; [James Long], 'The Kols, The Insurrection of 1832; and the Land Tenure Act of 1869', *Calcutta Review* 50 [title page mentions 49] (1869): 132. A dissenting voice one finds in 'The Kholes' *AJMR*, n.s., 8, (May–August 1832): 186.
[7] Binay Bushan Chaudhuri, *Peasant History*, 724.
[8] Roy, *The Mundas and Their Country*, 113–14.
[9] Jha, *The Tribal Revolt of Chotanagpur*, 164–65.
[10] Binay Bushan Chaudhuri, *Peasant History*, 724.
[11] John Davidson, 1839, in Sarat Chandra Roy, 'A Historical Document', *MII* 51, no. 3 (1971): 194.
[12] Virottam, *The Nagabanshis and the Cheros*, 190.

[13] Jha, *The Tribal Revolt of Chotanagpur*, 131, quoting the last statement from the petition of Raja Jagannath, 25 March 1832. However, Long gave the same statement as made in 1820 to Roughsedge. See [James Long], 'The Kols, The Insurrection of 1832; and the Land Tenure Act of 1869', 140.

[14] Elwin, quoting Hallet and McPherson's Ranchi District Gazetteer 1917, 35. See Verrier Elwin, 'The Kol Insurrection', *MII* 25, no. 4 (Rebellion Number, 1945): 260. For a discussion of the economic aspect of debtor servitude, that is, of tying the producer to the soil, see Gyan Prakash, *Bonded Histories: Genealogies of Labor Servitude in Colonial India*, South Asian Studies 44 (Cambridge: Cambridge University Press, 1990), 31–32.

[15] As early as 1823 Agent Cuthbert stated that a system of jurisprudence adapted to this 'distinct and uncivilized race of people' was desirable, and suggested to place it 'under the management and superintendence of an able and experienced commissioner, assisted by about four assistants, possibly military gentlemen, acquainted with this area'. See Jha, *The Tribal Revolt of Chotanagpur*, 65. Shakespear, too, stressed that the inhabitants of the Chotanagpur plateau, a 'rude and half civilized people', required 'a mild and conciliatory line of conduct'. See Memorandum Shakespear, 20 January 1826, quoted in Jha, *The Tribal Revolt of Chotanagpur*, 140, note 4.

[16] Roy, 'Ethnographical Investigation in Official Records', *JBORS* 7 (1921): 13.

[17] Cuthbert in 1827, but in the same report he noted 'the great number of inhabitants' (quoted in Roy, 'Ethnographical Investigation in Official Records' (1921): 16).

[18] Roy, 'Ethnographical Investigation in Official Records' (1921): 13.

[19] S. C. Sinha, Jyoti Sen, and Sudhir Panchbhai, 'The Concept of Diku among the Tribes of Chota Nagpur', *MII* 49, no. 2 (1969): 121–38; Sita Kant Mahapatra, 'The Insider Diku: Boundary Rules and Marginal Man in Santal Society', *MII* 56, no. 1 (1976): 37–49.
The Hos used the same word: 'dickoo' for 'foreigners in general'. See Samuel Richard Tickell, 'Vocabulary of the Ho Language', *JASB* 9, part 2 (1840): 1063.

[20] Jagdish Chandra Jha extensively covered the Kol Insurrection in a methodologically sound way. There is no need here to restate particulars which can be found in his seminal work. See Jha, *The Tribal Revolt of Chotanagpur*.
The affair of Bindrai's loan I take mainly from Jha, *The Tribal Revolt of Chotanagpur*, 170–72. See also Roy, *The Mundas and Their Country*, 113–23.

[21] C. P. Singh, *The Ho Tribe of Singhbhum*, 102–103.

[22] Jha, *The Tribal Revolt of Chotanagpur*, 171–72. Achet Singh in the original.

[23] Jha, *The Tribal Revolt of Chotanagpur*, 68–129.

[24] Jha, *The Tribal Revolt of Chotanagpur*, 70.

[25] Wilkinson to Neave, 20 January 1832, paraphrased in Jha, *The Tribal Revolt of Chotanagpur*, 78.

[26] Hundred troops in Ch. Metcalfe to Bentinck, 19 January 1932; 120 troops were mentioned in Ch. Metcalfe to Bentinck, 29 January 1832. See Cyril H. Philips ed., *The Correspondence of Lord William Cavendish Bentinck, Governor-General of India: 1832–1835*, 2 vols., (Oxford: Oxford University Press, 1977), 760; 763.

[27] B. K. Roy made much of the insurrection in Tori, as this movement 'cannot be branded as a movement of the tribal inhabitants of Chotanagpur against the non-tribal settlers [as] the chief participants . . . were non-Kols, i.e. non-tribals'. Hence, he stated that 'the anti-British movement in this area had assumed the character of a national uprising'. See B. K. Roy, 'Kol Movement of 1832 in Tori Parganah (Palamau District)', *JHR* 5, no. 1 (1962): 32–35. Uprising, against what? On 24 January, the Bhogta and Ghasi tribes of Tori rebelled. By the end of January Captain Maltby arrived in Tori with a hurriedly raised auxiliary force. By 8 February, the troops had withdrawn, and the 'lower classes' combined with the 'Coles' and recommenced 'burning, plundering and killing'. See Jha, *The Tribal Revolt of Chotanagpur*, 77, 79, 81, 89. Of course, the targets were the large landholders and tax farmers.

[28] In the first stages of the Insurrection, on the request of Cuthbert, Wilkinson and he were nominated Joint Commissioners. See Jha, *The Tribal Revolt of Chotanagpur*, 81. Later, Wilkinson and W. Dent became Joint Commissioners.

[29] Wilkinson to Adj. General, 4 February 1832, quoted in Jha, *The Tribal Revolt of Chotanagpur*, 106.

[30] 'A Kohl-killer', correspondent of the Bengal Hurkaru, spoke ('in rather unpleasant satisfaction' added Jha) of the 'jolly good drubbing' they had given the insurgents under Bhudu Bhagat in the village Sillagaon (Jha, *The Tribal Revolt of Chotanagpur*, 110, note 1). This episode shows how careful one must be in pronouncing moral judgements on the 'British' based on the material from just one source, such as 'a Kohl-killer'. Another writer, 'present at one of these attacks' wrote that he had been 'quite disgusted at being obliged to see the brutes shot and bayoneted'. He, as a professional, added, 'but the villains deserved all they got'. He sighed at seeing the heads of Buddhu Bhagat, his brother and his nephew: 'how horrid it is to see such sights'. See 'The Kholes', *AJMR* 8, (May–August 1832): 186–88.

[31] India Gazette, February 24, 1832, quoted in 'The Kholes', 186–88. J. C. Jha followed another account, by 'an Officer' in the Bengal Hurkaru, of 25 February 1832. He spoke of 4,000 people surrendering. See Jha, *The Tribal Revolt of Chotanagpur*, 109.

[32] Dalton, *Descriptive Ethnology of Bengal*, 173.

[33] Jha, *The Tribal Revolt of Chotanagpur*, 192; 202.

34 Jha, *The Tribal Revolt of Chotanagpur*, 127.
35 Jha, *The Tribal Revolt of Chotanagpur*, 123.
36 Jha gives 19 April 1832 as the date when Bindrai surrendered, referring to information from the Joint Commissioners of 26 April 1832. See Jagdish Chandra Jha, *The Tribal Revolt of Chotanagpur*, 127. So did Dalton. See Dalton, *Descriptive Ethnology of Bengal*, 173. At the same time, we know that on 19 April 1833 Achuta Singh handed over Bindrai Manki and others to Wilkinson in Saraikela. See Wilkinson to Macsween, 27 April 1833 (London: OIOC), BC 58,890. The evidence for a 1833 date is supported by Jha elsewhere. See J. C. Jha, *The Bhumij Revolt*, 155, esp. note 4. The difficulty disappears when we see that Bindrai surrendered twice. He surrendered the first time in 1832, when he was pardoned. See Macsween to Joint Commissioner in Jungle Mahals, 19 February 1833 (London: OIOC), BC 58,903. The second time he surrendered was exactly one year later near Saraikela.
37 Cuthbert had given a broad outline of its different peoples in his report of 1827. There were, he stated, 'three descriptions' of Kols, namely Kharias, Oraons and Mundas, 'these vary in language more than in manners'. The agent saw in them 'the lowest kind' of Indians and 'in their manners and customs . . . little removed from savages'. Cuthbert's savageness was both visual and female. 'The only covering worn by the women is a small piece of cloth passed between their thighs.' See S. T. Cuthbert (1827), quoted in Roy, 'Ethnographical Investigation in Official Records' (1921).
38 'Postscript to Asiatic Intelligence', *AJMR* 8, n.s., 8, (May–August 1832): 120.
39 'The Kholes', 186, 188; 'Account of the Kholes or Coles', *AJMR*, n.s., 8, (May–August 1832): 264–66; Jha, *The Tribal Revolt of Chotanagpur*, 25–26).
40 'Account of the Kholes or Coles', 264–66.
41 Roughsedge to Richards, 3 April 1821 (London: OIOC), Bengal Political, 24 April 1821, Cons. No. 25.
42 Dalton, *Descriptive Ethnology of Bengal*, 172. Singbhum in the original. The idea of Larka participation stuck. Even seventy years after the events, Mundas told the lawyer/anthropologist S. C. Roy with glee about the defeat of the British by the Larkas in the south of Chotanagpur. They performed a song about Larkas or Hos fighting near the small central town of Pithoria. Wilkinson had his headquarters here in 1831–32. See Roy, *The Mundas and Their Country*, 116–17. This idea was enlarged by D. N. Majumdar, who gave the Hos 'a leading part' in the 'rebellion of the Mundas'. See Dhirendra Nath Majumdar, *The Affairs of a Tribe: A Study in Tribal Dynamics* (Lucknow: Ethnographic and Folk Culture Society, 1950), 6. See also Murali Sahu, *The Kolhan Under British Rule* (Jamshedpur: Sushanta Kumar Sahu, 1985), 47–49. K. S. Singh mentioned rather rhetorically that the Insurrection spread like 'a prairie fire' and was led by 'a confederacy of many tribes', including—and here he was wrong—the 'militant Ho tribes'. See Kumar Suresh Singh, *Tribal Society in India: An Anthropo-historical Perspective* (New Delhi: Manohar Publications, 1985), 126.
43 *John Bull in the East*, 12 February 1832, quoted in 'The Disturbed Districts', *AJMR*, n.s., 8, (May–August 1832): 144–45.
44 Jha, *The Tribal Revolt of Chotanagpur*, 198.
45 Sahu, *The Kolhan Under British Rule*, 49. According to Paty, Bindrai was from Karaikela. See Chittaranjan Kumar Paty, *History of Seraikella and Kharswan States* (New Delhi: Classical Publishing Company, 2002), 29.
46 Metcalfe's Minute, New Delhi, NAI, Foreign Department, Secret, 6 August 1832, pros. 8–11. Singbhum in the original.
47 Roughsedge to Metcalfe, 9 May 1820 (London: OIOC), BC. 21,438. Singbhoom Coles in the original.
48 Metcalfe's Minute, New Delhi, NAI, Foreign Department, Secret, 6 August 1832, pros. 8–11. Singbhoom Coles in the original. Given these words, it is surprising that Jha found that Metcalfe 'failed to recognise . . . the strength of the Kol spirit of independence'. See Jha, *The Tribal Revolt of Chotanagpur*, 173.
49 'Account of the Kholes or Coles', 264–66.
50 As Wilkinson wrote to Neave on 29 January 1832. See Jha, *The Tribal Revolt of Chotanagpur*, 78.
51 Jha, *The Tribal Revolt of Chotanagpur*, 185.
52 'The Kholes', 188. Kholes, Lurka in the original.
53 Ch. Metcalfe to Bentinck, 4 March 1832, in Philips, *The Correspondence of Lord William Cavendish Bentinck*, 773. Singbhoom in the original.
54 Jha, *The Tribal Revolt of Chotanagpur*, 78, 185. An important grievance of these Larkas was the ill-treatment of their women who came to sell iron in this market in Sonapur. These were not Hos, but Mundas from Porahat. J. C. Jha called these women 'Larkas'. See Jha, *The Tribal Revolt of Chotanagpur*, 185. The locus of Sarat Chandra Roy which he used, mentioned 'Porahat Mundas'. Verrier Elwin quoted the Ranchi District Gazetteer of M. G. Hallet and T. S. McPherson (1917) and mentioned 'Munda women'. See Elwin, 'The Kol Insurrection', 259.
55 Unless you perform the magic practiced by S. B. Chaudhuri. Depending exclusively on tertiary sources, he failed to see the difference between the Mundas and the Hos. In line with that, the Kolhan campaign of 1836–37 was presented as a direct consequence of 'the explosion of the Kols', that is, the Kol Insurrection of 1831–32. See Sashi Bhusan Chaudhuri, *Civil Disturbances During the British Rule in India (1765–1857)* (Calcutta: The World Press, 1955), 100. Like the former an overview based on secondary and even tertiary sources was K. K. Datta's *Unrest against British Rule in Bihar* (Kali Kinkar Datta ed., *Unrest against British Rule in Bihar, 1831–1859*, prepared in the State Central Records Office, Political Department, Bihar, Patna (Patna: Superintendent Secretariat Press, Bihar, Patna, 1957), 10–16. It mainly followed Herbert Hope Risley,

Districts of Hazaribagh and Lohardaga, vol. 16 of *A Statistical Account of Bengal*, ser. ed. W. W. Hunter, (London: Trübner, 1877; repr., New Delhi: Concept, 1976). In Datta's concluding paragraph, he redefined the insurrection as directed against 'the replacement of their indigenous system of administration by the rapidly growing authority of their British Master'. See Datta, *Unrest against British Rule in Bihar*, 16. However, this 'indigenous system' was an import, dating from Mughal times.

[56] Statement Bindrae, enclosure Jt. Commissioners to Government, 12 February 1832 (London: OIOC), BC 54,227, quoted in Jha, *The Tribal Revolt of Chotanagpur*, 171–72.
R. Guha expressed ignorance 'at the present state of research' whether eating seized goods by insurgents was common. Maybe, he surmised, the Kols were sufficiently influenced by Hinduism to have acquired from these a fear of ritual pollution. See Ranajit Guha, *Elementary Aspects of Peasant Insurgency in Colonial India* (Delhi: Oxford University Press, 1983), 147–48. Singrai mentioned in his statement to Russell that Raja Jagannath of Chotanagpur had told the mundas and mankis to bring the riches of the thikadars to him and 'let their paddy rice and other eatable things be pillaged by the hungry and poor'. Quoted in P. C. Roy Chaudhury, 'A Forgotten Agrarian Disturbance in Chotanagpur', *BPP* 75 (1956): 62). Uncooked rice was not subject to ritual exclusion rules. See Barbara Verardo, 'Rebels and Devotees of Jharkhand, Social, Religious and Political Transformations among the Adivasis of Northern India' (PhD thesis, London School of Economics and Political Science, 2003), 196.

[57] Then they surrendered and delivered up their arms. 'Poor little boys with pellet bows and little twigs without heads for arms—the scene made my heart bleed. On one side a tremendous armed force, on the other a naked, helpless, defenceless rabble'. See *India Gazette*, 24 February 1832, quoted in 'The Kholes', 186–88. J. C. Jha followed an account by 'an Officer', in the *Bengal Hurkaru*, of 25 February 1832. He spoke of 4,000 people surrendering. See Jha, *The Tribal Revolt of Chotanagpur*, 109.

[58] Devendra N. Panigrahi, *Charles Metcalfe in India: Ideas and Administration, 1806–1835* (New Delhi: Munshiram Manoharlal, 1968), 194–216; Dayal Dass, *Charles Metcalfe and British Administration in India* (New Delhi: Criterion Publications, 1988), 127–49.

[59] *John Bull in the East*, quoted in 'The Kholes', 186.

[60] Jha, *The Tribal Revolt of Chotanagpur*, 122. Coles in the original.

[61] *John Bull in the East*, quoted in 'The Kholes', 186.

[62] In some circles, much has been made of the exclamation of Mr. Kurtz in Joseph Conrad's *The Heart of Darkness*, 'exterminate the brutes!' See Jan C. Breman, 'Civilisatie en racism, Een staat van terreur: Kongo rond de eeuwwisseling' [Civilization and Racism: A State of Terror: Congo around 1900], in Dutch, in: *Kolonialisme, racisme en cultuurpolitiek*, eds. Jan Breman and others, special issue, *De Gids* 154, no. 5–6 (1991): 448–93. For an imperialist like Kurtz, this was not a politically correct slogan. The imperialist was primarily concerned with the political and economic incorporation of the subject population. The program of the raja of Chotanagpur, however, was colonialism, that is, subjugating the original population and then, in great measure, marginalising them by mass immigration.

[63] Jha, *The Tribal Revolt of Chotanagpur*, 30. Pergunnah in the original.

[64] 'The Kholes', 186, 187.

[65] Roy Chaudhury, 'A Forgotten Agrarian Disturbance in Chotanagpur', 60–65; Jha, *The Tribal Revolt of Chotanagpur*, 157–63.

[66] Minute by Mr. Blunt, 4 April 1832, New Delhi, NAI, Foreign Department, Secret, 6 August 1832. See also: Roy, *The Mundas and Their Country*, 120–21; Jha, *The Tribal Revolt of Chotanagpur*, 173, 196. On the other hand, Kumar had Blunt say that the local government officials of Chotanagpur had been apathetic towards the original population. See Kumar, *History and Administration of Tribal Chotanagpur*, 31-32).

[67] Charles Metcalfe (1785–1846), who after 1806 had set up the Delhi system, was after the governor general the highest in the pecking order of the service. He was also credited with a rare grasp of the feelings of the Indian population. This might have been more of the upper classes, as he had two children with a high-caste Indian lady. He was not adverse to pressing this advantage and stated that he used his 'multifarious experiences during a long course of service, in various and distant parts of India, in British and foreign territories, in camps and in courts, in cities, and in hamlets, in personal intercourse with all classes from the prince to the peasant'. See Metcalfe's Minute (New Delhi: NAI), Foreign, Secret, 6 August 1832, pros. 8–11. My kind of guy.

[68] Jha, *The Tribal Revolt of Chotanagpur*, 173.

[69] The Kols, Metcalfe said, were industrious and peaceable subjects. True, he believed that there had been exaction, but the victims had not tried to obtain redress. Moreover, the Kols seemed to have acted 'with thorough unanimity and concert . . . They thoroughly cleared their own country of foreigners and interlopers'. See Ch. Metcalfe to Bentinck, 4 March 1832, in Cyril H. Philips ed., *The Correspondence of Lord William Cavendish Bentinck, Governor-General of India: 1832–1835*, 2 vols., (Oxford: Oxford University Press, 1977), 773. A few weeks later, he did not believe that the insurrection in Chotanagpur was caused, as Blunt thought, by specific grievances. No attempts had been made to seek redress from them, although Bengal and Calcutta itself were 'swarming' with Kols from Chotanagpur. See Metcalfe, 14 April 1832, New Delhi, NAI, Foreign Department, Secret, 8 August 1832, pros. 8–11.

70 Metcalfe's Minute, New Delhi, NAI, Foreign Department, Secret, 6 August 1832, pros. 8–11. Cole and Coles in the original. P. Kumar claimed that Metcalfe thought that the Kols 'wanted to demolish the British Empire'. See Kumar, *History and Administration of Tribal Chotanagpur*, 32. In fact, that is not what Metcalfe wrote. He merely wanted to impress that whatever the Company might do, the British would always be regarded as foreigners.

71 Metcalfe's Minute, New Delhi, NAI, Foreign Department, Secret, 6 August 1832, pros. 8–11. Singbhoom Coles in the original. Given these words, it is surprising that Jha found that Metcalfe 'failed to recognise ... the strength of the Kol spirit of independence'. See Jha, *The Tribal Revolt of Chotanagpur*, 173.

72 Metcalfe's Minute, New Delhi, NAI, Foreign Department, Secret, 6 August 1832, pros. 8–11.

73 Metcalfe's Minute, New Delhi, NAI, Foreign Department, Secret, 6 August 1832, pros. 8–11.

74 Jha, *The Tribal Revolt of Chotanagpur*, 126–28.

75 Judicial letter to the Court of Directors, 25 September 1832; quoted in B. K. Roy, 'An Official Account of the Outbreak and Suppression of the Kol Insurrection During January, 1832', *JHR* 9, no. 2 (1967): 36.

76 Jha, *The Tribal Revolt of Chotanagpur*, 222–23. Charles Metcalfe stated that 'the obnoxious part of the tax was then ordered to be abolished ... which [modifications] were represented as rendering it comparatively popular'. See Charles Metcalfe's Minute of 14 April 1832, New Delhi, NAI, Foreign Department Secret, 6 August 1832.

77 Kumar, *History and Administration of Tribal Chotanagpur*, 30–31.

78 John Master, who investigated the trials, found that many law officers had mechanically followed the Muslim law and, as a rule, had pronounced capital punishment for rebellion. This was, Master stated, much too strict. See Jha, *The Tribal Revolt of Chotanagpur*, 216–20.

79 Wilkinson to Swinton. March 11, 1832, New Delhi, NAI, Foreign Department, Political Branch, Consultations 26 March 1832, Cons. 34–35.

80 Peter Auber, *Rise and Progress of the British Power in India*, by Peter Auber, M.R.A.S., late Secretary to the Honourable the Court of Directors of the East-India Company, vol. 2 (London: Wm. H. Allen, 1837), 690.

81 Eric Stokes, *The English Utilitarians and India* (Oxford: Clarendon Press, 1959; repr., Indian paperback edition, Delhi: Oxford University Press, 1989), 79. Repeated attempts by the Board of Control, the English government body to oversee the East India Company's affairs, to get Bengal adopt the southern ryotwari system, in 1812, 1813, 1815 respectively, ran into fierce opposition. See Panigrahi, *Charles Metcalfe*, 80. As late as 1828, the Bengal government pointed out that it was impractical to deal with 360,000–440,000 village headmen. See Panigrahi, *Charles Metcalfe*, 187.

82 Bentinck quoted William Fraser in his Minute of 20 January 1832. See Panigrahi, *Charles Metcalfe*, 69. This lack of uniformity, it has been pointed out, could not be a viable future for Britain's Indian possessions in the longer run. In the 1860s and 1870s, we see that as part of the Empire, a much more unitary Indian state was created. In the end it was Cornwallis' insistence on private property which prevailed. See Panigrahi, *Charles Metcalfe*, 157.

83 To it belonged Vice-President of the Council Charles Metcalfe; Deputy Secretary of the Judicial Department James Thomason and Member of the Council W. Blunt. See Stokes, *The English Utilitarians and India*, 153. On Thomason, see Peter Penner, 'James Thomason's Role in Vernacular Education', chap. 6 of *The Patronage Bureaucracy in North India: The Robert M. Bird and James Thomason School, 1820–1870* (Delhi: Chanakya Publications, 1981), 141–69.

84 Minute by Mr Blunt, 4 April 1832, New Delhi, NAI, Foreign Department, Secret, 6 August 1832.

85 Panigrahi, *Charles Metcalfe*, 8, 96, 97–98; 173; Percival Spear, 'The British and the Indian State to 1830', in *Tradition and Politics in South Asia*, ed. R. J. Moore (New Delhi: Vikas, 1979), 165; Stokes, *The English Utilitarians and India*, 21–22, 94–95; John William Kaye, *The Administration of the East India Company: A History of Indian Progress* (London: Richard Bentley, 1853), 215-19. The earliest use of the phrase 'village republic' was by Munro in 1806. See Burton Stein, *Thomas Munro: The Origins of the Colonial State and His Vision of Empire* (Delhi: Oxford University Press, 1989), 130.

86 Panigrahi, *Charles Metcalfe*, 218–19.

Most of the discussions of Indian 'village republics', or 'communities' of the last decennia go back to Louis Dumont's admirable article. See Louis Dumont, 'The "Village Community" from Munro to Maine', chap. 6 of *Religion, Politics and History in India: Collected Papers in Indian Sociology*, Le monde d'outre-mer passé et present, Première serie—Etudes 34 (Paris/The Hague: Mouton, 1970), 112–32.

87 This was 'a passing idyll', thundered Stokes (Stokes, *The English Utilitarians and India*, 148).

88 Panigrahi, *Charles Metcalfe*, 131–33.

89 Stokes, *The English Utilitarians and India*, 153–54; Panigrahi, *Charles Metcalfe*, 129–30.

90 One can point to Munro, who in his reforming zeal was aware of the work of Cleveland in the 1770s and 1780s with the Mal Paharias. See Kaye, *The Administration of the East India Company*, 221, note. In the mid-1820s, in the west of India the young officer Outram formed the Khandesh Bhil Corps to pacify the hills. See Kaye, *The Administration of the East India Company*, 473–87; James M. Campbell ed., *Khandesh District*, vol. 12 of *Gazetteer of The Bombay Presidency* (Bombay: Government Central Press 1880; repr., by J. M. Torgal, [Bombay: Gazetteers Department, Government of Maharashtra], 1985), 258–59; 317–18; Arvind M. Deshpande, *John Briggs in Maharashtra: A Study of District Administration Under Early British Rule* (Delhi: Mittal, 1987); A. K. Prasad, *The Bhils of Khandesh: Under the British East India Company (1818-1858)* (Delhi:

Konark, 1991); Stuart Gordon, *Marathas, Marauders and State Formation in Eighteenth-Century India* (Delhi, Calcutta, Chennai, Mumbai: Oxford University Press, 1994), 159–60). The Malwa and the Rajasthan Bhil Corps followed. See Stuart Gordon, *Marathas, Marauders and State Formation*, 161. Dayal Dass gave 1835 for the 'Mewar battalion'. See Dass, *Charles Metcalfe and British Administration in India*, 17.

[91] Jha, *The Tribal Revolt of Chotanagpur*, 146–50.

[92] Sutherland to Government, n.d., quoted in Jha, *The Tribal Revolt of Chotanagpur*, 147.

[93] *Bengal Hurkaru*, 14 April 1832, quoted in Jha, *The Tribal Revolt of Chotanagpur*, 141.

[94] Jha, *The Tribal Revolt of Chotanagpur*, 224–32.

[95] W. Dent himself wrote a note of dissent. Experience, he stated, had shown that the Maharaja of Chotanagpur should not be entrusted with extensive powers, and certainly not with those over the police. Dent proposed to man the police stations in Chotanagpur with the principal inhabitants of the area concerned. However, a change of personnel was not enough in itself. From the 'great extent, the peculiar nature of the country and state of the population' followed that the Bengal regulations were not well applicable to Chotanagpur. From the same considerations followed that controlling European officer should reside within the area. See Jha, *The Tribal Revolt of Chotanagpur*, 229–30.

[96] Jha, *The Tribal Revolt of Chotanagpur*, 235–36.

[97] Jha, *The Tribal Revolt of Chotanagpur*, 234, 237, note 1. For the Arakan rules see W. Blunt, Special Commissioner, 'Rules for the Administration of Criminal Justice in the Province of Arakan' (Kolkata: WBSA), Bengal Judicial (criminal) Lower Provinces, 22 July 1833, proc. no 26, 3 July 1828.

[98] Jha, *The Tribal Revolt of Chotanagpur*, 244.

[99] Most of this section is taken from Hodson, *List of the Officers of the Bengal Army*, vol. 4, 472–73.

[100] 'Wilkinson', *Westmoreland Papers* (website), 2004-2011, accessed 1 December 2011, http://www.northofthesands.org.uk/westmoreland/parish/12/crosby_ravensworth.

[101] Autobiography of John Hearsay, in Hugh Pearse, *The Hearsays: Five Generations of an Anglo-Indian Family* (London: William Blackwood and Sons, 1905), 327–28. Hodson mentioned the *London Gazette* of 1 March 1819. See Hodson, *List of the Officers of the Bengal Army*, vol. 4, 473.

[102] Jha, *The Tribal Revolt of Chotanagpur*, 233–34.

[103] That is Hodson's view. P. Kumar gave at one locus 6 May 1830, at another 25 March 1830. See Kumar, *History and Administration of Tribal Chotanagpur*, 29–30, 47.

[104] There is considerable difficulty here, as it appears from J. C. Jha's account that Wilkinson was appointed Agent on either 6 or 9 December 1832. See Jha, *The Tribal Revolt of Chotanagpur*, 240–42. According to Hodson, Wilkinson became commissioner to the governor general in 1836. What happened in 1836 was probably that Wilkinson was relieved from his post as commander of the Ramgarh Battalion and remained agent to the governor general. See Hodson, *List of the Officers of the Bengal Army*, vol. 4, 473. Only Act XX of 1854 brought Chotanagpur under the control of the lieutenant governor of Bengal as a non-regulation province under a commissioner. See P. C. Roy Chaudhury, *Singhbhum*, Bihar District Gazetteers (Patna: Superintendent Secretariat Press, Bihar, Patna, 1958), 101; see also Roy, *The Mundas and Their Country*, 130, note 21.

[105] Roy, 'Ethnographical Investigation in Official Records' (1935): 232.

[106] That sounded good, but profited more specifically the top layer of the village society, and it made alienation of land easier. Thus, the loss of land by the original population continued. See Fidelis de Sa, *Crisis in Chota Nagpur: With Special Reference to The Judicial Conflict Between Jesuit Missionaries and British Government Officials, November 1889–March 1890* (Bangalore: A Redemptorist Publication, 1975), 49–55.

[107] John Hoffman[n], *The World of the Mundas*, vol. 1 (New Delhi: Critical Quest, 2005), 17.

[108] Tickell, 'Memoir', 807.

[109] Jha, *The Tribal Revolt of Chotanagpur*, 244, note 1.

[110] Court of Directors to Bengal Government, 16 September 1835, quoted in Jha, *The Tribal Revolt of Chotanagpur*, 257.

[111] 'A.D. 1833 Regulation XIII', in Records Department, *Bengal Regulations Revenue and Judicial 1826–1834*.

[112] On 6 September 1833. See Jha, *The Tribal Revolt of Chotanagpur*, 240.

[113] Wilkinson to C. Macsween, 13 January 1834 (London: OIOC), BC 58,890. Wilkinson to Ensign P. Nicolson, 7 January 1834, Extract from Fort William Judicial Consultation, 17 February 1834 (London: OIOC), BC 58, 892 *(From now on WINS in the notes.)*

[114] Wilkinson to C. Macsween, 13 January 1834 (London: OIOC), BC 58,890.

[115] The sets for Civil Justice and Criminal Justice were attached to Wilkinson to C. Macsween, 13 January 1834 (London: OIOC), BC 58,890. *(From now on: Rules for Civil Justice: WCIV, and Rules for Criminal Justice: WCRIM in the notes.)* WCIV, paras 21–24.

[116] WINS, para 26.

[117] The rules for Civil Justice still apply to the Kolhan Government Estate. See Consultative Committee Meeting of the Ministry of Home Affairs Held on 21 August 1984, Item No. 24, 25, 26 (Delhi: Ministry of Home Affairs, 1984).

[118] WINS, para 11. The station should have a treasurer, but Wilkinson thought that cash for one month would do. The treasurer's main work would be to receive the revenue, to send it on quickly and to take charge of the stamps for the official papers. See WINS, para 23.

[119] Wilkinson hoped that all this would not cost more than Rs. 1,200. See WINS, para 12.

[120] WINS, para 16.

[121] WINS, para 16.

[122] WINS, para 15. The judicial assistants, particularly, should not acquire any status in the eyes of the public. The assistant should never ask his staff for their opinion and 'whenever you have occasion to be displeased with your [judicial assistants] let your reprimands be in public' (WINS, para 15). Umlah in the original. Wilkinson expected that a few examples would be sufficient to show the litigators that they should expect nothing from fraternizing with or giving bribes to the staff. See WINS, para 14.

[123] WINS, para 14.

[124] WINS, para 14; See also Jha, *The Tribal Revolt of Chotanagpur*, 245. Outside the area of the East India Company, in Ceylon in 1808, Governor Maitland ordered his collectors to make 'frequent circuits' adding up to 'one complete circuit of the whole of the district'. The collector was to keep 'a most minute diary of his proceeding'. Quoted by S. D. S. in his Introduction to Leonard Woolf, *Diaries in Ceylon, 1908–1911, Records of a Colonial Administrator: Being the Official Diaries Maintained by Leonard Woolf while Assistant Government Agent of the Hambantota District, Ceylon*, edited and with a preface by Leonard Woolf, and, *Stories from the East: Three Short Stories on Ceylon*, by Leonard Woolf (1908–11), repr. by *The Ceylon Historical Journal* 9, nos. 1–4 (July 1959–April 1960), 2nd edition (Dehiwala: Tisara Press, 1983), xxx.

[125] Wilkinson to C. Macsween, 13 January 1834 (London: OIOC), BC 58,890.

[126] These instructions from WINS, para 14.

[127] Wilkinson's instructions for the annual tour and its emphasis on visiting the villages proved to be a breakthrough in the area. As we have seen, earlier tours tended to be either a military campaign or a series of visits to local rajas and potentates. In 1821, the annual tour by the registrar of the Ramgarh district and joint magistrate and assistant collector (all in one person) was again instituted. See Jha, *The Tribal Revolt of Chotanagpur*, 60. A few years later, in 1827, Cuthbert admitted that no European officer had visited Chotanagpur for nearly seven years. See S. T. Cuthbert in Roy, 'Ethnographical Investigation in Official Records' (1921): 22. The regular series of annual tours through the area started with Wilkinson's letter to his assistants on 7 January 1834. From Wilkinson's time, the rule of the annual tour was strictly adhered to and the habit kept up till the end of British rule. 'If 'the key note of British rule was indeed personal rule' rule it was best characterized by the Tour. Not only this was an essential duty for every official in the district, but it featured in one form or another in nearly every trade and occupation.' See Charles Allen (ed.), *Plain Tales from the Raj: Images of British India in the Twentieth Century*, ed. in association with Michael Mason; Introduction by Philip Mason (London: Futura Publications, 1976), 163.

[128] WCIV, paras 21–24.

[129] WCIV, para 23.

[130] WINS, para 23.

[131] WCIV, para 7.

[132] WINS, para 22. Kutcherry in the original.

[133] 'Rules for Civil Justice', paras 1, 4, 5 in Wilkinson to C. Macsween, 13 January 1834 (London: OIOC), BC 58,890. In *forma pauperis*: 'in the way destitute people do'. B. N. Sinha and S. K. Chattapadhayay mentioned here the 'forma paupers', and the 'forma papper'. See B. N. Sinha and S. K. Chattopadhayay, *Commentaries on the Chota Nagpur Tenancy Act 1908: With Rules, Notifications and other Allied Laws, Amended with Act No. 45 of 1982 and Bihar Finance Act No. 58, of 1982* (Allahabad: Rajal, 1985), 425. They were nearly as bad in Latin as I am in Sanskrit, I fear.

[134] WINS, paras 6, 7.

[135] WCIV, para 5.

[136] Sentences that were more severe had to wait for approval by the agent. To get this, the assistant should forward his original proceedings with notes in English for final judgement to the agent. This had to be done immediately after he gave the verdict. The powers of the assistant were further limited by the chain of appeals. See Wilkinson to P. Nicolson, 7 January 1834, 'Modification directed by Government of the Rules by Captain Wilkinson', para 3 (London: OIOC), BC 58,890.

[137] Wilkinson to P. Nicolson, 7 January 1834, 'Modification directed by Government of the Rules by Captain Wilkinson', para 2 (London: OIOC), BC 58,890.

[138] WCIV, paras 14–16.

[139] WCIV, para 30. However, the appeal and the case in the Sadar Nizamat Court would be in Persian, the language of the Bengal higher courts. The possibility of dispensing with the Persian language in judicial and revenue proceedings was enacted a few years later, in Act XXIX of 1837. See Records Department, *India Acts*, vol. 1, (Calcutta: William Thacker, 1834–40), no pagination.

[140] WCIV, para 12.

[141] WCIV, para 28.

[142] WCIV, para 27 and note.
[143] WCIV, para 28. To close the loophole of arrears of revenue as a reason for the sale of land, the rules saw to it that complaints 'relative to balances or undue exaction of rent or disputed Revenue Accounts' could be received on unstamped paper, and would be 'heard and decided by the Assistants; any parties who may be dissatisfied with the decision of an Assistant, being at liberty to institute an Appeal to the Agent'. See WCIV, para 7.
[144] Apart from the productive agricultural lands, the ancestral lands were of first importance to the community. 'Even if they die at a distance, their heirs consider it a necessary act of piety, to transport their bones to their own village, that they may be buried in the Hursali, or burying-ground of the village'. See John Davidson to J. R. Ouseley 29 August 1839, in Roy, 'Ethnographical Investigation in Official Records' (1935) : 231–50. Obviously to prevent trouble in this sensitive sphere, local personnel could not receive cases involving (ancestral) land held exempt from revenue. See WCIV, para 1.
[145] John Davidson to J. R. Ouseley 29 August 1839, in Roy, 'Ethnographical Investigation in Official Records' (1935): 241.

Chapter 7: Strategic Moves on the Ethnic Frontier

[1] Wilkinson to Mangles, 22nd August 1836 (London: OIOC), BC 66,546. Rani Mohan Kumari succeeded her husband in 1827. As the accession of a woman was a precedent, this caused an armed uprising. She was pensioned off to Khurdha in 1833. See Balabhadra Ghadei, 'Orissa in the Great Revolt of 1857', *Orissa Review* (August 2008): 10–11, accessed 14 August 2011, http://www.orissa.gov.in/e-magazine/Orissareview/2008/August-2008/engpdf/or-august-2008.pdf.
[2] Wilkinson to Swinton. 11 March 1832, New Delhi, NAI, Foreign Department, Political Branch, Consultations 26 March 1832.
[3] Wilkinson to Swinton. 11 March 1832, New Delhi, NAI, Foreign Department, Political Branch, Consultations 26 March 1832. Mahrattas in the original.
[4] Dass, *Charles Metcalfe and British Administration in India*, 175.
[5] Government to Joint Commissioners, 17 May 1832, quoted in Jha, *The Tribal Revolt of Chotanagpur*, 207.
[6] Singhbhum paid Rs. 101, Surguja Rs. 3,362 and Sambalpur Rs. 30,700. See Swinton to Macnaughton, 26 March 1832, New Delhi, NAI, Foreign Department, Political.
[7] Swinton to Macnaughton, 26 March 1832, New Delhi, NAI, Foreign Department, Political.
[8] Macnaughton to Swinton, 13 June 1832, New Delhi, NAI, Foreign, Political.
[9] Macnaughton, Secretary to Governor General, to George Swinton, Chief Secretary to Government, 13 June 1832, New Delhi, NAI, Foreign Department, Political. Anyway, Bentinck's plans for the redeployment of troops were shot down by the Court of Directors in 1836. See Dass, *Charles Metcalfe and British Administration in India*, 176.
[10] Wilkinson to Swinton, 31 October 1832 (London: OIOC), BC 58,902. Singhboom, Dindraee, Bundgaum in the original. Bandgaon was the northernmost part of the Porahat Singh state. It was a late addition to Singhbhum. See Roy Chaudhury, *Singhbhum*, 418–19.
[11] Macsween to the Joint Commissioner in Jungle Mahals, 19 February [1833], Extract Fort William Judicial Consultation of the 8th March 1833 (London: OIOC), BC 1503.
[12] Wilkinson to Swinton, 31 October 1832 (London: OIOC), BC 58,902. Coles in the original.
[13] Wilkinson to Swinton, 31 October 1832 (London: OIOC), BC 58,902. Coles, Singbhoom in the original.
[14] 'From the Kishenpoor lines'. Kishenpur was another name for Ranchi, but apparently here the Chakradharpur Lines are meant.
[15] Wilkinson to Swinton, 31 October 1832 (London: OIOC), BC 58,902.
[16] Wilkinson to Swinton, 26 December 1832 (London: OIOC), BC 58,902.
[17] Wilkinson to Swinton, 12 January 1833 (London: OIOC), BC 58,904. Coles, Pergunnah, Sonepoor Mankees, Moondas, Nagpoor in the original.
[18] Jagdish Chandra Jha, 'Ganga Narain the Hero of the Bhumij Revolt of 1832–33', *JHR* 5, no. 1 (1962): 25–31; but for the full story, see the excellent Jagdish Chandra Jha, *The Bhumij Revolt (1832–33): Ganga Narain's Hangama or Turmoil* (Delhi: Munshiram Manoharlal, 1967).
[19] Swinton to Wilkinson, 31 December 1832 (London: OIOC), BC 58,902.
[20] Wilkinson to Swinton, 12 January 1833 (London: OIOC), BC 58,904. Coles, Singbhoom in the original.
[21] Wilkinson to Swinton, 12 January 1833 (London: OIOC), BC 58,904.
[22] Swinton to Wilkinson, 28 January 1833 (London: OIOC), BC 58,904. Rajah, Singboom in the original.
[23] Dalton, *Descriptive Ethnology of Bengal*, 175.
[24] An officer, quoted in Jha, *The Bhumij Revolt*, 101, note 5.
[25] Wilkinson, 'List of Zemindars and Their Estates and of Pergunnahs Under the Koss Management of the Rajah of Singbhoom' (London: OIOC), BC 58,534, September 1832–August 1834.
[26] Wilkinson, 'List of Zemindars and Their Estates and of Pergunnahs Under the Koss Management of the Rajah of Singbhoom

(London: OIOC), BC 58,534, September 1832–August 1834.

[27] Wilkinson to Macsween, 27 April 1833 (London: OIOC), BC 58,890. The same story, but transposed to June 1833, in Kumar, *History and Administration of Tribal Chotanagpur*, 130–32. See also Jha, *The Bhumij Revolt*, 155. Wilkinson to Mangles, 22 August 1836 (London: OIOC), BC 66,546. Also paraphrased in K. K. Basu, 'The History of Singhbhum 1821–1836', *JBRS* 42 (1956): 295.

[28] Wilkinson to Macsween, 27 April 1833 (London: OIOC), BC 58,890. Ganganarain, Rajah in the original.
This must have been standard practice with Wilkinson. Wilkinson insisted that the use of the council and of private arbitration instead of the courts was to be encouraged. In his Rules he stated that after the plaint had been filed and the answer of the defendant received, the agent or his assistant could at their discretion refer cases to these councils. The meeting of the village council would be in the main station or any other place where the assistant happened to be. When meeting to determine justice, the participants should not be nominated until the plaintiff, defendant and witnesses had been assembled. The plaintiff and defendant should each be permitted to challenge any members of the council. After the council for this case was instituted, the plaintiff and defendant had to agree to abide by its decision. For boundary disputes between two villages or estates, councils would be chosen from the neighbourhood, investigate the dispute on the spot 'and place such boundary marks as will prevent further disputes'. See WCIV, para 23.

[29] Wilkinson to Macsween, 27 April 1833 (London: OIOC), BC 58,890.

[30] Wilkinson to Macsween, 27 April 1833 (London: OIOC), BC 58,890. Singboom, peers, Bamanghatty in the original.

[31] Wilkinson to Macsween, 27 April 1833 (London: OIOC), BC 58,890. Singboom, Rajah Achete Sin, Diwan Kisna in the original.

[32] Kumar, *History and Administration of Tribal Chotanagpur*, 132.

[33] Wilkinson to Macsween, 27 April 1833 (London: OIOC), BC 58,890. Acheyt Sing, Bessee, Jeynt, Bessee, Joomal Moonda, Sumbulpoor, Rajah, Rajoo in the original.

[34] Wilkinson to Macsween, 27 April 1833 (London: OIOC), BC 58,890; see also Sahu, *The Kolhan Under British Rule*, 44. The agreement is also mentioned by C. P. Singh, whose text suggested that the event took place in 1830, but whose notes indicated a date just before 27 April of 1833. See C. P. Singh, *The Ho Tribe of Singhbhum*, 96–97. Mankees, Moondas, Bessee in the original.

[35] Raghunath Bisi still had not returned to Jaintgarh in 1837. See Wilkinson to Mangles, 5 May 1837 (London: OIOC), BC 69,239; see also: Illegible [Wilkinson] to S. K. (S. R.) Tickell, 12 December 1838; Roy Chaudhury, *Singhbhum Old Records*, 14–16.

[36] On the Bamanghati dispute and its history up to 1834, I mainly follow Sahu, *The Kolhan Under British Rule*, 51–67. See also the rather confused account in C. P. Singh, *The Ho Tribe of Singhbhum*, 104–22. There is a short treatment, unfortunately blaming it all on the British, in Das Gupta, *Adivasis and the Raj*, 109–11. A useful guide to this complex period is Jagdish Chandra Jha, 'British Contact with Singhbhum, 1821–1831', *JBRS* 47 (1961): 124–28. For the events after 1834, I mainly followed the files in London, OIOC, BC 66,546.

[37] After 1774, Damodar Bhanj had tried to stay clear both of the Company and the Marathas, a course in which he only partially succeeded. When he died childless in 1796 there followed years of contention to the throne. The widow queen Sumitra Dei appealed to the Marathas for military help. It was extended to her on condition of her paying revenue. Still, in 1800, the Raja of Keonjhar placed his second son on the throne of Mayurbhanj. See L. N. Raut, 'The State of Mayurbhanj During the Years of Maratha Supremacy in Orissa', *OHRJ* 28, nos. 1 and 2 (1982): 88–107; Patnaik, *Feudatory States of Orissa*, 61. In 1803, the Company took Odisha and restored the power of *rani* Sumitra. She ruled till 1810. See Patnaik, *Feudatory States of Orissa*, 80–81, 101–04.

[38] Roughsedge to Metcalfe, 9 May 1820 (London: OIOC), BC 21,438. Dalton called the mahapater 'a Gond chief', apparently referring to his Dorawa extraction. See Dalton, *Descriptive Ethnology of Bengal*, 180.

[39] B. K. Roy, 'Kuchang in Singhbhum Politics During 1768–1773', *JHR* 4, no. 2 (1962): 5–10.

[40] Mohammed Laeequddin, *Census of Mayurbhanj State: 1931*, vol. 1, *Report,* published under the Authority of the State (Calcutta: Caledonian, 1937), 19.

[41] Jha, *The Bhumij Revolt*, 9.

[42] O'Malley, *Singhbhum*, 229, 248. See also B. K. Roy, 'Kuchang in Singhbhum Politics During 1768–1773', *JHR* 4, no. 2 (1962): 5–10; Dalton, *Descriptive Ethnology of Bengal*, 179; Roy Chaudhury, *Singhbhum*, 439; C. L. Philip, 'Confidential History of Seraikella State: Completed to 1927 by C. L. Philip', typescript, (Chaibasa: Tribal Research and Training Centre, 1927), 6.
The takeover by Saraikela around 1800 might well have had the implicit sanction of Mayurbhanj, as around 1800, Abhiram Singh was the father-in-law of the Bhanj raja of Mayurbhanj. See E. T. Dalton and Commissioner of Cuttack Division to H. L. Dampier, Secretary to Government of Bengal, 15th February 1868 (New Delhi, NAI, Indian Foreign, Political, July 1868), pros. 217–310.

[43] For the rulers of Mayurbhanj from 1688 on, see 'Mayurbhanj (Princely State), Present ruler, predecessors and short history', *Rootsweb* (website), accessed 14 May 2011,

http://freepages.genealogy.rootsweb.ancestry.com/~royalty/ips/m/mayurbhanj.html.

[44] Jagannath Patnaik omits the rule of *rani* Jamuna Dei and gives Bikram's name as 'Tribikram'. See Patnaik, *Feudatory States of Orissa*, 103.

[45] I follow for 1826 as the year of Niranjan's death, Jha, 'British Contact with Singhbhum, 1821–1831', 126. Das Gupta gives 1831. See Das Gupta, *Adivasis and the Raj*, 110. There is some confusion about the precise name of his successor. Wilkinson called him Madhoo Dass; Ross wrote Madhop Doss. Wilkinson to Mangles, 28 February 1837; A. Ross to Court of Directors, 1 March 1838, (London: OIOC), BC 69, 239.

[46] M. Sahu gives 1825 as the year of the May meeting. See Sahu, *The Kolhan Under British Rule*, 53.

[47] Patnaik, *Feudatory States of Orissa*, 104.

[48] Sahu, *The Kolhan Under British Rule*, 44–45.

[49] 'Translation of a Letter from Ruggonauth Busee Brahmin of Jyntgurh of Singboom dated the 8th and received the 18th February 1830 to the P.l Agent SW Frontier', enclosed in Wilkinson to A. Sterling (Stirling), 12 May 1830 (London: OIOC), Bengal Political Consultations, 28 May 1830.

[50] Wilkinson to Thomson, 6 May 1832, in Sahu, *The Kolhan Under British Rule*, 54.

[51] Das Gupta, *Adivasis and the Raj*, 111.

[52] Wilkinson to Thomson, May 6, 1832. See C. P. Singh, *The Ho Tribe of Singhbhum*, 109. See also Das Gupta, *Adivasis and the Raj*, 110.

[53] Das Gupta, *Adivasis and the Raj*, 110.

[54] K. K. Basu mentioned 16 December 1831 as the date of approval. See Basu, 'The History of Singhbhum 1821–1836', 294.

[55] Jha, 'British Contact with Singhbhum, 1821–1831', 128.

[56] C. P. Singh, *The Ho Tribe of Singhbhum*, 107–08; Sahu, *The Kolhan Under British Rule*, 55; Patnaik, *Feudatory States of Orissa*, 161.

[57] Das Gupta, *Adivasis and the Raj*, 110–11.

[58] Wilkinson to Mangles, 22 August 1836 (London: OIOC), BC 66,546.

[59] Metcalfe to Bentinck, 7 April 1832, Philips, *The Correspondence of Lord William Cavendish Bentinck*, 794.

[60] Postmaster-General to A. Bushby, Officiating Secretary to the Government in the General Department, 22 February 1833; Wilkinson to Postmaster-General, Calcutta, 19 April 1833 (London: OIOC), BC 58,906.

[61] But possibly Wilkinson, because here I follow an unsigned letter which J. C. Jha attributed to Wilkinson (Wilkinson to Government, London, OIOC, Home Miscellaneous, no. 724, 478–79). See Jagdish Chandra Jha, 'British Contact with Singhbhum, 1821–1831', *JBRS* 47 (1961): 127 and note 22. C. P. Singh, however, mentioned Stockwell as the author of the proposal to separate the 'four Kol Peers' from both Mayurbhanj and Bamanghati. See C. P. Singh, *The Ho Tribe of Singhbhum*, 108.
Henry Ricketts referred to the proposal as made by himself in 1833. See Ricketts to Master, 3 June 1834 (London: OIOC), BC 66,544.

[62] This is the direct quote, the 'man of energy' referring, of course, to a British officer. Cole in the original. While paraphrasing, C. P. Sing mistook him for 'an influential chief of the tribe'. See C. P. Singh, *The Ho Tribe of Singhbhum*, 108. M. Sahu took him in the plural for 'some influential Kol chiefs of the locality'. See Sahu, *The Kolhan Under British Rule*, 58.

[63] Paraphrased in Jha, 'British Contact with Singhbhum, 1821–1831', 127.

[64] Wilkinson to Mangles, 22 August 1836 (London: OIOC), BC 1666.

[65] Sahu, *The Kolhan Under British Rule*, 59–60.

[66] Patnaik, *Feudatory States of Orissa*, 161–62. K. M. Patra, *Orissa under the East India Company* (New Delhi: Munshiram Mahoharlal, 1971), 298.

[67] Patra, *Orissa under the East India Company*, 298.

[68] Sir Henry Ricketts, then thirty-one years old, was at the first stages of a splendid career in the Indian Civil Service. See [Alexander J. Arbuthnot], 'Ricketts, Sir Henry (1802–1886)', *Dictionary of National Biography*, vol. 16 (1921–22; repr. London: Oxford University Press, 1963–64), 1148–49. See also Prabhat Mukherjee, 'The Commissioners of Orissa I, Sir Henry Ricketts', *OHRJ* 11, no. 2 (1962): 106-113. In 1828, Ricketts was made Collector and Magistrate of the newly-instituted northern division of Orissa. He became commissioner of Cuttack in August 1835. See Pr. Mukherjee, 'The Commissioners of Orissa I, Sir Henry Ricketts', 107. J. Patnaik gave 1836. See Patnaik, *Feudatory States of Orissa*, 167. So did Patra. See Patra, *Orissa under the East India Company*, 299. In 1838, Ricketts saved the Black Pagoda from destruction by the raja of Khurda. In the more tribal sphere, his role in the actions to suppress Meriah sacrifices by the Gonds should be mentioned. Ricketts was instrumental in introducing examinations of the knowledge of local languages of young civil servants in 1853. In 1854, he carried out an investigation into the administration of Singhbhum. See Henry Ricketts, 'Report on the District of Singhbhoom', in *Selections from the Records of the Bengal Government* 16 (Calcutta: Military Orphan Press, 1857), 61–115. This 'admirable specimen of the best type of Haileybury civilian' had as his dying wish that his name and the date of his death be inscribed on the monument to his wife's memory in Balasore with the words: 'He never forgot Balasore and the Ooreahs.'. Below it was an Odia translation. See [A. J. Arbuthnot], 'Ricketts, Sir Henry (1802–1886)'.

[69] Prabhat Mukherjee, 'The Commissioners of Orissa I: Sir Henry Ricketts', 107.
[70] Wilkinson to Mangles, 22 August 1836, para 34 (London: OIOC), BC 66,546.
[71] H. Ricketts to John Master, 3 June 1834 (London: OIOC), BC 66,544.
[72] C. P. Singh, *The Ho Tribe of Singhbhum*, 113–14.
[73] H. Ricketts to John Master, Officiating Commissioner of Circuit for the 19th Division Balasore, 3 June 1834 (London: OIOC), BC 66,544. Mahdeb Doss Mohapater, Coles, Mohurbunge in the original.
J. Master to C. Macsween Esqr, Secretary to Government Judicial Department, 4 June 1834 (London: OIOC), BC 66,544.
[74] 'Urzee of Roop Sing a Government Servant stationed at Baminghatty dated the 13th of June and received the 17th June at Kishenpoor' (London: OIOC), BC 66,544.
[75] Dalton called them 'Dorawas', also 'Naiks', Gonds of the Singhbhum district, who 'formerly' were settled in Bamanghati. After the insurrection of the Mahapater, they were 'banished from Bamanghati and permitted to settle in Singhbhum'. See Dalton, *Descriptive Ethnology of Bengal*, 277.
[76] 'Urzee of Roop Sing a Government Servant stationed at Baminghatty dated the 13th of June and received the 17th June at Kishenpoor' (London: OIOC), BC 66,544. Doorwah in the original.
[77] 'Urzee of Roop Sing a Government Servant stationed at Baminghatty dated the 13th of June and received the 17th June at Kishenpoor' (London: OIOC), BC 66,544.
[78] In these sources 'sahibs' do not always indicate British, but also Company soldiers, or even simply 'soldiers'. These different meanings could be used in one and the same statement, see 'Translation of Cheytun Dobasheas statement, 22nd June 1834' (London: OIOC), BC 66,544.
[79] Rajahs in the original.
[80] 'Urzee of Roop Sing a Government Servant stationed at Baminghatty dated the 13th of June and received the 17th June at Kishenpoor' (London: OIOC), BC 66,544. Coles, Peers in the original.
[81] 'Translation of an Urzee from Kooar Ajimber Sing of Seriekela dated 2 of Assar (24) Bengally' (London: OIOC), BC 66,544. There is a mistake in the date, but from other letters I conclude that it was written on 27 June 1834.
'Translation of Urzie from Roop Sing dated 2nd July 1834' (London: OIOC), BC 66,544.
[82] Sahu, *The Kolhan Under British Rule*, 63.
[83] 'Urzee of Roop Sing a Government Servant stationed at Baminghatty dated the 13th of June and received the 17th June at Kishenpoor' (London: OIOC), BC 66,544. Echapeer, Koochang in the original. See also Sahu, *The Kolhan Under British Rule*, 66.
[84] B. K. Roy, 'Kuchang in Singhbhum Politics During 1768–1773', *JHR* 4, no. 2 (1962): 5–10; O'Malley, *Singhbhum*, 248; Roy Chaudhury, *Singhbhum*, 439.
[85] Singh Deo, *Singhbhum, Seraikella and Kharswan Through the Ages*, 44–46.
[86] Sahu, *The Kolhan Under British Rule*, 63.
[87] 'If we want things to stay as they are, things will have to change' (Giuseppe Tomasi di Lampedusa, *The Leopard*, [original *Il Gattopardo*] (1958; English trans., New York: Pantheon, 1991), 40. I am grateful to Dirk Vlasblom who drew my attention to this book.
[88] Wilkinson to Macsween, 23 June 1834 (London: OIOC), BC 66,544.
[89] Macsween to Wilkinson, 21 July 1834 (London: OIOC), BC 66,544.
[90] Macsween to Wilkinson, 29 October 1834 (London: OIOC), BC 66,544.
[91] Ricketts to Macsween, 1 November 1834 (London: OIOC), BC 66,544. Bamunghatty, Rajah in the original.
[92] Ricketts to Macsween, 1 November 1834 (London: OIOC), BC 66,544. Rajah, shews in the original.
[93] Ricketts to Macsween, 1 November 1834 (London: OIOC), BC 66,544. Coles in the original.
[94] Ricketts to Macsween, 1 November 1834 (London: OIOC), BC 66,544.
[95] Ricketts to Macsween, 1 November 1834 (London: OIOC), BC 66,544.
[96] Macsween to Ricketts, 10 November 1834 (London: OIOC), BC 66,544.
[97] Sahu, *The Kolhan Under British Rule*, 65. C. L. Philip gave 3 November 1835 as the date. See Philip, 'Confidential History of Seraikella State', 6.
[98] Wilkinson to R. D. Mangles, Secretary to the Government of Bengal, 4 June 1835 (London: OIOC), BC 66,545. Lurkas, Singboom, Pergs in the original.
[99] Government of India to Court of Directors, 12 October 1835 (London: OIOC), BC 66,544.
[100] Philip, 'Confidential History of Seraikella State', 6.
[101] Sahu, *The Kolhan Under British Rule*, 65–66; Wilkinson to Mangles, 22 August 1836 (London: OIOC), BC 66,546.
[102] Wilkinson to Mangles, 22 August 1836 (London: OIOC), BC 66,546.
[103] Ricketts to Mangles, 14 January 1836 (London: OIOC), BC 66,545.
[104] Mangles to Ricketts, 26 January 1836 (London: OIOC), BC 66,545. Coles in the original.
[105] Ricketts to Mangles, 14 January 1836 (London: OIOC), BC 66,545. Ajumber, Mahdeb Dass Mohapater, Rajah in the original.

[106] Wilkinson to Mangles, 22 August 1836 (London: OIOC), BC 66,546.

[107] Roy Chaudhury, *Singhbhum*, 443.

[108] Ouseley to Halliday, 12 August 1839, in Roy Chaudhury, *Singhbhum Old Records*, 19.

[109] As Jadunath Sing stated in 1839: 'It was contrary to usage for a pension to be given to a murderer by the heirs of the deceased'. Ouseley to Halliday, 12 August 1839, in Roy Chaudhury, *Singhbhum Old Records*, 20.

[110] Paty, *History of Seraikella and Kharswan States*, 34.

[111] Sahu, *The Kolhan Under British Rule*, 66.

[112] Wilkinson to Mangles, 22 August 1836 (London: OIOC), BC 66,546. Coles in the original. The letter was also used by Dalton. See Dalton, 'The "Kols" of Chota Nagpore', 167.

[113] Already in 1834, the 'greatest number of the Native Records whilst Major Roughsedge was Agent, were not in the Office'. See Wilkinson to Macsween, 29 October 1834 (London: OIOC), BC 66,544. This notwithstanding that Calcutta had a few years previously ago acted upon this defect. On 28 May 1830, Calcutta announced, that 'a list of the correspondence with your predecessors on the affairs in Singbhoom and the insurrection of the Coles in 1821 will be transmitted to you from this [Political] department and duplicates of such despatches be forwarded as are not forthcoming in your office'. See Swinton to Wilkinson, 28 May 1830 (London: OIOC), Bengal Political Consultations, No 68, 28 May 1830. Apparently, this was not enough.

[114] Coles, Peers, Rajah in the original.

[115] Chiefs for sirdars in the original.

[116] Wilkinson to Mangles, 22 August 1836, para 49 (London: OIOC), BC 66,546.

[117] Cole Peers, Ramghur, Sinbhoom, Peers, Gumla in the original.

[118] Wilkinson to Mangles, 22 August 1836 (London: OIOC), BC 66,546.

[119] Penelope Carson, 'An Imperial Dilemma, The Propagation of Christianity in Early Colonial India', *The Journal of Imperial and Commonwealth History* 18, no. 2 (1990): 179. The Evangelical revival in England stressed the role of education in the fight against superstition, and that view was extended to India. See Stokes, *The English Utilitarians and India*, 27–36.

[120] Mangles to Wilkinson, 5 September 1836 (London: OIOC), BC 66,546.

[121] Dass, *Charles Metcalfe and British Administration in India*, 194–95.

[122] J. C. Jha mentioned these friendships. See Jha, *The Tribal Revolt of Chotanagpur*, 244, note 1. At the time of this visit, the private secretary to Governor General Lord Auckland was John Colvin. See Emily Eden, *Up the Country, Letters Written to Her Sister from the Upper Provinces of India* (1866; repr., from the 1930 edition by Edward Thompson, with a new introduction by Elizabeth Claridge and notes by Edward Thompson, London: Virago Press, 1984), ix.

[123] 'Am.tg to C.os Rupees Three hundred and twenty /C.os Rupees 320'. Mangles to Wilkinson, 1 November 1836 (London: OIOC), BC 69,239.

[124] Mangles to Macnaughten, 19 September 1836 (London: OIOC), BC 66,546. Assim, Coles in the original.

[125] Mangles to Macnaughten, 19 September 1836 (London: OIOC), BC 66,546. Calculated, Coles in the original.

[126] Mangles to Macnaughten, 21 September 1836 (London: OIOC), BC 66,546.

[127] Extract Judicial Letter from India, dated 6 February (no. 3) 1837 (London: OIOC), BC 66,546.

[128] Mangles to Macnaughten, 19 September 1836 (London: OIOC), BC 66,546.

[129] Extract Judicial Letter from India, dated 6 February (no. 3) 1837 (London: OIOC), BC 66,546.

[130] Ricketts to the Secretary to Government in the Judicial Department Fort William, 13 November 1836 (London: OIOC), BC 69,239. Hazareebaugh, Mohapater, Bamunghattee, Captn, Mohurbunje, Rajah in the original.

[131] Mangles to Ricketts, 22 November 1836 (London: OIOC), BC 69,239. Singbhoom, Govt., Rajah, Govnt., Hazareebaugh in the original.

[132] Mangles to Ricketts, 22 November 1836 (London: OIOC), BC 69,239. Singbhoom, Govt., Rajah, Govnt., Hazareebaugh in the original.

[133] Wilkinson to Mangles, 22 August 1836 (London: OIOC), BC 66,546.

[134] Extract Judicial Letter from India, dated 6 February 1837 (no 3) 1837 (London: OIOC), BC 66,546.

[135] Wilkinson to Mangles, 5 November 1836 (London: OIOC), BC 69,239.

[136] Wilkinson to Mangles, 30 November 1836 (London: OIOC), BC 69,239.

[137] Wilkinson to Mangles, 30 November 1836 (London: OIOC), BC 69,239.

[138] The course of the campaign is taken from M. Sahu with additional information from C. P. Singh. See Sahu, *The Kolhan Under British Rule*, 72–77; C. P. Singh, *The Ho Tribe of Singhbhum*, 122–27.
When C. P. Singh characterised the campaign as one of 'the most modern army of its day, drilled and disciplined almost to perfection, equipped with technologically advanced weapons of war', he did not betray an intimate knowledge of military history. He mentioned the 'efficient command of Col. Richards and Capt. Wilkinson, who had acquired an unerring grasp of tactics of war together with an intimate knowledge of the topography of the country.' That goes rather far for a 'blank spot'. By the way, the force was not under command of Richards, who had headed the Second Kolhan Campaign in 1821. But why this unexpected praise of the Company army and its command? It is a case of impression management. On the other side was

'arrayed a rabble masquerading as an army'. Without mentioning the source, C. P. Singh had taken the 'rabble' image from a British officer who described the Kol Insurrection of a few years earlier and much further north. See 'The Kholes', *AJMR*, n.s., 8 (May-August 1832): 188. He was not the last one to be inaccurate, see also Sushila Mishra, *History of the Freedom Movement in Chota Nagpur (1885–1947)* (Patna: Kashi Prasad Jayaswal Research Institute, 1990), 127–28.

[139] Wilkinson to Mangles, 7 January 1837 (London: OIOC), BC 69,239.
[140] A. Ross to Court of Directors, 1 March 1838 (London: OIOC), BC 69,239.
[141] Wilkinson to Mangles, 18 December 1836 (London: OIOC), BC 69,239. This is the only direct reference to Colonel Richards that I could find on the conduction of the Kolhan Campaign III. It referred to events in 1821. The campaign of 1836–37 was called by several writers, on the authority of Dalton, Colonel Richards' Campaign. See Dalton, *Descriptive Ethnology of Bengal*, 182. However, Richards was the commander during the Second Kolhan Campaign of 1821. In 1836–37, he was commanding the Danapur Division. At the time, the Third Kolhan Campaign was called 'the Operations of Captn. Lawrence during the months of November and December 1836 and January and February 1837'.
[142] Wilkinson to Mangles, 18 December 1836 (London: OIOC), BC 69,239.
[143] Wilkinson to Mangles, 14 December 1836 (London: OIOC), BC 69,239.
[144] Wilkinson to Mangles, 7 January 1837 (London: OIOC), BC 69,239. Hon'ble, Daks in the original.
[145] Wilkinson to Mangles, 22 January 1837 (London: OIOC), BC 69,239.
[146] Sahu, *The Kolhan Under British Rule*, 74.
[147] Wilkinson to Mangles, 14 February 1837 (London: OIOC), BC 69,239.
[148] Sahu, *The Kolhan Under British Rule*, 74–76.
[149] Wilkinson to Mangles, 14 February 1837 (London: OIOC), BC 69,239. Gomarrea in the orginal.
[150] Wilkinson to Mangles, 14 February 1837 (London: OIOC), BC 69,239.
[151] Wilkinson to Mangles, 14 February 1837 (London: OIOC), BC 69,239. Coles, Bamunghatty in the original.
[152] Wilkinson to Mangles, 28 February 1837 (London: OIOC), BC 69,239. Mankies, Moondas, Singhboom Rajah, Peers in the original.
[153] Mangles to Wilkinson, 28 February 1837 (London: OIOC), BC 69,239. Hon'ble in the original.
[154] A. Ross to Court of Directors, 1 March 1838 (London: OIOC), BC 69,239.
[155] 'A.D. 1833 Regulation XIII', in Records Department, *Bengal Regulations Revenue and Judicial 1826–1834*, para VII.

Chapter 8: The Arrival of the Assistant

[1] Wilkinson to Mangles, 28 February 1837 (London: OIOC), BC 69,239.
[2] Wilkinson to Mangles, 28 February 1837 (London: OIOC), BC 69,239. Rajah(s), Baboos, paras, Augt, Colhan, Zemindars in the original.
[3] Kumar, *History and Administration of Tribal Chotanagpur*, 135–37. Kumar mentioned 'bottles of country wine'.
[4] Mangles to Wilkinson, 21 March 1837 (London: OIOC), BC 69,239.
[5] Wilkinson to Mangles, 22 August 1836, para 57 (London: OIOC), BC 66,546.
[6] Mangles to Wilkinson, 21 March 1837 (London: OIOC), BC 69,239. &, Govt. in the original.
[7] Wilkinson to Mangles, 30 March 1837 (London: OIOC), BC 69,239. Ltt., Ramghur, 2., Singbhoom, Capt., Lieutt., Coles in the original.
[8] Jha, *Bhumij Revolt*, 169. Jha gives R. Ouseley, but I take it to be John Ralph Ouseley.
[9] Wilkinson to Mangles, 5 May 1837 (London: OIOC), BC 69,239.
[10] 'Military Appointments, &c.', *The Calcutta Monthly Journal* 30 (May 1837, published 28th June 1837): 62, reprinted in *Calcutta Monthly and General Register of Ocurrences, Throughout the British Dominions in the East, Forming an Epitome of the Indian Press for the Year 1837*, 3rd series, vol. 3 (Calcutta: Samuel Smith, 1838). Colhan in the original.
[11] Mangles to Wilkinson, 9 May 1837 (London: OIOC), BC 69,239. Cos., Colhan in the original. See also 'Civil Appointments &c.', in 'Asiatic Intelligence, Calcutta', *AJMR*, n.s., 24 (September-December 1837): 96.
[12] Lieutt. Thos. Simpson to Mangles, 12 May 1837 (London: OIOC), BC 69,239. Mangles to Simpson, 23 May 1837 (London: OIOC), BC 69,239. Lieutt, Colhan in the original.
[13] Mangles to Wilkinson, 9 May 1837 (London: OIOC), BC 69,239; Wilkinson to Tickell, 12 May 1837; Wilkinson to Mangles, 13 May 1837, in Murali Sahu, 'Some Old Records Concerning Singhbhum', cyclostyled copy in the Tribal Research and Training Centre, Bara Guira, n. pl, n.d., 25, 4–5.
[14] Wilkinson to Mangles, 14 February 1837 (London: OIOC), BC 69,239.
[15] Mangles to Wilkinson, 28 February 1837 (London: OIOC), BC 69,239. Govt in the original.
[16] Macnaughten to Mangles, 13 March 1837 (London: OIOC), BC 69,239.
[17] Wilkinson to Mangles, 28 February 1837 (London: OIOC), BC 69,239. Koodabera, Chaibassa, Goomlagurh in the original.
[18] Wilkinson to Mangles, 30 March 1837 (London: OIOC), BC 69,239.

[19] Tickell, 'Memoir', 705. Chyebassa in the original.
[20] Wilkinson to Tickell, enclosure in Wilkinson to Mangles, 5 May 1837 (London: OIOC), BC 69,239.
[21] Wilkinson to Tickell, enclosure in Wilkinson to Mangles, 5 May 1837 (London: OIOC), BC 69,239. Hindoos, Lurkas in the original.
[22] Tickell, 'Memoir', 784.
[23] Tickell to Wilkinson, n.d (Patna: BSA), SOC. Indeed, no date, but from the place in the bound volume, I hazard May or early June 1837.
[24] G. G.'s Agent to Tickell, June 2, 1837, in Roy Chaudhury, *Singhbhum Old Records*, 7.
[25] Wilkinson to Tickell, enclosure in Wilkinson to Mangles, 5 May 1837 (London: OIOC), BC 69,239.
[26] Ricketts, 'Report on the District of Singhbhoom', 94.
[27] John Deeney, *Ho-English Dictionary* (Chaibasa: Xavier Ho Publications, 1978), 89.
Lionel B. Burrows gave only the 'encampment of many tents'. See Lionel B. Burrows, *The Grammar of the Ho Language* (Calcutta: Catholic Orphan Press,1915); reprinted as *The Grammer of the Ho Language: An Eastern Himalayan Dialect* (New Delhi: Cosmo Publications, 1980), 156. Sic: it is 'Grammar', of course; and Ho is not spoken in the eastern Himalaya, but in Jharkhand and Odisha.
[28] Dunbar, 'Some Observations on the Lurka Coles', 373.
[29] Dunbar, 'Some Observations on the Lurka Coles', 372.
[30] Kumar, *History and Administration of Tribal Chotanagpur*, 134.
[31] Wilkinson to Tickell, enclosure in Wilkinson to Mangles, 5 May 1837 (London: OIOC), BC 69,239.
[32] Ricketts, 'Report on the District of Singhbhoom', 97–98. See also S. N. Singh, 'A Short History of Jails in Chotanagpur During the Early British Rule', *JHR*, 4, no. 2 (Republic Day 1962): 35–39.
[33] Wilkinson to Mangles, 7 January 1837 (London: OIOC), BC 69,239.
[34] Wilkinson to Tickell, enclosure in Wilkinson to Mangles, 5 May 1837 (London: OIOC), BC 69,239. Coles, Ramghur in the original.
[35] Ricketts, 'Report on the District of Singhbhoom', 95.
[36] Samuel Richard Tickell, 'Manis Crassicaudata, (Auct) M. Pentadactyla (Ibid.), Short-tailed or thick-tailed Manis, In Hindustan, generally called "Bujjerkeet" –Orissa, "Bujjer-Kapta" and "Surooj Mookhee"–By the Lurka Koles, "Armoo"', *JASB* 11 (1842): 227–28.
[37] 'A.D. 1833 Regulation XIII' (London: OIOC), Bengal Regulations: Revenue and Judicial, 1826–1834.
[38] Wilkinson to Mangles, 28 February 1837 (London: OIOC), BC 69,239. Govt, 60 to 70 miles, 50 to 65 [miles] in the original.
[39] Wilkinson to Mangles, 28 February 1837 (London: OIOC), BC 69,239.
[40] Wilkinson to Tickell, enclosure in Wilkinson to Mangles, 5 May 1837, (London: OIOC), BC 69,239. Nagree, Peer in the original.
[41] Wilkinson to Mangles, 28 February 1837 (London: OIOC), BC 69,239. Rajah in the original.
[42] From Mayurbhanj: Thai, Bharbharia (or Nagra), Lalgarh and Anwla. From Porahat: Bar including Jaintgarh, (Sat) Bantaria including Jagannathpur, Kotgarh, Jamda, Latua, Charai, Gumra (Goomlapeer), Barkela, Ajodhya, 'Gopunathpore', Govindpore (Asantalia?); Kainua (Kalleenowahpeer), Kuldina, Rengra, Saranda. From Saraikela: Rajabasa, 'Oonchdeapeer', 'Purlongpeer' (Chiru or Gulkera?), Sidiu and Lota. See Wilkinson to Tickell, enclosure in Wilkinson to Mangles, 5 May 1837 (London: OIOC), BC 69,239.
[43] As a token of esteem, the Kunwar of Saraikela got Rs. 800; the Khandapater of Koraikela, Rs. 300; Lokhnath Singh of Kera, Rs. 250; the Mahapater of Chainpur, Rs. 200. See Wilkinson to Mangles, 28 February 1837 (London: OIOC), BC 69,239.
[44] Wilkinson to Tickell, enclosure in Wilkinson to Mangles, 5 May 1837 (London: OIOC), BC 69,239. Madhub Doss, Mohurbhunj, Rajah in the original.
[45] Wilkinson to Mangles, 28 February 1837 (London: OIOC), BC 69,239.
[46] A. Ross to Court of Directors, 1 March 1838. No. 8 of 1838, Judicial Department (London: OIOC), BC 69,239. See also J. R. Ouseley to F. I. Halliday, 12 August 1839, in Roy Chaudhury, *Singhbhum Old Records*, 21.
[47] Risley, *Singbhum District*, 137.
[48] J. R. Ouseley to F. I. Halliday, 12 August 1839, in Roy Chaudhury, *Singhbhum Old Records*, 18–22.
[49] J. R. Ouseley to F. I. Halliday, 12 August 1839, in Roy Chaudhury, *Singhbhum Old Records*, 18–22. Judonauth in the original.
[50] Wilkinson, 22 February 1838, in Ricketts, 'Report on the District of Singhbhoom', 111.
[51] C. V. Aitchison, *A Collection of Treaties, Engagements, and Sanads Relating to India and Neighbouring Countries*, vol. 2 (Calcutta: Government of India, Central Publication Branch, 1930), 343.
[52] Wilkinson to Tickell, enclosure in Wilkinson to Mangles, 5 May 1837 (London: OIOC), BC 69,239. Singbhoom in the original.
[53] Wilkinson to Tickell, enclosure in Wilkinson to Mangles, 5 May 1837 (London: OIOC), BC 69,239. Coles in the original.

[54] Henry Ricketts to Secretary to Government in the Judicial Department, Fort William, 31 May 1837; Mangles to Wilkinson, 6 June 1837 (London: OIOC), BC 69,239.

[55] Wilkinson to Mangles, 5 May 1837 (London: OIOC), BC 69,239. Zemindars in the original.
Thirty years later, this led to a lengthy discussion. It was not clear whether Mayurbhanj, or any other Tributary Mahal, was British territory or not. It was ultimately decided it was not. See New Delhi, NAI, Foreign, Political, July 1868; April 1872; June 1873; May 1874; July 1873; August 1884; February 1889; June 1891.

[56] Ricketts to Secretary to Government in the Judicial Department, 31 May 1837 (London: OIOC), BC 69,239. Colhan, Bamunghattee in the original.

[57] Mangles to Wilkinson, 6th June 1837 (London: OIOC), BC 69,239.
Calcutta had decided against the wishes of the raja of Mayurbhanj, who assumed that Wilkinson harboured ill feelings towards him. He petitioned to be always heard whenever Wilkinson sent a report concerning his state, and 'that any district of mine may not be included in the jurisdiction of Hazareebaugh, but may remain as it always has in the jurisdiction of Cuttack'. This letter with a request of his comments, was sent to Wilkinson, who had answered to Calcutta's satisfaction on 26 May 1837. See A. Ross to Court of Directors, 1 March 1838, no. 8 of 1838, Judicial Department (London: OIOC), BC 69,239.

[58] Tickell to Wilkinson, 4 January 1839 (Patna: BSA), SOC. Kolehan, Bammunghattee, Santal, Kole in the original.

[59] Governor-General's Agent to S. K. (*sic*) Tickell, 12 January 1839, in Roy Chaudhury, *Singhbhum Old Records*, 17. Coles in the original.

[60] Tickell to Wilkinson, 13 February 1839 (Patna: BSA), SOC. Rajah in the original.

[61] Tickell to Wilkinson, 4 January 1839 (Patna: BSA), SOC.

[62] Governor-General's Agent to S. K. (*sic*) Tickell, 12 January 1839, in Roy Chaudhury, *Singhbhum Old Records*, 17. Coles in the original.

[63] Tickell to Wilkinson, 4 January 1839 (Patna: BSA), SOC. Sontal in the original.

[64] Tickell to Wilkinson, 4 January 1839 (Patna: BSA), SOC. Koles, Bamunghattee Sontals in the original.

[65] Tickell to Wilkinson, 13 February 1839 (Patna: BSA), SOC. Koles in the original.
The attitude of these zamindars had bothered Tickell before. In September 1837, just a few months after he arrived in Chaibasa, a messenger had arrived from the raja of Mayurbhanj with a small list of names of Hos, who according to him were recent settlers from Thai *pir*. He asked permission to expel them. Tickell suspected that these Hos were, in fact, 'old residents' of Bamanghati, and that the raja 'wanted to get rid of them for other and private views'. So, he told the messenger that he would first make 'further enquiries'. See Tickell to Wilkinson, 8 September 1837 (Patna: BSA), SOC.

[66] Wilkinso[n] to P. R. Peckell (S. R. Tickell), 21 February 1839, in Sahu, 'Some Old Records Concerning Singhbhum', 29–30. Coles, malgoozaree, mohurbunge, Bamunghatty, Colehan, Cole, Coles, Cole, Colehan in the original.

[67] Wilkinson to Mangles, 28 February 1837 (London: OIOC), BC 69,239. Rajah, Cole, peers, Bamunghatty in the original. See also Roy Chaudhury, *Singhbhum*, 369.

[68] J. D. Sifton, *Final Report on the Survey and Settlement of the Manoharpur Estate in Singhbhum* (Bankipore: The Bihar and Orissa Secretariat Book Depot, 1914), 1.

[69] Wilkinson to Tickell, enclosure in Wilkinson to Mangles, 5 May 1837 (London: OIOC), BC 69,239.

[70] Tickell to Wilkinson, 6 June 1838. See Murali Sahu, *The Kolhan under British Rule* (Jamshedpur: Sushanta Kumar Sahu, 1985), 162.

[71] Roughsedge to Swinton, 14 April 1821 (London: OIOC, Bengal Political Consultations), 12 May 1821.

[72] Tickell, 'Memoir', 699.

[73] 'Such as Gowallas, Bhuiyas and Gonds'. Tuckey made a distinction between 'old' and 'new' diku holdings, the difference being registration before and after 1867. See Tuckey, *Final Report*, 24–25.

[74] 'the Kamars, Magadha Gowalas, Kumhars and Tantis'. See Tuckey, *Final Report*, 24–25.

[75] Wilkinson to Mangles, 5 May 1837, (London: OIOC), BC 69,239.

[76] Thomas Wilkinson, 'Wilkinson's Rules', appendix VI to N. N. Sinha and S. K. Chattopadhyay, *Commentaries on Chotanagpur Tenancy Act 1908: With Rules, Notifications and Other Allied Laws, Amended with Act no. 45 of 1982 and Bihar Finance Act no. 58 of 1982* (Allahabad: Rajal, 1985), 425–30.

[77] Wilkinson to Mangles, 5 May 1837, (London: OIOC), BC 69,239. *Wilkinson's Rules for Civil Justice for the Kolhan*. From now on: WR.

[78] WR, para 4.

[79] WR, para 7.

[80] WR, para 8.

[81] WR, para 11.

[82] WR, paras. 6, 8.

[83] WR, para 8.

[84] Wilkinson to Tickell, enclosure in Wilkinson to Mangles, 5 May 1837 (London: OIOC), BC 69,239.

[85] Wilkinson to Tickell, enclosure in Wilkinson to Mangles, 5 May 1837 (London: OIOC), BC 69,239.

[86] In addition, there would be the bearers and servants on the assistant's tours, such as the 'Nagpoor Dhangars' (probably Oraons) on Tickell's tour in 1839–1840. See Tickell, 'Memoir', 707.
[87] Wilkinson to Tickell, enclosure in Wilkinson to Mangles, 5 May 1837 (London: OIOC), BC 69,239.
[88] Wilkinson to Macsween, 27 April 1833 (London: OIOC), BC 58,890.
[89] Wilkinson to Ensign P. Nicolson, 7 January 1834, Extract from Fort William Judicial Consultation, 17 February 1834 (London: OIOC), BC 58, 892, paras 14, 16 and 19.
[90] Wilkinson to Mangles, 28 February 1837 (London: OIOC), BC 69,239. Coles in the original.
[91] Wilkinson to Tickell, enclosure in Wilkinson to Mangles, 5 May 1837 (London: OIOC), BC 69,239. Interpreters for Dobusheas in the original.
[92] Wilkinson to Tickell, enclosure in Wilkinson to Mangles, 5 May 1837 (London: OIOC), BC 69,239.
[93] John William Kaye, *The Administration of the East India Company: A History of Indian Progress* (London: Richard Bentley, 1853), 215.
[94] Wilkinson to Tickell, enclosure in Wilkinson to Mangles, 5 May 1837 (London: OIOC), BC 69,239.
[95] Tickell, 'Memoir', 807.
[96] Court of Directors to Government of India, 21 November 1838 (London: OIOC, India & Bengal Despatches, 5 September to 28 November 1838, letter 1 March (no. 8) 1838.
[97] Wilkinson to Tickell, enclosure in Wilkinson to Mangles, 5 May 1837 (London: OIOC), BC 69,239.
[98] Wilkinson to Tickell, 9 December 1838. See Sahu, 'Some Old Records Concerning Singhbhum', 29. mankee, Colehan in the original.
[99] 'No. LIII. Translation of Pottah given by Captain Tickell to Raoria, Mankee of Kowsillaposi in Bur Peer, dated 19th March 1839', in C. V Aitchison, *A Collection of Treaties, Engagements, and Sanads Relating to India and Neighbouring Countries: Containing the Treaties, etc., Relating to the Bengal Presidency, Assam, Burma and the Eastern Archipelago, Revised and continued Up to the present time by the Authority of the Foreign Department*, vol. 1, (Calcutta: Office of the Superintendent of Government Printing, India, 1892), 148–50. The deed to Jamedar Manki of Asura, given in Tuckey, *Final Report*, 13, is virtually the same.
[100] Roy Chaudhury, *Singhbhum Old Records*, 54–5.
[101] This was an essential point, strongly rephrased in Wilkinson's instructions to Tickell. See Wilkinson to Tickell, enclosure in Wilkinson to Mangles, 5 May 1837 (London: OIOC), BC 69,239). Rajah and, Zemindar in the original.
[102] Roy Chaudhury, *Singhbhum Old Records*, 54–5.
[103] Roy Chaudhury, *Singhbhum*, 332.
[104] Wilkinson to Tickell, enclosure in Wilkinson to Mangles, 5 May 1837 (London: OIOC), BC 69,239.
[105] Wilkinson to Tickell, enclosure in Wilkinson to Mangles, 5 May 1837 (London: OIOC), BC 69,239.
[106] Governor-General's Agent to S. K. (*sic*) Tickell, 10 December 1838, in Roy Chaudhury, *Singhbhum Old Records*, 12–13.
[107] 'No. LIII. Translation of Pottah given by Captain Tickell to Raoria, Mankee of Kowsillaposi in Bur Peer, dated 19th March 1839'. See Aitchison, *A Collection of Treaties*, vol. 1, 150.
[108] Wilkinson to Tickell, enclosure in Wilkinson to Mangles, 5 May 1837 (London: OIOC), BC 69,239. Coles, Punchayets in the original.
[109] Wilkinson to Tickell, enclosure in Wilkinson to Mangles, 5 May 1837 (London: OIOC), BC 69,239.

Chapter 9: Poto Ho's Resistance

[1] The south had 'suffered considerably'. See Depree, *Geographical and Statistical Report*, 37.
[2] Governor-General's Agent to S. K. (*sic*) Tickell, 10 December 1838, in Roy Chaudhury, *Singhbhum Old Records*, 12–13.
[3] Tickell to Wilkinson, 23 September 1837 (Patna: BSA), SOC.
[4] Tickell to Wilkinson 31 October 1837 (Patna: BSA), SOC.
[5] Tickell to Wilkinson, 18 September 1837, vol. 118 (Patna: BSA, SOC,) . The text is corrupted, the *pir*'s name is not clear.
[6] Tilsoon or Toonia was a *pir* of Porahat. See Birch to E. T. Dalton, 5 August 1858, referred to in Francisca Kujur, *Raja Arjun Singh of Porahat (1829 AD – 1890 AD)* (Allahabad: K.K. Publications, 2007), 2.
[7] Tickell to Wilkinson, 21 October 1837 (Patna: BSA), SOC. Kishenpur in the original.
[8] Pudmpoor in the original. See Tickell to Wilkinson, 23 October 1837 (Patna: BSA), SOC. It could be either the Padampur opposite the village of Siringsia or the village with the same name five km north-east of Jaintgarh.
[9] Tickell to Wilkinson 23 October 1837 (Patna: BSA), SOC. Burpeeree, Jeynt in the orginal.
[10] Tickell to Wilkinson 23 October 1837 (Patna: BSA), SOC.
[11] Tickell to Wilkinson 31 October 1837 (Patna: BSA), SOC; Mathew Areeparampil, *Struggle for Swaraj: A History of Adivasi Movements in Jharkhand (from the earliest times to the present day)* (Lupungutu, Tribal Research and Training Centre (TRTC), 2002), 121

12 Tickell to J. R. Ouseley, 7 May 1839 (Patna: BSA), SOC.
13 Tickell to Wilkinson, 31 October 1837 (Patna: BSA), SOC.
14 Areeparampil, *Struggle for Swaraj*, 121–22.
15 Tickell to Wilkinson, 31 October 1837 (Patna: BSA), SOC.
16 Tickell to Wilkinson, 31 October 1837 (Patna: BSA), SOC. Bora in the original.
17 Tickell to Wilkinson, 31 October 1837 (Patna: BSA), SOC.
18 Tickell to Wilkinson, 30 October 1837 (Patna: BSA), SOC.
19 F. G. Cardew, *A Sketch of the Services of the Bengal Native Army to the Year 1895* (Calcutta: Office of the Superintendent of Government Printing, 1903), 158. Cardew erroneously gave November 30th.
20 Sahu, *The Kolhan under British Rule*, 79.
21 Tickell to Wilkinson, 19 November 1837 (Patna: BSA), SOC. See also the short overview of these actions in F. C. Gardew (compiler), *A Sketch of the Services of the Bengal Native Army, To the Year 1895*, compiled in the office of the Adjutant General in India (Calcutta: Office of the Superintendent of Government Printing, India, 1903), 158. Also C. P. Singh, 'The Martyrs of Singhbhum', *Journal of the Bihar Research Society* 57 (1971): 151.
22 'Cole Insurrection', *AJMR*, n.s., 26 (May 1838): 19. 'about forty yards' in the original.
23 Areeparampil, *Struggle for Swaraj*, 123–24. Fr Mathew stated that the range of the long distance-bow would be one mile, but that is not the shooting range at Siringsia. Earlier, one of Roughsedge's officers, mentioned 200 yards. See 'Short Account of the Lurkacoles', *John Bull in the East*, reprinted in *AJMR*, 13 (January–June 1822): 137.
24 'Cole Insurrection', 19. Khundbund, yards in the original.
25 Tickell to Wilkinson, 19 November 1837 (Patna: BSA), SOC.
26 Tickell to Wilkinson, 19 November 1837 (Patna: BSA), SOC. Cardew followed the correspondent, though, but put the one dead on the British side, 'one man killed and 15 wounded'. See F. G. Cardew, *A Sketch of the Services of the Bengal Native Army to the Year 1895*, 158.
27 Tickell to Wilkinson, 19 November 1837 (Patna: BSA), SOC. Ghat, Koles in the original.
28 Sahu, *The Kolhan under British Rule*, 79. 'Gummu Munda of Dumuria village, . . . one of the mankis of Bar pir'.
29 The sources are not entirely clear here. Tickell mentioned 300 including 'native Comd. &no[n] Comd. Officers'. See Tickell to Wilkinson, 24 November 1837 (Patna: BSA), SOC. That would settle it, but Murali Sahu insists that it were the troops plus 300 allies, and he gives the breakdown of this number. See Sahu, *The Kolhan under British Rule*, 79–80. On tactical grounds, one is inclined to follow Sahu here. It would hardly make sense to go after 2,000 Hos with only a party of 300 local allies, who would not have an advantage of armaments and training.
30 Tickell to Wilkinson, 24 November 1837 (Patna: BSA), SOC. Areeparampil, *Struggle for Swaraj*, 124. Sahu, *The Kolhan under British Rule*, 79–80.
31 Areeparampil, *Struggle for Swaraj*, 125.
32 Lieutenant Thomas Simpson to Armstrong, 2nd in command of the Ramgarh Batallion, commanding troops in Singbhoom, 3 December 1837 (Patna: BSA), SOC.
33 Tickell to Wilkinson, 5 December 1837 (Patna: BSA), SOC.
34 Armstrong to Tickell, 8 December 1837 (Patna: BSA), SOC. Coles, *poot* in the original.
35 Armstrong to Tickell, 8 December 1837 (Patna: BSA), SOC.
36 Sahu, *The Kolhan under British Rule*, 80. Areeparampil, *Struggle for Swaraj*, 125, added the names of Borah, Nurrai, Narra, Pandua and Mangami. The precise date of Poto's capture is not entirely clear. OIOC, India and Bengal Despatches, no. 22, of 1837, 20 December 1837, gave 7 December. Sahu gave 8 December, and this tallies with Armstrong's, Simpson's and Tickell's accounts of these days.
37 Government Letter no. 1368, 5 December 1837, mentioned in Sahu, *The Kolhan under British Rule*, 80.
38 Areeparampil, *Struggle for Swaraj*, 125. Sahu, *The Kolhan under British Rule*, 80–81.
39 Tickell to Wilkinson, 15 January 1838 (Patna: BSA), SOC.
40 Tickell to Wilkinson, 17 January 1838 (Patna: BSA), SOC.
41 'Cole Insurrection', 20. Cole(s) in the original.
42 India & Bengal Dispatches, Bengal 4 December 1834 to 25 March 1840, Judicial ,12 March 1840. Fr. Mathew's copy in the Tribal Research and Training Centre, Guira. Singhboom in the original.
43 India & Bengal Dispatches, Bengal 4 December 1834 to 25 March 1840, Judicial ,12 March 1840. Fr. Mathew's copy in the Tribal Research and Training Centre, Guira.

Part III: The Establishment of the Estate, 1837–1842

Chapter 10: Post-Conflict Reconstruction

[1]

Table 1 Expenses Wilkinson's trip to Calcutta 1837.

	Rupees
Wilkinson's trip to Calcutta on duty and back to Kissenpur (Ranchi) Chota Nagpur	320
Expense for intelligence and apprehension of wanted people	1,411
Grain for the prisoners at Chaibasa	344"12"5
Compensation to the Hos of the village of Pooboduree for water-courses previously constructed by them on the site of the new cantonment in the Kolhan	100
Building of bridges for the troops and erection of the jail	461
Totalling	2,637"12"5

Wilkinson to Mangles, 28 February 1837 (London: OIOC), BC 69,239. Cole, Kissenpore, Chota Nagpore, Singbhoom, Coles, Choebassa, Colhan, in the original.

[2] Wilkinson to Mangles, 22 August 1836 (London: OIOC), BC 66,546.

[3] Wilkinson to Mangles, 28 February 1837 (London: OIOC), BC 69,239. Colhan, Singbhoom, Rajah, Baboos in the original.

[4] Wilkinson to Mangles, 28 February 1837 (London: OIOC), BC 69,239. Cole(s), Dussera, Devy pooja in the original.

[5] Tuckey, *Final Report*, 16.

[6] Wilkinson to Mangles, 28 February 1837 (London: OIOC), BC 69,239.

[7] Ricketts, 'Report on the District of Singhbhoom', 70–73. I have added the percentage increase.

[8] But in 1840 Tickell stated that the amount of rent was Rs. 6,500. See Tickell, 'Memoir', 700.

[9] Court of Directors to Government of India, 21 November 1838 (London: OIOC), India & Bengal Despatches, 5 September to 28 November 1838, letter 1 March (no 8) 1838.

[10] Governor-General['s Agent] to Lieutenant Simpson, 25 September 1838, in Roy Chaudhury, *Singhbhum Old Records*, 11.

[11] Tickell, 'Memoir', 806.

[12] Tickell to J. R. Ouseley, 7 May 1839 (Patna: BSA), SOC.

[13] Wilkinson to Tickell, enclosure in Wilkinson to Mangles, 5 May 1837 (London: OIOC), BC 69,239.

[14] Tickell, 'Memoir', 806. It was a success for the time being. Serious violence among the Hos along *kili* lines would not reappear till the Mutiny of 1857–61.

[15] Government v[ersus] Musummat Beerung, widow of Gergenday, age 22 years (London: OIOC), Extract Bengal Judicial Proceedings 7 August 1838, nos. 30–2. Musummat Beerung in the orginal. It is possible that she was from Seraikela, as her caste was given, rather unclearly, as 'Coondee Soveeklay Cole'.

[16] Government v[ersus] Musummat Beerung, widow of Gergenday, age 22 years (London: OIOC), Extract Bengal Judicial Proceedings 7 August 1838, nos. 30–32. Coles of Singbhoom in the original.

[17] Government v[ersus] Musummat Beerung, widow of Gergenday, age 22 years (London: OIOC), Extract Bengal Judicial Proceedings 7 August 1838, nos. 30–32.

[18] We might get a glimpse of her fourteen years later, when in 1852 the assistant reported as an example of the lack of discipline in the prison, one female prisoner who was 'the recognized concubine' of one of the guards. See Ricketts, 'Report on the District of Singhbhoom', 97.

[19] Tuckey, *Final Report*, 13. See also MacPherson, *Final Report on the Operations*, 108.

[20] Tickell, 'Memoir', 698, 699.

[21] Risley, *Singbhum District*, 75–76.

[22] Roy Chaudhury, *Singhbhum Old Records*, 331.

[23] Tuckey, *Final Report*, 14. 'According to the ideas and in the interests of the Hos', Tuckey added.

[24] Tickell to Wilkinson, 11 March 1838 (Patna: BSA), SOC. Moondas, Mankees, peers, mankees, peer in the original.

[25] [illegible] (Wilkinson) to Tickell, 10 December 1838, in Roy Chaudhury, *Singhbhum Old Records*, 12–13.

[26] There is early-twentieth-century evidence that a circle of villages under a manki did not cross the border of the *pir*. At that time, too, there was speculation about the connection between mankis and *pirs*. Under influence of the Khuntkati operations in Chotanagpur, MacPherson thought that 'the Jurisdiction of a Manki is known as a Pir'. See MacPherson, *Final Report on the Operations*, 108. So did Tuckey, who thought that 'originally there was probably one Manki for each Pir, but as the country developed, it became impossible for one Manki to do the work in the larger Pirs, and they were divided into suitable units'. See Tuckey, *Final Report*, 12. The *pirs* covered the whole of the Kolhan, but the further they were from the border with Porahat

the larger they tended to be. Probably it was there, furthest from Porahat, that Tickell found no manki. Institution of these was made more easy for him because the borders of the Kolhan followed ethnic lines.

[27] Wilkinson to Tickell, enclosure in Wilkinson to Mangles, 5 May 1837 (London: OIOC), BC 69,239.

[28] Wilkinson to Mangles, 28 February 1837 (London: OIOC), BC 69,239.

[29] Wilkinson to Tickell, enclosure in Wilkinson to Mangles, 5 May 1837 (London: OIOC), BC 69,239.

[30] Governor-General['s Agent] to Lieutenant Simpson, Official Assistant of the Political Agent, Colehan, Singhbhum, 25 September 1838, in Roy Chaudhury, *Singhbhum Old Records*, 10–11.

[31] Governor-General's Agent to S. K. (*sic*) Tickell, 10 December 1838, in Roy Chaudhury, *Singhbhum Old Records*, 12-13. Mankees, Peers in the original.

[32] Tickell to Wilkinson, 21 November 1838 (Patna: BSA), SOC. Doobashias in the orginial.

[33] Governor-General's Agent to S. K. (*sic*) Tickell, 10 December 1838, in Roy Chaudhury, *Singhbhum Old Records*, 12-13. Mankees, Peers in the original.

[34] Tickell, 'Memoir', 700.

[35] Tickell to Wilkinson, 21 November 1838 (Patna: BSA), SOC. Malgoozaree in the orginial.

[36] Wilkinson to Tickell, enclosure in Wilkinson to Mangles, 5 May 1837 (London: OIOC), BC 69,239. Cole in the original.

[37] Tickell to Wilkinson, 21 November 1838 (Patna: BSA), SOC. Biswee, Jynt, Koles, Koles in the original.

[38] Tickell to Wilkinson, 21 November 1838 (Patna: BSA), SOC. Ghuno Mankee, Gwallas & Bhoooians, mankees, ryots, Hindoos, Kolehan in the original. Tickell used 'race' here as used by Cuvier, whose work he knew well. In the 1817 French original of *The Animal Kingdom* Cuvier used the expression 'races' for 'conformations héréditaires'. The English translation of 1827, however, had 'varieties'. See Michael Banton, 'The classification of races in Europe and North America, 1700—1850', *International Social Science Journal* 39, no. 1 (February 1987): 51. Note that here Tickell used the word 'civilization' not to refer to 'British civilization' but to indicate the culture of the Bhuiyas and Goalas.

[39] Tickell to Wilkinson, 21 November 1838 (Patna: BSA), SOC.

[40] Tickell to Wilkinson, 21 November 1838 (Patna: BSA), SOC. Jynt, Biswee, Kolehan, peers, mankees, moondas in the original.

[41] Governor-General's Agent to S. K. (*sic*) Tickell, 12 December 1838, in Roy Chaudhury, *Singhbhum Old Records*, 14–15. Wilkinson's letter is, quite possibly, 'Tickell's list of abandoned villages' mentioned by Sen. See Asoka Kumar Sen, 'Reconstructing Adivasi Village History: Problems and Possibilities', *JAIS* 2, no 2 (August 2015): 32.

[42] Wilkinson to Tickell, enclosure in Wilkinson to Mangles, 5 May 1837 (London: OIOC), BC 69,239. Coles in the original.

[43] Tickell, 'Memoir', 804.

[44] Samuel Richard Tickell, 'Vocabulary of the Ho Language', *JASB* 9, part 2 (1840): 1063. See also John Deeney, *Ho-English Dictionary* (Chaibasa: Xavier Ho Publications, 1978), 241, 66, 80 and 191, respectively.

[45] Dunbar, 'Some Observations on the Lurka Coles', 373.

[46] Tickell, 'Memoir', 793.

[47] Samuel Richard Tickell, 'Vocabulary of the Ho Language', 1063–64.

[48] Wilkinson to Tickell, enclosure in Wilkinson to Mangles, 5 May 1837 (London: OIOC), BC 69,239. Practise in the original. He probably copied the lapse period from his earlier rulings in Chotanagpur proper.

The principle of limitation of legal memory came from English law. It was introduced in 1275, by the first Statute of Westminster, in which 'the time of memory was limited to the reign of Richard I (Richard the Lionheart), beginning 6 July 1189, the date of the King's accession'. See 'Time immemorial', *WP*, accessed 20 November 2014. In India, it was stated in Regulation II of 1805, Section 3, Clause 1. See John Clark Marshman, 'Limitation of Time for the Cognizance of Suits', addendum to *Guide to the Civil Law of the Presidency of Fort William: Containing all the Unrepealed Regulations, Acts, Constructions and Circular Orders of Government, to which is prefixed An Epitome of Every Act and Rule* (Serampore: Serampore Press, 1842), para 16, 526. That leaves the question, why Wilkinson gave such a short period of twelve years. Maybe he was following the —by then —legal convention in India. Maybe, he was just pragmatic, and thought that this was a solution of the land question which would bring quiet to a deeply disturbed area, and at the same time would not overburden the courts with old cases. Now 1822 was the year of the deaths of both Roughsedge and Raja Govind Nath, which started the de facto introduction of the Bengal regulations and the creation of a new class of immigrant landlords. See Kumar, *History and Administration of Tribal Chotanagpur*, 23. Also see Roy, *The Mundas and Their Country*, 107. The jury is still out on this question.

I am grateful to the philosopher of law Frans Niessen who drew my attention to the importance of limitation of legal memory.

[49] Governor-General's Agent to S. K. (*sic*) Tickell, 10 December 1838, in Roy Chaudhury, *Singhbhum Old Records*, 12–13. Mankees, Peers in the original.

[50] Wilkinson to Tickell, enclosure in Wilkinson to Mangles, 5 May 1837 (London: OIOC), BC 69,239.

[51] 'They never touch milk'. See Risley, *Singhbhum District*, 47.

[52] Tickell, 'Memoir', 805–6.

[53] Tickell, 'Memoir', 805.

54 Tickell, 'Memoir', 805. Michael Yorke informed me that the Hos of Saranda cultivated *asan* in gardens that were family property.
55 Tickell's letter, 1 February 1842, cited in Cook to Commissioner, 18 December 1911. See Das Gupta, *Adivasis and the Raj*, 247, note 3.
56 Dunbar, 'Some Observations on the Lurka Coles', 373.
57 Dunbar, 'Some Observations on the Lurka Coles', 373.
58 Tickell, 'Memoir', 806. As Tickell explained, the Ho language had a good system of counting. See Samuel Richard Tickell, 'Vocabulary of the Ho Language', *JASB*, new series, 9, part 2 (1840): 1065.
The habit of taking a handful was not unique to the Hos. It was also practiced in Ancient Greece, as the denomination of their coin, *drachma*, meant 'fistful'. See 'Greek drachma', *WP*, accessed 19 April 2013.
59 Wilkinson to Tickell, enclosure in Wilkinson to Mangles, 5 May 1837 (London: OIOC), BC 69,239.
60 Assistant to Governor-General's Agent and Commissioner, July 13, 1841, in C. P. Singh, *The Ho Tribe of Singhbhum*, 150.
61 'Second examination of Bajee Moond of Garia in Goomlah 28th April 1821 for the purpose of obtaining local information', appendix to: Roughsedge to Swinton, 7 August 1821 (London: OIOC), BC 21,439.
62 Tickell, 'Memoir', 805. 'Poory' in the original.
63 Taylor, *Pir Notes*, 20.
64 Tickell to J. R. Ousely, 17 November 1839 (Patna: BSA), SOC.
65 Tickell to J. R. Ousely, 17 December 1839 (Patna: BSA), SOC. Chyetchunder in the original.
66 Tickell, 'Memoir', 804.
67 Wilkinson to Mangles, 5 May 1837 (London: OIOC), BC 69,239.
68 Wilkinson to Tickell, enclosure in Wilkinson to Mangles, 5 May 1837 (London: OIOC), BC 69,239.
69 Mangles to Wilkinson, 6 June 1837 (London: OIOC, BC 69,239). Lurka Coles in the original.
70 Court of Directors to Government of India, 21 November 1838 (London: OIOC), India & Bengal Despatches, 5 September to 28 November 1838, letter no. 8, 1 March 1838.
71 Macaulay considered that 'all the historical information which had been collected from all the books written in the Sanskrit language is less valuable that what may be found in the most paltry abridgements used at preparatory schools in England'. Anyway, Macaulay was not an India buff. Compare this statement with this on fruits: 'all the tropical fruits together are not worth any of our commonest English productions – cherry, strawberry, currant, apple, pear, peach'. The mango 'eats like honey and turpentine, the plantain like a rotten pear'. Quoted in Zareer Masani, *Macaulay: Britain's Liberal Imperialist* (London: The Bodley Head, 2013), 99, 59 respectively. He was much opposed to continue giving importance to Sanskrit and Persian and Arab in education as well as in much of official life, and greatly in favour of teaching European knowledge in the English language. See John William Kaye, *The Administration of the East India Company: A History of Indian Progress* (London: Richard Bentley, 1853), 597. Also William Wilson Hunter, *Life of Brian Houghton Hodgson* (London: John Murray, 1896, also repr. New Delhi, Madras: Asian Educational Services, 1991), 312–13. About the realities and reactions, see the excellent David Kopf, *British Orientalism and the Bengal Renaissance: The Dynamics of Indian Modernization, 1773–1835* (Berkeley and Los Angeles: University of California Press, 1969), 236–72.
Governor-General William Bentinck's decision in favour of English education was a resounding defeat for the Orientalists, many of them in the Asiatic Society of Bengal, who had made much of India's culture available for modern study and appreciation. For Bentinck's and other Anglicists' ideological roots, see Charles Allen, *The Prisoner of Kathmandu, Brian Hodgson in Nepal 1820-43* (London: Haus, 2015), 117–19, 164–67.
72 Council of Education, quoted from James Long's introduction to Adam's *Reports on Education in Bengal (1835-38)* in Hunter, *Life of Brian Houghton Hodgson*, 320. See also Peter Penner, 'James Thomason's Role in Vernacular Education', Chapter 6 of *The Patronage Bureaucracy in North India: The Robert M. Bird and James Thomason School, 1820–1870* (Delhi: Chanakya Publications, 1981), 145–46. Both James Thomason and B. H. Hodgson came out strongly at the side of 'vernacular education', education in the modern Indian languages.
73 Tickell to Wilkinson, 11 March 1838 (Patna: BSA), SOC. Hindoo in the original.
74 Tickell to John Davidson, 1 April 1839 (Patna: BSA), SOC.
75 Wilkinson to Tickell, enclosure in Wilkinson to Mangles, 5 May 1837 (London: OIOC), BC 69,239.
76 Tickell, 'Memoir', 706.
77 Wilkinson to Tickell, enclosure in Wilkinson to Mangles, 5 May 1837 (London: OIOC), BC 69,239.
78 For a general introduction to witchcraft among the Hos and related peoples, see Sanjay Bosu Mullick, 'Gender Relations and Witches among the Indigenous Communities of Jharkhand, India', in *Gender Relations in Forest Societies in Asia: Patriarchy at Odds*, ed. Govind Kelkar, Dev Nathan and Pierre Walter (New Delhi: Sage, 2003), 119–46.
79 Wilkinson to Tickell, enclosure in Wilkinson to Mangles, 5 May 1837 (London: OIOC), BC 69,239.
80 Tickell to J. R. Ouseley, 7 May 1839 (Patna: BSA), SOC.
81 Tickell, 'Memoir', 802.
82 Wilkinson to Tickell, enclosure in Wilkinson to Mangles, 5 May 1837 (London: OIOC), BC 69,239.

[83] Wilkinson to Tickell, enclosure in Wilkinson to Mangles, 5 May 1837 (London: OIOC), BC 69,239.
[84] Wilkinson to Tickell, enclosure in Wilkinson to Mangles, 5 May 1837 (London, OIOC), BC 69,239.
[85] Wilkinson to Tickell, enclosure in Wilkinson to Mangles, 5 May 1837 (London: OIOC), BC 69,239. Coles in the original.
[86] Mangles to Wilkinson, 6 June 1837 (London: OIOC), BC 69,239. Coles in the original.
[87] Dunbar, 'Some Observations on the Lurka Coles', 374.
[88] Tickell, 'Memoir', 801.
[89] Tickell, 'Memoir', 801.
[90] Tickell, 'Memoir', 706.
[91] Tickell, 'Memoir', 801.
[92] M. W. R. (illegible) to J. R. Ouseley, 17 September 1840 (Patna: BSA), SOC.
[93] From 15 May 1839 until 30 September 1843, Thomas Wilkinson was Resident at Nagpur. He retired on 1 March 1844. In England, he became member of the Royal Asiatic Society of Great Britain and Ireland, and was mentioned as 'Wilkinson, Lieut.-Col. Thomas, Gravely, Lyndfield, Sussex'. See 'List of the Members of the Royal Asiatic Society of Great Britain and Ireland', *JRASGBI* 17 (1860): 12. He got the K.C.S.I. on 24 May 1866. Wilkinson died in London on 7 April 1867, aged 72. See Hodson, *List of the Officers of the Bengal Army*, vol. 4, 473. He was buried in the church of his native Crosby Ravensworth. He is remembered with an altar tomb and a plaque with the inscription 'Be ye doers of the work and not hearers only' (James 1: 22). See 'Wilkinson', *Westmorland Papers* (website), accessed 1 December 2011,
 http://www.northofthesands.org.uk/westmoreland/parish/12/crosby_ravensworth .
[94] Tickell, 'Memoir', 807.
[95] Roy, *The Mundas and Their Country*, 130.
[96] John Ralph Ouseley (1801–50) was the second son of Sir William Ouseley (1769–1842), oriental scholar—he was a Leiden alumnus—and traveller. J. R. Ouseley built the Agent's residence in Ranchi. In 1843 'certain irregularities' in a trial conducted by him, ending in a death sentence, and 'the loose inconsequential and confused nature of Major Ouseley's reply' proved him to be 'an officer not qualified to conduct judicial business of a difficult and important character'. See Secretary to the Government of Bengal in the Judicial Department to Secretary to the Government of India, Political Department, 10 April 1843, New Delhi, NAI, Foreign, Political, 2 September 1843. In its reply the governor general agreed, but found 'no evidence of how the other parts of his function are performed'. Therefore, he was 'prepared to take into consideration the separation [of] the judicial functions from the other administrative duties of the G. G. Agent on S. W. Frontier and the entrusting of them to a separate officer'. See Secretary to Government of India to J. Halliday, Secretary to Government of Bengal, ibid. In November 1844, he was 'removed from this appointment and ordered to join his regiment'. See Hodson, *List of the Officers of the Bengal Army*, vol. 4, 438–39. J. R. died in 1850, leaving an 'Indian widow'. See 'Papers, mainly concerning the estate of Lt-Col John Ralph Ouseley (1801-50), Bengal Army 1817-50', London (OIOC), Ms Eur D908. S. C. Roy gave 1839–49 as the term for J. R. Ouseley. See Roy, *The Mundas and Their Country*, 130–31.
[97] John Ralph's uncle was the diplomat William Gore Ouseley, who served in Washington, Rio de Janeiro, assisted to the creation of Argentina, and served in Buenos Aires. See 'William Ouseley', *WP*, accessed 7 February 2011; 'William Gore Ouseley', *WP* , accessed 7 February 2011. His father was a nephew of Joseph Walker Jasper Ouseley (1800–89) at the time superintendent of the Mysore princes and Persian translator under government, who became professor of Persian and Arabic at Haileybury (1844–59) and was Examiner in Oriental Languages to the Civil Service Commission from 1862 to 1883. See Hodson, *List of the Officers of the Bengal Army*, vol. 4, 439.
Joseph Walker was not Robert, as Kumar thought. See Kumar, *History and Administration of Tribal Chotanagpur*, 83. Robert was Joseph Walker's son. He 'stabbed a native' in October 1854 (ibid, 88), but was sent back to England as his crime was believed to have been brought about by a 'too strict attention to his studies'. After his arrival in England, his 'temporary insanity' was quickly gone. He was allowed to return to India in 1857. See Waltraud Ernst, *Mad Tales from the Raj: The European Insane in British India, 1800–1858* (London and New York: Routledge, 1991), 118–19.
[98] Dr John Davidson to Major J. R. Ouseley, [29 August] 1839 , in Sarat Chandra Roy, 'Ethnographical Investigation in Official Records', *JBORS*, 25 (1935): 243–44.

Chapter 11: Consolidation

[1] Asoka Kumar Sen, 'Reconstructing an Event, The Great Rebellion of 1857-8 and Singhbhum Indigenes', in *The Politics of Belonging in India: Becoming Adivasi,* edited by Daniel J. Rycroft and Sangeeta Dasgupta (London and New York: Routledge, 2011), 90.
[2] Wilkinson to Tickell, enclosure in Wilkinson to Mangles, 5 May 1837 (London: OIOC), BC 69,239. Singbhoom, Handea, Cole in the original.
[3] India & Bengal Dispatches, Bengal 4 December 1834 to 25 March 1840, Judicial 12 March 1840. Fr. Mathew's copy in the Tribal Research and Training Centre, Guira.

[4] '3/4 of a Seer of Rice, 1/8 of a Seer of dhal, one pice weight of Salt, and the same quantity of Tobacco'. See Wilkinson to Tickell, enclosure in Wilkinson to Mangles, 5 May 1837 (London: OIOC), BC 69,239.
The pice weight of salt and tobacco poses a problem. One standard seer was 2 lb. 0 oz, about 955 grammes. See H. H. Wilson, *A Glossary*, 474. If we take 1 pice as a fraction of a seer, it would make a pice = 0.0156, seeing that 1 pice = 1/4th anna = 1/16th of a rupee. That would give the prisoner 14,5 gm of salt and tobacco a day—and still little chance he would ever come out alive. I assume a writing mistake and take Tickell's pice as a pie. There were 3 pie in 1 pice. Thus I arrive at a pice of 4.86 gm, i.e., a little less than 5 gm.

[5] Five sheep for the prison, mentioned Ricketts in 1857. This bonanza should be viewed in the perspective of a maximum number of inmates of 250 normally and 200 in the hot season. See Henry Ricketts, 'Report on the District of Singhbhoom', 97–98.

[6] Tickell to Wilkinson, 13 June 1839 (Patna: BSA), SOC.

[7] Wilkinson to Tickell, enclosure in Wilkinson to Mangles, 5 May 1837 (London: OIOC), BC 69,239. Singbhoom, Handea, Cole in the original.

[8] Tickell to Wilkinson, 13 June 1839 (Patna: BSA), SOC.

[9] 'Affairs of Singbhoom', 24 October 1838, in Bengal Judicial, 21 November 1838, no. 12 (London, OIOC), India and Bengal Despatches, 5 September to 28 November 1838.

[10] Tickell to J. R. Ouseley, 7 May 1839 (Patna: BSA), SOC.

[11] Tickell to J. R. Ouseley, 22 May 1839 (Patna: BSA), SOC. Kolehan in the original.

[12] Tickell to J. R. Ouseley, 7 May 1839 (Patna: BSA), SOC.

[13] Tickell to J. R. Ouseley, 7 May 1839 (Patna: BSA), SOC. Koles in the original.

[14] Bengal Judicial 12 March 1840, in India & Bengal Dispatches. Bengal 4 December 1834 to 25 March 1840. Fr. Mathew's copy in the Tribal Research and Training Centre, Guira. Singboom Cole in the original.

[15] Wilkinson to Tickell, enclosure in Wilkinson to Mangles, 5 May 1837 (London: OIOC), BC 69,239. Coles in the original.

[16] Tickell to John Davidson, 1 April 1839 (Patna: BSA), SOC. Koles, Hindoos in the original.

[17] J. R. Ouseley's Tour-Diary of 1840 in K. K. Basu, 'Tour-Diary of J. R. Ouseley', *OHRJ* 5 (1956): 167.

[18] Roy Chaudhury, *Singhbhum Old Records*, 165.

[19] Ricketts, 'Report on the District of Singhbhoom', 105.

[20] Ricketts, 'Report on the District of Singhbhoom', 105. There were 16 annas to a rupee.

[21] Under-Secretary to the Government of Bengal to I. P. (*sic*) Ouseley, 16 April 1845, in Roy Chaudhury, *Singhbhum Old Records*, 64–65.

[22] Basu, 'Tour-Diary of J. R. Ouseley', 166–67; Jagdish Chandra Jha, 'Singhbhum under the South-West Frontier Agency, 1837-'54', *JBRS* 55 (1969): 152–53.

[23] Basu, 'Tour-Diary of J. R. Ouseley', 167.

[24] Basu, 'Tour-Diary of J. R. Ouseley', 166–67; Jagdish Chandra Jha, 'Singhbhum under the South-West Frontier Agency, 1837-'54', 152–53.
Five years later, in November 1845, Ouseley invited the Lutheran missionaries sent to India by Revd Gossner. With this the Christian mission in Chotanagpur started. See S. Mahto, *Hundred Years of Christian Missions in Chotanagpur Since 1845* (Ranchi: The Chotanagpur Christian Publishing House, 1971), 22–24. See also Joseph Bara, 'Tribal Education, the Colonial State and Christian Missionaries: Chhotanagpur, 1839-1870', in *Education and the Disprivileged: Nineteenth and Twentieth Century India*, ed. Sabyasachi Bhattacharya (Hyderabad: Orient Longman, 2002), 134.

[25] Penelope Carson, 'An Imperial Dilemma, The Propagation of Christianity in Early Colonial India', *The Journal of Imperial and Commonwealth History*, 18, no. 2 (1990): 182–83.

[26] Samuel Richard Tickell, 'Vocabulary of the Ho Language', *JASB*, new series, 9, part 2 (1840): 1089–90.

[27] Basu, 'Tour-Diary of J. R. Ouseley', 166. Bhooas in the original.

[28] J. R. Ouseley to F. I. Halliday, 12 August 1839, in Roy Chaudhury, *Singhbhum Old Records*, 18–22.

[29] J. R. Ouseley to F. I. Halliday, 12 August 1839, in Roy Chaudhury, *Singhbhum Old Records*, 18–22. Raja in the original.

[30] Tickell to J. R. Ouseley, 1 December 1839 (Patna: BSA), SOC.

[31] Tickell to J. R. Ouseley, 1 December 1839 (Patna: BSA), SOC. Kummer o'deen Hussein, baboos, Ranee, Porahaut in the original.

[32] Tickell to J. R. Ouseley, 1 December 1839 (Patna: BSA), SOC. Zamindaree, Ranee, in the original.

[33] The whole episode in I. K. Auseley (J. R. Ouseley) to H. J. Prinsep, 28 August 1839, in Roy Chaudhury, *Singhbhum Old Records*, 22–24. Quote is on p. 23.

[34] I. K. Auseley (J. R. Ouseley) to H. J. Prinsep, 28 August 1839, in Roy Chaudhury, *Singhbhum Old Records*, 24. Suttee, Pooree (Jugurnath), in the original.

[35] 'Sati Regulation XVII, A.D. 1829 of the Bengal Code: 4 December 1829', *Women in World History* (website), accessed 15 February 2011, http://chnm.gmu.edu/wwh/p/103.html.

[36] Tickell, 'Memoir', 799.

[37] T. C. Robertson to Thakoor Opunder Sing, 23 October 1839, quoted in C. L. Philip, 'Confidential History of Seraikella State: completed to 1927 by C. L. Philip', typescript (Chaibasa: Tribal Research and Training Centre, 1927), 4.
[38] Tickell to J. R. Ouseley, 4 January 1840 (Patna: BSA), SOC.
[39] Tickell to J. R. Ouseley, 11 January 1840 (Patna: BSA), SOC.
[40] Tickell to J. R. Ouseley, 24 March 1840 (Patna: BSA), SOC. Madhubchunder in the original.
Madhab Chandra Chowdry probably got his appointment after Tickell arrived in Chaibasa. Wilkinson's instructions to Tickell spoke of one English writer 'if procurable for 25 Rs.' See Wilkinson to Tickell, enclosure in Wilkinson to Mangles, 5 May 1837 (London: OIOC), BC 69,239. In 1841, he still had not got his rise. See Tickell to J. R. Ouseley, 1 May 1841 (Patna: BSA), SOC. Chowdry was to stay on for a long time. We find him again in 1854, still working in the hot, airless office, but then for a meagre Rs. 40 per month. See Ricketts, 'Report on the District of Singhbhoom', 101. During the Mutiny, he was still active in the Chaibasa establishment as the head English writer. See Ritambari Devi, *Indian Mutiny: 1857 in Bihar* (Delhi: Orient Publications, 1989), 165.
[41] Tickell to J. R. Ouseley, 30 March 1840 (Patna: BSA), SOC.
[42] New Delhi, NAI, India Foreign, 11 May 1840, Foreign Consultations 110–14.
[43] Extract Political Letter from the Governor General of India, No. 8, 16 October 1840 (London: OIOC), BC 80,492.
[44] Hodson, *List of the Officers of the Bengal Army*, vol. 4, 277; J. R. Ouseley to H. V. Baily, 30 May 1840, New Delhi, NAI, Foreign Consultations, 8 June 1840.
[45] Allen, *The Prisoner of Kathmandu*, 5.
[46] B. H. Hodgson to H. Torrents, July 23 1840, New Delhi, NAI, Foreign Consultations 10 August 1840, no. 59; New Delhi, NAI, Foreign Consultations, 27 July 1840, nos 40–41.
[47] Asst. Secretary to Resident at Khatmandu, 7 May 1840, New Delhi, NAI, Foreign, Political Consultation 111, 11 May 1840.
[48] Hunter, *Life of Brian Houghton Hodgson*, 183–84.
[49] Hunter, *Life of Brian Houghton Hodgson*, 188–89.
[50] Charles Allen connected the episode also to the outbreak of the Opium War, 'seized on by the Durbar as a new opportunity to test the Company's resolve'. See Allen, *The Prisoner of Kathmandu*, 207.
[51] Hunter, *Life of Brian Houghton Hodgson*, 188.
[52] Hunter, *Life of Brian Houghton Hodgson*, especially chapter IX. Also Allen, *The Prisoner of Kathmandu*, 207-11.
[53] [Gvt] to B. H. Hodgson, 10 August 1840, New Delhi, NAI, Foreign, Political, Consultation 60.
[54] Allen, *The Prisoner of Kathmandu*, 215-16.
[55] B. H. Hodgson to his father, in Hunter, *Life of Brian Houghton Hodgson*, 190–91.
[56] Hunter, *Life of Brian Houghton Hodgson*, especially chapter IX. For a critical reassessment of Hodgson's and Hunter's account, see John Whelpton, *Kings, Soldiers and Priest: Nepalese Politics and the Rise of Jang Bahadur Rana, 1830-1857* (Delhi: Manohar, 1991), 73–91; John Whelpton, 'The Political Role of Brian Hodgson', in *The Origins of Himalayan Studies: Brian Houghton Hodgson in Nepal and Darjeeling 1820-1858*, ed. David Waterhouse (Abingdon: RoutledgeCurzon, 1st Indian reprint, 2005), 30–31.
[57] 'Afterwards printed for the use of the Foreign Department'. See Hunter, *Life of Brian Houghton Hodgson*, 128, note 2.
[58] Ramesh K. Dhungel, *Brian H. Hodgson and his Nepali and Himalayan Manuscripts: at the British Library (Eur Mss Hodgson) (1/10/2007); At the Royal Asiatic Society (26/11/2007)*, SOAS, University of London and CNASS, TU, February 2008, (forthcoming), 2008.
I am grateful to Professor Dhungel to show me his working copy during our meeting in Kathmandu in 2009.
B. J. Hasrat called Tickell's Excerpts, 'a precise and matter-of-fact narrative, devoid of circumlocutions', but found it better on the internal politics than on the Nepalese foreign policy. See Bikrama Jit Hasrat, *History of Nepal, As Told by its Own and Contemporary Chroniclers* (Hoshiapur: V. V. Research Institute Press, 1970), lxix and 289, note.
[59] 'Appointment of [Tickell, Lt. S. R., 31st NI] as Assistant Agent, Rajpootana', Foreign proceedings, 11 January 1841, New Delhi, NAI, Foreign Consultations, nos 5–7.
[60] Though he appeared as stationed in 'Rajpootanah' in 'List of subscribers' in the *Calcutta Journal of Natural History and Miscellany of the Arts and Sciences in India* 2 (1842), n.p.
[61] Tickell had provided some details in February 1841. See MacPherson, *Final Report on the Operations*, 20.
[62] Hodson, *List of the Officers of the Bengal Army*, vol. 4, 277. See also New Delhi, NAI, Foreign Consultations, no. 32, 22 February 1841.
[63] Tickell to J. R. Ouseley 12 May 1841 (Patna: BSA), SOC.
[64] Tickell to J. R. Ouseley, 10 June 1841 (Patna: BSA), SOC. The affaire is briefly mentioned in MacPherson, *Final Report on the Operations*, 169.
[65] Tickell to J. R. Ouseley, 1 May 1841 (Patna: BSA), SOC.
[66] Tickell to J. R. Ouseley, 5 June 1841 (Patna: BSA), SOC.
[67] Tickell to J. R. Ouseley, 13 April 1841 (Patna: BSA), SOC. Raja, Ilakkidars, Juddoonath Singh, Chunder Deo, Roodar Singh, in the original.

[68] Tickell to J. R. Ouseley, 13 April 1841 (Patna: BSA), SOC.
[69] J. R. Ousley (*sic*) to F. I. Halliday, 12 August 1839, in Roy Chaudhury, *Singhbhum Old Records*, 21.
[70] MacPherson, *Final Report on the Operations*, 20.
[71] James H. Taylor, *Final Report on the Survey and Settlement Operations in the Porahat Estate, District Singhbhum, 1900–1903* (Calcutta: Bengal Secretariat Press, 1904), 20.
In the season 1840–1841, the estate of Kera was put on a quitrent at one-fifth of the gross produce. It came to Rs. 164-5-0. See Taylor, *Pir Notes*, 21. The Anandpur quitrent came at one third of the gross product, amounting to a meagre Rs. 97. See Taylor, *Pir Notes,* 34.
G. C. Depree gave 1/5th of the 'gross proceeds' as the rent for both Kera and Anandpur. The rent of Karaikela and Chainpur was 1/3rd of the gross proceeds. See Depree, *Geographical and Statistical Report*, 29. It is not clear whether this rent was fixed in 1840–41 or earlier.
The raja had some income from Bandgaon, one-third of its gross produce, but Jadunath tried to take the whole by dispossessing the fief holder. Tickell wanted to go with that, but he was overruled. See MacPherson, *Final Report on the Operations*, 226.
[72] MacPherson, *Final Report on the Operations*, 17.
[73] MacPherson, *Final Report on the Operations*, 20, 27.
[74] Tickell to J. R. Ouseley, 13 April 1841 (Patna: BSA), SOC. Raja in the original.
[75] Tickell to J. R. Ouseley, 27 May 1841 (Patna: BSA), SOC. Judhoonath, Raja, Baboos, Roodra, Ranee, Chunder in the original.
[76] Tickell to J. R. Ouseley, 27 May 1841 (Patna: BSA), SOC.
[77] Tickell to J. R. Ouseley, 1 June 1841 (Patna: BSA), SOC.
[78] In 1858, Dalton estimated the population of Porahat at 24,744. See Francisca Kujur, *Raja Arjun Singh of Porahat (1829 A.D. –1890 A.D.)*, (Allahabad: K.K. Publications, 2007), 7.
[79] That was how it was remembered in 1907 by Rusu Manki of Durka *pir* in an interview held on 24 January that year. See Barbara Verardo, 'Rebels and Devotees of Jharkhand, Social, Religious and Political Transformations among the Adivasis of Northern India' (PhD thesis, London School of Economics and Political Science, 2003), 98.
[80] Taylor, *Final Report*, 20.
[81] Tickell to J. R. Ouseley, 13 July 1841 (Patna: BSA), SOC. Malgoozaree, Chyebassa, Hazareebaugh, Bankoora in the original.
[82] Tickell to J. R. Ouseley, 31 August 1841 (Patna: BSA), SOC.
[83] Ricketts, 'Report on the District of Singhbhoom', 70–73. I have added the percentage increase.
[84] Bengal Revenue, 8 December 1842, in Board of Control Records, Bengal Public Department, no. 22 of 1844, 20 November 1844 (London: OIOC), E/4/784.
[85] Bengal Revenue, 8 December 1842, in Board of Control Records, Bengal Public Department, no. 22 of 1844, 20 November 1844 (London: OIOC), E/4/784.
[86] Tickell, 'On the Orál, or Singhbhoom Flying Squirrel, Pteromys Orál', *Calcutta Journal of Natural History and Miscellany of the Arts and Sciences in India* 2 (1841): 405–6.
[87] Tickell to Blyth, 19 January 1842, PASB, in JASB 11, part 1 (January to June 1842): 197.
[88] Blyth, monthly reports by the Curator, *PASB*, in *JASB* 11, part 1 (January to June 1842): 273, 444, 451, 453, 456-463, 588. With the Gaur Tickell stepped in the shoes of his predecessor Roughsedge.
[89] Tickell to Blyth, 19 January 1842, *PASB,* in *JASB* 11, part 1 (January to June 1842): 197.
[90] Tickell to J. R. Ouseley, 6 July August 1841 (Patna: BSA), SOC. Dassoo Baboo in the original.
[91] The maize showed some agricultural innovation, as this plant is native to America. It appeared in India in the fifteenth century. See Colin P. Masica, 'Aryan and Non-Aryan Elements in North Indian Agriculture', *Aryan and Non-Aryan in India,* edited by Madhav M. Deshpande and Peter Edwin Hook (Ann Arbor: Center for South Asian and Southeast Asian Studies, The University of Michigan, 1979), 105–6.
[92] Samuel Richard Tickell, 'Notes on the Bendkar, a People of Keonjur', *JASB* 11 (1842): 206.
[93] Samuel Richard Tickell, 'The Zoological Works of Samuel Richard Tickell', illustrated manuscript work in 14 volumes (London: Zoological Society of London, [1865–1873]). Oorkhia, Sarndapeer (singbhoom), Sontals or bhoomijes , Singbhoom, Keonjur, Sumbhulpoor, Gower in the original. Elsewhere in the manuscript, Tickell mentioned 'Oorkhia, Rengrapeer, Singbhoom' and the Baitarani river. Urkia is on the banks of the Koël, 2.5 km south west of Manoharpur on the opposite bank,.
[94] Tickell, 'Memoir', 783.
[95] Samuel Richard Tickell, 'Notes on the Bendkar', 205. Kotegurh, Burpeer in the original.
[96] But the memory remained clear. Many years later, on 3 August 1867, Tickell painted the owl in the very scene he had described (see Plate 5.5).
[97] Ball, *Jungle Life in India*, 334–35.
For the Manis Crassicaudata, see Urs Rahn, 'Modern Pangolins', in *Grzimek's Encyclopedia of Mammals*, ed. Sybil P. Parker vol. 2 (New York: McGraw-Hall, 1990), 630–41.

[98] Samuel Richard Tickell, 'Manis Crassicaudata., (Auct), M. Pentadactyla (Ibid.), Short-tailed or thick-tailed Manis, In Hindustan, generally called "Bujjerkeet" –Orissa, "Bujjer-Kapta" and "Surooj Mookhee"–By the Lurka Koles, "Armoo"', *JASB* 11 (1842): 221–30. Chyebasa in the original.

Afterglow: A Complete History of Indian Birds

[1] Tickell, 'Halcyon Smyrnensis (Linn.s), The Smyrna Kingfisher (Bengal variety)', in 'The Zoological Works', vol. 9, plate 39.
Listed as Indian White-breasted Kingfisher in G. Carmichael Low, Douglas Dewar, T. H. Newman, G. A. Levett-Yeats, 'A Classification of the Original Watercolour Paintings of Birds of India by B. H. Hodgson, S. R. Tickell, and C. F. Sharpe in the Library of the Zoological Society of London', *Proceedings of the Zoological Society of London* 100, issue 3 (London: Zoological Society of London, 1930): 600–601.
[2] Samuel Richard Tickell, 'Notes on a curious species of Tiger or Jaguar, killed near the Snowy Range, North of Darjeeling', *JASB* 12, part 2 (1843): 814. Letter from Captain Tickell to the Secretary, published in *Proceedings of the Asiatic Society*, *JASB* 12, part 2, (July-December 1843), 831.
[3] John Whelpton, 'The Political Role of Brian Hodgson', 34–35. Hodgson would return to India as a private individual in 1845.
[4] Tickell, 'The Zoological Works'.
[5] Hodson, *List of the Officers of the Bengal Army,* vol. 4, 277. See also *India office, Family History Search* (website), accessed 5 January 2011, http://indiafamily.bl.uk.
[6] Tickell's father-in-law was of a religious turn of mind, See Reginald Heber, quoted in unsigned review of '*Narrative of a Journey through the Upper Provinces of India, from Calcutta to Bombay, 1824—1825* by Reginald Heber', in *The British Critic: Quarterly Theological Review and Ecclesiastical Record* 4 (London, 1828): 203, *Google Books* (website), accessed 6 January 2011, http://books.google.nl/books.
[7] She died 16 May 1844. John William Templer resigned in 1847, went to England where he remarried in 1860. He got two more daughters. He died in Bath in 1873. See 'John William Templer, 23 Nov 1794–26 Mar 1873', *The Templer Family from Somerset, Devon and Dorset* (website), accessed 28 April 2016,
 http://my.rootsmagic.com/templerfamilycouk/individual.html#601
[8] Holmes à Court gives 25 September 1845, *Holmes à Court* (website), accessed 10 July 2009, http://holmesacourt.org.
The Templer Family website gave 8 August 1846, accessed 28 April 2016,
http://my.rootsmagic.com/templerfamilycouk/pedigree.html#64.
[9] Roy Chaudhury, *Singhbhum Old Records*, 31.
[10] Phillimore, R.H., ed. (1968). *Historical Records of the Survey of India. Volume V. 1844 to 1861.* (Dehra Dun: Survey of India)*, pp. 254, 255, 538.*
[11] Tickell's Treaty of Sugauli opens Charles Allen's remarkable *The Prisoner of Kathmandu: Brian Hodgson in Nepal 1820-43*, London: Haus, 2015, 1–2. The painting is reproduced opposite p. 152. Discussing it in his note on p. 283, Allen supposed that in 1849 Tickell gave the painting to Jung Bahadur Rana when he met him at Makwanpur on the Nepal border to escort him to Patna. There is no indication for that. Obviously, Tickell painted or sketched the landscape on the spot. Allen thinks that Tickell did so on his departure in 1841. See Allen, *The Prisoner of Kathmandu*, 214. Tickell could as well have done so during his enforced idleness on the border in 1840.
[12] Hodson, *List of the Officers of the Bengal Army*, vol. 4, 77. Hodson did not mention the Bhagalpur assignment.
[13] Valentine Ball, 'On the Avifauna of the Chutia (Chota) Nagpur Division, S.W. frontier of Bengal', *Stray Feathers: Journal of Ornithology for India and its Dependencies,* 2 (1874): 355–439.
[14] However, in the JASB Tickell is mentioned as 'Deputy Commissioner of Amherst, Tenasserim, in 1861'. See Samuel Richard Tickell, 'Memoranda Relative to Three Andamanese in the Charge of Major Tickell, when Deputy Commissioner of Amherst, Tenasserim, in 1861', *JASB* 33 (1864): 162.
[15] On the Big Boileau Chart, Ada Elizabeth is mistakenly mentioned as Ada Josephine, see Jane Alicia Innes, *Big Boileau Chart* (website), accessed 17 February 2011, http://burningviolin.org/family/WebCards/ps06/ps06_491.htm.
[16] Hodson, *List of the Officers of the Bengal Army*, vol. 4, 276. See also Medical declaration by C. K. Bond, Civil Surgeon, Moulmein, 6 November 1856 (New Delhi: NAI), Foreign, Political, 19 December 1856.
Captain H. Hopkinson to Cecil Breden?, 15 April 1858 (New Delhi, NAI), Foreign, Political, 14 May 1858.
[17] *India office, Family History Search* (website), accessed 17 May 2008, http://www.familysearch.org . The birth was announced in the *Bombay Times*, 5 October 1858.
[18] Samuel Richard Tickell, 'Memoranda Relative to Three Andamanese', 169.
[19] St John's Road, Trafalgar Terrace, St. Helier, Jersey. He was there in 1871. See Brother Anthony of Taizé, 'The Tickell Family', *An Sonjae* (website), accessed 10 July 2009,
http://hompi.sogang.ac.kr/anthony/GrigsbyTickell.htm.

[20] Barbara and Richard Mearns, 'Samuel Richard Tickell (1811—1875)', *Biographies for Birdwatchers: The Lives of Those Commemorated in the Western Palearctic Bird Names* (London, 1988), 381–83; 'Colonel S. R. Tickell', *The Ibis: Quarterly Journal of Ornithology*, Jubilee Supplement, 9th series, 11 (1908), *Internet Archive* (website), accessed 6 October 2009, http//www.archive.org/stream/ibias29brit_djvu.txt.

[21] 33, Montpellier Villas, Cheltenham.

[22] 'By descent to the sitter's grandson, Colonel Tickell, by whom sold, Christie's, 2nd May 1874, lot 73, bt. Agnew for BP 1,575 on behalf of Sir Charles Mills, bt., later Lord Hillingdon, and thence by family descent' ('Richard Tickell ca 1780', part of Lot 8: Thomas Gainsborough R.A. 1727-1788, Sotheby, November 27 2003, *Artfact* (website), accessed 10 January 2010, www.Artfact.com.

[23] Zoological Society of London, 'Proceedings of the Scientific Meetings of the Zoological Society of London for the Year 1874', London, 1875: 667, *Internet Archive* (website), accessed 14 November 2010, http://www.archiveorg/stream/proceedingsofgen74zool/proceedingsofgen74zool_djvu.txt.

[24] His grave bears the following inscription, 'In loving memory of Colonel Samuel Richard Tickell, Bengal Army. Born 1811. Died at Cheltenham 20 April 1875. And of Maria Georgiana, his wife, born 1825. Died at Ealing 23 June 1918. Also to the memory of their grandson Captain Templer Henry Scott, 87 Punjabis, who fell in action on 26 April 1915 near Ypres and was buried on the field of battle, aged 31 years.' See Brother Anthony of Taizé, 'The Tickell Family'.

[25] Arthur Walden, 'Notes on the late Colonel Tickell's manuscript Work entitled 'Illustrations of Indian Ornithology'', *The Ibis: Quarterly Journal of Ornithology*, series 3, 6 (July 1876): 337, *Internet Archive* (website), accessed 24 February 2011, http://www.archive.org/details/ibis63brit.

[26] He was the son of Samuel Richard's cousin-german General Richard Tickell. 'Cousin-german' or 'first cousin': the child of Ego's aunt of uncle.
For Edward Arthur Tickell, see Reginald Steward Boddington, *Genealogical Memoranda Relating to the Sparks and Tickell Families* (London: privately printed, 1877), 8. He was M.A. of Balliol College, Oxford. He died on 2 August 1897. See Herbert Robertson, 'Clonegald Churchyard', *Journal of the Memorials of the Dead* 6 (1904-05-1906): 198-99, on *County Carlow, Clonegald, Journal of the Memorials of the Dead* (website), accessed 1 March 2011, http://home.people.net.au/~ousie/county_carlow_memorials_of_the_dead_JPMD_Clonegald.htm.

[27] Council of the Zoological Society of London, *Report of the Council of the Zoological Society of London, the Year 1877: Read at the Annual General Meeting, April 29th, 1878*, (London: Taylor and Francis, 1878), 13, *Internet Archive* (website), accessed 20 February 2011, http://ia700404.us.archive.org/27/items/annualreportzool78zool/annualreportzool78zool.pdf. MS in the original.

[28] Zoological Society of London, 'Proceedings of the Scientific Meetings of the Zoological Society of London for the Year 1874', London, 1875: 667, *Internet Archive* (website), accessed 14 November 2010, http://www.archiveorg/stream/proceedingsofgen74zool/proceedingsofgen74zool_djvu.txt.
'The following were stated to be the contents of the seven volumes :—
Vol. I. Raptores diurni, with 41 plates and descriptions of 60 species.
Vol. II. Raptores nocturni, with 21 plates and descriptions of 24 species, also 1 plate of eggs containing figures of those of 9 species.
Vol. III. Zygodactyly with 46 plates and descriptions 'of 83 species also 1 plate of eggs containing figures of those of 7 species.
Vol. IV. Tenuirostres, with 32 plates and descriptions of 56 species, and 1 plate of eggs containing figures of those of 5 species.
Vol. V. Dentirostres (part l),with 38 plates and descriptions of 73 species, also 1 plate of eggs containing figures of those of 6 species.
Vol. VI. Dentirostres (part 2), with 30 plates and descriptions of 71 species
Vol. VII. Fissirostres, with 53 plates and descriptions of 81 species; also 1 plate of eggs containing figures of those of 15 species'.

[29] Samuel Richard Tickell, 'The Zoological Works of Samuel Richard Tickell', illustrated manuscript work in 14 volumes, London: Zoological Society of London, [1865–1873].

[30] Walden, 'Notes on the late Colonel Tickell's manuscript Work', 337, 339.

[31] Walden, 'Notes on the late Colonel Tickell's manuscript Work', 336.

[32] Cited in Walden, 'Notes on the late Colonel Tickell's manuscript Work', 340.

[33] Cited in Walden, 'Notes on the late Colonel Tickell's manuscript Work', 340–41. The article is Tickell, 'List of Birds'.

[34] Walden, 'Notes on the late Colonel Tickell's manuscript Work', 350.

[35] Barbara and Richard Mearns, **'Samuel Richard Tickell (1811–1875)'**, 383.

[36] For an overview, see G. Carmichael Low, Douglas Dewar, T. H. Newman, G. A. Levett-Yeats, 'A Classification of the Original Watercolour Paintings of Birds of India by B. H. Hodgson, S. R. Tickell, and C. F. Sharpe in the Library of the Zoological Society of London', *Proceedings of the Zoological Society of London* 100, issue 3 (London: Zoological Society of London, 1930): 549–625.

[37] Two of Tickell's paintings from the Hodgson Collection of the Natural History Museum in London are reproduced in Allen,

The Prisoner of Kathmandu, 215.

[38] 'A History of British Birds (1843)', *WP*, accessed 15 December 2013.

[39] I am grateful to Ms Ann Datta of the Library of the Zoological Society of London for these references.

[40] On the general preference for coloured bird plates, see Isabelline Brooks, 'Colour Prejudice and William Yarrel', 2004, *Ibooknet* (website), accessed 1 March 2011, http://www.ibooknet.co.uk/archive/news_april04.htm .

[41] C. W. Smith and Sir C. D'Oyly, *The Feathered Game of Hindostan* (Patna: Behar Amateur Lithographic Press, 1828).
C. W. Smith and Sir C. D'Oyly, *Oriental Ornithology* (Patna: Behar Amateur Lithographic Press, 1829).
For background, see, 'The Ornithological Library of Richard Howard', Lot 175 of Sothebys, auction 28, Smith (Christopher Webb) and Sir Charles D'Oyly, The feathered Game of Hindostan, April 1999, *Sotheby's* (website), accessed 19 December 2010, www.sothebys.com; 'Christopher Webb Smith (1793–1871) and Sir Charles William D'Oyly', sale 6807, 24 September 2003, *Christie's* (website), accessed 19 December 2010, www.Christies.com; 'Webb-Smith Collection', on *University of Cambridge*, Department of Zoology, Special Collections (website), accessed 19 December 2010, www.zoo.cam.ac.uk/library/webbsmith.hml.

[42] Walden, 'Notes on the late Colonel Tickell's manuscript Work', 337.

[43] Walden, 'Notes on the late Colonel Tickell's manuscript Work', 337–38.

[44] Walden, 'Notes on the late Colonel Tickell's manuscript Work', 357.

[45] Of course Bewick use blockprints, a medium very different from Tickell's pen sketches. See Julian Bell. 'England's Great Neglected Artist', review of *The Art of Thomas Bewick* by Diana Donald, *New York Review of Books* 62, no. 16 (22 October– 4 November 2015): 12–16.

[46] Walden, 'Notes on the late Colonel Tickell's manuscript Work', 338.

[47] Walden, 'Notes on the late Colonel Tickell's manuscript Work', 336.

[48] Edward Blyth, *Catalogue of the birds in the Museum Asiatic Society* (Calcutta: J. Thomas, 1849), 347.

[49] Edward Blyth, 'Blyth to Darwin [22 September 1855], University of Cambridge, *Darwin Correspondence Project* (website), letter 1755, accessed 24 October 2010, http://www.darwinproject.ac.uk/entry-1755. It gives 'Extracts from a letter from Capt. S. R. Tickell, Principal Asst. Commr Tenasserim Provinces dated Moulmein, Augt. 29/55'.

[50] Bikram Grewal, 'Samuel Tickell (1811–1875)', in 'Birdmen of India: The Pioneers', *Birds of India* (website), accessed 26 February 2011, http://www.kolkatabirds.com/birdmenpioneers.htm.

[51] John William Kaye, *The Administration of the East India Company: A History of Indian Progress* (London: Richard Bentley, 1853), 464.

[52] *Holmes à Court* (website), accessed 10 January 2010, http://holmesacourt.org. Scott became Consul in Tientsin in 1897–1899.

[53] Mary Louisa married 18 February 1865 in Hongkong to William Marsh Cooper. They moved to Swatow, where Philip Templer and Harry Ashley were born to them. In 1869, William became the British consul on Taiwan. In 1875, they got a son Alan Lesly. Finally in 1877, William Marsh Cooper became the Ningpo consul. He retired on grounds of ill health in 1888 and died in 1896 at Madeley Road, Ealing, Middlesex. Mary Louisa lived till the age of 92, and died in 1938 at Madeley Road.. See 'William Marsh Cooper, China Consular Service', in 'The British Consuls in South Formosa', in *The Takao Club* (website), accessed 12 January 1014, http://takaoclub.com/britishconsuls/william_marsh_cooper.htm. I assume the house is 74, Madeley Road, the house in which Mary Louisa, Ada Elizabeth Tickell and their mother Maria Georgiana Tickell, née Templer lived during the Census of 1911. See Brother Anthony of Taizé, 'The Tickell Family'.

[54] Samuel Richard Tickell, 'Original water-colour drawings and illustrated MS relating to Indian Birds', forming one of a set of volumes from which the illustrated MS work by Tickell on Mammals, &c. of India, in the Library of the Zoological Society of London was elaborated, [about 1870].
The inserted leaf mentioned, 'The manuscript ['Illustrations of Indian Ornithology'] is preserved in the library of the Zoological Society of London, but it has not yet been possible to trace the whereabouts of the remaining two folio and two quarto volumes of drawings. (presented by Mrs. Ada Elizabeth Scott, née Tickell) May 1947.' Apparently this text refers to an outdated source. Probably at this time, too, Ada Elisabeth donated a folio book 'Original water-colour drawings of Arakan fishes' with 64 water colour drawings to the London Museum of Natural History. See *Natural History Museum*, The Library and Archives Collection (website), accessed 10 September 2015,
http://www.nhm.ac.uk/our-science/departments-and-staff/library-and-archives/collections.html.

[55] See Appendix 'Impact of Tickell's articles' for an overview.

[56] Edward Tuite Dalton, 'The "Kols" of Chota Nagpore', Special Number on Indian Ethnology 1866, *JASB* 35, part 2 (1867): 153–98;
Edward Tuite Dalton, 'The "Kols" of Chota Nagpore', *Transactions of the Ethnological Society of London*, n.s., 6 (1868): 1–41;
Edward Tuite Dalton, 'The Coles of Chota Nagpore', 'The Ho Tribe: Otherwise Called the Lurka or Fighting Coles of Singbhoom' and 'Cole Christians: The Mission in Chota Nagpore' texts accompanying plates in John Forbes Watson and John William Kaye eds., *The People of India: A Series of Photographic Illustrations, with the Descriptive Letterpress, of the Races*

and Tribes of Hindustan, Originally Prepared under the Authority of the Government of India, and Reproduced by Order of the Secretary of State for India in Council*, vol. 1 (London: India Museum, 1868), no pagination.
Edward Tuite Dalton, *Descriptive Ethnology of Bengal*, Illustrated by Lithograph Portraits copied from Photographs (Calcutta: Office of the Superintendent of Government Printing, 1872; repr., *Tribal History of Eastern India* [New Delhi: Cosmo Publications, 1978]).

[57] Chaudhury, *Singhbhum*, 256–58.

[58] Asoka Kumar Sen, *Representing Tribe: The Ho of Singhbhum Under Colonial Rule* (New Delhi: Concept, 2011), 10, 13, 14, 30, 17, 31–32, 34, 35, 38, 39, 41, 43, 63, 105–6, 111, 112, 131;
Das Gupta, *Adivasis and the Raj*, 118.
Of Tickell's administrative work in Singhbhum, there is a sketchy overview in Kumar, *History and Administration of Tribal Chotanagpur*, 147.

[59] Tickell, 'Memoir', 787, 806.

[60] Aravind Adiga, *The White Tiger* (London: Atlantic Books, 2008), 253.

[61] Samuel Richard Tickell, 'Grammatical Construction of the Ho Language', *JASB* 9, part 2 (1840): 997–1007;
Samuel Richard Tickell, 'Vocabulary of the Ho Language', *JASB* 9, part 2 (1840): 1063–90.

Part IV: Tickell's Hodésum Articles of 1840

Chapter 12: The Rude Forefathers

[1] V. C. P. Hodson, *List of the Officers of the Bengal Army*, vol.4, 276–77.

[2] Hodson, *List of the Officers of the Bengal Army*, vol. 4, 276.

[3] Some data on Samuel Tickell's family can be found through the *India Office, Family History Search* (website), accessed 12 February 2010, http://indiafamily.bl.uk. See also *Family Search, International Genealogical Index* (website), accessed 17 May 2008, http://familysearch.org.

[4] See Hodson, *List of the Officers of the Bengal Army*, vol. 4, 276. See also Edward Dodwell, James Samuel Miles (compilers and editors), *Alphabetical List of the Officers of the Bengal Army: With the Dates of Their Respective Promotion, Retirement, Resignation, or Death, Whether in India or in Europe, From the Year 1760 to the Year 1834 Inclusive, Corrected to September 30, 1837* (London: Longman, Orme, Brown, [1838]), 256-57. Brother Anthony of Taizé mentioned that he died 'after a severe and lingering illness' near Berhampore. See Brother Anthony of Taizé, 'The Tickell Family', *An Sonjae* (website), accessed 10 July 2009,
http://hompi.sogang.ac.kr/anthony/GrigsbyTickell.htm.

[5] 'Commonplace-book, verse compiled by members of the Tickell family, in England and India', British Library Manuscript, add. MS 59656, circa 1787–1816.
The last poem is a lament for Samuel Tickell by his wife:
Belov'd and mourn'd ah! more than words can tell
My husband, guide, polestone, friend farewell!

[6] 'In both civil and military lines the bungalow was the commonest structure, single-storey, thatched roof, buildings made of sundried brick—though again set in lawns and gardens'. See Suresh Chandra Ghosh, *The Social Condition of the British Community in Bengal, 1757–1800* (Leiden: E. J. Brill, 1970), 108.

[7] William Linley (1771–1835), served the East India Company in 1790-5 and again in 1800-5, the first time as a writer in Madras, the second time in 'some occupation of profit and respectability'. He retired in 1810. See [W. L. Bowles], 'Linley, Wm, esq.', *The Annual Biography and Obituary 1836*, vol. 20 (London, 1836): 434-35.

[8] He bequeathed the collection which included the famous *The Linley Sisters* by Gainsborough to the Dulwich Picture Gallery. See 'William Linley', *WP*, accessed 13 July 2009; [W. L. Bowles], 'Linley, Wm, esq.', *The Annual Biography and Obituary 1836*, 20 (London, 1836): 435.

[9] Patrick Wood, 'Thomas Linley, Mozart's Boyhood Rival', *Early Music America* 15, no. 1 (Spring 2009): 34–37. See also the description of the drowning in 'Linley (Thomas), in John Gorton, *A General Biographic Dictionary: A New Edition Continued to the Year 1833*, in three volumes (London: Wittaker, 1833), vol. 2: n.p.

[10] The painting is in the Dulwich Picture Gallery. The sittings were interrupted by Elizabeth Anne's elopement with Richard Brinsley Sheridan. It was retouched in 1785. See 'Elizabeth and Mary Linley', *Dulwich Picture Gallery* (website), accessed 11 September 2015, http://www.dulwichpicturegallery.org.uk/explore-the-collection/301-350/elizabeth-and-mary-linley/.

[11] Mary Craven, 'Elizabeth Linley, Afterwards Mrs. Sheridan', in Mary Craven, *Famous Beauties of two Reigns: Being an Account of Some Fair Women of Stuart and Georgian Times* (With a Chapter on Fashion in Femininity by Martin Hume), (London: E. Nash, 1906), 174–76.

[12] Thomson Willing, 'Mrs. Sheridan, Portrait by Sir Joshua Reynolds', in Thomson Willing, *Some Old Time Beauties: After Portraits by the English Masters, with Embellishment and Comment by Thomson Willing* (Boston: Joseph Knight, 1895), 37–50.
[13] Craven, 'Elizabeth Linley, Afterwards Mrs. Sheridan', 180.
[14] Craven, 'Elizabeth Linley, Afterwards Mrs. Sheridan', 181–84.
[15] John George Robertson, 'Richard Brinsley Sheridan (1751–1816)', *Encyclopaedia Britannica*, vol. 4, 11th ed., (Cambridge: Cambridge University Press, 1911), 845–47, on *Theatrehistory.com* (website), accessed 12 July 2009, www.theatrehistory.com/irish/sheridan001.html.
[16] Willing, 'Mrs. Sheridan, Portrait by Sir Joshua Reynolds'.
[17] Robertson, 'Richard Brinsley Sheridan (1751–1816)'.
[18] Robertson, 'Richard Brinsley Sheridan (1751–1816)'.
[19] Wood, 'Thomas Linley, Mozart's Boyhood Rival', 34–37.
[20] 'Thomas Tickell', *WP*, accessed 17 May 2008.
[21] You are not mistaken if you see a connection with the setting of Jane Austen's 1813 *Pride and Prejudice*. 'Chatsworth is the Derbyshire home of the Dukes of Devonshire. The house dates from the Elizabethan era but the exterior was rebuilt under the 1st Duke around the start of the 18th century . . . It is thought that Jane Austen visited Chatsworth in 1811 and used it as the background for Pemberley'. See 'Jane Austen's Pemberly', *Orchard Gate Books* (Website), accessed 8 January 2011, http://www.orchard-gate.com/pemberly.htm.
[22] 'Miss B.' is mentioned in Stephen Jones, 'Richard Tickell', in *Biographia Dramatica; or, A Companion to the Playhouse*, 1812, reproduced in 'Spenser and the Tradition, 1713–1714', on *English Poetry 1579–1830* (website), accessed 3 May 2012, http://spenserians.cath.vt.edu/BiographyRecord.php?action=GET&bioid=34612.
A biting account of the affair and of Miss Barnes' character is given in 'Histories of the Tete-à-Tete Annexed; or Memoirs of Anticipator, and the Barn-door Fowl (no. 31, 32.)', *The Town and Country Magazine; or Universal Repository of Knowledge, Instruction and Entertainment*, vol. 18 (London: A. H. Junior, 1786): 569-70.
On Miss Barnes' theatrical career, see Philip H. Highfill, Kalman A. Burnim, and Edward A. Langhans, 'Barnes, Miss', *Biographical Dictionary of Actors, Actresses, Musicians, Dancers, Managers, and other Stage Personnel in London, 1660–1800*, vol. 1: Abaco to Belsille (Carbondale and Edwardsville: Southern Illinois University Press, 1973), 293-94.
[23] 'Richard Tickell ca 1780', part of Lot 8: Thomas Gainsborough, R.A. 1727–1788, Sotheby's (27 November 2003), *Sotheby's* (website), accessed 10 January 2010, www.Artfact.com.
[24] Craven, 'Elizabeth Linley, Afterwards Mrs. Sheridan', 192.
[25] Quote from John Taylor, *Records of My Life* (1823), in 'Richard Tickell ca 1780'.
[26] 'The Georgian Era', *The Mirror of Literature, Amusement, and Instruction: Containing Original Essays; Historical Narratives, Biographical Memoirs, Sketches of Society, Topographical Descriptions, Novels and Tales, Anecdotes, Select Extracts from New and Expensive Works, The Spirit of the Public Journals, Discoveries in the Arts and Sciences, Useful Domestic Hints, etc. etc. etc.*, vol. 19, no. 535 (25 February 1832): 122–24; no. 536 (3 March 1832): 137–39.
On the relation between Sheridan and Richard Tickell, as well as the care of Elizabeth for her sister's children, see Thomas Moore, *Memoirs of the Life of the Right Honourable Richard Brinsley Sheridan*, vol. 2 (London: Longman, Reese, Orme, Brown, and Green, 1826), 75–76, 80–81; 224–25.
[27] 'The Georgian Era', 138.
[28] William Dalrymple, 'Plain Tales from British India', *The New York Review of Books* 54, no. 7 (26 April 2007): 49.
[29] Robertson, 'Richard Brinsley Sheridan (1751–1816)'.
[30] 'Richard Sheridan', *Spartacus Schoolnet* (website), accessed 17 May 2008. www.spartacus.schoolnet.co.uk/PRsheridan.htm.
[31] 'But [Sheridan's] infidelities were notorious, driving her into the arms of Lord Edward Fitzgerald, by whom she eventually had a child, although they reconciled before her death. His second wife was treated just as badly. No wonder one his most famous quotations from his plays is "Tis safest in matrimony to begin with a little aversion"!'
See Chris Gosnell, 'The Sheridan Family', *Ocotillo Road: The Internet Home of Chris Gosnell and Family* (website), accessed 14 August 2015, http://ocotilloroad.com/geneal/sheridan1.html.
[32] Boddington, *Genealogical Memoranda Relating to the Sparks and Tickell Families*, 7.
[33] [William Smyth], *Memoir of Mr. Sheridan* (Leeds: J. Cross, 1840), 53-55. See also William Fraser Rae, 'Tickell, Richard'.
[34] S. T. Coleridge, one of the three Lake poets, quoted in [W. L. Bowles], 'Linley, Wm, esq.', 435.
[35] 'Theatre Royal, Drury Lane', *WP*, accessed 11 July 2009. In the fire many of Thomas Linley the Younger's compositions were lost.
In 1812, Sheridan lost his seat in parliament and creditors closed in on him. In gratitude for his support for America's independence, the US Congress offered him GBP 20,000, which he declined. See Robertson, 'Richard Brinsley Sheridan (1751–1816)'. The portrait of Elizabeth by Sir Joshua Reynolds, engraved by Bartolozzi, was 'the last valued possession to be parted with'. See Willing, 'Mrs. Sheridan, Portrait by Sir Joshua Reynolds'.

[36] Robertson, 'Richard Brinsley Sheridan (1751–1816)'.

[37] Frederick H. Armstrong, *Handbook of Upper Canadian Chronology*, revised edition (Toronto and London: Dundurn Press, 1985), 41, 127, 174.

[38] Richard Barnes Tickell figures in Simcoe's correspondence, where first he is named B.B. Tickle, and later B.B. Tickell. See Ernest Alexander Cruikshank, *The Correspondence of Lieut. Governor John Graves Simcoe, with Allied Documents*, collected by and ed. Brigadier-General E. A. Cruikshank, for the Ontario Historical Society, vol. 3 (1794–1795), (Toronto: Ontario Historical Society, 1925), 73–79, 97–100, 331. His death, but not the year of his demise, is related in John Arthur Roebuck, 'Autobiography', in Robert Eadon Leader (ed.), *Life and Letters of John Arthur Roebuck, P.O., Q.C., M.P.: with chapters of Autobiography* (London, New York: Edward Arnold, 1897), 11. There is a rather puzzling reference to R. B. Tickell, buried 10 October, 1799? in the church of St. Marks, Niagara. See [Janet C. Carnogan], *Centennial, St. Mark's Church, Niagara, 1792-1892* (Toronto: James Bain, 1892), 8.

[39] 'Ebenezer Roebuck and Zipporah Tickell who were married at St. George's, Hanover Square, London in 1795.' See, 'Roebuck Coat of Arms / Roebuck Family Crest', *Coat of Arms Store & Family Crests Gifts* (website), accessed July 2009, http://www.4crests.com/roebuck-coat-of-arms.html. The politician John Arthur Roebuck was their fifth son. On her second marriage, see John Arthur Roebuck, 'Autobiography', 3.

Her mother Miss Barnes, who had taken care of three of Zipporah's children when Zipporah was in India, accompanied her to Canada, where she, still 'a wondrous beauty', died within four years. On her and Zipporah's deaths, see John Arthur Roebuck, 'Autobiography', 16–17.

Zipporah's widower John Simpson died in Kingston, Ontario, on 27 April 1873. See John Beswarick Thompson, 'John Simpson', *Dictionary Canadian Biography Online* 10, 1871-1880 (website), accessed 10 July 2009, http://www.biographi.ca/009004-119.01-e.php?&id_nbr=5267.

[40] Craven, 'Elizabeth Linley, Afterwards Mrs. Sheridan', 191–92.

[41] April Alliston, 'Introduction', in Sophia Lee, *The Recess: Or A Tale of Other Times*, ed. April Alliston (Lexington: University Press of Kentucky, 2000), xxxiii. Sophia Lee lived from 1750 to 1824.

[42] John Arthur Roebuck, 'Autobiography', in *Life and Letters of John Arthur Roebuck, P.O., Q.C., M.P., with Chapters of Autobiography*, ed. Robert Eadon Leader (London, New York: Edward Arnold, 1897), 3–4.

Anne Boscawen died 1831 when she was eighty-six. See 'Memorial Stone in St James Church, Piccadilly, by Elizabeth Anne Tickell, dau of Richard Tickell', *Find a Grave* (website), accessed 14 August 2015, http://www.findagrave.com. 'This table is erected by a grateful and affectionate friend who enjoyed in her society for 50 years, a love like that of a parent.'

[43] 'In St Paul's, Covent Garden, is a tablet to his memory bearing the following inscription:

'In Memory of William Linley Esq. Who departed this life on 6th May 1835 Aged 64 years. The last of a family endowed with genius, He delighted in cultivating his own And in rewarding that of others. His religious feelings were humble and sincere. This tablet is erected by a grateful and affectionate niece whom in life he loved and in death remembered.'

See Clementine Black, *The Linleys of Bath* (London: Martin Secker, 1911), http://www.archive.org/stream/linleysofbath00blacuoft/linleysofbath00blacuoft_djvu.txt (retrieved 31 December 2010), 333). See also [W. L. Bowles], 'Linley, Wm, esq.', 435.

[44] In a book that was property of William Linley and later of Elizabeth Anne Tickell, there were inserted, among other things, 'Twelve original Water-color drawings, by Captain Richard Brinsley Tickell, Sheridan's nephew (named after him). Captain Tickell was in the Royal navy, and was killed at Travalgar. The drawings represent Nelson's ship, the Victory, revictualing, Battle of Cape St Vincent; Blockade of Cadiz; and various ships of the Royal Navy, in English and foreign waters.'

See J. W. Bouton, *The Havemeyer Library: Catalogue of the Extensive and Valuable Library, Formed by a Well-known Collector Who Has Devoted Many Years and a Large Expenditure of Money in its Formation, Comprising an Unusual Assemblage of Fine Art and Illustrated Works, Unique Extra Illustrated Copies, @ Standard Authors in all Departments of Literature, Now Offered for Sale at the Very Reasonable Prices Affixed by J.W. Bouton* (1125 Broadway, New York, NY: Printed for the publisher, 1889), 90–93.

[45] An interesting detail is that during a serious illness Samuel Linley was nursed by Emma Hart, the later Second Lady Hamilton and paramour of Nelson. See 'Samuel Linley', *WP*, accessed 13 July 2009. For the connection with Emma, the Second Lady Hamilton, see Clementine Black, *The Linleys of Bath*, 146. On Emma, see 'Emma, Lady Hamilton', *WP*, accessed 1 January 2011. The article mentions her work in the Drury Lane theatre, but not in the Linley family.

A movie after her life, 'That Hamilton Woman' (1941) with Vivien Leigh playing Emma, was a favourite of Winston Churchill.

[46] 4 May 1825, entry in Sydney Morgan, *Lady Morgan's Memoirs, Autobiography, Diaries and Correspondence*, 2 vols., 2nd rev. ed. (London: Wm. H. Allen, 1863), 216–17, markup and editing by David Hill Radcliffe (August 2010), on: *Lord Byron and His Times* (website), accessed 8 January 2012, http://lordbyron.org.

[47] Roebuck, 'Autobiography'.

We have a reference to: 'Eight Autograph Letters, Signed, addressed to Miss Tickell and the Hon. Mrs. Boscawen, by the Duchess of Cloucester, the Princess Elizabeth, and the Princess Sophia . . . Autographs of Earl St. Vincent, Braham, Lord

Normanby, the Princess Charlotte, William IV, Queen Adelaide, Lady Caroline Lamb, the Duke of Cambridge and Lord Russell.' Bouton, *The Havemeyer Library*, 90–93

[48] William Wordsworth, 'French Revolution as it Appeared to Enthusiasts at His Commencement', 4, in *The Complete Poetical Works* (London: Macmillan, 1888), on Bartleby.com, (website) 1999, accessed 16 May 2016, www.bartleby.com/145/.

[49] Ben Wilson, *Decency and Disorder: The Age of Cant, 1789–1837* (London: Faber and Faber, 2008).

[50] Her grandson does not name Miss Barnes, calling her just his grandmother. See Roebuck, 'Autobiography', 1–25. In 1914, the identity of Zipporah was wrongly exchanged for that of 'Betty Tickell . . . through her marriage with an Indian civil servant, mother of John Arthur Roebuck (1801–79), the politician'. See A. R. Bayley, 'A note on Sheridan', *Notes and Queries* 11-X, no. 239 (1914): 61.

[51] Roebuck, 'Autobiography', 3–4.

[52] While it is likely that they met, it is not likely that Samuel Richard Tickell and John Arthur Roebuck had much contact. Soon after his arrival John Arthur Roebuck became an utilitarian and a friend of John Stuart Mill. In 1832 he entered Parliament as a member for Bath. He was nominally a Whig, but already at his maiden speech fiercely independent. A few years later, he became a leading Chartist. See Asa Briggs, *The Age of Improvement, 1783-1867 (*1959, published with corrections and revised Note on Books, 9th impr., [London and New York: Longman 1991]), 304-5. By that time, Samuel Richard had long left England.

[53] Tickell, 'Memoir', 784.

[54] Thomas Moore, *Letters and Journals of Lord Byron: with Notices of his Life*, 2 vols. (London, 1830–1831), *Lord Byron and His Times* (website), accessed 2 January 2012,
http://lordbyron.org/monograph.php?doc=ThMoore.1830&select=AD1813.13#AD1813.13-2 .

[55] Tickell, 'Memoir', 803.
The Apollo Belvedere was a partially restored copy of a bronze original by the Greek sculptor Leochares, made sometime between 350–325 BC. Soane possessed a cast, made about 1719 in Italy for Lord Burlington. It was in the Cheswick house. See 'The Collections', *Sir John Soane's Museum* (website), accessed 10 January 2010, www.soane.org/collections.html.

[56] 'Samuel R. Tickell, Biography', *India Office, Family History Search* (website), accessed 5 January 2011, http://indiafamily.bl.uk.
The daughter of R. M. Barnard was Anne Boscawen's namesake. She married in 1829. See 'Marriages', *The Annual Register; or, A View of the History, Politics, and Literature of the Year 1829*, vol. 28 (London, 1830): 199. She died in 1833. See 'Obituary [Anne Boscawen Gowland, dau. of Robert Markland]', *The Gentleman's Magazine and Historical Chronicle* 103, part 2, from July to December 1833 (London: Sylvanus Urban, 1833): 94.

[57] Samuel Richard Tickell's Cadet Papers (London: OIOC), L/Mil/9/167/447-56.

[58] Hodson, *List of the Officers of the Bengal Army*, vol. 1, xxiv.

[59] Hodson, *List of the Officers of the Bengal Army*, vol. 4, 276–77.

[60] Samuel Richard Tickell's Cadet Papers, 8 June 1827 (London: OIOC), L/Mil/9/167/447-56.

[61] Madan Paul Singh, *Indian Army Under the East India Company* (New Delhi: Sterling, 1976), 143.

[62] Hodson, *List of the Officers of the Bengal Army*, vol. 4, 276–77.

[63] John Gould, *A Century of Birds from the Himalaya Mountains* (London, 1830–32).
Thomas Pennant, *Indian Zoology* (London, 1790).
John Latham, *A General History of Birds*, 11 vols. (London, 1821–24).
Thomas Bewick, *A History of British Birds* (1797–1804).
Georges Cuvier, *Règne Animal distribue d'après son Organisation pour servir de base à l'Histoire Naturelle des Animaux et d'Introduction à l'Anatomie Comparee* (1817. Tickell knew French, but he could have had the English translation: *The Animal Kingdom* (London, 1827).

[64] Tickell, 'Memoir', 706, 787, 783.

[65] Samuel Richard Tickell, 'Manis Crassicaudata, (Auct) M. Pentadactyla (Ibid.), Short-tailed or thick-tailed Manis, In Hindustan, generally called "Bujjerkeet" –Orissa, "Bujjer-Kapta" and "Surooj Mookhee"–By the Lurka Koles, "Armoo"', *JASB* 11 (1842): 227–28.

[66] Hodson, *List of the Officers of the Bengal Army*, vol. 4, 276–77. So did the *Alphabetical List*, which gave 7 November 1829. See also Edward Dodwell, James Samuel Miles (compilers and editors), *Alphabetical List of the Officers of the Bengal Army: With the Dates of Their Respective Promotion, Retirement, Resignation, or Death, Whether in India or in Europe, From the Year 1760 to the Year 1834 Inclusive, Corrected to September 30, 1837* (London: Longman, Orme, Brown [1838]), 262.

[67] 'Military Appointments, Promotions, &ca.', *AJMR*, n.s., 13, (January–April 1834): 200.

[68] Niall Ferguson, *Empire: How Britain Made the Modern World* (London: Allen Lane, The Penguin Press, 2003), 186.

[69] 12 March 1822, see: *AJMR* 14, (July– December 1822): 397. Also: *The East India Register and Directory for 1823*, 2nd ed., corrected to 16 September 1823 (London: A. W. Mason, Geo. Owen and G. H. Brown): 464.

[70] *India Office Family History Records*, http//indiafamily.bl.uk (retrieved on several occasions in 2010 and 2011). Also: 'Miscellaneous', *The Quarterly Oriental Magazine, Review and Register* 2 (Calcutta: Thacker, 1824): lix, lxiv.
In 1845, George King died in Brighton at the age of 62. See 'Deaths', *Allen's Indian Mail and Register of Intelligence for British and Foreign India, China, and All Parts of the East* 3 (London: W. H. Allen, 1845): 172.

[71] Emma Roberts, chapter 7 of *Scenes and Characteristics of Hindostan, with sketches of Anglo-Indian Society* (London, 1835), republished in *Carey's Library of Choice Literature: Containing The Best Works of the Day, in Biography, History, Travels, Novels, Poetry, &ca. &ca.*, vol. 1 (Philadephia, 1836): 165–69.

[72] Emily Eden, *Up the Country: Letters written to her sister from the Upper Provinces of India* (1866, reprinted from the 1930 edition by Edward Thompson, with a new introduction by Elizabeth Claridge and notes by Edward Thompson, London: Virago Press, 1984), 11-17.
Ms Eden was very conscious of the small number of Englishmen. Elsewhere she wrote that it was 'odd and rather awful', to have a gathering of sixty Christians, defended by '12,000 false worshippers' (the troops) and surrounded by millions 'who all despise and detest our faith'. See ibidem, 35.

[73] Reginald Heber, *Narrative of a Journey through the Upper Provinces of India:From Calcutta to Bombay, 1824–1825 (with Notes upon Ceylon), An Account of a Journey to Madras and the Southern Provinces, 1826, and Letters Written in India by the late Right Rev. Reginald Heber, D. D., Lord Bishop of Calcutta*, ed. Amelia Heber, vol. 1 (London: John Murray, 1828), 213–22.

[74] Heber, *Narrative of a Journey*, 213–14. Bankipoor in the original.
Unsigned review of *Narrative of a Journey through the Upper Provinces of' India, from Calcutta to Bombay, 1824—1825'*, in *The British Critic, Quarterly Theological Review and Ecclesiastical Record* 4 (London, 1828): 200, *Google Books* (website), accessed 6 January 2011, http://books.google.nl/books).

[75] On Charles D'Oyly, his connection to Brian Houghton Hodgson, and his stay in Patna, see Allen, *The Prisoner of Kathmandu*, 20–22, 56, 126–127, 202.

[76] W. R. Gilbert to Swinton, 27 April 1824 (London: OIOC), Bengal Political Consultations, 27 June 1823.

[77] William Wilson Hunter, *Life of Brian Houghton Hodgson* (London: John Murray, 1896; repr., New Delhi, Madras: Asian Educational Services, 1991), 28–30.
David Waterhouse ed., *The Origins of Himalayan Studies: Brian Houghton Hodgson in Nepal and Darjeeling 1820–1858* (Abingdon: RoutledgeCurzon, first Indian reprint 2005), 3.
I am grateful to Dr Ramesh Dhungel of the Centre for Nepal and South Asian Studies in Kathmandu who drew my attention to this book.

[78] Quotation from http://www.bl.uk/onlinegallery/onlineex/apac/other/019wdz000002060u00079000.html, accessed 22 May 2012.
D'Oyly could have taken the name 'School of Athens' from the title of the painting by Rafael in 1510–1511. A full sized copy of this painting, 4.25 by 8.40 m, was exhibited in the House of Hugh Smithson Percy, first Duke of Northumberland. It is now in the Victoria and Albert Museum. See, *V&A, Search the Collections* (website), accessed 22 May 2012. http://collections.vam.ac.uk/item/O89799/oil-painting-the-school-of-athens-after/. D'Oyly could well have seen this lively picture sometime between 1785 and 1798, when he was in London for studies.

[79] *Nob Kishen's nautch party*, painting by Sir Charles D'Oyly , 1825–28 , *V&A, Search the Collections* (website), accessed 15 May 2012, http://collections.vam.ac.uk/item/O18838/watercolour-illustration-nob-kishens-nautch-party/
The watercolour painting was intended for his *Tom Raw, the Griffin: a burlesque poem*, but it was omitted from the printed version of 1828.

[80] 'Wedding' *The Quarterly Oriental Magazine, Review and Register* 2, September and December (Calcutta Thacker, 1824): lxii.

[81] Smith, Christopher Webb and Sir Charles D'Oyly, *The Feathered Game of Hindostan* (Patna: Behar Amateur Lithographic Press, 1828).
Smith, Christopher Webb and Sir Charles D'Oyly, *Oriental Ornithology* (Patna: Behar Amateur Lithographic Press, 1829). D'Oyly retired in 1838 and Webb in 1842.

[82] Hodson, *List of the Officers of the Bengal Army*, vol. 4, 276–77.

[83] 'Military Appointments, Promotions, &c.', *AJMR*, n.s., 12, (September–December 1833): 110.

[84] Samuel Richard Tickell, 'List of Birds Collected in the Jungles of Barabhum and Dholbhum', *JASB* 2, part 2 (1833): 569–83. The list is partly reproduced in Henry Spry, *Modern India: With Illustrations on the Resources and Capabilities of Hindustan*, vol. 1 (London: Whittaker, 1837), 326–30.

[85] Maybe Brian Houghton Hodgson in Kathmandu and John Gould in London. It could also refer to Charles D'Oyly and Christopher Webb Smith.

[86] Tickell, 'List of Birds', 582–83.

[87] Tickell, 'List of Birds', 571–72.

[88] Tickell, 'List of Birds', 574–75.

[89] Tickell, 'List of Birds', 574–75.
[90] Tickell, 'List of Birds', 579–80. Saul, Subonrika in the original.
[91] Tickell, 'List of Birds', 579–80.
[92] Edward Dodwell, James Samuel Miles (compilers and editors), *Alphabetical List of the Officers of the Bengal Army*, 262.
[93] F.185/15 and F.59/32. See S. N. Prasad, *Catalogue of the Historical Maps of the Survey of India (1700–1900)* (New Delhi: The National Archives of India, 1975), 386, 157.
[94] 'Military Appointments, Promotions, &c.', *AJMR*, n.s., 22, (January–April 1837): 56.
[95] Wilkinson to Mangles, 22 August 1836; Mangles to Wilkinson, 5 September 1836 (London: OIOC), BC 66,546.
[96] 'Military Appointments, Promotions, &c.', *AJMR*, n.s., 22, (January–April 1837): 129.
[97] *Monthly Journal and General Register* (1836): 90.
[98] 'Proceedings of the Asiatic Society, Wednesday Evening, the 5th October, 1836', *JASB* 5 (1836): 587.
[99] Bengal Political Department, 7 March 1838, no. 6 (London: OIOC), E/4/754.

Chapter 13: The Hodésum Articles

[1] Samuel Richard Tickell, 'Memoir on Hodésum (Improperly Called *Kolehan*)', *JASB* 9, part 2 (1840), 694–710, 783–808.
Samuel Richard Tickell, 'Grammatical Construction of the Ho Language', *JASB* 9, part 2 (1840), 997–1007.
Samuel Richard Tickell, 'Vocabulary of the Ho Language', *JASB* 9, part 2 (1840), 1063–90.
Samuel Richard Tickell, 'Supplementary Note to the Memoir on the Hodésum, vol. ix, pp.649 and 783', *JASB* 10 (1841): 30.
[2] Samuel Richard Tickell, 'The Zoological Works of Samuel Richard Tickell' (London: Zoological Society of London, 1865–73), illustrated manuscript work in 14 vols.
Samuel Richard Tickell, 'Original Water-colour Drawings and Illustrated MS Relating to Indian Birds', forming one of a set of volumes from which the illustrated MS work by Tickell on Mammals, &c. of India, Library of the Zoological Society of London was elaborated, [abt. 1870].
[3] Tickell, 'Memoir', 1089.
[4] Tickell, 'Memoir', 806.
[5] Tickell, 'Memoir', 803.
[6] J. P. Lostly, 'The Architectural Monuments of Buddhism, Hodgson and the Buddhist Architecture of the Kathmandu Valley', in David Waterhouse ed., *The Origins of Himalayan Studies*, 94–95.
[7] Ann Datta and Carol Inskipp, 'Zoology . . . Amuses Me Much', in David Waterhouse ed., *The Origins of Himalayan Studies*, 137–38.
[8] Allen, *The Prisoner of Kathmandu*, 214–15.
[9] In 1819–20, at the beginning of his career, Hodgson assisted Traill in the settlement of the recently acquired Kumaon. See Hunter, *Life of Brian Houghton Hodgson*, 36–56, esp. 38. W. W. Hunter noted that Traill gave Hodgson 'the habit of systematic enquiry into the population, their history, language, social institutions, and economic conditions'. See Hunter, *Life of Brian Houghton Hodgson*, 52. That was an overstatement by a too admiring biographer. Actually, Traill gave little information on the population of Kumaon. He first published a lengthy 'Statistical Sketch' in 1828 in the Asiatick Researches. In 1832 followed a 'Statistical Report' on the Bhotia Mehals of Kamaon. The outstanding feature of the Sketch was an enumerative discussion of the ghosts of Kumaun. Traill's Statistical Report was more systematic, but rather superficial. With its list of products and discussion of trade, it reads like an economic brochure. See George William Traill, 'Statistical Report on the Bhotia Mehals of Kamaon', *AR* 17 (1832): 1–50.
[10] Hunter, *Life of Brian Houghton Hodgson*, 364.
[11] 'MSS EUR Hodgson/25 Ethnography and Languages 1830s–1850s', entry 7, *Hodgson Papers, Inventory of Hodgson's Private Papers at the British Library*, accessed 16 March 2014,
http://catalogue2.socanth.cam.ac.uk:8080/exist/servlet/db/Hodgson/hodgson.xq.
[12] There are few works on Hodgson. William Wilson Hunter's 1896 hagiographic *Life of Brian Houghton Hodgson* was based on a direct knowledge of the main character and on a proper study of his correspondence. Lately, Hodgsonian studies have speeded up with the encompassing collection of articles, edited in 2004 by David M. Waterhouse, *The Origins of Himalayan Studies*; and in 2015 with Charles Allen's *The Prisoner of Kathmandu: Brian Hodgson in Nepal 1820-43*.
[13] Hunter, *Life of Brian Houghton Hodgson*, 11, 69–71, 77. Allen, *The Prisoner of Kathmandu*, 109, 115–16, 120, 202.
[14] Hunter, *Life of Brian Houghton Hodgson*, 80. Allen, *The Prisoner of Kathmandu*, 186.
[15] Hunter, *Life of Brian Houghton Hodgson*, 83, 85.
[16] Hunter, *Life of Brian Houghton Hodgson*, 88.
[17] 'Mary Rose Tickell', *India Office Family History Search* (website), accessed 5 February 2010, http://indiafamily.bl.uk.
[18] Hunter, *Life of Brian Houghton Hodgson*, 88, 166–67.
[19] Hodgson's pay was GBP 4,000 a year. See Hunter, *Life of Brian Houghton Hodgson*, 84. The exchange rate was taken as 1

GBP = Rs. 10.

[20] 'Marriage: 1840 Jan 01 Thomas Lacminden [recte Lumisden] Strange, bachelor, Madras Civil Service, Son of Sir Thomas Andrew Strange, of Iver, m by lic & Mary Rosa Hodgson, Widow, of the Late Lieut W HODGSON Bengal Horse Artillery Iver witnesses: S. A. Ward, S. F. Ward, Philip W. Muir, R. Tripell (R. Tickell), (Col. Bengal Engineers)' See Mike Strange, 'Buckinghamshire—Strange and derivates', *Your Total Event* (website), accessed 21 March 2011, http://www.yourtotalevent.com/people/STRANGEinBuckinghamshire.htm.
For the father, see 'Thomas Andrew Lumisden Strange', *WP*, accessed 3 February 2010.

[21] Mary Rose was to have two more children and died in 1847, probably in India. Her youngest was born there the year before. See 'Mary Rose Tickell', 2007, *Lyons Family Tree Guide* (website), accessed 5 February 2010, http://lyons.familytreeguide.com/getperson.php?personID=I2342. Her widower became a fierce critic of irrational beliefs in Christianity till his death in 1884.

[22] In 1841, if we count actual residence, or at latest 1843 if we count twenty-five years of service. See Hunter, *Life of Brian Houghton Hodgson*, 176.

[23] Hunter, *Life of Brian Houghton Hodgson*, 167.

[24] B. H. Hodgson to H. Torrents, July 23 1840, New Delhi, NAI, Foreign Consultations 10 August 1840, no. 59; Foreign Consultations 27 July 1840, no 40-41.

[25] Hunter consistently mentioned the assistant resident 'Mr. J. R. Tickell', as the author. Hunter had not seen the printed volume, but had taken his excerpts and quotations from the manuscript (Secret) Consultations in the India Office. As in the writing of the time the S and the J were quite similar, a copying error must have caused this uncertainty. But then, 'Mr.' is not a military rank, so Hodgson must have left Hunter really in the dark about Tickell.

[26] Charles Allen called Tickell 'welcome company' to Hodgson and stated that 'the two saw each other as fellow enthusiasts and collaborators'. Allen, *The Prisoner of Kathmandu*, 213–14. He added no evidence.

[27] Allen, *The Prisoner of Kathmandu*, 215.

[28] Tickell, 'Memoir', 700.

[29] Tickell, 'Grammatical Construction of the Ho Language', 1000; Tickell, 'Vocabulary of the Ho Language', 1062.

[30] Tickell, 'Memoir', 797.

[31] Samuel Richard Tickell, 'Notes on the Bendkar, a People of Keonjur', *JASB* 11 (1842): 205; Tickell, 'Manis Crassicaudata', 226. 'Lurka Coles' in the original.

[32] Tickell, 'Grammatical Construction of the Ho Language', 1007.

[33] *PASB*, January–June (1841): 172–3.

[34] 'MSS EUR Hodgson/25 Ethnography and Languages 1830s–1850s', entry 7, *Hodgson Papers, Inventory of Hodgson's Private Papers at the British Library*, accessed 16 March 2014,
http://catalogue2.socanth.cam.ac.uk:8080/exist/servlet/db/Hodgson/hodgson.xq.

[35] This was the case also in England, as Virginia Woolf pointed out in her classic. See Virginia Woolf, *A Room of One's Own* (1928; republished, Harmondsworth: Penguin, 1967), 67.

[36] Tickell, 'Memoir', 783.

[37] Fr. Sanjay Ekka, Burigora, West Singhbhum, personal communication, 2010.

[38] Tickell, 'Grammatical Construction of the Ho Language', 997.

[39] Tickell, 'Grammatical Construction of the Ho Language', 997–98.

[40] Tickell, 'Grammatical Construction of the Ho Language', 997.

[41] In a written language 2,000 words would be a good practical base and 3,000 words would put you at reasonable ease; in a spoken language such as Ho, 2000 words would make you rather comfortable. See Paul Nation and Robert Waring, 'Vocabulary size, Text Coverage and Word Lists', [1997], *Université catholique de Louvain* (website), accessed 23 March 2011, http://www.fltr.ucl.ac.be/fltr/germ/etan/bibs/vocab/cup.html. Tickell with his 1650 words fell just short of that.
We talk here about very basic skills; in a highly literate society like in the Netherlands, the number of words people know upon leaving their primary education is 27,000, as was established in 2013. See
http://www.wetenschap24.nl/programmas/grootnationaalonderzoek/nieuws/Het-taal-onderzoek/Resultaten-GNO-Taal.html, accessed 15 December 2013.
Fr Deeney gave 'close to 12,000 entries' in his dictionary, a vast improvement on Burrow's 1800 Ho words. But he remarked that it was still 'far from being an exhaustive Ho-English Dictionary'. See John Deeney, *Ho-English Dictionary* (Chaibasa, Xavier Ho Publications, 1978), iii.

[42] Tickell, 'Vocabulary of the Ho Language', 1081.

[43] Tickell, 'Vocabulary of the Ho Language', 1080–87.

[44] Tickell, 'Vocabulary of the Ho Language', 1080. Before Tickell's parts, I have inserted '—'.

[45] Tickell, 'Grammatical Construction of the Ho Language', 997.

[46] Tickell, 'Grammatical Construction of the Ho Language', 997.

[47] Tickell, 'Grammatical Construction of the Ho Language', 997.

48 Tickell, 'Memoir', 788.
49 Tickell, 'Vocabulary of the Ho Language', 1090.
50 Tickell, 'Vocabulary of the Ho Language', 1081. Before the questions, I have inserted '—'.
51 Tickell, 'Memoir', 695, 807.
52 Tickell, 'Memoir', 709, note.
53 Dunbar, 'Some Observations on the Lurka Coles', 370–77.
54 Tickell, 'Memoir', 803.
55 Tickell, 'Memoir', 694–98, quotation on page 695.
56 Dalton, *Descriptive Ethnology of Bengal*, 178.
57 Tickell, 'Memoir', 696. Lurka Coles, Singbhoom, Kolehan in the original.
58 Tickell, 'Memoir', 803.
59 Tuckey, *Final Report*, 17–22. Tuckey's operations lasted from 1913 to 1918.
60 'or Kolehan of the Hindoos'. See Tickell, 'Memoir', 697. Ooria Bramins, Porahaut, Singbhoom in the original.
61 Therefore, he did not get much credit for his description from later archaeologists. In 1874, Beglar called it 'not always reliable', but in 1983, Joshi was more complimentary, Tickell's work belonged to a small number of 'valuable works of reference'. See Joseph D. Beglar, *Report of Tours in the South-Eastern Provinces in 1874–75 and 1875–76* (Calcutta, 1878; repr., Varanasi: Indological Book House, 1970), 69. See also Arjun Joshi, *History & Culture of Khijjingkotta under the Bhanjas* (Delhi: Vikas, 1983), 16.
62 Tickell, 'Memoir', 706–9.
63 Tickell, 'Memoir', 706, 707.
64 Singh Deo, *Singhbhum, Seraikella and Kharswan Through the Ages*, 29–30; 37–38.
65 M. A. Haque, 'Route of Firuz Shah's Invasion of Orissa in 1360 A.D.', *OHRJ* 15, nos. 3 and 4 (1967): 63;
L. N. Raut, 'The State of Mayurbhanj During the Years of Maratha Supremacy in Orissa', *OHRJ* 28, nos. 1 and 2 (1982): 88–89.
66 Tickell, 'Memoir', 708.
67 Tickell, 'Memoir', 707.
68 Tickell, 'Supplementary Note to the Memoir on the Hodésum'.
69 E. Ryan read a 'letter from Captain S. R. Tickell, with sketches of idols' on Thursday evening 11 November 1841. See *PASB*, in *JASB* 10 (1841): 399. I am grateful to Dr. Ata Malik for the trouble she took to try and trace – in vain - the sketches at the Asiatic Society of Bengal. It is possible that Tickell did mention the sketches in his letter, but did not include these. As in another case, 'Lieut. Tickell has not favoured us with the drawing alluded to, disappointed no doubt with our Calcutta lithographies of subjects of this nature'. See note to Samuel Richard Tickell, 'Remarks on the Moschus Memina', *Calcutta Journal of Natural History* 1 (1841): 420.
70 Tickell, 'Memoir', 697–98.
71 Tickell, 'Memoir', 698.
72 Tickell, 'Memoir', 807.
73 Tickell, 'Memoir', 689.
74 Tickell, 'Memoir', 679.
75 Tickell, 'Memoir', 803. Hindoos in the original.
76 Tickell, 'Memoir', 803. Hindoos in the original.
77 Tickell, 'Memoir', 806.
78 Tickell, 'Memoir', 788. Hindoostanee in the original.
79 Tickell, 'Memoir', 785–87. Singbhoom, Kolehan, Chota Nagpoor, Jankeebooroo, Soobernrekha, gowers, Thakoors, mechans, mechan in the original.
80 Tickell, 'Memoir', 785–87. Sarnda, Pugrees, scimetars in the original. The Dorawas were not mentioned.
81 Tickell, 'Memoir', 787. The quote is from Walter Scott, 'The Tale of Alice Brand' (1810), on *Tam Lin Balladry* (website), accessed 11 September 2015, http://tam-lin.org/stories/Alice_Brand.html.
82 Tickell, 'Memoir', 787.
83 Tickell, 'Memoir', 699. Sixty miles, thirty-five to sixty miles, in the original.
84 Tickell, 'Memoir', 699–702.
85 Tickell, 'Memoir', 702–5.
86 Tickell, 'Memoir', 702.
87 Tickell, 'Memoir', 702–3. Koles, Oorias in the original.
88 Samuel Richard Tickell, 'Remarks on the characters and habits of Ursus labiatus, with a figure, Plate VII', *Calcutta Journal of Natural History and Miscellany of the Arts and Sciences in India* 1 (1841): 200–205.
89 Tickell, 'Vocabulary of the Ho Language', 1084–85. Before Tickell's parts in the negotiation, I have inserted '-'.
90 Tickell, 'Memoir', 704. Tickell, 'Vocabulary of the Ho Language', 1068–70.

[91] Tickell, 'Memoir', 704. Unfortunately, to my knowledge this deficit has never been remedied. Even the indefatigable Fr. Deeney admitted: 'For insects we had no reference book'. See Deeney, *Ho-English Dictionary*, viii.
[92] 'Surprisingly in general Hos cannot distinguish snakes well, e.g. Ho high school boys cannot distinguish a wolf snake from a krait'. See Deeney, *Ho-English Dictionary*, vii–viii.
[93] Tickell, 'Memoir', 704. 'Gara bin' means 'river snake'. See Deeney, *Ho-English Dictionary*, 107, 36, respectively.
[94] Tickell, 'Memoir', 706. 'It is a nipping and an eager air', Shakespeare, *Hamlet*, 1.4: 2.
[95] Tickell, 'Vocabulary of the Ho Language', 1087.
[96] Tickell, 'Memoir', 706.
[97] Tickell, 'Memoir', 785.
[98] Tickell, 'Remarks on Pteropus Edulis, Geoffrey', *Calcutta Journal of Natural History and Miscellany of the Arts and Sciences in India* 3 (1843): 33.
[99] Tickell, 'Memoir', 783. 'four or five miles' in the original.
[100] Tickell, 'Memoir', 783. The citation is from Thomas Gray, *Elegy Written in a Country Churchyard* of 1751. See Thomas Gray, 'Elegy written in a Country Church Yard' [1751], *RPO: Representative Poetry Online* (website), accessed 23 November 2011, http://rpo.library.utoronto.ca/poem/882.html.
See also: Thomas Gray, 'Elegy Written in a Country Churchyard' (1751), Commentary, The Thomas Gray Archive: A Collaborative Digital Collection (website), accessed 11 September 2012, http://www.thomasgray.org/cgi-bin/display.cgi?text=elcc .
[101] Tickell, 'Memoir', 783.
[102] Tickell, 'Memoir', 806.
[103] Tickell, 'Memoir', 804.
[104] Tickell, 'Memoir', 805.
[105] Dunbar, 'Some Observations on the Lurka Coles', 372. Colehan in the original. *Sookool* for *Jookool*, as the *J* was an apparent spelling error.
[106] Tickell, 'Memoir', 784. In later years, that passage would be taken up to state that all the Hos were, or once were, nomads. Latham, who started the trend, even presented them as 'locomotive agriculturists'. See Robert Gordon Latham, *A Descriptive Ethnology*, vol. 2 (London: John van Voorst, 1859, reprinted as *Tribes and Races: A Descriptive Ethnology of Asia, Africa & Europe*, Delhi: Cultural Publishing House, 1983), 419.
[107] Tickell, 'Memoir', 784.
[108] Tickell, 'Memoir', 805.
[109] Tickell, 'Memoir', 804–5.
[110] Dunbar, 'Some Observations on the Lurka Coles', 371. Hindoos in the original.
[111] Tickell, 'Memoir', 805.
[112] Tickell, 'Memoir', 784; 803. Hindoos, Belvidere in the original.
[113] Tickell, 'Memoir', 784.
[114] Dunbar, 'Some Observations on the Lurka Coles', 372.
[115] Tickell, 'Vocabulary of the Ho Language', 1066–67.
[116] Tickell, 'Memoir', 805. Tusser in the original.
[117] Tickell, 'Vocabulary of the Ho Language', 1083–84. Before Tickell's parts in the negotiation, I have inserted '-'.
[118] Tickell, 'Vocabulary of the Ho Language', 1083–84. Before Tickell's parts, I have inserted '—'.
[119] Tickell, 'Memoir', 806.
[120] 'Vigesimal', WP, accessed 19 November 2015.
[121] Tickell, 'Vocabulary of the Ho Language', 1065.
[122] Tickell, 'Vocabulary of the Ho Language', 1066.
[123] Tickell, 'Vocabulary of the Ho Language', 1079.
[124] Tickell, 'Memoir', 806. Here, Tickell was way too optimistic. In twenty years, during the Mutiny old divisions would reappear.
[125] Tickell, 'Memoir', 803.
[126] Tickell, 'Memoir', 804. Later, this belief that there was a 'special virtue attached to the shadows of persons' was also noticed with the Mundas. See Hoffmann and Van Emelen, *Encyclopaedia Mundarica* 1: 62–63.
[127] J. R. Ouseley in 1840 See K. K. Basu, 'Tour-Diary of J. R. Ouseley', *OHRJ* 5 (1956): 167.
[128] Tickell, 'Memoir', 804.
[129] Tickell, 'Memoir', 803–4. Hindooised in the original.
[130] Tickell, 'Memoir', 805.
[131] Dunbar, 'Some Observations on the Lurka Coles', 372.
[132] Tickell, 'Memoir', 808.
[133] Tickell, 'Memoir', 804.

[134] Tickell, 'Memoir', 804.
[135] Tickell, 'Memoir', 808.
[136] Tickell, 'Memoir', 804.
[137] Dunbar, 'Some Observations on the Lurka Coles', 372–73. Mankie in the original.
[138] Tickell, 'Memoir', 788.
[139] Tickell, 'Memoir', 800–801.
[140] Tickell, 'Memoir', 801.
[141] Deeney, *Ho-English Dictionary*, 30–31.
[142] Tickell, 'Memoir', 800.
[143] Tickell, 'Memoir', 788.
[144] Tickell, 'Memoir', 784.
[145] Tickell, 'Memoir', 804.
[146] John William Kaye, *The Administration of the East India Company: A History of Indian Progress* (London: Richard Bentley, 1853), 215.
[147] Tickell, 'Memoir', 803.
[148] Tickell, 'Memoir', 797–99. Mankees in the original.
[149] Tickell, 'Memoir', 788–91. For the list of omens, see pages 791–93.
[150] Dunbar, 'Some Observations on the Lurka Coles', 375.
[151] Tickell, 'Memoir', 795–96.
[152] Dalton remarked that among the Hos ('Kols') he had not found any conception of the hereafter 'that may not be traced to Brahmanical or Christian teaching'. He added that anyway Hos did not give such stories unless prompted to 'often inadvertently'. See Dalton, *Descriptive Ethnology of Bengal*, 204.
[153] Tickell, 'Memoir', 708–9.
[154] Tickell, 'Memoir', 800.
[155] Wilkinson to Tickell, enclosure in Wilkinson to Mangles, 5 May 1837 (London: OIOC), BC 69,239.
[156] Tickell, 'Memoir', 801.
[157] Tickell, 'Memoir', 802.
[158] Tickell, 'Memoir', 801–3.
[159] Tickell, 'Memoir', 806.
[160] Tickell, 'Vocabulary of the Ho Language', 1083.
[161] Tickell, 'Memoir', 806.
[162] Tickell, 'Vocabulary of the Ho Language', 1087–88.
[163] Tickell, 'Vocabulary of the Ho Language', 1067.
[164] Tickell, 'The Zoological Works', vol.: 'Mammals of India', 62.
[165] Tickell, 'The Zoological Works', vol.: 'Mammals of India', 62. Singbhoom, Kole, Mankee, Chuckerdur singh, in the original.
[166] Tickell, 'Memoir', 803.
[167] Tickell, 'Memoir', 788.
[168] Tickell, 'Vocabulary of the Ho Language', 1076, 1077.
[169] Tickell, 'Memoir', 807.
[170] Tickell, 'Memoir', 808.
[171] Tickell, 'Vocabulary of the Ho Language', 1080.

Reflection: That Tickell Woman

[1] Allen J. Greenberger, *The British Image of India: A Study in the Literature of Imperialism, 1880–1960* (London: Oxford University Press, 1969).
[2] James Fenimore Cooper, *The Last of the Mohicans* (1826; rep.Harmondsworth: Penguin Books, 1994).
[3] For the difference between colonialism and imperialism, see Nirad C. Chaudhuri, *Thy Hand, Great Anarch! India: 1921-1952* (1987, Chatto and Windus, paperback edition, London: Hogarth Press, 1990), 779.
For a case contemporary to the establishment of the Kolhan Government Estate, see the 1838 Trail of Tears of the Cherokee nation. The Cherokees were banned from their villages and lands in south east USA to the near desert conditions of Oklahoma. In the forced and badly planned removal, out of 13,000 some 4,000 Cherokees died. See 'Trail of Tears', WP, accessed 23 April 2013.
[4] Li Shang-Yin, 'Written on the Monastery Wall', in *Poems of the Late T'ang*, trans. A. C. Graham (Harmondsworth: Penguin Books, 1968), 161.

[5] Tickell, 'Memoir', 784, 803.
[6] Tickell, 'Memoir', 706; Shakespeare, *Hamlet*, 1.4: 2.
[7] Tickell, 'Memoir', 787.
'Tis merry, 'tis merry in good green wood' is the opening line of Sir Walter Scott's 'The Tale of Alice Brand'. See Walter Scott, 'The Tale of Alice Brand', in *The Lady of the Lake* (1810), www.tam-lin.org/tales.tamlin5 .html (retrieved 16 April 2007).
[8] Walter Scott, 'The Life of Jonathan Swift D.D.', in Walter Scott, *The Complete Works of Sir Walter Scott: With a Biography and His Last Additions and Illustrations*, 7 vols., vol. 6 (New York: Conner and Cooke, Franklin Building, 1833), 48. Scott had received this assistance probably in 1811, as he gratefully mentioned a 'Mr. Tickell' in a letter. See Scott to Matthew Weld Hartstongue, 22 December 1811, in *The Letters of Sir Walter Scott*, edited by Herbert J. C. Grierson, vol. 3, p. 43 (London: Constable, 1932–37), on *The letters of Sir Walter Scott* (website), accessed 13 October 2012,
 http://www.walterscott.lib.ed.ac.uk/etexts/etexts/letters.html.
He referred to Thomas as 'Major Tickell' in his 1814 multivolume *Life and Editions of Swift*.
[9] Hodson, *List of the Officers of the Bengal Army 1758–1834*, vol. 4, 276.
[10] Tickell, 'Memoir', 783. That quotation was kind of Samuel Richard, as Gray himself had not much regard for his great-great-grandfather Thomas Tickell. He called him 'only a poor short winded imitator of Addison, who had himself not above three or four notes in poetry . . . However I forgive him for the sake of his ballad [Colin and Lucy], which I always thought the prettiest in the world'. See Thomas Gray, 'Thomas Gray to Horace Wadpole' (1748), in Grosse ed., *Works*, vol. 2 (1895), 219, *Spencer and the Tradition: English Poetry 1579-1830* (website), accessed 20 February 2011,
 http://spenserians.cath.vt.edu/CommentRecord.php?action=GET&cmmtid=1793.
Thomas Gray (1716–71) wrote the poem over long time, after he returned from his Grand Tour through Europe. *The Elegy*, published in 1751, was a great and instantaneous success. The celebration of the graves of humble and unknown villagers was a novelty. Still, Gray's depiction of village life started with the tolling of the village curfew, which was inspired by Dante's 1308–21 *La Divina Commedia, Purgatorio*, Canto 8, v–vi. See the text and commentary in *The Thomas Gray Archive, A Collaborative Digital Collection* (website), accessed 11 September 2012,
 http://www.thomasgray.org/cgi-bin/display.cgi?text=elcc .
For the agrarian background to Gray's 'Elegy', see Kenneth MacLean, *Agrarian Age: A Background for Wordsworth* (New Haven Connecticut: Yale University Press, 1950; repr., Hamden Connecticut: Archon Books, 1970), 47–48.
[11] Tickell, 'Memoir', 697, 787, 803.
[12] Tickell, 'Memoir', 807.
[13] Brian Houghton Hodgson, *Essay the First, On the Kocch, Bódo and Dhimal Tribes*, 3 parts (Calcutta: J. Thomas, Baptist Mission Press, 1847), 150.
[14] Hodgson, 'Aborigines of the Nilgiris, with Remarks on Their Affinities', *JASB* 25 (1856): 498.
[15] Hodgson, 'Aborigines of the Nilgiris, with Remarks on Their Affinities', 501.
[16] And, now greatly overstating his point, he found that their language, too, was the same as that of the Santhals, Mundas, Bhumij, Oraons, and even Gonds, 'not to speak of other and remoter tribes . . . having . . . Turanian tongues'. See Hodgson, 'Aborigines of the Nilgiris, with Remarks on Their Affinities', 501.
[17] After Hodgson retired in 1844, he placed his children in the care of his sister Fanny, who was married to Baron Pierre Nahuys, provincial governor at Arnhem in the Netherlands. Mehr-un-Nissa Begum was left behind in Nepal. Local lore had it that she was pregnant with a third child, but that is not confirmed. See Harihar Raj Joshi, 'Brian Houghton Hodgson – The Unsung Story', in David Waterhouse ed., *The Origins of Himalayan Studies*, 234-37. There seemed to have been some contact between Hodgson and his abandoned wife, but she did not join him in Darjeeling to which Hodgson repaired in 1845. The date of her death is unknown. Hunter, who did not mention her name, implied that she died just before or in 1853. See Hunter, *Life of Brian Houghton Hodgson*, 86. Hodgson (re)married in 1853 Ann Scott, whom he had met in Holland. His daughter Sarah had died in 1851 in the Netherlands; his son Henry would die in Darjeeling in 1856.
[18] New Delhi, NAI, Foreign Consultations, no. 32, 22 February 1841.
[19] This question was suggested to me by Jack Miles' discussion of Oedipus Rex and Hamlet. See Jack Miles, *God, A Biography* (New York: Vintage Books, 1996), 397–408.
[20] Tickell, 'Memoir', 702, 783. Byturni in the original.
[21] Tickell, 'Memoir', 704.
[22] Tickell, 'Memoir', 785.
[23] Tickell, 'Memoir', 704.
[24] Tickell, 'Memoir', 806.
[25] Tickell, 'Memoir', 788.
[26] Tickell, 'Memoir', 806.
[27] Eric Stokes, *The English Utilitarians and India* (Oxford: Clarendon Press, 1959; Indian paperback ed., Delhi: Oxford University Press, 1989), 242.

[28] Tickell, 'The Zoological Works'.

Conclusion: A People in Their Own Land

No notes

Appendix: Impact of Tickell's articles

[1] On Bhutan, the Khyen tribe, Assam, Arakan, once more Assam, some hills near Sylhet, the valley of Spiti in the Himalayas.
[2] Brian Houghton Hodgson, *Essay the First, On the Kocch, Bódo and Dhimal tribes*, 3 parts (Calcutta: J. Thomas, Baptist Mission Press, 1847), 150, footnote.
See also: Brian Houghton Hodgson, 'Aborigines of the Nilgiris, with Remarks on their Affinities', *JASB* 25 (1856): 498, 501.
[3] 'The Arian Race', in *Calcutta Review* 26 (1856): 537–39. This unsigned article used Tickell's remarks on the custom of the Hos to bury the burned remains of their dead under a huge flat stone, and to erect upright memorial stones for their dead, to connect the Hos to the 'Kasias' (Khasis) of the present-day Meghalaya state in North-eastern India. This habit connected them also to the 'cromlechs' on the British Isles.
[4] Robert Gordon Latham, *A Descriptive Ethnology*, vol. 2 (London: John van Voorst, 1859, reprinted as *Tribes and Races: A Descriptive Ethnology of Asia, Africa & Europe*, Delhi: Cultural Publishing House, 1983), 281–94, 415–58.
[5] Latham, *A Descriptive Ethnology*, vol. 2, 424, 425.
[6] Latham, *A Descriptive Ethnology*, vol. 2, 419.
[7] Dunschuud; D. C. Mackey; I. M. Grote to W. J. Allen, 10 March, 1855; D .C. Mackey; M. J. Grob; G. Sand to W. J. Allen [August or September 1855], quoted in Roy Chaudhury, *Singhbhum Old Records*, 77; 103.
[8] Emil Stöhr, 'Die Singhbhum-Abteilung der Provinz der Südwest-Grenze von Bengalen', *Petermann's Mittheilungen über wichtige neue Erforschungen auf dem Gesammtgebiete der Geographie*, 7. Band, Heft VI (The Singhbhum District of the South Western Frontier Province of Bengal, Petermann's Announcements on Important New Research in the Whole Field of Geography, vol. 7, part 6) (1861): 219–26, esp. 225–26.
[9] Edward Tuite Dalton, 'The "Kols" of Chota Nagpore', Special Number on Indian Ethnology 1866, *JASB* 35, part 2 (1867): 153–198. Dalton published the same article with the Ethnological Society of London. It was read there on January 8, 1867, and published in 1868 in the Transactions. See Edward Tuite Dalton, 'The "Kols" of Chota Nagpore', *Transactions of the Ethnological Society of London*, n.s., 6 (1868): 1–41.
[10] John Forbes Watson and John William Kaye eds., *The People of India: A Series of Photographic Illustrations, with Descriptive Letterpress, of The Races and Tribes of Hindustan, Originally Prepared Under the Authority of the Government of India, and Reproduced by Order of the Secretary of State for India in Council*, 8 vols., vol. 1 (London: India Museum, 1868–1875), pl. 18, 'Larka Cole, Aboriginal ("fighting Cole"), Chota Nagpoor'.
[11] Dalton, *Descriptive Ethnology of Bengal*, 185–86, 204.
[12] David Duncan, *Asiatic Races*, compiled and abstracted by Professor David Duncan, in Herbert Spencer ed., *Descriptive Sociology; or, Groups of Sociological facts*, classified and arranged by Herbert Spencer; compiled and abstracted by David Duncan, Richard Scheppig, James Collier, Division I, part 3-A (London and Edinburgh: Williams and Norgate, 1876), 11, 19, 37.
[13] Ball, *Jungle Life in India*, 168.
[14] E. Balfour, 'Kol', in *The Cyclopaedia of India and of Eastern and Southern Asia: Commercial, Industrial, and Scientific, Products of the Mineral, Vegetable and Animal Kingdoms, Useful Arts and Manufactures*, vol. 2, H-Nysa, 3rd ed. (London: Bernard Quaritch, 1885), 591.
[15] 'Kols – Funeral Ceremonies', *North Indian Notes and Queries: A Monthly Periodical* 2, no. 7 (1892): 123.
William Crooke, *An Introduction to Popular Religion and Folklore of Northern India* (Allahabad: Government Press North Western Provinces and Oudh, 1894; repr., New Delhi: Asian Educational Services, 1994).
[16] Hoffmann and Van Emelen, *Encyclopaedia Mundarica* 6: 1765, 1769.
[17] See Dhirendra Nath Majumdar, 'The Traditional Origin of the Hos: Together with a Brief Description of the Chief Bongas (or Gods) of the Hos', *JASB*, n.s., 20 (1924, published 1925): 193-97. See also Dhirendra Nath Majumdar, *A Tribe in Transition: A Study in Culture Pattern* (Calcutta: Longmans, Green, 1937), 5, 11–13; and from the same author, *The Affairs of a Tribe: A Study in Tribal Dynamics* (Lucknow: Ethnographic and Folk Culture Society, 1950).
[18] Joseph D. Beglar, *Report of Tours in the South-Eastern Provinces in 1874–75 and 1875–76* (Calcutta, 1878; repr., Varanasi: Indological Book House, 1970), 69, 77.
[19] Arjun Joshi, *History & Culture of Khijjingakotta under the Bhanjas* (Delhi: Vikas, 1983), 16.
[20] 'Tickell was most vocal in glorifying the ideal of the noble savage'. See Das Gupta, *Adivasis and the Raj*, 118. As we have

seen, romanticism is way too simple to characterise Tickell's approach.

At several places, Asok Kumar Sen made use of Tickell material. See Asoka Kumar Sen, *Representing Tribe, The Ho of Singhbhum Under Colonial Rule* (New Delhi: Concept, 2011), 10, 13, 14, 30, 17, 31–32, 34, 35, 38, 39, 41, 43, 63, 105–6, 111, 112, 131.

Padmaja Sen, finally, used Tickell's 'Vocabulary' to make her point that the Hos would have a 'culture of the present'. See Padmaja Sen, 'The Culture of the Present: An Understanding of the Adivasi Aesthetics, *JAIS* 1, no. 1 (2014): 34-5.

[21] Lieut. Tickell, *Memoir on the Hodésum (Kolehan)*, Kolkata: Baskey Publication, 2012. It does not seem to be on the market.

[22] Risley, *Singbhum District*, 24–26, 26–31, 70–71.

[23] Lewis Sidney Steward O'Malley, *Singhbhum, Saraikela and Kharsawan*, Bengal District Gazetteers (Calcutta: The Bengal Secretariat Book Depôt, 1910).

[24] Tuckey, *Final Report*, 13.

[25] Roy Chaudhury, *Singhbhum*, 256–58.

[26] Friedrich Max Müller, 'The last results of the researches respecting the non-Iranian and non-Semitic languages of Asia and Europe, or the Turanian family of language (letter of Professor Max Muller to Chevalier Bunsen, on the classification of the Turanian languages), quoted in Christian Charles Josias Bunsen, *Outlines of the Philosophy of Universal History, Applied to Language and Religion*, vol. 1 (London: Longman, Brown, Green and Longmans, 1854), 436. See also *Internet Archive* (website), accessed 8 June 2014,
https://archive.org/stream/outlinesphiloso01bunsgoog/outlinesphiloso01bunsgoog_djvu.txt.

[27] Francis Mason, 'The Talaing Language', *Journal of the American Oriental Society* 4 (1854): 283.

See also Charles James Forbes Smith Forbes, 'On the Connexion of the Móns of Pegu with the Koles of Central India', *JRASGBI* 10 (1878): 235–36.

[28] Samuel Richard Tickell, 'Language of the Kolarian Aborigines—Grammatical Construction of the Ho language', Special Number on Indian Ethnology 1866, *JASB* 35, part 2 (1867), 268–78.

[29] Friedrich Müller, *Allgemeine Ethnographie* [General Ethnography], (zweite, umgearbeitete und bedeutend vermehrte Auflage [2nd, revised and considerably augmented edition] 1st ed. 1873; repr., Wien: Alfred Hölder, 1879), 461–63.

[30] Th. Jellinghaus, 'Kurze Beschreibung der Sprache der Munda Kohls in Chota Nagpore besonders nach ihren den Volksstamm charakterisierenden Eigenthümlichkeiten' [Short Description of the Language of the Munda Coles in Chota Nagpore Especially of the Typical Characteristics of the Tribe], *Zeitschrift für Ethnologie: Organ der Berliner Gesellschaft für Anthropologie, Ethnologie und Urgeschichte* 5 (1873): 170.

It is, perhaps, an indication of the mutual isolation of the small circles of Europeans in Ranchi that apparently he was not aware of the article by Rakhal Das Haldar, 'An Introduction to the Mundárí Language', *JASB* 40, part 1, no 1 (1871): 46–67.

[31] Sten Konow, 'Mundás and Dravidas', *The Indian Antiquary* 33 (1904): 121.

See also Ferdinand Hahn, *Kurukh Grammar* (Calcutta: Bengal Secretariat Press, 1900), vi.

[32] Sudhubushan Bhattarcharya, *Studies in Comparative Munda Linguistics* (Simla: Indian Institute of Advanced Study, 1975), 27.

As I found out in Leiden, Tickell's efforts are still known to historical linguists of South Asia. In 1997 I had the privilege to attend a honorary banquet for F. B. J. Kuiper the then ninety-year old doyen of Leiden Sanskrit studies. When I recalled his work on proto-Munda words in Sanskrit and mentioned that I was working on the author of the first Munda grammar, he said immediately, 'That was Tickell, no?'

Index

(r = ruled, n = note)

Abhai Singh, 32, 136, 167

Abhiram Singh (r1743-1818), 30, 33, 72, 109, 280n42, 281n69, 307n42

Achuta Singh (raja abt 1215), 11

Achuta Singh II (r1827-39), 82-3, 104-108, 115; accession, 81, 82, 298n19; death, 118; 133, 163, 224; Kol Insurrection, 90-91; April 1833 meeting, 106-8, 301n36; Mayurbhanj, 223

agreement: East India Company with Ghanshyam Singh, 41, 42, 119; East India Company with the Hos in 1821, 62-3, 73, 119

agriculture: proto-Munda, 6, 267nn22-25; Ho,71 154, 204-5, 228; English, 217

Ajambar Singh (Saraikela, r1823-1837): assists Roughsedge 46; praised by Roughsedge, 287n19; accession, 79; feared by the Hos, 79, 225; Gilbert, 79-80; Kuchang, 114, 116; Mayurbhanj, 117; accused of poisoning Achuta of Porahat, 117; death, 133. *See also* Pauri Devi

Ajodhya *pir*, 28, 42, 42-43, 44, 47, 54, 59, 60, 66, 67, 69, 73, 74, 75, 78, 124, 279n18, 296n82

amnesty: Roughsedge's offer 1820, 42; Wilkinson's – in Chotanagpur 1833, 96; Wilkinson's – in Singhbhum 1833, 107; Tickell's – 1839, 161

Anandpur, 15, 32, 55, 73, 136, 167, 169, 201, 274n139, 279n15, 322n71. *See also* Abhai Singh

annual tour, 37-38, 99, 100, 172, 284n120, 305nn124-127

Anwla *pir*, 28, 82, 83, 130, 145, 200, 269n47, 279n18, 312n42; in Kolhan Campaign II 60, 61; in Bamanghati dispute, 109, 130, 111, 114, 118, 120; in Kolhan Campaign III, 121, 124-125

Arakan rules, 97, 304n97

Arjun Singh II. *See* Kala Arjun

Arjun Singh III, 16, 17, 153, 274n150, 281n73

Arjun Singh IV, 118, 133, 163, 166, 168, 170,

Armstrong, Lieutenant (later Captain), 129, 142, 144, 145, 167, 315n52

Asantalia *pir*, 15, 16, 28, 41, 54, 74, 124, 312n42

assistant's quarters (Chaibasa), 132

Asura (village), 74, 312n9

Austen, Jane, 327n21

Austroasiatic, 5-6, 266n19, 267n22

Auxiliaries. *See* Hos.

Bahuran (commander mercenaries), 74; arrival in Jaintgarh, 50; collection of rent in Chakradharpur, 52-3, 63-4, 72; killed in battle of Cheri, 53, 55, 58, 66; Maratha employment, 288n63; surrounded at Pokharia, 53, 74-5, 76, 297n73

Baji Munda, 71-72, 76, 77

Balandia, 13, 15, 16, 20, 28, 48, 50, 55, 59, 60, 61, 73, 74, 77, 108, 110, 120, 121, 124, 125-6, 223, 273n119, 275n155; attacks Jaintgarh, 49, 82, 108; burning of –, 48-9; in Poto resistance, 141-2, 150, 226

Bamanghati, 9, 16, 22, 26, 28-9, 42, 50, 55, 59, 60, 61, 62, 63, 65, 69, 74, 82, 84, 107-8, 123, 133, 134-6, 145, 156, 269n50, 270n62, 277n196, 309n75, 313n65;

Bamanghati dispute, 108-119, 201, 224. 307n36; debate on –, 112, 115-6, 308n61; Kolhan Campaign III, 124-6; Narsinhgarh arrangement, 112-3; Wilkinson's letter of 22 August 1836, 119-22

Bandgaon, 32, 68, 74, 90, 105, 106, 156, 163, 169, 201, 306n10, 322n71; in Kol Insurrection, 90, 92, 93, 95, 104

Bantaria *pir*, 28, 32, 48, 54, 58, 60, 61, 69, 73, 74, 114, 126, 269n47 271n81, 279n18, 312n42

Bar *pir*, 32, 58, 60, 61, 107, 126, 141, 142, 174, 224, 269n47, 271n81, 312n42, 315n28

Barnes, Miss, 186-187, 188, 219, 327n22, 328n39, 329n59; children with Richard Tickell, 185, 187

Barnes Tickell, Zipporah (1779-1842), 186, 187-188, 328n39, 329n50

barter, 155, 172, 207

Bendkars, 172, 196, 221, 228

Bengal regulations, 38, 89, 96, 97, 284n111, 285n147, 304n95, 347n48

Benisagar, 4, 8-9, 10, 200, 216, 222, 230, 269n36, 270n68, 271nn78-80

Bewick, Thomas, 178, 179, 189, 325n45, 329n63

Bhalbhadar Dandpal, 150. *See also Chari and Charum*

Bharbharia *pir*, 28, 224, 269n47, 312n42; - in Bamanghati dispute, 109, 110-11, 113, 115, 120; Kolhan Campaign II, 60-62; Kolhan Campaign III, 113-14, 121, 124-5; Tusa's meeting, 113

Bhim Deo (*mahapater* of Jagannathpur), 142

Bhuiyas, 6, 7, 9, 10-13, 14, 15, 16, 20, 32, 136, 153, 163, 172, 200, 201, 202, 222, 224, 271-2n86, 272n98-99, 273n127, 274n129, 274n134, 295n54, 313n73, 317n38

Bikram Bhanj (r1813-22), 108, 109-10, 114

Bikram Singh (bro. of Ranjit Singh), 12

Bikram I (Saraikela), 16, 30, 33, 274n150, 275n152-3

Bikram Singh II (r1818-23), 30, 33-4, 42, 44-5, 46, 53-4, 66, 69, 79, 84, 85, 280n42, 290n105, 289n12. *See also Pauri Devi.*

Bindrai (of Bandgaon): popular leader, 93, 104-5, 106, 107, 300nn20-45; Kol Insurrection, 90-2, 300n36; meeting in Lankah, 91, 94

Blunt, W., 95, 96, 97, 302nn66-69, 303n83, 304n97

blowing from the gun, 57, 290n4

Board of Control, 38, 161, 171, 291n4, 303n81

Body Guard (of the governor general), 59, 291n21

Bonga Buru, battle of, 47

Borah (Poto resistance), 144, 315n36

Boscawen, Anne, 183, 186, 187, 188, 328nn12-56

Brahmins, 9, 11, 68, 69, 70, 162, 169, 200, 201, 202, 208, 224, 271n78, 272n99, 282n92, 298n10

bride price, 71, 155, 207, 210-11, 295n58

Brown Bess, 46

British territory, 37, 58, 119, 279n19, 284n111, 313n55

Bungoo Thon (village), 76

burial (Ho), 198, 211-12, 217, 227, 229

Burrai (Poto resistance), 141, 142, 144, 315n36

Cattle, 7, 15, 29, 48, 59, 60, 71, 91, 92, 104, 105, 107, 113, 121, 124-6, 139, 141, 142, 144, 149-50, 155, 156, 204, 207, 208, 210-11, 223, 228

Chaibasa, 14, 46, 47, 50, 74, 126, 140, 151, 155, 156, 168, 169, 174, 179, 207, 228, 267n27, 271n82, 316n1; army base, 131, 134, 142, 163, 170, 179; choice as capital, 130-31, 226; construction programme, 131; Roughsedge in –, 45, 46; Tickell in –, 137, 150, 164, 167, 171, 172, 173, 174, 194, 199, 208, 217

Chainpur, 32, 54, 55, 57, 74, 106, 124, 144, 156, 169, 200, 281n61, 293n53, 297n93, 312n43, 322n71; battle of -, 53-4, 56, 58, 60, 61, 63, 66, 72, 74, 77, 86, 225, 289n85, 290n105

Chait Chandra (*mahapate*r), 156

Chaitan Singh (Kharsawan, (died 1839), 31, 40, 54, 79, 81, 92, 106-7 117, 149, 164, 165, 289n96. *See also* Chainpur; Opender; *sati*

Chakradharpur, 15, 17, 22, 31, 32, 52, 54-5, 58, 60, 61, 71-2, 74, 79, 105, 106, 107, 118, 133, 156, 163, 268n27, 272n88, 293n2, 306n14

Chakradhar Singh (r1837-85), 81, 106-7, 118, 133-4, 156, 164, 202, 215, 225, 298n21

Chalmers, Dr, 168

Chandra Deo, 168; in Calcutta, 169

Chari (village), 150. *See also* Bhalbhadar Dandpal

Charum (village), 150. *See also* Bhalbhadar Dandpal

Cheri, 28; battle of, 53-54, 55, 58, 74; *See also* Bahuran

Chhatrapati Singh, 13, 14-15, 223, 274n150

Chiru *pir*, 14, 28, 53, 312n42

cholera, 81, 140, 159, 168

Chotanagpur plateau, 5-6, 11, 20, 36, 58, 69, 92, 95, 156, 159, 167, 175, 178, 192, 199-200, 202, 219, 223, 268nn26-27-32-33, 269n50, 277n201, 279n15, 300nn27-30-31

Chotanagpur (state), 14, 16, 17, 26, 28, 32, 36-8, 39, 40, 58, 89-90, 91, 94, 95-9, 102, 103, 104, 121, 122, 132, 137, 138, 139, 201, 273n128, 275nn161-167, 283nn96-97-102-103-106, 283nn111-118, 285n145, 292n38, 300nn13-14-15, 301n42, 302nn56-57-62, 304n95-104, 305n127, 316n26, 320n24. *See also* Kol Insurrection

Chowdry, Madhab Chandra (English writer at Chaibasa), 164-5, 168, 321n40

Christianity, 122, 162, 310n199, 332n21

Chronicle (*Vamsa*) of Singhbhum, 9, 10-16, 20, 22, 200, 222, 272n90, 273n127, 275nn152-160

Civilization, savage, (Hos), 25, 28, 41, 42, 45, 47, 51, 56, 57, 67, 68, 69, 70, 71, 116, 117, 123, 138, 141, 146, 150, 153, 170, 171, 225, 226, 300n15, 337n20

civilization (Hindus), 30, 57, 60, 67, 68, 69, 71, 78, 157, 172, 317n38

clearings (of land), 7, 12, 20, 135, 136, 172, 173, 179, 205, 206

Cleveland, August (1754-84), 97, 98, 303n90

Climate, weather (of Hodisum), 36, 50, 61, 104, 112, 197, 204, 285n135

cloth, 22, 44, 53, 67, 71, 72, 82, 129, 145, 156, 160, 172, 206, 301n37

colonialism, 302n62, 335n3. *See also* imperialism

Colvin, A. J. Colvin, 56, 67, 285n147, 290n116, 310n122 *See also* Tamar

coora (supply base), 60, 291n17

Cuvier, Georges, 189, 294n39, 317n38, 329n63

dances (Ho), 110, 193, 209, 210, 220, 226, 227

dances (English), 190, 210, 220

Darbila (village), 141

Darwin, Charles, 179

Davidson, John, 102, 129, 159, 161, 305n144

Debi (leader of Balandia), 141

Debt, 38, 90, 96, 195, 300n14, 195, 218

Deeney, John (1922-2010), 21, 265n4, 268n34, 274n137, 276nn191-194, 332n41, 334n91-3

Delhi, 12, 14, 36, 96-7, 203, 302n67

diku (*dickoo*), 90, 136, 295n54, 300n19, 313n73

divani of Bengal, 18, 36, 283n110

DNA, 4-6, 266n17-19

Doom Sirdar, 76

Doormoo (Guira), 77

Dopai (village), 42, 46, 47, 53. *See also* Singrai.

Dorawas, 111, 113, 114, 125, 136, 307n38, 309n75, 333n80

D'Oyly, Charles (1781-1849), 178, 190, 330n75-81

dress, clothing (Ho), 2, 22, 44, 53, 67, 68, 71, 72, 82, 129, 131, 145, 156, 160, 161, 203, 206, 210, 215, 294n27

Dripnath Sahi, 17, 36, 274n161-163, 283n106

dual parentage, 85, 229, 299n10. *See also* Silva, Roland

Dulposee (village), 141

Dumriya (village), 143, 150, 226

Dunbar, William, 130, 131, 155, 158, 199, 206, 207, 208, 210, 286n2

education (in Kolhan Government Estate), 156, 157, 161-2

epidemics, 159, 227. *See also* cholera; smallpox

ethnic frontier, 22, 223, 271n77, 283nn99-100; in Bamanghati, 108, 135; in Chotanagpur, 35, 36, 90, 92, 94, 224; in Singhbhum, 22, 28, 63, 80, 123, 135, 138, 201, 216, 222, 223

'*Eyá, goikiddáing*' (death of Kapur), 214

Ferguson, John, 17-19, 276n175

Festivals, 201, 209, 220, 224

finances (Porahat), 168

finances (Kolhan Government Estate), 122, 129, 137-8, 150

food (Ho), 59-60, 157, 160, 170, 199, 204, 208, 210, 219, 227

Frobisher, Thomas, 59, 60, 75

Gainsborough, Thomas: *The Linley Sisters*, 184, 326n8; *Richard Tickell*, 176, 186, 324n22

Gamharia, 126

Ganga Narain, 105, 106, 107, 191

Ganja and bhang, 131

Gangpur, 18, 29, 120, 201, 275n160, 275n163

Garra bing, 204

gaur, 69, 171, 173, 191, 202, 203, 294nn38-39, 322n88. *See also* wild buffalo

Ghanshyam Singh (r?-1827), 49, 54-5, 78; accession, 31, 280n46; area under control of –, 28, 31, 45, 48, 58, 74; death, 80, 298n19; description of Singhbhum, 22, 26, 28, 66, 74-6, 278n12, 291n8, 296n77; negotiations with East India Company, 25, 39-42, 84, 85, 223, 286n157, 299n7; Pauri Devi, 25, 33-4, 39, 42, 45, 79,-80, 84, 85, 119, 190; plunder of Gumra, 51-3, plunder of Hodisum, 60, 61;

relation with the Hos, 29, 31-2, 34, 48, 50, 73-5, 86, 297n93, 298n12; relation with Saraikela, 30, 33-34, 46

Ghasi Singh (Anandpur), 167

Ghasi Singh (Chakradharpur), 31, 52, 64, 66, 67, 69, 74, 106, 133, 280n48, 289nn80-84, 293n53

Ghatsila, 18, 19, 109, 112

Ghunnoo (manki of Gumuriya), 82, 153-4. *See also* Raghunath Bisi

Gilbert, Walter Raleigh, 66, 79-80, 83, 85, 86, 110, 114, 116, 190, 281n74, 292n43, 297n6, 298n19

Goalas (cowherds), 113, 114, 153, 155, 202, 208, 293n14, 317n38

Gonds, 7, 10, 97, 113, 196, 308n68, 309n75, 313n73, 336n16. *See also* Dorowas

Gosain, Dharam Das, 55, 74

governor general, 17, 30, 38, 40, 41, 50-51, 56, 57, 59, 84, 94, 96, 100, 104, 105, 119, 127, 130, 145, 162, 175, 190, 291n4, 318n71, 319n96

governor of Bengal, 123, 125, 127, 129, 304n104

Govind Nath Shah, 37, 89, 90, 275n16, 317n48

grand strategy of the East India Company, 38, 118, 150, 216, 223, 284n130; buffer states, 19, 20, 36, 37, 39, 120; chain of command, 2, 85-6; client states, 39, 104; containment, 56, 63, 86, 109; *cordon sanitaire*, 51, 55, 114, 117, 119; discussion on how to dispose of the Hos, 109, 116-117; forward defence, 15, 36-7, 51; interference, 29, 40, 85, 86, 103, 115, 117, 120, 134; non-interference, 58, 118, 162; other people's war, 85; pacification, 109; sole superpower, 38, 111, 121, 223, 224; under East India Company management, 62, 97, 111-2, 121, 124, 128, 129-30, 135, 138, 149, 153, 163, 300n15

Gray, Thomas, 189, 217, 336n10

Guira (village), 76, 77

Gumra *pir*, 22, 28, 31-2, 43, 44, 45, 47, 52, 55, 60, 61, 69, 74, 77, 106, 107, 114, 121, 124, 125, 126, 140, 224, 271n81, 279n18, 296n69, 297n93, 298n28, 312n42

Gumuriya (village), 48, 73, 141, 153

Guntiya massacre, 46-47, 73

Hart, Emma (second Lady Hamilton), 328n45

Heesterman, J. C., 22, 299n11

health (Ho), 83, 105, 112, 115, 130, 157, 159, 160, 168, 205

Hos: appearance, 5, 69-70, 206-07, 210, 217, 188, 218; armaments, 46-7, 287n27; battle tactics, 45-6, 47, 48-9, 53-4, 125, 126, 143-4; auxiliaries to the EIC, 47, 53-4, 74, 124, 144, 223, 314n29; bravery, 46, 47, 61; character, 132, 142, 161, 199, 215; cooperation of villages, 21, 76, 82, 225-6; divisions, 2, 73, 73, 74, 77-8, 82, 86, 110, 114, 124, 151, 225; exclusiveness, 2, 17, 18, 22, 28, 42, 48, 65, 68, 69, 153, 208, 224, 225, 226, 283n99; expansion of the Ho area, 10, 13, 15, 16, 20, 28-9, 135-6, 227; *kilis* (clans), 7, 20, 21, 65, 66, 77-8, 81, 82, 139, 150, 199, 207, 225-6, 227-8, 269n34, 275n155, 216n14; number of -, 32, 297n91, 41, 58, 136, 227; 281n76; religion and spirits, 7, 11, 21, 70, 76, 78, 120, 157-8, 162-3, 193, 199, 210, 211-3, 214, 224, 227, 230, 277n201; village life, 205, 209, 217, 219

Hodisum: Dunbar on, 206, 286n2; Roughsedge on, 44, 67-8, 78, 227, 286n2, Tickell on, 130-1, 203

Hodgson, Brian Houghton (1801-94), 166-7, 175, 190, 194, 196, 219, 318n72, 321n56, 323n3, 330nn75-85, 331nn9-12-19, 332n22, 336n17; Tickell staying with –, 165-7, 194, 215, 332nn25-26; disagreement with Tickell, 194-6, 218, 229, 336n16. *See also* Mehr-un-Nissa Begum

Hodgson, William (1805-1838), 194-5

hospital, 158, 168

house (Ho), 42, 53, 71, 74, 76, 125, 131, 132, 158-9, 174, 196, 197, 205, 210, 213, 227, 228

hunt, 69-70, 163, 172, 175, 195, 203-4, 206, 208, 209, 214, 218, 219, 226, 294n38; great hunt, 180, 198, 202-3, 217, 224, 231

Hunter, W. W., 195, 283n111, 276n179, 321n56, 331nn9-12, 332n25, 336n17

Hygiene (filth), 168, 208, 215, 220

ili. *See* rice beer

illness (Ho), 157-8, 213, 224

imperialism, 216, 224, 302n62, 335n3. *See also* colonialism

interpreters, 52, 64, 67, 82, 105, 108, 124, 137-8, 152-3, 196, 197, 210, 288n84, 293n14, 295n60

irrigation (water works), 44, 54, 70, 154, 175, 206

Jackson, James Nesbitt, 26, 39, 84, 123, 279n18

Jackson's Road, 26, 29, 50, 51, 55, 58, 63, 81, 111, 120, 123, 279n17, 293n51

Jadunath Bhanj (r1822-1863), 110, 111-15, 118, 119, 224

Jadunath Singh (*divan* of Porahat), 118, 133-4, 163, 168-9, 202, 310n109, 322n71

Jagannathpur, 12, 15, 20, 22, 48, 74, 108, 126, 140, 142, 143, 145, 150, 272n86, 312n42

Jagannath Dhal, 18, 19

342 | A Land of Their Own

Jagannath Shah (Chotanagpur, (r1822-1869), 89, 90, 275n167, 300n13, 302n56,

Jagannath Singh III, 16, 275nn152-153

Jagannath Singh IV, 17-19, 31, 32, 275n160, 298n19

Jail, 131-2, 151, 156, 160, 161, 168, 316n1

Jaintgarh, 15-16, 22, 26, 28, 29, 32, 33, 41, 48, 49, 51, 60, 61, 66, 68, 70, 73, 74, 81, 82, 105, 106, 111, 225, 271n82, 272n86, 274n148, 279nn15-18, 288n52, 293n53, 312n42; first burning, 49-50, 73; second attack, 80-2, 86, 110, 128, 223, 224, 307n35; third attempt at, 140-2; pacification of the area, 63, 107, 124, 125, 126, 150, 153; Raghunath versus Ghunnoo, 153, 202. *See also* Raghunath Bisi

Jagu (divan), 107-8

Jamda *pir*, 14, 114, 126, 140, 269n47, 271n85, 274n137, 312n42

Jha, J. C., 92, 93, 97, 265n2, 276n176, 279n19, 283n99, 284nn111-118, 289n80, 293n53, 300nn13-15-20-27-30-31, 301nn36-48-54, 302n57, 303nn71-95, 305n127, 306n18, 307n36, 308nn45-61, 310n122, 311n8,

Jotong (Poto resistance), 141

Jonko (Poto resistance), 141

Jumal Munda (Pingua), 82, 108, 298n31

Jamuna Dei (Mayurbhanj, dau. of Abhiram of Saraikela (r1810-13), 109, 308n44

Jung Bahadur Rana, 175, 323n11

jungle (Singhbhum), 2, 4, 7, 18, 19, 20, 29, 40, 48, 54, 56, 91, 99, 105, 106, 123, 125, 130, 135-6, 141, 143, 144, 145, 154, 155, 159, 170, 171, 172-3, 176, 179, 190-2, 200, 201, 202-04, 206-07, 214, 216, 218, 219, 221, 227, 283n96, 284n111, 285n135, 286n2

Kala Arjun (Singh raja), 15-16, 20, 22, 33, 222, 274nn139-150, 275n153-55, 281n73

Kapur. *See* 'Eyá, goikiddáing'

Karaikela, 32, 74, 91, 92, 106, 124, 143, 156, 163, 169, 201, 271n84, 301n45, 322n71

Kashiram Singh II (r abt 1641), 13, 14, 15, 16, 20

Kathkaranjia, 63, 81, 82, 120, 293n51

Keonjhar, 8, 9, 11, 12, 14, 15, 17, 18, 29, 32, 49, 53, 58, 63, 82, 108, 109, 111, 120, 134, 141, 142, 156, 164, 173, 197, 271n77, 272nn98-99, 274n143, 275nn160-163-165, 307n37

Kera, 32, 73, 91, 105, 106-8, 114, 124, 143, 156, 163, 169, 201, 275n153, 312n43, 322n71

Keetee (leader from Thai pir), 77

Khairpal (village), 48, 73

Khandband (village), 143-4

Kharsawan, 16, 22, 25, 29, 30, 31, 34, 40, 41, 42, 43, 54, 63, 68, 74, 79, 81, 92, 105-6, 107, 114, 115, 117-8, 119, 120-21, 133, 134, 143, 164-5, 201, 278n5, 279n19, 281n76, 286n157. *See also* Chaitan Singh

Khiching, 8-11, 200, 222, 265n1, 270nn51-61-66-68, 271nn73-74, 272n99

Khunti, 6, 7, 8, 21, 91, 265n4, 268n32

kilis (clans). *See under* Hos

Khuntpani (village), 74

Khuntpani Gorge, battle of the, 60

Kochey (Poto resistance), 141

Kol Insurrection, 89, 90, 90-92, 94, 96-100, 102, 103, 104, 107, 111, 223, 291n38, 300n20, 301n55, 311n138; the force from Singhbhum, 92-3; meeting at Lankah, 90, 92, 105. *See also* Bindrai

Kols, 11-15, 18, 20, 21, 32, 33, 56, 58, 61, 66, 68, 70, 71, 73, 74, 79, 81, 82, 83, 91, 92-95, 97, 104-6, 116, 120-121, 123, 126, 128, 132, 133, 135, 141, 145, 149, 161, 168, 191, 203, 218, 222, 225, 229, 230, 271nn78-90, 274n134, 277n194, 281n74, 281n76, 290n116, 292n38, 300n27, 301nn37-55, 302nn56-69, 303n70, 335n152

Kolhan, 7, 12, 16, 17, 21, 26, 28, 29, 44, 48, 50, 51, 52, 57, 58, 60, 63, 64, 65, 66, 68, 69, 72, 73, 76, 81, 83, 99, 108, 111, 113, 128, 129, 130, 133, 134, 135, 136, 142, 145, 149, 153, 155, 158, 200, 201, 203-4, 206, 208, 225, 271n80, 272n86, 279n18, 297n91, 333n60

Kolhan Campaign I, 25, 35, 44-9, 50, 65, 66, 67, 68, 73, 74, 79, 85, 125, 128, , 279n15, 287n11, 290n1, 294n35

Kolhan Campaign II, 25, 56, 57, 58-59, 59-61, 63, 65, 66, 74, 75, 77, 79, 85, 295n50. *See also* Richards, William

Kolhan Campaign III, 120, 123, 124, 125-6, 131, 133, 140, 149, 150, 192, 199, 224, 286n2, 301n55, 310n138, 311n141. *See also* Bamanghati: Bamanghati dispute.

Kolhan Government Estate, 1-3, 127, 128, 130, 134, 138, 140, 149, 154-9, 161-3, 201, 224, 273n109; assistant, 129-30, 134, 149, 174, 175, 321n61; borders, 152, 226; compensation to chiefs for -, 133, 163, 167; ethnicities of its inhabitants, 7, 10, 132, 133, 134, 135, 136-7, 153, 154, 201, 222, 224, 226, 228; *pirs* of, 121, 122, 133, 136; staff; 108, 131, 137, 165-6, 167, 320n40; unprofitability of the KGE, 149-150. *See also* Chaibasa; Manki-Mundas; Wilkinson system

Kotgarh, 106, 114, 126, 140, 173, 269n47, 271nn81-85, 312n42

Krishna (*diwan* of Porahat), 81, 82, 83, 91, 108, 298n37

Kuchang, 30, 105, 109, 114-6, 118, 200

343 | A Land of Their Own

Kuiper, F. B. J. (1907-2003), 231, 267n25, 338n32

Kulke, Hermann, 14, 271n77, 272n92, 273nn126-127

Kundubera (village), 130

Kunta (leader of Tamar), 56, 290n116

Kuntu Pater ('Coondoo Pater, a Sirdar of Coorea'), 53, 63-4, 66, 67, 74, 76, 107

labour (Ho), 58, 101, 131, 154, 155, 170, 171, 177, 206, 271n78

Lalgarh pir, 28, 51, 60, 61, 77, 82, 83, 109, 110, 111, 112, 114, 118, 120, 124, 125, 126, 200, 201, 269n47, 271n81, 279n18, 312n42

Lalkant Singh (bro. of Ghasi Singh), 52, 53, 74

land (agricultural - in Hodesum), 99, 123, 157; Hos do not rent out – to foreigners, 170, land question, 99, 316n8, 317n48; land market, 154-5, 101, 223; rent, 12, 15, 31, 44, 52-53, 101, 104, 105, 109, 110, 111, 122, 139, 140, 150, 152, 153, 170, 201

language (Ho), 1-2, 5, 28, 62, 67, 70, 71, 78, 117, 154, 157, 160, 162, 196-7, 198, 209, 216-7, 219, 221, 226, 229, 231, 265nn4-6, 269n46, 318n58, 332n41, 336n16; Roughsedge on-, 67. *See also under* Tickell, Samuel Richard

language policy, 40, 57, 98, 101, 117, 157, 196, 231, 318n71

Larka Kol (people and country), 21, 42, 67, 231, 277n194

Latham, Robert Gordon, 229-30

Lee, Sophia, 187-8, 328n41

legal memory, 155, 317n48

Li Shang-Yin, 217, 335n4

Linley, Elizabeth Anne, 184-5, 186, 219, 327n35

Linley, Mary, 183, 184, 186, 187

Linley, Thomas the elder and family, 183-186, 328n45

Linley, Thomas the younger, 184, 185, 327n35

Linley, William, 184, 188, 189, 326nn7-8, 328n43

lone frontier man, 216

Loknath Singh (Kera), 156, 312n43

Luttwak, Edward, 85, 284n130

Macaulay, Thomas Babington, 157, 317n71

Macleod, Captain, 61

Madhu Das, 110, 111, 112, 113-4, 116, 118, 133, 224. *See also* Bamanghati

Maguni Rout, 13

Mahadei, 67, 107, 225

Maillard, John Peter, 45-7, 48-9, 286nn12-13, 287nn46-49

Manguee Naik (seller of charms), 141

Manguee Patnaick (informant of Tickell), 168

Manki (Ho), Chhatrapati, 15; Ho mankis, 17, 21, 124, 268n43, 277n196, 316n26; Kala Arjun, 15; Roughsedge, 62, 76; Tickell, 138-9, 140, 141, 142, 143, 151-2, 153-4, 196, 205, 209, 210, 211, 212, 215, 228, 230, 314n99, 315n28, 317n26; Wilkinson, 104, 105, 106, 107, 108, 113, 118, 121, 122, 124, 126; See also: Wilkinson System.

Manki (Munda), 90, 91, 92, 93, 95, 96, 98, 301n36, 302n56

Man Singh (Mughal general), 12, 14, 36, 222

Raj Man Singh (B. H. Hodgson's painter), 194

maps: Arrowsmith, Aaron, 278n15, , 257; Jackson, James Nesbitt, 26, 28, 39, 84, 123, 278nn17-18; Rennell, James, 26, 278n15; Tickell, Samuel Richard, 192

Marathas 17-8, 19, 20, 26, 30, 36, 37, 38, 39, 84, 104, 114, 275nn158-165, 282n97, 283n109, 303n90, 306n37

market (Hodisum), 15, 22, 155, 156, 171, 207, 224

market (Chotanagpur), 36, 37, 38, 301n54

Markland Barnard, Robert, 188-9, 329n56

marriage (Ho), 65, 77, 139, 151, 155, 171, 208, 210, 211, 228, 230

Mary Morris (mo. of Samuel Richard Tickell), 183, 189

Marwar (*also* Marwaris), 7, 200, 201, 273n125

Masum Thakoor (doctor in Saraikela), 164

Mata Pingua (Balandia), 48, 50, 58, 60, 61, 74, 82, 108, 223, 288n45, 289n84, 298n31. *See also* Balandia

Mayurbhanj, 8, 9, 11-12, 14, 15, 17, 18, 30, 39, 58, 61, 107, 108-25, 133, 134-6, 145, 164, 168, 201, 224, 265n1, 270n54, 271n78, 272nn98-99-100, 273nn108-126, 274nn158-160, 277n196, 307nn37-42-43, 308n61, 312n42, 313nn55-57-65. *See also* Bamanghati; Jadunath Bhanj; Khiching; Kuchang

Medicine, 112, 141, 158-9, 291n21

megaliths, 6, 276n29, 368n29

Mehr-un-Nissa Begum, 219, 336n17

'Memoir on the Hodésum (Improperly Called Kolehan)', 1, 180, 188, 189, 193-4, 196, 198-9, 200, 201, 203, 215, 217, 229-31, 269n37, 271n78, 295n54, 333n81, 334nn100-106, 336nn7-10; omissions in -, 199, 203, 204, 211, 218, 220. *See also* Tickell, Samuel Richard

Measurements (*coss, kundee, seers, pie*), 276n80, 280n150, 298n24

Metcalfe, Charles, 40, 50, 66, 70, 93, 94, 96, 97, 98, 111, 117, 119, 122, 162, 281n91, 302nn67-69; Metcalfe's Minute, 93, 95, 300n48, 303nn70-71-76

Midnapur, 18, 19, 26, 30, 39, 56, 57, 59, 84, 99, 105, 111, 112, 191, 273n108, 276n173, 279nj19, 283n96

migration (also immigration, invasion), 6, 7, 12, 20, 36, 90, 200, 265n15, 266n19, 267n22, 277n189, 302n62

military tenures, 12, 13, 15, 153, 168

milk, 53, 155, 317n51

Mir Kumir Ud-din Hussain, 163, 166

Mohan Kumari (rani of Sambalpur), 103, 285n134, 288n4, 306n1

money (with the Hos), 52, 53, 63, 72, 82, 128, 129, 131, 139, 154, 155, 156, 160, 163, 168-9, 170, 171, 201, 207, 208, 224, 318n58

Mon-Khmer (language group), 5, 265n6

Mozart, Wolfgang Amadeus, 184

Munda (language), 5-6, 12, 13, 16, 67, 196, 231, 264nn4-5, 266nn23-26, 277n191, 336n16, 338n32

Munda (people), 6, 7, 8, 10, 20, 21, 29, 32, 38, 66, 68, 69, 90, 92, 93, 105, 199-200, 203, 218, 266nn19-22, 268n32, 269n35, 291n38, 3301nn37-55

Munda (village leader), 44, 62, 71, 75, 76-7, 82, 95-6, 98, 106, 108, 113, 118, 122, 126, 137, 138-9, 140, 141, 152, 153, 154, 196, 205, 228, 268n43, 296n89, 302n56, 314n28

Musammat Birang, 151

Nakia Munda, 82

Nandu (head interpreter of Wilkinson), 105

Narra (Poto resistance), 144, 153, 315n36

Narayan Singh, 39-41, 48, 49

Narsanda massacre, 45-7, 73, 225

Nepal, 35, 165, 183; Hodgson in –, 167, 174, 190, 194-5; Tickell in –, 165, 167, 175, 177, 194, 220, 321n58, 323n11

Niessen, Frans, 317n48

Niranjan Das (Bamanghati), 62, 109-10

Nizam Ruia (village), 143

non-regulation system, 89, 97, 98, 99, 127, 132, 162, 216, 220, 223, 303n82

oath, 11, 53, 107, 128, 137, 139

omens, 210, 230, 335n49

Opender (son of Chaitan Singh), 164-5

Opender Bissoï (informant of Tickell), 168

Oraons, 7, 12, 38, 69, 91, 92, 199, 200, 269n36, 301n37, 314n86, 336n16

Ouseley, John Ralph, 129, 159, 162-3, 164-5, 175, 208, 319nn96-97, 320n24, 320n40

Padampur (village), 142, 314n8

Pallottino, Massimo, 21, 277n192

Pandua (Poto resistance), 145, 315n36

Pangolin, 132, 173

Pardhan (Poto resistance), 141

Pat Dumuria (village), 141

Panda, Deepak, 197n3

Patna, 178, 183, 184, 189, 190, 200, 283n111, 291n4, 323n11, 330n75

Pauri Devi, 10, 11, 12, 13, 16, 25, 33-34, 39, 42, 45, 50, 72, 79, 80, 84, 85, 119, 190, 223, 272n86, 273n124, 274n129, 281n69

Perdhar ('Sirdar of Gutilpee'), 76

phoot (supply base), 59, 291n17

Pingua *kili*, 48, 59, 77, 81, 82, 110, 128, 141, 225-6, 227, 275n155

Pir system, 14-15, 16-17, 21, 28, 50, 52, 60, 61, 65, 66, 74, 75 map), 75-6, 77, 78, 94, 106, 107, 109-13, 114, 117, 121, 122, 133, 135, 138, 151-2, 154, 199, 223, 227, 269n47, 277n196, 296nn76-82, 315n27, 316n26. *See also under* Kolhan Government Estate

Pitamber Sing, description by –, 18-19, 22, 279n19

population figures, 34, 50, 71, 136, 169, 281n76, 295n54, 322n78

Pokam (village), 141

Pokharia, battle of- , 14, 53, 57, 59, 225, 297n93

Politics, 20, 65, 73, 75, 78, 167, 185, 274n142, 321n58. *See also under* Ho

Porahat, 1, 7, 10-11, 13, 15, 16, 17, 20, 22, 25, 26, 28, 29-34, 39-42, 43, 49, 50, 51, 52-5, 60, 61, 63, 64, 66, 68, 69, 73, 74, 78, 79, 80, 81, 82-3, 84-6, 90, 103, 105, 106, 107, 108, 115, 118, 119, 124, 133-4, 135-6, 140, 163-4, 166, 167-9, 190, 199-201, 222, 224, 225, 272nn86-88-99, 274n148, 275n160, 279nn15-18-21, 281nn61-69-74, 281n76, 286n160, 297n73, 298n37, 301n54, 306n10, 312n42, 314n6, 316n26, 322n78

Potel Gopari (Poto resistance), 141

Poto Ho, 141-5, 150, 199, 224, 226, 228, 315n36

Potters, 71, 154

Private property, 38, 94, 101, 154, 155, 156, 207, 303n82, 318n54

Priyangu, 8

puja (ceremony), 77, 141, 150, 224, 289n94

Purushottam Singh II, 16, 275nn152-153

Queen of Porahat (widow of Achuta Singh), 118, 134, 163, 202

Raghunath Bisi, 22, 26, 27, 31, 48, 49-50, 58, 63, 66, 70, 75, 76, 77, 78, 80-3, 103, 128, 140, 142, 153-4, 193, 202, 223, 225, 228, 280n58, 293n53, 298n24, 307n35

raids, 19, 28-9, 50, 58, 71, 82, 91, 104, 105, 106, 109, 115, 119, 120, 124, 151, 155, 223, 228, 286n157, 290n116

Rajabasa (*pir*), 28, 44, 60, 118, 121, 279n18, 312n42

Rajabasa (village in Rajabasa *pir*), 53, 73

Rajabasa (village north of Jaintgarh), 141, 143, 226

Rajput, 13-14, 32, 36, 42, 70, 222, 271n71, 273nn125-126-127, 274n130, 275n160, 277n196, 282n92

Raju Mahapater (Padampur), 108, 141

Ramgarh Battalion, 35-6, 37, 38, 48, 56, 58, 59, 77, 79, 80, 98, 104, 120, 121, 124, 126, 128, 130, 132, 144, 149, 284n112, 287n12, 304n104; armament, 47; ethnic composition, 281n92

Ranjit Singh, 12-13, 14

Ratan's rout, 53, 54, 58, 60, 72

records (in the South West Frontier Agency), 119, 125, 132, 199, 200, 201, 222, 265n2, 269n41, 280n57, 285n155, 300n37, 301n55, 305nn127-139, 306n144, 310n113

religion (Ho). *See under* Ho

Renfrew, Colin, 268n30, 277n189

Rengra *pir*, 121, 124, 126, 312n42, 322n93

revenue (Bamanghati), 108, 110, 112, 224, 307n37. *See also* Bamanghati

revenue (Chotanagpur), 37, 38, 95, 96, 97, 99, 175, 283nn109-111, 285n145, 305n118, 306n143-144

revenue (Kolhan Government Estate), 112, 116, 119, 128, 136, 139, 149-50, 152-3, 154, 167, 170, 171, 193 222, 226, 228

revenue (Porahat), 15, 18, 19, 21, 31, 48, 52, 69, 72, 73, 76, 79, 82, 83, 93, 133, 163, 164, 167, 169, 225, 227, 280n55, 288n71

rice beer (ili, hanria), 71, 89, 110, 127, 160, 208-9, 215, 227, 311n2

Richards, William, 25, 56, 58, 59, 61, 63, 65, 71, 74, 125, 289n15, 290n1, 310n138, 311n141

Ricketts, Henry, 112-3, 115, 116-7, 121, 122, 123-4, 132, 133-4, 308n61, 316n18 320n5, 321n40; life, 308n68

Roads, 4, 10, 18, 42, 43, 46, 49, 51, 60, 62, 68-9, 73, 80, 108, 143, 156, 178, 192, 226, 228, 279n15; Tickell's road to Chotanagpur, 156. *See also* Jackson's road

Roebuck, John Arthur, 188, 328n39, 329n52

romanticism, 337n20, 200, 216, 217. *See also* Gray, Thomas; Scott, Walter

Roughsedge, Edward (1774-1822), life and death, 34-6, 45, 68, 79, 227, 281-2n77-79, 285n134, 297n3; agreement with Hos, 62-3; agreement with Singhbhum, 41-2, 223, 278n5; Chotanagpur Tributary States, 38,39, 285n147; commander Ramgarh Battalion, 35, 37; conflicts with civil line of the administration, 37, 38, 56, 89, 284nn112-113; description Singhbhum, 26, 28, 31-3, 279n21; description of the Hos, 26, 28, 42-3, 44, 65-71, 225, 294n35; Hos on Roughsedge, 79, 224, 288n36; interrogating the Hos, 66, 72, 76, 293n2; language skills, 67, lectured by Hastings, 50-1, 56; negotiations with Singhbhum, 25, 39-42; 286n157; political agent on the South Western Frontier, 36, 58; periods spent in Hodisum, 65; proposal to blow Hos from the gun, 57, 291n4; relation with Saraikela, 25, 30, 34, 40, 41, 42, 43, 45, 46, 64, 103, 281n69, 287n19; Sambalpur, 26, 35-6, 38, 39, 43, 49, 50, 56, 63, 66, 79, 285n134; strategic objectives in Chotanagpur, 36, 37, 38, 278n6, 283-4n111, 287n15; strategic objectives with the Hos, 50-1, 58, 68, 78, 119-20; strategic objectives in Singhbhum, 30, 85, 51, 55, 55-6, 58, 84; *See also* Chotanagpur (state); Kolhan Campaign I; Kolhan Campaign II, maps; Pauri Devi. *See also under* Sambalpur

Ruddell, David (lieutenant, later captain), 28, 39, 40, 41-2, 299n7

Rudra Singh (emissary Porahat to Calcutta, 1841), 168, 169

Ruia (village), 143

Sahib, 94, 98, 113, 141, 203, 207, 225

Sambalpur, 10, 17, 18-19, 26, 36, 38-9, 81, 84, 103, 104, 108, 111, 120, 173, 275nn160-163, 283n98, 285n134, 286n163, 291n18, 197n3, 306n6; Roughsedge and Sambalpur, 35, 39, 43, 49, 50, 56, 57, 59, 61, 63, 66, 79

Santhals, 5, 7, 110, 114, 135, 172, 173, 202, 336n16

Saraikela, 1, 8, 16, 17, 22, 25, 30, 31, 33-4, 42,44-6, 53-4, 64, 66, 69, 72, 73, 74, 79-80, 81, 84-6, 92, 106-8, 119, 121, 124, 125, 128, 134, 136, 137, 140, 142, 144, 149, 156, 164, 165, 201, 202, 223, 224-5, 272n86, 275nn152-160, 279nn18-19, 281nn69-74 -76, 286n157-169, 290n105, 298n21, 301n36, 312nn42-43 ; strategic importance, 29, 30, 34, 40-1, 43, 57, 85-6, 91, 92, 106,

109, 114-7, 118-9, 120, 130, 133, 224, 307n42. *See also* Kuchang; Pauri Devi

Saraks (Sarawaks), 7, 10, 12, 13, 200, 201, 206, 222, 271nn80-82

Saranda pir, 13, 15, 21, 32, 34, 60, 106, 126, 136, 140, 172-3, 203, 269n44, 271n81-85, 279n18 312n42, 318n54

sati, 162, 164-5

Scott, Walter, 189, 217, 333n81, 335nn7-8

Seringsia, battle of, 141, 142-3

Sheridan, Richard Brinsley (1751-1816), 183-7, 326n10, 327nn26-31-35

Silli (dependency of Chotanagpur), 94, 95

Silva, Roland, 85, 299n10

Simpson, Thomas, 129, 144, 315n36

Singh Pokharia, 14

Singrai (of Bandgaon), 90, 93

Singrai (of Dopai), 42, 43, 53, 66, 73, 74, 223, 286n164

smallpox, 159

Smith, Nathaniel, 56, 89

snow leopard, 174

sokas, 141, 157

Sonapur (in Chotanagpur), 28, 91, 93, 94, 95, 96, 98, 104, 105, 201, 301n54

songs (Ho), 2, 22, 197, 209, 219, 220, 223, 226, 268n33, 277n201

Sonoo Kunda (of Karaikela), 156

South West Frontier Agency, 35, 39, 98-99, 100, 101, 103, 111, 119, 127, 134, 139, 156, 174, 192

spirits (Ho). *See under* Ho

Stirling, Andrew, 70, 272n109, 294n46

Stockwell, George, 111-12, 307n61

Suban Pingua, 77, 80, 82, 225, 297n100

Sumitra Dei (Mayurbhanj, (r1796-1810), 109, 307n37

Surgeon, 49, 129, 130, 155, 158, 166, 189, 199, 209, 294n38, 323n16

Tamar, 17, 30, 40-1, 43, 55, 58, 91, 92, 95, 105, 155, 156, 201, 202, 224, 273n108, 278nn5-15, 285nn145-146-147-153, 290n116; Tamarians, 68, 93-94. *See also* Colvin

tamarind tree, 205, 217

Tandar (munda of Asura), 75

Tantis (weavers), 11, 67, 71, 140, 202, 206, 224, 271n78, 293n14, 295n54, 313n74

tasar (silk), 155, 156, 207

taxes. *See* revenue

Tebo Ghat, 20, 21, 275n168

Templer, John William, 175, 323n7

Tent, 59, 80, 100; Roughsedge's -, 25, 36, 69; Tickell's -, 165, 179

Thai *pir*, 28, 42, 49, 51, 60, 61, 62, 63, 69, 74, 77, 107, 109, 110, 111, 113, 114-5, 118, 120, 121, 124-5, 269n47, 279n18, 312n42, 313n65

Tickell, Edward Arthur, 176, 324n26

Tickell, Elizabeth Anne, 183, 186, 187-188, 328nn42-43-44. *See also* Tickell, Samuel Richard: children

Tickell, Mary Rose, 183, 189, 194-5, 332nn20-21. *See also* Hodgson, William

Tickell, Richard, 184, 185-7, 188, 327n26; *See also* Barnes, Miss; Boscawen, Anne; Linley, Mary; Sheridan, Richard Brinsley

Tickell, Richard Samuel, 217

Tickell, Samuel, 183, 187, 326nn3-4-5

Tickell, Samuel Richard (1811-1875), 1, 2, 176, 183-4. 226-7, 231, 324n24; 338n32; annual tour to Saranda, 172-3; appointment as junior assistant, 129-30, 167, 192; archaeologist, 4, 7, 8, 200-01, 271n78, 333nn61-69; assistant, 128-9, 134, 166-7, 174, 175, 192, 303n12, 325n58; breakdown of relations with the Hos, 170-71; career (military): Cadet, Ensign, Lieutenant, 189, 191, 192; in Chaibasa, 130-31, 171-2, 313n65, 321n40; communication with the Hos, 121, 138, 160, 193-4, 214, 215 218; children, 175, 176, 180, 323n15, 325nn53-54; *darbars* (with Wilkinson), 128-9, demarcation of the borders of the Kolhan Government Estate, 124-5, Burma, 175-6; descriptions of landscape, jungle, 191-2, 172-3, 191, 203, 204, 219; feuds among the *kilis*, 150-51, 'Grammatical Construction of the Ho Language', 193, 194, 196; great hunt, 199, 202-03, 217, 231; Hindus (Brahmins), 199, 200-02, 220; history of Singhbhum, 7, 199-201, 271n78; 'Ho' (appellation), 196; Ho auxiliaries, 142, 144; Hodésum articles, 170, 193, 217-8, 221; hunting, (of birds, bear, tiger), 162, 175, 202-03, 214-5, 218, 226, 221; intellectual baggage on leaving for India, 188, jokes, 215, 218; Kathmandu, 166-7, 194, 195, 196, 215, 218-9, 220, 226; last night in Hodisum jungle, 172-3, 322n96; 'List of Birds Collected in the Jungles of Borabhum and Dholbhum', 191-2; learning the Ho language, 160 196-7, 332n41; leave at the Cape, 174, 221; leaves the Kolhan, 165, 173; living quarters in Chaibasa, 132, 171; market (– on the), 156; marriage with Maria Georgiana Templer, 175, 325n53; member

Asiatic Society of Bengal, 192; 'Memoir on the Hodésum (Improperly Called Kolehan)', 193, 198-9, 229; 'Memoranda Relative to Three Andamanese', 176; Nepal, 167, 175, 178, 194, 195, 220, 321n58, 323n11; ornithologist, 178, 179-80, 220; painter, 2, 176, 177, 178-9, 193, 204, 226; Porahat, 133, 163-4, 166, 168-70 322n71; retirement, 174, 176, 177, 179; salary, 129, 149, 166; sermon (Tickell's), 162-3, 197, 214; taxidermist of -, 171, 172; survey in Kol country, 102, 123; survey of Kolhan, 133, 136, 152; visit to Calcutta, 174; views on civilization, 153, 213-4, 220-01; visit to Darjeeling, 174; 'Vocabulary of the Ho Language', 180, 193-4, 196-8, 204, 206, 208, 214, 215, 230, 300n19, 338n20; 'The Zoological Works of Samuel Richard Tickell', 176-8, 180, 193, 324n28-36, 325n54. *See also* Bendkars, Hodgson, Brian Houghton, Hos; Kolhan Government Estate; language; Manki (Ho): Tickell; Poto Ho; revenue (Kolhan Government Estate); *sati*, Seringsia, battle of –; Wilkinson: manki-Munda system

tiger, 31, 173, 196, 202, 204, 214-5, 221, 227

tiger's den, 22, 42, 44, 69, 294n35

Tikoo (village in Chotanagpur),94

Thakurani (title of a deity or a lady), 9, 164, 271nn71-73, 272n86

Tondanghatu (village), 143

Toonia (*pir* in Porahat), 140, 314n6

Tope (Poto resistance), 141

Toreeparre (village), 141

Trade (domestic, foreign), 15, 18, 22, 66, 71-2, 131, 155, 156, 199, 206, 207, 224, 269n50, 275n160. *See also* market

Trail of Tears (Cherokee, USA 1838), 335n3

Traill, George William, 331n9

Tributary States, 38, 104, 285n147

Tuckey, A. D., 7, 10, 136, 152, 200, 230, 269nn41-42-44-47, 271nn81-82, 272n91, 274n137, 295n54, 296n82, 313n73, 316n23-26

Utilitarianism, 220, 221, 329n52

Van Troy, Joseph, 6, 268m32, 269nn35-49

Vansittart, George, 17, 19, 279n19

Verelst, Harry, 18-19

village republics (history of –), 96, 303nn86-87

village (Ho), 7, 9, 10, 13, 15, 16-7, 20, 21, 28, 31, 32, 34, 35, 42, 44, 48, 49, 52-3, 59, 60-1, 62-3, 65-6, 67, 70, 71-3, 74, 76, 77, 78, 86, 93, 105, 110, 114, 119, 121-2, 123, 125, 131, 133, 135-6, 138-9, 140, 141-2, 150, 151, 152, 153, 154-5, 157, 169, 174, 178, 179, 205-06, 209-10, 210, 214, 215, 217, 220, 224-5, 227-8, 269n44, 295nn54-56, 295n69, 297n91, 316n1, 316n41; not necessarily a political unit, 76, 121, 126, 129, 142, 296n89; informally a tax unit, 154-5

weavers. *See* Tantis

Wenskus, Reinhard, 269n46

wild buffalo, 69-70, 202, 203, 225

Wilkinson, Thomas (1795-1867), appointment as political agent on the South Western Frontier, 98, 129, 304n104; April 1833 meeting at Saraikela, 92, 106-08, 301n36, 306n34, 307n27; March 1837 *darbars* in the Kolhan Government Estate, 128-9; lectured by Calcutta,, 145-6; leaves Chotanagpur, 159; letter of 22 August 1836, 119-22, 124, 192; Kol Insurrection, 91-2, 96-7, life and death 98, 390n93; networker, 98, 122; November-December 1835 meeting in Saraikela, 118; Tickell and -, 98, 128-30, , 138, 159, 192, 201; visit to Calcutta, 122-3, 316n1;. *See also* Kolhan Campaign III; Kolhan Government Estate; Kol Insurrection; non–regulation system; Poto Pingua; Wilkinson system; witches

Wilkinson System; caste councils, 139, court language, 67, 101; - introduced in Chotanagpur, 99, 100-02, 223; - introduced in Kolhan Government Estate, 99, 153, 130, 151-3, 224, 226, 228, 317n48; jurisdiction over the border, 134; land question, 99, 100-01, 317n48; Manki-Munda system, 136-7, 151-2; staff, 99, 100, 132, 137-8, 305n122; stamp duty (*in forma pauperis*), 99, 101, 305n118, 306n143; village councils, 99, 100, 121-2, 138, 139, 305n133, 307n28; Wilkinson's Rules, 96, 97, 99, 100, 101, 125, 130, 136-9, 146, 223, 304nn97-117, 305n136. *See also* manki (Ho): Wilkinson; manki (Hos): Tickell; manki (Munda)

Wine, 131, 186, 187, 208, 210, 283n134

witches, 40, 105, 120, 157, 158, 213, 215, 227, 318n78. *See also* sokas

जलाद्रक्षेत्तैलाद्रक्षेद्रक्षेच्छिथिलबन्धनात् ।
मूर्खहस्ते न मां दद्यादिति वदति पुस्तकम् ॥

'Save me from water, protect me from oil and from loose binding,

And do not give me into the hands of fools!' says the manuscript.

www.ingramcontent.com/pod-product-compliance
Lightning Source LLC
LaVergne TN
LVHW081535070526
838199LV00006B/366